PUBLIC PAPERS OF THE PRESIDENTS

OF THE UNITED STATES

PUBLIC PAPERS OF THE PRESIDENTS

OF THE UNITED STATES

Harry S. Truman

Containing the Public Messages, Speeches, and
Statements of the President

JANUARY 1 TO DECEMBER 31, 1947

1947

UNITED STATES GOVERNMENT PRINTING OFFICE

WASHINGTON : 1963

PUBLISHED BY THE
OFFICE OF THE FEDERAL REGISTER
NATIONAL ARCHIVES AND RECORDS SERVICE
GENERAL SERVICES ADMINISTRATION

For sale by the Superintendent of Documents, U.S. Government Printing Office
Washington, D.C., 20402 - Price $5.52

FOREWORD

THE IMPORTANCE OF this series lies in the extraordinary character of the office of President of the United States.

A President's written and spoken words can command national and international attention if he has within him the power to attract and hold that attention. It is partly through the use of this power that leadership arises, events are molded, and administrations take their shape.

It is this power, quite as much as powers written into the Constitution, that gives to the papers of Presidents their peculiar and revealing importance.

Harry Truman

PREFACE

IN THIS VOLUME are gathered most of the public messages and statements of the President of the United States that were released by the White House during 1947. Similar volumes are available covering 1945 and 1946, the administration of President Eisenhower, and the first two years of the Kennedy administration. Volumes covering the period January 1, 1948–January 20, 1953, and the year 1963 are under preparation.

This series was begun in 1957 in response to a recommendation of the National Historical Publications Commission. An extensive compilation of the messages and papers of the Presidents, covering the period 1789 to 1897, was assembled by James D. Richardson and published under congressional authority between 1896 and 1899. Since that time various private compilations were issued, but there was no uniform, systematic publication comparable to the *Congressional Record* or the *United States Supreme Court Reports*. Many Presidential papers could be found only in mimeographed White House releases or as reported in the press. The National Historical Publications Commission therefore recommended the establishment of an official series in which Presidential writings and utterances of a public nature could be made promptly available.

The Commission's recommendation was incorporated in regulations of the Administrative Committee of the Federal Register issued under section 6 of the Federal Register Act (44 U.S.C. 306). The Committee's regulations, establishing the series and providing for the coverage of prior years, are reprinted at page 559 as "Appendix D."

Preface

The text of this book is based on Presidential materials issued during 1947 as White House releases and on transcripts of news conferences. A list of White House releases from which final selections were made is published at page 539 as "Appendix A."

The full text of President Truman's news conferences is here published for the first time, since direct quotation of the President's replies usually was not authorized. Addresses and speeches have been printed as actually delivered.

Proclamations, Executive orders, and similar documents required by law to be published in the *Federal Register* and *Code of Federal Regulations* are not repeated. Instead, they are listed by number and subject under the heading "Appendix B" at page 550.

The President is required by statute to transmit numerous reports to Congress. Those transmitted during the period covered by this volume are listed at page 557 as "Appendix C."

The items published in this volume are presented in chronological order, rather than being grouped in classes. Most needs for a classified arrangement are met by the subject index. For example, a reader interested in veto messages will find them listed in the index under the heading "veto messages."

The dates shown at the end of item headings are White House release dates. In instances where the date of the document differs from the release date that fact is shown in brackets immediately following the heading. Other editorial devices, such as text notes, footnotes, and cross references, have been held to a minimum.

Remarks or addresses were delivered in Washington, D.C., unless otherwise indicated. Similarly, statements, messages, and letters were issued from the White House in Washington unless otherwise indicated.

Preface

Original source materials, where available, have been used to protect against substantive errors in transcription. In maintaining the integrity of the text, valuable assistance was furnished by Dr. Philip C. Brooks and Philip D. Lagerquist of the Truman Library.

The planning and publication of this series is under the direction of David C. Eberhart of the Office of the Federal Register. The editor of the present volume was Warren R. Reid, assisted by Mildred B. Berry. Frank H. Mortimer of the Government Printing Office developed the typography and design.

Wayne C. Grover
Archivist of the United States

Bernard L. Boutin
Administrator of General Services
October 18, 1963

CONTENTS

LIST OF ITEMS

List of Items

xv

List of Items

List of Items

List of Items

List of Items

List of Items

List of Items

List of Items

List of Items

List of Items

Harry S. Truman

1947

99–438—63——3

1 Letter Accepting Resignation of Bernard M. Baruch as U.S. Representative on the United Nations Atomic Energy Commission. *January 4, 1947*

Dear Mr. Baruch:

The Secretary of State has handed me your letter of resignation as the Representative of the United States on the Atomic Energy Commission.

At first I was reluctant to accept the resignation. However, upon reflection, I have to agree with the correctness of the conclusions stated in your letter. The recent action of the General Assembly of the United Nations placed the responsibility for the consideration of disarmament proposals primarily upon the Security Council, where Senator Austin will represent the United States. I am impressed by the fact that, with one exception, the governments represented on the Security Council have the same representatives on the Atomic Energy Commission.

I know how tremendously interested you have been in the accomplishment of the task assigned you, and when you tell me that you believe your task is completed and that the work should now be taken over by Senator Austin, I accept your decision.

I wish to congratulate you most heartily on having secured the acceptance by the Commission of the United States proposal. It is inevitable that members of the Commission representing many governments should have differences of opinion as to the best approach to a solution of this problem. That our proposal should finally be accepted by a vote of ten to nothing, with two states abstaining, is a tribute to the fairness of our proposal. At the same time, it is convincing evidence of your skill and patience in presenting the proposal.

I wish you would extend to those who have been associated with you in this most important service my sincere appreciation of their efforts. Your own efforts in this matter only furnish additional evidence of your unselfish devotion to your country.

Very sincerely yours,

HARRY S. TRUMAN

NOTE: Mr. Baruch served as U.S. Representative on the United Nations Atomic Energy Commission from April 6, 1946, to January 4, 1947. His letter of resignation, released with the President's reply, was accompanied by "The First Report of the United Nations Atomic Energy Commission," dated December 31, 1946 (Government Printing Office, 101 pp.).

2 Annual Message to the Congress on the State of the Union. *January 6, 1947*

[As delivered in person before a joint session]

Mr. President, Mr. Speaker, Members of the Congress of the United States:

It looks like a good many of you have moved over to the left since I was here last!

I come before you today to report on the State of the Union and, in the words of the Constitution, to recommend such measures as I judge necessary and expedient.

I come also to welcome you as you take up your duties and to discuss with you the manner in which you and I should fulfill our obligations to the American people during the next 2 years.

The power to mold the future of this

Nation lies in our hands—yours and mine, and they are joined together by the Constitution.

If in this year, and in the next, we can find the right course to take as each issue arises, and if, in spite of all difficulties, we have the courage and the resolution to take that course, then we shall achieve a state of well-being for our people without precedent in history. And if we continue to work with the other nations of the world earnestly, patiently, and wisely, we can—granting a will for peace on the part of our neighbors—make a lasting peace for the world.

But, if we are to realize these ends, the Congress and the President, during the next 2 years, must work together. It is not unusual in our history that the majority of the Congress represents a party in opposition to the President's party. I am the twentieth President of the United States who, at some time during his term of office, has found his own party to be in the minority in one or both Houses of Congress. The first one was George Washington. Wilson was number eighteen, and Hoover was number nineteen.

I realize that on some matters the Congress and the President may have honest differences of opinion. Partisan differences, however, did not cause material disagreements as to the conduct of the war. Nor, in the conduct of our international relations, during and since the war, have such partisan differences been material.

On some domestic issues we may, and probably shall, disagree. That in itself is not to be feared. It is inherent in our form of Government. But there are ways of disagreeing; men who differ can still work together sincerely for the common good. We shall be risking the Nation's safety and destroying our opportunities for progress if we do not settle any disagreements in this spirit, without thought of partisan advantage.

THE GENERAL DOMESTIC ECONOMY

As the year 1947 begins, the state of our national economy presents great opportunities for all. We have virtually full employment. Our national production of goods and services is 50 percent higher than in any year prior to the war emergency. The national income in 1946 was higher than in any peacetime year. Our food production is greater than it has ever been. During the last 5 years our productive facilities have been expanded in almost every field. The American standard of living is higher now than ever before, and when the housing shortage can be overcome it will be even higher.

During the past few months we have removed at a rapid rate the emergency controls that the Federal Government had to exercise during the war. The remaining controls will be retained only as long as they are needed to protect the public. Private enterprise must be given the greatest possible freedom to continue the expansion of our economy.

In my proclamation of December 31, 1946, I announced the termination of hostilities. This automatically ended certain temporary legislation and certain executive powers.

Two groups of temporary laws still remain: the first are those which by Congressional mandate are to last during the "emergency"; the second are those which are to continue until the "termination of the war."

I shall submit to the Congress recommendations for the repeal of certain of the statutes which by their terms continue for the duration of the "emergency." I shall at the same time recommend that others within this classification be extended until the state of war has been ended by treaty or by legislative action. As to those statutes which continue until the state of war has been terminated, I urge that the Congress promptly consider each statute individually, and repeal such emergency legislation where it is advisable.

Now that nearly all wartime controls have been removed, the operation of our industrial system depends to a greater extent on the decisions of businessmen, farmers, and workers. These decisions must be wisely made with genuine concern for public welfare. The welfare of businessmen, farmers, and workers depends upon the economic well-being of those who buy their products.

An important present source of danger to our economy is the possibility that prices might be raised to such an extent that the consuming public could not purchase the tremendous volume of goods and services which will be produced during 1947.

We all know that recent price increases have denied to many of our workers much of the value of recent wage increases. Farmers have found that a large part of their increased income has been absorbed by increased prices. While some of our people have received raises in income which exceed price increases, the great majority have not. Those persons who live on modest fixed incomes—retired persons living on pensions, for example—and workers whose incomes are relatively inflexible, such as teachers and other civil servants—have suffered hardship.

In the effort to bring about a sound and equitable price structure, each group of our population has its own responsibilities.

It is up to industry not only to hold the line on existing prices, but to make reductions whenever profits justify such action.

It is up to labor to refrain from pressing for unjustified wage increases that will force increases in the price level.

And it is up to Government to do everything in its power to encourage high-volume production, for that is what makes possible

good wages, low prices, and reasonable profits.

In a few days there will be submitted to the Congress the Economic Report of the President, and also the Budget Message. Those messages will contain many recommendations. Today I shall outline five major economic policies which I believe the Government should pursue during 1947. These policies are designed to meet our immediate needs and, at the same time, to provide for the long-range welfare of our free enterprise system:

First, the promotion of greater harmony between labor and management.

Second, restriction of monopoly and unfair business practices; assistance to small business; and the promotion of the free competitive system of private enterprise.

Third, continuation of an aggressive program of home construction.

Fourth, the balancing of the budget in the next fiscal year and the achieving of a substantial surplus to be applied to the reduction of the public debt.

Fifth, protection of a fair level of return to farmers in post-war agriculture.

LABOR AND MANAGEMENT

The year just past—like the year after the First World War—was marred by labor-management strife.

Despite this outbreak of economic warfare in 1946, we are today producing goods and services in record volume. Nevertheless, it is essential to improve the methods for reaching agreement between labor and management and to reduce the number of strikes and lockouts.

We must not, however, adopt punitive legislation. We must not, in order to punish a few labor leaders, pass vindictive laws which will restrict the proper rights of the rank and file of labor. We must not, under the stress of emotion, endanger our American freedoms by taking ill-considered action which will lead to results not anticipated or desired.

We must remember, in reviewing the record of disputes in 1946, that management shares with labor the responsibility for failure to reach agreements which would have averted strikes. For that reason, we must realize that industrial peace cannot be achieved merely by laws directed against labor unions.

During the last decade and a half, we have established a national labor policy in this country based upon free collective bargaining as the process for determining wages and working conditions.

That is still the national policy.

And it should continue to be the national policy!

But as yet, not all of us have learned what it means to bargain freely and fairly. Nor have all of us learned to carry the mutual responsibilities that accompany the right to bargain. There have been abuses and harmful practices which limit the effectiveness of our system of collective bargaining. Furthermore, we have lacked sufficient governmental machinery to aid labor and management in resolving their differences.

Certain labor-management problems need attention at once and certain others, by reason of their complexity, need exhaustive investigation and study.

We should enact legislation to correct certain abuses and to provide additional governmental assistance in bargaining. But we should also concern ourselves with the basic causes of labor-management difficulties.

In the light of these considerations, I propose to you and urge your cooperation in effecting the following four-point program to reduce industrial strife:

Point number one is the early enactment of legislation to prevent certain unjustifiable practices.

First, under this point, are jurisdictional strikes. In such strikes the public and the employer are innocent bystanders who are injured by a collision between rival unions. This type of dispute hurts production, industry, and the public—and labor itself. I consider jurisdictional strikes indefensible.

The National Labor Relations Act provides procedures for determining which union represents employees of a particular employer. In some jurisdictional disputes, however, minority unions strike to compel employers to deal with them despite a legal duty to bargain with the majority union. Strikes to compel an employer to violate the law are inexcusable. Legislation to prevent such strikes is clearly desirable.

Another form of inter-union disagreement is the jurisdictional strike involving the question of which labor union is entitled to perform a particular task. When rival unions are unable to settle such disputes themselves, provision must be made for peaceful and binding determination of the issues.

A second unjustifiable practice is the secondary boycott, when used to further jurisdictional disputes or to compel employers to violate the National Labor Relations Act.

Not all secondary boycotts are unjustified. We must judge them on the basis of their objectives. For example, boycotts intended to protect wage rates and working conditions should be distinguished from those in furtherance of jurisdictional disputes. The structure of industry sometimes requires unions, as a matter of self-preservation, to extend the conflict beyond a particular employer. There should be no blanket prohibition against boycotts. The appropriate goal is legislation which prohibits secondary boycotts in pursuance of unjustifiable objectives, but does not impair the union's right to preserve its own existence and the gains made in genuine collective bargaining.

A third practice that should be corrected is the use of economic force, by either labor or management, to decide issues arising out of the interpretation of existing contracts.

Collective bargaining agreements, like other contracts, should be faithfully adhered to by both parties. In the most enlightened union-management relationships, disputes over the interpretation of contract terms are settled peaceably by negotiation or arbitration. Legislation should be enacted to provide machinery whereby unsettled disputes concerning the interpretation of an existing agreement may be referred by either party to final and binding arbitration.

Point number two is the extension of facilities within the Department of Labor for assisting collective bargaining.

One of our difficulties in avoiding labor strife arises from a lack of order in the collective bargaining process. The parties often do not have a clear understanding of their responsibility for settling disputes through their own negotiations. We constantly see instances where labor or management resorts to economic force without exhausting the possibilities for agreement through the bargaining process. Neither the parties nor the Government have a definite yardstick for determining when and how Government assistance should be invoked. There is need for integrated governmental machinery to provide the successive steps of mediation, voluntary arbitration, and—ultimately in appropriate cases—ascertainment of the facts of the dispute and the reporting of the facts to the public. Such machinery would facilitate and expedite the settlement of disputes.

Point number three is the broadening of our program of social legislation to alleviate the causes of workers' insecurity.

On June 11, 1946, in my message vetoing the Case Bill, I made a comprehensive statement of my views concerning labor-management relations. I said then, and I repeat now, that the solution of labor-management difficulties is to be found not only in legislation dealing directly with labor relations, but also in a program designed to remove the causes of insecurity felt by many workers in our industrial society. In this connection, for example, the Congress should consider the extension and broadening of our social security system, better housing, a comprehensive national health program, and provision for a fair minimum wage.

Point number four is the appointment of a Temporary Joint Commission to inquire into the entire field of labor-management relations.

I recommend that the Congress provide for the appointment of a Temporary Joint Commission to undertake this broad study.

The President, the Congress, and management and labor have a continuing responsibility to cooperate in seeking and finding the solution of these problems. I therefore recommend that the Commission be composed as follows: twelve to be chosen by the Congress from members of both parties in the House and the Senate, and eight representing the public, management and labor, to be appointed by the President.

The Commission should be charged with investigating and making recommendations upon certain major subjects, among others:

First, the special and unique problem of nationwide strikes in vital industries affecting the public interest. In particular, the Commission should examine into the question of how to settle or prevent such strikes without endangering our general democratic freedoms.

Upon a proper solution of this problem may depend the whole industrial future of the United States. The paralyzing effects of a nationwide strike in such industries as transportation, coal, oil, steel, or communications can result in national disaster. We have been able to avoid such disaster, in recent years, only by the use of extraordinary war powers. All those powers will soon be gone. In their place there must be created an adequate system and effective machinery in these vital fields. This problem will require careful study and a bold approach, but an approach consistent with the preservation of the rights of our people. The need is pressing. The Commission should give this its earliest attention.

Second, the best methods and procedures for carrying out the collective bargaining process. This should include the responsibilities of labor and management to negotiate freely and fairly with each other, and to refrain from strikes or lockouts until all possibilities of negotiation have been exhausted.

Third, the underlying causes of labor-management disputes.

Some of the subjects presented here for investigation involve long-range study. Others can be considered immediately by the Commission and its recommendations can be submitted to the Congress in the near future.

I recommend that this Commission make its first report, including specific legislative recommendations, not later than March 15, 1947.

RESTRICTION OF MONOPOLY AND PROMOTION
OF PRIVATE ENTERPRISE

The second major policy I desire to lay before you has to do with the growing concentration of economic power and the threat to free competitive private enterprise. In 1941 the Temporary National Economic Committee completed a comprehensive investigation into the workings of the national economy. The Committee's study showed that, despite a half century of anti-trust law enforcement, one of the gravest threats to our welfare lay in the increasing concentration of power in the hands of a small number of giant organizations.

During the war, this long-standing tendency toward economic concentration was accelerated. As a consequence, we now find that to a greater extent than ever before, whole industries are dominated by one or a few large organizations which can restrict production in the interest of higher profits and thus reduce employment and purchasing power.

In an effort to assure full opportunity and free competition to business we will vigorously enforce the anti-trust laws. There is much the Congress can do to cooperate and assist in this program.

To strengthen and enforce the laws that regulate business practices is not enough. Enforcement must be supplemented by positive measures of aid to new enterprises. Government assistance, research programs, and credit powers should be designed and used to promote the growth of new firms and new industries. Assistance to small business is particularly important at this time when thousands of veterans who are potential business and industrial leaders are beginning their careers.

We should also give special attention to the decentralization of industry and the development of areas that are now underindustrialized.

HOUSING

The third major policy is also of great importance to the national economy—an aggressive program to encourage home construction. The first Federal program to relieve the veterans' housing shortage was announced in February 1946. In 1946 one million family housing units have been put

6

under construction and more than 665,000 units have already been completed. The rate of expansion in construction has broken all records.

In the coming year the number of dwelling units built will approach, if not surpass, the top construction year of 1926. The primary responsibility to deliver housing at reasonable prices that veterans can afford rests with private industry and with labor. The Government will continue to expedite the flow of key building materials, to limit nonresidential construction, and to give financial support where it will do the most good. Measures to stimulate rental housing and new types of housing construction will receive special emphasis.

To reach our long-range goal of adequate housing for all our people, comprehensive housing legislation is urgently required, similar to the non-partisan bill passed by the Senate last year. At a minimum, such legislation should open the way for rebuilding the blighted areas of our cities and should establish positive incentives for the investment of billions of dollars of private capital in large-scale rental housing projects. It should provide for improvement of housing in rural areas and for the construction, over a 4-year period, of half a million units of public low-rental housing. It should authorize a single peacetime Federal housing agency to assure efficient use of our resources on the vast housing front.

FISCAL AFFAIRS

The fourth major policy has to do with the balancing of the budget. In a prosperous period such as the present one, the budget of the Federal Government should be balanced. Prudent management of public finance requires that we begin the process of reducing the public debt. The budget which I shall submit to you this week has a small margin of surplus. In the Budget Message I am making recommendations which, if accepted, will result in a substantially larger surplus which should be applied to debt retirement. One of these recommendations is that the Congress take early action to continue throughout the next fiscal year the war excise tax rates which, under the present law, will expire on June 30, 1947.

Expenditures relating to the war are still high. Considerable sums are required to alleviate world famine and suffering. Aid to veterans will continue at peak level. The world situation is such that large military expenditures are required. Interest on the public debt and certain other costs are irreducible. For these reasons I have had to practice stringent economy in preparing the budget; and I hope that the Congress will cooperate in this program of economy.

AGRICULTURE

The fifth major policy has to do with the welfare of our farm population.

Production of food reached record heights in 1946. Much of our tremendous grain crop can readily be sold abroad and thus will become no threat to our domestic markets. But in the next few years American agriculture can face the same dangers it did after World War I. In the early twenties the Nation failed to maintain outlets for the new productive capacity of our agricultural plant. It failed to provide means to protect the farmer while he adjusted his acreage to peacetime demands.

The result we all remember too well. Farm production stayed up while demand and prices fell, in contrast with industry where prices stayed up and output declined. Farm surpluses piled up, and disaster followed.

We must make sure of meeting the problems which we failed to meet after the first World War. Present laws give considerable stability to farm prices for 1947 and 1948, and these 2 years must be utilized to maintain and develop markets for our great productive power.

The purpose of these laws was to permit an orderly transition from war to peace. The Government plan of support prices was not designed to absorb, at great cost, the unlimited surpluses of a highly productive agriculture.

We must not wait until the guarantees expire to set the stage for permanent farm welfare.

The farmer is entitled to a fair income.

Ways can be found to utilize his new skills and better practices, to expand his markets at home and abroad, and to carry out the objectives of a balanced pattern of peacetime production without either undue sacrifice by farm people or undue expense to the Government.

HEALTH AND GENERAL WELFARE

Of all our national resources, none is of more basic value than the health of our people. Over a year ago I presented to the Congress my views on a national health program. The Congress acted on several of the recommendations in this program—mental health, the health of mothers and children, and hospital construction. I urge this Congress to complete the work begun last year and to enact the most important recommendation of the program—to provide adequate medical care to all who need it, not as charity but on the basis of payments made by the beneficiaries of the program.

One administrative change would help greatly to further our national program in the fields of health, education, and welfare. I again recommend the establishment of a well-integrated Department of Welfare.

VETERANS

Fourteen million World War II servicemen have returned to civil life. The great majority have found their places as citizens of their communities and their Nation. It is a tribute to the fiber of our servicemen and to the flexibility of our economy that these adjustments have been made so rapidly and so successfully.

More than two million of these veterans are attending schools or acquiring job skills through the financial assistance of the Federal Government. Thousands of sick and wounded veterans are daily receiving the best of medical and hospital care. Half a million have obtained loans, with Government guarantees, to purchase homes or farms or to embark upon new businesses. Compensation is being paid in almost two million cases for disabilities or death. More than three million are continuing to maintain their low-cost National Service Life Insurance policies. Almost seven million veterans have been aided by unemployment and self-employment allowances.

Exclusive of mustering-out payments and terminal leave pay, the program for veterans of all wars is costing over seven billion dollars a year—one-fifth of our total Federal budget. This is the most far-reaching and complete veterans program ever conceived by any nation.

Except for minor adjustments, I believe that our program of benefits for veterans is now complete. In the long run, the success of the program will not be measured by the number of veterans receiving financial aid or by the number of dollars we spend. History will judge us not by the money we

8

spend, but by the further contribution we enable our veterans to make to their country. In considering any additional legislation, that must be our criterion.

CIVIL RIGHTS

We have recently witnessed in this country numerous attacks upon the constitutional rights of individual citizens as a result of racial and religious bigotry. Substantial segments of our people have been prevented from exercising fully their right to participate in the election of public officials, both locally and nationally. Freedom to engage in lawful callings has been denied.

The will to fight these crimes should be in the hearts of every one of us.

For the Federal Government that fight is now being carried on by the Department of Justice to the full extent of the powers that have been conferred upon it. While the Constitution withholds from the Federal Government the major task of preserving peace in the several States, I am not convinced that the present legislation reached the limit of Federal power to protect the civil rights of its citizens.

I have, therefore, by Executive order,[1] established the President's Committee on Civil Rights to study and report on the whole problem of federally-secured civil rights, with a view to making recommendations to the Congress.

NATURAL RESOURCES

In our responsibility to promote the general welfare of the people, we have always to consider the natural resources of our country. They are the foundation of our

[1] Executive Order 9808 (3 CFR, 1943–1948 Comp., p. 590).

life. In the development of the great river systems of America there is the major opportunity of our generation to contribute to the increase of the national wealth. This program is already well along; it should be pushed with full vigor.

I must advise the Congress that we are rapidly becoming a "have not" Nation as to many of our minerals. The economic progress and the security of our country depend upon an expanding return of mineral discovery and upon improved methods of recovery. The Federal Government must do its part to meet this need.

FOREIGN AFFAIRS

Progress in reaching our domestic goals is closely related to our conduct of foreign affairs. All that I have said about maintaining a sound and prosperous economy and improving the welfare of our people has greater meaning because of the world leadership of the United States. What we do, or fail to do, at home affects not only ourselves but millions throughout the world. If we are to fulfill our responsibilities to ourselves and to other peoples, we must make sure that the United States is sound economically, socially, and politically. Only then will we be able to help bring about the elements of peace in other countries—political stability, economic advancement, and social progress.

Peace treaties for Italy, Bulgaria, Rumania, and Hungary have finally been prepared. Following the signing of these treaties next month in Paris, they will be submitted to the Senate for ratification. This Government does not regard the treaties as completely satisfactory. Whatever their defects, however, I am convinced that they are as good as we can hope to obtain by agreement among the principal wartime Allies. Further dispute and delay would gravely jeopardize political stability in the countries concerned for many years.

During the long months of debate on these treaties, we have made it clear to all nations that the United States will not consent to settlements at the expense of principles we regard as vital to a just and enduring peace. We have made it equally clear that we will not retreat to isolationism. Our policies will be the same during the forthcoming negotiations in Moscow on the German and Austrian treaties, and during the future conferences on the Japanese treaty.

The delay in arriving at the first peace settlements is due partly to the difficulty of reaching agreement with the Soviet Union on the terms of settlement. Whatever differences there may have been between us and the Soviet Union, however, should not be allowed to obscure the fact that the basic interests of both nations lie in the early making of a peace under which the peoples of all countries may return, as free men and women, to the essential tasks of production and reconstruction. The major concern of each of us should be the promotion of collective security, not the advancement of individual security.

Our policy toward the Soviet Union is guided by the same principles which determine our policies toward all nations. We seek only to uphold the principles of international justice which have been embodied in the Charter of the United Nations.

We must now get on with the peace settlements. The occupying powers should recognize the independence of Austria and withdraw their troops. The Germans and the Japanese cannot be left in doubt and fear as to their future; they must know their national boundaries, their resources, and what reparations they must pay. Without trying to manage their internal affairs, we can insure that these countries do not re-arm.

INTERNATIONAL RELIEF AND DISPLACED PERSONS

The United States can be proud of its part in caring for the peoples reduced to want by the ravages of war, and in aiding nations to restore their national economies. We have shipped more supplies to the hungry peoples of the world since the end of the war than all other countries combined!

However, insofar as admitting displaced persons is concerned, I do not feel that the United States has done its part. Only about 5,000 of them have entered this country since May, 1946. The fact is that the executive agencies are now doing all that is reasonably possible under the limitation of the existing law and established quotas. Congressional assistance in the form of new legislation is needed. I urge the Congress to turn its attention to this world problem, in an effort to find ways whereby we can fulfill our responsibilities to these thousands of homeless and suffering refugees of all faiths.

INTERNATIONAL TRADE

World economic cooperation is essential to world political cooperation. We have made a good start on economic cooperation through the International Bank, the International Monetary Fund, and the Export-Import Bank. We must now take other steps for the reconstruction of world trade and we should continue to strive for an international trade system as free from obstructions as possible.

ATOMIC ENERGY

The United States has taken the lead in the endeavor to put atomic energy under effective international control. We seek no monopoly for ourselves or for any group of nations. We ask only that there be safeguards sufficient to insure that no nation will be able to use this power for military purposes. So long as all governments are not agreed on means of international control of atomic energy, the shadow of fear will obscure the bright prospects for the peaceful use of this enormous power.

In accordance with the Atomic Energy Act of 1946, the Commission established under that law is assuming full jurisdiction over domestic atomic energy enterprise. The program of the Commission will, of course, be worked out in close collaboration with the military services in conformity with the wish of the Congress, but it is my fervent hope that the military significance of atomic energy will steadily decline. We look to the Commission to foster the development of atomic energy for industrial use and scientific and medical research. In the vigorous and effective development of peaceful uses of atomic energy rests our hope that this new force may ultimately be turned into a blessing for all nations.

MILITARY POLICY

In 1946 the Army and Navy completed the demobilization of their wartime forces. They are now maintaining the forces which we need for national defense and to fulfill our international obligations.

We live in a world in which strength on the part of peace-loving nations is still the greatest deterrent to aggression. World stability can be destroyed when nations with great responsibilities neglect to maintain the means of discharging those responsibilities.

This is an age when unforeseen attack could come with unprecedented speed. We must be strong enough to defeat, and thus forestall, any such attack. In our steady progress toward a more rational world order, the need for large armed forces is progressively declining; but the stabilizing force of

American military strength must not be weakened until our hopes are fully realized. When a system of collective security under the United Nations has been established, we shall be willing to lead in collective disarmament, but, until such a system becomes a reality, we must not again allow ourselves to become weak and invite attack.

For those reasons, we need well-equipped, well-trained armed forces and we must be able to mobilize rapidly our resources in men and material for our own defense, should the need arise.

The Army will be reduced to 1,070,000 officers and men by July 1, 1947. Half of the Army will be used for occupation duties abroad and most of the remainder will be employed at home in the support of these overseas forces.

The Navy is supporting the occupation troops in Europe and in the Far East. Its fundamental mission—to support our national interests wherever required—is unchanged. The Navy, including the Marine Corps, will average 571,000 officers and men during the fiscal year 1948.

We are encountering serious difficulties in maintaining our forces at even these reduced levels. Occupation troops are barely sufficient to carry out the duties which our foreign policy requires. Our forces at home are at a point where further reduction is impracticable. We should like an Army and a Navy composed entirely of long-term volunteers, but in spite of liberal inducements the basic needs of the Army are not now being met by voluntary enlistments.

The War Department has advised me that it is unable to make an accurate forecast at the present time as to whether it will be possible to maintain the strength of the Army by relying exclusively on volunteers. The situation will be much clearer in a few weeks, when the results of the campaign for volunteers are known. The War Department will make its recommendations as to the need for the extension of Selective Service in sufficient time to enable the Congress to take action prior to the expiration of the present law on March 31st. The responsibility for maintaining our armed forces at the strength necessary for our national safety rests with the Congress.

The development of a trained citizen reserve is also vital to our national security. This can best be accomplished through universal training. I have appointed an Advisory Commission on Universal Training to study the various plans for a training program, and I expect that the recommendations of the Commission will be of benefit to the Congress and to me in reaching decisions on this problem.

The cost of the military establishment is substantial. There is one certain way by which we can cut costs and at the same time enhance our national security. That is by the establishment of a single Department of National Defense. I shall communicate with the Congress in the near future with reference to the establishment of a single Department of National Defense.

National security does not consist only of an army, a navy, and an air force. It rests on a much broader basis. It depends on a sound economy of prices and wages, on prosperous agriculture, on satisfied and productive workers, on a competitive private enterprise free from monopolistic repression, on continued industrial harmony and production, on civil liberties and human freedoms—on all the forces which create in our men and women a strong moral fiber and spiritual stamina.

But we have a higher duty and a greater responsibility than the attainment of our own national security. Our goal is collective security for all mankind.

If we can work in a spirit of understanding and mutual respect, we can fulfill this solemn obligation which rests upon us.

The spirit of the American people can set the course of world history. If we maintain and strengthen our cherished ideals, and if we share our great bounty with war-stricken people over the world, then the faith of our citizens in freedom and democracy will be spread over the whole earth and free men everywhere will share our devotion to those ideals.

Let us have the will and the patience to do this job together.

May the Lord strengthen us in our faith.

May He give us wisdom to lead the peoples of the world in His ways of peace.

NOTE: The President spoke at 1 p.m. His address was carried on a nationwide radio broadcast.

3 Letter Accepting Resignation of James F. Byrnes as Secretary of State. *January 7*, 1947

My dear Jim:

I have weighed carefully the considerations set forth in your letter of December 19, 1946, and in your letter of April 16, 1946, each emphasizing your desire to retire from the office of Secretary of State. Because I know how vital these considerations are, I must accede to your desire.

I accept, therefore, with great reluctance and heartfelt regret, your resignation effective at the close of business on January 10, 1947, or upon the qualification of your successor.

I realize full well how arduous and complex have been the problems which have fallen to you since you took office in July,

1945. Big events were then impending and the months that have ensued have presented problems of the utmost moment, with all of which you have dealt with rare tact and judgment and—when necessary—firmness and tenacity of purpose.

Yours has been a steadying hand as you have met the difficult problems which have arisen with such unvarying succession.

For all that you did during the war, and in the making of the peace, you have earned the thanks of the Nation. So I say: well done, in the hope that we can continue to call upon you for the counsel which you can give out of so rich and varied an experience.

With every good wish,

Very sincerely yours,

HARRY S. TRUMAN

NOTE: Mr. Byrnes served as Secretary of State from July 3, 1945, to January 21, 1947. His letters of resignation dated April 16, 1946, and December 19, 1946, were released with the President's reply.

4   Special Message to the Congress: The President's First Economic Report. *January 8, 1947*

To the Congress of the United States:

As the year 1947 opens America has never been so strong or so prosperous. Nor have our prospects ever been brighter.

Yet in the minds of a great many of us there is a fear of another depression, the loss of our jobs, our farms, our businesses.

But America was not built on fear. America was built on courage, on imagination and an unbeatable determination to do the job at hand.

The job at hand today is to see to it that America is not ravaged by recurring depressions and long periods of unemployment, but that instead we build an economy so fruitful, so dynamic, so progressive that each citizen can count upon opportunity and security for himself and his family.

Nor is prosperity in the United States important to the American people alone. It is the foundation of world prosperity and world peace. And the world is looking to us.

I believe that the American people have the wisdom and the will to use our abundant resources so that all may prosper. I reject, and I know the American people reject, the notion that we must have another depression. I am not referring to minor detours and bumps in the road ahead—these we know we shall have. I am referring to economic collapse and stagnation such as started in 1929. This need not happen again, and *must* not happen again.

The Congress passed the Employment Act of 1946 by an overwhelming bipartisan vote. This Act wisely provided for a Council of Economic Advisers to the President, men who as a result of training, experience, and attainments are exceptionally qualified to analyze and interpret economic developments, to appraise programs and activities of the Government and to formulate and recommend national economic policy.

The Congress also provided for a permanent joint committee to receive and analyze this annual Economic Report of the President and to submit recommendations concerning it to both Houses.

In transmitting this first Economic Report, I am conscious of its significance as the beginning of a series of reports that will serve the Executive and the Congress as the basis for an orderly and continuing review of the economic state of the union and for integrated and comprehensive steps to ensure the permanent economic health of the Nation.

The Economic Report is an opportunity for national self-examination and self-criticism. It is a challenge to the President and the Congress to determine the causes of whatever problems we face in our economic life and to find the solutions to those problems. It provides an opportunity for all our citizens to judge the merits of the analysis and proposed action. It is a new and splendid tool to help us in our tasks. And like all governmental tools, its effectiveness will increase year by year as we learn by doing.

Prosperity cannot be the concern of one party or of one group. It cannot be attained without the goodwill and the cooperation of all.

To build a greater America we must approach the task with unity of purpose, with patience, with wisdom, and with determination to overcome all obstacles. If we do this—and we must—I have no doubt about the ability of Americans to build, on a firm basis of security and political and economic freedom, a country in which the rewards we enjoy can be doubled within the life span of many of those now living.

I. REVIEW OF 1946

EMPLOYMENT

During 1946, civilian employment approached 58 million. This was the highest civilian employment this Nation has ever known—10 million more than in 1940 and several million higher than the wartime peak. If we include the military services, total employment exceeded 60 million. Unemployment, on the other hand, remained low throughout the year. At the present time it is estimated at about 2 million actively seeking work. This is probably close to the minimum unavoidable in a free economy of great mobility such as ours.

Thus, at the end of 1946, less than a year and a half after VJ-day, more than 10 million demobilized veterans and other millions of wartime workers have found employment in the swiftest and most gigantic changeover that any nation has ever made from war to peace. At its peak during 1946 aggregate employment was substantially in accord with the objectives stated by the Congress in the Employment Act.

PRODUCTION

Total production turned out by the Nation's farmers and workers likewise mounted to new peacetime levels. In 1946 it was about 50 percent above the 1939 predefense level and only 15 percent below the wartime high. However, production is not yet at its peak in relation to our present plant and manpower resources. Bottlenecks, shortages of materials and components, labor-management disputes, and other reconversion difficulties have had their retarding influence.

But with all these obstacles, production in the second half of 1946 reached a higher rate than in any peacetime year. Goods scarce during the war began to fill dealers' shelves. The American people were eating more food per capita than in any previous year, even though in some cases they were unable to buy exactly the kind of food they wanted. In total, people were supplied with more goods and services than ever before. This indicates that when all our resources are fully marshalled for peacetime pursuits, the whole American people will be able to enjoy a standard of living far surpassing any that we have ever known.

PURCHASING POWER

The Congress, by setting maximum purchasing power as an objective of National policy in the Employment Act, pointed to the importance of purchasing power in keeping our economy fully employed and fully productive. When people stop buying, business stops producing and employment drops. It is therefore of the utmost importance that at all times we be concerned as to the volume of purchasing power of the Nation and its relation to the volume of production of goods and services.

Purchasing power, of course, depends upon current cash income, the use of savings, and the use of credit. It also depends upon prices. As we all know, when prices go up the purchasing power of the dollar goes down.

In 1946 the problem of linking maximum purchasing power with maximum employment was not completely solved. To be sure, cash and credit were available to purchasers in extraordinary amounts. This was due to high agricultural and industrial earnings, large accumulated savings, considerable extension of credit, and the payment of veterans' allowances and mustering-out pay. In the face of continuing shortages of many kinds of goods and services, this led to an inflationary pressure. When price controls were relaxed and finally dropped, this pressure resulted in a substantial increase in the general price level.

The rise in prices that occurred in the latter half of 1946 greatly reduced the purchasing power of the current incomes received by the large majority of people. It is true that some groups in the population received increases in income that for them balanced or more than balanced the rise in prices. But the large mass of consumers did not enjoy such offsets. How to effect a mutual adjustment of incomes and prices which will provide purchasing power adequate to sustained maximum production in the years ahead thus becomes a central problem for private enterprise and Government.

II. PRICES, WAGES, PROFITS IN 1946

The relation of wages, prices, and profits is the key to the maintenance of purchasing power. If prices are too low in relation to wages, they squeeze or eliminate profits, stifling the initiative of business, interfering with production, and reducing or retarding employment. If prices are too high in relation to wages, they restrict the market and reduce employment, as well as causing suffering to individual consumers.

PRICES

During the war years prices were on the whole successfully kept in check under the "hold the line" policy, with farm and food prices rising somewhat more than most others. Between VJ-day and the middle of last year when the lapse in price control occurred, prices rose moderately, chiefly due to price increases granted to speed production or to take account of wage rises. The average increase in wholesale prices from VJ-day to mid-1946 was 7 percent, and in retail prices was 3 percent, although textiles and clothing rose considerably more than the average.

But between June and December wholesale prices jumped an additional 24 percent, while the consumer price index climbed 15 percent. The sharpest increases were for the most part in farm and food products, textiles, clothing, and in residential construction.

The Congress made clear its intent that decontrol be speeded. In fact, after the new price-control law was passed, the direct control of prices soon became virtually impossible. It was no longer a question of whether it was in the interest of the workers, businessmen, farmers, and the public to control prices; it was a question whether price controls were any longer workable. It was the advice by late fall of labor, business, the farm groups, and my Cabinet that general price control be dropped.

Two things immediately happened. Prices rose sharply. Goods that had been produced under price control but withheld in the hope of decontrol appeared on shelves.

The increase in consumer prices has substantially reduced the purchasing power of the great majority of consumers.

WAGES

After VJ-day, direct wage controls, with the exception of those in the building trades, were dropped in order to permit a return, so far as possible, to collective bargaining. Indirect wage controls were, however, maintained until general price decontrol.

Between July 1945 and July 1946 the average wage-rate increase in manufacturing was about 10 percent. Nearly half of this increase was offset by reductions in overtime, declines in piecework earnings, and the shift of workers from higher-paid wartime to lower-paid peacetime jobs. Thus, for manufacturing as a whole, the average hourly earnings of labor last July were 6 percent above what they were the year before. Because of the reduction in the workweek during 1945 and 1946, weekly take-home pay declined in many industries and rose but moderately elsewhere in spite of the increase in wage rates.

Since July 1946 there has been some further increase in wage rates, average hourly earnings, and average take-home pay, but less than the increase in prices. Thus real earnings have fallen.

PROFITS

Business profits began to rise in many lines of nondurable goods and in most trades and services soon after VJ-day. This rise reflected the increased volume of civilian sales. Price increases during the past year and removal of the excess-profits tax added still further to profits after taxes. In most of the soft goods and service lines, profits after taxes in the second quarter of 1946 were already above the levels of 1944 and 1945. Further increases were reported for the third quarter.

But profits have been extremely uneven as between industries. In many of the reconversion industries, especially where volume was slow in getting underway, profits at first were low and in many cases there were actual losses, many of which, however, were alleviated by the carry-back provision of the tax law.

Third-quarter reports showed increased profits in most of the durable-goods industries, although price ceilings had not yet been generally removed. Profits increased further during the fourth quarter with the removal of price control.

We should not infer that all industries or all firms in a given industry were operating at a highly profitable level or that none were incurring losses. We must also remember that the purchasing power of the business dollar as well as the consumer dollar has been diminished by the price rise. Nevertheless, taking account of all of these considerations, it is plain that business in general is receiving exceptional profits.

III. The Nation's Economic Budget

The volume of employment and production in any given period depends upon the volume of expenditures. These expenditures are of four types:

1. Consumer Buying.
2. Business Buying.
3. Foreign Buying.
4. Government Buying (Federal, State, and local).

In order that we may have a better idea of the size of the job ahead and the relative proportion of our goods and services going to consumers, business, foreign markets, and Government, I here set forth the Nation's Economic Budget.

The Nation's Economic Budget shows the distribution of income and expenditures among consumers, business, and Government, and imports and exports. It sheds light upon whether price and wage policies and other public policies are encouraging an alignment among these four component parts which is favorable to sustained high levels of economic activity, or which threatens us with an economic decline. The Economic Budget also indicates whether a given level of economic activity is being achieved mainly by private expenditures, or by public expenditures, and in what proportion. By comparing budgets for different periods, we can discern favorable and unfavorable trends.

The Nation's Economic Budget is primarily a device for the measurement of our economic activity. Use of this device is not wedded to any particular economic theory. The Economic Budget is an objective summary statement of our economy in action at a given time, as reflected by the income and expenditures of its major parts. It reflects the aggregate actions of millions of consumers and businesses and of the Federal, State, and local governments.

By way of illustration, Table I contrasts the Nation's Economic Budget during the last pre-defense year 1939 with the Budget during the war year 1944, and with the Budget during the transition year 1946.

POSTWAR TRANSFORMATION

The figures for the years 1939, 1944, and 1946 show that a transformation has taken place in our economy since the last predefense year. The great increase in the total Economic Budget reflects the change-over from an economy of substantial unemployment and moderate production to an economy of unparalleled employment and production. Great significance lies in the fact that the Economic Budget for the year 1946 was almost as high as during the war year 1944, and more than twice as high as during the predefense year 1939. Even allowing for price changes, we have made such great strides forward in wealth and productivity that our thinking for the future can no longer be bound by the distant past.

The changes in the composition of the Nation's Economic Budget during these years also deserves attention.

During the war year 1944, Government expenditures were more than half the total Economic Budget.

Business responded to the Government's demand with record production.

Private income derived from production doubled the predefense level, even after allowance for the increase in taxes.

Consumer expenditures increased, but due to the shortages of civilian goods, effective price control, and patriotic motives for saving, they did not increase nearly as much as they otherwise would have, the difference going into savings.

In the transition year 1946, the expenditures of business and consumers once more took the lead, as the Government's wartime expenditures were drastically reduced. Business spent large sums for reconverting, overhauling, and modernizing plants and equipment and for replenishing depleted

TABLE I.—THE NATION'S ECONOMIC BUDGET, 1939, 1944, AND 1946

[Billions of dollars; current prices]

Economic Group	Predefense Calendar Year 1939			War Calendar Year 1944			Reconversion Calendar Year 1946 [1]		
	Receipts	Expenditures	Excess (+), Deficit (−)	Receipts	Expenditures	Excess (+), Deficit (−)	Receipts	Expenditures	Excess (+), Deficit (−)
CONSUMERS									
Income after taxes	68			133			142		
Expenditures		62			99			127	
Savings (+)			+6			+34			+15
BUSINESS									
Undistributed profits and reserves	8			11			11		
Gross capital formation [2]		10			4			27	
Excess of receipts (+) or capital formation (−)			−2			+7			−16
INTERNATIONAL									
Net imports									
Net exports		1			−2			5	
Net expenditures on foreign account			−1			+2			−5
GOVERNMENT (Federal, State, local)									
Receipts from the public other than borrowing	15			59			57		
Payments to the public		18			104			55	
Excess of receipts (+) or payments (−)			−3			−45			+2
ADJUSTMENTS									
For Government transfers to public [3]	−2	−2	0	−5	−5	0	−16	−16	0
For Government transfers abroad [4]					−2	+2		−4	+4
Total, Gross National Product	89	89	0	198	198	0	194	194	0

[1] Preliminary.

[2] Includes residential construction, but excludes net exports.

[3] Includes transfers of funds which are included in private receipts and Government expenditures but do not involve addition to the Nation's output, such as unemployment compensation, veterans' readjustment allowances, mustering-out pay, etc.

[4] Includes loans to foreign governments, subscriptions to international organizations, reimbursable lend-lease, etc.

pipe lines of inventories. High business activity resulted in high levels of consumer income and expenditures. Consumer spending was further increased by the use of wartime savings and expanding installment credit, and in the case of veterans by mustering-out pay and readjustment allowances.

As a point of departure for examining our objectives for this year, it is useful to present tentative estimates of the rates at which expenditures and receipts in the Nation's Economic Budget were running at the end of 1946. This is shown in Table II.

In comparing preliminary estimates for the fourth quarter of 1946 with those for the year as a whole, the significant changes may be summarized as follows:

1. Government expenditures were reduced. This was highly desirable, but it meant that much higher private expenditures were needed to sustain maximum employment and production.

2. Business expenditures increased, but a part of the increase reflected higher prices rather than increased production.

3. Consumer expenditures rose, but practically all of the increase was attributable to the price rise. Consumer incomes rose less than expenditures and actually declined in real terms.

This trend in the position of consumers becomes of central importance as we turn to a consideration of our prospects for 1947.

IV. GOALS FOR 1947

The Employment Act requires that this Economic Report set forth the levels of employment, production, and purchasing power needed to carry out the policy of the Act. This policy is to create and maintain "conditions under which there will be afforded useful employment opportunities, including self-employment, for those able, willing, and seeking to work, and to promote maximum employment, production, and purchasing power."

EMPLOYMENT OBJECTIVES

We do not know exactly how many people will want jobs during 1947. Our labor force fluctuates by several million during the course of any year, with the changing seasons, with boys and girls of school age going back to the classroom, and with part-time workers coming into and going out of the labor force. The purposes of the Act would be substantially achieved if during 1947 we sustain employment at about the 1946 levels

TABLE II.—THE NATION'S ECONOMIC BUDGET DURING THE 4TH QUARTER OF THE CALENDAR YEAR 1946
[Preliminary estimates; billions of dollars]

Economic Group	4th Quarter Seasonally Adjusted Annual Rates			Year as a Whole		
	Receipts	Expenditures	Excess (+) or Deficit (−)	Receipts	Expenditures	Excess (+) or Deficit (−)
Consumers	148	135	+13	142	127	+15
Business	14	33	−19	11	27	−16
International	....	4	−4	....	5	−5
Government	56	51	+5	57	55	+2
Adjustments: Transfer Payments	−13	−18	+5	−16	−20	+4
Gross national product	205	205	0	194	194	0

or slightly higher.

In maintaining a high level of total civilian employment, we must also achieve a better distribution between localities of labor scarcity and labor surplus; between occupations that are short of workers and occupations that are overcrowded. The proper use of our workers is equally important both to the economy and to the individual.

PRODUCTION OBJECTIVES

During the last quarter of 1946, total national production is estimated to have reached an annual rate of 205 billion dollars. We know, however, that we are not yet turning out goods as fast as we are capable of doing with our present plant, manpower, and material resources. Bottlenecks in the supply of certain parts and materials have slowed down production. So have labor-management disputes. With maximum employment in 1947, we should be able to increase our total output significantly, although limits may be imposed by shortages of basic materials.

It is not yet clear that our basic industries are fully adjusted to a 200-billion-dollar peacetime economy. It will become increasingly important that capacity goals in the basic industries such as steel, power, and transportation be set high enough so as not only to sustain present and foreseeable levels of economic activity, but also to permit their expansion.

It is not practical to state in physical terms just exactly how much our production should be during 1947 because of the great variety of goods and services which our economy produces. To state production in terms of dollars is of doubtful usefulness at the present time because price levels may move up or down and any dollar figure set forth now

might prove to be misleading. We do know, however, that a labor force of the anticipated size can be expected to produce more goods and services during 1947 than were produced during the past twelve months. Perhaps an over-all increase of 5 percent might be a reasonable objective for maximum production.

A considerable amount of last year's production went into the rebuilding and re-equipping of our manufacturing plant and the replenishing of producers' and dealers' inventories. We can expect an increased flow of consumer goods during 1947 even if there were to be no increase in total output. Hence, a 5-percent increase in total production would mean a greater proportionate increase of consumer goods.

The question, therefore, will become one of the ability of consumers to buy the total supply of products offered to them.

PURCHASING POWER OBJECTIVES

Consumer purchasing power depends upon the flow of money into consumers' hands as current income. It depends also on the use of past savings and the rate of current saving. It depends on the use of credit and it depends upon what money will buy; that is, upon the level of prices.

No attempt will be made to set a dollar figure on the purchasing power needed to buy the goods and services which the Nation will produce in 1947. It is plain, however, that if employment is to remain high and if production is to increase in 1947, real purchasing power must rise sufficiently to take the increased production off the market.

It has been stated that maximum production for 1947 would give us an over-all increase of some 5 percent above the level reached during the last quarter of 1946.

This increase would be due only in small part to a slight rise in the number of workers employed, and principally to the increased efficiency of the productive process as the lingering impediments to maximum production are eliminated.

What are the chances that consumers could buy an additional several billion dollars' worth of product if present prices and pay rates were maintained? Only a minor portion of the value of the additional goods and services produced in 1947 would be reflected in additional consumer income. The greater part of the additional income would be represented in the surpluses of governments and in reserves of business concerns. Thus it follows that consumers would have to buy considerably more goods and services with only slightly increased income. This could be done only if consumers made still freer use of credit, or if they reduced the rate of their new savings and drew heavily upon their past savings. Although consumer credit has not yet reached prewar levels, it has already expanded greatly, and still freer use might build up difficulties of the future. The rate of net savings, as shown elsewhere in this Report, has receded to a point below which it can hardly be expected to fall. Increasing consumer purchasing power in this way could at best be only a temporary solution, and certainly not a desirable one.

Another method by which the markets could be cleared of the enlarged volume of goods and services produced in 1947 would be to enlarge the real purchasing power of the consumers by increasing their incomes. It would be unrealistic, however, to expect that this increase in real purchasing power of consumers could occur solely through a corresponding increase in *money* incomes. An attempt to raise income by the amount necessary would mean such large increases

in money wages and salaries at certain points as to threaten curtailments of production or wage-price spirals. Further, there is no practical way to distribute such wage and salary increases throughout the whole population in such a manner as to effect the desired supports to the market. The groups of wage and salary earners whose purchasing power has been most reduced are the very ones who are likely to participate least in an increase of money earnings. Such concentration of pay increases within particular groups would make even more difficult the task of obtaining a sufficient total increase to sustain maximum employment, production, and purchasing power.

Thus it follows that we could not expect to attain the economic objectives for this year solely by an increase in money incomes. A major approach to bringing real purchasing power of consumers into balance with productive capacity this year must be through reduced prices.

The emphasis on price reduction as a major route for an increase in consumers' purchasing power does not overlook the desirability of increases in pay rates in some sectors.

It follows that only through adjustments both in the price and pay structure, made with discriminating regard for specific circumstances rather than on an over-all national basis, can we achieve a sustained demand for the maximum output which the American economy is able to produce this year.

V. FAVORABLE AND UNFAVORABLE FACTORS IN 1947

Because the health of our economy depends on the acts of 140 million people with millions of separate enterprises, including farming, business, and professional, it is not possible to forecast the precise course of events a year in advance in a report of this kind. Indeed, the Employment Act contemplates that the state of the Nation's economic health must be constantly watched so that timely policies may be adopted during the course of the year as conditions change. We can, however, appraise in advance some of the favorable and unfavorable factors affecting the expenditures of consumers, business, foreign buyers, and Government.

CONSUMER INCOME AND EXPENDITURES

The main facts about consumer income, expenditures, and purchasing power are given in Appendix B, Tables II, III, and V. Here I shall comment briefly upon a few of the favorable and unfavorable factors.

Favorable factors in consumer demand

Consumer demand has been at very high levels since VJ-day. This has been due largely to two factors: First, the pent-up demand for many goods that have been scarce in recent years; and, second, a level of incomes and purchasing power substantially higher than in prewar years.

Some of the pent-up demands are gradually being met, but during this year we can anticipate continued high demand for a number of items that have been scarce, including housing, automobiles, appliances, and many housefurnishings.

With larger supplies of durable goods coming on the market this year, an increased proportion of consumer expenditures may be made for these items and a smaller proportion for nondurable goods and services. Such a shift may be listed as a favorable factor because it will tend to-

ward the reduction of the prices of many nondurable goods and services which were raised to extraordinarily high levels in 1946 because of the concentration of consumer expenditures in these fields.

The most solid and permanent foundation for consumer demand is current disposable income. In this there has been great improvement since the prewar period, even when account is taken of the increase in consumers' prices. The following table illustrates this:

TABLE III.—PER CAPITA DISPOSABLE INCOME

Year or Quarter	Actual Dollars	1944 Dollars
1935–39 (average).............	497	623
1944......................	995	995
1945......................	1,000	978
1946 [1]...................	1,026	925
Seasonally Adjusted Annual Rates:		
First quarter..............	983	950
Second quarter...........	1,008	958
Third quarter.............	1,054	921
Fourth quarter........... [1]	1,060	880

[1] Preliminary estimates based on incomplete data.

The American public had a "disposable" income (after taxes) of 145 billion dollars in 1946. This represents an average of $1,026 per capita. In the prewar period, 1935–39, the corresponding figure was $497. It is true that a large part of this increase in income was absorbed by higher prices. The Consumer Price Index in 1946 averaged 39 percent above the 1935–39 level. This index measures the increase in the retail prices of most of the goods and services bought by families with low to moderate incomes. It provides a rough measure of the general rise in prices paid by consumers as a whole. Thus, it appears that average per capita incomes rose considerably more than prices. This means that the average per capita real purchasing power in 1946 was substantially greater than in the prewar period.

In consequence of these improvements, and in spite of some continued shortages, the average American family is buying more food, clothing, and other things than ever before. The total volume of consumption of these and other things, particularly durable goods, need to be maintained and expanded if 1947 is to be a year of maximum production.

Unfavorable factors in consumer demand

Despite the continuance of many favorable factors, the recent trends in consumer

purchasing power are disturbing. Many groups of consumers suffered a larger drop in purchasing power in the latter half of 1946 than is indicated by the trends in average per capita disposable income shown in Table IV. The purchasing power of wages has dropped seriously, especially during the past six months. The $46 weekly take-home pay of the average factory worker in October 1946 bought only about as much as the $35 he received in April 1942.

In consequence of these developments, and the appearance of more goods on the market, there has been a marked change in saving by consumers, indicated in the following table:

TABLE IV.—TRENDS IN CONSUMERS' SAVINGS

Year or Quarter	Disposable Income	Less: Consumer Expenditures	Equals: Savings	Percent of Disposable Income	
				Spent	Saved
	(Billions of dollars)				
1935–39 average	64.3	58.8	5.5	91.4	8.6
1940	72.9	65.7	7.3	90.1	9.9
1941	88.7	74.6	14.2	84.1	15.9
1942	110.6	82.0	28.6	74.1	25.9
1943	124.6	91.3	33.3	73.3	26.7
1944	137.4	98.5	38.9	71.7	28.3
1945	139.6	106.4	33.1	76.2	23.8
1946 [1]	144.5	127.0	17.5	87.9	12.1
Seasonally Adjusted Annual Rates:					
First quarter	138.0	120.9	17.1	87.6	12.4
Second quarter	141.8	122.0	19.8	86.0	14.0
Third quarter	148.4	129.4	19.0	87.2	12.8
Fourth quarter [1]	149.7	135.5	14.2	90.5	9.5

[1] Preliminary estimate based on incomplete data.

NOTE.—Detail will not necessarily add to totals because of rounding.
Source: Department of Commerce.

In the war year 1944, consumers saved about 28 percent of their total disposable income. A major part of this saving reflected shortages of civilian goods, effective price ceilings, and patriotic bond purchases. The rate of savings has fallen substantially

since then, and by the end of 1946 had dropped to a little less than 10 percent of this disposable income. This was only slightly above the level of savings in the prewar years 1935–39. It is doubtful whether the rate of consumer savings will or even can be reduced much further except by adversity.

In spite of the high rate of savings during the war, it is unsafe to assume that most American families still have enough savings in hand to supplement current income for any considerable length of time. Recent surveys indicate that 24 percent of American families held no war bonds or bank accounts in 1945, and 29 percent held less than $500 of savings in these forms. Available data point to the fact that past savings have been used to supplement current incomes during this past year.

Another element in current trends is the rapid increase in installment and credit buying during recent months. Consumer credit totaled almost a billion and a half dollars more in November 1946 than in March. But undue extension of deficit financing on the part of millions of American families can gravely hurt our business system and lead in the end to deficit financing by the Government. In the long run, consumers must rely on current incomes for purchasing power.

If consumer incomes should remain at current levels, we would expect savings to drop little, if any. Consequently we would not expect consumers as a whole to spend much more money than they were spending at the end of the year, without considerable expansion in consumer credit, unless total consumer incomes are increased.

Some of my short-range recommendations bear upon this problem.

BUSINESS INCOME AND OUTLAYS

Business investment, as the term is used in the Nation's Economic Budget, includes investment in industrial plant and equipment, in inventories, in commercial construction, and in residential construction. To maintain maximum production and employment in 1947 it is desirable that business investment be at an annual rate at least equal to the annual rate prevailing in the last quarter of 1946.

Plant and equipment

During the war years, a large deferred demand for industrial and commercial construction and equipment had been accumulating.

In 1946, business investment in plant and equipment approximated 15 billion dollars as compared to 12 billion dollars in 1929 and about 7 billion dollars in 1939. Even with allowances for a substantial rise in costs, it is evident that the most recent rate of investment in plant and equipment is much higher than before the war and the defense program.

For the long run, continuation of expenditures for privately financed productive facilities at anywhere near the recent levels will depend upon the size of our peacetime market, investment incentives, and the rate of technological progress, rather than upon backlog.

Inventories

Business inventories increased six to seven billion dollars in 1946, and at the end of the year were worth about 33 billion dollars. Although this sum is not disproportionate to total sales, there may be a decline in the rate of accumulation in 1947. As uncertainties in supply and price clear up, inventories will become more stable. A reduction in the rate of inventory accumulation will mean a lower level of business investment in this area and raises the question of whether or how it is to be offset by increases in other forms of investment or consumer expenditures.

Commercial construction

During 1946, the volume of commercial construction, although limited by the shortage of materials and by the requirements of the Veterans' Emergency Housing Program, reached one billion dollars. The Civilian Production Administration was obliged to defer a large proportion of the nonresidential building applications so that demand for commercial buildings remains high.

In addition, the distributors of goods and services as a whole, although with individual exceptions, have enjoyed record profits during the past year and apparently are in a position to finance an expansion of their capital facilities. However, the high costs of construction tend to offset in some degree the favorable outlook created by the continued existence of substantial demand.

At the present time not only have new residential areas been built up without a corresponding building up of commercial facilities, but substantial additional residential construction would create still further demand for commercial facilities.

Residential construction

Investment in residential construction, which totaled about 3⅓ billion dollars in 1946, would need to approximate 6 billion dollars in 1947 at the current price level in order to maintain a satisfactory level of activity in this field. As a result of the Veterans' Emergency Housing Program in 1946 the supply of materials has been increased sufficiently to permit the building of at least 1,000,000 houses in 1947.

However, the price problem in housing is even more serious than in other lines because the gap between consumer income and housing prices is so great. While material prices may fall substantially this year, the gap will still remain dangerously high, especially for the lower income groups. But even if the backlog demand provides a ready market for all the housing which is produced in 1947, this superficially satisfactory situation would plant the seeds of a collapse in residential construction within a few short years because the number of families who can afford high-priced houses comprises only a small part of the population.

Favorable factors in business demand

The prospects for business investment are brightened by several clear elements of strength. The first of these is the availability of abundant aggregate funds including ample bank credit.

The second favorable factor is that profits in most lines of industry and business have been highly rewarding during 1946 and have been rising quarter by quarter. The profits outlook for 1947 suggests adequate motive for investment in plant, equipment, and inventory to meet the wants of a people functioning at maximum employment.

Still another favorable factor is the backlog demand for construction.

Unfavorable factors in business demand

Threatening the continuation and expansion of business investment is the fear that a drop in general consumer demand may be in the offing.

Another main factor that could adversely affect business confidence, and thus business demand, would be the recurrence of serious management-labor disputes. Also, the high

25

cost of housing constitutes an adverse factor. Finally, business demand may be somewhat restricted by shortages of certain basic materials.

INTERNATIONAL TRANSACTIONS

The net balance of international transactions in 1946 was about the same as we can anticipate for 1947. Some changes in the components of that balance and in the methods of financing it, however, are both desirable and likely to occur.

Intense demand of foreign countries for goods available only or chiefly in this country has been one of the factors accounting for a high level of employment, production, and purchasing power in the United States during 1946.

Our receipts from the sales of goods and services abroad have recently been running at a rate of about 15 billion dollars a year, compared with only 4 billion dollars prior to the war.

Foreign demand for United States goods at present is associated with the incompleteness of reconstruction in war-devastated areas, and it will continue to be high during 1947, even though some countries may be reluctant to purchase at our current high prices. Sufficient resources will be available to foreign countries to finance urgently needed purchases from us. Any recession in domestic demand would permit us to meet some of the now unsatisfied foreign demand, with a resulting increase in exports. Even if this should be confined to a rise in quantities rather than in the dollar values it would be a factor cushioning the effects of any dip in domestic production and employment.

Should fears concerning our willingness and ability to buy and lend abroad increase, however, foreign countries may husband their dollar resources so as to make them available over a longer period. In this event our exports would be reduced.

GOVERNMENT BUDGETS

In the Budget Message, I review in detail expenditures and receipts for the current fiscal year, and transmit recommendations for the next fiscal year. There is no need to repeat those details in this Economic Report. It should be noted that the Government receipt and expenditure figures used in the Economic Report are not identical with the conventional figures of budget estimates, because they refer to the calendar year rather than to the fiscal year and because they are on a consolidated and cash basis in order to measure the economic impact of Government transactions on the economy.

With an outlook of high economic activity for the current year, the revenue policies are designed to balance the budget and achieve a surplus toward the retirement of the national debt. The expenditure policies are designed exclusively to cover the essential cost of national defense and war liquidation, to meet our international commitments and the obligations to war veterans under existing law, to carry forward programs required by the Congress, and to take some small but essential further steps toward fulfilling the duties of alert and progressive government.

Nevertheless, it is obvious that Government transactions, which—including Federal, State, and local government—total more than a fourth of our national product, profoundly affect the whole economy. An analysis of the economic impact of Government expenditures is facilitated by a break-down of the totals according to the type of recipients and character of the payments. Federal payments to the public are classified along lines of economic significance in the following estimates:

TABLE V.—FEDERAL CASH PAYMENTS (INCL. NET LOANS) TO THE PUBLIC

[Billions of dollars]

Payments to—	Calendar year 1946	1947	Change
1. Active Federal personnel:			
Civilian...	5.2	4.3	—0.9
Military...	6.1	3.6	—2.5
Total..	11.4	7.9	—3.5
2. Individuals (other than active Federal personnel):			
Civilian...	4.1	3.7	—0.4
Military...	7.8	6.5	—1.3
Total..	11.9	10.2	—1.7
3. Farmers (incl. food subsidies) [1].................................	1.0	1.2	+0.2
4. Business [1]...	1.8	1.0	—0.8
5. Holders of the Federal debt (interest payments)........................	3.9	3.7	—0.2
6. State and local governments..	1.0	1.5	+0.5
7. International organizations, foreign governments and U.S. exporters.........	2.1	3.9	+1.8
8. Producers of goods and services, transportation, and miscellaneous..........	11.6	9.7	—1.9
Total..	44.7	39.0	—5.7

[1] Excluding payments for purchase of goods and services.

Detail will not necessarily add to totals due to rounding.   Calendar year 1947 is estimated.

While Federal cash expenditures are expected to decline by about 6 billion dollars from calendar year 1946 to calendar year 1947, State and local expenditures are expected to increase by approximately 1 billion dollars, largely because of a probable increase in expenditures for public works, veterans' bonuses, and an increase in pay rates.

Thus there will be a net reduction in governmental expenditures on all levels by about 5 billion dollars. As has been shown in Table II above, a considerable decline in Federal expenditures took place during the calendar year 1946, and only a small further decline is expected for this year as compared with the end of last year. The economy seems already to have adjusted itself to the decline in Federal spending that took place during the first three quarters of 1946 without a net loss in employment or production. This testifies to the effectiveness of reconversion policies.

During the war, State and local payments were reduced below prewar level whereas receipts from the public increased somewhat. The total of State and local gross debt was reduced by about 4 billion dollars.

Since VJ-day, State and local expenditures have steadily increased. This trend is likely to continue in 1947.

State and local revenues in 1947 will probably not be greatly different from those in 1946 unless there is a sharp drop in economic activity or prices. Payments to and receipts from the public of State and local governments will be in approximate balance during this year.

VI. SUMMARY OF ECONOMIC CONDITIONS
AND TRENDS

On the plus side of the economic ledger we possess a fabulous wealth of resources. Our industrial plant is larger and, in many cases, better than ever before. Funds for business expansion are ample and profit incentives are high in most lines. Our labor force has greatly increased its number of semiskilled and skilled workers. The spending power of consumers, as a whole, is much higher than it ever was before the war. Consumer desires are fortified by a backlog of unsatisfied wants, particularly for housing, commercial construction, automobiles, household appliances, furnishings, and other durable goods. There are long-deferred and needed public works—Federal, State, and local. There is a strong and sustained foreign demand. More than that, we can be optimistic about the desire to buy, because of the higher standards of living which almost all of our people have recently enjoyed and which they do not want to forego.

While these favorable factors in our economic situation are fundamental, it is more practical and profitable to examine weaknesses that need corrections than to congratulate ourselves upon the blessings which we already enjoy.

1. Chief among the unfavorable factors is the marked decline in real purchasing power of great numbers of consumers, resulting from the large price increases in the second half of last year. Maximum production and employment this year would yield a substantial increase in the available supply of consumer goods and services, especially in the area of durable goods. This requires higher real purchasing power to take the goods off the market.

If price and wage adjustments are not made—and made soon enough—there is danger that consumer buying will falter, orders to manufacturers will decline, production will drop, and unemployment will grow—unless consumers resort to large additional borrowing and use of past savings to buy the increased supply of goods. These temporary expedients are limited in power and even if available would merely postpone the day of reckoning.

2. Weakening of the activity of investment might operate also as an obstacle to maximum employment, production, and purchasing power. If industrial and commercial construction slackens, and prices for residential construction remain high as compared with incomes of laborers and white-collar workers, our maximum employment objective might be threatened this year or soon thereafter.

3. Labor-management strife, with severe work stoppages, remains a possibility. This would directly interfere with production or employment by creating or intensifying shortages of materials, parts, or equipment. Through creation of uncertainties about demand or supply and costs of materials, it might lead to reductions in business outlays for plant, equipment, and inventories.

That is why in my State of the Union Message I placed so much stress upon successful labor-management relations.

During this year, the underlying favorable factors are strong enough to maintain high prosperity. But this year brings us face to face with maladjustments and unfavorable possibilities which, if not corrected or prevented, could cause a recession in production and employment. The Government will watch this situation and be prepared for action if needed.

I shall now proceed to discuss the contribution labor, business, agriculture, and the Government can make to the solution of these basic problems, along with recommendations related to other elements in a "national economic policy" as called for by the Employment Act.

VII. RECOMMENDATIONS

SHORT-RANGE PROGRAM

My short-range recommendations have long-range significance as well. But they merit immediate attention from the Congress and from the people as a whole because of their influence upon economic conditions in 1947.

1. Prices and wages

Removal of emergency price and wage controls has restored the main responsibility for prices and wages to business, labor, farmers, and consumers. The Government can point out dangers seen from the perspective of the whole economy, but the correctives must largely be applied by others.

Business should reduce prices wherever possible in order to bring about the necessary increase in consumer purchasing power to bolster their markets. Price reductions are especially needed in the case of goods such as many articles of food, clothing, housefurnishings, and building materials, whose prices have risen out of line. If business makes these reductions in a timely and orderly way, it will help sustain markets rather than destroy them.

Farmers must realize that last year's exceptional farm prices will fall somewhat as world food supplies increase and as consumers find a more ample supply of durable goods to purchase. Existing price supports afford protection against a severe price decline.

Labor, on its part, must recognize that high volume at low costs and low prices requires high productivity and the absence of restrictions on production. For its own advantage as well as that of the country at large, labor should refrain from demands for excessive wage increases that would require price increases or would prevent price reductions that are necessary to sell the capacity output of the product.

Management in turn should recognize that increased productivity permits wage increases in some cases as well as price reductions; and that wages and salaries need to be raised where they have lagged substan-

tially behind the increase in living costs in the past few years or where they are substandard.

But just as there can be no universal or uniform rule to govern price reductions, so there can be no uniform rule relating to wages. Both price adjustments and wage adjustments are necessary in the ensuing months. Wage adjustments, like price adjustments, need to be made with a discriminating regard for individual situations throughout the economy.

The Government can help in several ways to maintain a balance between prices and wages. Procurement agencies will avoid policies that stimulate price increases or prevent reductions. Disposal of surplus goods will be speeded. The antitrust laws will be applied vigorously to prevent and eliminate restrictive practices and pricing abuses.

The Congress should take steps at once to extend rent control beyond next June. A large increase in rents would substantially reduce consumer purchasing power.

On the wage side, the Congress should extend the coverage of the Fair Labor Standards Act to classes of workers in interstate commerce now excluded, and should raise the minimum wage in view of the substantial rise in the cost of living and in the national production since it was enacted.

2. Social security

I shall treat generally of the social-security program in a subsequent section dealing with long-range programs and recommendations. In view of current economic trends, however, certain action is desirable at once. I urge the Congress to take immediate steps to revise benefit payments under the social-security system. The Congress has already authorized a temporary increase in public assistance benefits. This legislation expires by the end of this year and new legislative action is required. Benefits under the old-age and survivors' insurance system should also be adjusted. These measures are necessary to alleviate real hardship which has been aggravated by increases in the cost of living. Beyond that, adequate social-security benefit payments provide a desirable support to mass purchasing power.

3. Housing

More than a million additional housing units need to be started in 1947. This goal will not only furnish badly needed shelter to our veterans and other citizens, but will result in a sizable contribution of the housing industry toward employment and purchasing power. At the lowest cost levels foreseeable this year, one million additional housing units will approximate an investment of 6 billion dollars during 1947.

As shortages of materials and manpower disappear, the main threat to a high volume of housing is the high level of current housing prices relative to the volume of consumer income.

To reduce the cost of housing on all fronts and by all desirable methods, we must start as promptly as possible a long-range housing program. Such a program can stimulate large investments in land acquisition and preparation for development. It can start the flow of new types of private investment into housing ventures. It can bring the traditional home-building industry into rental housing as well.

No subject has received more protracted study by the Congress leading to more uniform conclusions. Nonpartisan housing legislation was introduced in the Seventy-ninth Congress and passed the Senate by a large majority.

On several occasions, I have urged enactment of this program which was developed within the Congress itself. I again urge enactment of this program at the earliest possible moment.

4. Taxation

Expert and lay opinion is in agreement on the rule of sound public finance that calls for a surplus in Government revenues over expenditures while employment is high and the total of income is large. In the present economic situation, it is clear that it would be unsound fiscal policy to reduce taxes.

Everyone is agreed that the tax burden is great and should be reduced as soon as possible. When reductions come, it will be important that they be fairly and equitably distributed, that they contribute to the maintenance of purchasing power by reducing the burden on the mass of consumers, and that they help provide the work and business incentives essential for a high level of production. There are various ways of accomplishing these objectives of tax policy and of making an equitable reduction of taxes fairly distributed over all levels of income. These problems should receive careful study so that we are adequately prepared for wise action when the time comes.

5. Labor-management relations

I have transmitted to the Congress, in my State of the Union Message, recommendations covering the broad field of labor-management relations, and need not dwell further on them here.

It is important, however, to emphasize once more, in relation to our goal of a permanent high-production, high-employment economy, the key responsibility that both management and labor have in helping to achieve this goal. Sound collective bargaining is essential.

In order to build an enduring prosperity for ourselves and our children, we must and we shall solve the problem of making necessary adjustments in wages and working conditions without round after round of crippling and futile halts in production.

The war has left us a tremendously increased productive potential, and further increases are in store. In order to keep our expanding economic activity in line with our growing capacities, the extraordinary postwar demand that we enjoy today must be transformed into sustained demand of an expanding peacetime economy.

Elimination of wartime controls does not mean that we want to go back to the size of economy we had before the war. The possibilities and requirements of a sustained 200-billion-dollar economy differ from those of an unstable 100-billion-dollar economy.

A variety of measures will be needed to fortify the basic structure of the American economy before the transformation from war and reconversion to a high-consumption peacetime economy is completed. We are still at the threshold in formulating a program of consistent polices designed to give business, agriculture, and labor the opportunities which are envisaged in the Employment Act.

A long-range program designed to strengthen the structure of the American economy should include policies toward:

1. Efficient utilization of the labor force;
2. Maximum utilization of productive resources;
3. Encouragement of free competitive enterprise;
4. Promoting welfare, health and security;
5. Cooperation in international economic relations;
6. Combating economic fluctuations.

1. Efficient utilization of the labor force

The Nation's labor force is its greatest productive asset. Prudent use of our human resources requires a working population not only large and well-trained, but enjoying high American standards of health, education, security, and personal and political freedom.

We must develop and utilize fully the skills of our labor force. We must improve productive efficiency through industrial training and counseling focused on employment opportunities in various occupations, industries, and localities. I am directing the Federal agencies concerned to initiate a study of these programs, in cooperation with State and local authorities, in order to improve such training and services and to remedy inconsistencies and gaps.

The return of the Employment Service to State administration should not result in its disintegration into 48 disconnected pieces, nor in the subordination of the placement service to unemployment insurance. An efficient placement service requires uniform minimum standards and an integrated interstate system for disseminating job information and placing workers across State lines.

We must end discrimination in employment or wages against certain classes of workers regardless of their individual abilities. Discrimination against certain racial and religious groups, against workers in late middle age, and against women, not only is repugnant to the principles of our democracy, but often creates artificial "labor shortages" in the midst of labor surplus. Employers and unions both need to reexamine and revise practices resulting in discrimination. I recommend that, at this session, the Congress provide permanent Federal legislation dealing with this problem.

2. Maximum utilization of productive resources

In our free-enterprise system, we rely mainly upon private initiative to expand the productive base of the economy. Our productive capacity has grown not only through technological developments, but also through a steady stream of additions to plant and equipment. Output per man-hour has increased on the average some 3 percent per year over the decades.

The whole history of America indicates that this progress can be entrusted mainly to the initiative and inventiveness within our business system. But we do need Nation-wide concerted action to remove the fear that demand will periodically be inadequate to absorb maximum production. This is what puts brakes upon inventiveness and initiative.

Even in times of prosperity, aside from war, a substantial portion of our productive facilities has been idle. Recurrent depressions have brought paralysis to as much as one-third or even one-half of our plants and machines.

While the Government has a function in the encouragement of new industries and the development and dissemination of research, the greatest incentive that the Government can provide for business productivity is through helping to prevent depressions. If production incentives are adequate, business will expand without hesitancy when markets for its products are reasonably assured through a successful Nation-wide program for continuous maximum employment, production, and purchasing power.

Agriculture.—The soil is one of the most valuable economic assets of the Nation. Most effective utilization and conservation of this resource should be an important aim of the agricultural program of the Government.

We have experienced amazing technological progress in agriculture and further progress is to be expected. This progress necessitates adjustments in farming, adjustments in the processing and manufacture of foods and clothing, and in the process of distribution.

American agriculture suffered a severe depression in the years following the First World War. This situation was generally recognized by all groups. It resulted in large-scale governmental programs to help the farmer get incomes more nearly in line with the incomes of other groups.

The long-range agricultural policy of the Government should be aimed at preserving the family-sized farm and preventing another agricultural depression as we go through the readjustments following the Second World War. It should help to see that farmers' incomes do not fall below those earned by other comparable productive groups. This should involve the least possible interference in the management of actual farming operations. It should be accomplished without use of subsidies so far as feasible. We should seek to make it possible for farmers to earn good incomes through their own efforts.

Above all, the long-range agricultural policy of the Government should be based upon the principle of plenty and not upon the encouragement of scarcity. The term "maximum production" in the Employment Act applies to the farm as well as to the factory. This basic policy is inconsistent with a policy of production restriction, though we must take a realistic view of the proportion that agriculture as a whole bears to the economy and also of the relative amount of effort devoted to the several lines of production. Our domestic capacity to absorb the products of our farms—if farmers are encouraged to turn their productive efforts in the right directions—will be enormous as we get nearer to solving the problems of sustained employment and high purchasing power. How much of an export surplus from the United States the markets of the world will be able to absorb will depend in part on our international economic policies, notably as to industrial imports and overseas investments.

Agricultural production increased more than 30 percent during the war. Technological improvements in farming and in food distribution would make it possible not only to continue this high rate of production, but also to increase it substantially during the next few years.

The high rate of agricultural production during and since the war has been supported by unusually high rates of food and fiber consumption. For the satisfactory solution of our agricultural problems during the next several years it is essential that we maintain these high rates of consumption, or even increase them. This is desirable not only from the farmer's point of view, but from the point of view of American diets and standards of living.

The Congress has recently authorized a permanent school-lunch program in cooperation with the States. I hope this program will be expanded until we are sure that every American school child gets an adequate diet. In addition, we should study carefully the possible need for food and nutrition programs to reach low-income families.

The Congress also recently authorized a broad and strengthened program to improve the marketing and distribution of farm products. This includes the strengthening of research and educational work, as well as the improvement of the various marketing services performed by the Government. We shall need to give increasing emphasis to marketing during the next few years. Better marketing can go a long way toward maintaining adequate rates of consumption, with benefit to farmers and the public alike.

We must honor the Government's commitment to support farm product prices during the period of readjustment to a stabilized peacetime basis. However, experience within the past year has demonstrated, on a small scale, some of the dangers that may result from holding the support level for any commodity too high. This only leads to maladjustments within agriculture, to the wastage of food, and to unnecessarily large Government expense.

The Government's long-range program to support farm incomes at reasonable levels must be kept flexible. It should be designed to encourage adjustments of production in line with the capacity of markets to take products at a price remunerative to efficient farming. It should promote well-managed use of our vast resources of farm land, machinery, and agricultural labor in such ways as to be profitable to farmers and of maximum benefit to the public as a whole.

The standard of living on farms depends on more than the amount of money income received by farmers. Farm communities have never received comparable treatment with cities in such matters as education, housing, medical care, health, nutrition, and social security. Federal and State programs in these fields should give increasing attention to the needs of rural areas.

Regional development.—Wide regions of this country still hold the promise of tremendous economic development. The Government should examine particularly the contribution it can make toward this development by stimulating production and distribution of low-cost hydroelectric energy,

33

by developing flood control and navigation, by improving roads, by enforcing fair competitive rates of transportation, by removing barriers to truck transportation, by land drainage and irrigation projects. We need to rebuild croplands, grazing areas, and forests. Future programs of resource and industrial development should be prepared so that we can move ahead rapidly at the appropriate time.

Even under today's full employment conditions, there are a few chronically depressed areas, and some areas left stranded by the end of the war. These problem areas were created by the interplay of Nation-wide forces, and our Government has the responsibility of assisting these communities in developing ways and means of improving their positions. The Council of Economic Advisers will give particular attention to these problems.

Federal-aid programs.—The Federal Government is engaged in several programs of grants-in-aid to State and local governments involving large amounts of money. Further programs are planned. These programs, particularly those related to health and education, public works, and road and airport construction, contribute greatly toward bringing all sections of the country up to the levels of productivity consistent with American standards of living.

I have asked the Council of Economic Advisers to cooperate with the Bureau of the Budget and other Federal agencies concerned, and with State and local advisory committees, to undertake a study of Federal grants to State and local governments to determine to what extent revised standards for the distribution of these grants may take into account more fully the needs for support that exist in various parts of the country.

Public works.—Aggregate expenditures for public works are large. They obviously have a considerable effect upon the whole

economy. Further, since many public-works projects are not related to the daily problems of business operations nor to the daily needs of consumers, they are subject to adjustment in their time of commencement and their rate of progress. This had led, particularly in recent years, to an overemphasis upon the prospects of stabilizing our whole economy through the bold use of public works.

There are valid reasons why public works cannot accomplish as much toward stabilization as some have supposed. In the event of severe unemployment, they cannot be generated in sufficient volume to avoid supplementation by other means. In a period of mild recession, they cannot be generated on time to be fully effective. If the tempo of the public-works program is geared to some business index, the reserves accumulated for emergency use may be used after they are needed and they then become inflationary rather than stabilizing. Even if advance preparations are made through the completion of plans, the acquisition of sites, and the accumulation of funds, there will be an inevitable time lag between calling the emergency program into operation and the employment of men on the job.

These comments are substantiated by experience. The chief lesson to be learned is that no one device constitutes an adeqaute safeguard against recession or an adequate fighting apparatus against depression. All useful devices need to be thought through in advance and blended into a consistent program.

Instead of regarding public works as the first and foremost device to restore our whole economy when it sags, we should attempt to stabilize public-works construction according to our long-term needs. Increasing regularization of public-works expenditures at all levels of governmental activity over a long period will offer an assurance of a demand for capital, of a market for materials and equipment, and of a field for employment which will assist in stabilizing that segment of the business world. This approach to public works will have the further advantage of appraising their size and character in terms of our total national needs.

This policy by no means forestalls the expansion of public works as a sustaining factor if recessions or depressions should unfortunately develop despite our best efforts to avoid them. The very procedure necessary for long-term regularized expenditure will pave the way for more effective emergency use than in the past.

Research and patents.—The United States will this year invest more than 1 billion dollars in research. In order to protect national security and the development of the domestic economy, I have established by Executive Order [1] a Presidential Research Board to survey Federal research and development programs. The continuance of a research program of large magnitude for many years to come, together with the fact that many of the inventions resulting from it will be patentable, calls for action to protect the public interest in inventions and discoveries resulting from expenditures of public funds. I hope that suitable legislation for a uniform patent policy will be enacted by the Congress at this session.

3. Encouragement of free competitive enterprise

It is imperative that there be no restrictions on free competition resulting in curtailment of production and employment, or in maintenance of high prices, or in interference with freedom to invest funds, or in hampering the entry of new firms to any line of production or trade. I recommend

---

[1] Executive Order 9791 (3 CFR, 1943–1948 Comp., p. 578).

that the Congress review the studies made by the Temporary National Economic Committee and by other Congressional Committees with a view toward supplementing or strengthening existing legislation in this field. Among the steps to be taken is the extension of Section 7 of the Clayton Act to prohibit mergers by the acquisition of assets, as well as by the acquisition of stock control.

Enforcement of existing antitrust laws.— The Antitrust Division of the Department of Justice and the Federal Trade Commission have both labored under inadequate appropriations. They should be better supplied with funds so that their activities can be more closely integrated. Accordingly, I am recommending in the Budget Message increased appropriations for the control of monopolistic practices.

Encouragement of small business.—The Government should take affirmative action to enlarge the opportunities for efficient and enterprising small businesses.

I believe that the Government should study ways and means of facilitating the availability of long-term credit and equity capital to small and promising business enterprises.

The Department of Commerce has developed, and will further develop, business service programs providing businessmen with such information on markets and technical and commercial facts as only large establishments can provide by their own staffs.

Consideration should be given to the impact which existing taxes have upon small and growing businesses.

4. Promoting welfare, health, and security

There are certain programs of Government which have come to be looked upon as "welfare programs" in a narrow sense. This has placed them in an insulated compartment. They have not been sufficiently related to the needs of the economy as a whole. In fact, they are a part of the problem of maximum employment, production, and purchasing power.

The Employment Act presents the opportunity to abandon this insulation, and to put these programs back in the economic setting from which they must draw their sustenance.

Unemployment insurance is designed to take care of the unemployed as a matter of right rather than of charity, but it also provides purchasing power as a cushion against recessions, and its tax features are of general economic significance. Retirement and pension systems exist to take care of workers who have given of their years in factory, field, or office. But these systems, both on the income and outgo side, have a profound effect upon volumes of purchasing power, and the retirement age needs to be adjusted to the size and composition of our labor force and the trend of improved technologies. Health insurance relates clearly to the efficiency of workers and thus to the productivity of industry and agriculture. And this is even more true of education, which must be reshaped continuously to meet the changing demands and job opportunities of the machine age—or, some day, of the atomic age.

The total amounts of public outlays for these and other purposes need to be measured against the total size of our economy— its wealth and resources today, and the trends and policies which shape its future. Many of these programs have been born of a depression psychology. They have proceeded from the assumption that our enterprise system will necessarily fail to employ given numbers of people from time to time, and that these other programs must be brought forward to prime the pump or fill in the gaps. Here, too, we need a restatement. We should regard them rather as an inescapable obligation of an enlightened people, and we should expand them as our resources permit.

The relationship between these welfare programs and general economic conditions has been inadequately explored. Proposals for maximum employment, production, and purchasing power, and proposals traditionally regarded as being in the general-welfare area, should be integrated because they are interrelated. Further studies will provide the basis for this integration.

Public health and education programs.— Among those whose income is less than the minimum necessary for a decent subsistence are those who cannot earn their living because of physical unfitness or lack of educational training.

A combination of public health, nutrition, education, and regional development programs would create additional job opportunities and supply workers fit to fill these jobs. Relatively small Government expenditures for health and education yield a high national dividend. It is more economical to prepare people to earn a decent living than to care for them through relief.

The Federal Government is now spending a large amount of money for health and education programs for war veterans, but general expenditures in these fields are relatively small. I urge the Congress to give early consideration to expanded peacetime programs of public health, nutrition, and education.

Social security.—Although maximum employment would protect wage earners generally from the effects of prolonged mass unemployment, the individual is still exposed to many hazards of economic insecurity.

Our social security program has not kept pace with the times, nor with our increase in general living standards. Many individuals are not covered by the present provisions of the Act, and the benefit payments to those covered are inadequate under today's conditions.

I recommend that the Congress, cooperating with the States, take action that will lead to increasing the amount and duration of unemployment benefits. Present unemployment reserve funds are ample to support such increases.

I recommend that the Congress amend the social-security laws to extend the benefits of old-age and survivors' insurance to the occupational groups now excluded, and to include under unemployment compensation the employees of all establishments, regardless of size, in the industries now covered by the Unemployment Compensation Tax Act. In expanding general social security, the Congress should not overlook the railway workers, whose protection is under separate laws.

While we compensate workers for loss of wages due to unemployment arising from lack of work opportunities, we do not insure them against the risks of loss of earnings from temporary or permanent disability, nor against the costs of medical care. This represents not only a heavy loss for the individual but a great waste of productive manpower.

There is an urgent need to spread the risks arising from sickness and disability by insuring workers against the loss of income and by providing, through social insurance, ready access to essential preventive and curative medical services. I have, in a previous message, presented recommendations for a program of medical care and disability benefits. I urge early consideration of this program.

Our present social insurance system is financed by employee and employer contributions. We must recognize, however, that the employees' contributions and the employers' pay-roll tax curtail mass purchasing power and increase businessmen's costs. From an economic point of view, it would be desirable to finance a part of the social security system out of the general budget. Therefore, I propose that the Congress, in working out a system of financing an expanded social security program, give full consideration to the economic as well as the social import of various methods of taxation for this purpose.

5. Cooperation in international economic relations

While most of this Report has necessarily been devoted to the domestic aspects of employment, production, and purchasing power, we must bear in mind that we are part of a world economy. Our sales of goods and services abroad, amounting to about 15 billion dollars in 1946, played an important role in the maintenance of domestic production, employment, and purchasing power and may be expected to do so this year. Such a high level of exports reflects in large part the war destruction of productive capacity in other countries. If we are to maintain a well-balanced prosperity over a long period, our foreign trade must be established on a more permanent basis.

In the long run we can sell to other countries only if we are willing to buy from them, or to invest our funds abroad.

Both foreign trade and foreign investment are vital to maintaining a dynamic economy in this country.

The shortages we have suffered during the war and are even now experiencing have proved to us our need for foreign imports. We will continue to need imports not only to add richness and variety to our standard of living but also as a means of conserving strategic materials. We do not have to fear so-called foreign competition when we have maximum production, employment, and purchasing power. We must not, of course, indulge in indiscriminate reduction of barriers to imports. Such a policy is not contemplated.

For a few years we cannot expect to buy as much from abroad as other countries buy from us. We will find it profitable to invest a part of our savings in developing the world's productive resources through sound loans and investments of equity capital abroad. This is important not only in the first instance as an immediate outlet for our goods and services, the supply of which will be increasing in the coming years, but also as a means of permanently increasing foreign markets for our farmers and businessmen. The quickest demonstration of this can be seen by the fact that nations that are industrialized are our best customers.

Many countries fear economic depression in the United States as a threat to their own stability. If faced with the alternatives of smaller trade and economic insulation on the one hand or close relations with an unstable American economy on the other, many might prefer some insulation as the lesser evil.

In preference to either of these alternatives, these countries would choose closer relations with a stable American economy operating at high levels. They have already begun to cooperate toward achieving these related goals: economic stability and expansion of world trade. The International Monetary Fund, designed to stabilize exchange rates, and the International Bank for Reconstruction and Development, set up to facilitate the international flow of capital, have already started to operate. At our initiative, experts of 18 important governments recently worked out a tentative charter for an International Trade Organization. This charter embodies principles of commercial conduct designed to enlarge the beneficial flow of world trade, to reenforce the domestic employment and development programs of the cooperating governments and, by intergovernmental commodity agreements, to remove the depressing effects of burdensome world surpluses. This charter represents the first major effort in the field of trade to replace unilateral action—which often injured other countries and provoked retaliation—by cooperation, and joint action under a set of common principles. Continued progress in the formation of the International Trade Organization represents the most important step that we can take to reestablish a high volume of foreign trade on a sound basis.

The willingness of many other countries to enter the proposed trade organization will depend to a great extent on our attitude in connection with the reciprocal tariff negotiations scheduled for this year. In return for our own tariff concessions, we can hope to secure not only reduction of foreign tariffs and discriminations but also elimination of a mass of restrictions, in particular, rigid import quotas preventing our access to foreign markets. Thus we should press forward with our program to secure the reciprocal reduction of trade barriers.

If we fail to do our part in putting international economic relations on a healthier basis, it is quite likely that some other countries will feel compelled to increase their own controls. Such a development would tend to break the world into trading blocs and could have profound effects upon world politics and the prospects for creating an enduring peace.

6. *Combating economic fluctuations*

Only by blending all practicable programs in wise proportions can we be successful in stabilizing our economy at the highest feasible levels. The long-range policies I have outlined are designed to strengthen the structure of the economy and to reinforce its resistance to economic fluctuations.

The greater this power of resistance, the less need there will be for some of the limited and specialized stabilizing devices which have received much attention in recent years.

I have directed the Council of Economic Advisers and the other appropriate Government agencies to make a continuing study of the stabilization devices that may become necessary and to recommend their being placed in operation in ample time to insure the anticipated effect.

Among these devices are a well-integrated program of employment stabilization; improvements in the process by which workers find jobs and employers find workers; improvements in the tax structure; wise management of the public debt; and a flexible credit policy.

Continuing policy cannot be extemporized from month to month or even from year to year; most policies designed to increase the stability of the economy are of long-range character. Fortunately, we have time in which to plan deliberately and wisely, and in which to secure the cooperation of all our citizens in driving toward our common goal: an expanding economy of maximum production, employment, and purchasing power under a system of free competitive enterprise, with full recognition of the duties and responsibilities of forward-looking government.

HARRY S. TRUMAN

NOTE: The message and the complete report are published in "Economic Report of the President to the Congress, January 8, 1947" (Government Printing Office, 1947, 54 pp.). As printed above the charts and appendixes have been omitted.

5　Memorandum Concerning the Red Cross Campaign. *January 8*, 1947

Memorandum for the Heads of Executive Departments, Commissions, and Agencies:

The American Red Cross during the five years of World War II gave a full measure of devotion to the relief of human suffering and the welfare of our countrymen and allies in all parts of the world. In the past year the immense activities of this agency have been rechanneled from demands of war to the complex problems of peace and our great responsibilities in binding up the wounds of war.

During the coming year the war-related activities of the Red Cross will continue to be very extensive. Large numbers of men will still be in uniform. There are millions of veterans to whom the Red Cross has an obligation. Tens of thousands will be in Army, Navy and Veterans' hospitals for a long time to come. The Red Cross is trained

and equipped through its thousands of Home Service workers to give the service needed, but it is imperative that the necessary funds be obtained to continue Red Cross operations on behalf of the Army, Navy and the Veterans.

In communities of all sizes the health and educational services of the Red Cross reaching millions of homes with projects in First Aid, Water Safety, Accident Prevention, Home Nursing and Nutrition for the welfare and conservation of life are greatly needed. When disasters threaten the neighborhood or the nation as a whole we look to the American Red Cross for prompt and effective emergency help.

To help raise the funds essential to finance this vast program, I desire that all departments of the Government cooperate wholeheartedly through the creation of an effective organization for the solicitation of their gifts. I have designated the Secretary of the Interior, The Honorable Julius A. Krug as Chairman of the Government Unit for the Metropolitan Area of Washington.

The American people during the war years have given to the American Red Cross the largest sums ever entrusted to any humanitarian agency. Our gifts in this 1947 Red Cross Fund I am confident will continue this magnificent support. I assure you that the Red Cross will continue to discharge with fidelity and integrity those responsibilities to which it is committed. The cooperation of all citizens of goodwill will fully guarantee success of this great cause.

HARRY S. TRUMAN

6 The President's News Conference on the Budget. *January 8*, 1947

THE PRESIDENT. Sit down, gentlemen, please. Let anybody in who wants to come.

Mr. Ross: In the meantime, we have here mimeographed—prepared by the Budget—a sort of synopsis of it.

This is the so-called Budget Seminar, as you know. The information given here may be used, but without attribution. This is for background purposes only, except where the President may specifically state otherwise. The preliminary statement he will make, however, will be on the record, and copies of it will be made later and passed out to those who wish them, in mimeographed form.

Q. Will we be able to get them late this afternoon?

Mr. Ross: Yes, after the conference.

Q. On the record, Charlie, as a press conference would be?

Mr. Ross: Yes.

THE PRESIDENT. The statement will be on the record and will be handed out to you in the form in which it is, as a statement.

Are you ready?

Well, I am going to sit down and talk into this microphone, because this is—has every chance to be quite a long session.

[1.] The Budget which I shall transmit to Congress on Friday is a balanced budget. If our estimates are realized, the budget will be in balance for the first time since 1930. The President sent down a balanced budget in 1938, but the recession came on, if you remember, and receipts fell off, and the relief appropriations had to be increased, and so 1938 finally wound up with a deficit.

It is realistic and as complete as we know how to make it. It is based on a careful study of the needs of the various departments, and the funds required to carry out the obligations of the Federal Government under programs established by the Congress.

It is a tight budget. I believe it is fair to say that no department or agency feels that its needs are fully met. They are all quarreling about the meanness with which they have been treated by the President. In its preparation I instructed the Director of the Budget to require thorough and conclusive justification for every item which he recommended to me. There isn't an article—an item in this budget that has not been thoroughly and completely justified. In every borderline case the decision has been to eliminate expenditures rather than to include them. It has been necessary for us to be more hard-boiled in making many decisions than I like to be. I hope I am not naturally hard-boiled. We have had to reduce sharply requests for a number of programs which in my opinion would be worthwhile were it not for our urgent need to reduce expenditures.

[2.]   Those of you who have studied the Budget Message have found, I am sure, the answers to most of your questions. However, the table shows the major categories of expense which are included. And they are as follows: several certain fixed charges which will be reduced, and you know how much they amount to? Within just a few millions of $33 billion.

The first category of those fixed charges, of course, is Interest on the Public Debt, Refunds, Veterans Pensions and Insurance, Employees Retirement and Workmen's Compensation, Philippine War Damage Commission, and so forth. That amounts to 4 billion—$10,499 million.

[3.]   And the next item is National Defense, the Army, the Navy, Terminal Leave for Enlisted Personnel—amounts to $11,256 million.

[4.]   And then commitments, largely uncontrollable, is the next item in that fixed set up; that is, grants to States and cities, government and relief of occupied areas, international commitments and loans, domestic loans, subsidies and contributions, veterans readjustment benefits and hospital care and administration; and the total for veterans runs about 7 billion, in this budget. And if anybody feels that he can reduce that to any extent, he is much better than I give him credit for being.

The issuance and payment of Government obligations, revenue collections, and net postal operations, legislative, judicial, and the General Accounting Office—that is the pay for Senators and Congressmen—and for charges and things of that sort, and that amounts to $11,228 million. That makes a total of $32,983 million. And the total budget is $37,528 million. I have been told by my staff that this budget has been more difficult to prepare than any ever issued before, and I can believe it.

[5.]   Corporations and war agencies have been included in detail in the Budget for the first time. Last year we sent up three budgets at different periods of the year—the Annual Budget, the War Supplement, and the Corporation Budget. This year they have all been integrated into one budget. For 4 years the war agencies have been presented in a special budget and in supplements in the spring, and only the preliminary estimate of their total was included in the January budget.

[6.]   In this year's budget, expenditures and appropriations are grouped under a new functional classification, in order to present to the Congress and the people a clearer picture of the purposes for which Federal funds are intended. I hope the press will use the new classification. We have put the figures for 10 years, 1939 to 1948, on this basis. The new classification is a part of a continuing effort to make the budget understandable in spite of its inherent complexities.

Now we are living in a new age, so far as Government expenditures and taxes and things of that sort are concerned. I can remember, when I was a very small boy, when the first billion dollar Congress came along. I don't think that anybody in this audience is old enough to remember that. That was in 1892, and I remember the terrific campaign that was made for the re-election of Grover Cleveland on that billion-dollar Congress.

Well, now we are living in the days of the $40-billion-a-year—not a $40 billion Congress, but a $40-billion-a-year expenditure for the Government of the United States; and for your information, we are not going back to a billion-dollar Congress. We are going to meet this age as we faced—just as we are going to adjust ourselves to the machine age, which we have not succeeded in doing.

[7.]   I have got a chart here that is a most interesting thing, that I would like for all of you to look at when we get through. That's [*indicating*] what the balance of the budget, which I didn't read to you, is expended for. That's the executive branch of the Government. You see the President up there in the ring with all the various people who are responsible to him and who have to report to him in operating the Government of the United States. If I should see one of these individuals each day, it would take me 3 months to see them all, right straight along, day after day. Of course, the President works from 5 o'clock in the morning until 12 o'clock at night, every day, and still it is almost impossible to get on top of the things that have to be done.

I have had three separate and distinct messages for preparation for the Congress at this time, for the first time in the history of the layout, and those three messages have to be in harmony. The Message on the State of the Union, the Economic Report of the President, which contains some 54 pages, and the Budget, which is, I think—is thicker this year than it has ever been in the history of the country because of those comparisons that had to be made over the 10-year period. Yet the President is supposed to know all about the contents of each single one of them.

And for your information, he is as well informed as it is possible for one man to be on the subject! [*Laughter*] And for that reason I want you to be exceedingly painstaking and careful in the study of this Budget Message. This Summary which has been gotten out for your benefit, I think answers nearly all the questions, technical and otherwise; and then the preliminary statement which is in the first part of the Budget, and which is the Message on the Budget, covers the rest of the situation. I think it has been more clearly set out this year than it ever has been in history, in the history of my

connection with the Government.

I have been working on these budgets since 1935. I was on the Appropriations Committee of the Senate from January 3d, 1935, until I became Vice President, and then President; and I have had a lot of experience with those things. And I think this is the most comprehensive budget statement that has ever been gotten out in my memory. And I hope you will study it carefully. It is a very important document and it ought to be read in conjunction with the Economic Report and with the Message on the State of the Union, which was read to the Congress on the 6th.

And now then, any questions you want to ask—I have got the technical staff here to answer them in detail and in total—any way you want.

[8.] Q. Mr. President, in the Budget résumé, the figures as set up do not conform either to the receipts and revenues as they would be under existing law as it now is, or under your recommendations.

THE PRESIDENT. Why don't they?

Q. I don't know.

THE PRESIDENT. Well——

Director Webb: I think Mr. Jones, who is head of our Fiscal Division, can give you the answer on that.

Mr. Jones: There is a footnote, isn't there? That's the two exceptions. Otherwise it does reflect existing——

Q. The thing I couldn't follow was why——

Mr. Jones: Would you read the first three paragraphs. He indicates there that he did not take those two recommendations into his budget.

Q. Why wasn't it? Why not?

THE PRESIDENT. Because I don't want to take them in there until they are facts.

Q. Well, the transfer of corporate funds is taken in, Mr. President.

THE PRESIDENT. That's right.

Q. It isn't a fact yet.

THE PRESIDENT. It will be.

Q. It will require legislation, will it?

THE PRESIDENT. I don't think so. If it does, why we will get that legislation, because everybody is interested in that.

Q. I have a question on the same point, Mr. President. In the first paragraph it says that revenues under existing law are—actually the phrase is "existing tax laws at 37.7 billions." In the Budget résumé it says based on existing legislation the revenues will be 37.531. Now to my way of thinking laws on the books are sound, and there are two figures for the same thing.

THE PRESIDENT. One of them is the postal deficit. One of them counts, the other doesn't.

Q. The difference is $379 million, which is to be added under proposed legislation?

THE PRESIDENT. That's right.

Director Webb: That's right.

Q. But it is included in existing laws in the one case and excluded in the other.

THE PRESIDENT. No. I think you are mistaken. It is included in the budget, which a President has a right to include when he asks for legislation. It is not included in existing laws because it will require a law to balance the postal deficit, if we are going to meet that situation.

Q. The Congress can change then—can consider this the balanced budget, despite the fact that it will require some transfers——

THE PRESIDENT. Of course.

Q. ——to be balanced?

THE PRESIDENT. That's it. The President has the right to take into consideration the fact that he is asking for things that will create the situation.

[9.] Q. In your estimates here for National Defense, for the Army and Navy, sir, are you contemplating the saving that could

be effected by merger? I believe you told the Congress Monday that a substantial saving could result, and I wonder——

THE PRESIDENT. No, no. I am including in the Army and Navy budget what the Army and Navy asked for and what I finally concluded to give them.

Q. Could you tell us, sir, how much you think might be saved by merger?

THE PRESIDENT. No, I cannot.

Q. Any figures been—put out?

THE PRESIDENT. No. No, they have not.

Q. Would you tell us what the Army figure is, what they originally asked for?

THE PRESIDENT. No, no—the Army and Navy figure is what they asked for and what I finally concluded to give them, which is not nearly what they asked for.

[10.] Q. Mr. President, what is the type of additional revenue sought for the Post Office Department?

THE PRESIDENT. Well, the—there's a certain subsidy in the Post Office Department.

Q. Second-class mail?

THE PRESIDENT. Yes, which ought not to be paid by the Government. The people who profit by that subsidy are the ones who quarrel about other people having subsidies.

Q. Will you send a recommendation of any kind to Congress on the matter?

THE PRESIDENT. I am asking the Congress to meet that deficit.

Q. Your message doesn't indicate by what means——

THE PRESIDENT. No, that is up to the Congress.

Q. Mr. President, have they given you any figures on the cost of that second-class subsidy?

THE PRESIDENT. No, I have no figures.

Q. Always a controversy——

THE PRESIDENT. That has always been a matter of controversy, that's true.

[11.] Q. Mr. President, can you give us

the figure, that is, the difference between the military's request and the budget figures, sir?

THE PRESIDENT. Oh, it's—how much was it?—I think about $3 or $4 billion—13 billion they asked for, was it?

Director Webb: No, considerably more than that. Just one minute—I can give you that. It's complicated. Let Mr. Martin give you that figure.

Mr. Martin: The original estimates for the War Department, my recollection tells me, is about 9 billion, two.

THE PRESIDENT. They got 6 billion, 658.

Mr. Martin: Yes, sir.

Q. Is that appropriations?

Mr. Martin: Now some of that difference is because we are classifying occupied areas as other than military, and also the Manhattan Project, or the Atomic Service is being classified under Natural Resources. The Navy figure, I believe, was somewhat over 6 billion, four.

THE PRESIDENT. They will get 4 billion, 423.

Q. Are you speaking of appropriations in both cases?

Mr. Martin: Expenditures.

THE PRESIDENT. Expenditures.

[12.] Q. Mr. President, I would like—one point I am still not clear on are your receipts. You include, as I understand it, in your net budget receipts your changes under proposed legislation, referring that to the postal deficit.

THE PRESIDENT. That is correct.

Q. I am not clear on why the distinction, if we are including that number, including the additional excise taxes which you also ask for, in other words which is also proposed legislation?

THE PRESIDENT. Well, the additional excise taxes will amount to about a billion, two or three—I think—a billion, two or three hundred million dollars, and my proc-

lamation of December 31st would eliminate them beginning on July 1st. I am asking the Congress to restore them. Congress is talking about taking them off right now. I don't know what they are going to do. So I wanted to show that even without that we would still be in balance, but if we get that we will have a billion, two or three hundred million dollars to be applied on the debt, which I hope will take place.

Director Webb: The postal deficit, too, you haven't included it.

THE PRESIDENT. Any one of the legislative requests have been included in the figure for arriving at the balance.

Q. That is gravy stuff then?

THE PRESIDENT. No it isn't gravy. It all ought to be done, in my opinion.

Q. I mean it's gravy—surplus——

THE PRESIDENT. In my opinion—only one man's opinion.

Q. It makes the surplus larger?

THE PRESIDENT. It makes the surplus larger. Would go to reduce the debt which, if we only reduce the debt at the rate of a billion and a half a year—259 billion—will take a long time to pay off. [*Laughter*]

[13.] Q. Mr. President, have those corporate funds been extended?

THE PRESIDENT. I am hoping the Congress will legislate on the subject and will make arrangements——

Q. That is what's baffling me, that they are included in this résumé.

THE PRESIDENT. Well, we have got the money. The money is in the Treasury. All it needs is a bookkeeping proposition to transfer it to the general fund.

Secretary Snyder: Not a matter of raising any money.

THE PRESIDENT. It's not a matter of raising any money.

Q. I don't understand that. It does require legislation, doesn't it?

Director Webb: Yes it does, Mr. President,

but there has been no controversy.

THE PRESIDENT. He tells me that it does, but there has been no controversy about it. Well, I hope you will become unconfused. If you will read all this and keep asking us questions, we will try to clear your mind up.

Q. We will question you as much as we can.

[14.] Q. Mr. President, what has that military figure been adjusted to, without the Manhattan Project and the Occupied Areas?

THE PRESIDENT. M a n h a t t a n Project amounts to $443 million, and the—what's that?——

Director Webb: Occupied Areas.

THE PRESIDENT. 645—amounts to 645 million—that would be about a billion——

Q. A billion, 80.

THE PRESIDENT. A billion, 80 million dollars.

Q. Mr. President, on that basis, if you subtract the atomic energy cost and the occupied areas cost from your military defense cost, it seems to me that you have a figure for military defense which is running higher than the figure for military defense in your last budget.

THE PRESIDENT. No it doesn't. Read the last budget. Doesn't do anything of the kind. Couldn't possibly run that much because we have reduced the number of men from 11 million—more than that—it is less than 2 million now.

Q. Mr. President, I am honestly confused. On page M16 (p. 63)[1] of your Budget Message the estimate for 1948 is 6 billion, 658——

THE PRESIDENT. For the Army, and 4 billion, 423 for the Navy. Now turn to last year's budget and see what it was.

Q. On that same page the estimate for 1947 was 6.741 and Navy was 5.588. Now you divide——

THE PRESIDENT. With the same things out as are out this year.

Q. Atomic Energy and Areas out?

THE PRESIDENT. Taken out here for comparison purely.

Director Webb: Let's let Mr. Martin clear that up.

Mr. Martin: In addition, you must add to that 6 billion, seven in the 1947 column approximately 1 billion, 500 thousand, which represents the amounts which the War Department will expend in 1948 from funds which the Treasury Department had charged the War Department with in the fiscal year 1946. In other words, it's a Treasury assessment there, in order to account for the—for the cash in both European currency and United States currency in the hands of disbursing officers abroad which were charged as expenditures in 1946, but the payments will be made in 1947.

Q. Is that military defense category, or international defense category?

Mr. Martin: Military defense category. There's a footnote on there about national defense which will explain that, as well as the paragraph in the President's Message.

Q. Mr. Martin, one more question. On that page, is that 6.741 figure for the military and military defense—does that include Atomic Energy, Manhattan, Occupied Areas?

Mr. Martin: No sir. Manhattan, as you notice—I believe it is 179 million—that shows right below it——

THE PRESIDENT. That's right.

Mr. Martin: ——and that carries Manhattan up to the first half of the year, and the second half of the year when the Atomic Energy takes over. It is included under Natural Resources, both the second half of 1947 and all of 1948.

---

[1] Page references in parentheses, throughout this news conference, indicate where the subjects referred to may be found in the Budget Message as printed herein (Item 7); all other references correspond to the page numbers in the Budget as published in House Document 19 (80th Cong., 1st sess.).

Q. Incidentally, while I have the Budget open to the page, I would like to direct your attention to the third paragraph on page M17 (p. 64), right opposite that table which you are talking about—the supplement legislation in that paragraph. I would like to know whether that is supplemental legislation that has been enacted or supplemental legislation for the enactment of which you are asking Congress?

Mr. Martin: Well, prior to the war it was a practice for the Army and Navy to appear before legislative committees of the Congress and obtain specific authorization for public works projects. During the war that procedure was abandoned because of the speed with which you had to handle public works. The President has directed that now we will go back to the previous practice. We will make allowances in the Budget for these projects but will consider them as items for specific authorization before we will send up the estimates.

Q. In other words, if Congress should fail to give the supplemental authority, these projects will not be undertaken?

Mr. Martin: Correct.

Q. Mr. President, can we have some explanation of the rather substantial increases in the amount of money to be spent for atomic energy, from 355 to 445?

THE PRESIDENT. I don't think it's really a substantial increase. It's all in one pot is what makes——

Mr. Martin: One reason is because the War Department withheld certain replacement work both in facilities and equipment when they knew the atomic energy would be taken over before long; and for that reason the 1947 expenditures are lower than 1948 because they will now go ahead with those increased facilities.

[15.] Q. I would like to ask a question. Apparently the budget contains a new re-

vision of the 1947 fiscal year budget as a whole.

Director Webb: That is correct.

Q. And your August revision places Government expenditures at 41.5 billions. Current revisions place them at 42.5 billions, despite the fact that there are anticipated supplemental appropriations totaling 3.980 million. That is a 1-billion-dollar increase as opposed to a 4-billion item, and I wonder what the explanation of that is?

Mr. Martin: In both cases we have always taken into consideration the estimate of supplementals that will come along every time we get a figure as to our estimated expenditures. We try to forecast every probable expenditure that will be included.

Q. In other words, the August revision contained part of the supplementals?

Mr. Martin: That's right.

THE PRESIDENT. That's correct, but——

Q. Mr. President, a year ago you said that you wanted to get the budget down to $25 billion——

THE PRESIDENT. I hope that the time would come when we could have a $25 billion budget. It is not in sight. Not in sight yet. I read you what the fixed charges are now. If there is any way in the world that those fixed charges could be lowered, I don't know how to do it. My—maybe those informed in Congress can tell me. [*Laughter*]

Q. I just wanted to get up to date on that.

THE PRESIDENT. Of course we want the budget to be as low as we can possibly make it, and I have cut this one to the bone myself. I don't know how much further the Congress will want to cut it, but I don't see how they can cut it and run the Government.

[16.] Q. You have got $500,000 for emergency funds for the White House, which says fund assistance and also unforeseen expenditures.

THE PRESIDENT. Well, last year, I think that figure last year was 5 million, and before that it was a hundred million.

Q. This is just a continuation of that?

THE PRESIDENT. That's all it is—for emergency purposes that may come along, and that fund is audited by the Comptroller General whenever it is necessary. It's open to Congress any time they want to see it.

Q. Nothing of any importance contemplated under that?

THE PRESIDENT. No.

Q. Could you give us an example of the general type of thing that comes under that heading?

THE PRESIDENT. Well, during the war there were—it was all war emergency items that came under it. During the last year the operation of the coal mines and the operation of the Montgomery Ward came out of that fund—and wherever there was a deficit—and whenever it is necessary to—whenever it was necessary to take over any of those things, a fund had to be set up to begin with—to operate. It came out of that money. In many cases it was paid back. There really wasn't a great deal of expenditure. I think in the $5-million fund that I had last year there was about a—one million and a quarter spent for the jobs like the ones I have named to you.

Q. The balance goes back?

THE PRESIDENT. Goes back in the Treasury.

[17.] Q. Mr. President, you have mentioned both a "balanced budget" and a "budget in balance." Those are technical terms which I don't understand.

THE PRESIDENT. This is a balanced budget. That's right. There are two situations with regard to the budget. One is cash and one is bookkeeping. For instance, if you yourself have a certain income and you borrow a lot of money at the bank, you may take in more than you pay out, but you still owe what's in the bank—what the note calls for in the bank. In the case of the Federal budgets there is a certain cash expenditure, and I will say to you that the cash expenditures and cash intake of the Treasury was greater in 1947 than the cash outgo in 1947, but it is more than 4 billion greater. The income in the Treasury is $4 billion greater. But we still have obligations created in 1947 that have not been paid and have to be charged on the bookkeeping budget. In 1948 the income will be $3 billion greater than the outgo, but we will, according to the bookkeeping figures, we will be within a few hundred millions—we will be over only a few hundred million dollars. It is an actual bookkeeping balanced budget as well as a cash balanced budget, which was not the case in 1947.

Q. 1947 was a cash balance?

THE PRESIDENT. 1947 was a cash balance, but not a bookkeeping balance.

Q. That is what Congress is going to take advantage of.

THE PRESIDENT. How do you mean?

Q. Well, what I mean is the fact that your budget has been balanced for some time in cash——

THE PRESIDENT. But still those obligations have to be paid.

[18.] Q. Aren't those mostly social security obligations, Mr. President?

THE PRESIDENT. No. It was the pay to the soldiers. Social security is part of it—social security is part of it.

Secretary Snyder: The reserves set up for social security are part of it.

THE PRESIDENT. The Secretary of the Treasury tells me the reserves set up for social security are part of it, but the big item in the 1947 budget was the terminal leave pay.

[19.] Q. Didn't the Treasury refinancing in this calendar year retire about $20 billion on the public debt?

THE PRESIDENT. We retired $20 billion on the public debt, but it was retired out of the cash balance by the sale of bonds.

[20.] Q. Mr. President, on the opening page of your Message here, at the bottom (p. 56, col. 1), you speak of the effect of a deficit on income and spending. You say it will cause tax yields to drop, also raise expenses for certain costs. Then you add, "Should such a recession occur, there will be a temporary slump growing out of the transition period difficulties, and would call for no revision in our budget policy."

THE PRESIDENT. That's right.

Q. That is a little unclear to me. How do you mean it would not call for revision when it would both affect your income— reduce it——

THE PRESIDENT. I have revised the budget to its extreme limit so far as I am concerned. There is nothing more I can do to it.

Q. You mean—would it affect your totals?

THE PRESIDENT. Well of course, if the situation develops so that we couldn't collect the taxes that we anticipate, naturally there would be a deficit. I am hoping that won't happen.

Director Webb: He is thinking more about figures. You spoke in terms of policy. You seem to be thinking in terms of actual budgeting expenditure receipts. The President in his Message is speaking about budget policy.

Q. Mr. President, in that same general connection, on page M12 (p. 60), you estimate that receipts from direct taxes on individuals in the 1948 fiscal year will be appreciated and increased from higher income from those individuals. On what figure is the estimate of higher income in fiscal 1948 based?

THE PRESIDENT. Based on $166-billion national income.

Q. That's the overall national income?

THE PRESIDENT. That's right.

[21.] Q. Mr. President, where, in the Veterans accounting, does the enlisted men's terminal leave pay appear?

THE PRESIDENT. It's in National Defense.

Q. Not under Veterans?

THE PRESIDENT. No, National Defense.

Mr. Martin: Military expenses.

[22.] Q. Mr. President, what was the 1947 figure on national income as revised in this Message?

THE PRESIDENT. $160 billion, so the Secretary of the Treasury tells me. That's 1947.

Q. 1947, yes.

Q. Mr. President, if I recall in the August revision, it was said that it was 165.

THE PRESIDENT. I think 165 is the right figure.

Q. The 1947 figure.

THE PRESIDENT. 1947—165—that's correct. 165 was the figure.

Q. That's for the fiscal year, Mr. President?

THE PRESIDENT. Fiscal year.

Q. 1948—166.

THE PRESIDENT. 166—1948.

[23.] Q. You said in your Message that the budget has been reduced by 20 billion this year, sir, and I can't quite figure that, when I look at table 5 on page A8. It looks like 9 billion.

THE PRESIDENT. Well, the public debt at the end of the war was about $280 billion, and now it is $259 billion. So if I can subtract correctly in my head, it's in the neighborhood of 20 billion. We have paid $20 billion in cash on the public debt.

Mr. Jones: The statement says we have reduced the debt from its peak by about 20 billion, doesn't it?

THE PRESIDENT. Yes.

Mr. Jones: And this is a redemption in this year 1947–48 that you are looking at.

Q. This is calendar year?

Mr. Jones: Fiscal year.

Q. Fiscal year. In other words, it went up and down in the same year, isn't that what it adds up to? Up to the peak and down in the same year?

Mr. Jones: It got to the peak on my birthday, if I remember rightly. [*Laughter*] Got to the peak and started right down.

THE PRESIDENT. It went up anyway just before the war—then it went to the top just before the Japanese folded up. I think we said in February they folded up in April— then it began to go down, and when we had the last bond drive, we had 25 billion, didn't we?

Mr. Martin: 25 or 26 billion in cash.

THE PRESIDENT. And we paid it on the national debt.

Q. Mr. President, I wonder if you would permit direct quotation of your remarks regarding the $25 billion budget, simply saying——

THE PRESIDENT. No, no. I am talking off the record except for the statement that I made.

Mr. Ross: Except for that part which will be mimeographed.

THE PRESIDENT. It will be mimeographed and handed out to you.

Q. When is that released?

Mr. Ross: That will be released in connection with the release of the Message— simultaneous release.

THE PRESIDENT. I am talking to you frankly and freely and I don't want to be quoted.

Q. Now this is all off the record?

THE PRESIDENT. Everything I have said. All except what I have read to you is off the record. This is only done for your information, and I am talking very frankly to you because I want you to know exactly what is in my mind on this subject. But I don't want to be quoted on this directly except so far as the statement is concerned.

[24.] Q. Mr. President, several times, in fact many times in this Message you make recommendations and say that there should be legislation. For instance, there is one on farm subsidies, and one on roads. Will you make a special—send a message on that, or is this Message considered notification?

THE PRESIDENT. This Message is considered notification.

Q. No further messages needed on those points?

THE PRESIDENT. Not unless it's absolutely necessary. I might find it necessary to write letters to the chairmen of the various committees.

Q. This is the particular notice——

THE PRESIDENT. This is the particular notice and notification right here.

[25.] Q. Mr. President, on page M61 (p. 96) of the Message—what in Heaven's name is antibiotic?

THE PRESIDENT. Well, you will have to ask some expert. Tell him what it is—[*to Mr. Webb*]—I don't know. [*Laughter*]

Director Webb: Germ control.

Q. Well, why not say so?

Q. Mr. President, on page 19——

THE PRESIDENT. We wouldn't have had that good question if that item hadn't been in there! [*Laughter*]

What was that question back there?

[26.] Q. On page M19 (pp. 66, 67) you say you have to provide some modest relief program for a few countries that are still in desperate straits, providing on page M20 (p. 66) an item there of $326 million, but you don't name the countries. Are you going to send a special message on that item to Congress?

THE PRESIDENT. That matter will be explained as soon as we know what is necessary in regard to it. It was an estimate as to what we may anticipate. You gentlemen are as well acquainted with the difficulties in Europe and Asia as I am and know what the—which countries are likely to be the ones that will be benefited by that.

[27.] Q. Mr. President, on page M20 (p. 66), beneath International Affairs and Finance, which of those items are fixed and which of them might be subject to revision by Congress?

THE PRESIDENT. I will let the experts answer that for you.

Mr. Martin: This word "fixed" is a pretty relative term.

Q. It has become so, yes sir.

Mr. Martin: The Treasury loan to the United Kingdom, would you call that fixed?

THE PRESIDENT. That is fixed by legislation, of course.

Director Webb: The only variation in that would be the amount they draw down on the loan. This is the estimate on the amount they will draw during the fiscal year 1948. That was done on consultation with them.

Q. Perhaps I should clarify my own question. By "fixed" I mean established by law by Congress, such as the British loan.

THE PRESIDENT. The amount of the British loan is established by law.

Mr. Martin: I am going to say everything but the last three items have been established by law would be the answer, I think.

Q. In the sums as presented, sir?

Mr. Martin: The sums of what would be withdrawn may be.

Q. How about UNRRA?

Mr. Martin: That is fixed.

Q. War Department and occupied countries. Neither of those is actually fixed by existing statutes.

Mr. Martin: Now with regard to UNRRA, that 305 is really unliquidated obligations already made, so they are bound to go in winding up UNRRA.

Mr. Jones: Already on the books to be paid—Philippine Aid has been approved

by the Congress, Membership in the International Organizations are fixed. State Department—those last three you might——

Q. How about that War Department figure?

Secretary Snyder: That is Occupied Areas.

Mr. Jones: Occupied Areas have to be appropriated for.

THE PRESIDENT. Have to be appropriated for, but it is a fixed charge. You can't get out of it.

Q. How about the last item, 326 million?

Director Webb: Proposed legislation.

Mr. Jones: Not fixed.

THE PRESIDENT. That is the item the gentleman was talking about a minute ago, what we may have to hand out for relief to those countries that can't support themselves.

Q. Occupied relief?

THE PRESIDENT. No. No, that doesn't necessarily—is not necessarily confined to occupied countries. We don't occupy Greece.

Q. That figure would be in addition to the occupied territories administered by the Army?

THE PRESIDENT. That's right.

Q. Is the Export-Import Bank figure of $730 million actually obligated by legislation up to this point, or is that something you estimate that they will estimate?

Director Webb: That they will expend.

THE PRESIDENT. That is what they will hand out during the year. We estimate that is what they will hand out.

Director Webb: Congress has already provided for it.

THE PRESIDENT. The money is already in the bank.

Q. Is it committed?

Director Webb: It has been committed, yes.

THE PRESIDENT. It has been committed. It has been committed, yes.

[28.] Q. Mr. President, on page M56 (p. 93) right under Federal Civilian Personnel, "Federal Agencies have reduced their civilian personnel to 2 million, three," where is the figure as to the cost of that— annual cost of that 2 million, three; because I understand Mr. Knutson is going to take a million off of it?

THE PRESIDENT. Well, I will give him "good" if he can do it.

Q. Scattered?

THE PRESIDENT. In every department, that is.

Q. Has it been broken down?

THE PRESIDENT. No.

Q. This is 3 million——

THE PRESIDENT. Three million! You have got to speak in billions when you talk about the budget. [*Laughter*]

Q. But there was a compilation as to the cost of that?

THE PRESIDENT. No, except in each department you will find an item which sets out what the personnel calls for. You can take each item and add them all up. The Budget Director tells me that the final figure will be 2,100,000 at the end of fiscal year 1948.

Q. Is that the figure for the cost of all civilian departments including personnel?

THE PRESIDENT. That's the total number of personnel, 2,100,000—the total number of people.

Director Webb: Civilians.

THE PRESIDENT. Civilians who will be on the Government payroll at the end of 1948.

Q. What is the total cost of the Government departments?

THE PRESIDENT. 37—500—or 700—whatever the total is. Read it!

Q. I mean the cost of running the Treasury Department and RFC?

THE PRESIDENT. You can go through the Budget and pick them all out. They are set out in detail. I haven't got them in my head. All you have to do is read the Budget. I will give you the whole book if you want it.

Q. Mr. President, how does this figure of 2,100,000 employees compare with prewar?

THE PRESIDENT. I don't know what last year's——

Director Webb: About 900,000 is the figure most people use.

Q. What is it?

Director Webb: About 900,000, the figure most generally accepted.

Q. Prewar?

THE PRESIDENT. Prewar.

Q. As of 1939?

Director Webb: Approximately 1939, yes.

Secretary Snyder: 1938.

Q. You give us the figure of nearly 33 billion as being fixed charges?

THE PRESIDENT. Yes. It's about—that figure is about correct for fixed charges.

Q. You were good enough to tell us some of the items in that. Can you tell us a few of the items that fall outside of that?

THE PRESIDENT. That's all the civil sections of the Government that are necessary to make it run. The President's Office is one of them, and this row of things you see around here [*indicating the chart previously referred to*]. The President, as I told you, is in the center of the executive branch of the Government. You will have a chance to look at this, and you will see all these things here.

Q. Congressional employees too?

THE PRESIDENT. Congressional employees, and the cost of the legislative government, and everything of that sort.

[29.] Q. In that category then, is it correct to say whether the Army and Navy figure has been cut so near to the bone that it can be considered as a fixed figure?

THE PRESIDENT. It is, in my mind. I don't know what the Congress will think about it.

I have had a terrible lot of weeping and wailing and gnashing of teeth over that thing. The Secretary of the Navy and the Secretary of War, and the Chief of Staff of the Army and the Chief of Naval Operations have been on my neck from time to time. In fact, I had almost in every one of these instances to personally pass on the amount of money that each department should have, and it wasn't in anywhere—not anywhere nearly in the neighborhood of what they thought they ought to have.

[30.] Q. Mr. President, I would like to ask Mr. Webb a question, to clarify something. As I understand it——

THE PRESIDENT. Sure.

Q. —— the number of employees, civilian employees, including those outside the United States, will be down to 2,100,000 at the end of the 1948 fiscal year. Now the comparable prewar figure was 900,000?

Director Webb: I am sure that is comparable. Just when it was—is that '38 or '39? We will have people on duty at the Bureau to better give you accurate information like that.

Q. It says here 900,000 at the end of 1939.

THE PRESIDENT. This young man says that the next paragraph says it was 900,000 at the end of 1939.

Q. Mr. Webb, was the 2 million, 1 at the end of fiscal year 1947 or 1948?

THE PRESIDENT. Fiscal 1948.

[31.] Q. Mr. President, on M58 (p. 94) you speak of extending statutory authority for RFC and that a new charter is to be submitted. What will be the form of that presentation—will it be a special message to Congress?

THE PRESIDENT. Well, when the Finance Committee meets—I mean when the Ways and Means Committee in the House and the Finance Committee meets in the Senate, I will send them the information, if they want it; and I know they will want it.

Q. Will this be the same draft that was proposed at the time Mr. Allen[1] resigned?

THE PRESIDENT. I can't say as to that. We are still working on it.

[32.] Q. Mr. President, could a minor item be clarified? The appropriations for the Secretary of War went up 11 million and the Secretary of the Navy went down 10 million——

THE PRESIDENT. I don't think that happened.

Q. It says back here in the table——

THE PRESIDENT. No, no, I don't think that happened at all.

Q. The office——

THE PRESIDENT. It couldn't have happened——

Director Webb: Let's let Mr. Martin——

THE PRESIDENT. ——because they were treated exactly alike proportionately. I think—I am sure he has his figures mixed up, because they were treated alike so far as——

Q. The figures I am speaking about, sir, are on the page— table— 639 and 825.

THE PRESIDENT. You experts look at that and see what's the matter with the table.

Director Webb: While Mr. Martin is looking that up, I would like to check one item. You mentioned that the Legislative and Judicial expenditures were down in this General Government group. They have been excluded in the——

THE PRESIDENT. They are not in the lower group. I said Judicial were in. They are not. It's only this big table here that's in the middle group.

[33.] Q. Mr. President, could you elaborate at all on the ideas on page M12 (p. 61)? You say, "For example, I believe that a reasonable share of the cost to the

---

[1] George E. Allen, a Director of the Reconstruction Finance Corporation.

Federal Government for providing specialized transportation facilities, such as airways, should be recovered."

THE PRESIDENT. That's true. Everybody who rides at Government expense ought to pay his way. We have been hauling a lot of people around all over the world, including your boss. [*Laughter*]

Q. Yes sir. [*More laughter*]

THE PRESIDENT. And I think he ought to pay his way.

Q. Airways?

THE PRESIDENT. That also has to do with airways.

Q. Including trucks in that?

THE PRESIDENT. Yes.

Q. Retroactive, is it?

THE PRESIDENT. Everything.

Q. All these newspaper junkets are going to be recovered?

THE PRESIDENT. Well, why not? I am making Congressmen and Senators pay their way.

Q. Being a taxpayer, I would just as soon have you recover.

THE PRESIDENT. I think you are right.

Q. Not referring to mileage, were you, Mr. President?

THE PRESIDENT. How's that?

Q. Not referring to mileage?

THE PRESIDENT. No, not necessarily.

[34.] Director Webb: Mr. Martin will answer your question.

THE PRESIDENT. Mr. Martin will answer your question now. Go ahead.

Mr. Martin: For the Office of the Secretary of the Navy there were several increases offset by some decreases, resulting in a net minus of $10 million. The increase is four and a half million for Miscellaneous Expense, five and a half for Island Governments, decreases of 10 million in Research, and 9 million, 600 for the Petroleum Reserves. War Department, 11 million increase is all in contingencies of the Army.

Q. Thank you.

THE PRESIDENT. There was no favoritism shown in that. They were treated exactly alike.

[35.] Q. On M12 and M13 (pp. 60, 61) you have got around $700 million in employment taxes, and on page M13 (p. 61) you say this is due mostly to increases—larger payrolls and mostly to increases in rates as provided by law. There have been many recommendations to freeze that law for the last 5 years.

THE PRESIDENT. That has been Senator Vandenberg's pet every year to freeze that law. I hope he won't do that this time.

Q. You assume that he will let the law——

THE PRESIDENT. If this fund is going to remain solvent, the law has got to go into effect.

Q. In other words, 700 million—I was going to say 700 million——

THE PRESIDENT. That's right.

Q. —— if they freeze it again, you are going to be out $700 million?

THE PRESIDENT. It's a trust fund which the Budget Director tells me has no effect on the total budget, but it should be allowed to go into effect so as to make that fund solvent.

Q. It wouldn't unbalance the budget?

THE PRESIDENT. Has no effect on the budget.

Q. Doesn't affect balancing the budget?

THE PRESIDENT. That's right. Those are trust funds and they go into the trust fund figure in the Treasury Department.

[36.] Q. I have not been able to find an estimate in here, although there is one, I am sure, of how much tax refunds there are going to be to corporations during 1948 fiscal year as a result of the excess profits tax carried back. I just haven't been able to find that figure. I wonder if——

THE PRESIDENT. Can any of you experts tell anything about that figure?

Director Webb: I tell you, if you will call the Budget Bureau, we will get that for you.

THE PRESIDENT. The Secretary of the Treasury says about 21 billion.

Secretary Snyder: Let him check it.

Director Webb: I think it's a little more than that.

THE PRESIDENT. We will send the—we are going to have the Bureau's office open as usual to answer all your detail questions.

Q. What's that phone number again?

THE PRESIDENT. Executive 3300—extension 118.

[37.] Q. Mr. President, may I ask an overall question? I was a little confused at some of these questions earlier. Is there any legislation needed to make this a balanced budget?

THE PRESIDENT. The legislation to restore the Post Office deficit and the legislation to restore these luxury taxes is needed, but it will not—the budget will still be in balance if they don't pass either one of those items.

Q. That would merely add another billion?

THE PRESIDENT. That would merely add a billion and a half to the Budget so that we could pay some on the national debt. As I said, with 289 billion, if we only pay it off a billion dollars a year, you and I won't be here when we finish it.

[38.] Q. To go back to that question, that means no legislation is required to transfer corporate funds?

THE PRESIDENT. You are the expert on that.

Q. I have been confused by——

THE PRESIDENT. This one is an attempt to be as little confusing as possible.

Mr. Jones: I think it does need some legislation to transfer those corporate funds.

Some of it is Federal Reserve, FDIC. Funds are available.

THE PRESIDENT. The money is all in the Treasury. Doesn't affect the budget.

Q. Might affect the budget—would affect the bookkeeping——

THE PRESIDENT. Might. Might.

Director Webb: Really no controversial issue. The money is there. It's a question of what the Government does with the money.

Q. That's the whole point, sir. It's the same thing that had me confused, too, and that is this: that the items of 379 are composed of repayments by the FDIC and Federal Reserve Bank and the Treasury ultimately, and the money now lies in the FDIC and the Federal Reserve Bank which is part of the Government, and yet when it is paid into the Treasury it results in receipts of that amount.

THE PRESIDENT. That's right.

Q. And those receipts are required to bring the budget into balance. Therefore, is it correct to consider those actual receipts in a balanced budget or is the money already there and it really is not a balanced budget, be off by about——

THE PRESIDENT. The budget is balanced when the President makes the recommendations in the budget for legislation to meet that situation.

Director Webb: There are a good many recommendations here for increases in expenditure. They are all totaled on page M61 (p. 96) under Proposed Legislation. The proposal deals with both sides of the budget.

THE PRESIDENT. You take it off both ways. If they don't comply with what you request you have the situation of expenditures and receipts about coming out even.

Q. Simply taking it out of one pocket and putting it into another?

THE PRESIDENT. That's all.

Q. So it isn't actual receipts to Government?

THE PRESIDENT. Yes they are.

Director Webb: Up to now, when the Government put up the money for the FDIC, that was charged out as an expense and it has been carried outside. Now, if they pass this legislation and permit it to be paid back into the Treasury, it will be shown as receipts, although the money has been right in the Treasury all the time.

THE PRESIDENT. Certain appropriations are estimated in there. You will come out even, anyway.

Director Webb: If you are disturbed about that, we will give you a statement about it. Give us a ring on it. Come over and see us.

THE PRESIDENT. It's complex if you want to make it that way, but it isn't complex to me. *I* understand it. [*Laughter*]

[39.] Q. On the bottom of page M17 (p. 64), expenditures for the War and Navy Departments, on estimates, include contemplated projects of highest priority at overseas bases and in the continental United States. I am curious to know what a high priority at overseas base might be?

THE PRESIDENT. I can't tell you. It's a diplomatic secret, and until we find out ourselves—[*laughter*]. I will tell you one of these days, but not now.

[*Pause*]

Well gentlemen, are you out of questions? That's a mighty thick book to be over with so quickly. [*Laughter*]

Mr. Ross: I would like to repeat—may I repeat that the attributable part of the President's statement I will have mimeographed and give out this afternoon. Only that part may be attributed directly.

Reporter: Thank you, Mr. President.

NOTE: President Truman's ninety-fourth news conference was held in the Movie Projection Room in the East Wing at the White House at 3 o'clock on Wednesday afternoon, January 8, 1947. The President was assisted in presenting information on the budget by Secretary of the Treasury John W. Snyder and by James E. Webb, Director of the Bureau of the Budget, J. Weldon Jones, Assistant Director in Charge of the Fiscal Division, and L. C. Martin, Assistant Director in Charge of Estimates.

7 Annual Budget Message to the Congress: Fiscal Year 1948. *January* 10, 1947

[Released January 10, 1947. Dated January 3, 1947]

To the Congress of the United States:

I am transmitting the Budget for the fiscal year 1948. It includes recommendations for the entire Federal program.

Expenditures under existing and proposed legislation are estimated at 37.5 billion dollars and revenues under existing tax laws at 37.7 billion dollars, leaving a very slight margin of surplus.

I strongly recommend that the Congress take early action to continue throughout the fiscal year 1948 the war excise-tax rates, which, under the present law, will expire July 1, 1947. My declaration of the end of hostilities on December 31, 1946, was not issued in order to achieve tax reduction. I considered it essential that war excise-tax rates be retained, but I also considered it necessary to terminate the "state of hostilities" as soon as it became possible to do so.

I also recommend that the Congress increase postal rates sufficiently to wipe out the postal deficit.

These recommendations would reduce expenditures to 37.1 billion dollars and increase revenues to 38.9 billion dollars. We would then have a budget surplus of 1.8 billion dollars.

As long as business, employment, and national income continue high, we should maintain tax revenues at levels that will not only meet current expenditures but also leave a surplus for retirement of the public debt. There is no justification now for tax reduction. At today's level of economic activity, our present revenue system will not yield so much in 1948 as in the current year. We shall no longer collect large sums from the excess-profits tax, and sales of surplus property will decline.

Revenue estimates are, of course, to a very large extent determined by the level of business activity. In this Budget, it has been assumed that, with minor fluctuations, business activity will average slightly higher than in the calendar year 1946. A recession in business would cause tax yields to drop. In addition, the cost of supporting agricultural prices and payments to unemployed veterans would increase. Should such a recession occur, it would be a temporary slump growing out of transition period difficulties and would call for no revision in our budget policy.

For the fiscal year 1947, it now appears that receipts will amount to 40.2 billion dollars and expenditures to 42.5 billion dollars. The 1-billion-dollar increase in expenditures over the August estimate occurred largely in veterans' programs. For example, many more veterans than had been expected decided to go to college or enroll for job training. We cannot regret this demand for education, but it illustrates the kind of uncertainty that cannot be eliminated in preparing our estimates.

The deficit for the current fiscal year would have been larger if Executive action had not been taken to place expenditure ceilings on some activities and to hold them well below the amounts available under appropriations already made. The way the various departments and agencies of the Government, particularly the War and Navy Departments, have succeeded in cutting their expenditures is gratifying. Although public works could not be cut so deeply as anticipated in August without causing a wasteful stoppage of work already under way, we shall still show a substantial saving in this fiscal year for these programs.

This Budget meets our basic requirements for Federal programs at home and abroad for the fiscal year 1948. The Federal Government must not only fulfill its contractual obligations; it must also provide the services that are necessary for the welfare and the progress of the Nation. We have to carry our proper share of the expense of building world organization. We must make effective provision for national defense.

We have many other commitments, both international and domestic, that must be honored. In fact, a very large part of all our expenditures in the fiscal year 1948 will be required to meet commitments already made. The Budget is designed to meet these needs, and to execute every program with strict economy.

The reconversion of wartime military and civilian services was far advanced during the calendar year 1946. Of 26 emergency war agencies in operation shortly before VJ-day, only 5 remain, and 3 of these are winding up their work. Two others—the War Assets Administration and the Office of Temporary Controls—have been added to help close out the war program. The 1948 Budget assumes a reduction of civilian employment in the Government as a whole to less than three-fifths of the wartime peak number—in addition to the heavy shrinkage of the armed forces.

The Government has been exerting every effort in the wake of the war demobilization to strengthen and make more efficient its internal organization and administrative methods. It is essential that citizens receive maximum service for their tax dollars, and the Administration plans further intensive measures to improve the administrative practices, organization, and efficiency of the departments and agencies.

But the cost of peacetime services has risen strikingly as compared to these costs before the war. Prewar figures can no longer be used as a yardstick. Although Government wages have not been raised so much as private wages, the cost of supplies has risen in line with the cost of goods in private markets. Further, the population to be served has grown since 1939 by 10 million people, adding proportionately to the demand for many public services. Many normal maintenance items had to be postponed on account of the war, and cannot be further neglected. Normal services which were cut during the war have to be restored.

Let me now review the expenditure side of the Budget, taking first the large items which practically determine the size of the total.

1. Interest on the national debt will be 5 billion dollars. This is an obligation that must be met.

2. Refunds due under the tax laws are estimated at 2.1 billion dollars. These are fixed obligations under present law.

These two items total 7.1 billion dollars.

3. National defense is estimated at more than 11.2 billion dollars, almost all for the operating expenses of the Army and Navy. Though we expect the United Nations to move successfully toward world security, any cut in our present estimate for 1948 would immediately weaken our international position. This large part of the Budget, in my judgment, represents a proper balance between security and economy.

The total so far is 18.3 billion dollars.

4. International affairs and finance will call for 3.5 billion dollars, a sharp reduction

from the 6.4 billion dollars required in the fiscal year 1947. We still have contractual commitments to make good in connection with our loan agreement with the United Kingdom and under the reconstruction lending program of the Export-Import Bank. We must discharge our occupation responsibilities in Europe and the Far East. We must provide for war damage restoration in the Philippines and for the relief and resettlement of displaced people of Europe. We must continue to give relief to some other countries which are most urgently in need.

The work of the United Nations and the specialized organizations associated with it is of the highest importance. We must not fail in our support. The Department of State, for which increased appropriations are requested, must be prepared to carry an increasing load of work in the growing field of American foreign relations.

Our international affairs budget is important for peace, security, and our own prosperity. To reduce it would delay the restoration of a peaceful and prosperous world.

The total of these four items is 21.8 billion dollars.

5. Veterans' services and benefits will cost more than 7.3 billion dollars. This country has provided generously for the successful return of veterans to civilian life and for the care of the disabled. While the cost looms large in the Budget, much of it goes to provide education and rehabilitation which will add to our national strength and prosperity. The cost for veterans' education, pensions, and hospitals will increase in the fiscal year 1948; but if employment remains high, the unemployment payments should be smaller. Veterans' benefits under present law appear to be adequate.

These five items—interest, refunds, national defense, international affairs, and veterans—require expenditures of 29.2 billion dollars, or almost four-fifths of the total Budget.

6. Programs for regulation and improvement of the transportation and communications systems and for development of natural resources will amount to 2.6 billion dollars. The largest single item is 443 million dollars for the Atomic Energy Commission. Our major effort now must be to exploit to the full the peacetime uses of this great discovery.

About 1.2 billion dollars of the expenditures on these two programs is for public works construction, and much of the rest is for the promotion of our merchant marine and other aids to transportation.

The expenditure for the Federal-aid program for highways rests on the Federal Government's agreements with the States. Air transport will be seriously retarded unless new air-navigation facilities are promptly supplied. River basin development and harbor improvement cannot be neglected without impairing efficiency in private enterprise. Most of the public construction projects are already under way. A few additional projects, not yet started, have been provided for in 1947 appropriations.

Public construction in these and other fields contributes to the productive capacity and taxpaying ability of the country. The postponement of public works in good times and their expansion in hard times will make their contribution even greater. All postponable public works should be deferred at the present time. But the need to protect and improve our natural resources has become acute as a result of the war, and we must carry out the works included in this Budget if we are to avoid waste.

7. Our agricultural program will amount to 1.4 billion dollars. This includes the price supports guaranteed by law, the conser-

vation of farm land, and our investments in rural electrification. In addition, the Department of Agriculture will continue its program to promote research in agriculture and better marketing methods.

This brings the total to 33.2 billion dollars.

8. The Budget programs for social welfare, health, and security, and for education and general research amount to 1.7 billion dollars. This total excludes unemployment compensation and old-age and survivors insurance, which are financed through trust-account operations that do not appear in Budget expenditures. It does include 481 million dollars in payments to the railroad retirement trust fund. More than half of the remaining expenditures is for aid to the aged and other dependent persons. The rest is largely for protection of public health, for crime control, and for grants to States for vocational education.

9. The Federal housing program is estimated at 539 million dollars. The bulk of the housing expenditures is for purchase by the Reconstruction Finance Corporation of guaranteed home loans to veterans and for continued operation of revenue-producing war housing in overcrowded communities.

Our social-security program and our education and housing programs can hardly be considered adequate. Improvements in these fields are seriously needed. Although this Budget does not contemplate major extensions in the next fiscal year, I recommend that the Congress lay the legislative ground work now for the needed improvements, including general health insurance and a long-range housing program.

The costs of social welfare, education, and housing bring the cumulative total above 35.4 billion dollars.

The remainder of the Budget totals 2.1 billion dollars. Nearly one-third is for war liquidation, including the overhead cost of disposing of surplus property. The rest is for services to business and labor through the Commerce Department and Labor Department, for general functions of the Treasury, the General Accounting Office, the legislative branch, the judicial branch, and the Executive Office of the President, and for many other items. These services, with a total cost of less than 5 percent of the Budget, are an indispensable part of the machinery of the Government.

The Budget total of expenditures thus comes to 37.5 billion dollars.

It has always been the Government's duty to provide whatever assistance is required to afford private enterprise a chance to prosper. In the nineteenth century a principal economic service of the Federal Government was the opening of the West. The Government acquired the territory, granted lands to settlers, gave military protection, and subsidized railroads and highways—thereby opening opportunities for the private initiative of the American people.

Today, our great new frontiers are in river-valley developments, in air transport, in new scientific discoveries, and in application of the new science and technology to human progress. These new frontiers can be developed only by the cooperation of Government and private enterprise.

Our expenditures on developmental projects are a good investment for the Government. They increase the productive power of the country and make for higher living standards. Directly or indirectly, the Government recovers the cost in the form of either service charges or increased revenue yields to the Treasury.

The Federal Government promotes improvements in agricultural methods. It provides many services to private enterprise that could not be organized except by Government. The Bureau of Standards, for example, furnishes basic scientific data. The Weather Bureau supplies information used by thousands of farmers and business concerns and has a rapidly developing field of work in aviation weather reporting. Maps and charts, as well as lighthouses, beacons, and other physical aids to navigation, are supplied by the Federal Government. Many kinds of statistical reports, required by American business, are also provided.

Since 1939, our complex system for the production of goods and services has grown so much that more services than ever are required from the Government. We cannot risk retarding our growth by lack of roads, electric power, air-navigation facilities, engineering data, maps, education, surveys of resources, weather reports, protection against disease, or any other necessary instrument of progress. There is a multitude of Government activities which the whole Nation takes for granted and on which our prosperity depends.

Let me now review briefly the appropriation side of the Budget.

This Budget recommends appropriations of 31.3 billion dollars for the fiscal year 1948 under existing and proposed legislation. It recommends that authority of 1.5 billion dollars be granted certain agencies to contract for services and supplies, such as aircraft and construction. Payments under such authority will be financed from appropriations to be made in subsequent years.

The expenditures for 1948 still reflect a portion of the cost of our tremendous war program for which appropriations were made in previous years. They also reflect certain large international commitments likewise previously authorized. These two factors in large measure explain why estimated expenditures for 1948 are so much more than the appropriations recommended for that year.

Existing appropriations available for obligation in 1948 and subsequent years are again under review. As these appropriations become unnecessary, their withdrawal will be recommended to the Congress.

The Federal Government, as shown by the size of its Budget, has far greater obligations than at any time before the war. Although the Budget reflects the urgent need for rigorous economy in the execution of every program, expenditures are inevitably large. The American people surely will not shirk their new responsibilities at home and abroad. They will supply the necessary funds to meet these responsibilities.

RECEIPTS

As previously indicated, I cannot recommend tax reduction. The responsibilities of the Federal Government cannot be fully met in the fiscal year 1948 at a lower cost than here indicated. Even if the cost were less it would be desirable in our present economic situation to maintain revenues in order to make a start toward the repayment of the national debt. At the present time, in my judgment, high taxes contribute to the welfare and security of the country.

Under the wartime tax system, millions of taxpayers with small incomes are called upon to pay high taxes. When the time comes for taxes to be reduced, these taxpayers will have a high priority among the claimants for tax relief.

I have recommended that the war excise-tax rates due to expire July 1, 1947, be continued. When the time comes for excise-tax revision, the Congress should review the entire group of excise taxes rather than concentrate attention on those that were imposed or increased during the war.

Our long-run tax program must be designed to maintain purchasing power and provide incentives for a high level of production.

In the corporation section of this Message, legislation is recommended which will require return to the Treasury as miscellaneous receipts of certain capital funds totaling 379 million dollars.

I also recommend that the Congress reconsider the extent to which fees should be charged for services rendered by the Federal Government. While it is not sound

BUDGET RECEIPTS

[Fiscal years. In millions]

Source	Actual, 1946	Estimate, 1947	Estimate, 1948
Direct taxes on individuals....................................	$19,008	$18.637	$19,120
Direct taxes on corporations.................................	12,906	9,227	8,270
Excise taxes..	6,696	7,283	6,118
Employment taxes...	1,714	1,955	2,694
Customs..	435	496	517
Miscellaneous receipts:			
Present law...	3,480	3,987	2,620
Proposed legislation......................................	....	....	379
Total receipts...	44,239	41,585	39,717
Less net appropriation to old-age and survivors insurance trust fund..	1,201	1,355	1,987
Budget receipts...	43,038	40,230	37,730
Proposed continuation of war excise rates (not included in Budget receipts)..	....	37	1,130

public policy to charge for all services of the Federal Government on a full cost basis, and many services should be provided free, the Government should receive adequate compensation for certain services primarily of direct benefit to limited groups. For example, I believe that a reasonable share of the cost to the Federal Government for providing specialized transportation facilities, such as airways, should be recovered.

Receipts from direct taxes on individuals are estimated to decrease from the fiscal year 1946 to 1947 because of the lower effective individual income tax rates in the Revenue Act of 1945, and to increase from the fiscal year 1947 to 1948 because of higher incomes. Direct taxes on corporations decline in the fiscal year 1947 and further in 1948 largely because of repeal of the excess-profits tax.

The excise-tax estimates increase in 1947 because of increased consumer demand and increased production, and decline under present law in 1948 because of the expiration of the war tax rates of the Revenue Act of 1943. The employment-tax estimates show increases in both fiscal years, due in 1947 mostly to larger pay rolls, and in 1948 mostly to increases in rates as provided by law. Miscellaneous receipts increase in 1947 over 1946 largely because of increased receipts from disposition of surplus property and decline in 1948 largely because of a decline in surplus-property receipts.

Borrowing and the Public Debt

The public debt reached a peak last February at 279 billion dollars. During the remainder of the calendar year, the debt was reduced by over 20 billion dollars and stood near 259 billion dollars at the end of December. Most of the securities retired were held by banks. This reduction was accomplished by drawing down the Treasury cash balance to a level more in line with peacetime requirements.

We propose to continue the sale of savings bonds. The proceeds will be available to redeem marketable securities—particularly those held by the banking system. It is important that every citizen in a position to do so help to maintain a sound economic situation by purchasing and holding United States savings bonds.

The annual interest charge of about 5 billion dollars is less than 3 percent of our current national income. It is well within our capacity to pay, particularly if we keep up a high volume of national production. The best method of keeping down the burden of the debt is to maintain prosperity. A single year of depression can lay more burdens on the people than many years of gradual debt reduction can relieve.

Our debt-management policy is designed to hold interest rates at the present low level and to prevent undue fluctuations in the bond market. This policy has eased the financial problems of reconversion for both business and Government. The stability of the Government bond market has been a major factor in the business confidence which has been of such value in achieving full production. Low interest rates have also relieved the burden on the taxpayer. The Treasury and the Federal Reserve System will continue their effective control of interest rates.

Expenditure Programs

In this year's Budget, expenditures are grouped under a new functional classification in order to present to the Congress and the people a clearer picture of the purposes for which Federal funds are spent. To facilitate comparison, figures for previous years are also given on the new basis.

The Budget classifications and Budget

BUDGET EXPENDITURES BY MAJOR PROGRAMS

[Fiscal years.   In millions]

	Expenditures			
Program	Actual, 1946	Estimate, 1947	Estimate, 1948	Appropriations, 1948
National defense..................................	$45,012	$14,726	$11,256	$9,493
International affairs and finance...................	1,464	6,394	3,510	1,169
Veterans' services and benefits.....................	4,414	7,601	7,343	7,009
Social welfare, health, and security................	1,113	1,570	1,654	1,877
Housing and community facilities...................	—180	544	539	179
Education and general research.....................	88	71	88	85
Agriculture and agricultural resources..............	752	1,117	1,381	824
Natural resources.................................	257	728	1,101	779
Transportation and communication.................	824	905	1,530	1,196
Finance, commerce, and industry...................	30	83	426	116
Labor..	104	124	118	118
General government...............................	972	1,545	1,492	1,341
Interest on the public debt........................	4,748	4,950	5,000	5,000
Refunds of receipts	3,119	2,155	2,065	2,065
Reserve for contingencies..........................	....	10	25	25
Adjustment to daily Treasury statement basis........	997	....	....	....
Total.....................................	63,714	42,523	37,528	31,276
From—				
General and special accounts.....................	65,019	42,698	36,699	31,276
Corporation accounts............................	—1,305	—175	829	....
Total......................................	63,714	42,523	37,528	31,276

totals reflect all transactions in the general and special accounts and the excess of expenditures over receipts of wholly owned Government corporations. For the first time, the net expenditures of wholly owned corporations are classified on a functional basis. The Budget totals do not include the operations of trust accounts. However, such transactions, when significant, are discussed in connection with the various Budget programs.

NATIONAL DEFENSE

Expenditures for "National defense" remain by far the largest category in the Budget. The cost of maintaining the military, air, and naval forces necessary in the fiscal year 1948 will be high. The present defense establishment requires larger forces, more complex mechanized equipment, more intensive use of equipment, and more extensive developmental activity than before the war.

However, in the fiscal year 1948 these expenditures will be but one-eighth of the outlays in the peak wartime fiscal year, 1945. This drastic cut reflects a corresponding reduction in the size of the armed forces. Outlays for munitions have been reduced even more.

Despite these reductions, our defense establishment will not have fallen to its ultimate peacetime level by the end of the fiscal year 1948. We still have large responsibilities arising out of the war. Military occupation in Europe and the Far East must continue. The lines of communication and supporting installations for the occupation forces must be maintained. Recruits must be trained as replacements.

The high cost of our defense establishments requires that the program be operated with the utmost efficiency. In the estimates for 1948 emphasis has been placed on eliminating as much duplication and overlapping in activities as is possible under present conditions. In my State of the Union Message I have again urged establishment of a single department of national defense. This

is an important step in the search for economy and efficiency in organization and administration of the armed services.

I recently appointed an advisory commission to study the need for a universal training program. We still have available from the war much of the equipment and installations which will be needed for such a program. The program, after it has been worked out and approved, will still require considerable time to get under way. Estimates for it have, therefore, not been included in this Budget. Since plans are not complete for the training program, a small

NATIONAL DEFENSE

[Fiscal years. In millions]

Program or agency concerned	Expenditures			
	Actual, 1946	Estimate, 1947	Estimate, 1948	Appropriations, 1948
Military defense:				
Military.................................	$24,846	$6,741	$6,658	$5,942
Atomic energy..............................	430	179	....	....
Naval defense................................	16,763	5,588	4,423	3,540
Terminal leave for enlisted personnel................	....	1,900	250	....
Activities supporting defense:				
Lend-lease (excluding War and Navy Departments):				
Treasury Department..........................	672	333	34	....
Maritime Commission and War Shipping Administration.................................	1,045	411	....	....
Agriculture Department........................	1,003	5	....	....
Other.......................................	45	35	....	....
Stock piling of strategic and critical materials:				
Treasury Department..........................	....	177	243	....
Reconstruction Finance Corporation.............	....	−87	−210	....
Reconstruction Finance Corporation (other)........	−53	−337	−121	....
War Shipping Administration (other).............	187	−250	−34	....
Other...	74	30	13	10
Total........	45,012	a 14,726	11,256	9,493
From—				
General and special accounts.....................	45,066	a 15,149	11,587	9,493
Corporation accounts............................	−53	−424	−331	....
Total..	45,012	a 14,726	11,256	9,493

a Excludes disbursements of approximately 1,500 million dollars for the War Department and 250 million dollars for the Navy Department which have appeared as Budget expenditures in previous years.

amount has been included in the Budget to cover the cost of induction machinery whenever provision is made for it.

Expenditures.—"National defense," as used in this Budget, is much less inclusive than the category used last year. For example, War Department expenditures of 645 million dollars in 1948 for supplies to and administration of occupied areas (other than Army pay, subsistence, and related items) are now in "International affairs and finance." Likewise, expenditures for the atomic energy activities of the Manhattan District project beginning January 1, 1947, when the Atomic Energy Commission took control, are shown in "Natural resources." For the fiscal year 1946 and the first 6 months of the fiscal year 1947 this program remains in "National defense."

The level of expenditures for "National defense" in 1947 would have been 1.7 billion dollars higher, and the reduction from 1947 to 1948 correspondingly greater, except for certain adjustments—1.5 billion dollars in War Department accounts and 250 million dollars in Navy accounts. Some funds withdrawn from the Treasury in 1946 and earlier years, and reported as expenditures at the time, were not used until 1947. Also some expenditures by the War Department in 1947 were offset by credits from funds which had accumulated in trust accounts during the war.

The expenditure estimate of 11.1 billion dollars in 1948 for the Army and Navy for military purposes reflects the reductions from the current fiscal year in the number of military personnel and in war-liquidation outlays—such as mustering-out payments (reduced by 370 million dollars), contract termination (700 million dollars), and surplus property handling. On the other side, the estimate reflects greater procurement in the fiscal year 1948, as war inventories cease to be available to supply current needs.

The estimated expenditures of 6.7 billion dollars for the War Department in the fiscal year 1948 include 132 million dollars for public works under supplemental legislation. The Navy expenditures of 4.4 billion dollars also include 77 million dollars for ship construction and public works under supplemental legislation. In both instances the objective is to return to the peacetime procedure of obtaining specific legislative authority for these programs.

Taken together, the War and Navy Department expenditures estimated for the fiscal year 1948 provide for an average military strength of 1,641,000 men and officers. Of this, Army strength is projected at 1,070,000 throughout the year; Navy and Marine strength will begin the year at 598,000 and average 571,000. These figures compare with an average strength in the fiscal year 1947 of 2,108,000. Pay, subsistence, travel, welfare, training, clothing, and medical expenditures for military personnel are estimated at 5.2 billion dollars in the fiscal year 1948, as against 6.7 billion dollars in the current year. Average annual costs per man for these purposes—about 3,100 dollars in 1948—have increased markedly since VJ-day. Fully 45 percent of Army and Navy expenditures in 1948 are in this category.

Expenditures by the War and Navy Departments for all other military purposes are estimated at 5.9 billion dollars in the fiscal year 1948. This sum covers procurement, research and development, construction, operation and maintenance, and citizen-reserve activities. The estimates for 1948 contemplate proceeding with construction projects of highest priority at overseas bases and in the continental United States, and limiting procurement to those items essential for the current operation, maintenance, and training of the military forces, except for aircraft and limited quantities of newly developed items.

Effective defense under modern conditions requires us to push ahead in scientific and technological fields. Toward this end, expenditures for research and development by the Army and Navy are projected at 530 million dollars in the fiscal year 1948—slightly above their 1947 rate. Similarly, we must keep alive the knowledge of military skills among our citizens. To provide for an orderly expansion of citizen-reserve organizations, expenditures of 308 million dollars are projected in 1948—about two-thirds more than the outlays in the current fiscal year when these programs are getting under way. The reserve organizations of the Army will still be below planned strength at the end of 1948.

The bulk of the terminated Army and Navy contracts has already been settled, with creditable dispatch. For all agencies, total commitments canceled on 318,000 prime contracts exceed 65 billion dollars. After deducting credits due the Government, total payments to contractors under the entire program are estimated at about 6.5 billion dollars. Of this total, about three-fourths of a billion dollars remained for payment at the beginning of the fiscal year 1947. Most of this has now been paid in final settlements or in advances pending settlement.

Applications for terminal-leave payments to enlisted military personnel have been smaller than expected. It is now estimated that 1.9 billion dollars will be paid in 1947 and only 250 million dollars in 1948.

Lend-lease expenditures in the fiscal year 1947 from funds appropriated to the President are largely interappropriation adjustments and payments for articles procured and services rendered in previous years. In 1948 there will be very small expenditures—all for closing out the program.

Except for some military aid to China and minor items, lend-lease was terminated after VJ-day. Since then, lend-lease goods valued at over 1 billion dollars have been sold to foreign countries on a cash or credit basis. Much progress has been made in effecting settlements with the countries which received about 50 billion dollars of lend-lease aid and extended almost 8 billion dollars of reciprocal aid. Final settlements have now been negotiated with the United Kingdom, Australia, New Zealand, India, France, Belgium, and Turkey, and discussions with the Netherlands, Norway, and the Union of South Africa are nearing completion.

The military program for stock piling of strategic materials has been reviewed carefully to minimize interference with business requirements. New stock piling is estimated at 90 million dollars in the fiscal year 1947 and 33 million dollars in 1948. In addition, excess metals and materials, amounting to 87 million dollars this year and 210 million dollars in the fiscal year 1948, will be transferred from Reconstruction Finance Corporation stocks to the Treasury military stock pile. Apart from stock piles transferred to the Treasury, the receipts of the Reconstruction Finance Corporation in its war activities reflect largely the rental and disposal of excess war plants, together with the sale of metals, minerals, and other commodities to the public.

Appropriations.—To finance the expenditure program outlined above, appropriations of 9.5 billion dollars and new contract authorizations of 541 million dollars will be necessary in the fiscal year 1948. These totals include 262 million dollars of supplemental appropriations and 91 million dollars of contract authorizations under legislation shortly to be submitted. The new appropriations needed in 1948 are about 2 billion dollars lower than the estimated expenditures, which include provision for payment of substantial amounts of unliquidated obligations of prior years.

INTERNATIONAL AFFAIRS AND FINANCE

The budget for our international program is designed to contribute to a peaceful world and a stable world economy. We have definite responsibilities to our wartime allies and in occupied countries. Our international lending program is an essential part of our efforts to achieve a world economy in which private trade will flourish.

The period when large-scale general relief is required for our allies is almost over. With the termination of the United Nations Relief and Rehabilitation Administration, there will remain, however, the urgent question of refugees and displaced persons. I urge the Congress to provide adequate support for the International Refugee Organization, now in process of being formed under the United Nations. It is also neces-

INTERNATIONAL AFFAIRS AND FINANCE

[Fiscal years. In millions]

	Expenditures			
Program or agency concerned	Actual, 1946	Estimate, 1947	Estimate, 1948	Appropriations, 1948
Reconstruction and stabilization:				
Subscriptions to International Fund and Bank......	$159	$1,426	....	....
Treasury loan to United Kingdom................	....	1,500	$1,200	....
Reconstruction Finance Corporation loans to United Kingdom................................	−39	−39	−40	....
Export-Import Bank loans.......................	464	1,025	730	....
Aid to China...............................	120	....	....	....
U.S. Commercial Company.....................	−118	20	....	....
Foreign relief:				
United Nations Relief and Rehabilitation Administration.....................................	743	1,515	305	....
War Department (occupied countries).............	....	556	645	$725
Other.......................................	4	3	....	....
Philippine-aid program...........................	28	105	137	144
Membership in international organizations..........	2	15	18	18
Foreign relations:				
State Department.............................	81	140	173	197
Other.......................................	20	12	15	9
Proposed legislation.............................	....	116	326	76
Total.....................................	1,464	6,394	3,510	1,169
From—				
General and special accounts:				
Purchase of capital stock in Export-Import Bank..	674	325	....	....
Philippine-aid program.........................	28	30	137	144
Other.......................................	1,129	5,283	2,683	1,025
Corporation accounts:				
Issuance of Export-Import Bank capital stock....	−674	−325	....	....
Export-Import Bank loans.......................	464	1,025	730	....
Reconstruction Finance Corporation loan to Philippines....................................	....	75	....	....
Other.......................................	−157	−19	−40	....
Total.....................................	1,464	6,394	3,510	1,169

66

sary that we provide a modest relief program for a few countries which are still in desperate straits. I recommend that the Congress speedily enact legislation to authorize these expenditures for which I am making provision in this Budget. In addition, I recommend that the Congress authorize participation in the World Health Organization and the proposed International Trade Organization and have included the small amounts needed for their support.

Expenditures.—The sharp decline in total expenditures in the fiscal year 1948 is due chiefly to the fact that in 1947 we shall complete our payment to the International Monetary Fund and our basic cash subscription to the International Bank for Reconstruction and Development. Further liabilities to the International Bank will arise only if we are called upon, within the limits of our total subscription, to join with other countries in making good any defaults by borrowers from the Bank.

More than half of our expenditures in the international field in the fiscal year 1948 will be loans for reconstruction or trade expansion. Disbursements will be predominantly under existing commitments. By the end of the fiscal year 1948 we shall have discharged about three-fourths of our commitments under our loan agreement with Britain. Since the International Bank is now ready for business, new authorizations for reconstruction loans by the Export-Import Bank are being sharply curtailed. In the future, the Export-Import Bank will be primarily concerned with loans to finance United States trade and small developmental loans in which we have a special interest. Outlays by the Export-Import Bank in the fiscal years 1946 and 1947 have been financed to a considerable extent by the sale of capital stock to the Treasury. Since the Treasury subscription is now complete, future net

outlays will be financed entirely by sale of notes to the Treasury.

The existing appropriation for United Nations Relief and Rehabilitation Administration expires at the end of the current fiscal year. Estimated expenditures in 1948 are entirely to wind up the program.

During the fiscal year 1948, the War Department will incur expenditures for administration and relief in Germany, Japan, Korea, and the Ryukyus and for administration in Austria. We must continue to provide subsistence to prevent disease, hunger, and unrest, and to provide proper administration, if these lands are eventually to become democratic and self-supporting. Moreover, shipments of food and other supplies are required to maintain the working efficiency of the populations and to stimulate production. Resulting increases in exports from these areas will furnish a growing source of funds to pay for necessary imports and thus help eliminate the need for financial assistance.

The recent agreement for economic unification of the British and United States zones in Germany will increase exports from those zones and help to make them self-sufficient by the end of the calendar year 1949. All costs incurred for the support of the German economy are to be repaid out of future German exports as quickly as recovery permits.

An important contribution to the economic revival of the occupied areas is being made by Federal agencies such as the U.S. Commercial Company in temporarily financing exports from these areas. Net dollar proceeds are currently being used primarily to purchase raw materials and equipment needed for a further expansion of exports in order to hasten the time when the occupied areas will become fully self-supporting. To aid in this program, I urge that the Congress authorize the U.S. Commercial Company to continue operations beyond June 30, 1947, the present expiration date.

Aid for the Philippine Republic includes assistance in rebuilding its economy, payments to fulfill our pledge to compensate partially for war damage, and maintenance of training programs for Philippine citizens. The 1947 total includes a Reconstruction Finance Corporation loan of 75 million dollars for aid in financing the current budget of the Republic.

Estimated expenditures of 18 million dollars for our membership in international organizations consist primarily of our share of the administrative budgets of the United Nations and its affiliated specialized organizations. In view of the immense tasks we have entrusted to the international organizations, this is a modest sum. Our contribution to the International Refugee Organization and funds for additional relief are included under proposed legislation.

Expenditures by the State Department are expected to increase in the fiscal year 1948. It is of utmost importance that the Department be equipped with sufficient funds and an adequate staff to make its maximum contribution to international peace. In 1948 there will be an increase of expenditures to carry on the improved Foreign Service program authorized under the Foreign Service Act of 1946. The Budget estimate for the Foreign Service buildings fund provides for the purchase of real property obtained by the Office of the Foreign Liquidation Commissioner in lend-lease and surplus property settlement agreements with other nations. Payment for these properties by the State Department increases miscellaneous receipts of the Treasury by a corresponding amount.

Appropriations.—Appropriations for the fiscal year 1948 total 1,169 million dollars, mainly for the administration and relief of occupied countries and for various State De-

partment programs. Funds for loans by the Export-Import Bank in the fiscal year 1948 will be obtained under its current borrowing authority. Advances to the United Kingdom will be made under the existing authorization. The appropriations total includes 11 million dollars of anticipated supplementals for the State Department and 76 million dollars for proposed legislation.

VETERANS' SERVICES AND BENEFITS

The Servicemen's Readjustment Act provides education and training benefits, unemployment and self-employment allowances, and loan guarantees. National service life insurance is an additional tangible benefit. For those who suffered disabilities, the best of medical care is provided. Pension rates for disabled veterans and for dependents of veterans were increased by the last Congress. In addition to the veterans' program, our servicemen have been assisted in resuming civilian life by mustering-out payments and terminal-leave payments.

Since the main purpose of our veterans' program is to reestablish former servicemen in civilian life, we must carefully avoid types of assistance which would encourage, or unnecessarily prolong, dependence upon Government subsidy. Any other policy would not only put an intolerable burden upon the taxpayer, but would be a great disservice to veterans themselves.

Although some amendments to veterans' legislation may still be required, no major new programs of assistance appear necessary. The job is now primarily one of effective administration. The Veterans' Administration has made great progress in establishing machinery that will administer this comprehensive program with speed and equity.

Expenditures.—The readjustment benefits program as a whole will continue in 1948 at its present level, as reductions in unem-

VETERANS' SERVICES AND BENEFITS

General and special accounts

[Fiscal years. In millions]

Program or agency concerned	Expenditures			Appropria-tions, 1948
	Actual, 1946	Estimate, 1947	Estimate, 1948	
Readjustment benefits, Veterans' Administration..	$1,350	$3,467	$3,462	$3,484
Pensions, Veterans' Administration...............	1,261	2,165	2,492	2,492
Insurance, Veterans' Administration...............	1,395	979	73	73
Hospitals, other services, and administrative costs:				
Construction:				
Veterans' Administration......................	27	37	84	43
Federal Works Agency..........................	....	40	50	25
War Department...............................	....	37	290	....
Current expenses:				
Veterans' Administration......................	377	870	890	892
Federal Works Agency..........................	3	6	1	....
War Department...............................	....	....	1	1
Total....................................	4,414	7,601	7,343	7,009

ployment allowances will be offset by increases in education and loan-guarantee expenditures. These estimates assume continuing prosperity and present legislation.

In the fiscal year 1947, almost 1,100,000 veterans, on the average, are drawing unemployment allowances and more than 200,000 are receiving self-employment allowances, at a time when total unemployment in the United States is less than 2,500,000. The turn-over on the allowance rolls has been rapid. Almost one-half of the 14,000,000 discharged from the services have already drawn unemployment or self-employment allowances. In recent months tightened administration and a more positive job-placement program by the employment service have contributed to a reduction in the numbers on the allowance rolls. In the fiscal year 1948 it is expected that about 900,000 veterans on the average will receive nearly one billion dollars in these allowances.

On the average 2,000,000 veterans are receiving education and training benefits in the fiscal year 1947. In 1948 possibly 2,100,000 will participate at a cost of over 2.3 billion dollars. We have had to meet an acute situation with respect to educational and housing facilities in universities, colleges, and schools throughout the country. In the fiscal year 1948 the Federal Works Agency will largely complete the conversion of war surplus facilities for educational purposes.

The number of trainees receiving on-the-job training has increased sharply to over 600,000. To guard against misuse of public funds, the Congress, in its last session, wisely provided limitations on subsistence allowances to veterans whose earnings exceed fixed monthly amounts and also clarified the standards to be used by the States in approving training establishments. Such limitations on subsistence allowances are essential to assure equity for veterans and taxpayers alike.

Amendments liberalizing the loan-guarantee program have brought a sharp increase in the number of loans guaranteed and in the average size of the guarantee. During the fiscal year 1947, new loans will be guaranteed for 750,000 veterans; in 1948, for

69

possibly 1,000,000. Roughly, 90 percent of these loans are made to finance home purchases by veterans. Expenditures in 1948 will be somewhat higher than in 1947—just over 100 million dollars for payment of the first year's interest on the guaranteed portion of the loan and for losses which are still relatively small.

Pension payments to disabled veterans and to dependents of veterans rose sharply from 1946 to 1947, as claims arising in World War II were granted. The increase in 1947 expenditures also reflects the 20 percent rise in pension rates approved by the last session of the Congress. Estimated expenditures of 2.5 billion dollars for pensions in 1948 include about 150 million dollars for subsistence allowances to disabled trainees and students. An average of 3,150,000 individuals will receive pensions and compensation in 1948—50 percent more than in 1946. This program will continue to increase for years to come.

Expenditures for insurance, which are mostly transfers to the national service life insurance trust fund, will decline sharply in 1948 with a corresponding decline in the trust funds accumulations. The total cost to the Government for servicemen's insurance in World War II will approach 3.7 billion dollars by the end of 1948 with small additional costs to come later.

The most extensive hospital and domiciliary construction program in the history of this Nation is now under way. The construction of veterans' hospitals and domiciliary facilities now authorized and recommended for authorization aggregates 1 billion dollars. Such construction, chiefly under the direction of the Corps of Engineers, will continue to increase in the fiscal year 1948. Less than half of the total program, however, will be completed by the end of that year.

In the fiscal year 1948 the operating and general administration expenses for veterans' programs as a whole will be somewhat higher than in the present year, chiefly because of the expansion of hospital facilities and improvement of medical care.

General administrative expenses for programs other than hospital and medical care are estimated in 1948 at about the 1947 level. The number of veterans participating in the readjustment, pension, and insurance programs will be higher, but the work load will fall as the number of entrants drops off.

The Administrator of Veterans' Affairs is carrying out a decentralization program aimed at attaining more effective administration through more direct contact with veterans in their communities.

Appropriations.—For these veterans' programs, this Budget recommends appropriations of 7,009 million dollars and contract authorizations of 220 million dollars to cover obligations to be incurred in the fiscal year 1948.

VETERANS' SERVICES AND BENEFITS

Trust accounts

[Fiscal years. In millions]

Item	Actual, 1946	Estimate, 1947	Estimate, 1948
Receipts:			
Transfers from general and special accounts.....................	$1,382	$974	$53
Premiums, interest, and other................................	1,085	641	653
Expenditures for benefits, refunds, and other (deduct).............	340	298	371
Net accumulation..	2,127	1,317	335

SOCIAL WELFARE, HEALTH, AND SECURITY

In spite of the achievements of the past 11 years in promoting the health, welfare, and social security of the American people, much remains to be done. Our present program affords but partial protection against the major causes of insecurity; large segments of the population are excluded from its benefits. We have not yet done enough to secure good health for the Nation.

The Federal Security Agency has recently been given broader jurisdiction over the social-welfare activities of the Government. As previously recommended, I favor creating a well integrated, yet flexible, Cabinet department of health, education, and social security to supersede this agency.

I hope that the studies already undertaken by congressional committees will result in the prompt expansion and integration of the present social-security system. There is, for example, serious need to correct inequalities between States in public assist-

ance payments and to extend the scope of Federal aid to include general assistance programs. The temporary increase in Federal grants for public assistance enacted in the last session of Congress will expire December 31, 1947; the Congress should now consider permanent legislation in this field. The estimated expenditures for the fiscal year 1948 include provision for such legislation.

The old-age and survivors insurance system at present leaves out 40 percent of those who earn their living. Even greater numbers are outside the unemployment compensation program. It is unjust to deny these agricultural workers, public employees, and other excluded groups the protection of social insurance. The system should be extended to cover them. At the same time, retirement benefits for the aged should be liberalized to reduce the necessity for piecing out insurance benefits with public-assistance payments.

Recent legislation for hospital construc-

SOCIAL WELFARE, HEALTH AND SECURITY

General and special accounts

[Fiscal years. In millions]

Program or agency concerned	Actual, 1946	Estimate, 1947	Estimate, 1948	Appropriations, 1948
Unemployment and accident compensation:				
Federal Security Agency............................	$75	$74	$72	$72
Railroad Retirement Board.........................	13	14	15	13
Retirement and dependency insurance:				
Railroad Retirement Board.........................	294	507	487	691
Federal Security Agency and other................	24	4	4	4
Assistance to aged and other special groups..........	436	702	720	727
Promotion of public health:				
Federal Security Agency............................	169	158	164	198
Federal Works Agency, Interior and War Departments..	10	12	17	15
Crime control and correction.......................	78	81	85	75
Other..	13	18	16	8
Proposed legislation................................	....	....	74	74
Total...	1,113	1,570	1,654	1,877

tion, for increased activities in mental health, and for expanded maternal and child-health services are substantial achievements toward improving the substandard health level of a large part of the population. But the major problem of financing health care still persists. Therefore, I again urge the Congress to enact a health-insurance program which will make adequate medical care available to everyone and provide protection against the economic hardships of sickness. Such a program should be al-

most entirely self-financing through pay-roll contributions.

Expenditures.—A large part of the social-insurance program is financed through trust-account operations which are not included in Budget expenditures. Pay-roll taxes collected by the States to finance unemployment compensation are deposited directly in a Federal trust account. The proceeds of Federal pay-roll taxes to cover old-age and survivors insurance are deducted from the receipts side of the Budget and do not ap-

SOCIAL WELFARE, HEALTH, AND SECURITY
Trust accounts
[Fiscal years.   In millions]

Fund and item	Actual, 1946	Estimate, 1947	Estimate, 1948
Unemployment trust fund:			
Receipts:			
Deposits by States....................................	$1, 010	$977	$1, 124
Railroad unemployment taxes........................	116	129	114
Transfers from general and special accounts...................	10	9	9
Withdrawals (deduct):			
State benefit payments.....................................	1, 128	800	700
Railroad unemployment benefit payments....................	17	36	49
Net accumulation..	—9	279	498
Federal old-age and survivors insurance trust fund:			
Net appropriation from general fund receipts....................	1, 201	1, 355	1, 987
Benefit payments and administrative expenses (deduct)...........	321	436	543
Net accumulation..	880	919	1, 444
Railroad retirement account:			
Transfers from general and special accounts....................	292	502	481
Benefit payments (deduct).....................................	152	198	270
Net accumulation..	140	304	211
Federal employees' retirement funds:			
Receipts:			
Transfers from general and special accounts (from general government)......................................	247	223	246
Deductions from salaries and other income....................	280	228	182
Annuities and refunds paid (deduct).........................	266	244	168
Net accumulation..	261	207	260

pear as Budget expenditures. For the railroad retirement system, however, the payroll tax receipts are included in net Budget receipts and the amounts transferred to the trust account appear in Budget expenditures. Similarly, the Government contribution to the Federal employees' retirement funds is a transfer included in Budget expenditures.

Trust fund withdrawals by the States to pay unemployment benefits depend not only on the number of unemployed in covered employment, but also on the rate of turnover. Budget expenditures for unemployment and accident compensation are mainly Federal grants to the States for administrative expenses of unemployment compensation. With high employment, accumulations in the trust fund will continue and administrative expenses will remain low.

Withdrawals from the trust fund for old-age and survivors insurance will continue to increase over a long period. As the program matures, the number of beneficiaries and the average benefit will gradually rise. A large estimated increase in receipts of this fund in the fiscal year 1948 is based on the assumption that the employment tax will rise from the present 2 percent rate on employers and employees to 5 percent on January 1, 1948, in accordance with present law.

Estimates for Budget expenditures for retirement and dependency insurance reflect the action of the last Congress in broadening the Railroad Retirement Act by adding survivors insurance and liberalizing benefits. Employer and employee tax rates were increased, resulting in larger payments to the trust account. These payments, which vary according to the railroad-pay-roll level, are expected to continue high. The major part of administrative expenses for old-age and survivors insurance is now paid directly from the old-age and survivors insurance trust fund and is therefore not included in Budget expenditures after the fiscal year 1946; this

change is responsible for a sharp drop in the Budget item for the Federal Security Agency for retirement and dependency insurance.

Federal payments for assistance to the aged and other special groups are expected to increase in the fiscal year 1948 because of a continuing long-term rise in benefit levels and case loads. A sharp rise in the expenditures in the fiscal year 1947 results from the higher public assistance benefits under temporary legislation and the inclusion of the school-lunch program in this category beginning this year.

Expenditures for promotion of public health are estimated slightly higher than in the current year. Although the total for the fiscal year 1948 includes expanded research and State-aid programs, including the Federal-State hospital program, these additions are largely offset by reductions of 24 million dollars owing to termination of the nurses' training program and of the maternity and infant-care program for families of servicemen.

Appropriations.—For the fiscal year 1948 the Budget includes appropriations of 1,877 million dollars, of which 74 million dollars are for proposed legislation. The recommended appropriation for the Railroad Retirement Board for the fiscal year 1948 exceeds the estimated expenditures to permit transfer to the trust account of taxes and income from 1947 and previous years; this transfer will take effect in the current fiscal year. The recommended appropriation for the hospital construction program is greater than the estimated expenditures because the program is just getting under way.

HOUSING AND COMMUNITY FACILITIES

I have urged the Congress to enact the essential features of the general housing bill which was passed by the Senate last year. The most urgent immediate requirements

73

HOUSING AND COMMUNITY FACILITIES

[Fiscal years.   In millions]

	Expenditures			
Program or agency concerned	*Actual,* 1946	*Estimate,* 1947	*Estimate,* 1948	*Appropriations,* 1948
Aids to private housing:				
Home Owners' Loan Corporation..................	—$275	—$245	—$210	....
Mortgage purchases (Reconstruction Finance Corporation)......................................	—45	233	443	....
Premium payments (Reconstruction Finance Corporation)......................................	2	60	....	....
Federal Housing Administration and other.........	—13	19	17	....
Public housing programs:				
Veterans' re-use (Federal Public Housing Authority)......................................	29	369	30	$8
War housing (Federal Public Housing Authority and other)...................................	34	29	135	142
Low-rent and other (Federal Public Housing Authority).................................	14	—10	18	8
Other housing services: Housing Expediter, and Administrator, National Housing Agency............	3	11	13	12
Provision of community facilities:				
Federal Works Agency.........................	68	53	35	4
Reconstruction Finance Corporation and other.....	3	25	44	....
Proposed legislation..............................	....	....	14	5
Total.............................	—180	544	539	179
From—				
General and special accounts.....................	158	526	225	179
Corporation accounts............................	—337	18	314	....
Total.............................	—180	544	539	179

are for incentives and aids to private lenders and builders to provide lower cost housing, especially rental housing, for assistance to local communities in their programs for urban redevelopment and low-rent housing, and for a permanent agency to supervise the major housing activities of the Federal Government.

Expenditures.—In our housing program we shall continue to rely primarily upon private housing construction. During the past year, with the assistance of many public and private agencies, we have succeeded in securing a rapid expansion in the supply of building materials available for construction

of veterans' housing. With the increased materials flow now evident, emphasis in the coming year will be focused on a few key materials, on acceleration of programs for recruitment and training of labor, and on provision of ample financing facilities for builders and prefabricators, as well as veterans and other purchasers. Particular attention will be given to measures to expand construction of rental housing. Many of these operations to aid private housing construction are reflected in expenditures of the Office of Temporary Controls, the Department of Labor, the Veterans' Administration, and the Reconstruction Finance

Corporation, as part of programs classified elsewhere.

The programs of the Federal Housing Administration and the Federal Home Loan Bank Administration involve relatively small net expenditures, but are of major importance in stimulating private construction. In the fiscal year 1948 the Federal Housing Administration expects to guarantee loans on 325,000 homes and apartments, most of them for new construction. During the same period savings and loan associations which are members of the Federal Home Loan Bank System will make an estimated 300,000 loans for financing new homes.

From an expenditure standpoint, the chief aids to private housing in the fiscal year 1948 will be provided by Reconstruction Finance Corporation purchases of mortgages guaranteed by the Veterans' Administration and the Federal Housing Administration. In the fiscal year 1948, purchases of veterans' home loans are expected to account for the great bulk of all mortgages purchased by the Reconstruction Finance Corporation. With the rapid rise in guaranteed loans to veterans (see "Veterans' services and benefits"), the Federal Government has recognized that its responsibility to the veterans can be realized only by assuring private financial institutions the same ready market for these obligations that they already possess for mortgages insured by the Federal Housing Administration. The lending institutions in turn have a responsibility to make sure that their loans will benefit the veterans and will not burden them with impossible future obligations.

Reconstruction Finance Corporation funds have also been employed to make premium payments to increase the supply of critically scarce building materials. In view of the rapid expansion in output and the decontrol of prices, it appears that these

programs can be terminated before the close of the current fiscal year.

The repayment of Home Owners' Loan Corporation loans will taper off in 1948 as its outstanding loans shrink. With its profits in recent years, we can now safely predict that this Corporation—which refinanced the loans of more than a million distressed borrowers during the depression—will liquidate without any loss to the Federal Government.

Expenditures on public housing programs are now concentrated almost entirely on liquidation of war housing activities and provision of emergency housing units for war veterans. Conversion of barracks and other types of temporary war structures—the largest expenditure item in 1947—will be substantially completed in the current year. Under this program an estimated 255,000 units are being provided for veterans and their families—more than half for veterans in educational institutions.

The continued housing shortage in many industrial areas has made it necessary for the Government to continue operating many temporary war housing units longer than previously expected. More than half of these units are occupied by veterans and servicemen. Expenditures in the fiscal year 1948 for management and disposition of war housing show an apparent increase primarily because receipts from the program are now deposited in miscellaneous receipts, rather than credited against expenditures. Payments of 85 million dollars also are forecast to transfer previous net receipts from rentals and sales into the general receipts of the Treasury. If allowance is made for these transfers and nonrecurring net receipts of 64 million dollars in 1947 from liquidation of the Defense Homes Corporation, program expenditures for war housing will decline substantially in 1948 from 1947 levels.

75

Receipts from the low-rent housing program will temporarily exceed expenditures in the current fiscal year because of anticipated repayments of loans by local housing authorities. Annual contributions to local housing authorities required by previous contracts will rise gradually as wartime tenants are replaced by low-income occupants.

Expenditures of the Federal Works Agency for defense public works will be virtually completed in the fiscal year 1948. Disbursements to localities for detailed planning of local public works will be limited to previous commitments under existing legislation.

On the other hand, disbursements on Reconstruction Finance Corporation loans to local agencies for construction of self-liquidating projects will be increased as materials become available to resume urgently needed work. To make sure that funds are adequate for these disbursements, I request that the present 100-million-dollar limitation on Reconstruction Finance Corporation loans for these purposes be increased to 125 million dollars.

Appropriations.—Of the total of 179 million dollars in appropriations estimated for the fiscal year 1948, an estimated 150 million dollars will be from current rental and disposition receipts of the veterans' re-use and war housing programs. Most of the 1948 expenditures will be made from Corporation funds or from unexpended balances of previous appropriations.

EDUCATION AND GENERAL RESEARCH

Our generous provision for education under the veterans' program should not obscure the fact that the Federal Government has large responsibilities for the general improvement of educational opportunities throughout the country. Although the expenditure estimates for the coming fiscal

year are limited to present programs, I have long been on record for basic legislation under which the Federal Government will supplement the resources of the States to assist them to equalize educational opportunities and achieve satisfactory educational standards.

The relationship of the Federal Government to higher education also demands serious consideration. The veterans' readjustment program, which compelled a rapid emergency expansion of facilities to meet immediate needs, has focused attention on this fundamental problem. A Presidential commission on higher education is studying the matter because of its great importance to the future of the Nation.

Many agencies of the Federal Government carry on research as a part of their regular programs. But we need a central agency to correlate and encourage the research activities of the country. While freedom of inquiry must be preserved, the Federal Government should accept responsibility for fostering the flow of scientific knowledge and developing scientific talent in our youth. To accomplish this, I recommend again that a National Science Foundation or its equivalent be established. The Scientific Research Board appointed in October 1946 is now making a study of the research program of the entire Federal Government in its relation to all other research activities planned or in progress. Its report will undoubtedly be of service in establishing a proper program for the new agency. It is assumed that no additional expenditures will be required during the fiscal year 1948.

Expenditures.—Federal expenditures for promotion of education, apart from the veterans' education program, now consist almost entirely of vocational grants to States, support of land-grant colleges, and general administration of the Office of Education. The Federal Works Agency will complete

EDUCATION AND GENERAL RESEARCH

[Fiscal years.   In millions]

	Expenditures			
Program or agency concerned	*Actual, 1946*	*Estimate, 1947*	*Estimate, 1948*	*Appropriations, 1948*
Promotion of education:				
Office of Education, Federal Security Agency.......	$27	$28	$35	$35
Federal Works Agency...........................	....	4	3	....
Educational aid to special groups (except veterans):				
Bureau of Indian Affairs (Interior)................	11	12	12	12
Other agencies..................................	2	3	6	6
Library and museum services.......................	6	8	17	18
General-purpose research:				
Office of Scientific Research and Development......	34	4	....	....
Commerce Department...........................	8	11	14	14
Other agencies..................................	....	....	1	1
Total..	88	71	88	85

during the fiscal year 1948 its expenditures for the maintenance and operation of schools in war-affected communities. Corresponding expenditures prior to the current fiscal year are classified in "Housing and community facilities."

In August 1946, the Congress increased the authorization for vocational education by 15 million dollars. It is not possible at this time, however, for the State and local governments to make firm commitments on the availability of matching funds for the development of new programs of vocational education or the expansion of existing programs. Therefore, although the estimates of appropriations and expenditures for the fiscal year 1948 include an anticipated supplemental appropriation under this authorization, it may be necessary to increase the amount on the basis of later information from State and local governments. Money for this purpose has been included in the reserve for contingencies.

Expenditures for educational aid to special groups include funds for education of Indians through the Department of the Interior and smaller amounts for assistance to the blind and the deaf and to Howard University through the Federal Security Agency. The major part of the estimated increase in expenditures is for construction of four buildings at Howard University, for which Congress has already appropriated money for drawing plans. Their construction is made urgent by the pressure of enrollment upon all existing facilities.

The increase in expenditures for library and museum services is due chiefly to the general expansion of activities of the Library of Congress.

Research is inherent in many Federal programs and consequently the bulk of such expenditures is included in the specific programs to which the research relates. The principal items of continuing expenditure for those research programs which serve several purposes or are general in character are in the Bureau of the Census, the Bureau of Standards, and the Coast and Geodetic Survey—all within the Department of Commerce. Some expansion of these activities is contemplated in the estimates for the fiscal year 1948. The Office of Scientific Research and Development, which was devoted to research in support of the war effort, will be almost completely liquidated in the fiscal year 1947.

Appropriations.—The total of appropriations for education and general research is 85 million dollars for the fiscal year 1948—3 million dollars less than the estimated expenditures. This total includes a tentative estimate of the amount which will be required under the new authorization for vocational education.

AGRICULTURE AND AGRICULTURAL RESOURCES

Because of high consumer incomes in the United States and the continuing world shortage of many foods, the demand for farm products will doubtless remain strong throughout the fiscal year 1948. Agricultural production goals for the 1947 crop year, with a few exceptions, will call for another year of maximum output.

The demand for American farm products, however, cannot be counted upon to continue indefinitely at the present high level. Under present legislation the Department of Agriculture is required to support prices of most agricultural commodities until December 31, 1948.

We must design our agricultural policies to work toward a better balance of supply with demand and so avoid excessive expenditures for price support. We should facilitate the transfer of unnecessary farm labor and resources from agriculture to industrial and other pursuits. We shall need also to devise ways of supporting farm income which will retain export markets for wheat, cotton, and tobacco, and at the same time give the American consumer the benefit of increasing efficiency in farm production.

The authority of the Commodity Credit Corporation expires on June 30, 1947. Since the Corporation now has a State charter, I am recommending that it be rechartered by act of Congress and that its present borrowing authority of 4,750 million dollars be renewed.

Expenditures.—By the fiscal year 1948 the program of the Commodity Credit Corporation will be limited almost entirely to price support for agricultural commodities. Reimbursements from lend-lease, United Nations Relief and Rehabilitation Administration, and foreign governments will be largely completed in the next 6 months. Liquidation of inventories is tapering off. For the present, the high level of farm prices has made price-support outlays unnecessary except for a few commodities such as potatoes and eggs.

In 1948, however, even with continued general prosperity, an estimated 330 million dollars will be spent to support agricultural prices. Larger outlays will be required should markets weaken seriously. In addition, loans by commercial banks guaranteed by the Commodity Credit Corporation will probably be substantial. The present borrowing authority, if renewed, will be ample to support agricultural prices during the fiscal year 1948.

Receipts from other corporate transactions in the Department of Agriculture are expected to be lower in 1947 and 1948 than in 1946. In 1946 there were unusually large repayments to the farm credit agencies and large receipts in revolving funds of the Treasury from return of capital of mixed-ownership corporations. In view of the large repayments and refinancing of the loans of the Federal Farm Mortgage Corporation, this Budget recommends that the Corporation's borrowing authority of 2 billion dollars be reduced to an amount more nearly commensurate with foreseeable needs. This recommendation should be considered when the Farm Credit Administration sub-

Agriculture and Agricultural Resources

[Fiscal years.   In millions]

	Expenditures			
Program or agency concerned	Actual, 1946	Estimate, 1947	Estimate, 1948	Appropria- tions, 1948
Loan and investment programs:				
Department of Agriculture:				
Price support, supply, and purchase programs (Commodity Credit Corporation)............	−$1,329	−$79	$330	....
Other corporate transactions..................	−261	−73	−50	$23
Farmers' Home Administration................	30	40	154	172
Rural Electrification Administration...........	11	12	25	31
Reconstruction Finance Corporation:				
Loans to Rural Electrification Administration....	74	200	300	....
Other loans................................	−24	10	−17	....
Other financial aids:				
Department of Agriculture:				
Conservation and use........................	311	352	311	202
Exportation and domestic consumption.........	75	80	66	148
Sugar Act..................................	54	52	53	55
Other......................................	3	5	7	9
Food subsidies (Commodity Credit Corporation and Reconstruction Finance Corporation)............	1,634	325	6	....
Agricultural land and water resources..............	39	52	53	49
Development and improvement....................	134	139	142	135
Total......................................	752	1,117	1,381	824
From—				
General and special accounts:				
Postwar price support........................	500	....	....	....
Cancellation of notes of Commodity Credit Corporation...............................	....	921	830	....
Other......................................	535	661	773	824
Corporation accounts:				
Postwar price support........................	−500	....	....	....
Cancellation of notes of Commodity Credit Corporation...............................	....	−921	−830	....
Other......................................	217	456	608	....
Total......................................	752	1,117	1,381	824

mits its report on the mortgage-loan programs of the Corporation and the Federal land banks.

The rural rehabilitation and farm tenant programs, formerly under the Farm Security Administration, and the Crop and Feed Loan Division of the Farm Credit Administration have been merged to form the new Farmers' Home Administration. This program shows an apparent increase in 1948, solely because of the changed method of financing required in the Farmers' Home Administration Act of 1946.

The increased estimates for Rural Electrification Administration loans will permit expansion of a program that is urgently needed by farmers but has been held back during the war years.

Commitments for payments to farmers under the Agricultural Adjustment Administration conservation and use program for the 1947 crop year have already been made as provided by the 1947 appropriation act. Expenditures for this program, including administrative expenses, are estimated at 311 million dollars in the fiscal year 1948.

A year ago the Budget Message recommended gradual reduction of these payments, and that recommendation is now renewed. More than 60 percent of the total payments go to about one-eighth of the Nation's farmers. Most of this money thus is being paid to farmers who, because of their strong position in American agriculture, would undoubtedly continue the best farm management practices without the persuasion of a bonus from the Treasury.

We should shift our effort from this kind of subsidy to providing technical guidance to all farmers for soil conservation and management, along the lines of the Soil Conservation Service and the Extension Service. I therefore propose that the appropriation act limit the conservation and use program for the crop year 1948 to 200 million dollars instead of the 300-million-dollar program to which we are committed for the crop year 1947. This will not affect expenditures materially until the fiscal year 1949.

Expenditures to encourage exportation and domestic consumption of farm products are financed under section 32 of the act of August 24, 1935, by a permanent appropriation equal to 30 percent of customs receipts. In the fiscal year 1946 expenditures for the school-lunch program were financed by this appropriation. These have been transferred to "Social welfare, health, and security" in later years. The remaining expenditures in 1947 and 1948 are for export subsidies, diversion of surplus commodities to new uses, and purchase and distribution of surplus agricultural commodities to State welfare agencies. Addition of the cotton export subsidy program previously financed by the Commodity Credit Corporation and other increases offset the transfer of the school-lunch program.

Almost all wartime food subsidy programs of the Commodity Credit Corporation and the Reconstruction Finance Corporation have now been discontinued. Subsidy payments from corporate funds in the fiscal year 1948 will be limited to sugar, which is expected to remain in short supply. In addition, payments to sugar growers in the United States under the Sugar Act program will remain at approximately the present level.

Expenditures for agricultural land and water resources, which include the Soil Conservation Service, upstream erosion and flood control, water conservation and utilization, and the submarginal land program, are estimated to increase slightly in 1948.

Expansion of agricultural research under the Research and Marketing Act of 1946 will cost an additional 18 million dollars in the fiscal year 1948. The farm labor supply program will decrease by about 16 million dollars. Other general programs for the development and improvement of agriculture, such as the Extension Service, the scientific research agencies, and the staff agencies of the Department of Agriculture, will remain at about the present level. Thus, the programs in this category as a whole will increase by 3 million dollars.

Appropriations.—To carry out our agricultural programs, I recommend that the Congress appropriate 824 million dollars for the fiscal year 1948. In addition, since not all of the permanent appropriation of section 32 funds will be required to subsidize exportation and domestic consumption of sur-plus agricultural commodities, the trans-fer of 100 million dollars to the Agricultural Adjustment Administration program for conservation and use of agricultural land resources is recommended. In 1947, 42.5 million dollars of section 32 funds were so transferred. In view of the probable need for these funds after 1948 for surplus dis-posal programs, however, we cannot look forward to their continued annual use for the conservation and use program.

The operations of the various agricultural corporations and the agricultural programs of the Reconstruction Finance Corporation will be financed out of corporate funds bor-rowed from the Treasury. It is estimated that 830 million dollars of notes owed the Treasury by the Commodity Credit Corpora-tion will be canceled in 1948 pursuant to the appraisal of the assets of the Corporation as of June 30, 1946. This cancellation of notes will be an expenditure under general and special accounts and a receipt under corporation accounts, and thus will have no net effect on Budget expenditures or on the appropriations recommended for 1948.

NATURAL RESOURCES

The natural resources program has been increasing to fill some of the gaps arising from wartime deferments and depletions. The estimated expenditures for the fiscal year 1948 represent a further expansion over the current year. They do not contemplate ini-tiation of large new projects.

The harnessing of atomic energy was a war achievement, and it remains of major mili-tary significance. With the appointment of the Atomic Energy Commission last fall we have entered on a new phase of development. This Commission has assumed direction of the Manhattan Engineer District project. Our aim is to bring the benefits of atomic

research to industry and medicine and to enrich standards of well-being.

In line with the shift in emphasis, the atomic energy program, since December 31, 1946, is classified in "Natural resources." This transfer in the middle of the current fiscal year and the inclusion on a full-year basis in 1948 are major reasons for the increases in expenditures for resource de-velopment in both years.

Expenditures.—In order to push forward basic research in development and use of atomic energy, I am recommending a pro-gram which will involve expenditures of 444 million dollars in the fiscal year 1948. This compares with total outlays of 385 million dollars in the current fiscal year, of which 179 million dollars are shown in "National defense."

Much of the productive future of this Na-tion lies in the effective development of our river basins. Under the Bureau of Reclama-tion and the Corps of Engineers, this work will go forward in 1948 at a somewhat in-creased expenditure rate. The estimates pro-vide for continuation of projects under way and starting those projects for which 1947 appropriations were made, but which have been temporarily deferred.

The only appropriations now recom-mended are for projects partly provided for in previous appropriation acts. A substan-tial portion of the expenditures is for multi-ple-purpose projects which, in addition to flood control, navigation, and irrigation benefits, will supply needed power for in-dustry and agriculture.

Some expansion of transmission facilities is needed by the Bonneville Power Admin-istration to market the hydroelectric power generated at certain of the Government's multiple-purpose dams. Receipts of 25 mil-lion dollars from the sale of power by this agency and the Southwestern Power Ad-ministration will be paid into miscellaneous

NATURAL RESOURCES NOT PRIMARILY AGRICULTURAL

[Fiscal years. In millions]

Program or agency concerned	Expenditures			Appropriations, 1948
	Actual, 1946	Estimate, 1947	Estimate, 1948	
Atomic energy:				
Atomic Energy Commission.....................	....	$201	$443	$250
Other agencies...............................	....	5	1	....
Land and water resources:				
Corps of Engineers (War)......................	$89	192	255	189
Bureau of Reclamation (Interior)...............	62	145	176	151
Bonneville and Southwestern Power Administrations (Interior)........................	9	20	27	23
Tennessee Valley Authority.....................	5	36	47	27
International Boundary and Water Commission (State).................................	1	4	10	9
Other (Interior).............................	10	12	15	15
Forest resources:				
Forest Service (Agriculture)...................	40	53	53	54
Department of the Interior.....................	3	3	3	3
Mineral resources:				
Department of the Interior.....................	18	21	23	20
Navy Department............................	3	6	4	....
Recreational use of resources (Interior).........	5	15	19	13
Other resources (Interior)....................	12	17	24	26
Total.....................................	257	728	1,101	779
From—				
General and special accounts:				
Tennessee Valley Authority...................	21	33	45	27
Other.......................................	254	694	1,054	752
Corporation accounts:				
Tennessee Valley Authority...................	—16	3	2	....
Reconstruction Finance Corporation............	—2	—2	....	....
Total.....................................	257	728	1,101	779

receipts of the Treasury in the fiscal year 1948.

Expenditures of the Tennessee Valley Authority will increase in the fiscal year 1948 as work progresses on the two large dams provided for in the 1947 appropriations. By the end of 1948 construction of the major dams will be almost complete; thereafter, the principal activity will be directed toward the effective utilization of local resources for industrial and agricultural improvement within the valley. The

Tennessee Valley Authority finances its power operations and transmission facilities from its own revenues. The Authority will continue the practice started in the last fiscal year of making payments to the Treasury.

Expenditures by the International Boundary and Water Commission for the United States share of the construction of dams and other water improvements on the Rio Grande, in cooperation with the Mexican Government, will be expanded in 1948, pursuant to the 1944 treaty.

Among the other expenditures by the Department of the Interior for land and water resources in 1948, the major portion is for the use, protection, and improvement of the public lands which it manages. The estimated expenditures for 1948 for grazing activities contemplate restoration of the program to approximately the 1946 level. Appropriations for the fiscal year 1947 were cut to a level that does not permit adequate protection and conservation of these grazing resources. The Department of the Interior is investigating the feasibility of raising grazing fees to cover the operating costs of the Grazing Service and also service charges on the cost of capital improvements.

Because of critical needs for lumber, our forests, both public and private, must be administered to yield the maximum immediate supply without unduly impairing future timber resources. Expenditures for the Forest Service for the fiscal year 1948 provide for increased timber-sale administration and forest-fire control. These increases are offset by decreases in other phases of the work.

Our mineral resources have been seriously depleted during the war. Substitutes or new sources of supply must now be found. As part of our military program we are accumulating a strategic stock pile of critical materials from both domestic and foreign sources. To plan this program successfully and to assure adequate supplies for industrial and consumer use, it is essential that we have full information on our domestic resources. Consequently, the Bureau of Mines and the Geological Survey will make small expansions in their mineral resource programs in 1948.

During the war the national park system has been maintained on virtually a custodial basis only. Increased expenditures are required in 1948 to provide the most needed improvements in roads, parkways, buildings and utilities, and for general administration and protection.

Other resource programs of the Department of the Interior will increase by 7 million dollars in 1948. General surveys and topographical mapping activities by the Geological Survey must be accelerated to provide basic data needed for natural resources programs and industrial development. Expenditures for conservation and development of fish and wildlife resources reflect a small increase in operating costs.

Some progress has been made in the development of Alaska, but only a beginning. Included in several of these programs are expenditures for the investigation and development of the natural resources of this vast area.

Appropriations.—Appropriations of 779 million dollars for resource development in the fiscal year 1948 include an estimated supplemental of 4 million dollars for the Forest Service. The total is substantially below estimated expenditures for that year. Postponement of some of the public works projects for flood control and reclamation in the current year will leave available in 1948 substantial balances from earlier-year appropriations. Similarly, the curtailment of other resource development activities has resulted in some carry-over of appropriations for these programs. A smaller amount from 1948 appropriations will be available to finance expenditures in later years.

In the case of the Atomic Energy Commission, the Budget recommendation includes contract authority in the amount of 250 million dollars in addition to the 250 million dollars of recommended appropriations. The appropriations to discharge obligations under this contract authority will be made in future years when the payments become due.

TRANSPORTATION AND COMMUNICATION

Six years of deferred maintenance and improvement must be made up before the basic postwar needs of motor and water transportation are met. The highway system, particularly, has fallen far behind the standards which should prevail under conditions of rapidly growing use. Urban congestion is again becoming a serious problem. Likewise, the enormous expansion of civil aviation since VJ-day has thrown an increasing burden upon inadequate airway and airport facilities. An expanded program is essential if undue hazards in the air are to be avoided and if the development of aviation is to continue without serious technical impediment. At the same time it is hoped to restore prewar service standards in the postal service. The enforcement of regulatory standards, particularly those designed for accident prevention in all types of transport, should be restored, at least to prewar levels.

It is the policy of the Government to withdraw from ship operation as rapidly as possible and to dispose of vessels in a manner that will promote a large and effective merchant fleet under our flag. But, since private operators see little prospect of profit in the coastwise trade and much of the overseas

TRANSPORTATION AND COMMUNICATIONS

[Fiscal years. In millions]

| | Expenditures | | | |
Program or agency concerned	Actual, 1946	Estimate, 1947	Estimate, 1948	Appropriations, 1948
Promotion of the merchant marine (Maritime Commission)	$374	−$117	$204	$6
Provision of navigation aids and facilities:				
War Department	93	124	152	120
Coast Guard	....	168	157	149
Provision of highways:				
Federal Works Agency	77	268	393	300
Other	13	33	35	33
Promotion of aviation:				
National Advisory Committee for Aeronautics	32	38	44	36
Commerce (Civil Aeronautics Administration)	62	92	149	152
Other	5	2	....	....
Regulation of transportation	22	25	15	15
Other services to transportation:				
Reconstruction Finance Corporation (railroad loans)	−43	−31	−3	....
Other	17	19	21	22
Postal service (Post Office Department)	161	276	352	353
Regulation of communications (Federal Communications Commission), and other services to communications	11	7	9	9
Total	824	905	1, 530	1, 196
From—				
General and special accounts	866	936	1, 533	1, 196
Corporation accounts	−43	−31	−3	....
Total	824	905	1, 530	1, 196

traffic is regarded as temporary, Government operations have continued. The Maritime Commission reconversion program, the lay-up of vessels in the reserve fleet, and the preparation of war-built vessels for sale are under way.

Expenditures.—The Maritime Commission, by its petition before the Interstate Commerce Commission, is attempting to obtain revision of the railroad rate structure in order to permit resumption of domestic shipping under private auspices. We must look to the domestic trade to provide the active core of our merchant fleet reserve, since we cannot hope to maintain in the foreign trade alone a merchant fleet adequate for the Nation's security. Because the long-run needs of foreign trade are not yet clear, the expenditure estimates contemplate only a moderate expansion in operating subsidies. Construction of new vessels is limited to those for which private purchasers are available and those essential to meet specialized needs for which war-built vessels cannot be adapted. I hope that the rate of ship disposition and liquidation of Government operations can be expedited.

Under the War Department are two major functions relating to transportation—the Panama Canal and the rivers and harbors work of the Corps of Engineers. To make up deferred maintenance, to continue at a minimum rate river and harbor construction projects already under way, and to make a slow beginning on projects authorized under the 1947 appropriation it is necessary to expand the expenditures during the fiscal year 1948.

Other aids to navigation are those maintained and operated by the Coast Guard (in the Treasury Department). The large decrease in the fiscal year 1948 reflects the return to a normal program, the completion of previously deferred work during 1947 and early 1948, and some reduction in Coast Guard aviation. In the interest of reducing expenditures, the installation of the Loran system of radio navigation aid will be spread over a number of years.

Most Federal expenditures for highways are concentrated in the Federal-aid program under the Federal Works Agency. This is a matching program in which Federal expenditures depend upon the level of State activity within the authorized annual rate of 500 million dollars established for each of the first three postwar years by the Federal-Aid Highway Act of 1944. Materials shortages, contracting difficulties, and high costs have delayed this program, but the situation should ease by next year. Sums apportioned to the States, however, are available only for a year after the close of the fiscal year for which they are authorized, and the rate of expenditure has thus far been well below congressional authorizations. States are, therefore, under pressure to obligate these funds at once. As has been urged by many of the States, it is recommended that the Congress extend for one additional year the period during which these funds may be expended. Moderate increases for the Agriculture and Interior Departments are included to begin to overcome the long deferment of work on the forest roads and trails and Indian roads.

The sharp upward trend in expenditures by the Department of Commerce for civil aviation results from the rapid expansion of the industry. Inadequate facilities and services have caused serious congestion and a threat to air safety. The expansion and modernization of the airways system provided in these estimates is essential for the continued progress of the industry and could not be reduced without great risk.

As the rapid growth of aviation continues, I believe it is unwise to place the entire burden of expanding, improving, and maintaining the airways upon the general taxpayer. Instead, civil aviation should bear a reasonable share. The Department of Commerce is considering the feasibility of various methods to recover part of the expenses from the users.

Substantial expenditures for grants-in-aid to airports under the 1946 legislation are anticipated for the first time, increasing from 7 million dollars in the fiscal year 1947 to 50 million dollars in 1948. This will be channeled as far as possible into urgent work designed to relieve bottlenecks in air transport, but the apportionment formula will limit the discretion of the Civil Aeronautics Administration in scheduling first the most needed projects.

Unless legislative action is taken to revise postal rates, the Post Office deficit threatens to be the largest in history. Mail volume has expanded enormously, but current operating costs have increased even more rapidly. This is the chief cause of the deficit. Further temporary additions to expenditures result from the need to take up deferred maintenance and replace equipment. The Post Office Department is studying its operations with a view to introducing economies. I am instructing the Postmaster General to institute all operating economies consistent with reasonable service and to prepare a comprehensive recommendation for rate revision sufficient to wipe out the deficit.

Appropriations.—Appropriations of 1,196 million dollars are included in the Budget for the fiscal year 1948 for "Transportation and communication," compared with estimated expenditures of 1,530 million dollars. Unobligated balances in Maritime Commission revolving funds are adequate for all expenditures with the exception of an appropriation of 6 million dollars recommended for the maritime training fund and aid to State marine schools. War Department and Federal Works Agency appropriations fall below expenditure estimates because of the

deferral to 1948 of work for which appropriations were already made in 1947. The appropriations total includes 50 million dollars for the Civil Aeronautics Administration as an estimate of the appropriation request that will be made for the airport program as soon as the plans of the Agency are sufficiently matured. Contract authorizations of 500 million dollars are included for the Federal-aid postwar highway construction program.

FINANCE, COMMERCE, AND INDUSTRY

By the end of the current fiscal year, almost all wartime controls of business will have ended. I recommend that the Congress extend the authority for rent control; price control on sugar and sirups, and rice; sugar rationing; export and import controls; priority and allocation controls on a few commodities still in extremely short supply; and a few other minimum controls which are indispensable for the time being.

Now that we are returning to a peacetime economy that depends for its success on private enterprise, the Government should resume and expand its services to business, including both financial and nonfinancial aids. In addition, free enterprise depends on positive Government action to preserve competition and control monopolies—proper functions that a democratic government must not neglect.

Expenditures.—During the rest of this fiscal year, the Office of Temporary Controls will discontinue as rapidly as possible direct controls over business operations previously administered by the Civilian Production Administration and the Office of Price Administration. Although a few essential controls should be retained a little longer, these, too, will be terminated as soon as conditions permit.

Among the other regulatory agencies, For-

FINANCE, COMMERCE, AND INDUSTRY

[Fiscal years. In millions]

	Expenditures			
Program or agency concerned	Actual, 1946	Estimate, 1947	Estimate, 1948	Appropriations, 1948
Promotion or regulation of business:				
Office of Temporary Controls.....................	$184	$133	$55	$52
Commerce Department...........................	11	22	28	31
Others (Federal Trade Commission, Federal Power Commission, etc.)............................	15	15	13	13
Business loans and guarantees:				
Reconstruction Finance Corporation loans to business................................	−111	−21	57	....
Retirement of Smaller War Plants Corporation capital stock...................................	....	....	100	....
War damage insurance (War Damage Corporation)....	−2	1	211	....
Aids to private financial institutions (Reconstruction Finance Corporation).........................	−72	−73	−55	....
Control of private finance (Securities and Exchange Commission).................................	5	5	6	6
Proposed legislation.............................	....	....	10	14
Total.....................................	30	83	426	116
From—				
General and special accounts.....................	216	176	112	116
Corporation accounts...........................	−185	−93	314	....
Total.....................................	30	83	426	116

eign Funds Control (Treasury) and Solid Fuels Administration (Interior) will also cease operations this year.

The peacetime regulatory agencies, however, must be strengthened from low levels justified during the war by the existence of other direct controls. This Budget, therefore, provides for the necessary increases in such essential agencies as the Federal Trade Commission, the Federal Power Commission, the Antitrust Division (Justice), and the Tariff Commission.

The Antitrust Division will concentrate its efforts on major violations of the antitrust laws. The Federal Trade Commission will increase its effectiveness by operating on an industry-wide basis, rather than through the slower procedure of individual complaints. It will also sponsor a larger number of industry conferences designed to locate and eliminate unfair trade practices through cooperative action.

In the past year, we have made a fine start in building up the business service programs of the Department of Commerce from their low wartime levels. To provide necessary information for business, provision of funds is recommended for a census of manufactures (already authorized by law) and likewise for a census of business to be authorized by proposed legislation. No census has been taken in either area since 1939 and present information is badly out of date. A small but necessary increase in the business service activities of the Bureau of Foreign and Domestic Commerce is also recommended.

The Patent Office urgently needs increases in personnel to cope with the growing backlog of patent applications and to handle registrations under recent trade-mark legislation.

The Reconstruction Finance Corporation estimates assume that repayment of outstanding wartime loans to business enterprises will continue in the fiscal year 1948, but at a slower rate. In its peacetime business loan program, the Corporation has been authorizing about 1,000 loans a month, chiefly to small business. Ninety percent of them are in amounts of 100,000 dollars or less. The new program also emphasizes guarantees of private credit rather than direct Government loans. These guarantees will not require disbursements in any large amount unless there should be an economic recession. In this event the Reconstruction Finance Corporation stands ready to purchase the loans offered by participating banks.

Since January 1946, the Reconstruction Finance Corporation has been administering the loan and lease program of the Smaller War Plants Corporation. Disbursements on previously authorized Smaller War Plants Corporation loans are nearly finished and outstanding loans are gradually being repaid. In the fiscal year 1948 the Reconstruction Finance Corporation plans to retire an estimated 100 million dollars in Smaller War Plants Corporation capital stock.

The War Damage Corporation, a Reconstruction Finance Corporation subsidiary, which at its peak had a total of 140 billion dollars of war damage insurance in force, is also terminating its operations. By 1948 it will be in full liquidation. The Reconstruction Finance Corporation has been directed to return to the Treasury the 210 million dollars of net profits from this operation.

The expenditures of 310 million dollars for retirement of Smaller War Plants Corporation capital and return of War Damage Corporation profits will be paid into miscellaneous receipts and thus have no net effect on the total Budget. With these transfer items eliminated, the net increase of expenditures under this function in 1948 is 33 million dollars.

Federal and State bank supervisory authorities are making special efforts to encourage banks and insurance companies to complete repayment of their prewar obligations to the Reconstruction Finance Corporation. By June 30, 1948, the outstanding volume of such loans and investments will be down to 100 million dollars out of a total of about 3.5 billion dollars disbursed since 1932.

With stock market activity and new security issues far above wartime levels, the Securities and Exchange Commission requires additional funds to rebuild its depleted staff and thus provide more adequate protection for the millions of investors.

Appropriations.—To finance the expenditures for these programs, estimated appropriations in the fiscal year 1948 of 116 million dollars include anticipated additional appropriations of 53 million dollars required by proposed extension of the existing authority of the Office of Temporary Controls and the authority of the Department of Commerce to control exports. They also include 14 million dollars for new censuses under proposed new legislation.

LABOR

The facilities of the Federal Government for dealing with the welfare of labor and with labor-management disputes provide for the encouragement of collective bargaining, administration of laws and regulations to protect the working force, assistance to States

LABOR

[Fiscal years. In millions]

Program or agency concerned	Expenditures			Appropriations, 1948
	Actual, 1946	Estimate, 1947	Estimate, 1948	
Mediation and regulation:				
Labor Department...........................	$14	$11	$9	$9
National Labor Relations Board.................	4	5	8	8
Other.......................................	6	3	4	4
Training and placement:				
Public employment offices.....................	71	90	78	78
Other.......................................	1	3	3	3
Labor information and statistics and general administration	8	12	14	14
Proposed legislation.............................	....	....	3	3
Total....................................	104	124	118	118

in promoting employment opportunities, and gathering of basic labor information.

In my message on the State of the Union, I have asked that the machinery in the Department of Labor for facilitating collective bargaining and expediting the settlement of labor-management disputes be amplified and strengthened. I have included administrative funds for this purpose under proposed legislation.

I recommend also that the Congress authorize grants to States through the Department of Labor for programs fostering safe working conditions. The toll resulting from industrial hazards reduces the productive capacity of the labor force. The new program should be administered by State departments of labor under Federal standards. Funds for this purpose have likewise been included under proposed legislation.

Expenditures.—The National Labor Relations Board has an accumulation of unresolved cases awaiting action owing to the increased incidence of representation cases and unfair labor practice cases and to the reduced appropriations available for the Board's work this year. Delay in settling such cases is in itself a cause of labor disturbance. Apart from the backlog of un-

settled cases, the number of cases brought before the Board for settlement has increased. The program submitted in this Budget is designed to reduce the backlog and keep the Board more nearly current in handling cases. This should diminish the incidence of strike action by labor organizations which is encouraged by tardy handling of cases.

The public employment service system, although now composed of the coordinated employment office facilities of the several States, is still financed in full by the Federal Government. Expenditures for these offices for the fiscal year 1947 are estimated at 90 million dollars. This includes the increased cost of State operation and 11 million dollars of nonrecurring terminal-leave pay for Federal employees upon the return of the employment service to the States. It is my hope that the public employment service system will maintain the high standard of operations and the efficient procedures which have proved essential for facilitating the flow of workers to areas where they are needed.

I propose also increased expenditures for labor information and statistics to facilitate collective bargaining and meet the more important needs of labor, business, Government, and the general public for current data concerning employment, wages, prices, and the like.

Appropriations.—For 1948, I recommend appropriations of 118 million dollars, including the amount for proposed legislation.

GENERAL GOVERNMENT

The principal types of expenditures in "General government" are for (1) legislative and judicial activities, and executive management and control; (2) the Government payment toward civilian employees' retirement; (3) other services covered by appro-

priations which relate to more than one function; and (4) a few special programs necessitated by the war, such as disposal of surplus property, which do not logically belong in any other category.

Expenditures for these functions in the fiscal year 1948 are expected to decline only moderately from the comparable total for 1947, because they will still include a substantial amount for war liquidation. Such activities will account for more than one-third of all the expenditures in this category.

Expenditures.—The work load of the Treasury Department remains at a high level. For example, in the Bureau of Internal Revenue tax returns for previous

GENERAL GOVERNMENT
[Fiscal years. In millions]

| | Expenditures | | | |
Program or agency concerned	Actual, 1946	Estimate, 1947	Estimate, 1948	Appropriations, 1948
Legislative functions.................................	$23	$29	$29	$25
Judicial functions....................................	13	17	17	18
Executive direction and management...............	8	7	7	7
Federal financial management:				
Treasury Department............................	350	357	361	365
General Accounting Office......................	38	41	37	37
Other...	9	5	5	1
Government payment toward civilian employees' general retirement system........................	245	220	244	244
Other general government:				
Reconstruction Finance Corporation..............	−17	62	66	....
War Assets Administration......................	98	494	393	328
Federal Works Agency..........................	61	79	81	70
Commerce Department..........................	25	30	34	38
Justice Department............................	35	39	39	39
Interior Department...........................	48	22	25	21
War Department civil functions (cemeteries).......	2	78	60	58
Other...	33	66	94	91
Total..................................	972	1,545	1,492	1,341
From—				
General and special accounts....................	989	1,483	1,427	1,341
Corporation accounts...........................	−17	62	66	....
Total..................................	972	1,545	1,492	1,341

years remain to be audited, pending excess-profits-tax cases must be investigated and settled, special efforts are continuing to reduce tax evasion, and the number of tax returns to be reviewed is increasing as war veterans revert to civilian status. Further, with the resumption of foreign trade and passenger travel and the designation of new airfields in the United States and Alaska as ports of entry, the staff requirements of the Bureau of Customs are above the level of 1946.

The Government payment toward the Federal civilian employees' general retirement system will be larger in the fiscal year 1948 than in the current year. About half of the increase reflects the advance in salary rates which took effect July 1, 1946, and was not covered in the appropriation for 1947. The remainder of the increase applies against previous liabilities of the Government to the retirement system.

The surplus property disposal program, under the War Assets Administration, is at its peak during the current fiscal year. Henceforth, it will be tapering off, but disposal will be relatively more difficult as Government stocks of scarce items are reduced and as civilian production increases. The statutory provisions governing the sale of surplus property which give preference to certain groups of purchasers have greatly complicated the disposal program, slowing down sales and augmenting administrative costs to such an extent that Congress might well reconsider these provisions. The expenditures of the War Assets Administration cover only part of the handling of surplus property; many other Federal agencies participate in this program. The proceeds from sales of surplus property are included in miscellaneous receipts of the Treasury.

The return of war dead from overseas is a civil function of the War Department which is just getting under way. The total cost of this program is estimated at 234 million dollars. Efforts will be made to complete this work in the next 2 years.

Public buildings construction programs of the Federal Works Agency will remain at a low level, but certain expenditures for repair and maintenance of buildings cannot be delayed. Together with expenses for current operation of the buildings, these constitute a sizable portion of "General government" expenditures.

Appropriations.—The appropriation total of 1,341 million dollars for the fiscal year 1948 includes 75 million dollars for anticipated supplemental appropriations. The total is well below the estimated expenditures, mainly because the War Assets Administration will be paying obligations incurred against earlier appropriations.

INTEREST ON THE PUBLIC DEBT

The volume of interest payments on the public debt reflects the magnitude and composition of the debt, as well as the level of interest rates. As long as prosperity permits, our objective should be a steady retirement in the outstanding debt. Interest rates will be kept at present low levels through continued cooperation between the Treasury Department and the Federal Reserve System.

The estimated increase of 50 million dollars in interest payments in 1948 over 1947 is due principally to (1) increased interest payments on the larger volume of special issues held by trust funds which pay relatively high rates; (2) increased accruals on savings bonds, owing to a large volume of bonds reaching higher accrual brackets; and (3) the change from semiannual to annual payment of interest on certificates of indebted-

INTEREST ON THE PUBLIC DEBT
[Fiscal years. In millions]

| Agency | Expenditures | | | |
	Actual, 1946	Estimate, 1947	Estimate, 1948	Appropriations, 1948
Treasury Department...........................	$4,748	$4,950	$5,000	$5,000

ness, effective September 1, 1946. The net effect of these factors has been to increase interest costs in 1948, even though the debt has been declining since its peak on February 28, 1946.

Interest payments are made on the basis of a permanent appropriation. The amount shown under recommended appropriations is equal to the estimated expenditures.

REFUNDS OF RECEIPTS

Tax refunds will be a large item in the Budget for some years to come, largely because of overpayment of individual income tax under the current payment system and settlement of the wartime income- and profits-tax liabilities of corporations. The overpayments made each year under the current payment system are in the main refunded during each immediately succeeding year. The refunds to corporations, attributable to wartime tax liabilities, will be spread over the next several years because of the time required to effect final settlement in many cases where the various carry-back and other relief provisions are applicable. If the war excise-tax rates are continued, refunds in 1948 will be 123 million dollars lower.

CIVIL PUBLIC WORKS

In the Budget, construction projects are listed in the programs which they serve. In total the expenditures for civil public works are estimated at 2.1 billion dollars in 1948 compared with 1.7 billion dollars in 1947.

Federal public works provide capital assets from which the Nation derives benefits over a long period of time. During the past decade the responsibility of the Federal Government, both directly and through grants to the States, has increased. Public construction is essential to our veterans, natural resources, transportation, social welfare, and housing.

Construction programs have to be scheduled over a number of years. The work done in any one year is largely controlled by legislation and appropriations in prior years. For these reasons the program for 1948 is larger than that for 1947. While curtailment orders in August 1946 slowed down the program, they could not alter the trends already established by legislation.

The recommendations for the fiscal year 1948 for grant and loan programs allow those programs to continue at rates consistent with

REFUNDS OF RECEIPTS
[Fiscal years. In millions]

| Agency | Expenditures | | | |
	Actual, 1946	Estimate, 1947	Estimate, 1948	Appropriations, 1948
Treasury Department...........................	$3,119	$2,155	$2,065	$2,065

the authorizing legislation.

Direct Federal construction of long-term projects will be confined to those for which appropriations have already been made. Short-term projects such as provision of national park facilities, forest roads and trails, and institutional facilities will be limited to those of an urgent character.

The Budget contemplates the construction at a conservative rate of all projects for flood control, navigation, and reclamation for which initial appropriations were made in prior years. It does not provide initial appropriations for any new projects under these three programs. Even so, expenditures will be greater in the fiscal year 1949 than in 1948.

This upward trend in public construction deserves careful consideration by the Congress.

FEDERAL CIVILIAN PERSONNEL

This Budget reflects the continuing decline in Federal civilian employment. Federal agencies have reduced their civilian personnel to 2,300,000—including those in the Territories and possessions and in foreign countries—from a wartime peak of 3,770,000 in June 1945. The Budget estimates contemplate further reductions.

Total civilian personnel of the War and Navy Departments is far below the wartime peak. Personnel in the emergency war agencies has been cut drastically except in the War Assets Administration, which is at the height of its work.

Three agencies—the Veterans' Administration, the Post Office, and the Treasury—together have almost as many employees as the 1939 total of 900,000 for the whole Federal Government. Personnel requirements of the Veterans' Administration are large because it must administer a great variety of programs for millions of veterans. The rise

in the number of postal employees reflects the growth of the population and the even larger increase of business and industry. Increased employment in the Treasury results mainly from the greater complexity and coverage of the tax system and the wide distribution of public-debt ownership.

Total employment in all the other Government departments and agencies combined is lower than in June 1945 even though certain functions of emergency war agencies have been returned to the peacetime agencies from which they were transferred and other permanent functions have been added.

The personnel reductions were facilitated by the statutory limitations on personnel and provisions for detailed personnel ceiling determinations enacted by the Seventy-ninth Congress. When we began to convert to a peacetime basis and appropriations greatly exceeded expenditures, this legislation served a useful purpose. By the Legislative Reorganization Act the Congress has in effect decided that the extent of Federal activities, and hence personnel, should be determined by the usual appropriations process. The statutory limitations and personnel ceilings constitute a separate and possibly conflicting method of controlling the number of employees. The appropriations process, to my mind, is far preferable to the personnel ceilings and limitations, since these place undue emphasis upon the number of employees and put a premium on contractual arrangements and other measures to get the necessary work done without exceeding numerical limitations.

I therefore recommend the repeal of the statutory limitations on personnel and provisions for personnel ceiling determinations.

GOVERNMENT CORPORATIONS

With the termination of wartime programs, net expenditures of corporations in

93

the fiscal year 1948 will be focused in a few major areas—chiefly purchase of veterans' housing mortgages, loans to finance rural electrification, price-support outlays for farm commodities, and disbursements on Export-Import Bank loans to foreign borrowers. These programs represent, in the main, capital items recoverable over a period of years. As long as high levels of business activity continue, disbursements in all other major areas will be held to low levels and will be partly or wholly offset by receipts.

In the fiscal year 1948 net expenditures from corporation accounts alone will amount to 829 million dollars, compared with net receipts of 175 million dollars in 1947. But if we take into account reduced payments by the Treasury to the corporations and increased repayment of capital funds to the Treasury by the corporations, net withdrawals from the Treasury for these programs will remain almost unchanged, despite the sharp shift in the methods of financing them.

At present certain wholly owned Government corporations have authority to issue obligations whose principal and interest are guaranteed by the Federal Government. During the war the Treasury, because of its tremendous public debt operations, requested the corporations to obtain their funds directly from it rather than issue obligations on the market. I now recommend that the authority of Government corporations to issue guaranteed obligations to the public be repealed and that such agencies be authorized to obtain their funds solely by borrowing from the Secretary of the Treasury.

During the war, the Treasury has been advancing funds to the corporations at an interest rate of 1 percent. This low rate was based in part on the general level of interest rates in the market and in part on the fact that a large proportion of corporation activities—like subsidies and preclusive buying—was non-income-producing.

From now on most corporation programs will be revenue-producing. Accordingly, I recommend that corporations be required to reimburse the Treasury for the full cost to it of money advanced to the corporations. Interest paid on borrowings from the Treasury should be based upon the current average rate on outstanding marketable obligations of the United States—now about 1.8 percent. Dividends should be paid on capital stock, if earned. While these changes in the amount of intragovernmental transactions will not affect the Budget deficit or surplus, they will cause the corporations' records to reflect more nearly the true costs of their operations.

I recommend that the statutory authority of the Reconstruction Finance Corporation be extended beyond the present expiration date of June 30, 1947. Such extension is assumed in the expenditure estimates in this Budget. The new charter to be submitted will provide for the repeal of all powers not required for peacetime activities. It will also provide for a reduction of 2.5 billion dollars in the Corporation's borrowing authority. With the receipts anticipated from liquidation of war activities the reduced authority should prove adequate.

I have already recommended extension of the authority of the U.S. Commercial Company and reduction in the borrowing authority of the Federal Farm Mortgage Corporation.

In this Budget, I am also recommending return of capital to the Treasury by certain mixed-ownership corporations. The Federal land banks will complete retirement of Government-owned capital stock during the fiscal year 1947. In the fiscal year 1948, it appears that they can repay the outstanding paid-in surplus of 37 million dollars. These transactions will return the land banks to the status of cooperative institutions owned by the farmers they serve. In addition, I recommend a further small retirement of the capital stock of the Federal home loan banks.

The Corporation Supplement to the 1947 Budget indicated that the Federal Deposit Insurance Corporation could soon begin to retire its capital stock. The continuing rapid growth in the Corporation's resources and the exceptionally strong position of the insured banks now make it possible to propose a substantial amount of capital redemption in the fiscal year 1948. Accordingly, I recommend that the Congress authorize the Corporation to repay all of the 139 million dollars of capital furnished by the Federal Reserve System. Since the Reserve banks have already replaced these funds from earnings in recent years, the Board of Governors of the Federal Reserve System has proposed that the Congress at the same time authorize the payment to the Treasury of the 139 million dollars. I also recommend that the Congress authorize the Corporation to repay 100 million dollars of the 150 million dollars furnished by the Treasury Department.

By the close of the fiscal year 1948, after these repayments, the Corporation will still have capital surplus and reserves of about 1 billion dollars—the objective set several years ago.

The Board of Governors has made a further recommendation, in which I also concur, that the Congress repeal the existing, largely dormant, authority of the Federal Reserve banks to make direct loans to industry, releasing to the Treasury the funds reserved for this purpose. The gold increment fund now includes 112 million dollars reserved for such loans, and an added 28 million dollars has been advanced to the Federal Reserve banks. These sums will be transferred to miscellaneous receipts.

These transfers from the Federal Deposit Insurance Corporation, the Federal Reserve banks, and the gold increment fund will add a total of 379 million dollars in miscellaneous receipts in the fiscal year 1948.

The Government Corporation Control Act requires that no wholly owned Government corporation not now possessing a Federal charter shall continue after June 30, 1948, unless reincorporated before that time by act of Congress. Of the 16 such corporations in operation when the act was approved, the following six are already in process of liquidation: Defense Homes Corporation, Federal Surplus Commodities Corporation, Inter-American Navigation Corporation, Institute of Inter-American Transportation, Prencinradio, and the U.S. Spruce Production Corporation.

This Budget recommends the liquidation of five other State-chartered corporations: Inter-American Educational Foundation, The RFC Mortgage Company, Rubber Development Corporation, Tennessee Valley Associated Cooperatives, and the Warrior River Terminal Company. The residual functions of the Rubber Development Corporation and the program of The RFC Mortgage Company will be assumed by their parent corporation, the Reconstruction Finance Corporation. The Warrior River Terminal Company will be absorbed by the Inland Waterways Corporation, of which it is now a subsidiary.

This Budget also recommends that three nonfederally chartered corporations be reincorporated by act of Congress: Commodity Credit Corporation, Export-Import Bank of

Washington, and the Virgin Islands Company. The act establishing the Commodity Credit Corporation as an agency of the United States expires in June. It, therefore, needs early consideration.

Recommendations on the Panama Railroad Company and the Institute of Inter-American Affairs have necessarily been postponed. The Department of State is reviewing the program of the Institute and a recommendation regarding its future status will be forthcoming soon.

Activities of the Panama Railroad Company have become closely interwoven with those of The Panama Canal in the 42 years since the Government purchased this Company. While its major functions obviously must be continued, a careful reexamination and reappraisal of the respective roles of the Company and The Panama Canal are required. As soon as studies are completed, my recommendations will be transmitted to the Congress.

In addition to examination of the nonfederally chartered corporations, studies are under way, in accordance with the provisions of section 107 of the Government Corporation Control Act, regarding those corporations whose fiscal affairs could be handled more appropriately in the same manner as those of regular Federal agencies. These and future studies will be useful, not only in

developing recommendations concerning specific corporations, but also in establishing a consistent pattern for use of Government corporations.

While the general role of the Government corporation has been accepted in the laws of this country for more than 30 years, the standards for use of this instrument are not fully developed and will be subject to many refinements. Experience indicates that the corporate form of organization is peculiarly adapted to the administration of governmental programs which are predominantly of a commercial character—those which are revenue producing, are at least potentially self-sustaining, and involve a large number of business-type transactions with the public.

In their business operations such programs require greater flexibility than the customary type of appropriation budget ordinarily permits. As a rule the usefulness of a corporation lies in its ability to deal with the public in the manner employed by private business for similar work. Necessary controls are or can be provided under the Government Corporation Control Act. Further study may well indicate not only that some existing corporations ought to be converted into agencies, but also that some existing agencies might administer their programs more effectively if they had some or all of the attributes of corporations.

PROPOSED LEGISLATION

The new legislation and the extension of existing legislation, proposed in this Message, for which funds are required in the fiscal year 1948 are as follows:

	Estimated expenditures, 1948
I. PROPOSED NEW LEGISLATION:	
International affairs and finance:	
Contributions to the support of new international organizations....................	$75, 718, 000
Relief program for foreign countries...	250, 000, 000
Social welfare, health, and security:	
Increase in public assistance benefits...	73, 500, 000
Antibiotics control...	242, 000
Housing and community facilities:	
Long-range housing program..	14, 000, 000

I. Proposed New Legislation—Continued.

Transportation and communication:

Upward revision in postal rates to meet the Post Office Department's operating deficit. . —$352, 000, 000

Finance, commerce, and industry:

Census of business.. 10, 150, 000

Census of mineral industries... 218, 000

Labor:

Grants to the States for programs fostering safe working conditions................ 1, 300, 000

Strengthened machinery for facilitating the settlement of industrial disputes........ 1, 295, 000

II. Proposed Extensions of Existing Legislation:

National defense:

Interim universal training operation.. 10, 250, 000

Social welfare, health, and security:

Continued benefits for United States civilians injured by enemy action.............. 138, 000

Finance, commerce, and industry:

Extension of rent control, price control on sugar and sirups, and rice, sugar rationing, export and import controls, priority and allocation controls on a few commodities, and a few other minimum controls.. 47, 610, 700

III. Proposed Extensions of Corporation Authority:

United States Commercial Company:

Extension beyond June 30, 1947.

Commodity Credit Corporation:

Extension beyond June 30, 1947.

Federal Farm Mortgage Corporation:

Reduction of borrowing authority.

Reconstruction Finance Corporation:

Extension beyond June 30, 1947.

Reduction of borrowing authority.

Increase in the present limit on loans to States or local public authorities for construction purposes.

In this Message every effort has been made to present the Federal Budget Program with as much clarity as its complexities permit. All citizens have an interest in the Budget. Both sides of the Budget touch their everyday lives. I consider it my duty to give them full information on what their Government proposes to do.

HARRY S. TRUMAN

NOTE: The message was transmitted to the Senate and to the House of Representatives on January 10.

As printed above, references to special analyses appearing in the budget document have been omitted.

8 Statement by the President on Highway Safety.
January 15, 1947

THE PROBLEM of reducing the death rate on the Nation's highways remains one of the most serious problems in our daily life. It is an appalling fact that 34,000 American citizens were killed in automobile accidents in 1946. I therefore call upon every State and every community in the land to work unceasingly throughout 1947 to promote highway safety.

A continuing safety campaign began in May 1946, with the organization of the President's Highway Safety Conference and the State safety conferences that resulted.[1] The gains that have been made are indicative of what can be accomplished by intensive effort.

---

[1] See 1946 volume, this series, Item 106.

We are faced with a challenge which every motor vehicle driver should take as a personal responsibility. Eternal vigilance, conscientious care and maintenance of the motor vehicle, respect for traffic laws and signals—all those can play a part in saving the lives of thousands.

Legislatures of all but eight of the States are now in session or soon will be. It is my hope that the recommendations of the President's Highway Safety Conference with respect to uniform traffic regulations, especially in the licensing of drivers, and strict impartial enforcement of traffic codes, will have early attention. Much of our difficulty is due to lack of uniformity in traffic laws and to unstandardized warning and directional signs which often confuse and mislead.

I ask that all through the year State and local public officials who are charged with legal responsibility in matters of highway safety, and all interested organizations, redouble their efforts. I urge every motorist to remember at all times that highway safety is his personal concern. Laws and regulations will be of little avail unless the individual driver holds himself strictly accountable to his own conscience.

9   Remarks to Members of the President's Committee on Civil Rights.   *January 15, 1947*

YOU HAVE a vitally important job. We are none of us entirely familiar with just how far the Federal Government under the Constitution has a right to go in these civil rights matters.

I want our Bill of Rights implemented in fact. We have been trying to do this for 150 years. We are making progress, but we are not making progress fast enough. This country could very easily be faced with a situation similar to the one with which it was faced in 1922. That date was impressed on my mind because in 1922 I was running for my first elective office—county judge of Jackson County—and there was an organization in that county that met on hills and burned crosses and worked behind sheets. There is a tendency in this country for that situation to develop again, unless we do something tangible to prevent it.

I don't want to see any race discrimination. I don't want to see any religious bigotry break out in this country as it did then.

You people can, I think, make a real contribution here, with the assistance of the Attorney General and the Office of the President, that will get us tangible results. Our work has got to start at the grassroots, and in starting at the grassroots, it has got to start in the hearts of the people themselves.

I appreciate highly your willingness to spend your time on a matter of this kind. You may get more brickbats than bouquets. Your willingness to undertake the job shows that your hearts are in the right place.

I know you will go to work in earnest and I hope that you will bring me something tangible by which we can accomplish the purposes which we have been trying to accomplish for 150 years, ever since the adoption of the Constitution.

[*At this point Charles E. Wilson, Chairman of the Committee, stated that the members realized "the complexities of the job" being assigned to them, "but," he said, "we will do our best to work something out and hope it will be helpful." The President then resumed speaking.*]

I am sure it will be. I have been very much alarmed at certain happenings around the country that go to show there is a latent spirit in some of us that isn't what it ought to be. It has been difficult in some places to enforce even local laws. I want the Attorney General to know just exactly how far he can go legally from the Federal Government's standpoint. I am a believer in the sovereignty of the individual and of the local governments. I don't think the Fed-

eral Government ought to be in a position to exercise dictatorial powers locally; but there are certain rights under the Constitution of the United States which I think the Federal Government has a right to protect. It's big job. Go to it!

NOTE: The President's Committee on Civil Rights was established on December 5, 1946, by Executive Order 9808 (3 CFR, 1943–1948 Comp., p. 590).

10 Letter to Secretary Patterson and Secretary Forrestal Concerning Unification of the Armed Services. *January* 16, 1947

Gentlemen:

I am exceedingly pleased to receive your joint letter of January 16 in which you advise that you have reached full and complete agreement on a plan for the unification of the armed services.

I recognize that each of the services has made concessions in the effort to reach this agreement, and I feel that it constitutes an admirable compromise between the various views that were originally held.

The agreement provides a thoroughly practical and workable plan of unification and I heartily approve it.

You have both worked ably and effectively, with your respective staffs, in bringing about this result. I appreciate your fine efforts and I congratulate you upon an accomplishment which, I am sure, will contribute greatly to the efficiency of our national defense.

Very sincerely yours,

HARRY S. TRUMAN

[The Honorable Robert P. Patterson, The Secretary of War; The Honorable James Forrestal, The Secretary of the Navy]

NOTE: The Secretaries' joint letter of January 16 and an attached draft of a proposed Executive order prescribing the functions of the Armed Forces were released with the President's reply.

In their letter the Secretaries referred to the President's letter of June 15, 1946, in which he had

stated his position on the essential points of disagreement between the military services. They were now pleased to report, the Secretaries said, that the views of the two departments had been resolved "within the scope and the spirit" of the President's stated position. They also said that they agreed to support legislation with the following points incorporated:

"a. There shall be a Council of National Defense, a National Security Resources Board and a Central Intelligence Agency (which already exists) as agreed by the Secretary of War and the Secretary of the Navy in their letter to the President of 31 May 1946.

"b. The armed forces shall be organized under a Secretary of National Defense so as to place the Army, the Navy (to include the Marine Corps and Naval Aviation), and the Air Force, each with a military chief, under the Departments of the Army, the Navy, and the Air Force respectively. Each shall be under a Secretary and, under the overall direction of the Secretary of National Defense, shall be administered as an individual unit. The Secretary of any of the three departments may, at any time, present to the President, after first informing the Secretary of National Defense, any report or recommendation relating to his department which he may deem necessary or desirable.

"c. A War Council shall be created consisting of the Secretary of National Defense as Chairman and with power of decision, the Secretary of the Army, the Secretary of the Navy and the Secretary of the Air Force, and the military heads of the three Services. The War Council will concern itself with matters of broad policy relating to the armed forces.

"d. There shall be a Joint Chiefs of Staff consisting of the military heads of the three Services, and also the Chief of Staff to the President if that office exists. Subject to the authority and direction of the Secretary of National Defense, the Joint Chiefs of Staff will provide for the strategic direction of the military forces of the United States, will formulate strategic plans, assign logistic responsibilities to the

Services in support thereof, integrate the military requirements and, as directed, advise in the integration of the military budget.

"e. There shall be a full-time joint staff to consist initially of not over 100 officers to be provided in approximately equal numbers by the three Services. The Joint Staff, operating under a Director thereof, shall carry out policies and directives of the Joint Chiefs of Staff.

"f. The Secretary of National Defense shall head the armed forces establishment, shall be vested with authority, under the President, to establish common policies and common programs for the integrated operation of the three departments and shall exercise control over and direct their common efforts to dis-

charge their responsibility for national security."

The Secretaries also stated that they had agreed on the terms of an Executive order which they were attaching for the President's consideration. They recommended issuance of the order concurrently with approval of the recommended legislation. On July 26 the President approved the National Security Act of 1947 (61 Stat. 495) and issued Executive Order 9877 "Functions of the Armed Forces" (Item 159, below).

The full text of the Secretaries' letter of January 16 is printed in the Congressional Record (vol. 93, p. A204). For the President's letter of June 15, 1946, see 1946 volume, this series, Item 138.

11 White House Statement Concerning the President's Recommendation of an Additional Repeal of Authorized Appropriations. *January 17, 1947*

THE PRESIDENT today recommended to the Congress the repeal of appropriations totaling $563,888,579. Contract authorizations of $132 million involved in those appropriations, were also recommended for rescission.

These amounts are in addition to five previous rescissions which reduced the net authorized Federal program by more than $64 billion.

The President's action is in accord with objectives expressed by the Congress—to maintain a continuous review of unrequired appropriation balances with a view to their recovery.

The major sum recommended for rescission is $325 million, made available to the Maritime Commission and not required because of the liquidation of wartime shipbuilding programs. Involved is the $132 million for which the Congress had given the Commission contractual authority as well as the appropriations.

The reduction in four Navy items accounts for the return of $119 million. These include: $50 million not needed to

meet contract termination costs; $50 million of War Department funds advanced to the Navy for the purchase of aircraft materiel and ordnance; $15 million in the Navy's public works program and $4 million no longer needed for emergency ship facilities.

The Atomic Energy Commission reported to the President that $40 million of the present funds will not be needed in the current year.

War Department rescissions total $33.5 million. Of this total, $17.5 million had been intended for the construction of buildings and utilities and the purchase of equipment; an additional $15 million represented a net gain to the Government in the form of interest on guaranteed loans to wartime contractors; most of the balance was earmarked for defense housing, seacoast defenses and similar items.

The Treasury Department reported that $10 million, originally intended for the acquisition of vessels and shore facilities by the Coast Guard, could now be returned to the surplus fund.

The President recommended the rescission

of $2.5 million of the $5 million emergency fund appropriated for his use by the Congress.

The President's recommendations for rescissions were taken into consideration in estimating expenditures in the 1948 budget.

The President stated that by administrative action he was ordering returned to the Treasury unneeded Lend-Lease funds, not available for obligation after June 30, 1946. Approximately $805 million of the unexpended balance of Lend-Lease appropriations, is being withdrawn from various agencies and carried to the surplus fund of the Treasury. There is also being deposited currently in the Treasury approximately $114 million of funds received from foreign governments in accord with section 6(b) of the Lend-Lease Act.

Amounts no longer required for the financing of certain public works projects by the Bureau of Reclamation, Department of the Interior, are to be recovered and returned by administrative action to the Reclamation fund where they will be available for appropriation by the Congress. It is estimated that $1,522,659 will be involved in this action.

Amounts in excess of current requirements, totaling $213,741,215 now available in special accounts for replacing military equipment and supplies hitherto sold by the War Department, are being carried to the Treasury surplus fund immediately, rather than permitting them to remain available for obligation until June 30, 1947.

Appropriations made to the President for United States participation in UNRRA were not included in the items to be considered for rescission action. Obligation of these funds ceases by law on June 30, 1947. The Congress has appropriated for UNRRA operations a total of 2 percent of the estimated national income for the year ending June 30, 1943, which amounts to $2.7 billion. Other major contributors have done likewise and are making their contributions available in full. The President expressed the belief that it is an obligation of this Government to make its full share available in appropriate goods and services, if this can be done within administrative requirements and the legal time limits for fund obligation. Any other course, he indicated, would not only constitute failure to meet this obligation but would seriously jeopardize UNRRA relief programs vital to the economic and political stability of vast areas in the world.

NOTE: The President's recommendations together with a letter of the Director of the Bureau of the Budget setting forth the details of the proposal are printed in House Document 55 (80th Cong., 1st sess.).

For the five previous rescissions see the 1945 volume (this series), Items 124, 134, 146, and the 1946 volume, Items 10, 130.

---

12 Letter to the President of the Senate and to the Speaker of the House Concerning Creation of a Department of National Defense. *January 18, 1947*

My dear ————:

In the State of the Union Message of January 6, 1947, I stated that I would communicate with the Congress in the near future with reference to the establishment of a single department of national defense.

For many months the Secretary of War and the Secretary of the Navy have been endeavoring to settle the differences existing between the services on this question.

I am gratified to advise that success has crowned their efforts and the armed services have reached an agreement on a plan of unification. I enclose herewith copy of a letter, signed by the Secretary of War and the Secretary of the Navy under date of January 16, 1947, containing the basic elements of this agreement. I enclose also copy of my reply to them on the same date.

In addition I submit a copy of a proposed executive order, agreed upon by the services, which presents the functions of the armed forces. It is contemplated that this order would be issued after the passage of appropriate legislation by the Congress upon this subject.

Representatives of my office and of the armed services are engaged in drafting a bill

to be submitted to the Congress for its consideration. These men, of course, are available to you at any time for consultation.

Very sincerely yours,

HARRY S. TRUMAN

NOTE: This is the text of identical letters addressed to the Honorable Arthur H. Vandenberg, President pro tempore of the Senate, and to the Honorable Joseph W. Martin, Jr., Speaker of the House of Representatives.

For the Secretaries' joint letter of January 16 and the President's reply of that date see Item 10.

On July 26 the President approved the National Security Act of 1947 creating a National Military Establishment (61 Stat. 495). On the same date he issued Executive Order 9877 "Functions of the Armed Forces" (Item 159, below).

13 Exchange of Messages With the President of France.
January 22, 1947
[Released January 22, 1947. Dated January 17, 1947]

ON THE OCCASION of your election as President of the French Republic I extend my most sincere congratulations and best wishes. May the period of your incumbency bring the fruits of peace and prosperity to the French people and strengthen the traditional bonds of friendship in democracy which unite them with the people of my country.

HARRY S. TRUMAN

[His Excellency, Vincent Auriol, Paris]

NOTE: President Auriol's reply, dated January 21, 1947, follows:

Your cordial message, Mr. President, has deeply touched me.

The warmth of your congratulations, the good wishes which you have expressed for the future of my country will go straight to the heart of all Frenchmen.

Be assured that I will spare no effort to strengthen the bonds already so close and so abiding that unite our two countries in a common faith for the future of democracy.   VINCENT AURIOL

14 The President's News Conference of
January 23, 1947

THE PRESIDENT. Well, gentlemen, I have no announcements to make, so I am open for questions.

[1.] Q. Mr. President, in the light of changing economic conditions, do you think you will favor any change in rent controls in the near future, sir?

THE PRESIDENT. They're — Congress is making an investigation of that situation now, and it's their move to act upon it.

[2.] Q. Mr. President, would you give us any information on your talk with Secretary Marshall today?

THE PRESIDENT. Yes. It was the usual

conversation with the Secretary of State, and covered a number of things.

[3.] Q. Mr. President, is there anything you can say now about the status of the congressional cooperation plan?

THE PRESIDENT. Well, it's in effect and working right along.

Q. Right along? I wondered how it was after yesterday's voting, and so forth?

THE PRESIDENT. I don't know what you refer to.

Q. The voting by which the Republicans voted to continue the special investigation——

THE PRESIDENT. Oh well, that's a matter for the Senate itself to decide upon, and I did not have a hand in that at all.

[4.] Q. Mr. President, Senators Brewster and White have suggested the appointment of Marion Martin to the Federal Communications Commission——

THE PRESIDENT. I have her under consideration. I will tell you about that when I get ready to make the appointment.

Q. Mr. President, is there anyone else under consideration?

THE PRESIDENT. A lot of people under consideration.

[5.] Q. Mr. President, would you care to say what the number of things were that you discussed with Secretary Marshall?

THE PRESIDENT. Well, yes, I will be glad to tell you what they were. We discussed China. We discussed South America. We discussed Germany. We discussed Palestine, and anything else around the world that happened to come by us. [*Laughter*]

Q. Has he decided, Mr. President, whether he will go to Moscow?

THE PRESIDENT. I have not discussed that matter with him as yet.

[6.] Q. Mr. President, in an interview last week with Dr. Grau in Havana, he told me that General Damera, head of the army for Cuba, had been up here talking to the chiefs of the Army, about a joint plan for hemispheric defense against communism.

THE PRESIDENT. I know nothing about it— I know nothing about it. That's the first I've heard of it.

Q. He said he was up here for that purpose.

THE PRESIDENT. I didn't talk to him. I didn't even know he was in the country.

[7.] Q. Mr. President, on rent control, is your attitude still as it was when last previously expressed?

THE PRESIDENT. I think we ought to hold the line on rent control, but of course the Congress will have to act on that.

[8.] Q. Mr. President, reports from Mexico City say that President Alemán may come up here to confer with you. Can you say anything about it?

THE PRESIDENT. I have invited him to pay a visit to the President of the United States, and I hope he accepts.

[9.] Q. Mr. President, in your Economic Message you indicated you thought it might be a propitious time for reducing prices. I notice that Ford has reduced prices but some have increased them. Have you any comment on that?

THE PRESIDENT. I am very happy that Mr. Ford in his statement says that he was following out the suggestion that I made in the message, and I appreciate it very highly. I think he made a proper move, and I hope a lot more people will do the same thing.

[10.] Q. Mr. President, did you see in advance the speech that John Foster Dulles made?

THE PRESIDENT. No, of course not.

Q. Did you see him in advance, sir?

THE PRESIDENT. I did not.

Q. You did not discuss the speech?

THE PRESIDENT. No, I never discussed the speech. He is a free agent. [*Laughter*]

[11.] Q. Mr. President, do you have any comment on Mr. May's indictment?

THE PRESIDENT. I did not know he was indicted, and I have no comment.

[12.] Q. Mr. President, have you heard anything from the RFC on the Lustron prefabricated homes?

THE PRESIDENT. No, I haven't.

[13.] Q. Mr. President, in your message to Congress you said you would submit recommendations for the elimination of emergency laws. Are they prepared yet?

THE PRESIDENT. They are in the course of preparation and will be submitted as soon as ready.

[14.] Q. Mr. President, we understand from the Governor General of Puerto Rico that he told you of their appeal for aid for Puerto Rico on account of the high basic prices——

THE PRESIDENT. We discussed the whole Puerto Rican situation when he was in here this morning. We shall discuss it again at the Cabinet meeting tomorrow, in an effort to help the Puerto Ricans to help themselves.

[15.] Q. Mr. President, has Secretary Marshall agreed on any changes in personnel in the State Department?

THE PRESIDENT. We haven't. General Marshall has asked the top-ranking personages in the State Department to stay.

Q. Including the Assistant Secretaries?

THE PRESIDENT. I don't know anything about that. You had better ask General Marshall. He has a free hand over there.

Q. Mr. President, the New York Times said this morning that you had directed General Marshall to make an immediate investigation of the differences between Mr. Braden and Mr. Messersmith. Is that correct?

THE PRESIDENT. The matter was discussed with General Marshall.

Q. Can you tell us anything about it?

THE PRESIDENT. No.

Q. Mr. President, is Senator Mead under consideration for a diplomatic post?

THE PRESIDENT. No, he is not.

Q. Mr. President, would you tell us something about your meeting with Assistant Secretary Braden last Friday?

THE PRESIDENT. Well, he was—it was the customary meeting with an Assistant Secretary of State who requested to see the President. We discussed the things in which he was interested.

[16.] Q. Mr. President, has the Postmaster General reported to you since——

THE PRESIDENT. Yes he has. I had a fine interview with Mr. Hannegan the day he got back here; and he looks fine.

Q. Is he going to stay on?

THE PRESIDENT. I urged him to stay.

[17.] Q. Mr. President, can you say anything about any special subjects which you and President Alemán would discuss?

THE PRESIDENT. That's a matter for us to agree on when the President comes up here; and I am not expected to tell the President of Mexico what he wants to talk to me about. [*Laughter*]

[18.] Q. Mr. President, was that Mr. Hannegan's Cabinet post, or both things?

THE PRESIDENT. Both.

Q. Mr. President, you said you urged him to stay. Do you mean that he suggested that he leave?

THE PRESIDENT. I urged him to stay on as National Chairman. I thought he was a good one, and I still think so.

Q. Do you think he will be able to, sir?

THE PRESIDENT. I hope he will. I can't answer that question until it is—his health situation is finally worked out, as it has further to go before complete recovery.

Q. What about the Postmaster Generalship? Do you want him to stay on?

THE PRESIDENT. I sure do.

Q. Mr. President, anybody else around here unhealthy?

THE PRESIDENT. I don't know. I am not,

Miss May.[1] [*Laughter*] They have a great—it's a great strain on people that are around the White House, and in more ways than one it seems to have a worse effect on all of them than it does on the President himself, from a physical standpoint.

[19.] Q. Mr. President, would you care to give us your views on an early confer- ence of the American Republics in Rio?

THE PRESIDENT. I have not discussed that with General Marshall as yet. I will give you my views as soon as I have had a chance to discuss it with him.

[20.] Q. Mr. President, last week you talked with Mr. De Gasperi, who has been given a mandate to appoint a new Italian Government. Have you any comment on that, sir?

THE PRESIDENT. No I haven't.

[21.] Q. Mr. President, getting back to the rent control thing, we get constant rumors that you do plan to make some ad- justments in rent——

THE PRESIDENT. That's the reason for the investigation in the committees of Congress. That's a matter that the Congress will have to pass upon.

[22.] Q. Mr. President, I just wanted to get clear on this Hannegan thing, had he asked you to give up—that he was—he would like to give up either one or both of his offices?

THE PRESIDENT. No. There have been so

many rumors and speculations around the United States as to whether he was going to quit or not, and so the first thing I told him when he came in the door was that "I want you to stay as Chairman and Post- master General." And that is as far as the conversation went.

Q. Is that here?

THE PRESIDENT. Right here in this chair. [*Laughter*]

Q. What did he say?

THE PRESIDENT. He was very much pleased and he said he would give me his answer as soon as he was sure that his health was all right.

[23.] Q. Mr. President, there has been some question about your visit to the Na- tional Theatre last night.

THE PRESIDENT. Yes?

Q. The Committee on Racial Democracy saying that Jim Crow——

THE PRESIDENT. ——I saw it in the paper for the first time. First time I heard of it, and I didn't know it was being picketed. I wanted to see that show. I wanted to see that for 20 years, so I went down there and saw it. [*Laughter*]

Q. The first time you have seen "Blos- som Time"?

THE PRESIDENT. That's the first time I have seen "Blossom Time."

Reporter: Thank you, Mr. President.

NOTE: President Truman's ninety-fifth news con- ference was held in his office at the White House at 4 o'clock on Thursday afternoon, January 23, 1947.

---

[1] Mrs. May Craig of the Portland (Maine) Press Herald.

15   Letter to the President of Italy Following Prime Minister
de Gasperi's Visit to the United States. *January 25, 1947*

[Released January 25, 1947. Dated January 20, 1947]

My dear Mr. President:

Upon the occasion of the departure from the United States of Prime Minister de Gasperi, I should like to reassure you, Mr.

President, that the United States Govern- ment is constantly mindful of the economic difficulties with which the Italian Govern- ment is faced and that sincere efforts are being made by our officials to find means to alleviate your country's most urgent needs.

Signor de Gasperi's recent visit in Washington has afforded us a most pleasurable opportunity to review questions of interest to our two Governments. In particular, our officials have received a better understanding of Italy's present requirements and of the outstanding job of reconstruction which your Government and people are undertaking.

In your communication of November 26, 1946, you informed me of the grave emergency with which your Government was confronted due to difficulties in the fulfillment of the UNRRA grain program. That problem has been receiving the most urgent attention of our officials and remains under constant consideration and review. I have authorized a number of emergency measures to ensure that every possible effort shall be made to expedite the delivery of grains to the peoples of the war-torn countries of Europe and Asia. As we have informed Signor de Gasperi, shipments of wheat have been diverted from other areas to meet the immediate requirements of Italy, and we have every expectation of being able to increase scheduled shipments of wheat to Italy beginning next month. Your Prime Minister will inform you of the other measures discussed with him which we fully anticipate will prove mutually beneficial to our two countries.

The American people have many close bonds with the Italian people and it is our sincere desire, in a spirit of fraternal cooperation, to do what we can to assist your country in its efforts to rebuild and strengthen a peaceful, prosperous and democratic Italy.

Very sincerely yours,

HARRY S. TRUMAN

[His Excellency, Enrico de Nicola, Provisional President of the Italian Republic, Rome]

16 Message to the King of Sweden on the Death of Prince Gustaf Adolf. *January* 27, 1947

I AM deeply shocked and grieved to learn of the death of Prince Gustaf Adolf. Please accept my heartfelt sympathy in your sorrow.

HARRY S. TRUMAN

[His Majesty Gustaf V, King of Sweden, Stockholm]

17 Radio Remarks on Behalf of the March of Dimes Campaign. *January* 30, 1947

[Broadcast from the White House at 11:45 p.m.]

Fellow Americans:

Again it is my privilege to speak to you about a movement that should have the heartfelt support of all of us. I refer to the continuing fight against the scourge of infantile paralysis.

Franklin D. Roosevelt, himself a victim of the disease, saw the need for an organization to wage the fight, and so, in 1938, he brought into being the National Foundation for Infantile Paralysis. We can do our part by giving to the March of Dimes. The

National Foundation, supported by your gifts, reaches into every corner of the country to find and help the stricken.

Let me show you by an example what the National Foundation for Infantile Paralysis has achieved.

Within 30 years there have been two appalling epidemics of the disease in the United States. The first epidemic, raging chiefly along the eastern seaboard, caught the country unprepared. There was not enough help, not enough knowledge; no one knew what to do. The poor suffered most, not because infantile paralysis strikes more often among the poor, but because those cases lacked funds for medical care. As the total cases mounted, panic spread; fantastic cures were advertised, for sale and not for sale. The total of dead for that epidemic was more than 20 percent of the victims, most of whom were young children. And most of those who survived were permanently crippled.

The second of the two epidemics struck last year—first in Florida, then in Alabama, Texas, Minnesota, Colorado, Missouri, Kansas, the Dakotas, Wisconsin, California, Illinois, and all along the Mississippi Valley. Last year the disease was more widespread. The cost of treating the stricken had risen very high—but thousands achieved complete recovery, and only 5 percent died.

The country, this time, was *not* caught unprepared. The National Foundation for Infantile Paralysis had educated the public in knowledge of the disease. Doctors knew what to do—and not only doctors but nurses and physical therapists—because the National Foundation had financed training for personnel at many hospitals and universities throughout the land. The poor did not suffer most, because the National Foundation was ready, through its county chapters, to provide funds for the care and treatment of every victim. There was no shortage of medical experts, equipment, supplies, or funds even in the hardest hit areas, because into those areas the National Foundation rushed extra help of every kind.

No organization but a great national nonprofit organization could have handled so huge a task. In coming to our rescue through last year's epidemic, the National Foundation exhausted its funds from the 1946 March of Dimes and drew heavily upon its resources. The millions spent last year on medical care and treatments, on research and education, must be replaced if the fight is to go on.

If there is one of you who has not yet joined the March of Dimes, I urge you to go now and enlist.

18 Special Message to the Congress on Extension of the Second War Powers Act. *January 31, 1947*

To the Congress of the United States:

During the past eighteen months the Nation has almost completed its great task of reconverting from all-out wartime production to a peace-time economy. As reconversion has proceeded, we have found it increasingly possible to dispense with many controls that were essential during active hostilities and immediately thereafter. We can now foresee the day when no further use of these powers will be necessary. But it has become apparent that the effective completion of reconversion will, in a few instances, require the continued use of powers granted by the Second War Powers Act after March 31, 1947, the expiration date of this law.

I stated to the Congress in my recent

State of the Union Message that after the termination of hostilities was proclaimed on December 31, 1946, there were two groups of temporary laws that still remained, namely, those which were to last during the "emergency" and those which were to continue until the "termination of the war." The study of these two groups of laws is proceeding and I shall submit recommendations on them in the near future.

This present message is directed solely to the Second War Powers Act because the powers existing under such Act expire on March 31, 1947.

Since the fighting ceased, it has been my avowed policy to terminate all emergency controls that were no longer necessary or workable. By November 1946, we had removed all manpower and wage controls, and all price ceilings except those on rent, sugar and sirups, and rice. Almost all the priority and allocation regulations based on Title III of the Second War Powers Act have been eliminated. As early as last May, the Senate Committee on the Judiciary, in reporting out the last extension of the Second War Powers Act, made the following findings in this connection:

"The record clearly shows that there has been a rapid lifting of the controls which have been exercised over our economy during the war, and a progressive abandonment of the rigid provisions of the original War Powers Act, evidencing what your committee regards as a sincere purpose and intention by the Office of War Mobilization and Reconversion, by the Civilian Production Administration, and by all the other agencies concerned, to return as rapidly as possible to the normal processes of our economy."

The House Committee on the Judiciary in its Report also referred favorably to the record of reductions in controls by the Government.

Speedy decontrol under the Second War Powers Act has continued since these reports were made. From a wartime peak of about 700 orders and schedules, the Civilian Production Administration (Office of Temporary Controls) by January 27, 1947, had in effect only 24 orders and 3 schedules, and this number will be still further reduced in the immediate future. The Department of Agriculture had left by January 27 only 19 war food orders, of which 9 are merely administrative or procedural, and still further reductions are planned by the Department between now and March 31. The Office of Defense Transportation has eliminated all but 3 transportation orders, and the Office of Price Administration (Office of Temporary Controls) now rations only sugar.

After March 31, 1947, moreover, it will be possible to dispense entirely with the use of the broad powers granted by Title III of the Second War Powers Act. Thenceforth only a few controls coming under this title will be needed, over a progressively diminishing list of commodities of which the supply is seriously deficient, both domestically and throughout the world, and the affected final products are critically important to industry or the public. Power to allocate under the Second War Powers Act is requested only for the specific cases described in this Message and for national emergencies declared by the President.

The few orders that would remain would be limited to clearly manageable controls in an economy freed of most emergency restrictions. They afford positive aids to business and the public which we must not withdraw prematurely, and they assist us in meeting international understandings and obligations.

The first area in which I believe continued authority is essential is in connection with foods still in critically short supply throughout the world. I consider that current import and export controls must be kept after March 31 to assure this country a proportionate share of the commodities in which we are deficient while carrying out our international food allocation arrangements. In a subsequent communication to the Congress I shall state whether there will be any need for continuing the Export Control Act beyond June 30, 1947, its present expiration date. We must also continue some controls on domestic use and distribution of grains and grain products, rice, sugar and edible molasses.

Grain: World cereal supplies are still far short of essential needs. Stated world import requirements for grain total about 38 million tons. Only about 24 million tons will be available from all exporting countries. This deficit will become most serious in the next few months. The most careful allocation of the available supplies, including those from the United States, which is the largest exporter, will be essential to avoid extreme hardship in the war-devasted countries. The United States has, in addition, a special responsibility in Germany and Japan, where heavy imports are required to maintain food supplies at least at a level sufficient to prevent disease and unrest. If this is not done, our troops would be jeopardized and our policy of encouraging the growth of democracy in these occupied countries would be endangered.

The United States has announced an export goal of at least 10½ million short tons of grain and flour. To reach this target, controls may continue necessary after March 31 to insure the movement of the grain to seaboard and to insure economies in the non-food uses of cereals in this country.

Special controls may also continue to be necessary on rice. World export supplies are even more short than other grains, and the United States has export responsibilities

to areas of particular concern to us, such as Puerto Rico, the Philippines and Cuba.

Sugar and Related Products: Because of our heavy dependence on imports, the world shortage of sugar and related products is of outstanding concern to the United States. Total sugar available for shipment to the United States, Canada and all western European countries in 1947 is expected to be only about 7½ million tons compared with average net imports before the war of about 8½ million, and 1946 imports of 6¾ million.

The United States will continue to receive its share of these supplies. Our share in past years has been sufficient to permit us to maintain, along with Canada and the United Kingdom, a considerably higher proportion of our pre-war consumption than other importing countries. Supplies in 1947 will be larger than in 1946. Nevertheless, 1947 supplies for the United States will still be below pre-war per capita supply and even farther below estimated demand.

In this situation, both our domestic and international interests require continuation of domestic and import controls over sugar and edible molasses and sirups and import controls only over other sugar-containing products and inedible molasses.

Domestically, unless current controls are continued, there would be inequitable distribution of the limited supply among various users; much sugar would be held for speculative purposes; and it is probable that sugar would go to a greater extent to industrial users, resulting in a lower proportion for household consumers than they now receive.

The cost of sugar used in the United States during 1947 will exceed one billion dollars. Although the extent to which prices would rise under premature decontrol is uncertain, there is grave danger that this cost might multiply several times, with serious results to consumers and sugar-using industries and eventually to sugar producers and refiners similar to those experienced after World War I.

Internationally, decontrol would make it extremely difficult for us to carry out the understanding under which the United States, since 1942, has acted as agent to buy the Cuban export supply for distribution among the importing countries in accordance with the recommendations of the International Emergency Food Council.

Fats and Oils: Fats and oils are among the commodities in shortest world supply. World import demand for the current calendar year amounts to about 6 million short tons, which is almost equal to pre-war trade in these commodities. However, only about half of this will be available. The production of coconut and palm oils in many parts of the Far East is still far below pre-war levels, and the European production of animal fats is also far below levels of pre-war years. As a consequence, all importing countries are forced to consumption levels of from 75 to 90 per cent of their pre-war levels. Only by maintaining careful distribution between countries, therefore, will it be possible to avoid serious inequities.

This situation requires the continuation of import and export controls to insure that we and other countries receive a proportionate share of this short world supply.

Other Foods: There are other agricultural commodities over which continued import controls also appear to be necessary as a result of continuing serious world shortages. These controls are necessary to carry out international understandings. The commodities they cover are: meat and meat products, dairy products, peas and beans, canned fish and protein foods.

Imported Industrial Materials: At the same time there are other commodities which we import for industrial purposes over which some form of allocation control will be necessary after March 31, 1947. These are cinchona bark and cinchona alkaloids, rubber, manila (abaca) and agave fiber and cordage, tin and antimony.

Cinchona bark and alkaloids are chiefly supplied by the Netherlands East Indies. Adequate imports from this source are uncertain. The estimated civilian deficiency for the year ending July, 1947, is over three million ounces of quinine and seventy thousand ounces of quinidine. So long as such a shortage continues, the most vital medical uses must be given top priority.

Natural and Synthetic Rubber: Natural rubber will probably continue in short supply throughout the world in 1947. At the same time, it is important to the national defense that a minimum synthetic rubber industry be maintained in the United States pending consideration of permanent legislation by the Congress. Consequently, continued allocation control over rubber, except for import controls over natural rubber, is necessary.

Manila and other hard cordage fibers are of basic importance, because from them are made rope, binder, baler and wrapping twines, paper, and padding. The supply in prospect from all sources for the next twelve months is no more than half our annual requirements. The termination of allocation control over manila would seriously impede agricultural and other essential production.

Tin and antimony are also basic materials which we must import. The supply of tin will not approximate demand until some time in 1948. In the case of antimony, we must wait for resumption of shipments from China, the primary pre-war source. Continued allocation of tin, tin plate and other tin products, and antimony is an important positive aid to our domestic industries and in carrying out our international understandings.

DOMESTIC SHORTAGES

Housing: The allocation powers of the Veterans Emergency Housing Act and of the Second War Powers Act were instrumental in increasing the flow of building materials to which the veterans housing program in large measure owes its progress to date. This achievement made possible the recent reduction in the number and scope of these controls.

During the balance of 1947, I anticipate a further reduction in the use of these powers, but it will be necessary to continue some limits on construction and to continue assistance to the producers of some bottleneck materials.

I understand that voluntary arrangements are being made with a number of producers to meet the needs of the building materials industries so that the use of allocation powers can be held to a minimum. To the extent that formal action may prove necessary, the Congress has wisely provided that materials and facilities for building construction may be allocated under the Veterans Emergency Housing Act until December 31, 1947. Accordingly, Title III need not be extended for the purposes of the housing program.

Freight Cars: There is at the present time an extremely serious freight car shortage. The shortage will increase as the Nation's production increases. The reported average daily freight car shortage now amounts to approximately 22,000 cars. For a number of months car loadings have been heavier than at any period since 1930, including the war years. The American railroads have about 521,000 fewer cars now than in 1930,

and about 31,100 fewer serviceable cars than they had on V-J Day. The number of freight cars being removed from service each month because of their being worn out exceeds on the average the number of new freight cars delivered to the railroads.

The load our railways must carry is growing while the facilities for handling the load are dwindling. To cope with this problem with any measureable degree of success requires a provident use of rail transportation facilities. Allocation is therefore necessary if we are to use the railway freight cars and other equipment and facilities that we have at all efficiently in this period just ahead.

Other Shortages: The only other current domestic shortages sufficiently serious to require continued allocation control beyond March 31 are streptomycin, automobiles, and tractors. Limited distribution of streptomycin for civilian use was begun in September, 1946, but it is at present impossible to determine requirements or to plan production of this drug. In the case of automobiles and tractors, it may be necessary for a time to continue to carry out the purpose of the Export Control Act by limiting production in this country of automobiles and tractors designed for export.

Some critical materials and equipment freed from distribution controls will remain short after March 31. In a very few cases this will mean that essential export requirements will not be met unless priorities are used. Priorities assistance should therefore be given, where necessary, to expand the production in foreign countries of materials critically needed in the United States, and, upon certification of the Secretaries of State and Commerce, to meet international understandings and responsibilities.

Because of the distortions and uncertainties generated by war conditions, we may encounter a National emergency that we do not now foresee. The extension of Title III should provide for allocation authority in a National emergency of this kind, but only if there is a declaration by the President that such a National emergency has arisen. Although I do not anticipate that such an emergency will occur, it is imperative that the government should have the power, during the remainder of the reconversion period, to deal with major unforeseen contingencies of this character.

RECOMMENDATIONS

When first adopted, the Second War Powers Act had 14 substantive titles, of which seven have been either enacted into permanent legislation or have been permitted to lapse. Only three of the remaining titles—I, III and V—will be needed after March 31, 1947. Although some of the programs remaining under these titles can and will be terminated during the next few months, it would be unsafe to act on the assumption that this can be done with all of them. I therefore recommend that the Congress extend for one year, to March 31, 1948, Titles I and V, and, in addition, Title III for the limited purposes enumerated in this Message.

The necessity for extending Title III, I have discussed at length. I shall briefly state the reasons for extending Titles I and V.

Title I permits the United States Maritime Commission to operate certain shipping lines and the Army and the Navy to supply local transportation to personnel where public facilities are inadequate. This title will be necessary until the Maritime Commission is in a position to settle with companies whose ships they have taken over and operated.

Title V permits the operation of ships under less restrictive rules as to equipment and manning than would otherwise be the case. This title is necessary for troops stationed abroad, both for their demobilization and the transportation of supplies, and in connection with repatriation programs. Its extension is urged by the State, Treasury, War and Commerce Departments, and by the Maritime Commission. The Navy's vessels are already covered by permanent legislation.

It is unsettling, both for business and for the general public, to be obliged to wait until the last possible moment for decision by the Congress on emergency legislation. I urge the Congress to give immediate and favorable consideration to the limited extension of the Second War Powers Act I have requested.

For ready reference, I attach hereto an Appendix setting forth a summary of the titles of the Second War Powers Act, together with a brief comment on each.

HARRY S. TRUMAN

APPENDIX—SUMMARY OF TITLES, SECOND WAR POWERS ACT

Recommended for extension: Titles I, III and V.

Title I. Emergency Powers of the Interstate Commerce Commission over Motor and Water Carriers. Extended until March 31, 1947. Further extension is recommended.

Title II. Acquisition and Disposal of Property. Extended until March 31, 1947, only as to the disposal of property. Further extension is not necessary.

Title III. Priorities and Allocation Powers. Extended until March 31, 1947 (until June 30, 1947, for building materials and related facilities). This title establishes priorities, rationing and allocation powers. Further extension is recommended.

Title IV. Purchase by Federal Reserve Banks of Government Obligations. Extended until March 31, 1947. The Federal Reserve Board and the Treasury Department will recommend permanent legislation covering this subject. Hence, further extension is not necessary.

Title V. Waiver of Navigation and Inspection Laws. Extended until March 31, 1947. Further extension is recommended.

Title VI. Power to Requisition. This title has expired.

Title VII. Political Activity. Extended until March 31, 1947. This title exempts employees serving part time and without compensation or with only nominal compensation from certain restrictions prohibiting participation in political activity (Hatch Act). No recommendation is made for further extension.

Title VIII. Protection of War Industries and Protection of Resources Subject to Hazards of Forest Fires. This title has expired.

Title IX. Free Postage for Soldiers, Sailors and Marines. This title has been repealed and replaced by permanent legislation.

Title X. Naturalization of Persons Serving in the Armed Forces in the United States during the Present War. This title has been made permanent legislation.

Title XI. Acceptance of Conditional Gifts to Further the War Program. This title has expired.

Title XII. Coinage of 5-Cent Pieces. This title has expired.

Title XIII. Inspection and Audit of War Contractors. This title has been made permanent legislation.

Title XIV. Utilization of War Information. Extended until March 31, 1947. Further extension is not necessary.

19   The President's News Conference of *February* 1, 1947

THE PRESIDENT. [1.] I have an important statement to make to you this morning which I think is one of the most important that I have made in a good while.

You will recall that in my statement of November 9th accompanying the action removing all wage controls and all but a few price controls, I concluded by saying that the responsibility for working out agreements for the adjustment of differences, without interruptions to production, now rested squarely upon labor and management.

I have a joint letter from the Associated General Contractors of America and the Building and Construction Trades Department of the American Federation of Labor. The Associated General Contractors represent management while the Building and Construction Trades Department represents nineteen international unions and approximately two million workers.

The letter encloses an agreement setting up a plan of industrial peace for the construction industry.

Let me read you a few excerpts from the letter.

All these documents are being mimeographed and will be available for you as you go out, in toto.

"We are enclosing a copy of a plan"—this is the quotation from the letter—

"We are enclosing a copy of a plan to provide a National Joint Conference Committee in the building and construction industry for the settlement of any dispute or disagreement which may arise and which is voluntarily submitted to the Committee by mutual agreement of the parties involved in the dispute.

"Having established this voluntary machinery to settle disputes in this important industry without stoppage of work by lock-out or strike, our organizations intend to exert every effort to see that these procedures are used wherever possible to settle any dispute that may arise—over the terms of new contracts or over the interpretation of existing agreements.

"This important industry is anxious to accept its responsibility—both labor and management. We will make our contribution toward providing the highest possible measure of industrial peace."

Now you will get the full text of those agreements mimeographed.

In my Message to the Congress on the State of the Union, I said: "We have established a national labor policy in this country based upon free collective bargaining as the process for determining wages and working conditions. This is still the national policy; it should continue to be the national policy." That is the end of the quotation from the message.

The agreement signed by the Associated General Contractors of America and the Building and Construction Trades Department of the A.F. of L. is a significant step forward in industrial relations in this country.

We have had good labor news during the past 10 days. The Steelworkers and the steel producing subsidiaries of the United States Steel Corporation have reached a final agreement on the problem of eliminating wage rate inequities—a highly complicated problem on which they had been working for over 2 years. The same parties have also reached an agreement to postpone the expiration date of their present contract until April 30.

The United States Rubber Company and the rubber workers union of the CIO have also recently reached agreement on a significant contract.

The making of these agreements indicates a widespread willingness to resolve industrial disputes without resort to force. We are moving closer and closer to our ideals of free collective bargaining.

Now for questions, if you have any.

Q. Do you think that may extend into other industries as well—beyond the building trades, Mr. President?

THE PRESIDENT. I hope it will—I hope it will.

Q. Mr. President, does that take in the things that you mention, such as jurisdictional strikes——

THE PRESIDENT. Yes, it takes in all those things. Yes it does.

Q. Secondary boycotts?

THE PRESIDENT. That takes in all those things. I think that you will find the statement has well set out all those things, when you get the mimeographed copies of the complete agreement.

Q. Thank you, Mr. President. [*The questioner then started to leave.*]

Voices: Wait a minute—wait a minute!

Q. Wait a minute! [*Laughter*]

THE PRESIDENT. Wait a minute, Bob.[1] It's all right, if *you* want to go. [*More laughter*]

[2.] Q. Mr. President, can you tell us anything about this rent situation? Is any penalty to be imposed on General Fleming for having made this——

THE PRESIDENT. There is not. General Fleming stated the case exactly, and General Fleming, I think, is a member of the Government. He stated the case in exactly the truth. That's all there is to it.

Q. Mr. President, had you talked with General Fleming before then?

THE PRESIDENT. I did not. The only time I saw General Fleming was at the Cabinet meeting, and I did not talk to him then.

---

[1] Robert G. Nixon of International News Service.

[3.] Q. Mr. President, I would like to ask you a question about something you probably don't—aren't aware of, but——

THE PRESIDENT. Go ahead.

Q. ——you have got yourself into an awful lot of trouble with the cat lovers of America. [*Laughter*]

THE PRESIDENT. With what?

Q. The cat lovers of America.

THE PRESIDENT. Cat lovers?

Q. Published reports of one of your speeches have been interpreted by all the cat people that terrible—cast terrible aspersions on cats.

THE PRESIDENT. What's that?

Q. I thought you might like to say a kind word for cats. [*More laughter*]

THE PRESIDENT. I don't know what you are talking about.

Q. I think it was your reference to National Cat Week?

THE PRESIDENT. Oh, yes. That was at an off-the-record meeting where I read the requests that—if you remember—for all the weeks. Well, one of the requests was for a national cat week, and I thought it was funny!

Q. You are not against cats?

THE PRESIDENT. No. Neutral. I am neutral on cats. Certain sort of cats that I am against, but they have two legs. [*Laughter*]

[4.] Q. If we might go back to this——

THE PRESIDENT. Sure.

Q. ——statement a second, sir, how did it happen that that was announced from the White House?

THE PRESIDENT. Because I thought it was of sufficient importance that it should be announced from the White House.

[5.] Q. Well, Mr. President, are you in another cat fight—you don't mean all two-legged cats are feminine, do you? [*Laughter*]

THE PRESIDENT. No indeed! Very small part of them are feminine.

Q. Would you say you are in favor of tom cat week? [*More laughter*]

THE PRESIDENT. No. I am drawing no line.

[6.] Q. Mr. President, is your stand on rents still the same as it was?

THE PRESIDENT. It is exactly the same as it was on Thursday at the press conference, and if you will get out the record of that press conference, there has been absolutely no change in that stand.

Q. In other words, you don't favor any general increase?

THE PRESIDENT. I certainly do not.

[7.] Q. Mr. President, are you considering a Republican for the Court of Claims vacancy?

THE PRESIDENT. I am considering at least a dozen people. I think three or four of them are Republicans.

[8.] Q. Mr. President, are arrangements being made to evacuate American citizens from Palestine?

THE PRESIDENT. Not that I know of.

[9.] Q. Mr. President, Mr. Stalin was quoted as saying that he called for not only another Big Three conference but several Big Three conferences. Do you agree with that?

THE PRESIDENT. I would be very much pleased to see Mr. Stalin and Mr. Attlee here in Washington. I don't expect to leave the United States to attend the Big Three conference.

Q. Do you think there is need for one now, sir, here?

THE PRESIDENT. I don't know of any need for it.

[10.] Q. Have you made a decision on the district attorney for the Eastern District of Missouri?

THE PRESIDENT. No, I have not.

[11.] Q. Mr. President, in view of the state visit of the Governor General of Canada, have you any idea of reciprocating by visiting——

THE PRESIDENT. Well, I might have. I haven't been invited to go there yet.

Q. You will, now!

[12.] Q. Mr. President, there have been several columnists who have written stories to the effect that you will make no "lame-duck" appointments. Is there a policy on your part——

THE PRESIDENT. I haven't inaugurated any policy, but I haven't as yet appointed any so-called "lameducks."

Q. I thought, Mr. President, that at some one time you had said you wouldn't do that.

THE PRESIDENT. I may have said that to somebody in a private conversation, but I made no public statement——

Q. I thought you had——

THE PRESIDENT. ——and I do not expect to make one.

[13.] Q. Mr. President, there was a Time story attributed to White House sources which quoted you as having decided to make a poll of the individual Governors of all States, whenever you were faced with an issue that you considered of national importance.

THE PRESIDENT. I never heard of that before. If it came out of the White House it didn't come from the President. It might have come from some of the "fixtures"—something like that—maybe it was one of the "cooks." [*Much laughter, as the President looked in the general direction of the couch*]

[14.] Q. Some days ago, sir, Mr. Ross announced that the White House staff was working on the question of state papers, and at that time it was pointed out that you had some very definite views on official papers and personal papers. I wondered, sir, if you would give us your definition of the distinction between those two?

THE PRESIDENT. That matter is under consideration. It will be presented to the Congress, at which time you will get my views in toto. I am not ready yet to make an expression.

[15.] Q. Mr. President, have you made any recommendations on the St. Louis airport fight?

THE PRESIDENT. No, I haven't.

Q. It has been called to your attention?

THE PRESIDENT. It has been called to my attention, yes.

[16.] Q. Mr. President, on your trip to Mexico City, will you make any stops—accept any invitations——

THE PRESIDENT. There will be no stops on the trip to Mexico City. There will be one stop coming back and that will be at Baylor.

Q. You will fly all the way? [*Laughter*]

Q. Are you going to make it in about 8 hours—8½ hours is it to Mexico City?

THE PRESIDENT. I don't know what time. I guess you can find out from Hank Myers.

Q. That mean an all-night flight?

THE PRESIDENT. I don't know how long it will take.

Q. Have you decided when you leave?

THE PRESIDENT. It hasn't been worked out yet, no.

Q. Mr. President, the Secret Service are reported as worried about your flying. Are you worried?

THE PRESIDENT. No, it hasn't occurred to me to worry. I like to fly. If your name is up it doesn't make any difference whether you are on a train or anywhere, you will get it anywhere.

[17.] Q. Mr. Churchill has stated in the House of Commons that Britain should withdraw from Palestine unless the United States were willing to share 50–50 on such——

THE PRESIDENT. Mr. Churchill is entitled to his opinion. I have no comment on it.

Q. There has been no official communication——

THE PRESIDENT. None whatever.

Q. Mr. President, have you been in touch with the Prime Minister on the Palestine problem?

THE PRESIDENT. I didn't hear the question. Will you——

Q. I said, sir, have you been in touch with the Prime Minister at all on the Palestine problem?

THE PRESIDENT. No, I have not.

[18.] Q. Mr. President, has the Secret Service indicated to you any worry on your flying?

THE PRESIDENT. No. No, they haven't. They haven't said anything to me about it.

Q. There is a suggestion at the Capitol that instead of building any new airports, that some of the money should be diverted to safety equipment on existing airfields. Do you have any opinion on that?

THE PRESIDENT. I have no opinion to express on that. We have been trying, ever since I have been in the White House, to get the Congress to inaugurate a policy for air, both national and international, and they have never yet been able to agree on a policy. The policy that is now in effect is one that was made by Executive order. I am hoping that the Congress will inaugurate a policy for air, and of course one of the first things necessary in that policy is safety.

Q. Mr. President, Congressman Bloom wants a separate air safety board. Would that be included——

THE PRESIDENT. I don't want to discuss anything of that kind until it is put up to me officially.

Reporter: Thank you, Mr. President.

THE PRESIDENT. You're welcome.

NOTE: President Truman's ninety-sixth news conference was held in his office at the White House at 10:40 a.m. on Saturday, February 1, 1947.

20   Letter to Leaders of Labor and Management in the Building and Construction Industry.   *February* 1, 1947

[Released February 1, 1947.   Dated January 31, 1947]

Gentlemen:

I congratulate the International Unions affiliated with the Building and Construction Trades Department, AFL and the Associated General Contractors of America on the plan that you have just concluded providing for a National Joint Conference Committee. I am also delighted to know that the specialty contractors have their own machinery or are setting up comparable procedures, or may have access to the flexible machinery provided in your plan.

No industry was more important to the war effort, and no industry has a greater contribution to make to the maintenance of a high level of employment. The year ahead presents a great challenge to your industry, calling for united and determined effort, if we are to achieve the great needs of the country for building and construction. Your industry, with approximately 2 million employees has just taken a far reaching and constructive step.

I recall that the government procurement agencies and the international unions comprising the Building and Construction Trades Department, AFL entered into agreements in July 1941 and May 1942 which provided for stabilization of wages and conditions at a time when we were at the critical tooling up stage of the war effort. The machinery established by those agreements, subsequently modified to include the contractors, served us well during the war. The combined efforts of labor, management, and government yielded an outstanding record of uninterrupted production.

Now that most of the war-time controls have been removed, it is appropriate that in the American tradition labor and management assume their full responsibility. You have negotiated the present plan without government participation. The public and the government look to you to make it work.

The agencies of government stand ready to be of all possible assistance to you in this new venture. The Secretary of Labor informs me that the Conciliation Service of the Department of Labor will cooperate with the Joint Conference Committee in every possible way on any disputes that may arise. The statistical services of the government agencies, and in particular those of the Bureau of Labor Statistics, stand ready to be of assistance to you. The splendid record of cooperation with the Davis-Bacon Division of the Department of Labor will no doubt be continued.

You have taken a notable step along the road to industrial peace. I know that with the full support of the members of all your organizations—both management and labor—your industry and the nation will achieve a higher level of production and greater stability.

Very sincerely yours,

HARRY S. TRUMAN

NOTE: This is the text of identical letters sent to Herbert E. Foreman, Managing Director, and James D. Marshall, Assistant Managing Director, of the Associated General Contractors of America, and to Richard Gray, President, and Herbert Rivers, Secretary-Treasurer, of the Building Trades Department, AFL. The text of the joint letter to the President from Mr. Foreman, Mr. Marshall, Mr. Gray, and Mr. Rivers was released with the President's reply, together with the text of an agreement between the organizations providing for a National Joint Conference Committee. The purpose of the Committee, as stated in the agreement, was to set up machinery in the building and construction industry "for the settlement of any dispute or disagreements which may arise and which is voluntarily submitted to the Committee by mutual agreement of the parties involved in the dispute thereby furnishing adequate machinery for the settlement of such disputes or disagreements in an orderly manner without any stoppage of work by lock-out or strike."

---

21 Message to the Congress Transmitting First Annual Report on U.S. Participation in the United Nations. *February 5, 1947*

To the Congress of the United States:

In accordance with the provisions of the United Nations Participation Act of 1945 I submit herewith my first annual report to the Congress on the activities of the United Nations and the participation of the United States therein.[1]

The Charter of the United Nations came into force as a fundamental law for the peoples of the world on October 24, 1945.

The General Assembly convened for the first time in London in January 1946. It elected the Secretary-General and brought into being the Security Council, the Economic and Social Council and the International Court of Justice.

In December 1946, at the Second Part of its First Session, in New York, the General Assembly completed its main organizational tasks by establishing the Trusteeship Council. Thus all of the principal organs of the United Nations have now been established. All of them, except the Trusteeship Council, have been working on their appointed tasks during most of the past year.

---

[1] On Mar. 19, 1946, I transmitted to the Congress the Report submitted to me by the Secretary of State on the First Part of the First Session of the General Assembly in London. [See 1946 volume, this series, Item 65.]

The policy of the United States, as I told the General Assembly in New York on October 23, 1946, is to "support the United Nations with all the resources that we possess . . . . . not as a temporary expedient but as a permanent partnership."

That policy—in season and out—in the face of temporary failure as well as in moments of success—has the support of the overwhelming majority of the American people. It must continue to have this support if the United States is to fulfill its appointed role in the United Nations, if the United Nations is to fulfill its purposes and if our land is to be preserved from the disaster of another and far more terrible war.

In the work of the United Nations during the past year the United States has sought constantly to carry out that policy. Our representatives have spoken for the whole Nation. They have been Democrats and Republicans, members of both the executive and legislative branches of our Government, men and women from private life.

The work of the United Nations during the past year has been the work of building foundations for the future.

First of all, there have been the structural foundations. The Assembly, the Councils, the Court and the Secretariat have had a vast amount of organizational work to do in order to establish themselves as functioning agencies of the international community. Much of this has been pioneering work. The whole structure of the United Nations is a far more extensive endeavor in international cooperation than the nations have ever before attempted.

The essential parts of this structure include not only the principal organs established by the Charter. They include equally the specialized agencies, such as the Food and Agriculture Organization, the International Labor Organization, the United Nations Educational, Scientific and Cultural Organization, the International Civil Aviation Organization, the International Bank for Reconstruction and Development, the International Monetary Fund, the proposed World Health Organization and International Trade Organization and several others. Each of these specialized agencies operates in a specific field under its own constitution. Each is or will be related to the central structure of the United Nations through the Economic and Social Council and the General Assembly. There is scarcely a field of activity having a common interest for the peoples of the world for which continuing instruments of international cooperation have not been developed during the past year.

Perhaps the most immediately significant development of the past year in this direction was the General Assembly's demonstration of its power to influence the policies of nations and to bring about greater understanding among them. The Assembly possesses few definitive powers. It makes recommendations that can be translated into effective law only by the action of the nations concerned. But the Assembly during its meetings in New York expressed a higher sovereignty of the people's will in a manner which promises much for its development as a dominant power for peace and progress in the world.

The building of the structural foundations of the United Nations during the past year has been accompanied by action over a very broad field toward giving life and meaning to the purposes and principles of the Charter.

There has been progress toward building security from war. Step by step we have advanced the first part of the way toward agreement on the essential principles of a truly effective international system of control over the means of destruction that science has placed in the hands of mankind.

The initiative in the control of atomic energy and other major weapons adaptable to mass destruction was taken by the United States. The resolution creating the Atomic Energy Commission was adopted at the First Meeting of the General Assembly in London. The United States presented in the Atomic Energy Commission last June its proposal for international control of atomic energy. The Soviet Union opposed these proposals, but the Commission worked throughout the summer and fall to build the bases for agreement.

In October the Soviet Union introduced in the General Assembly proposals on the general regulation and reduction of armaments that seemed at first far removed from the United States position. Nevertheless, seven weeks later the Assembly was able to adopt unanimously a resolution reaffirming all the principles of the Atomic Energy Resolution and reflecting for the first time unanimous agreement on the essential principle of a system of international control and inspection established by treaty and not subject to any veto in its operations.

Two and a half weeks later, on December 31, the Atomic Energy Commission transmitted its first report to the Security Council. The Report had been adopted by the Commission by a vote of 10 to 0, the Soviet Union and Poland abstaining.

Many months of hard work and difficult negotiation in the Security Council and the Atomic Energy Commission lie ahead. Not all the essential principles have yet been agreed upon. The problem of enforcement must still be resolved. All the principles must be given specific and practical application in treaties and conventions unanimously agreed upon.

This is one of the main tasks before the United Nations in the coming year. To succeed, we must at the same time build the other essential foundations of a general system of collective security. The nations can safely lay aside their arms only in so far as their security is protected by other means.

An essential element of collective security will be the ability of the Security Council to fulfill its primary responsibility for the maintenance of international peace and security. In its consideration of international disputes during its first year the Council demonstrated increasing power to ameliorate situations that otherwise might have become dangerous and to influence the policies of nations in the direction of upholding the purposes and principles of the Charter. This was generally true even when the five permanent members failed to reach the required unanimity for definitive action. The Security Council's application on a continuing basis of the public and peaceful methods of the council chamber to the settlement of disputes between nations is a new development in international relations, the significance of which gives every promise of becoming more apparent in the year ahead.

Important steps have been taken by the United Nations during the past year toward economic reconstruction and toward establishing the necessary basis for an expanding peace-time trade and employment.

A draft Trade Charter establishing principles and practices aimed at increasing the volume of world trade and employment by reducing or eliminating artificial trade barriers and restrictions has been proposed by the United States and is now being developed by a Preparatory Committee of 18 nations. One of the primary United Nations' tasks of the year ahead is the adoption of such a Charter and the creation of an International Trade Organization to carry it out.

The General Assembly has unanimously asked the Economic and Social Council to act on recommendations for the reconstruction and integration of the European economy and establishment of an Economic Commission for Europe. This Commission would unite all the interested countries, including the Soviet Union on the East and the United States on the West, in a common program. Steps toward economic reconstruction and development in the Far East will also be undertaken by the Economic and Social Council this year.

Progress has also been made by the Economic and Social Council and the specialized agencies during the past year in many other respects. It is not too much to say that the establishment and maintenance of lasting peace will depend in large part upon the ability of the United Nations to carry through to a successful conclusion the work it has begun toward world economic recovery and cooperation.

The promotion and protection of basic human rights for all peoples is a fundamental purpose of the United Nations. Active support for the wider realization of these rights and freedoms has been and should continue to be a primary objective of United States policy in the United Nations.

During the past year our representatives in the Assembly and the Economic and Social Council took the initiative in writing a charter for the International Refugee Organization under which the right to freedom and another chance for a decent life of a million victims of war and racial, political, or religious oppression would be preserved. I shall recommend to the Congress prompt acceptance of the constitution of the IRO and appropriation of our share of the expenses of its program.

The United States believes that freedom of information must be realized on a far wider basis than exists in the world today if the United Nations is to succeed. We have strongly supported the policy of public debate of all issues in the United Nations because this promotes public knowledge and understanding and gives the peoples of the world a more direct opportunity to influence the results. We have also asked for action to break down the barriers to a wider, freer flow of information in the world. Preparations are now going forward for a world conference on freedom of information before the end of this year as one step in this direction.

The provisions of the Charter relating to dependent peoples offer to those hundreds of millions who do not yet govern themselves their best hope for attainment of this and other basic human rights and freedoms. The United States Representatives took a leading part in the General Assembly in bringing about the establishment of the Trusteeship System in the face of sharp disagreements and other major difficulties that might have caused indefinite delay. The United States will support further steps during the coming year toward strengthening the Trusteeship System.

America has long been a symbol of freedom and democratic progress to peoples less favored than we have been. We must maintain their belief in us by our policies and our acts.

One of the important long-range achievements of the General Assembly's First Session was the adoption of resolutions introduced by the United States on the codification and development of international law.

The General Assembly unanimously directed its committee on codification to give first attention to the charter and the decision of the Nuremberg Tribunal, under which aggressive war is a crime against humanity for which individuals as well as states must be punished. The Assembly also agreed that genocide—the deliberate policy of extermination of a race or class or any other human group—was a crime under international law. These developments toward the application of international law to individuals as well as to states are of profound significance to the state. We cannot have lasting peace unless a genuine rule of world law is established and enforced.

The justifiable hope and confidence to which the great progress of the United Nations in the past year has given rise can be betrayed and lost. The difficulties and dangers that lie before us are many and serious. They are strewn across the road that leads to the final peace settlements, to the establishment and maintenance of collective security, to the control of atomic energy and regulation and reduction of other arms, to the attainment of economic recovery and an expanding world economy, and to the wider realization of human rights.

Our policy of supporting the United Nations "with all the resources that we possess" must be given effective practical application on a genuinely national, bipartisan basis in every activity of the United Nations. This is just as necessary in the economic and social field as it is in the political field. We must

pursue without hesitation bipartisan policies of economic cooperation with the rest of the world in such matters as economic reconstruction and development and the expansion of world trade and employment. Because of the interdependence of the economy of nations, it will also be vital to world recovery as well as to our own prosperity that we maintain at home a stable economy of high employment.

The responsibility of the United States is a particularly heavy one because of the power and influence that our history and our material resources have placed in our hands. No nation has a higher stake in the outcome than our own.

HARRY S. TRUMAN

NOTE: The report is printed in House Document 81 (80th Cong., 1st sess.).

For the President's address of October 23, 1946, to the United Nations General Assembly, see 1946 volume, this series, Item 236.

22 Letter to the President of the Senate and to the Speaker of the House on Succession to the Presidency. *February 5, 1947*

My dear Mr. ————:

On June 19, 1945, I sent a Message to the Congress of the United States suggesting that the Congress should give its consideration to the question of the Presidential succession.

In that Message, it was pointed out that under the existing statute governing the succession to the office of President, members of the Cabinet successively fill the office in the event of the death of the elected President and Vice President. It was further pointed out that, in effect, the present law gives to me the power to nominate my immediate successor in the event of my own death or inability to act.

I said then, and I repeat now, that in a democracy, this power should not rest with

the Chief Executive. I believe that, in so far as possible, the office of the President should be filled by an elective officer.

In the Message of June 19, 1945, I recommended that the Congress enact legislation placing the Speaker of the House of Representatives first in order of succession, and if there were no Speaker, or if he failed to qualify, that the President pro tempore of the Senate should act until a duly qualified Speaker was elected.

A Bill (H.R. 3587) providing for this succession was introduced in the House of Representatives and was passed by the House on June 29, 1945. It failed, however, to pass the Senate.

The same need, for a revision of the law of succession, that existed when I sent the

Message to the Congress on June 19, 1945, still exists today.

I see no reason to change or amend the suggestion which I previously made to the Congress, but if the Congress is not disposed to pass the type of bill previously passed by the House, then I recommend that some other plan of succession be devised so that the office of the President would be filled by an officer who holds his position as a result of the expression of the will of the voters of this country.

It is my belief that the present line of succession as provided by the existing statute, which was enacted in 1886, is not in accord with our basic concept of Government by elected representatives of the people.

I again urge the Congress to give its attention to this subject.

Very sincerely yours,

HARRY S. TRUMAN

NOTE: This is the text of identical letters addressed to the Honorable Arthur H. Vandenberg, President pro tempore of the Senate, and to the Honorable Joseph W. Martin, Jr., Speaker of the House of Representatives.

On July 18 the President approved a bill (61 Stat. 380), providing for the performance of the duties of the office of the President in case of removal, resignation, death, or inability both of the President and the Vice President.

23   Statement by the President on the Death of O. Max Gardner. *February 6, 1947*

THE NATION mourns the untimely passing of O. Max Gardner. Great as were his achievements in public and in private life, he was on the threshold of what all his friends were confident would be a career of distinction and further usefulness, in the field of diplomacy.

Whether he turned his talents to the law, to business and industry, or to government, so great and so versatile were his talents that his achievements at once became outstanding.

In Washington, particularly from the war years onward, his counsel was invaluable. In his last official post, that of Under Secretary of the Treasury, his advice was always helpful, particularly in the approach to the solution of those manifold problems of finance and fiscal affairs which reconversion presented.

Keen, kindly, courteous always, rich in humor, delightful as a raconteur, he had also a prodigious capacity for work. To these qualities he added a tact and urbanity which would have served him admirably had he been permitted to assume his duties as our Ambassador to Great Britain.

In his passing I have lost a loyal and devoted personal friend and the country has lost a great American.

24   Special Message to the Congress on Rubber. *February 7, 1947*

To the Congress of the United States:

In my recent message to the Congress requesting the extension of certain titles of the Second War Powers Act for continued controls in a few specific areas, I pointed out the importance of natural and synthetic rubber to the national security. In that connection, I urged the Congress to continue allocation controls over rubber pending consideration of permanent legislation that would insure the maintenance of a minimum synthetic rubber industry in the United States.

I am sure that the Congress will wish to consider carefully all aspects of the problem before enacting permanent legislation. During the period of such consideration, however, I urge that there be no break in the continuity of policy and administrative action concerning both natural and synthetic rubber. I therefore wish to review, in somewhat fuller detail than was possible in my previous message, the character of this problem, and to suggest actions that seem desirable for the Congress to take at this time.

The problem has not been a matter of immediate concern up to the present time, because world supplies of natural rubber have been so critically short that it has been necessary for us to make fullest practicable use of our facilities for producing synthetic rubber. As I stated in my previous message, the world supply of natural rubber is still inadequate to meet world needs. We must, however, recognize that the time is rapidly approaching when this condition will no longer prevail. According to the best evidence that I have been able to obtain, it appears that perhaps in late 1947, and almost certainly by early 1948, natural rubber production will have increased to the point where it will be possible to satisfy world rubber needs largely from natural rubber. With an adequate world supply of natural rubber and a free choice of materials by industry, the use of synthetic rubber in the United States might fall substantially below the permanent production goals considered to be minimum for the needs of national security. This would be even more likely if at some time in 1948 the world supply of natural rubber should begin to exceed the total world demand for all rubber.

The Congress has already made provision,

by means of the Strategic and Critical Materials Stock Piling Act of 1946, for the accumulation of a stockpile of natural rubber within the borders of the United States. The physical properties of rubber, however, and the necessity of stockpile rotation, place limits which make the largest feasible Government stockpile of natural rubber inadequate in itself to meet the demands of a national emergency. The stockpile must be supplemented by an assured production of American-made rubber.

Appropriate action should be taken now to assure that adequate facilities for the production of American-made rubber of the highest quality continue to be available. Part of this productive capacity should continue in effective operation, and the techniques required for the efficient processing of synthetic rubber in the manufacture of rubber products should be maintained and improved.

The Congress will recall the extraordinary measures that had to be taken in the early days of the recent war to meet the emergency caused by the sudden unavailability of our normal supplies of rubber. At the direction of President Roosevelt a Rubber Survey Committee was created which outlined vigorous measures to be taken by both industry and Government. We were fortunate in having time to carry out the program outlined by this Committee, for the shortage of rubber could have caused the collapse of our war effort and of our domestic economy.

On another occasion we might not be so fortunate. The security of the United States and the essential needs of its citizens must never again be jeopardized by inadequate or uncertain rubber supplies.

In recognition of this fact, the Director of War Mobilization and Reconversion created an Interagency Policy Committee on Rubber in September, 1945. This committee made an exhaustive study of the problem, in cooperation with industry and the executive agencies concerned, and submitted two reports which were transmitted to the Congress on March 8 and July 22, 1946. These reports outline the dimensions of the problem and suggest various methods of meeting it.

The Congress should deal with all aspects of this matter during the present session because of its vital effect upon our national security. Meanwhile, it is imperative that the Congress extend authority to continue controls over rubber under the Second War Powers Act, as I requested in my previous message. Prompt action by the Congress will provide the basis for continuity of operation in rubber controls, and will permit their simplification and orderly relaxation or removal. It will also greatly aid the agencies concerned in planning production in Government-owned synthetic rubber plants and such action will contribute to the disposal of these plants to private industry.

The time will soon arrive when it will no longer be necessary to use these controls to insure equitable distribution of natural rubber or to produce the maximum number of commodities from synthetic rubber. When this time comes, continued controls would be used only for the purpose of insuring the maintenance of a minimum synthetic rubber industry in the United States. Controls should be used for such maintenance of a synthetic rubber industry only if specific authority is provided for that purpose.

I therefore recommend that the Senate and the House of Representatives, by Joint Resolution, make a declaration of policy to the effect that it is the firm intention of the Government to maintain a synthetic rubber industry in the United States, adequate to the minimum needs of national security.

I further recommend that the Senate and the House of Representatives act expeditiously in establishing appropriate committee arrangements to consider the problems involved in maintaining a synthetic rubber industry in the United States and to draft such legislation as is found to be necessary to accomplish this objective.

I repeat my recent recommendation that the authority to continue allocation controls on rubber be continued for one year under Title III of the Second War Powers Act, in order that the Congress may have an opportunity to consider this problem and to enact such permanent legislation as in its judgment is necessary and appropriate.

The program of action I have outlined has the unanimous and vigorous support of all agencies of Government concerned with this problem. I am instructing these agencies to give all possible assistance to the Congress in its consideration of the problem, and to make available, on request, the statistical material and other information which they have collected.

HARRY S. TRUMAN

NOTE: On March 29 the President approved a joint resolution providing for the maintenance of a domestic rubber-producing industry and extending the allocation control authority contained in title III of the Second War Powers Act (61 Stat. 24).

25 Message to Admiral Stone Commending Him on His Service With the Allied Commission for Italy. *February 7, 1947*

[Released February 7, 1947. Dated February 4, 1947]

ON THE OCCASION of the abolition of the Allied Commission for Italy, with which you have been intimately associated since its inception and of which you have been Chief Commissioner since July, 1944, I wish to express to you the sincere appreciation of the United States Government for the splendid service which you have rendered your country and the very real contribution which you have made to the Allied cause.

The purpose of the Allied Commission was only partially to insure security in the theater of a great battle. Equally important has been the guidance and assistance which the Commission has given to the new Italy in its work of reconstruction and its rebirth as a true democracy. With the support and cooperation of your British and American colleagues you have made an outstanding contribution to the achievement of both these high purposes of the Allied Commission in Italy.

[Rear Admiral Ellery W. Stone, USNR, Rome, Italy]

NOTE: Admiral Stone served as Acting Chief Commissioner of the Allied Commission for Italy from November 10, 1943, to July 1944, then as Chief Commissioner to February 7, 1947.

26 Letter to the President of the Senate and to the Speaker of the House Concerning Gifts to the United Nations. *February 7, 1947*

[Released February 7, 1947. Dated February 6, 1947]

My dear ————:

An offer of $8,500,000 has been made to the United Nations for acquisition of a headquarters site in the city of New York, on the condition that the gift should be free of Federal Gift Taxes.

The United Nations desires to take advantage of this generous offer and has requested that the United States comply with the condition attached to this gift.

I heartily recommend that this government comply with this request. It would appear that the most desirable method by which this gift could be freed from such taxes would be to amend the appropriate sections of the Internal Revenue Code. In addition to accomplishing the purpose of complying with the above offer, the effect of such an amendment would be to encourage other public-spirited citizens to make gifts to the United Nations.

I enclose herewith, for your consideration, copy of a suggested joint resolution which would accomplish the desired purposes.

I consider that the passage of such a resolution is definitely in the public interest and I suggest that you bring this to the attention of the Congress at your earliest convenience.

Very sincerely yours,

HARRY S. TRUMAN

NOTE: This is the text of identical letters addressed to the Honorable Arthur H. Vandenberg, President pro tempore of the Senate, and to the Honorable Joseph W. Martin, Jr., Speaker of the House of Representatives.

On February 26 the President approved a joint resolution (61 Stat. 6), providing for the granting, in the case of income, estate, and gift taxes, of deductions for contributions to the United Nations.

27 Statement by the President Announcing Further Steps in Aid of Highway Safety. *February 8, 1947*

AT THE President's Highway Safety Conference in Washington last May, an "Action Program" was formulated to unite all States and communities in a campaign for safe and efficient highway transportation. Three national committees were established, representing State officials, civil organizations, and the Federal agencies concerned with highway matters, to coordinate the efforts of their respective groups.

These committees have suggested to me the desirability of following up the conference this year with a meeting to appraise progress and to devise whatever additional plans may be necessary to promote wider adoption of the "Action Program" recommendations.

Accordingly, I have asked Major General

Philip B. Fleming, the Federal Works Administrator, who served as Conference Chairman, to reconstitute the Committee on Conference Reports as an "Action Program" group for this purpose, and to arrange a meeting in Washington during June.

At that time, most of the 44 State legislatures meeting this year will have completed their work. The meeting therefore will provide each State with a timely opportunity to report its progress toward enactment of uniform laws on driver licensing and other matters vital to safety, as recommended in the "Action Program."

I have written to all Governors requesting their continued cooperation in this important campaign.

28 Statement by the President on the Increasing Incidence of Heart Disease. *February 8, 1947*

THE HEALTH of the Nation is a matter of paramount concern to all our citizens. Good health is, after all, a priceless asset to the Nation and to the individual. Perhaps it is our greatest national asset.

This country was spared many of the ravages of war which have left in less favored countries a heritage of disease and the ills of pestilence and famine, inevitably following in the wake of war.

We have been inconvenienced, but the national health has not suffered because of short rations. But we do have a health problem which arises out of the increased tempo of our modern American life.

All thoughtful citizens must be alarmed by the increasing incidence of heart disease. The physician knows, and the rank and file of our citizens should understand, that heart disease is now the leading cause of death. It is an alarming portent that 400,000 Americans will die of heart disease this year, and it is distressing to know that 1 out of every 20 persons now suffers from serious diseases of the heart and blood vessels.

In the face of these grim facts, I appeal to all my countrymen to cooperate with every agency and organization and every individual doctor in fighting the present-day national peril—heart disease.

29 Statement by the President Urging Extension of Authority To Ship Emergency Supplies to Europe. *February* 13, 1947

THIS GOVERNMENT stands ready to do everything within its power to relieve the plight of the British people in their present fuel emergency.

Although we have received no request from England for aid, I have directed Captain Granville Conway, Coordinator of Emergency Export Programs, to determine how quickly and in what quantity coal can be landed at British ports. It would take a minimum of 15 days to ship coal from this country to England. Such shipments might very well arrive too late to help England in the present emergency.

There are, however, a number of colliers at sea in the vicinity of the British Isles carrying coal to other European countries. It may be possible to divert some of these colliers to English ports.

In view of the present emergency in England, the United States representative on the European Coal Organization which sits in London has been instructed to support a request for a reallocation of the shipments of coal now at sea, if this is the British desire. It is understood, of course, that coal diverted from other countries would be made up as rapidly as shipping schedules can be readjusted.

A remarkable job has been done in stepping up our export shipments of coal. In December, 1.8 million tons were shipped; in January, 2.5 million tons; and this month we plan to ship 2.9 million tons. In March, we hope to do even better, for these shipments are vital to the rehabilitation of Europe and other war-torn areas.

To meet these future schedules it is imperative that uncertainty over continuation of the authority of the Maritime Commission to operate Government-owned ships be dispelled as quickly as possible. This authority, unless extended by the Congress, will expire on March 1.

On January 21, I asked the Congress to adopt a joint resolution extending the authority to June 30. I am gratified that the House Committee on Merchant Marine and Fisheries is holding hearings on this resolution today.

I cannot emphasize too strongly the need for quick action by the House and the Senate on this legislation because without it our emergency export programs for fuel and grain will break down completely at the end of this month. Every day that action is delayed means further disruption of February schedules for shipments of coal and wheat to Europe. Because of the uncertainty now prevailing tanker shipments of fuel oil to the East Coast ports have already slowed down.

I urge the Congress to act promptly to extend the authority of the Maritime Commission to operate the ships which are so vitally needed.

NOTE: On February 26 the President approved a joint resolution (61 Stat. 6), providing for the continuation of the authority of the Maritime Commission to operate vessels until July 1, 1947.

On February 14 the White House released a message from Prime Minister Clement Attlee expressing appreciation for the offer of help in the coal shortage but declining to ask that cargoes be diverted to English ports in view of the need for coal in Europe.

30   Toasts of the President and the President-Elect of Uruguay.
February 13, 1947

WE ARE very fortunate today to have as our guest the President-elect of Uruguay, our good friend. We appreciate very much his being here today. We want him to enjoy his visit in the United States. We want to contribute to that enjoyment all we can. I have always been curious to see his country. I hope some time that I shall have a chance to do it.

The President brought me a booklet today, with pictures of his farm, and his son and his grandson; and he has grapes just like these. He says they are even better than California grapes ever pretend to be. I should like to go some time and sample them.

But I am sure that he does just what he says he does. We are indeed glad to have him in the United States, and I should like to propose a toast to the President-elect of our neighboring Republic.

NOTE: The President proposed the toast at a luncheon at the White House. President-elect Berreta's response, as translated directly afterward, follows:

Mr. President, President-elect Tomás Berreta expresses his profound thanks for being present here as a guest of the President of the United States. He feels particularly moved because his country has made a cult of democracy, a cult of the principle of government of, by and for the people. When he comes into this house with the pictures of Lincoln and Washington—leaders who brought democracy to the entire hemisphere—and he sits alongside the President of the United States, surrounded by his advisers, he is indeed grateful for this opportunity.

Moreover, he says that the fine touch of having grapes on the table he takes as a symbol of the fact that the President of the United States, like himself, comes from an agricultural region as a worker—a worker of the ground. Therefore, he expresses profound thanks to be in this country.

31   The President's News Conference of
February 13, 1947

THE PRESIDENT. [1.] Gentlemen, and ladies, some of you, I think, haven't—you were not in here yesterday when we were showing the picture here, which is, I think, a treasure. Now it is public property. We have closed the deal on it on Lincoln's birthday, and are able to announce that it is public property. And I hope to hang it out in the lobby where a lot of people can see it, or in the National Gallery of Art. I just put it up there—[*indicating the wall*]—temporarily so the picture men could take pictures of it. It is very interesting. If you haven't read the release that we put out on it, I would suggest that everyone read it, because it is an interesting thing. That picture of Lincoln there, that is the original of the official picture that hangs over the mantel in the State Dining Room in the White House.[1]

[1] On February 12 the White House announced that the President had authorized the purchase by the Government of a historical painting, "The Peacemakers," depicting President Lincoln, Generals Grant and Sherman, and Admiral Porter in conference aboard the steamship "River Queen" during the last days of the Civil War. The picture, the work of George P. A. Healy, the release stated, was painted shortly after the war. The artist was not present at the meeting near Richmond. However, he had previously painted individual portraits of the four and he had obtained the data from which he worked from General Sherman.

The portrait of President Lincoln in the State Dining Room, also the work of Mr. Healy, the release added, is believed to have been a replica of the one in the group picture. Robert Todd Lincoln, in a letter to a friend many years later, described the history of both pictures in some detail. Of the portrait he wrote, "I have never seen a portrait of my father which is to be compared with it in any way."

I have no special announcements to make, and if anybody wants to ask questions, I will listen.

[2.] Q. Mr. President, you last week— or early this week, I forget the exact date— stressed the necessity for maintaining the synthetic rubber industry in this country, even when the supply of natural rubber becomes more plentiful. Could you give us any details on how that industry would be maintained?

THE PRESIDENT. No. That's a matter that we'll have to work out. I went into the whole rubber situation while I was in the Senate, and made the report which finally wound up as the rubber policy of the United States Government. Of course, I think it is necessary for us to maintain and stand by synthetic plants so that we will not be caught as we were in the—in this Second World War, although we all hope and are working toward the end that there will be no more world wars.

[3.] Q. Mr. President, are you going to accept Mr. Hannegan's nomination for 1948? [*Laughter*]

THE PRESIDENT. I thought, Bert [1]—I thought you might come out with something like that, so I will read you a statement that covers the thing categorically.

Q. Slowly, Mr. President.

THE PRESIDENT. I will read this slowly, but it is ready for handing out——

Q. That has been mimeographed, sir?

THE PRESIDENT. Yes, it has been mimeographed.

"In view of certain comment regarding the Presidency, I wish to say that there has been no change in my attitude since the statement I read to you November 11, 1946.

"The Presidency is being conducted now just as it was then. It will continue to be so conducted. That is to say, I intend to

––––––––––
[1] Bert Andrews of the New York Herald Tribune.

continue to act in this office as the agent of the American people, without regard to my personal political fortunes. I repeat what I said on November 11, when I pledged the Executive to cooperate in every proper manner with the Congress:

"'As President of the United States, I am guided by a simple formula: to do in all cases, from day to day, without regard to narrow political considerations, what seems to me to be best for the welfare of all of our people.'"

That's all the answer I have for you, Bert.

Q. It's a good answer.

[4.] Q. Mr. President, what is your opinion of this projected Republican $6 billion cut in the budget?

THE PRESIDENT. The budget that I sent to the Congress is the budget which is necessary for the operation of the country. I have no comment to make on any statement that the Republicans may make, for I know nothing about the details.

Q. Can you comment on the $2½ billion on national defense cut—proposed cut?

THE PRESIDENT. I think Secretary Patterson answered that very effectively yesterday.

Q. Do you endorse his statement, sir?

THE PRESIDENT. I do.

[5.] Q. Mr. President, are you considering Mr. Ed Pauley for Ambassador to England?

THE PRESIDENT. I am not.

[6.] Q. Mr. President, can you tell me why the Democrats are going to have a Jefferson Dinner instead of a Jackson Day Dinner this year?

THE PRESIDENT. Well, they are holding it in April instead of January. That's the only reason that I know of.

Q. They gave me two reasons in the Committee when I asked——

THE PRESIDENT. Well, the Committee ought to know. I didn't. [*Laughter*]

Q. But one reason was that the only date

they could get the hotel was nearer Jefferson than Jackson. Then they said they had had Jefferson Dinners for 13 or 14 years, and it was time for a change.

THE PRESIDENT. You mean Jackson. No. You see, the battle of New Orleans was fought on the 8th day of January, and that is usually the time for the Jackson Day Dinners. There is one in Missouri every year on the 8th of January. Jefferson's birthday, as you know, is on the 13th of April; and if we hold dinners in April—Jefferson Day Dinners, there isn't any difference. They accomplish the same purpose.

Q. Is there not a difference between Jefferson and Jackson democracy?

THE PRESIDENT. Not a bit.

[7.] Q. Mr. President, can you tell us something about your meeting with the President-elect of Uruguay?

THE PRESIDENT. Yes. I had a very pleasant meeting with the President-elect of Uruguay, and we had luncheon over at the White House at one o'clock. And he is a very charming gentleman. And he is a farmer, and he and I speak the same language. He doesn't speak English and I don't speak Spanish, but we speak the farm language. [*Laughter*]

[8.] Q. Would you like to comment on the attack on Mr. Lilienthal?

THE PRESIDENT. Mr. Lilienthal is fully and thoroughly equipped for the position to which I appointed him, and I shall stay with him straight through.

[9.] Q. Mr. President, there has been a big vacancy on the FCC for a good many months.

THE PRESIDENT. Yes.

Q. Is there any chance it will be filled?

THE PRESIDENT. It will probably continue for some time to come yet. I haven't found the man I want to put on that.

[10.] Q. Following this press confer-

ence, Governor Warren of California is due to visit you. Would you accede to his request for 40 billion—for the 20 billion—million, rather—State Central Valley Authority project?

THE PRESIDENT. .I don't know whether he is going to ask me that or not. I will talk to him about it when he comes in.

[11.] Q. Mr. President, what do you think of Senator McKellar's charges that Lilienthal either is a Communist or flirts on the fringe?

THE PRESIDENT. They are absolutely unfounded.

Q. Can we quote that, sir?

THE PRESIDENT. Yes—verbatim.

[12.] Q. Mr. President, there are reports that Mr. John Small is going to be appointed to the presidency of one of the corporations seized by the Alien Property Custodian. Is there any truth in that?

THE PRESIDENT. News to me.

[13.] Q. Mr. President, that—is the appointment of an Ambassador to Britain—could you tell us anything about it? Have you settled on anybody?

THE PRESIDENT. No, we have not. As soon as I have decided, and we find that the gentleman will—or lady—will accept——

Q. Lady?

THE PRESIDENT. I will let you know immediately.

Q. You mean there is a possibility that you might appoint a lady Ambassador?

THE PRESIDENT. I said that for the benefit of May.[1] [*Laughter*]

Q. I would like to repeat that question, sir. Is there a possibility that one will be named to that diplomatic post?

THE PRESIDENT. There is of course a possibility of a woman getting any job, but not that one.

---

[1] Mrs. May Craig of the Portland (Maine) Press Herald.

[14.] Q. May I ask if you haven't found the man you want for the FCC, does that preclude Miss Martin?

THE PRESIDENT. No, not necessarily. Doesn't preclude a woman. You know, they take that "man" to mean the whole species.

[15.] Q. Mr. President, is General Eisenhower among those under consideration for the appointment to London?

THE PRESIDENT. He is not. I need General Eisenhower right where he is.

Q. Secretary Forrestal on the list?

THE PRESIDENT. I need Secretary Forrestal right where he is.

[16.] Q. Do you have any further comment on the British economic crisis? [1]

THE PRESIDENT. No, I have no comment. I am sorry to see it happen, but I have no comment on it.

Q. Mr. President, have you received any assurance from the leaders on the Hill that the authority of the Maritime Commission to operate ships will be extended? I understand it expires the last of this month.

THE PRESIDENT. I understand a bill for extension has been reported out.

[1] See Item 29.

[17.] Q. Mr. President, is Mr. Clayton being considered for Ambassador to England?

THE PRESIDENT. Who?

Q. Mr. Clayton?

THE PRESIDENT. No.

[18.] Q. Mr. President, do you plan to ask Congress for extension of the draft?

THE PRESIDENT. I will issue a statement on that in a few days.

[19.] Q. Is John Nicholas Brown being considered, just to give you another name for the ambassadorship?

THE PRESIDENT. I am not going to tell you anything about it. You could ask me everybody in the United States, and I will say not until I get ready to announce it will I give it to you.

[20.] Q. Mr. President, do you have any word on when former President Hoover is returning from Europe?

THE PRESIDENT. No, I haven't. He will return as soon as he finishes his job over there.

Q. Thank you, Mr. President.

NOTE: President Truman's ninety-seventh news conference was held in his office at the White House at 4 o'clock on Thursday afternoon, February 13, 1947.

32 Statement by the President on the Famine in Rumania. *February 17, 1947*

I HAVE just been informed by American officials in Rumania that 500,000 people are now starving in Moldavia, the Northern Province of Rumania. Thousands have already died, hundreds are dying daily, and conditions are steadily worsening.

In the circumstances, I have asked the American Red Cross to finance and supervise distribution of 4,500 tons of 10-in-1 rations and 2,500 tons of beans to these starving people. These supplies, already on the water, will be diverted by the United States Army and should reach Constanza, Rumania, within 10 days. They are sufficient to provide 1,000 calories per day for 500,000 people for approximately 16 days. The Rumanian Government is being requested to make available transportation and other facilities to enable the Rumanian Red Cross, under supervision of the American Red Cross, to distribute this food without charge and with guarantees against discrimination on political, racial, religious, or social grounds.

At the same time, despite the magnitude of world demands on existing stocks and transportation facilities, urgent attention is being given to the possibilities of providing additional food supplies, in the form of cereal grains, for purchase by Rumania, and in that connection the Rumanian Government has been asked to give immediate assurances that measures will be taken so that food thus furnished, as well as remaining indigenous food, will be utilized effectively to prevent the recurrence of such an emergency situation as has now arisen. Among the assurances desired are guarantees that, so long as the present famine continues, (1) Rumania will not employ any grain for the payment of reparations, (2) Rumania will not export or permit the export of any grain from Rumania for the repayment of grain loans from other countries, for trade purposes, or for any other reasons, and (3) United States representatives in Rumania will be free to observe, in such manner as they see fit, the distribution within Rumania of grain from United States sources, which distribution will likewise be effected without political, racial, religious, or social discrimination.

I have taken this action on humanitarian grounds. It is in the tradition of the American people to take all possible steps to alleviate the present suffering of the people of Rumania, no matter what may be the cause of the dire emergency in which these people now find themselves.

NOTE: On March 26 the White House released a message to the President from Brig. Gen. Cortlandt V. Schuyler, U.S. Military Representative, Allied Control Commission in Rumania, who had just returned from a 6-day inspection trip through the famine area. General Schuyler reported that he was convinced "that this program has been highly successful, that the food was distributed quickly and efficiently to those who needed it most without regard to political, racial, or religious considerations." He also stated that he believed the prompt action by the American relief agencies had saved many thousands who would otherwise have died of starvation.

33 Citation Accompanying Legion of Merit Awarded to the King of Saudi Arabia. *February 18, 1947*

CITATION TO ACCOMPANY THE AWARD OF
THE LEGION OF MERIT
DEGREE OF CHIEF COMMANDER

TO

ABDUL AZIZ IBN ABDUR RAHMAN AL FAISAL
AL SAUD

HIS MAJESTY Abdul Aziz Ibn Abdur Rahman al Faisal Al Saud, King of Saudi Arabia, rendered exceptionally meritorious service to the war effort of the United Nations. He led his country in an unwavering course of support and encouragement to the cause of the Allies, a course which culminated in a declaration of war against the Axis in March 1945. As Commander-in-Chief of Saudi Arabia, he kept the land, sea and air routes under his control open for use, and by his attitude of wholehearted cooperation, he enabled American forces to accomplish a program of construction and resource development in the country that derived benefits of major proportions for the prosecution of the war. Through his unswerving loyalty, and by his dynamic leadership at the head of his nation in the support of the cause, King Abdul Aziz Ibn Saud made a notable contribution to the successful war effort of the United Nations.

HARRY S. TRUMAN

34 Citation Accompanying Legion of Merit Awarded to the Crown Prince of Saudi Arabia. *February 18, 1947*

CITATION TO ACCOMPANY THE AWARD OF
THE LEGION OF MERIT
DEGREE OF COMMANDER

TO

AMIR SAUD IBN ABDUL AZIZ BIN ABDUL RAHMAN
AL FAISAL AL SAUD

HIS ROYAL HIGHNESS Amir Saud Ibn Abdul Aziz bin Abdul Rahman al Faisal Al Saud, Crown Prince of Saudi Arabia, rendered exceptionally meritorious service to the war effort of the United Nations. Acting as Deputy to the King, he helped to lead his country in an unwavering course of support and encouragement to the cause of the Allies, a course which culminated in a declaration of war against the Axis in March 1945. In control of the armed forces of Saudi Arabia, he skillfully carried out the policy of his government in keeping the land, sea and air routes open for use, and by his active support and cooperation, he greatly aided American forces in accomplishing a program of construction and resource development in the country that derived benefit of major proportions for the prosecution of the war. Through his able and effective manner in actively carrying out the high policies of his country, Amir Saud, Crown Prince of Saudi Arabia, contributed substantially to the successful war effort of the United Nations.

HARRY S. TRUMAN

35 Special Message to the Congress on Termination of Emergency and Wartime Powers. *February 19, 1947*

To the Congress of the United States:

During the year and a half that have elapsed since the defeat of our last enemy in battle, we have progressively eliminated the great majority of emergency controls over the Nation's economy. The progress of reconversion now makes it possible to take an additional step toward freeing our economy of war-time controls.

Accordingly, I am recommending that the Congress repeal certain temporary statutes still in effect by virtue of the emergencies proclaimed by the President in 1939 and 1941, and I have requested the executive departments and agencies to cease operations under powers derived from certain permanent statutes that are effective only during emergencies, to the extent that such operations are related to the 1939 and 1941 emergencies.

The recommendations I here present for the consideration of the Congress will, if accepted, materially assist in further freeing the country of war controls and will help make possible an early ending of the emergencies. I have under continuing study the question of terminating the emergencies proclaimed in 1939 and 1941, and intend to take action as soon as circumstances permit.

In my recent message to the Congress on the State of the Union I outlined the following program with respect to the termination of emergency and war-time powers:

"Two groups of temporary laws still remain: The first are those which by Congressional mandate are to last during the 'emergency'; the second are those which are to continue until the 'termination of the war'.

"I shall submit to the Congress recommendations for the repeal of certain of the statutes which by their terms continue for the duration of the 'emergency.' I shall at the same time recommend that others within this classification be extended until the state of war has been ended by treaty or by legislative action. As to those statutes which continue until the state of war has been terminated, I urge that the Congress promptly consider each statute individually, and repeal such emergency legislation where advisable."

Accordingly, I now submit recommendations with respect to more than 100 laws which are affected by the limited emergency declared September 8, 1939, or the unlimited emergency declared May 27, 1941.

In the case of these statutes that remain in force until termination of the war, I have directed the executive departments and agencies to assist the Congress in its consideration of these statutes, individually, by making available full information concerning them to the appropriate Congressional committees. The work done on this subject in the 79th Congress by the Committees on the Judiciary of both Houses, with the assistance of the Office of War Mobilization and Reconversion, the Department of Justice, and other Government agencies should offer valuable aid to the Congress in accomplishing the task which remains. At a later date it may prove desirable to send a further communication to the Congress concerning these statutes.

Emergency laws dealt with in this message fall into five broad classes: (a) Temporary statutes which are no longer needed, and which consequently should be repealed forthwith; (b) Permanent statutes under which operations related to the 1939 or 1941 emergencies have been or are being discontinued, but which should remain for possible use during future emergencies; (c) Statutes appropriating funds, which should,

when the funds are no longer required, be handled by rescission of funds rather than by repeal of the statutes; (d) Statutes which should be temporarily extended by the Congress pending consideration of permanent legislation or other dispositions as indicated below; (e) Statutes which should continue in force for the period or purpose stipulated.

In appendices to this message the statutes under reference are enumerated according to the above classifications.

A. Temporary Statutes Which Should Be Repealed

I recommend the outright repeal of the 24 statutes or portions thereof specified in Appendix A. To a greater or lesser degree, all these statutes were designed to meet special problems of the war which no longer face us. It should be noted, however, that repeal of one of these laws will restore customs duties over certain commodities. In repealing it, the Congress should provide for the customary thirty days' notice before duty changes become effective.

B. Permanent Statutes Effective Only During An Emergency

The 36 laws enumerated in Appendix B are permanent legislation but come into force only during emergencies. Many of them were enacted during or before the first World War. Nothing requires their removal from our body of permanent law at this time, and it is preferable that operations conducted under them by virtue of the 1939 and 1941 emergencies should lapse rather than that the statutes should be repealed.

I have requested the head of each executive department and agency to discontinue at the earliest possible moment and in any event not later than March 15, 1947, the exercise of such powers as are derived, from these statutes, by virtue of the existence of the emergencies of 1939 and 1941.

C. Statutes Appropriating Funds

When appropriated funds are no longer required, it is the established procedure of the Congress to rescind these funds rather than to repeal the appropriation acts. On six occasions since the surrender of Japan I have recommended that the Congress rescind certain appropriated funds, and I shall continue to make recommendations for rescission of funds whenever possible.

Dependent upon the emergencies of 1939 and 1941 are 20 appropriation provisions listed in Appendix C. Expenditures under two of these acts have already ceased. Expenditures under twelve others will be terminated as rapidly as possible, and appropriate recommendations for rescission will be made.

In the case of four acts making appropriations for roads under the Defense Highway Act of 1941, after the end of the emergency these funds will continue to be needed by the Federal Works Agency for maintenance of access road projects until June 30, 1947, completion of access road projects now under construction, strategic network projects, and necessary advance engineering. I shall shortly transmit a budgetary communication in the usual form for this purpose.

In the case of the appropriation acts by which funds were provided for clerical assistance to Senators and for the Capitol police force, this is, of course, a matter which exclusively concerns the Congress.

D. Statutes Which Should Be Temporarily Extended

In the case of most of the 12 statutes listed in Appendix D, the Congress may wish to consider permanent legislation. In order to preserve existing activities and conditions until the Congress has had an opportunity to consider such legislation, I recommend the temporary extension of these statutes until June 30, 1948. In a few cases, termination on an indicated date appears desirable even though permanent legislation

is not contemplated. The reasons for temporary extension in each case, the period of extension requested, and the executive departments and agencies interested are set forth in Appendix D.

E. Statutes Remaining in Force for the Period or Purpose Stipulated

Of the remaining 10 statutes affected by the existence of the emergencies, five will continue in force for a stipulated period after the emergencies have been declared at an end, and two have no termination provisions. The remaining statutes consist of one mandatory law under which operations cannot be discontinued during the emergencies (Act of July 2, 1940); and another two laws which are needed until the end of the emergencies (Act of June 29, 1936, and Act of March 8, 1946). The five statutes with terminal provisions beyond the emergencies should be allowed to remain in force for the periods stipulated by their terms; the two statutes without termination provisions should continue for the limited purposes provided; and the remaining statutes should be permitted to lapse according to their terms.

These statutes are enumerated in Appendix E, which states the purpose for which each of these laws will be needed and lists the executive departments or agencies concerned.

HARRY S. TRUMAN

APPENDIX A—STATUTES WHICH SHOULD BE REPEALED

Act of June 11, 1940, title II (54 Stat. 265, 293). Authorizes the Secretary of the Navy to exceed the statutory limit, under the Bureau of Engineering and the Bureau of Construction and Repair (consolidated into the Bureau of Ships by Act of June 20, 1940 (54 Stat. 492)), on repair and alterations to vessels commissioned or converted "to meet the existing emergency."

Act of June 26, 1940 (54 Stat. 599). Authorizes employment of Dollar-A-Year men "until such time as the President shall declare the present emergency at an end."

Act of April 1, 1941 (55 Stat. 62, 71). Permits foreign service officers unable to serve abroad to serve in other posts "during the period of the existing state of emergency proclaimed by the President on September 8, 1939."

Act of July 11, 1941, sec. 3 (55 Stat. 585; 50 U.S.C. Supp. V, App. 1181). Authorizes the Secretary of the Treasury "during the national emergency declared by the President on September 8, 1939, to exist," to negotiate construction and repair contracts for the Coast Guard subject to the provisions of section 2 of the act of June 28, 1940, and to waive the provisions of the act of August 24, 1945 (49 Stat. 793), relating to performance and payments bonds.

Act of November 19, 1941, sec. 6, in part, as amended (55 Stat. 766) authorization to appropriate certain funds for the access road program "during the continuance of the emergency declared by the President on May 27, 1941."

Act of December 23, 1941 (55 Stat. 855, 856). Authorizes the Secretary of Agriculture to procure, transport, and distribute agricultural and other commodities and supplies to meet the emergency requirements of the territories and possessions of the U.S., appropriation for which "shall remain available for expenditure . . . until six months . . . after termination of the unlimited national emergency declared . . . on May 27, 1941."

Act of January 2, 1942 (55 Stat. 881). Permits the employment of U.S. nationals on public works in Hawaii "during the national emergency declared by the President on May 27, 1941."

Act of January 24, 1942 (56 Stat. 17). Permits the withdrawal of alcohol for industrial purposes without tax during "the unlimited national emergency proclaimed May 27, 1941."

Act of February 7, 1942, title III, sec. 301 (56 Stat. 53, 82; 22 U.S.C., Supp. IV, 412, note). Authorizes, within a total monetary limitation, the disposition under the Lend-Lease Act (22 U.S.C. Supp. IV, 411, et seq.) of ships appropriated for in whole or in part under the heading "Increase and Replacement of Naval Vessels, Emergency Construction," for a period not exceeding "the duration of the existing national emergency."

Act of February 7, 1942 (56 Stat. 63) providing that "no officer of the Navy or Marine Corps who has been, or heretofore may be, adjudged fitted shall be involuntarily retired prior to six months subsequent to the termination of the existing national emergency."

Act of February 21, 1942, title I (56 Stat. 98, 101; 39 U.S.C. 321b, note). Suspends the requirement, so far as the Selective Service System is concerned, to submit to the Postmaster General quarterly reports of mail transmitted under the penalty mail privilege during the period of the emergency declared by the President on May 27, 1941.

Act of March 27, 1942 (56 Stat. 187). Permits removal and transfer of alcohol for redistillation without tax during the unlimited national emergency proclaimed May 27, 1941.

Act of June 5, 1942 (56 Stat. 323), sec. 4. Permits the lease or sale of public lands by the Secretary of the Interior for the manufacture of munitions. "This Act shall cease to be operative six months after the termination of the unlimited emergency proclaimed by the President in the proclamation of May 27, 1941."

Act of July 8, 1942 secs. 1 and 4 (56 Stat. 649; 10 U.S.C. Supp. V 299a, 299d). Creating for the AAF the title of "Flight Officer," authorizing flight officers to be appointed, and upon appointment, to be commissioned in the Army of the U.S. under the provisions of the Act of September 22, 1941. (The Act of September 22, 1941 (55 Stat. 728), as amended by the Act of July 7, 1943, sec. 1 (57 Stat. 380; 10 U.S.C. Supp. IV, 484, note) authorizes temporary appointments of certain persons to be made as officers in the Army of the U.S. "during the present emergency", and further provides that any appointment may be vacated at any time by the President and, if not sooner vacated, "shall continue during the present emergency and six months thereafter.")

Act of September 29, 1942 (56 Stat. 760). Makes transportation and storage facilities available for military use by authorizing the removal of merchandise in customs' custody, "until the expiration of 6 months after the termination of the unlimited national emergency proclaimed by the President on May 27, 1941."

Act of December 17, 1942 (56 Stat. 1052). Amends the annual leave act of March 14, 1936 (49 Stat. 1161), to permit the accumulation of 90 days' annual leave for Government employees during the national emergency declared by the President of the United States on September 8, 1939.

Act of December 24, 1942 (56 Stat. 1080). Permits any holder of oil or gas leases on the public domain who discovers a new oil or gas field to have his royalty computed at a flat rate of 12½ percent during the period of the national emergency proclaimed by the President on May 27, 1941.

Act of June 22, 1943 (57 Stat. 161), amending sec. 353(b) of the Communications Act of 1934, amended to suspend the requirement of 6 months prior service for radio officers on certain cargo ships "during the emergency proclaimed September 8, 1939."

Act of July 9, 1943 (57 Stat. 390). Relieves newspapers or other periodicals that suspended publication because of war conditions from payment of second-class application fees upon resumption of publication, if regular publication is resumed "prior to the end of the 6th month following the expiration of the unlimited national emergency proclaimed by the President on May 27, 1941."

Act of July 12, 1943 (57 Stat. 520). Permits the use of butter substitute at St. Elizabeths Hospital "during the present national emergency." (This has now been otherwise provided for.)

Naval Appropriation Act of 1945, June 22, 1944 (58 Stat. 301, 308; 34 U.S.C. Supp. IV, 1042 note). Authority to appoint qualified enlisted men of the Navy, Naval Reserve, and Marine Corps to the Naval Academy after 9 months of service "during the present emergency."

Act of September 21, 1944, title II, sec. 207 (58 Stat. 734, 736). Amends section 2 of the Clarke-McNary Act of June 7, 1924 (16 U.S.C. 565). Provides that for each fiscal year "during the existing emergency" the Secretary of Agriculture may authorize expenditures not to exceed $1,000,000 from certain prior appropriations, for protection against forest fires, without requiring an equal expenditure by the State and private owners.

Act of December 20, 1944 (58 Stat. 817, 19 U.S.C., Supp. IV, 1001, par. 758, note) suspending duty on coconuts for unlimited national emergency of May 27, 1941.

Act of May 29, 1945 (59 Stat. 208, Public Law 62, 79th Cong. 1st sess.). Provides in appropriation to the Navy Department, Bureau of Supplies and Accounts, that "during the present emergency" qualified enlisted men of the Navy, Naval Reserve, and Marine Corps may be appointed to the Naval Academy after 9 months of service.

APPENDIX B—PERMANENT STATUTES EFFECTIVE ONLY DURING AN EMERGENCY

Act of July 5, 1884 (23 Stat. 109), as amended. Authorizes certain discretion in the purchase of supplies for the Army "in cases of emergency."

Act of July 5, 1884 (23 Stat. 110), as amended. Waives the requirement of advertising for the purchase of means of transportation by the Quartermaster Corps "in cases of extreme emergency."

Act of August 1, 1892, sec. 1 (27 Stat. 340), as amended. Prohibits employment of laborers and mechanics by the United States or the District of Columbia in connection with dredging or rock excavation in any river or harbor of the United States or the District of Columbia for more than 8 hours a day "except in case of extraordinary emergency."

Act of April 11, 1898 (30 Stat. 737). Exempts lands acquired "in case of emergency" for the erection of an urgently needed temporary fort or fortification from formalities and procedures which, under other Acts, would delay payment therefor.

Act of February 2, 1901, sec. 18 (31 Stat. 752). Authorizes the Surgeon General of the Army with the approval of the Secretary of War to appoint as many contract surgeons as may be necessary "in emergencies."

Act of March 2, 1901 (31 Stat. 905). Authorizes purchase of supplies of the Army without advertising "in cases of emergency."

Act of March 17, 1916 (39 Stat. 36). Organizations of the Army below the maximum enlisted strength authorized by law may be raised to that strength "when in the judgment of the President an emergency arises which makes it necessary."

Act of June 3, 1916, as amended, sec. 35 (41 Stat. 780; 10 U.S.C. 426). No member of the Enlisted Reserve Corps shall be ordered to active duty in excess of the number permissible under appropriations made for this specific purpose, nor for a longer period than 15 days in any one calendar year, without his own consent, "except in time of a national emergency expressly declared by Congress."

Act of June 3, 1916, sec. 38, as amended by the act of June 19, 1935, sec. 1 (49 Stat. 391). "Except in time of a national emergency expressly declared by Congress," no officer of the National Guard of the United States shall be employed on active duty for more than 15 days in any calendar year without his own consent.

Act of June 3, 1916, sec. 37a, as amended by the act of June 4, 1920, sec. 32 (41 Stat. 776). Employment of reserve officers on active duty is restricted to 15 days a year without such officers' consent, "except in time of a national emergency expressly declared by Congress."

Act of June 3, 1916, sec. 69 (39 Stat. 200), as amended. "In the event of an emergency declared by Congress" the period of enlistment in the National Guard which otherwise would expire may be extended by Presidential proclamation for a period of six months after the termination of the emergency.

Act of August 29, 1916 (39 Stat. 602). Authorizes the President "whenever in his judgment a sufficient national emergency shall exist" to transfer to the Navy Department or the War Department vessels, equipment, and personnel of the Coast Guard.

Act of March 4, 1917 (39 Stat. 1192). Authorizes the President to suspend the provisions of law prohibiting more than 8 hours' labor in any one day of persons engaged in work covered by contracts with the United States "in case of national emergency."

Act of May 22, 1917, sec. 16 (40 Stat. 87). Relates to transfer of personnel, equipment, etc., of Coast and Geodetic Survey to jurisdiction of the War or Navy Departments "in time of national emergency."

Act of June 15, 1917, title II, sec. 1 (40 Stat. 220). Authorizes the Secretary of the Treasury (or the Secretary of the Navy when the Coast Guard operates as a part of the Navy) to assume control over foreign or domestic vessels in United States ports "whenever the President by proclamation or Executive Order declares a national emergency to exist by reason of actual or threatened war, insurrection or invasion, or disturbance or threatened disturbance of the international relations of the United States."

Act of July 1, 1918 (40 Stat. 714), as amended. Authorizes the President to increase to a stated figure the authorized enlisted strength of the active list of the Regular Navy "whenever in his judgment a sufficient emergency exists."

Act of May 24, 1924 (43 Stat. 146), sec. 19, renumbered sec. 27 and amended. Authorizes the President to recall any retired foreign-service officer temporarily to active service "in the event of public emergency."

Act of March 3, 1925 (43 Stat. 1110). Authority to close Fort McHenry Military Reservation in Maryland, "in case of a national emergency," and use it for military purposes during the period of such emergency and as long thereafter as necessary.

Act of April 12, 1926 (44 Stat. 241). Authorizes the Secretary of War to lease to the city of Tucson, Ariz., certain lands for a municipal aviation field. The Government of the United States may assume absolute control of the management and operation of the field for military purposes "in case of emergency," or in event it shall be deemed advisable.

Act of May 29, 1926 (44 Stat. 677). Authorizes an exchange of certain lands and the establishment of an aviation field near Yuma, Ariz. The War Department may assume absolute control of the management and operation of the field "in case of emergency" or in the event that it shall be deemed advisable by the Secretary of War.

Act of May 14, 1930, sec. 10 (46 Stat. 329, 332). Authorizes the Secretary of the Navy to lease the floating drydock and waterfront accessories at the naval station, New Orleans (Algiers), for periods "not exceeding ten years," any lease to be revocable at his discretion "in case of national emergency declared by the President."

Act of May 29, 1930 (46 Stat. 479). Authorizes the Secretary of the Navy to lease the naval destroyer and submarine base at Squantum, Mass., for periods not exceeding 25 years, any lease to be revocable at the discretion of the Secretary of the Navy "in case of national emergency declared by the President."

Act of March 3, 1931, as amended by the Act of August 30, 1935, sec. 6 (49 Stat. 1011, 1013). Authorizes the President to suspend certain provisions of the Act of March 3, 1931, as amended, relating to the rate of wages for laborers and mechanics under public contracts "in the event of a national emergency."

Act of February 28, 1933, sec. 4 (47 Stat. 1367, 1368). Possession of certain property authorized to be conveyed to the county of Arlington, Va., for highway purposes may be resumed "whenever in the judgment of the President an emergency exists that requires the use and appropriation of the same for the public defense."

Act of March 9, 1933, sec. 4 (48 Stat. 2). Forbids the Federal Reserve banks to transact business except under regulations prescribed by the Secretary of the Treasury with the approval of the President, "during such emergency period as the President . . . by proclamation may prescribe."

Act of June 15, 1933, sec. 7 (48 Stat. 156). An extension by the President of enlistment terms of the National Guard 6 months "in the event of an emergency declared by Congress."

Act of May 15, 1936 (49 Stat. 1278, 1292). Authorizes and directs the Secretary of War to convey to the city of Little Rock, Ark., certain lands for public purposes. Provides that "in time of national emergency," upon request of the Secretary of War the municipality shall turn over to the United States complete control and operation of the property without rental or other charge, for use for such length of time "as the emergency shall require," in the discretion of the Secretary of War.

Act of May 27, 1936 (49 Stat. 1387). Authorizes the Secretary of Commerce to convey the Charleston Army Base Terminal to the city of Charleston, S.C. Any deed is to contain a condition that "in the event of a national emergency" the property may be taken upon order of the President by the United States for the use of the War Department "during the period of such emergency."

Act of June 19, 1936 (49 Stat. 1535). Authorizes the Secretary of War to transfer certain lands to the Territory of Hawaii, the conveyance to contain a condition and a reservation reserving the right to resume and occupy the land whenever in the judgment of the President "an emergency exists that requires the use and appropriation of the same for public defense."

Act of June 29, 1936, Merchant Marine Act, 1936, sec. 712(d) (49 Stat. 2010), as amended. Termination of charters. Power exercisable "whenever the President shall proclaim that the security of the national defense makes it advisable, or during any national emergency declared by proclamation of the President."

Act of February 16, 1938, title III, sec. 371, as amended (52 Stat. 64). Authorizes the Secretary of Agriculture to cause an immediate investigation when he has reason to believe the marketing quota for corn, wheat, cotton, rice, tobacco, or peanuts should be increased or terminated "because of a national emergency" or because of a material increase in export demand.

Act of June 21, 1938, sec. 3 (52 Stat. 833, 834). Authorizes the Maritime Commission to sell or lease the Hoboken pier terminal to the city of Hoboken, N.J. In the event of any sale, the deed is to contain a covenant that the property may be taken upon order of the President "in event of a national emergency" for use of the War Department "during the period of such emergency."

Act of August 7, 1939 (53 Stat. 1254). Permits the requisition of United States owned vessels, "whenever the President shall proclaim that the security of the U.S. makes it advisable or during any national emergency declared by proclamation of the President."

Act of June 14, 1940, sec. 10 (54 Stat. 394, 395). Makes applicable to naval public utilities projects in the 14th Naval District (Pearl Harbor, Hawaii) provisions of the Act of April 25, 1939 (53 Stat. 590, 592). Authorizes contracts upon a cost-plus-a-fixed-fee basis in certain cases, "during the period of any national emergency declared by the President to exist."

Act of July 2, 1940 (54 Stat. 724). Authorizes the President "in the event of declared national emergency," to set aside the requirement that the natural features of Barro Colorado Island are to be left in their natural state for scientific observation and investigation.

Act of December 16, 1941 (55 Stat. 807). Authorizes the Secretary of the Treasury (or the Secretary of the Navy "in the event the Coast Guard should operate as a part of the Navy") to purchase (without regard to 41 U.S.C. 5) or accept gifts of motorboats, yachts, and similar vessels for Coast Guard use, "during any period of national emergency."

APPENDIX C—STATUTES APPROPRIATING FUNDS

(a) *Statutes under which expenditures have ceased.*

Act of December 23, 1941 (55 Stat. 855–856). Authorizes the appropriation to the Department of Agriculture, Surplus Marketing Administration, and proceeds from certain sales and other receipts from operations, to be deposited to the credit of the appropriation made in this statute, such appropriation including such deposits to remain available for expenditure for the purposes authorized "until six months have elapsed after the termination of the unlimited national emergency declared by the President on May 27, 1941."

Act of July 3, 1945 (59 Stat. 318, 319). Appropriation made to the Department of the Interior Division of Geography ($25,000), to be available "during the emergency declared by the President on May 27, 1941, and for a period not exceeding 30 days thereafter."

(b) *Statutes under which expenditures will cease as rapidly as possible.*

Act of October 14, 1940 Lanham Act (54 Stat. 1125). Appropriations available under this act to the Federal Works Administrator for war housing and not rescinded by the First Supplemental Appropriations Rescission Bill 1946, by its terms remains available until the termination of the emergency declared by the President on September 8, 1939.

Act of December 23, 1941 (55 Stat. 855–856). Appropriations to the Federal Works Agency for national defense housing ($300,000,000) and for defense public works (community facilities) ($150,000,000), to remain available "during the continuance of the unlimited national emergency declared by the President on May 27, 1941." Appropriations in the same statute to the Department of the Interior (Government in the Territories) for relief and civilian defense in Alaska, Virgin Islands, and Puerto Rico, to remain available "for the duration of the unlimited national emergency declared by the President on May 27, 1941."

Act of April 28, 1942 (56 Stat. 226, 235–236). Appropriation made to the Federal Works Agency for emergency safeguarding of public buildings and property ($12,500,000) and additional contract authorization to the Public Roads Administration for the construction and improvement of access roads and for replacing existing highways and highway connections ($25,400,000), the first to remain available, and the second to continue, "during the existence of the emergency declared by the President on May 27, 1941."

Act of July 2, 1942 (56 Stat. 633, 634). Appropriation made to the Federal Works Agency for war public works ($17,500,000) to remain available "during the continuance of the unlimited national emergency declared by the President on May 27, 1941."

Act of October 26, 1942 (56 Stat. 990, 1000). Appropriation made to the National Housing Agency for war housing ($600,000,000) to remain available "during the continuance of the unlimited national emergency declared by the President on May 27, 1941."

Act of July 12, 1943 (57 Stat. 537, 540, 541). Appropriations made to the Federal Works Agency for war public works, community facilities ($50,000,000) and to the National Housing Agency for war housing ($100,000,000), to remain available "during the continuance of the unlimited national emergency declared by the President on May 27, 1941."

Act of December 23, 1943 (57 Stat. 611, 618). Appropriation made to the National Housing Agency for war housing ($50,-000,000), to remain available "during the continuance of the unlimited national emergency declared by the President on May 27, 1941."

Act of April 1, 1944 (58 Stat. 150, 153). Appropriation made to the Federal Works Agency for war public works, community facilities ($115,000,000), and appropriation to the National Housing Agency for war housing ($7,500,000), to remain available "during the continuance of the unlimited national emergency declared by the President on May 27, 1941, and shall not be available for obligation for new projects after June 30, 1945."

Act of June 22, 1944, sec. 114 (58 Stat. 301, 321). Appropriations for the Naval Establishment, fiscal year 1945, for payment of claims up to $1,000, resulting from the administration or operation of the naval service "during the existing national emergency."

Act of June 28, 1944 (304, 58 Stat. 597, 604). Supplemental appropriation made to the National Housing Agency for temporary war housing, of not to exceed $7,500,000 of unexpended balances of certain previous appropriations, to remain available "during the continuance of the unlimited national emergency declared by the President on May 27, 1941, and shall not be available for obligation for new projects after June 30, 1945."

Act of December 22, 1944 (58 Stat. 853, 857–859). Appropriation made to the National Housing Agency ($15,000,000) for purposes of title I of the Lanham Act, as amended, and to Federal Works Agency ($12,000,000) for community facilities "during the continuance of the unlimited national emergency declared by the President May 27, 1941, but not to be available for new projects after June 30, 1945."

Act of April 25, 1945 (59 Stat. 77, 80, 81, 82). Appropriation made to the Federal Works Agency for war public works, community facilities ($20,000,000) and appropriation to the National Housing Agency for war housing ($84,373,000), to remain available "during the continuance of the unlimited national emergency declared by the President on May 27, 1941, but not to be

available for obligation for new projects after June 30, 1945."

(c) *Statutes under which the appropriations should remain available by legislation.*

Act of December 17, 1941 (55 Stat. 810, 821). Appropriation made to the Federal Works Agency, Public Roads Administration, for certain road and flightstrip construction under secs. 6 and 8 of Defense Highway Act of 1941, and authorization given to obligate further funds for such road construction, to remain available "during the continuance of the emergency declared by the President on May 27, 1941."

Act of June 26, 1943 (57 Stat. 169, 180). Appropriations totaling $88,000,000 made to the Federal Works Agency for various purposes specified under provisions of the Defense Highway Act of 1941, to remain available "during the continuance of the emergency declared by the President on May 27, 1941."

Act of June 27, 1944 (58 Stat. 361, 371). Appropriations totaling $54,000,000 made to the Federal Works Agency for various purposes specified under provisions of the Defense Highway Act of 1941, to remain available "during the continuance of the emergency declared by the President on May 27, 1941."

Act of May 3, 1945 (59 Stat. 106, 117–118). Appropriations totaling $48,000,000 made to the Federal Works Agency for various purposes specified under provisions of the Defense Highway Act of 1941, to remain available "during the continuance of the emergency declared by the President on May 27, 1941."

(d) *Statutes exclusively of concern to the Congress.*

Act of June 13, 1945 (59 Stat. 238, 241, 250). Legislative Branch Appropriation Act, 1946. Under the title "Clerical Assistance to Senators," provides for certain additional clerks for Senators, to be employed only "during the period of the emergency." Under the title "Capitol Police," an appropriation for additional protection applies "during the present emergency."

Act of July 1, 1946 (Public Law 479, 79th Cong., 2nd Sess.). Legislative Branch Appropriation Act, 1947. Appropriations for additional police protection for the Capitol Buildings and Grounds, etc., during the present emergency.

Statute; comment and interested agency; and proposed effective period.

Act of June 20, 1940 (54 Stat. 492, 494), authorizing the appointment of an Under Secretary of the Navy "during any national emergency."

This law should be retained pending permanent legislation—Navy Department.

June 30, 1948.

Lanham Act, October 14, 1940 (54 Stat. 1125), as amended, January 21, 1942 (56 Stat. 11), war housing, including authority for temporary re-use housing, to maintain and repair buildings; and to adjust rents in exceptional cases. "When the President shall have declared that the emergency declared by him on September 8, 1939 to exist has ceased, (a) the authority [for war housing] shall terminate except with respect to contracts previously entered into . . . and (b) the removal of property acquired or constructed . . . shall in any event be accomplished not later than two years after the President declares that the emergency declared by him on September 8, 1939, has ceased to exist, with the exception only of such housing as the Administrator, after consultation with local communities finds is still needed in the interest of the orderly demobilization of the war effort."

Retention of this Act is needed to permit operations authorized on temporary re-use housing for veterans, servicemen, and their distressed families. The portions of the Act containing the general authority to provide housing for war workers may and will become inoperative as to war housing upon the end of the emergency, but the statute must be kept in effect for the purposes of re-use housing program.—National Housing Administration.

When the President shall have declared that the emergency declared by him on September 8, 1939, has ceased to exist, the authority for the war housing program shall terminate except to the extent that the powers granted are necessary to carry on the temporary re-use housing program for service men, veterans, and their families; provided, however, that the Administrator may continue, with funds derived from the rental or operation of projects acquired or constructed under this Act or under the temporary shelter acts, any interest heretofore acquired in lands pursuant to the Act, and may acquire any further interest in such lands whenever the Administrator determines that such aquisition is necessary to protect the Government's investment, or to maintain the improvements constructed thereon or that the obligation of the Government to restore the property to its original condition would exceed the cost of acquiring the title thereto.

Act of July 29, 1941 (55 Stat. 606), relating to the retirement or discharge of certain Army officers "during the time of the national emergency announced by the President on May 27, 1941."

This law should be continued pending permanent legislation.—War Department.

June 30, 1948.

Act of September 22, 1941 (55 Stat. 728), as amended by the Act of July 7, 1943 (57 Stat. 380), authorizes temporary appointments of officers in the U.S. Army without regard to any particular component of the Army "during the present emergency . . . (the appointments) shall continue during the present emergency and six months thereafter."

This law should be continued pending legislation on peacetime Army organization.—War Department.

June 30, 1948.

Act of November 17, 1941 (55 Stat. 764–765), permitting arming of American merchant vessels "during the unlimited national emergency proclaimed by the President on May 27, 1941."

This law should be continued pending action on permanent legislation.—Navy Department.

June 30, 1948.

Act of March 13, 1942 (56 Stat. 171), suspending import duties on scrap iron, scrap steel, relaying and rerolling rails, or nonferrous metal scrap during the unlimited emergency proclaimed by the President on May 27, 1941.

This law should be continued in view of the present shortage of the materials involved.—Civilian Production Administration.

June 30, 1948.

Act of June 27, 1942 (56 Stat. 461–462), permits the free importation of articles for members of the armed forces of the United Nations in the United States; of articles made by members of United States armed forces who were prisoners of war; and of articles addressed to enemy prisoners of war and enemy civilian internees in the U.S. (in accordance with the Geneva Convention). "Shall be effective as to articles entered for consumption or withdrawn from warehouse for consumption . . . before the expiration of 6 months after the termination of the unlimited national emergency, proclaimed by the President on May 27, 1941."

This act should be retained as part of a reciprocal arrangement, pending permanent legislation, to assist members of U.N. forces still in this country; to provide for United States personnel who were formerly prisoners and are still abroad; and to provide for the few remaining enemy prisoners in the United States.—War and Navy Departments.

June 30, 1948.

Act of October 26, 1942 (56 Stat. 990, 1000), permitting designation of PBA employees as special policemen "during continuance of the unlimited national emergency declared by the President on May 27, 1941."

This law should be retained for the protection of present Federal properties pending permanent legislation.—Federal Works Agency.

June 30, 1948.

Act of October 26, 1942 (56 Stat. 990, 1006), amending the Act of September 9, 1940 (54 Stat. 884), suspends the requirement that the head of each department and agency submit quarterly reports on the weight of mail sent free of postage "during the period of the national emergency declared by the President on September 8, 1939."

This law should be extended for the War and Navy Departments until June 30, 1947, at which time these departments wish simultaneously to begin making this report and another required by the Act of June 28, 1944 (58 Stat. 394), on mail sent free of postage. The requirement of the latter report, as to the Army and Navy only, is suspended for the duration of the war and 6 months, but it is proposed to begin both series of reports as of the intermediate date given above.—Navy and War Departments.

Until June 30, 1947.

Act of June 23, 1943 (57 Stat. 162), as amended August 8, 1946 (Public Law 660, 79th Cong.), establishing re-employment rights for persons entering the Merchant Marine after May 1, 1940, and before the termination of the unlimited "national emergency declared by the President on May 27, 1941."

This law should be continued during the shortage of maritime personnel and so long as men are being inducted under the Selective Service law and obtaining similar rights.—Selective Service.

The Act should be extended to protect any person entering the service before termination of the present war but not later than March 31, 1947 [present end of draft inductions], or such later date as persons may be inducted under the provisions of the Selective Service Act of 1940, as amended.

Act of July 1, 1943 (57 Stat. 371), providing for appointment of commissioned officers of the WAC, the appointments to continue during the present emergency and 6 months thereafter under the Joint Resolution of September 2, 1941 (55 Stat., 728), "during the present emergency . . . provided that any appointment . . . shall continue during the present emergency and 6 months thereafter."

This law is needed to maintain existing Army staff pending legislation on organization of the peacetime Army.—War Department.

June 30, 1948.

Act of May 22, 1944 (58 Stat. 324–326), authorizing temporary appointments of members of the Army Nurse Corps, female dietetic and physical therapy personnel as officers in the U.S. Army, "during the present emergency . . . provided that any appointment . . . shall continue during the present emergency and 6 months thereafter."

This law is needed, pending permanent legislation, to maintain the present Army staff.—War Department.

June 30, 1948.

APPENDIX E—STATUTES WHICH SHOULD BE CONTINUED FOR THE PERIOD OR PURPOSE STIPULATED

Statutes and reason for continuation and interested agency.

Act of June 3, 1916, National Defense Act, sec. 30 (10 U.S.C. 658), as amended by the Act of April 25, 1938 (52 Stat. 221). Members of the Regular Army Reserve may be ordered to active duty only in case of emergency declared by the President, and shall be placed in an inactive status or be discharged "within six months after the termination of an emergency declared by the President."

The Army will require the services of officers under this law for an indefinite period pending the establishment of its peacetime organization.—War Department.

Act of June 29, 1936, sec. 302 (49 Stat. 1992). Authorizes the President to suspend provisions dealing with citizenship of officers and crews of certain vessels "during a national emergency."

Operations under this law are being continued in view of the present shortage of personnel.—Coast Guard.

Act of July 2, 1940, sec. 4(b) (54 Stat. 714). Provides that the regular hours of laborers and mechanics employed by the War Department in the manufacture or production of military equipment shall be 8 hours per day or 40 hours per week, during the period of any national emergency declared by the President to exist.

This law is mandatory in its effect and operation cannot be discontinued before termination of the national emergency.— War Department.

Act of July 30, 1941, sec. 9 (55 Stat. 610), as amended by act of June 30, 1943 (57 Stat. 270), and act of June 8, 1945 (Public Law 78, 79th Cong.). Authority to construct; and right to use petroleum pipelines, the latter to terminate upon "The expiration of one year after the termination of the unlimited national emergency proclaimed . . . on May 27, 1941."

Pending final disposition of pipelines now held as war assets, this law is required to authorize arrangements for their use.—War Assets.

Act of November 19, 1941, sec. 5 (55 Stat. 766) as amended by act of July 13, 1943 (57 Stat. 560). Provides that certain Federal funds shall remain available for obligation by the States on secondary or feeder roads and for the elimination of grade crossings on Federal aid highways during the continuance of the emergency declared by the President on May 27, 1941, and for a period of one year thereafter.

This law should continue in effect according to its terms pending the completion of programs now being carried on by the States.—Federal Works Agency.

Act of July 14, 1945 (Public Law 147, 79th Cong.). Extends the times for commencing and completing construction of a bridge across the St. Croix River to be built by the States of Minnesota and Wisconsin, jointly or separately, "until the end of one and three years, respectively, after the date of the termination of the unlimited national emergency proclaimed by the President on May 27, 1941."

The continued extension of the period for this construction is regarded as highly desirable.—Federal Works Agency.

Act of February 28, 1945 (59 Stat. 9), amending Agriculture Adjustment Act of 1938 and Soil Conservation and Domestic Allotment Act to provide that the Secretary of Agriculture may regard certain farms as farms producing cotton, wheat, or peanuts for any crop year during the present emergency because the production of war crops or service by the owner or operator in the armed forces caused the production history of the farm to be non-representative of its normal production.

This law is needed to give continued authority in the specified cases for determining production history.—Department of Agriculture.

Act of March 8, 1946 (Public Law 321, 79th Cong.), sec. 9(c)(3). Requires agreement by purchaser of vessel of Maritime

Commission that if vessel is used by United States prior to termination of national emergency declared by the President on May 27, 1941, the compensation for use shall be limited to 15 percent per annum of statutory sale price.

This statute provides the measure of compensation in the cases specified.—Maritime Commission.

Act of May 18, 1946 (Public Law 385, 79th Cong.), sec. 2. Establishes time limit of two years after the end of the limited emergency for removal of temporary housing erected on lands owned by the United States or the District of Columbia in the District of Columbia.

In order to provide for the orderly termination of the authorized program this law should expire according to its terms.—National Housing Agency.

Act of August 10, 1946 (Public Law 720, 79th Cong.), sec. 3. Provides that active duty performed by certain enlisted men of the Fleet Reserve "during any period of national emergency declared by the President" shall be considered for purposes of computing retainer or retired pay.

This act authorizes the crediting of certain active duty during any national emergency for retainer or retirement pay purposes.—Navy Department.

NOTE: On July 25 the President approved a joint resolution (61 Stat. 449) terminating certain emergency and war powers.

36 The President's News Conference of *February* 20, 1947

THE PRESIDENT. Good morning. How are you all?

Q. How are you?

Q. Quite a snowfall.

THE PRESIDENT. I was just watching it. They tell me that the streets are as slick as glass.

[1.] Q. You didn't take your morning walk this morning, did you?

THE PRESIDENT. Yes I did! I walked before the snow started. No, I didn't miss it.

Q. You must have been early.

THE PRESIDENT. Well, I always leave the White House between half past 6 and a quarter to 7. It snowed about 10 minutes after 7. Sure did. I hardly ever miss.

Q. What?

THE PRESIDENT. I hardly ever miss, unless it's pouring down rain.

I have no particular announcements to make. If you have any questions, I will try to answer them.

[2.] Q. Mr. President, when you visit Puerto Rico, do you plan to discuss any political questions with the leadership there?

THE PRESIDENT. I do not.

Q. Do not?

THE PRESIDENT. Just paying an official visit to Puerto Rico to see how they are getting along in their native government.

[3.] Q. Mr. President, Mr. Lippmann seems to feel that the reason poison gas was not used in the last war was because everybody had it, and that the same thing would apply to the atomic bomb.

THE PRESIDENT. Mr. Lippmann is entitled to his opinion the same as anybody else. I have no comment to make on it.

[4.] Q. Mr. President, when will you send up your message on the universal training and selective service?

THE PRESIDENT. It will be some time yet before it will be ready. I have that special committee, as you know, getting all the facts together, and as soon as that special committee makes the report, then I shall send up the message.

Q. Mr. President, then you plan no message on the draft?

THE PRESIDENT. That is under consideration, and will—at a later date I will make an announcement on it.

[5.] Q. Mr. President, do you plan to send a message on export controls to the Hill in the near future?

THE PRESIDENT. I do not.

[6.] Q. Any prospects of announcements on Ambassadors to India and England?

THE PRESIDENT. As soon as I have made the decision I will make the announcements immediately.

[7.] Q. You are still for universal training?

THE PRESIDENT. Yes indeed. I have always been for it ever since 1905, and that's a long time. I demonstrated that I was for it because I immediately went into training when I was 21 years old.

[8.] Q. Mr. President, has the shortage of boxcars been brought to your attention?

THE PRESIDENT. Time and again. Time and again.

Q. What is the situation, so far as you are concerned?

THE PRESIDENT. We are working it out. We have been working on it all the time to the best of our ability.

Q. It's a very vital thing.

THE PRESIDENT. It's a vital thing. Of course it's vital. We have been working on it all the time—doing everything we can to alleviate it.

[9.] Q. Did I understand you to say that you went into training when you were 21? There was no universal——

THE PRESIDENT. National Guard.

Q. National Guard.

THE PRESIDENT. When I was 21.

[10.] Q. Mr. President, would you give us your opinion on the bill in Congress for permission to study reorganization of the executive department of the Government?

THE PRESIDENT. I always give my opinion on bills when they come to my desk for signature, and not before that time.

[11.] Q. Mr. President, Representative Landis says that unless you take some immediate action about calling a conference between mine operators and the unions, there is going to be another disastrous strike April 1. Have you any comment on that?

THE PRESIDENT. No comment.

[12.] Q. Mr. President, what will be the impact on your foreign policy in the event the economy program of the Republicans is carried out in Congress, particularly with reference to occupied countries?

THE PRESIDENT. I will comment on that when that situation develops. It has by no means developed yet.

[13.] Q. Mr. President, could you comment on this? I understand that Senator Taft thinks that tax reduction should come before debt reduction. What do you think of the principle of that, sir?

THE PRESIDENT. Well sir, I would prefer not to comment on that. Senator Taft is entitled to his opinion. I will give you my comments when those matters come to my desk. I will give them to you in no uncertain terms.

[14.] Q. Mr. President, I ask a lot of questions this morning.

THE PRESIDENT. It's all right.

Q. But have you noticed that the Treasury cash surplus has reached $1,700 million—a record figure in our history?

THE PRESIDENT. Yes. It is going to be much greater than that when we get through collecting all the taxes.

Q. Do you think we are going to be able to get the budget you pledged this year?

THE PRESIDENT. We are going to come mighty close to it. I don't want to make any comment on it until we have got all the figures in, but we will have a cash balance. But whether the budget will show a balance or not, I don't know. They are two entirely different things.

[15.] Q. Mr. President, are you considering any emergency action on rent control, in the event OPA is allowed to die?

THE PRESIDENT. I have not yet come to the conclusion that OPA is going to die.

[16.] Q. Mr. President, are you planning any changes in the Embassy in Cairo, Egypt?

THE PRESIDENT. No.

[17.] Q. Mr. President, when do you expect to send up the unification bill?

THE PRESIDENT. In a very short time. Just as soon as it is ready, I will make it public and send it up.

[18.] Q. Mr. President, if the Republicans in Congress don't pass your proposals on the finishing up of the Second War Powers, what effect do you think it will have on the condition of the country?

THE PRESIDENT. I think I stated that in the statement in the message at the time. If you will read that message I think you will find just exactly what I think about it.

[19.] Q. Is there any way the OPA can be kept alive if it doesn't get the deficiency which you have been requesting?

THE PRESIDENT. I will cross that bridge when I get to it.

[20.] Q. Mr. President, it has been reported from Tokyo that the Army Commissioner of Reparations has reached conclusions drastically different than those submitted to you by Ambassador Pauley. Has that been brought to your attention?

THE PRESIDENT. I hadn't heard about it. I don't know how they could reach any conclusions because they don't know anything about the whole picture.

Q. But he remarked on the statement——

THE PRESIDENT. I don't know anything about that. I haven't seen or heard of it.

[21.] Q. What do you hear from the Hill on Mr. Lilienthal's chances of confirmation?

THE PRESIDENT. I am still behind Mr. Lilienthal 100 percent, and I think he will be confirmed.

Q. [*Aside*] So do I.

THE PRESIDENT. I hear a comment, and so do I. [*Laughter*]

[22.] Q. Mr. President, you remarked a little while ago that ever since this summer you took long walks. Would you care to tell us this time which way you went?

THE PRESIDENT. Well, I got up early enough so that it wasn't snowing when I left. I left the White House about 20 minutes of 7 and got back about a quarter after. I went up 17th to Rhode Island, over to 15th Street and back to the White House——just about 2 miles.

Q. Thank you, sir.

[23.] Q. Mr. President, this morning someone asked you about export controls. You said that you were not going to send a message about it. That was included, I believe, that subject, in the message you sent to Congress on the subject of many controls.

THE PRESIDENT. That's right.

Q. As far as I can find out, that message has been lost in committee up there. Nobody seems to be doing anything about it on the Hill.

THE PRESIDENT. Well, of course, they are busy with other things. They don't have time to look at the emergencies closely. But they will probably get around to it. I hope they will.

[24.] Q. Mr. President, there have been some stories out of the War Department to indicate that the administration has definitely made up its mind to ask no extension of the draft.

THE PRESIDENT. That matter is under consideration. As soon as a decision has been reached, the announcement will be made on it.

[25.] Q. Mr. President, it has been reported the Navy is withdrawing from China. Is that true?

THE PRESIDENT. I haven't heard about it.

[26.] Q. Mr. President, it has been reported that you are against "lameduck" appointments. Is that true?

THE PRESIDENT. That is a matter on which I don't want to make any comment. The actions will speak for that.

Q. Are you contemplating any actions in the near future?

THE PRESIDENT. Well, not immediately. Not in the immediate future.

Q. Anything about — [*inaudible*]?

THE PRESIDENT. No. Same condition it has been all the time.

[27.] Q. Mr. President, you haven't decided on an Ambassador to London, did I hear you say?

THE PRESIDENT. No sir, I have not. I will make the announcement to you just as soon as the decision is reached.

Reporter: Thank you, Mr. President.

THE PRESIDENT. You're welcome.

NOTE: President Truman's ninety-eighth news conference was held in his office at the White House at 10:30 a.m. on Thursday, February 20, 1947.

---

37 Special Message to the Congress Requesting Appropriations for Aid to Liberated Countries. *February* 21, 1947

To the Congress of the United States of America:

I recommend that the Congress authorize the appropriation of not to exceed $350 million to assist in completing the great task of bringing relief from the ravages of the war to the people of the liberated countries.

The period of full scale supply operations by the United Nations Relief and Rehabilitation Administration is rapidly drawing to a close. In some of the liberated countries UNRRA will have achieved its objective fully, for these countries will once again be self-supporting so far as the basic essentials of life are concerned. In other liberated countries, however, this is not yet the case. Compared with what has already been done, what remains to be done is relatively small and limited in time and scope, but none-the-less vitally important.

On humanitarian grounds, and in the light of our own self-interest as well, we must not leave the task unfinished. We cannot abandon the peoples still in need. To do so would be to replace hope with despair in the hearts of these peoples and thus to undermine the spiritual and economic stability upon which our own hopes for a better world must rest. Others will help but such is the preponderance of our economic resources that success cannot be achieved without us. If we fail to do our part, millions of human beings will be denied the elemental necessities of life. Their strength and recuperative powers, which have been slowly growing, will be undermined. The time, now in sight, when they can once more exist without help and make their contributions to the peace, prosperity and progress of the world, will be indefinitely postponed.

I recommend that this relief assistance be given directly rather than through an international organization, and that our contribution be administered under United States control. International cooperation in the program and the necessary coordination of our relief activities with those of other contributors can be achieved by informal consultations with all nations concerned through the mechanism of the United Nations and otherwise. I believe that our relief contribution should be used only for providing the basic essentials of life, such as medical supplies, food and items which will aid in the production of foodstuffs.

The authorization recommended is designed for the urgent relief needs for the balance of the year. The most critical period will be in the spring and summer months, when UNRRA shipments will cease and the harvests are not yet available. Swift legislative action is necessary if our help is not to come too late.

The United States, in keeping with our traditions of immediate and whole-hearted response to human need, has stood in the forefront of those who have checked the forces of starvation, disease, suffering and chaos which threatened to engulf the world in the wake of the war. The task is nearly finished. I urge the Congress to act promptly to insure that we do not stop short of the goal; that we do not endanger the permanence of the gains we have helped to achieve.

HARRY S. TRUMAN

NOTE: On May 31, 1947, the President approved a joint resolution (61 Stat. 125) providing for relief assistance to the people of countries devastated by war.

38 Special Message to the Congress on U.S. Participation in the International Refugee Organization. *February 24, 1947*

To the Congress of the United States of America:

I recommend that the Congress authorize the United States to participate as a member of the International Refugee Organization.

As an aftermath of the war, there are more than one million displaced persons remaining in Germany, Austria and Italy. Almost two-thirds of these are under United States care and control. The Allied military victory over the Axis Powers brought with it a practical and moral responsibility with reference to these victims of the Axis.

The General Assembly of the United Nations has considered the problem of these displaced persons carefully and at great length. At the first session in London, certain basic principles were established. It was agreed that this problem is international in scope and nature; that every effort should be made to facilitate the repatriation of displaced persons who desire to return to their homelands; that displaced persons who have valid objections to return should not be forced to do so, but should be cared for by an international agency until new homes can be found for them elsewhere. Between the January and October sessions of the General Assembly, the Economic and Social Council made a detailed study of the entire problem and recommended the establishment of an International Refugee Organization which would provide an integrated and effective solution. At the meeting of the General Assembly in New York which ended in December, the draft constitution recommended by the Economic and Social Council was adopted. The United States representative to the United Nations, Senator Warren Austin, signed the constitution of the International Refugee Organization subject to subsequent approval by the Congress.

This constitution represents an earnest effort by the United Nations to solve one of the most poignant and difficult problems left in the wake of the war. The organization to be created will have no governmental powers. It can in no way alter the statutes of any of its members. It can obtain funds only by appropriations by the constitutional processes of its members. It will be solely a service organization to aid in the solution of a common problem. I am confident that with the full support of the United States, the International Refugee Organization will demonstrate the practical effectiveness of co-operation and understanding among nations. The participation of this Nation in the Organization was proposed in my Budget Message for the fiscal year 1948, and pro-vision was made for the necessary funds within the proposed budget.

With respect to those displaced persons in our own areas of occupation, the United States Army has an excellent record of per-formance in a field which is not traditionally the responsibility of soldiers. The Army from the first recognized the need for mak-ing the maximum use of international civil-ian agencies, and has done so. With the forthcoming termination of the supply of civilian personnel from other organizations now used in the care and supply of displaced persons, I believe that it is of the utmost importance that the International Refugee Organization be established as soon as pos-sible. It would indeed be serious if it were not in a position to begin operations on July 1, of this year.

It is not unreasonable that many of the other potential members of the International Refugee Organization should watch closely the attitude of the United States before making their own definite commitments. I feel sure that with the firm and prompt leadership of the United States, this orga-nization will be in a position to function as an international body to perform an es-sentially international service.

HARRY S. TRUMAN

NOTE: On July 1 the President approved a joint reso-lution (61 Stat. 214) providing for membership and participation by the United States in the Inter-national Refugee Organization.

39 Statement by the President Upon Issuing Order on the Administration of the Reciprocal Trade Agreements Program. *February 25, 1947*

I WISH to reaffirm the faith of this admin-istration in the Cordell Hull Reciprocal Trade Agreements Program which became effective in 1934 and which has been ex-tended by Congress all these years. This program is based on the principle of nego-tiation between this and other countries for the reduction of trade restrictions and elim-ination of discriminations on a mutually advantageous basis; for each concession granted by the United States, a correspond-ing concession is received. This program has become an integral part of our foreign policy, and has widespread support from in-dustry, labor, and farmers.

I am today issuing an Executive order which formalizes and makes mandatory cer-tain existing trade agreements procedures and which, in addition, makes some pro-cedural changes. I wish to make clear that the provisions of the order do not deviate from the traditional Cordell Hull principles. They simply make assurance doubly sure that American interests will be properly safeguarded.

This order is the result of conversations between Under Secretaries of State Acheson and Clayton and Senators Vandenberg and Millikin, and has been carefully considered by the interdepartmental trade agreements organization. This organization is composed of representatives of the Departments of State, War, Navy, Treasury, Agriculture, and Commerce, and the Tariff Commission.

The United States is preparing to meet with 18 other nations in Geneva on the 10th of April to negotiate on policies affecting world trade. We plan to complete the draft of a charter establishing common principles of world trade policy and setting up an international trade organization. We also shall negotiate the reduction of tariffs, the removal of other barriers to trade, and the elimination of discriminatory practices. I am very happy that Senators Vandenberg and Millikin agree that we should go forward with the Geneva negotiations.

All of us must now recognize that bipartisan support of our foreign economic policy, as well as of our foreign policy in general, is essential. If we are to succeed in our efforts, through the United Nations, to organize the world for peace, we cannot refuse our cooperation where economic questions are involved. Here, as elsewhere in our foreign relations, we must abandon partisanship and unite in our support of a foreign policy that serves the interests of the Nation as a whole.

NOTE: The text of Executive Order 9832 "Prescribing Procedures for the Administration of the Reciprocal Trade Agreements Program" (3 CFR, 1943–1948 Comp., p. 624) was released with the President's statement.

40 Message to the Congress Transmitting First Report of the Air Coordinating Committee. *February 26, 1947*

To the Congress of the United States:

I transmit to the Congress, for its information and consideration, the First Report of the Air Coordinating Committee, for the calendar year 1946.

The Committee was established by Executive Order on September 19, 1946, in order to achieve full development and integration of United States aviation policies and activities, and includes representatives of the executive agencies primarily concerned with aviation. Through its Aviation Industry Advisory Panel, the Committee draws upon

the experience and the views of the air transport and aircraft manufacturing industry, of organized labor, and of other aviation interests.

It is my hope that the Report may prove useful to the Congress in its deliberations on aviation matters, which are of such great concern to our country's welfare.

HARRY S. TRUMAN

NOTE: The report, dated January 31, 1947, and released with the President's message, is printed in House Document 148 (80th Cong., 1st sess.).

41 White House Statement in Response to Foreign Secretary Bevin's Remarks Relating to U.S. Interest in Palestine. *February 26, 1947*

THE IMPRESSION that has arisen from yesterday's debate in the British Parliament that America's interest in Palestine and the

settlement of Jews there is motivated by partisan and local politics is most unfortunate and misleading.

The President's statement of October 4, 1946, which was referred to in that debate, merely reaffirmed the attitude toward Palestine and Jewish immigration into Palestine which the United States Government has publicly expressed since the summer of 1945. This attitude was and is based upon the desire of the President to advance a just solution of the Palestine problem. Our position on this subject was communicated to the British Government by the President in his letter to Prime Minister Attlee on August 31, 1945, which was publicly released by the President on November 13,

1945, when he announced the establishment of the joint Anglo-American Committee of Inquiry. The statement of October 4, 1946, reiterated this Government's position, which was already fully known to all parties to the Palestine negotiations.

America's interest in Palestine is of long and continuing standing. It is a deep and abiding interest shared by our people without regard to their political affiliation.

NOTE: For the President's statement of October 4, 1946, see 1946 volume, this series, Item 227; for his letter of August 31, 1945, to Prime Minister Attlee, see 1945 volume, Item 188.

42 Letter to the President of the Senate and to the Speaker of the House Transmitting Draft of National Security Act. *February 26, 1947*

My dear ———:

On January 17, 1947, I informed you that representatives of my office and of the armed services were engaged in drafting a bill to be submitted to the Congress for its consideration concerning a plan of unification. This draft, entitled "National Security Act of 1947", has now been completed and I am enclosing herewith a copy of it.

This proposed bill has the approval of the Secretary of War, the Secretary of the Navy and the Joint Chiefs of Staff.

It is my belief that this suggested legislation accomplishes the desired unification of the services and I heartily recommend its enactment by the Congress.

Very sincerely yours,

HARRY S. TRUMAN

NOTE: This is the text of identical letters addressed to the Honorable Arthur H. Vandenberg, President pro tempore of the Senate, and to the Honorable Joseph W. Martin, Jr., Speaker of the House of Representatives. The text of the draft bill was released with the President's letter.

On July 26 the President approved the National Security Act of 1947 (61 Stat. 495).

43 Remarks to Representatives of the American Council of Voluntary Agencies for Foreign Service. *February 27, 1947*

THE AMERICAN people during and following World War I developed a tradition of help to the war afflicted through public and private support. Throughout World War II, and now in this trying postwar

period, we are maintaining this tradition of humanitarianism.

A large need continues for public and private help. Congress has before it my recommendations for direct help, and I have asked also that we share the responsibility with other countries of the United Nations in meeting the needs of refugees.

While the provisioning of whole populations and the settlement of refugees is primarily a public task, voluntary help should continue as in the past. This form of help is essential to complement the public programs, whether carried out by our Government on its own responsibility or through the United Nations.

44 Special Message to the Congress Requesting Funds for Rental Housing for Veterans. *February 28, 1947*

To the Congress of the United States:

A significant contribution to the amount of rental housing so direly needed by veterans and their families at rentals they can afford has been made during the past year by the temporary re-use program under Title V of the Lanham Act.

Under this program, Army barracks and other military or civilian wartime structures are converted into temporary dwellings. Many of these are re-used on their sites; others are moved and set up on the campuses of universities for the use of student veterans. Still others have been placed on new sites in cities where the housing shortage is desperate.

These educational institutions, municipalities and other public bodies have used their own funds to provide sites for these temporary re-use homes. In many cases, also, they have provided the necessary utilities. The Federal Government, through the Congress, made two appropriations, totaling $445,627,000, to finance its part of this program.

Originally, it was planned to convert war structures into 200,000 temporary units under this program. This would of course have provided accommodations for many more than 200,000 persons. Rising costs of labor and building materials, as well as rising costs caused by the increased time required for completion due to shortages, have made it necessary for the Government several times during the past year to cut back the temporary re-use program.

Prior to February 1, 1947, allocations had been made for 158,834 units, but the rising costs of building and the scarcity of materials made it necessary recently to suspend 8,357 of these. With cutbacks which had been ordered earlier, it now appears that it will be possible, out of the Federal appropriations, to provide for only about 150,000 units, or approximately 25 per cent fewer than was planned. Of these 95,451 units have been completed and around 55,000 including suspended units are under construction.

No more allocations out of the funds available under the Lanham Act can be made. Prior to the time cutbacks and suspensions were ordered, as a result of the approaching exhaustion of funds, however, many local groups such as city governments and educational institutions, already had obligated or spent considerable funds of their own, as required under the Lanham Act. This was done to acquire sites, provide utilities or community facilities to accommodate the housing which they confidently expected would be set up. In some instances they also spent funds on a reimbursable basis, to provide utilities and perform other necessary work in connection with these houses. When it became obvious that some temporary re-use units could not be completed at Federal expense, many local bodies set aside funds of their own in order to bring these units to completion.

The result is that in order for the Federal Government to fulfill its contractual obligations a further appropriation by the Congress of $50,000,000 is necessary.

These obligations fall into four categories:

1. Completion of all units now under contract, including approximately 8,357 units suspended since December 14, 1946.

2. Completion of approximately 4,869 units which were cancelled in previous cutbacks.

3. Reimbursement of public bodies for expenditures of their own funds for the completion of approximately 400 units which otherwise would have been cancelled.

4. Reimbursement of public bodies for the cost of utility and other on site work performed by them in connection with veterans' temporary housing on a reimbursable basis.

The Federal Government must carry out contractual obligations accepted in good faith by educational institutions, municipalities and other local bodies.

It is recommended, therefore, that the authorization contained in section 502(d) of the Lanham Act be increased by $50,000,000 and that the funds subsequently appropriated under the increased authorization be available to meet the four obligations specified above.

Over and above these contractual obligations, we have obvious responsibilities to those who served their country in the armed forces. Under our program about half of the temporary re-use housing is made available to colleges and other institutions of learning to house veterans while they are studying under the terms of the G.I. Bill of Rights. The other housing is set up in crowded cities, where otherwise many of our returned servicemen would be unable to find accommodations. Rentals of these temporary structures average $30 per family unit. I am sure I do not need to stress the urgency of the completion of this program to alleviate the stringent housing shortage faced by so many of our veterans.

I urge the Congress to make a further appropriation of $50,000,000 in order that the Government may meet its contractual obligations referred to and in order that this phase of our continuing program of aid to veterans may be carried out.

HARRY S. TRUMAN

NOTE: On May 31 the President approved a bill (61 Stat. 128) to provide additional funds for national defense housing.

45   Statement by the President Upon Signing Bill for Cooperation With Mexico in Control of Livestock Diseases.
February 28, 1947

SIGNING of this bill marks a new forward step in Western Hemisphere cooperation. For many years two of the world's most devastating livestock diseases—foot-and-mouth disease and rinderpest—have increasingly plagued the New World. I am glad to support this worthy legislation which Congress has wisely and quickly enacted.

It means that the United States now becomes the ally of Mexico in fighting off these highly infectious animal diseases, costly to livestock producers and consequently to the consumers of livestock products.

NOTE: As enacted, the bill (S. 568) is Public Law 8, 80th Congress (61 Stat. 7).

46 The President's News Conference of
February 28, 1947

THE PRESIDENT. [1.] I have no particular announcements to make to you today except that at—a little later there will be a release for morning papers of a report on the food—from the food board—the Cabinet food committee.

Any questions?

[2.] Q. Mr. President, in your 1947 budget and in the fiscal 1948 are there sufficient funds provided to carry out your recommendations?

THE PRESIDENT. No, there are not.

Q. How much would you have to have?

THE PRESIDENT. The $350 million that was asked for to continue the work that had been carried out by the letter that is contained in this year's budget.

Q. That's right.

THE PRESIDENT. And I can't remember what the figure is.

Q. 725 in the Army budget.

THE PRESIDENT. That's right.

Q. But there is no breakdown of that 725 in the Army budget, and that is for all the occupied areas.

THE PRESIDENT. Yes, and we haven't heard—we are making a survey in the Far East now, and I can't give you any accurate data on that until the Far East survey comes in. I think Mr. Hoover made a good report, and that he did a good job on that.

Q. Now, as I understand the 350 million, that was for the liberated countries, not for Germany alone?

THE PRESIDENT. That's right.

Q. And have you any idea how much you will require to carry our Mr. Hoover's recommendations for the current year?

THE PRESIDENT. I can't answer that until we have the whole picture, then we will make a survey of it and as soon as——

Q. That goes for fiscal 1948 as well?

THE PRESIDENT. That's right—that's right.

[3.] Q. Mr. President, can you make any comment on the situation in Greece as it is affected by the British—general British economic setup?

THE PRESIDENT. I have no comment to make.

[4.] Q. Mr. President, Mr. Hoover on the Hill this morning advocated that the relief to the liberated countries be paid back by those countries, which was not in your message that went to the Hill.

THE PRESIDENT. Well, I haven't seen Mr. Hoover's testimony, and until I have read the record, I can't comment on it.

Q. It's in the report, Mr. President.

THE PRESIDENT. How's that?

Q. That recommendation is in the report.

THE PRESIDENT. Yes, but that does not—the report does not refer to any 350 million.

Q. No sir.

THE PRESIDENT. That report is for food for enemy countries. I know that Mr. Hoover recommended that it might be made a charge against the future income of that country so that it could be paid back. There is nothing wrong with that.

Q. That was in your message.

THE PRESIDENT. Sure.

Q. Will the Army distribute the 350 million? Is that planned? Or might it be done by some United Nations organization?

THE PRESIDENT. We have not yet made up the—have not decided yet how that will be done. I'll find out whether they are going to get it or not before we make any arrangements.

[5.] Q. Mr. President, could we pursue the subject of Greece a little further? There are reports from London today—supposed to come from a Foreign Office spokesman—to the effect that the British Government has asked this Government to aid either financially in Greece or to take over the occupation of Greece itself.

THE PRESIDENT. I have no comment on that.

[6.] Q. Mr. President, is there any foundation in that report that has been broadcast——

THE PRESIDENT. There is no comment on that report.

[7.] Q. Mr. President, has the Potsdam agreement still—are we still supposed to be——

THE PRESIDENT. I stand by the Potsdam agreement.

[8.] Q. Mr. Hoover advocated also this morning——

THE PRESIDENT. Well now, I can't comment on anything Mr. Hoover said until I see the record.

[9.] Q. Mr. President, are you planning any new assignment for Jimmy Byrnes?

THE PRESIDENT. Not at the present.

Q. How about the near future?

THE PRESIDENT. Well, I have no comment on that now. If a place comes along where Mr. Byrnes can be used, and he is willing to do it, of course I will make use of him. I always have.

[10.] Q. Mr. President, this is a repeater from last week, but Dr. Nourse seems to be talking to some interested people on the question of export controls. An earlier message of yours I believe, sir, said you would make recommendations to Congress on that subject. Do you plan such recommendations in the near future?

THE PRESIDENT. We will have recommendations on that. I don't know how "near future" it will be, but when it is necessary we will make the recommendations.

Q. Does it expire, sir, on June 30th?

THE PRESIDENT. That's right.

[11.] Q. Mr. President, do you care to comment on that conference that you had yesterday with the congressional leaders?

THE PRESIDENT. No comment.

[12.] Q. Mr. President, could you tell us now anything about the draft? They have been putting that off for some weeks.

THE PRESIDENT. I will have a message on the draft sent down very shortly. As soon as that is ready, why I will see that you get it.

Q. Is that Selective Service or universal training?

THE PRESIDENT. Selective Service.

[13.] Q. Can you give us any clue as to whether we are going to continue the draft or not?

THE PRESIDENT. I will let the message speak for itself.

[14.] Q. Mr. President, could we have a clue as to who the four Republicans are you don't like?

THE PRESIDENT. Well now, I didn't know anything about that. That's the first time I ever heard that, Miss May.[1] [*Laughter*]

Q. You are quoted as having said at the last congressional reception that there are only four you didn't like.

THE PRESIDENT. Well, I don't remember that comment. I don't remember that comment.

Q. Would it be only four, Mr. President?

THE PRESIDENT. Well, I wouldn't like to limit it to four. [*Laughter*]

Q. How about Democrats, Mr. President?

THE PRESIDENT. Well, let's not comment on the Democrats. I am not commenting on the Republicans, you understand. And those four don't necessarily have to be in Washington, Mrs. Craig.

Q. Oh, I understood they were there.

THE PRESIDENT. Well, I say I am not limiting the four to Washington, so you can go way back in my political career and figure that out.

---

[1] Mrs. May Craig of the Portland (Maine) Press Herald.

[15.] Q. Mr. President, are you asking Mr. Pauley to take another job in the Administration, now that you have accepted his resignation?

THE PRESIDENT. No, I am not.

Q. You are not?

THE PRESIDENT. I have not offered him another job.

[16.] Q. Mr. President, is Congressman Tarver of Georgia being considered for the Court of Claims?

THE PRESIDENT. Mr. Tarver has been recommended by the Georgia delegation.

Q. And you——

THE PRESIDENT. I have him under consideration.

[17.] Q. Mr. President, any likelihood of an early appointment to fill the vacancy on the Federal Communications Commission?

THE PRESIDENT. Yes, I think we will have that appointment ready to send down very shortly now. I will let you know what it is when I make up my mind.

[18.] Q. Mr. President, the Senate Committee today rejected the nomination of Mr. Clapp to the TVA.

THE PRESIDENT. Well, I have been—I was in the Senate for 10 years and I have seen that happen on several occasions, and the member was still approved by the Senate. Mr. Clapp is a career public servant, and a good one, and he contributed as much as anybody else to the success of TVA; and I think that he is perfectly fitted for the job, and I shall stay behind him to the finish, just as I am doing with Mr. Lilienthal.

[19.] Q. Mr. President, have you had any further word from Mr. Bevin since the White House statement concerning his public [1] ——

THE PRESIDENT. I never did have any word from Mr. Bevin.

Q. You don't expect——

THE PRESIDENT. Don't expect any. [*Laughter*]

Q. Any personal comment you would like, Mr. President, to add to the White House statement in regard to Mr. Bevin's——

THE PRESIDENT. No comment.

[20.] Q. Mr. President, going back for a moment to that draft situation, is it your opinion that we should continue the mechanics of Selective Service?

THE PRESIDENT. I shall take that up in the message, and when the message is ready, I will furnish you with a copy that covers the whole thing.

[21.] Q. Mr. President, is any increase in the export-import loan authority anticipated—contemplated?

THE PRESIDENT. If it becomes necessary to ask for that increase, we will ask for it. We haven't considered it immediately.

[22.] Q. Mr. President, this is on a light note, but I notice in your recommendations for repeal of the laws that you propose the repeal of the dollar-a-year-men law.

THE PRESIDENT. Will you ask that question again, I didn't hear——

Q. Your bill—you submitted—the laws that you submitted for repeal—the revision—you proposed to repeal the law permitting employment of dollar-a-year men. I just wondered what was behind that, if anything?

THE PRESIDENT. Nothing whatever. Probably——

Q. Retrenchment?

THE PRESIDENT. Just—it might be—it might be retrenchment. I don't remember that detail in the recommendations. There was nothing sinister about it at all. The dollar-a-year men made a great contribution

---

[1] See Item 41.

to the war effort, which nobody knows better than I do.

[23.] Q. Mr. President, you have been owing Sumner Pike 50 cents ever since 1940. He never got paid. [*Laughter*]

THE PRESIDENT. The Federal Government owes me 66 cents for a dollar-a-year job which I never did get! [*More laughter*]

[24.] Q. Mr. President, are you going to appoint John McCloy president of the World Bank?

THE PRESIDENT. I think John McCloy—I don't appoint him——

Q. I mean, are you going——

THE PRESIDENT. I want him to be appointed.

Q. You will?

THE PRESIDENT. Yes.

Q. Or have you?

THE PRESIDENT. I have.

[25.] Q. Mr. President, you have been invited to visit Salem College, North Carolina, at some time on your way back from Mexico. Will you have time for that?

THE PRESIDENT. I don't think I will have a chance to stop there. I hope to pay that visit there some day, though.

[26.] Q. Mr. President, have you received an invitation from Canada yet?

THE PRESIDENT. Yes I have.

Q. Are you going?

THE PRESIDENT. Well, I have it under consideration. I never can make a firm appointment until just a short time before I find I can get away. I would like very much to go.

Q. When will that be, Mr. President?

THE PRESIDENT. Some time in the—next summer.

Q. What is the occasion? Any particular occasion?

THE PRESIDENT. No particular occasion—just a friendly visit.

[27.] Q. Mr. President, any significance in the resignation of Mr. Sam O'Neal?

THE PRESIDENT. Not that I know of.

[28.] Q. Mr. President, could you give us any notion of what is going to happen to rent control, in view of the Senate Committee——

THE PRESIDENT. I have, I think——

Q. ——and the OPA?

THE PRESIDENT. ——on four different occasions I have stated my position on rent control, and it hasn't changed.

Q. You still feel hopeful about OPA's survival?

THE PRESIDENT. I have nothing to say on that. I can tell you about that when Congress acts.

Q. Mr. President, in that connection, there was a story yesterday that you were considering the deal offered by Senator Hawkes to continue a 50-percent increase in rents?

THE PRESIDENT. I make no deals. When the bills come up here for consideration, I take them on their merits. They are not made on deals.

Reporter: Thank you, Mr. President.

NOTE: President Truman's ninety-ninth news conference was held in his office at the White House at 4 o'clock on Friday afternoon, February 28, 1947.

47 Statement by the President on the World's Food Needs.
February 28, 1947

I HAVE received from the Cabinet Committee on World Food Programs a report on our progress in exporting grain this year.

It is heartening for all of us to know that if we keep up our present rate of shipments, we shall have shipped the 400 million bushels of grain and flour by the end of April that we had originally expected to ship by the end of June.

The possibility of reaching this goal 2 months ahead of time gives us no grounds for complacency, however, for the battle of food is by no means over.

Mr. Hoover's survey of conditions in the countries he has just visited, as well as many reports which have come to me, reveal the tragic conditions of hunger under which many millions of people all over the world are still living. Even after the last of the grain we originally promised for this year has left our shores, millions will still be weakened and wasted by hunger. The next few months before the new harvests are gathered in Europe and in other countries to which a part of our exports are going, will be most critical ones.

It is essential to economic and political reconstruction overseas that a new food crisis be averted. We must go beyond our program and continue to ship as much grain in May and June as we can, in the interest of world stability and freedom, as well as in the long-range interest of the United States. At the same time we must continue to export as much coal as possible, since the need for fuel in many countries is second only to the need for food. This will take some sacrifice and considerable effort on our part.

We have the problem of transportation and to a lesser extent the problem of procurement. But neither of these is a new problem, and neither is insurmountable. It was because of these and related problems that I set up the Cabinet Committee on Food last September and asked it to maintain a continuous review of the world food situation and to recommend actions which should be taken by this Government to fulfill its responsibilities in meeting world demands for food.

Last December, on the recommendation of the Cabinet Committee, I asked Captain Granville Conway, former War Shipping Administrator, to undertake once more the task he so ably performed last spring in coordinating Government activities relating to the movement of emergency food and fuel exports. All agencies of Government, especially the Department of Agriculture, the Office of Defense Transportation, and the Maritime Commission have put forth tremendous effort. As a result of their activities and the full cooperation of American farmers, the grain and flour trades, the railroads and shipping lines, our exports have mounted to an alltime high for this season.

In addition to everything that the executive branch of Government can do, action by the Congress is required to carry this program forward. Funds must be provided to assist countries formerly aided by UNRRA and for the War Department's program for the occupied areas. Furthermore, if we are to maintain the international food allocation system so vital to the success of this whole food program, extension of certain limited portions of the Second War Powers Act, as already requested, will be necessary.

I know that it is a source of gratification to the people of our country, as it is to me, that we have been able to supply needed food to many of our wartime allies, and that at the same time we have been able to make substantial shipments to Italy, Switzerland, Austria, Eire, Finland, and other countries whose needs have also been great.

I am sure that I express the opinion of all Americans in pledging that we will continue the policy of sharing out of our abundance with those in dire need. Every additional pound of grain we can export is a contribution to human welfare, to reconstruction, and to world peace.

NOTE: The report of the Cabinet Committee on World Food Programs, in the form of a three-page letter dated February 28, was released with the President's statement. The report summed up the grain export situation as follows:

"1. Early program difficulties have been largely overcome through the full cooperation of many agencies and services, and the rate of export is now at just about the highest practicable level.

"2. Nearly 300 million bushels of grain and grain products have already been shipped from the United States since last July 1.

"3. If all goes well, the original 400 million bushel 1946–47 grain export goal should be met in full around the first of May and the goal will be exceeded by the additional shipments which can be moved out during May and June.

"4. Little additional wheat out of the 1946 crop is expected to be purchased for export pending final appraisal of 1947 wheat crop prospects.

"5. In spite of the success of our program so far, needs overseas are still urgent and growing. We must not and will not relax our efforts.

"6. If our present plans can be carried out, the United States shipments of grain to meet critical world needs during 1946–47 will set a new record, becoming the greatest single year for food grain exports in history."

The report was signed by Clinton P. Anderson, Secretary of Agriculture, who served as chairman, William C. Foster, Acting Secretary of Commerce, and Dean Acheson, Under Secretary of State.

48 Remarks Upon Presenting the Wendell Willkie Awards for Journalism. *February 28, 1947*

THESE AWARDS are in recognition of journalistic endeavor of a high order. The idea of a free press is fundamental to the freedoms that we cherish as Americans. While there are limitations on all our freedoms, including the freedom of the press, we can say without fear of challenge that we have a press that is freer than any other in the world today.

Our press in general has outgrown the provincialism, the narrow isolationism, of another era. It has accepted as its province Wendell Willkie's "One World." It is doing a valiant service in educating us to understand that we must live in that "one world." As they did during the war, reporters go to distant and perilous parts of the earth to bring us the news. The news-gathering apparatus of our press is farflung and highly efficient.

The more than 60 Negro newspapers in our country form an important part of that press. These newspapers show an understandable concern with the problems of relationship between the races. From the columns of the Negro press example after example can be cited of reporting and editorial writing which deal with these problems in the courageous and constructive manner that we expect of the best of our journalism.

One of the newspapers given an award tonight prepared the way for a much-needed improvement in the Negro schools of its community. Still another accepted the challenge of equal rights in citizenship and urged Negro citizens to assume their responsibilities. A third exposed an example of intolerable discrimination. The entries considered by the awards committee covered a wide range, including reporting both at home and overseas. They maintained, I am told by the committee, a very high standard.

We are living in a time of profound and swiftly moving change. We see colonial peoples moving toward their independence. It is a process that we, as Americans, can understand and sympathize with, since it parallels our own struggle for independence. We, as Americans, will want to supply guidance and help wherever we can. One way in which we can help is to set an example of a nation in which people with different backgrounds, with different origins work peacefully and successfully alongside one another. That is one meaning of this meeting here tonight and I congratulate those of you who are responsible for our coming together on this occasion.

More and more we are learning, and in no small measure through the medium of the press, how closely our democracy is under observation. We are learning what loud echoes both our successes and our failures have in every corner of the world. That is one of the pressing reasons why we cannot afford failures. When we fail to live together in peace, the failure touches not us, as Americans, alone, but the cause of democracy it-

self in the whole world. That we must never forget.

I thank you very much.

NOTE: The President spoke in the National Press Club Auditorium at a ceremony presided over by Dr. Douglas S. Freeman, editor of the Richmond News Leader and biographer of Robert E. Lee. Recipients of the awards were P. Bernard Young, Jr., editor, Norfolk Journal and Guide; Frank L. Stanley, editor, Louisville (Ky.) Defender; C. C. Dejoie, Louisiana Weekly; Ralph Matthews, editor, National Bureau of the Afro-American; Enoch P. Waters, Chicago Defender; Louis R. Lautier, Chief, Negro Newspaper Publishers Association News Service; William O. Walker, editor, Cleveland Call-Post; Lewis Jones, Houston Informer; and Robert Durr, Birmingham Weekly Review. A special certificate of merit was presented to the Chicago Defender and to Radio Station WBBM of the Columbia Broadcasting System for collaboration on a weekly program, "Democracy, U.S.A.," prepared by H. Leslie Atlas of CBS and Charles P. Browning of the Chicago Defender.

49   Radio Remarks Opening the Red Cross Campaign. *February 28, 1947*

[Broadcast from the White House at 10 p.m.]

My Fellow Citizens:

Recently there came to my desk a small pamphlet with a four-word title, "This Is Our Story." I opened it to find inside one of the really great stories of our time. Its pages unfolded a simple and moving story of the American Red Cross, geared now to peacetime requirements, yet remaining at the side of our occupation troops and in hospital wards with our servicemen and veterans.

The far-reaching work of the Red Cross is, indeed, *our* story. It is a story in which all of us can take deep pride. For we the people have built the Red Cross—an organization which translates dollars into helpful deeds, which transcends all barriers of race, creed, or color, which concerns itself only with human needs.

This narrative deals not with nameless

millions, but with the boy who will no longer deliver papers down the street because he's lying paralyzed in a hospital, with the athlete whose mind was wiped clean of memory, with a little girl in France whose bare feet were frozen in the snow. It deals, too, with a Red Cross disaster worker who toiled with the injured throughout the night while his wife and only child lay among the dead.

This is an inspiring record of hope relit and comfort given. It is a story from the hearts of the millions who helped and were helped by the Red Cross during one 12-month period.

As the Nation's official disaster relief agency and as an auxiliary to our Armed Forces, the Red Cross must maintain direct access to the American people in order to render maximum service under its congressional charter. It can best serve the national interest and retain necessary freedom of action when emergency strikes by conducting an independent appeal for membership and financial support once a year.

The 1947 Red Cross Campaign begins tomorrow. Nearly 3 million volunteers have enlisted to help carry its message to the entire citizenship. I fervently hope these unselfish workers will be welcomed in every home and business establishment of the land.

Let us remind ourselves that many times a year the people turn to the Red Cross— once a year the Red Cross turns to the people. That time is now at hand.

Every dollar contributed will be multiplied in usefulness. Let us keep the Red Cross at full strength. Let us all respond proudly and generously to this call.

50   Special Message to the Congress on Discontinuing the Selective Service.   *March 3, 1947*

To the Congress of the United States:

The Selective Service and Training Act will expire on March 31, 1947. The only assured way of maintaining the Army and the Navy at their required strengths during the Fiscal Year 1948 is through resort to Selective Service. I have decided, however, after most careful consideration and consultation with the Secretary of War and the Secretary of the Navy, and with the earnest desire of placing our Army and Navy on an entirely volunteer basis at the earliest possible moment, that I should not recommend an extension of the Act at this time. In order that my position may be better understood, the following facts are submitted.

The strength of the Army, including the Air Forces, must be maintained throughout the next fiscal year at 1,070,000 and the Navy, including the Marine Corps, must be maintained at a strength of 571,000 if this nation is to have reasonable assurance of security. These requirements are absolute, and we must not divest the War and Navy Departments of the means of meeting any material shortages.

Personnel losses from the Army through separation during fiscal year 1948 can be computed with a reasonable degree of accuracy. They will reach a total of 360,000, or an average of 30,000 per month. Gains, on the other hand, cannot be so accurately determined. A recruiting campaign for volunteers for the Army was initiated in September, 1945, but shortages in recruiting have heretofore forced the War Department to fill the gap through Selective Service. The last two months of 1946 provided an average of 18,000 recruits per month. During January 1947, however, they rose to some 35,000 enlistments and during the first two weeks of February were about 13,000. Giving weight to the fact that past records prove January to be the best recruiting month of the year, it is estimated by the War Department that if present efforts to obtain volunteers are continued, it can count with a fair degree of certainty on an average of 20,000 enlistments and re-enlistments per month during the coming fiscal year. If only 20,000 recruits per month are obtained, the deficit in required strength will be about 120,000 by July 1, 1948. However, there is a reasonable expectation that better results may be obtained.

The War Department is now engaged in reducing the Army to the strength of 1,070,-000, on June 30, 1947, provided for in the budget. In effecting this reduction, it will shortly direct the discharge of all non-volunteers.

The Navy Department is also reducing the Navy to the strength provided for in the budget for the next fiscal year. To maintain an average strength of 571,000 during the fiscal year 1948, the Navy will require approximately 150,000 recruits. Without the incentive of Selective Service, it is not certain that this number of recruits can be obtained.

The Army and the Navy are still reducing their forces and the Army is not using inductees for the full term the law allows; consequently, an extension of Selective Service at this time would be solely on the basis of predicted shortages during the next year. With a recent brightening in recruiting prospects, this appears to be the logical time to shoulder the risks involved.

Therefore, I recommend that no extension of Selective Service at this time be made, but with the understanding that:

First, the War and Navy Departments will request the re-enactment of a Selective Service Act at a later date if they are unable to maintain the Army at a strength of 1,070,-000 men and the Navy at a strength of 571,000 through voluntary enlistments.

Second, the Army and Navy be authorized from appropriated funds to employ temporarily the necessary civilian personnel over and above those specifically authorized and appropriated for by the Congress to the extent necessary to balance any shortage of enlisted personnel when strength may fall below the required levels.

The efforts of the War Department to reach the desired goal of an entirely volunteer Regular Army are worthy of the maximum support on the part of the Administration, the Congress and the people.

HARRY S. TRUMAN

NOTE: For the President's statement upon expiration of the Selective Training and Service Act, see Item 63.

51 Address in Mexico City.
March 3, 1947

Mr. President, distinguished guests:

My presence here today as the guest of the great Republic of Mexico is one of the truly happy occasions of my career. I might say, incidentally, that I never had such a welcome in my life. I am deeply moved to be here again, among my friends and neighbors. I have wanted to return to Mexico ever since November 1939, when I visited this city and enjoyed the memorable hospitality of the Mexican Congress. To my good friend President Miguel Alemán, and to all the people of Mexico, I say from the bottom of my heart: Thank you for your gracious welcome.

It is a common failing of many people to complain of hardships and overlook their good fortune. In the international sphere, many people emphasize the disagreements that separate nations and forget the large areas of agreement that bring nations together in mutual understanding. It would be foolish to pretend that fundamental differences in political philosophies do not exist. The task of achieving permanent peace and security for all mankind is not easy, but I am certain that permanent peace and security are the goal of all peoples everywhere, whatever their language, or nationality, race, or creed. Because of my belief that the peoples of the world have peace as a common objective, I refuse to be discouraged by apparent difficulties. Difficulties are a challenge to men of determination.

Mr. President, you refer to 1847. We did have tragic difficulties then. In fact, we had difficulties with our northern neighbor Canada in 1814. We also had a terrible quarrel between our own States. But, Mr. President, we have learned the hard way that peace is best at home and abroad with our neighbors. We have fought two world wars within a generation. We have found that the victor loses in total war as well as the vanquished.

If a realistic view of the world takes full account of the differences that separate nations, it must also take full account of the common beliefs that unite nations. Nowhere is this element of unity—unity of heart and mind—more evident than in the neighborly community of the American Republics. Here we recognize clearly that, as you have stated so concisely and eloquently, Mr. President, "together we must live and together we must prosper." Therefore, we must have world peace.

Here in the Western Hemisphere we have already achieved in substantial measure what the world as a whole must achieve. Through what we call our Inter-American System, which has become steadily stronger for half a century, we have learned to work together to solve our problems by friendly cooperation and mutual respect.

We have a good-neighbor policy in common and, as a result of this sincere application of that policy, we form a good neighborhood. Our example has a salutary effect upon the whole world. The success of our cherished Inter-American System is a source of inspiration for the developing system of the United Nations, of which we are all members.

We are united by more than the common procedures and agencies of inter-American cooperation. All our peoples have a common belief which we call democracy. Democracy has a spiritual foundation because it is based upon the brotherhood of man. We believe in the dignity of the individual. We believe that the function of the state is to preserve and promote human rights and fundamental freedoms. We believe that the state exists for the benefit of man, not man for the benefit of the state. Everything else that we mean by the word democracy arises from this fundamental conviction. We believe that each individual must have as much liberty for the conduct of his life as is compatible with the rights of others. To put this belief into practice is the essential purpose of our laws.

We know that the maximum freedom and dignity of the individual cannot be attained under a dictatorship. Freedom and dignity of the individual can be attained only under a system of law which protects the rights of individuals, and through a government made up of freely elected representatives of the people. When we have this, we have a democratic government—one that is suited to the democratic way of life.

This is a simple, fundamental truth.

The good-neighbor policy, which guides the course of our inter-American relations, is equally simple. It is the application of democracy to international affairs. It is the application of the Golden Rule.

The good-neighbor policy applies to international relations the same standards of conduct that prevail among self-respecting individuals within a democratic community. It is based upon mutual respect among nations, the respect that each accords to the rights of the other, without distinction of size, wealth, or power. It is an expression of that bond of common belief which we call democracy.

It is the only road into the future that will lead us to our goal of universal peace and security. Along that road we shall persevere.

The good-neighbor policy specifically includes the Doctrine of Nonintervention. This assures each nation freedom for its own development. My country, in common with all the American Republics, pledged itself at the Conference of Montevideo in 1933 and the Conference of Buenos Aires in 1936 to observe the Doctrine of Nonintervention. What it means is that a strong nation does not have the right to impose its will, by reason of its strength, upon a weaker nation. The wholehearted acceptance of this doctrine by all of us is the keystone of the Inter-American System. Without it we could not exist as a community of good neighbors. It is a binding commitment under the good-neighbor policy. It is part of the basic international law recognized by all the American Republics. My own country will be faithful to the letter and to the spirit of that law.

Nonintervention does not and cannot mean indifference to what goes on beyond our own borders. Events in one country may have a profound effect in other countries. The community of nations feels concern at the violation of accepted principles of national behavior by any one of its members. The lawlessness of one nation may threaten the very existence of the law on which all nations depend.

In our domestic civil life we long ago recognized that the alternative to the rule of the strong was law established by the community. For some years now we have been seeking, with increasing success, to apply this basic concept to international relations. It is no coincidence that the effort to achieve collective world security has been concurrent with the growing acceptance of the Doctrine of Nonintervention. It is in-spiring to note the progress we have made toward establishing a community of nations with authority to enforce the law on delinquents. The Charter of the United Nations specifically invests the world community of nations with a measure of such authority. Within the good-neighbor community of the 21 American Republics we have witnessed and are witnessing a similar constructive development, beginning at Buenos Aires in 1936 with unanimous acceptance of the principles of consultation. The development of the Inter-American System was accelerated by the great work done in this city at the 1945 Conference on Problems of War and Peace, where the plan of a reorganized and strengthened System was created.

International relations have traditionally been compared to a chess game in which each nation tries to outwit and checkmate the other. I cannot accept that comparison with respect to the relations between your country and mine, Mr. President. The United States and Mexico are working together for the mutual benefit of their peoples and the peace of the world. You have made me feel, what I could not have doubted in any case, that I stand here, in the midst of the great people of Mexico, as a trusted friend and a welcome guest.

To you and to the people of Mexico I bring a message of friendship and trust from the people of the United States. Though the road be long and wearisome that leads to a good neighborhood as wide as the world, we shall travel it together.

Our two countries will not fail each other. Thank you.

NOTE: The President spoke at 9:35 p.m. in the Palacio Nacional. His opening words "Mr. President" referred to President Miguel Alemán of Mexico. The address was carried on a nationwide radio broadcast.

52 Address on Foreign Economic Policy, Delivered at Baylor University. *March 6, 1947*

President Neff, ladies and gentlemen, members of the faculty of this great school and its pupils:

I can't tell you how very much I appreciate this honor which you are conferring upon me.

I am particularly touched by your remembrance of my mother.

It is with a real sense of gratification that I meet with you today on the beautiful campus of Baylor University in Waco. I congratulate you on the outstanding achievements of this great university during the one hundred and one years of its existence. I am sincerely grateful for the degree of Doctor of Laws that you have bestowed upon me, and I am honored to become a fellow alumnus of the distinguished men and women of this institution who have contributed so much to make our country great.

At this particular time, the whole world is concentrating much of its thought and energy on attaining the objectives of peace and freedom. These objectives are bound up completely with a third objective—reestablishment of world trade. In fact the three—peace, freedom, and world trade—are inseparable. The grave lessons of the past have proved it.

Many of our people, here in America, used to think that we could escape the troubles of the world by simply staying within our own borders. Two wars have shown how wrong they were. We know today that we cannot find security in isolation. If we are to live at peace, we must join with other nations in a continuing effort to organize the world for peace. Science and invention have left us no other alternative.

After the First World War, the United States proposed a League of Nations, an organization to maintain order in the world. But when our proposal was accepted and the League was established, this country failed to become a member.

Can any thoughtful person fail to realize today what that mistake cost this Nation and cost the world?

This time we are taking a different course. Our country has taken a leading part in building the United Nations, in setting up its councils, its committees and commissions, and in putting them to work. We are doing everything within our power to foster international cooperation. We have dedicated ourselves to its success.

This is not, and it must never be, the policy of a single administration or a single party. It is the policy of all the people of the United States. We, in America, are unanimous in our determination to prevent another war.

But some among us do not fully realize what we must do to carry out this policy. There still are those who seem to believe that we can confine our cooperation with other countries to political relationships; that we need not cooperate where economic questions are involved.

This attitude has sometimes led to the assertion that there should be bipartisan support for the foreign policy of the United States, but that there need not be bipartisan support for the foreign *economic* policy of the United States.

Such a statement simply does not make sense.

Our foreign relations, political and economic, are indivisible. We cannot say that we are willing to cooperate in the one field and are unwilling to cooperate in the other. I am glad to note that the leaders in both parties have recognized that fact.

The members of the United Nations have renounced aggression as a method of settling their political differences. Instead of putting armies on the march, they have now agreed to sit down around a table and talk things out. In any dispute, each party will present its case. The interests of all will be considered, and a fair and just solution will be found. This is the way of international order. It is the way of a civilized community. It applies, with equal logic, to the settlement of *economic* differences.

Economic conflict is not spectacular—at least in the early stages. But it is always serious. One nation may take action in behalf of its own producers, without notifying other nations, or consulting them, or even considering how they may be affected. It may cut down its purchases of another country's goods, by raising its tariffs or imposing an embargo or a system of quotas on imports. And when it does this, some producer, in the other country, will find the door to his market suddenly slammed and bolted in his face.

Or a nation may subsidize its exports, selling its goods abroad below their cost. When this is done, a producer in some other country will find his market flooded with goods that have been dumped.

In either case, the producer gets angry, just as you or I would get angry if such a thing were done to us. Profits disappear; workers are dismissed. The producer feels that he has been wronged, without warning and without reason. He appeals to his government for action. His government retaliates, and another round of tariff boosts, embargoes, quotas, and subsidies is under way. This is economic war. In such a war nobody wins.

Certainly, nobody won the last economic war. As each battle of the economic war of the thirties was fought, the inevitable tragic result became more and more apparent. From the tariff policy of Hawley and Smoot, the world went on to Ottawa and the system

of imperial preferences, from Ottawa to the kind of elaborate and detailed restrictions adopted by Nazi Germany. Nations strangled normal trade and discriminated against their neighbors, all around the world.

Who among their peoples were the gainers? Not the depositors who lost their savings in the failure of the banks. Not the farmers who lost their farms. Not the millions who walked the streets looking for work. I do not mean to say that economic conflict was the *sole* cause of the depression. But I do say that it was a *major* cause.

Now, as in the year 1920, we have reached a turning point in history. National economies have been disrupted by the war. The future is uncertain everywhere. Economic policies are in a state of flux. In this atmosphere of doubt and hesitation, the decisive factor will be the type of leadership that the United States gives the world.

We are the giant of the economic world. Whether we like it or not, the future pattern of economic relations depends upon us. The world is waiting and watching to see what we shall do. The choice is ours. We can lead the nations to economic peace or we can plunge them into economic war.

There must be no question as to our course. We must not go through the thirties again.

There is abundant evidence, I think, that these earlier mistakes will not be repeated. We have already made a good start. Our Government has participated fully in setting up, under the United Nations, agencies of international cooperation for dealing with relief and refugees, with food and agriculture, with shipping and aviation, with loans for reconstruction and development, and with the stabilization of currencies. And now, in order to avoid economic warfare, our Government has proposed, and others have agreed, that there be set up, within the United Nations, another agency to be concerned with problems and policies affecting world trade. This is the International Trade Organization.

This organization would apply to commercial relationships the same principle of fair dealing that the United Nations is applying to political affairs. Instead of retaining unlimited freedom to commit acts of economic aggression, its members would adopt a code of economic conduct and agree to live according to its rules. Instead of adopting measures that might be harmful to others, without warning and without consultation, countries would sit down around the table and talk things out. In any dispute, each party would present its case. The interest of all would be considered, and a fair and just solution would be found. In economics, as in international politics, this is the way to peace.

The work of drafting a world trade charter was begun by the United States. It was carried forward by a Preparatory Committee of eighteen nations meeting in London last fall. It should be completed at a second meeting of this Committee in Geneva, beginning on April tenth.

The progress that has already been made on this project is one of the most heartening developments since the war.

If the nations can agree to observe a code of good conduct in international trade, they will cooperate more readily in other international affairs. Such agreement will prevent the bitterness that is engendered by an economic war. It will provide an atmosphere congenial to the preservation of peace.

As a part of this program we have asked the other nations of the world to join with us in reducing barriers to trade. We have not asked them to remove all barriers. Nor have we ourselves offered to do so. But we *have* proposed negotiations directed toward the reduction of tariffs, here and abroad, toward the elimination of other restrictive measures and the abandonment of discrimination. These negotiations are to be undertaken at the meeting which opens in Geneva next month. The success of this program is essential to the establishment of the International Trade Organization, to the effective operation of the International Bank and the Monetary Fund, and to the strength of the whole United Nations structure of cooperation in economic and political affairs.

The negotiations at Geneva must not fail.

There is one thing that Americans value even more than peace. It is freedom. Freedom of worship—freedom of speech—freedom of enterprise. It must be true that the first two of these freedoms are related to the third. For, throughout history, freedom of worship and freedom of speech have been most frequently enjoyed in those societies that have accorded a considerable measure of freedom to individual enterprise. Freedom has flourished where power has been dispersed. It has languished where power has been too highly centralized. So our devotion to freedom of enterprise, in the United States, has deeper roots than a desire to protect the profits of ownership. It is part and parcel of what we call American.

The pattern of international trade that is most conducive to freedom of enterprise is one in which the major decisions are made, not by governments, but by private buyers and sellers, under conditions of active competition, and with proper safeguards against the establishment of monopolies and cartels. Under such a system, buyers make their purchases, and sellers make their sales, at whatever time and place and in whatever quantities they choose, relying for guidance on whatever prices the market may afford. Goods move from country to country in response to economic opportunities. Governments may impose tariffs, but they do not dictate the quantity of trade, the sources of imports, or the destination of exports. Individual transactions are a matter of private choice.

This is the essence of free enterprise.

The pattern of trade that is *least* conducive to freedom of enterprise is one in which decisions are made by governments. Under such a system, the quantity of purchases and sales, the sources of imports, and the destination of exports are dictated by public officials. In some cases, trade may be conducted by the state. In others, part or all of it may be left in private hands. But, even so, the trader is not free. Governments make all the important choices and he adjusts himself to them as best he can.

This was the pattern of the seventeenth and eighteenth centuries. Unless we act, and act decisively, it will be the pattern of the next century.

Everywhere on earth, nations are under economic pressure. Countries that were devastated by the war are seeking to reconstruct their industries. Their need to import, in the months that lie ahead, will exceed their capacity to export. And so they feel that imports must be rigidly controlled.

Countries that have lagged in their development are seeking to industrialize. In order that new industries may be established, they, too, feel that competing imports must be rigidly controlled.

Nor is this all. The products of some countries are in great demand. But buyers outside their borders do not hold the money of these countries in quantities large enough to enable them to pay for the goods they want. And they find these moneys difficult to earn. Importing countries, when they make their purchases, therefore seek to discriminate against countries whose currencies they do not possess. Here, again, they feel that imports must be rigidly controlled.

One way to cut down on imports is by curtailing the freedom of traders to use foreign money to pay for imported goods. But recourse to this device is now limited by the terms of the British loan agreement and by the rules of the International Monetary Fund. Another way to cut down on imports is by raising tariffs.

But if controls over trade are really to be tight, tariffs are not enough. Even more drastic measures can be used. Quotas can be imposed on imports, product by product, country by country, and month by month. Importers can be forbidden to buy abroad without obtaining licenses. Those who buy more than is permitted can be fined or jailed. Everything that comes into a country can be kept within limits determined by a central plan. That is regimentation. And this is the direction in which much of the world is headed at the present time.

If this trend is not reversed, the Government of the United States will be under pressure, sooner or later, to use these same devices to fight for markets and for raw materials. And if the Government were to yield to this pressure, it would shortly find itself in the business of allocating foreign goods among importers and foreign markets among exporters and telling every trader what he could buy or sell, and how much, and when, and where. This is precisely what we have been trying to get away from, as rapidly as possible, ever since the war. It is not the American way. It is not the way to peace.

Fortunately, an alternative has been offered to the world in The Charter of the International Trade Organization that is to be considered at Geneva in the coming month. The Charter would limit the present freedom of governments to impose detailed administrative regulations on their foreign trade. The International Trade Organization would require its member nations to confine such controls to exceptional cases, in the immediate future, and to abandon them entirely as soon as they can be abandoned.

The trade-agreement negotiations that will accompany consideration of the Charter, should enable countries that are now in difficulty to work their way out of it by affording them readier access to the markets of the world. This program is designed to restore and preserve a trading system that is consistent with continuing freedom of enterprise in every country that chooses freedom for its own economy. It is a program that will serve the interests of other nations as well as those of the United States.

If these negotiations are to be successful, we ourselves must make the same commitments that we ask all other nations of the world to make. We must be prepared to make concessions if we are to obtain concessions from others in return. If these negotiations should fail, our hope of an early restoration of an international order in which private trade can flourish would be lost. I say again, they must not fail.

The program that we have been discussing will make our foreign trade larger than it otherwise would be. This means that exports will be larger. It also means that imports will be larger. Many people, it is true, are afraid of imports. They are afraid because they have assumed that we cannot take more products from abroad unless we produce just that much less at home.

This is not the case. The size of our market is not forever fixed. It is smaller when we attempt to isolate ourselves from the other countries of the world. It is larger when we have a thriving foreign trade. Our imports were down to a billion dollars in 1932; they were up to five billion in 1946. But no one would contend that 1932 was a better year than 1946 for selling goods, or making profits, or finding jobs. Business is poor when markets are small. Business is good when markets are big. It is the

purpose of the coming negotiations to lower existing barriers to trade so that markets everywhere may grow.

I said to the Congress, when it last considered the extension of the Trade Agreements Act, and I now reiterate, that domestic interests will be safeguarded in this process of expanding trade. But there still are those who sincerely fear that the trade agreement negotiations will prove disastrous to the interests of particular producing groups. I am sure that their misgivings are not well founded. The situation briefly is this:

(1) The Reciprocal Trade Agreements Act has been on the books since 1934. It has been administered with painstaking care and strict impartiality. Some 30 agreements with other countries have been made. And trade has grown, to the great benefit of our economy.

(2) This Government does not intend, in the coming negotiations, to eliminate tariffs or to establish free trade. All that is contemplated is the reduction of tariffs, the removal of discriminations, and the achievement, not of free trade, but of freer trade.

(3) In the process of negotiations, tariffs will not be cut across the board. Action will be selective; some rates may be cut substantially, others moderately, and others not at all.

(4) In return for these concessions, we shall seek and obtain concessions from other countries to benefit our export trade.

(5) Millions of Americans—on farms, in factories, on the railroads, in export and import businesses, in shipping, aviation, banking, and insurance, in wholesale establishments and in retail stores—depend upon foreign trade for some portion of their livelihood. If we are to protect the interests of these people, in their investments and their employment, we must see to it that our

trade does not decline. Take one of these groups as an example: we exported in 1946 over three billion dollars worth of agricultural products alone, mostly grain, cotton, tobacco, dairy products, and eggs. If we should lose a substantial part of this foreign market, the incomes of over six million farm families would be materially reduced and their buying power for the products of our factories greatly curtailed.

(6) There is no intention to sacrifice one group to the benefit of another group. Negotiations will be directed toward obtaining larger markets, both foreign and domestic, for the benefit of all.

(7) No tariff rate will be reduced until an exhaustive study has been made, until every person who wishes a hearing has been heard, and careful consideration given to his case.

(8) In every future agreement, there will be a clause that permits this Government— or any other government—to modify or withdraw a concession if it should result, or threaten to result, in serious injury to a domestic industry. This is now required by the Executive order [1] which I issued on February the 25th, following extensive conferences between officials in the Department of State and the majority leaders in the Senate.

All these points—the history of trade-agreement operations, the way in which negotiations are conducted, the protection afforded by the safeguarding clause—should provide assurance, if assurance is needed, that domestic interests will not be injured.

The policy of reducing barriers to trade is a settled policy of this Government. It is embodied in the Reciprocal Trade Agreements Act, fathered and administered for many years by Cordel Hull. It is reflected in the Charter of the International Trade Organization. It is one of the cornerstones of our plans for peace. It is a policy from which we cannot—and must not—turn aside.

Those among us—and there are still a few—who would seek to undermine this policy for partisan advantage and go back to the period of high tariffs and economic isolation, I can only say this: Times have changed. Our position in the world has changed. The temper of our people has changed. The slogans of 1930 or of 1896 are sadly out of date. Isolationism, after two world wars, is a confession of mental and moral bankruptcy.

Happily, our foreign economic policy does not now rest upon a base of narrow partisanship. Leaders in both parties have expressed their faith in its essential purposes. Here, as elsewhere in our foreign relations, I shall welcome a continuation of bipartisan support.

Our people are united. They have come to a realization of their responsibilities. They are ready to assume their role of leadership. They are determined upon an international order in which peace and freedom shall endure.

Peace and freedom are not easily achieved. They cannot be attained by force. They come from mutual understanding and cooperation, from a willingness to deal fairly with every friendly nation in all matters— political and economic. Let us resolve to continue to do just that, now and in the future. If other nations of the world will do the same, we can reach the goals of permanent peace and world freedom.

NOTE: The President spoke at 1 p.m. on the campus of Baylor University in Waco, Tex., immediately after receiving an honorary degree from the university. His opening words referred to Pat Morris Neff, president of the university. The address was carried on a nationwide radio broadcast.

---

[1] Executive Order 9832 "Prescribing Procedures for the Administration of the Reciprocal Trade Agreements Program" (3 CFR, 1943–1948 Comp., p. 624).

53   Letters Concerning the OWMR Advisory Board's Report on the Guaranteed Wage.   *March 8,* 1947

[Released March 8, 1947.   Dated March 7, 1947]

To the Chairman of the Council of Economic Advisers:

My dear Dr. Nourse:

The Advisory Board of the Office of War Mobilization and Reconversion has transmitted to me the Report on the Guaranteed Wage. In its letter of transmittal the Board said, "The Report represents a major contribution to the sum of knowledge in this field and deserves serious consideration by Government, labor, management and the public."

Although the Board pointed out that guaranteed wage plans should not be the subject of legislative action, it did make clear the responsibility of the Government for maintaining a continuing study of the guaranteed wage and for supplying data and information to those interested in wage guarantees.

Accordingly, I request that the Council of Economic Advisers study the economic implications of the guaranteed wage, particularly as a device for helping to stabilize employment, production, and purchasing power. This study should consider existing legislation in the fields of social insurance, minimum wages, fiscal and tax policies, and other laws that affect the inauguration or operation of guaranteed wage plans.

Since there are particular functions which other Federal agencies can best undertake to provide current information on guaranteed wage plans and advice concerning their applicability and operation, I am also requesting the Secretary of Commerce and Secretary of Labor to assume certain responsibilities. Copies of these letters are enclosed.

Very sincerely yours,

HARRY S. TRUMAN

[Honorable Edwin G. Nourse, Chairman, Council of Economic Advisers, Washington, D.C.]

To the Secretary of Commerce:

My dear Mr. Secretary:

When we discussed the Report on the guaranteed wage study made to me last month by the OWMR Advisory Board, you expressed an interest in providing industry with current information on wage guarantees in relation to the stabilization problems of various industries. This will be a useful service and the Department of Commerce should undertake this responsibility.

I am also asking the Secretary of Labor to continue to survey guaranteed wage plans and to make data on the various types available to other Government departments and agencies and to the public. In addition, the Council of Economic Advisers is being asked to study the economic implications of the guaranteed wage.

Very sincerely yours,

HARRY S. TRUMAN

[The Honorable The Secretary of Commerce, Washington, D.C.]

To the Secretary of Labor:

My dear Mr. Secretary:

The work so far done by the Department of Labor has contributed greatly to the value of the guaranteed wage study recently transmitted to me by the OWMR Advisory Board.

The interests of the general public and of

labor and industry will be served if the Department of Labor continues the compilation of information on guaranteed wage plans, and makes its findings available. Accordingly, I ask you to assume this responsibility.

I am also asking the Secretary of Commerce to provide industry with current information on wage guarantees in relation to the stabilization problems of various industries, and the Council of Economic Advisers to study the economic implications of the guaranteed wage.

> Very sincerely yours,
>
> HARRY S. TRUMAN

[The Honorable The Secretary of Labor, Washington, D.C.]

NOTE: The report, entitled "Guaranteed Wages," is dated January 31, 1947 (Government Printing Office, 473 pp.).

54   Special Message to the Congress Recommending Establishment of an Office of Selective Service Records.   *March 10, 1947*

To the Congress of the United States:

In my message of March 3, 1947, to the Congress, I recommended that there be no extension of the Selective Training and Service Act at this time. Because I am confident that the Congress and the Nation stand ready both now and in the future to take such action as may be necessary to assure the security of the Nation, and because there are now reasonably good prospects of maintaining at adequate strength the Army and Navy without resort to Selective Service, I believe we can liquidate the Selective Service System, except for its records. Since the Act expires on March 31, 1947, we are faced with the immediate need of providing for the consolidation and preservation of records and providing for liquidation of the Selective Service System.

In order to provide for the orderly and expeditious liquidation of the Selective Service System, and to take care of storage and servicing of the records of the System, I recommend the establishment of an "Office of Selective Service Records." It will be the duty of this office to begin immediately the liquidation of all local board offices, and to centralize at suitable locations in each State the valuable accumulation of records for safekeeping, in the event such records are needed in the future. It would not be the part of wisdom to destroy such records until their value has disappeared.

In the immediate future there are certain values to the veterans themselves and to the Nation in retaining and servicing the records apart from reasons of National Security. During the last six months of 1946, the Selective Service System complied with more than 1,000,000 requests from State and Federal agencies for information about veterans. A large number of these requests were in the interest of veterans as individuals. It is desirable to continue to make use of the records in this manner, while at the same time assuring that the confidential nature of these records should not be violated.

I recommend, therefore, the enactment of a law providing for:

(1) The establishment of an Office of Selective Service Records which will (a) liquidate the Selective Service System, and (b) establish and maintain federal record depots in the several states, the District of Columbia, and the territories and possessions of the United States;

(2) Transfer to the Office of Selective Service Records all property, records, per-

sonnel, and unexpended balances of appropriations of the Selective Service System; and

(3) The continuance of the confidential nature of Selective Service records transferred to the Office of Selective Service Records with a provision for penalties for violations thereof.

HARRY S. TRUMAN

NOTE: On March 31 the President approved an act providing for the establishment of an Office of Selective Service Records (61 Stat. 31).

55 Letter to Members of the Advisory Committee on the Merchant Marine. *March 11, 1947*

Dear Mr. —————:

As an aftermath of the war, the United States faces critical problems in connection with the construction, modernization, and maintenance of an adequate fleet of passenger and freight vessels. With no new passenger liners and few cargo vessels scheduled to be built in the immediate future, the Nation is not assured of the existence of a balanced and modern merchant fleet. This is a matter that concerns not only our commerce and trade, but our national security as well.

Even before the war, we had few passenger vessels. When we entered the war, we shifted to the construction of mass-produced cargo ships, in order to carry America's great production of war material overseas. We used all our pre-war passenger vessels, one-third of which were more than 20 years old, as transports or fleet auxiliaries. Some of these were sunk or badly damaged, and many others were so drastically altered for war use that their complete reconversion to peacetime needs it not economically justified.

Although our present need is primarily for passenger ships, our ship construction program as a whole merits careful consideration. As an important element of national security in connection with preparation for expansion in case of emergency it is essential that shipbuilding skills be maintained by shipbuilders through an orderly replacement program of all types of vessels. Latest technological developments must be incorporated into our future cargo and combination cargo-and-passenger vessels, as well as into passenger liners, if the United States is to maintain a well-balanced modern merchant fleet to meet trade as well as security requirements.

I feel that the whole problem should be carefully studied in all its phases by a group of citizens equipped by background and training to counsel the Government and assist it in formulating a program to strengthen our merchant marine. Accordingly, I have established an Advisory Committee on the Merchant Marine, and ask you to serve upon it. The Committee should meet with representatives of the Navy Department, the United States Maritime Commission, and the leading authorities in the ship operation and shipbuilding industries. After studying the problem, the Committee should present for my consideration its recommendations as to the number and types of merchant vessels to be constructed annually under a stable, long-range program, as well as any other recommendations that the Committee feels will prove helpful. Its findings will assist me in developing a sound merchant marine policy and in formulating proposals to the Congress for any necessary legislation. The heads of the executive departments and agencies concerned stand ready to give you all possible aid.

Sincerely yours,

HARRY S. TRUMAN

NOTE: This is the text of identical letters addressed to the following appointees to the Advisory Committee: K. T. Keller, President, Chrysler Corp., Detroit, Mich.; Marion B. Folsom, Vice Chairman, Business Advisory Council for the Department of Commerce, and Treasurer, Eastman Kodak Co., Rochester, N.Y.; Andrew W. Robertson, Chairman

of the Board, Westinghouse Electric Corp., Pittsburgh, Pa.; James B. Black, President, Pacific Gas & Electric Co., San Francisco, Calif.; and Vice Adm. Edward L. Cochrane, formerly Chief, Bureau of Ships, U.S. Navy, and President, The Society of Naval Architects and Marine Engineers. Mr. Keller was appointed Chairman, and Mr. Folsom, Vice Chairman of the Committee.

The letter and the list of appointees were part of a White House release announcing that the President had that day established the Advisory Committee on the Merchant Marine.

56 Special Message to the Congress on Greece and Turkey: The Truman Doctrine. *March* 12, 1947

[As delivered in person before a joint session]

Mr. President, Mr. Speaker, Members of the Congress of the United States:

The gravity of the situation which confronts the world today necessitates my appearance before a joint session of the Congress.

The foreign policy and the national security of this country are involved.

One aspect of the present situation, which I present to you at this time for your consideration and decision, concerns Greece and Turkey.

The United States has received from the Greek Government an urgent appeal for financial and economic assistance. Preliminary reports from the American Economic Mission now in Greece and reports from the American Ambassador in Greece corroborate the statement of the Greek Government that assistance is imperative if Greece is to survive as a free nation.

I do not believe that the American people and the Congress wish to turn a deaf ear to the appeal of the Greek Government.

Greece is not a rich country. Lack of sufficient natural resources has always forced the Greek people to work hard to make both ends meet. Since 1940, this industrious, peace loving country has suf-

fered invasion, four years of cruel enemy occupation, and bitter internal strife.

When forces of liberation entered Greece they found that the retreating Germans had destroyed virtually all the railways, roads, port facilities, communications, and merchant marine. More than a thousand villages had been burned. Eighty-five percent of the children were tubercular. Livestock, poultry, and draft animals had almost disappeared. Inflation had wiped out practically all savings.

As a result of these tragic conditions, a militant minority, exploiting human want and misery, was able to create political chaos which, until now, has made economic recovery impossible.

Greece is today without funds to finance the importation of those goods which are essential to bare subsistence. Under these circumstances the people of Greece cannot make progress in solving their problems of reconstruction. Greece is in desperate need of financial and economic assistance to enable it to resume purchases of food, clothing, fuel and seeds. These are indispensable for the subsistence of its people and are obtainable only from abroad. Greece must have help to import the goods necessary to restore

176

internal order and security so essential for economic and political recovery.

The Greek Government has also asked for the assistance of experienced American administrators, economists and technicians to insure that the financial and other aid given to Greece shall be used effectively in creating a stable and self-sustaining economy and in improving its public administration.

The very existence of the Greek state is today threatened by the terrorist activities of several thousand armed men, led by Communists, who defy the government's authority at a number of points, particularly along the northern boundaries. A Commission appointed by the United Nations Security Council is at present investigating disturbed conditions in northern Greece and alleged border violations along the frontier between Greece on the one hand and Albania, Bulgaria, and Yugoslavia on the other.

Meanwhile, the Greek Government is unable to cope with the situation. The Greek army is small and poorly equipped. It needs supplies and equipment if it is to restore authority to the government throughout Greek territory.

Greece must have assistance if it is to become a self-supporting and self-respecting democracy.

The United States must supply this assistance. We have already extended to Greece certain types of relief and economic aid but these are inadequate.

There is no other country to which democratic Greece can turn.

No other nation is willing and able to provide the necessary support for a democratic Greek government.

The British Government, which has been helping Greece, can give no further financial or economic aid after March 31. Great Britain finds itself under the necessity of reducing or liquidating its commitments in several parts of the world, including Greece.

We have considered how the United Nations might assist in this crisis. But the situation is an urgent one requiring immediate action, and the United Nations and its related organizations are not in a position to extend help of the kind that is required.

It is important to note that the Greek Government has asked for our aid in utilizing effectively the financial and other assistance we may give to Greece, and in improving its public administration. It is of the utmost importance that we supervise the use of any funds made available to Greece, in such a manner that each dollar spent will count toward making Greece self-supporting, and will help to build an economy in which a healthy democracy can flourish.

No government is perfect. One of the chief virtues of a democracy, however, is that its defects are always visible and under democratic processes can be pointed out and corrected. The government of Greece is not perfect. Nevertheless it represents 85 percent of the members of the Greek Parliament who were chosen in an election last year. Foreign observers, including 692 Americans, considered this election to be a fair expression of the views of the Greek people.

The Greek Government has been operating in an atmosphere of chaos and extremism. It has made mistakes. The extension of aid by this country does not mean that the United States condones everything that the Greek Government has done or will do. We have condemned in the past, and we condemn now, extremist measures of the right or the left. We have in the past advised tolerance, and we advise tolerance now.

Greece's neighbor, Turkey, also deserves our attention.

The future of Turkey as an independent and economically sound state is clearly no less important to the freedom-loving peoples of the world than the future of Greece. The circumstances in which Turkey finds itself today are considerably different from those of Greece. Turkey has been spared the disasters that have beset Greece. And during the war, the United States and Great Britain furnished Turkey with material aid.

Nevertheless, Turkey now needs our support.

Since the war Turkey has sought additional financial assistance from Great Britain and the United States for the purpose of effecting that modernization necessary for the maintenance of its national integrity.

That integrity is essential to the preservation of order in the Middle East.

The British Government has informed us that, owing to its own difficulties, it can no longer extend financial or economic aid to Turkey.

As in the case of Greece, if Turkey is to have the assistance it needs, the United States must supply it. We are the only country able to provide that help.

I am fully aware of the broad implications involved if the United States extends assistance to Greece and Turkey, and I shall discuss these implications with you at this time.

One of the primary objectives of the foreign policy of the United States is the creation of conditions in which we and other nations will be able to work out a way of life free from coercion. This was a fundamental issue in the war with Germany and Japan. Our victory was won over countries which sought to impose their will, and their way of life, upon other nations.

To ensure the peaceful development of nations, free from coercion, the United States has taken a leading part in establishing the United Nations. The United Nations is designed to make possible lasting freedom and independence for all its members. We shall not realize our objectives, however, unless we are willing to help free peoples to maintain their free institutions and their national integrity against aggressive movements that seek to impose upon them totalitarian regimes. This is no more than a frank recognition that totalitarian regimes imposed upon free peoples, by direct or indirect aggression, undermine the foundations of international peace and hence the security of the United States.

The peoples of a number of countries of the world have recently had totalitarian regimes forced upon them against their will. The Government of the United States has made frequent protests against coercion and intimidation, in violation of the Yalta agreement, in Poland, Rumania, and Bulgaria. I must also state that in a number of other countries there have been similar developments.

At the present moment in world history nearly every nation must choose between alternative ways of life. The choice is too often not a free one.

One way of life is based upon the will of the majority, and is distinguished by free institutions, representative government, free elections, guarantees of individual liberty, freedom of speech and religion, and freedom from political oppression.

The second way of life is based upon the will of a minority forcibly imposed upon the majority. It relies upon terror and oppression, a controlled press and radio, fixed elections, and the suppression of personal freedoms.

I believe that it must be the policy of the United States to support free peoples who are resisting attempted subjugation by armed minorities or by outside pressures.

I believe that we must assist free peoples to work out their own destinies in their own way.

I believe that our help should be primarily through economic and financial aid which is essential to economic stability and orderly political processes.

The world is not static, and the *status quo* is not sacred. But we cannot allow changes in the *status quo* in violation of the Charter of the United Nations by such methods as coercion, or by such subterfuges as political infiltration. In helping free and independent nations to maintain their freedom, the United States will be giving effect to the principles of the Charter of the United Nations.

It is necessary only to glance at a map to realize that the survival and integrity of the Greek nation are of grave importance in a much wider situation. If Greece should fall under the control of an armed minority, the effect upon its neighbor, Turkey, would be immediate and serious. Confusion and disorder might well spread throughout the entire Middle East.

Moreover, the disappearance of Greece as an independent state would have a profound effect upon those countries in Europe whose peoples are struggling against great difficulties to maintain their freedoms and their independence while they repair the damages of war.

It would be an unspeakable tragedy if these countries, which have struggled so long against overwhelming odds, should lose that victory for which they sacrificed so much. Collapse of free institutions and loss of independence would be disastrous not only for them but for the world. Discouragement and possibly failure would quickly be the lot of neighboring peoples striving to maintain their freedom and independence.

Should we fail to aid Greece and Turkey in this fateful hour, the effect will be far reaching to the West as well as to the East.

We must take immediate and resolute action.

I therefore ask the Congress to provide authority for assistance to Greece and Turkey in the amount of $400,000,000 for the period ending June 30, 1948. In requesting these funds, I have taken into consideration the maximum amount of relief assistance which would be furnished to Greece out of the $350,000,000 which I recently requested that the Congress authorize for the prevention of starvation and suffering in countries devastated by the war.

In addition to funds, I ask the Congress to authorize the detail of American civilian and military personnel to Greece and Turkey, at the request of those countries, to assist in the tasks of reconstruction, and for the purpose of supervising the use of such financial and material assistance as may be furnished. I recommend that authority also be provided for the instruction and training of selected Greek and Turkish personnel.

Finally, I ask that the Congress provide authority which will permit the speediest and most effective use, in terms of needed commodities, supplies, and equipment, of such funds as may be authorized.

If further funds, or further authority, should be needed for the purposes indicated in this message, I shall not hesitate to bring the situation before the Congress. On this subject the Executive and Legislative branches of the Government must work together.

This is a serious course upon which we embark.

I would not recommend it except that the alternative is much more serious.

The United States contributed $341,000,-000,000 toward winning World War II. This is an investment in world freedom and world peace.

The assistance that I am recommending for Greece and Turkey amounts to little more than $1/10$ of 1 percent of this investment. It is only common sense that we should safeguard this investment and make sure that it was not in vain.

The seeds of totalitarian regimes are nurtured by misery and want. They spread and grow in the evil soil of poverty and strife. They reach their full growth when the hope of a people for a better life has died.

We must keep that hope alive.

The free peoples of the world look to us for support in maintaining their freedoms.

If we falter in our leadership, we may endanger the peace of the world—and we shall surely endanger the welfare of this Nation.

Great responsibilities have been placed upon us by the swift movement of events.

I am confident that the Congress will face these responsibilities squarely.

NOTE: For the President's statement upon signing the bill endorsing the Truman Doctrine, see Item 100.

57 Statement by the President Concerning Greek Reaction to His Message. *March* 15, 1947

I HAVE just received two warm and appreciative messages from Greece, one from Prime Minister Maximos and one from Mr. Themistocles Sophoulis, leader of the Parliamentary Opposition. Both of these messages welcome the prospect of the kind of American assistance which I recently requested Congress to authorize, and pledge the wholehearted support of the Greek people in devoting any aid that may be forthcoming to the purpose of constructive rehabilitation and the cause of peace and freedom. These two statements bear witness to the fact that all of the Greek Parliament, including the Opposition as well as those parties now represented in the Coalition cabinet, are prepared to cooperate unreservedly with the United States Government in its desire to assist Greece in restoring those basic conditions of economic stability and internal order which will allow the Greek people to build their future in peace and security.

I sincerely hope that these evidences of good will mark the beginning of a happier era for Greece, in which all loyal citizens will contribute their share toward the restoration of a country of whose democratic history they may be proud. It is also my profound hope that those Greeks who have taken up arms against their government will accept with confidence the amnesty which the Greek Government is extending to all except those guilty of crimes against the common law. The Greek people, aware of the sympathetic interest of the American people, will, I am sure, rally their strength to vitalize their national life, forgetting past excesses and looking courageously toward a hopeful future.

NOTE: The messages to the President from Demetrios Maximos, Prime Minister of Greece, and Themistocles Sophoulis, the leader of the Opposition Committee, were released with the President's statement.

58 Special Message to the Congress on Export Controls.
March 19, 1947

To the Congress of the United States:

In my message to the Congress on January 31, 1947, concerning the extension of specified parts of the Second War Powers Act, I stated that it was desirable to delay any communication on the subject of the control of this country's exports until it became clear whether or not an extension of such controls would be necessary, beyond June 30, 1947.

Further review of domestic and world supplies has now convinced me that this Government must continue its control over the export of products in critically short supply here and abroad, in order to protect the economy of the United States as well as to discharge our international responsibilities. The situation, although essentially temporary in character, will certainly remain acute for some time to come.

As a result of the war, many nations have been stripped of essential supplies and their productive capacity has been curtailed. Foreign demands for these supplies are therefore extremely large. Prices of many commodities in other countries are far above present levels in the United States. Uncontrolled exports of food products would result in a marked increase in the already substantial burden of living costs borne by the American people. Unlimited export of feeds, seeds and fertilizers would make extremely difficult the achievement of the food production goals which we have asked American farmers to meet and would increase the cost of production of farm products.

This country is the great undamaged center of industrial production to which the whole world looks for materials of every kind. Our steel, lumber, building materials, industrial chemicals and many other basic industrial commodities are sought throughout the world. Shortages of many of these commodities restrict our own domestic production of other essential products. Unrestrained export would inevitably limit the level of our own industrial production and employment. Furthermore, there are instances in which we wish to direct exports to those countries which produce commodities essential to our own economy. Thus, limited amounts of equipment have been directed to certain countries to increase the production of tin, hard fibres, sugar, and fats and oils.

Serious as would be the effect of unlimited and completely undirected exports upon a nation still troubled by many shortages, our domestic problems are not the only ones which lead me to urge upon the Congress a further extension of export controls. The United States has become a nation with world-wide responsibilities. During a period of world shortages, the distribution of this country's exports has serious international significance. If we retain the ability to channel commercial exports of critically scarce materials, we can permit export of these products to countries whose need is greatest while still protecting the United States from excessive export drains. Our international responsibilities cannot be fulfilled without this machinery. In its absence, foreign purchasing would tend to be concentrated on those commodities in greatest world shortage. Not only would our domestic supply and price structure be seriously affected, but the commodities would go to destinations where the need is comparatively less pressing.

Furthermore, we have granted loans and other monetary aid to nations whose existence must be preserved. These loans will accomplish their purpose only if the recipient nations are able to obtain critically needed supplies from this country. Export control is an important instrument in carrying out the purpose of these loan programs.

The record clearly shows that this authority over exports has been exercised in the past only with respect to those commodities in critically short supply and that, as rapidly as the supply situation has improved, commodities have been removed from control. The list of items subject to export control has been reduced from a wartime peak of over 3,000 to approximately 725 on October 1, 1946, and approximately 500 at the present time. We will continue to remove export controls as rapidly as the supply situation permits. I look forward to the day when the United States and other countries can remove these interferences to the free flow of commodities in world trade. But the danger of immediate and complete decon-

trol in the face of continuing domestic and world scarcities is too great for this nation to undertake at this time.

I therefore, recommend that the authority derived from the Export Control Act be extended for a period of one year beyond its present expiration date, June 30, 1947. It is essential that this extension be made well in advance of this date. Delay would prove unsettling to business and would handicap the planning and execution of our food and other export programs. Effective administration of the export control orders requires the assurance of continuity in operations. I urge upon the Congress prompt action in extending this authority.

HARRY S. TRUMAN

NOTE: An extension to July 15, 1947, of certain export controls was provided for by a joint resolution approved by the President on June 30, 1947 (61 Stat. 214), and a further extension to February 29, 1948, by the Second Decontrol Act of 1947, approved July 15, 1947 (61 Stat. 321).

59 Special Message to the Congress on U.S. Participation in the World Health Organization. *March* 21, 1947

To the Congress of the United States:

I am transmitting herewith for your consideration a suggested Joint Resolution providing for United States membership and participation in the World Health Organization. I also am enclosing a memorandum from the Secretary of State with reference to United States membership in the World Health Organization.

I have been impressed by the spirit of international good will and community of purpose which have characterized the development of the Constitution of this Organization. I am sure that it will make a substantial contribution to the improvement

of world health conditions through the years.

In view of the significance and urgency of international health problems, I consider it important that the United States join the World Health Organization as soon as possible. Therefore, I hope that the suggested Joint Resolution may have the early consideration of Congress.

HARRY S. TRUMAN

NOTE: The joint resolution was approved by the President on June 14, 1948 (62 Stat. 441).

Secretary Marshall's memorandum, enclosed with the President's message, is printed in House Document 177 (80th Cong., 1st sess.).

60 Statement by the President Upon Signing the Urgent Deficiency Appropriation Bill. *March 22, 1947*

I HAVE today approved the Urgent Deficiency Appropriation Bill, 1947 (H.R. 1968). This bill provides deficiency funds that I requested for such critically important activities as the Veterans Administration, the Office of Defense Transportation, and the Division of Disbursement of the Treasury. It also includes rescissions of funds for a number of agencies.

The bill also contains certain provisions affecting the functions of the Office of Temporary Controls and two of its constituent agencies—the Office of Price Administration and the Civilian Production Administration. In signing the bill I am mindful of its effect upon the rent control and sugar rationing programs which are so important to the welfare of the American people. I believe that a brief explanation of the bill is necessary so that the country may be fully aware of the danger in which it places these programs and what needs to be done to protect the public interest.

The Urgent Deficiency Bill requires the complete liquidation of the Office of Temporary Controls, which is now administering these programs, by June 30, 1947. The Congress has not, however, decided that rent control and sugar rationing are to end by that date. On the contrary, the Congress is now considering legislation to extend sugar rationing beyond March 31 and rent control beyond June 30, 1947.

Although I believe that the establishment of the Office of Temporary Controls was a prudent method of carrying through to the end these wartime controls and of effecting their rapid liquidation through keeping them in a temporary agency, my principal concern at this time is not what agency of the Government shall be entrusted with the administration of these programs. My present concern is that these programs be continued effectively until such time as they are no longer necessary.

I have already directed that the utmost economies be made in the administration of these programs, but I know it is not the intent of the Congress to cripple rent control and sugar rationing before the policy of the Congress is determined with regard to the extension of these programs. Accordingly, I have requested the Temporary Controls Administrator to continue these programs on an effective basis, with the expectation that the Congress will take further timely action on rent control and sugar rationing. Legislation to authorize continuation of these programs is now before the Congress and prompt action is urgently needed to insure continuity. If the programs are to be maintained with full effectiveness, the legislation should include authorization to make available to the new administering agencies for operating purposes such amounts as are necessary out of funds already appropriated.

The Urgent Deficiency Bill rescinds $2,400,000 from the appropriations to the Civilian Production Administration and requires the liquidation of that agency by June 30, 1947. In the light of this action, it is necessary for that agency to terminate its important activities in support of the Veterans' Emergency Housing Program by March 31, 1947. These functions include the limitation of nonresidential construction and increasing the production of critical building materials.

It is of the utmost importance that an effective housing program be continued. Moreover, it is clear that the Congress did not intend that these important functions be discontinued. Accordingly, I am issuing an order today transferring these functions to the Housing Expediter, who is authorized under existing law to carry them out. These few but essential controls will be continued

by him as long as they are necessary and will be fully enforced.

NOTE: As enacted, H.R. 1968 is Public Law 20, 80th Congress (61 Stat. 14).

61 Message to Secretary General Trygve Lie on the Anniversary of the United Nations First Meeting in the United States. *March 25, 1947*

ON THIS, the first anniversary of the first meeting in the United States of an organ of the United Nations, I send you greetings on behalf of the Government and people of the United States. The American people are deeply grateful that the Seat of the United Nations has been located in their country. They believe in the future of the United Nations with firm conviction. During its first year in the United States the United Nations has made a good beginning upon the great and difficult task of building a

peaceful world. The United States, in all its acts, seeks to add strength to the United Nations and to give effect to the principles and purposes of the United Nations Charter. May I add a personal word of thanks to you, Mr. Secretary General, for the strong and steadfast manner in which you have performed the high duty entrusted to you as the impartial servant of the United Nations and its 55 Member Countries in the cause of peace.

HARRY S. TRUMAN

62 The President's News Conference of *March 26, 1947*

THE PRESIDENT. [1.] Well gentlemen, this is the hundredth press conference that I have held. I have nothing special to tell you because all the announcements have all been made, but I thought you might have a question or two you might like to ask me so I'd let you in.

[2.] Q. Mr. President, what is the purpose of your conference today with the AFL leadership?

THE PRESIDENT. They asked for the conference, and I guess they will state what the purpose is when they get here.

[3.] Q. Mr. President, will former Ambassador Lane have your approval when he speaks out openly against the tragedy in Poland?

THE PRESIDENT. He is speaking for himself. My letter answers that question.[1]

[4.] Q. There is a report that the Ambassador of Honduras, Mr. Erwin, is being

_____

[1] On March 25 the White House released an exchange of letters between the President and Arthur Bliss Lane, Ambassador to Poland. Mr. Lane offered his resignation, effective March 31, stating his belief that he could do more for U.S.-Polish relations "if I should revert to the status of a private citizen and thus be enabled to speak and write openly, without being hampered by diplomatic convention, regarding the present tragedy in Poland." In accepting Mr. Lane's resignation the President said, "I am well aware of the difficulties which confronted you in the performance of your mission to Poland and appreciate the vigorous efforts which you made to persuade the Polish Provisional Government to fulfill its pledges with respect to the holding of free elections in Poland."

recalled. Anything you can say on that?

THE PRESIDENT. No comment.

[5.] Q. What about Mr. Patterson of Yugoslavia? Is he going back?

THE PRESIDENT. No.

Q. He isn't going back?

THE PRESIDENT. He isn't going back.

[6.] Q. Mr. President, is Mr. Pawley going back—Brazil—Mr. Pawley?

THE PRESIDENT. Who? Yes, I am sure he will go back.

[7.] Q. Mr. President, I would like to have your comment on us after a hundred conferences?

THE PRESIDENT. On you? [*Laughter*]

Q. Yes.

THE PRESIDENT. Well, you really put me on the spot, Miss May,[1] but I enjoy these press conferences immensely, and I want to say to you that I think you have been eminently fair to me ever since we started, and I can't tell you how much I appreciate it. I think everybody here has tried his best to give the facts as they are. I have no quarrel with you at all.

[8.] Q. Mr. President, do you intend to appoint successors soon to Mr. Lane and Mr. Patterson, or leave those posts vacant for the time being?

THE PRESIDENT. As soon as we possibly can, we will appoint successors, and I will announce those immediately so that you will have them right away.

Q. Mr. Patterson remaining in the diplomatic service, or is he dropping out?

THE PRESIDENT. Well, that is up to him. I don't know whether he is going to remain or not.

[9.] Q. Mr. President, can you tell us anything about your talk yesterday with Ambassador Pawley?

THE PRESIDENT. I had a very pleasant talk

---

[1] Mrs. May Craig of the Portland (Maine) Press Herald.

with Mr. Pawley on conditions in Brazil, and it is—that was about all there was to it. He was just making a report to me on conditions as they are—very optimistic report.

[10.] Q. Mr. President, both the Democratic and Republican leadership up on the Hill say that the Greek bill will not be through by the deadline, it is going to take some weeks longer. Do you favor a stopgap loan from the RFC or something——

THE PRESIDENT. Well, I sincerely hope that the Congress will act as promptly as possible and that it will not be necessary to have the stopgap.

Q. But if it doesn't get through?

THE PRESIDENT. Then we will take that matter up when it confronts us.

[11.] Q. Mr. President, Gael Sullivan got into something of an uproar while you were away, by proposing that the two national chairmen sign a statement on foreign policy. Had Mr. Sullivan consulted with you before he did that?

THE PRESIDENT. The first time I saw it was in the paper.

[12.] Q. Mr. President, in your talk with Senator Austin yesterday, can you say whether or not he is to present the view of your position and the view of this country on the Greek-Turkish situation in the U.N.?

THE PRESIDENT. I don't like to anticipate Senator Austin's speech. He is going to make a speech Friday, which will cover the whole situation.

[13.] Q. Mr. President, did you speak to Gael Sullivan about his letter?

THE PRESIDENT. He spoke to me about it.

Q. Afterward?

THE PRESIDENT. Afterward.

Q. Did you speak anything to him?

THE PRESIDENT. You had better ask Gael!

Q. Mr. President, does Gael have any intention of resigning now as executive director?

THE PRESIDENT. No, I think not.

[14.] Q. Mr. President, some Sherlock Holmes in the shoe factory—he is sending the shoes that they say you are going to bowl in—and from deducing something or other, he says you are a left-handed bowler. Is that correct?

THE PRESIDENT. Yes, I always was left-handed.

Q. How can the shoes——

THE PRESIDENT. I don't know what effect the shoes have on it. We'll find out, maybe, when they come.

[15.] Q. Mr. President, have you any thoughts now on prices generally?

THE PRESIDENT. I hope that prices will not continue to rise. I sincerely hope that business will see the handwriting on the wall and hold prices so there will be no spiral later.

Q. Would you like to see some of them reduce prices, Mr. President?

THE PRESIDENT. Yes I would. A great many of them have been doing that. For instance, International Harvester Company, and Ford, and one or two others—which I have seen in the paper.

[16.] Q. Mr. President, will you sign the portal-to-portal pay bill as it stands?

THE PRESIDENT. I will talk to you about that when it comes to me. I don't know what is in it and I don't know what will be in it until it gets to my desk. I will give you the answer when it comes.

[17.] Q. On that price thing once more, sir, you said "handwriting on the wall." Would you mind explaining that a little bit?

THE PRESIDENT. What was that?

Q. You said that you hoped some of the other business people would see the handwriting on the wall——

THE PRESIDENT. Well, I mean by that I don't want to see a spiral in prices which will cause inflation and which will cause another round of clamoring for wage in-

creases. It just never stops, unless we can stop it now.

Q. Are you concerned with the price rises?

THE PRESIDENT. I have been concerned all along.

Q. Were you concerned last year when you asked them to continue price control, Mr. President?

THE PRESIDENT. Yes, of course. That's the reason I asked for it. The situation, I think, though, will build up along lines that will be for the best interests of the country. That is my opinion now. And the Economic Council is making a complete survey of the situation on which they will make a report to me very shortly.

Q. The price situation?

THE PRESIDENT. Yes.

[18.] Q. Are you concerned over the wage demands now pending, Mr. President?

THE PRESIDENT. I beg your pardon?

Q. Are you concerned over the wage demands now in negotiation?

THE PRESIDENT. Well, I think the negotiations are going forward in good shape. The settlement in the rubber situation did not cause an increase in prices, and I hope that the other negotiations will end up the same way.

[19.] Q. Mr. President, what do you think about actions like Congress in cutting off the salaries of persons appointed in the executive departments? Do you think that is proper procedure?

THE PRESIDENT. I never have thought so. But that bill hasn't reached me yet. It still has to pass the Senate.

Q. Mr. President, that bill is an appropriation bill, I suppose?

THE PRESIDENT. Yes, it is.

Q. And that—you didn't say so, but to veto an appropriation bill doesn't restore the amount of money, of course, does it?

THE PRESIDENT. Oh no, it has——

Q. Do you want to give us any instruction what you might—what might happen?

THE PRESIDENT. No, I would rather discuss that when the bill is before me. You see, it isn't—it hasn't passed——

Q. It hasn't passed?

THE PRESIDENT. —— it hasn't become a matter of legislation, and I don't like to comment on things that are pending in the Congress. Only one time that I made a comment on things pending in the Congress and that was when I suggested Congress should raise their salaries, if you remember, last year. [*Laughter*]

[20.] Q. Mr. President, was Secretary Schwellenbach speaking for the administration when he recommended outlawing the Communist Party?

THE PRESIDENT. I have no comment on that. He was speaking for himself, however. That is pending in Congress, and I will attend to that when it comes down before me.

[21.] Q. Mr. President, one of the big issues that is being debated ever since you made your speech to the joint Congress, which is now called the Truman Doctrine,[1] is the question of whether your policy for the United States will lead to peace or to war. I wondered if you had any comment to elaborate on that particular——

THE PRESIDENT. I think the speech speaks for itself. I think it was made very clear, that the speech was made hoping that it would contribute to peace.

[22.] Q. Mr. President, would your position on pending legislation prevent you from commenting on the tax reduction bill before the House today?

THE PRESIDENT. Well, there isn't any bill pending as yet. When it comes up here, I will comment on it. I have made comments on it in the Message, I think, on the State of the Union.

Reporter: Thank you, Mr. President.

NOTE: President Truman's one hundredth news conference was held in his office at the White House at 10:30 a.m. on Wednesday, March 26, 1947.

---

[1] Item 56.

---

63 Statement by the President on the Expiration of the Selective Training and Service Act. *March* 31, 1947

THE Selective Service System has rendered the Nation a service of incalculable value. Those who made possible its accomplishments during the emergency—the vast majority of whom served without compensation—deserve the country's gratitude.

The Selective Training and Service Act expires at midnight. Its records and personnel will be transferred to the newly created Office of Selective Service Records.

Since enactment of the Selective Training and Service Act September 16, 1940, the Selective Service System has furnished to the Armed Forces more than ten million men. Those fighting men, comprising approximately two-thirds of all our Armed Forces, were selected by local boards through the most democratic process ever created for the purpose.

But that only begins to indicate the accomplishments of the local boards and other units of the Selective Service System. For every man who was selected to fight, many others had to be selected to stay at home to make the guns and mold the bullets for the successful prosecution of the war. Others had to stay to secure the domestic economy and to care for the health and safety of the civilian nation. How well the process of Selective Service was carried out is recorded not alone by victories won on battlefields, but by the statistics showing the production figures in agriculture and industry—the highest in history.

I extend my heartfelt appreciation on be-

half of the Nation to the Selective Service System, not only to the unpaid officials but to the thousands of loyal clerks who have worked so faithfully through those long years.

64 Statement by the President Upon Signing the Sugar Control Extension Act. *March* 31, 1947

I AM TODAY signing the Sugar Control Extension Act of 1947 which continues through October 31, 1947, the authority to control the price, allocation and rationing, importation, and exportation of sugar and related materials. Through this legislation the Congress has recognized the urgent need of continuing this authority beyond March 31, 1947, and has taken action which to that extent is in the national interest.

It is necessary that I sign this measure in order to avoid any lapse in sugar distribution controls after March 31. I sign it with reluctance, however, in view of the fact that October 31 appears to be too early for the termination of sugar controls. This fact was recognized by many members in both Houses of the Congress, both in Committee and in debate.

As I explained in my message to the Congress on January 31, 1947, regarding the extension of certain powers granted in the Second War Powers Act, there is a continuing world shortage of sugar. While our supplies in 1947 will be larger than those available last year, they will still be substantially below prewar per capita supply and still further below estimated demand.

I should like to emphasize the fact that sugar supplies in the United States normally approach a low level early in the fall. If controls are ended on October 31, the situation may be as dangerous as if they had been allowed to lapse today.

In setting the October 31 termination

date, the Congress apparently assumed that supplies by that time might be materially larger than those now definitely in prospect. It is true that domestic sugar production is being greatly expanded, especially in our beet sugar areas, as a result of the Government's program to increase supplies, and that under the Commodity Credit Corporation's purchase program we shall obtain our share of the greatly increased Cuban production. However, we shall not benefit substantially by an increase in new crop supplies until early in 1948. In addition, normally large export producers, such as the Philippine Islands, Java, and Formosa, are still practically out of production as a result of war devastation. Recovery will be slow, although the favorable production factors for this year in those areas have been considered in allocation and rationing calculations.

Sugar controls are of concern not only to domestic producers and users but have international implications as well. As the purchaser of the Cuban sugar crop, this country acts as the agent of friendly nations to make sure that other countries as well as our own receive their fair share of the world's sugar supply. We must continue to fulfill our pledge of dealing fairly with other nations while guaranteeing to the American consumers the maximum amount that our share of total world supplies permits this year. A premature ending of controls over sugar would bring about a scramble of competing countries for the inadequate supplies now in prospect. A period of soaring sugar prices and unrestrained competition in the world market might, after a brief period of false prosperity, result in disastrous economic consequences for the sugar-producing countries.

In view of all these factors, the provisions in the bill originally reported out by the Senate Banking and Currency Committee for continuation of controls through March 31, 1948, with provision for earlier termination by the Secretary of Agriculture if the supply situation made such action possible, would have been preferable to the earlier mandatory termination date of this Act.

If it becomes apparent later in the year that hopes for supply increases are not materializing, and that discontinuance of sugar controls by October 31 would not be in the public interest, I shall ask the Congress to reconsider the present terminal date for sugar control authorization. Such action would be in accordance with the possibilities which were clearly recognized by members of the Congress in the course of debate on the current extension.

I have been informed that the appropriated funds available for continued sugar controls are inadequate to carry out these controls effectively for the rest of this fiscal year. No administrative agency can be expected to administer these controls without sufficient funds. The Congress should see to it that necessary financial provisions are made, both for the rest of this fiscal year and for the period of operation and liquidation in the next fiscal year.

NOTE: The Sugar Control Extension Act of 1947 is Public Law 30, 80th Congress (61 Stat. 35).

---

65 Special Message to the Congress Recommending Extension of Rent Controls. *April* 1, 1947

To the Congress of the United States:

Public Law 548 of the 79th Congress provides:

"On or before April 1, 1947, the President shall report to the Congress what, if any, commodities or classes of commodities, including housing accommodations, are in such critically short supply as to necessitate, in his judgment, the continuance of the powers granted by this Act as to them after June 30, 1947, together with his recommendations as to established departments or agencies of the Government (other than the Office of Price Administration) which should be charged with the administration of such powers."

On November 12, 1946, price controls were eliminated on all commodities except sugar, sugar solutions derived from sugar cane or sugar beets, corn syrup and corn sugar, blended syrups, and rough and milled rice. Since the Sugar Control Extension Act of 1947 has become law, it is unnecessary for me to repeat the views I have already expressed with respect to the subject matter of that Act.

Despite the rapid upswing in residential construction during 1946 the Nation is still faced with a critical housing shortage. Dwelling accommodations, particularly rental units, are still radically out of balance with demand. In 88 cities surveyed by the Bureau of Labor Statistics and the Bureau of the Census during 1946, vacancies in rental units were virtually non-existent. The vacancy rates in habitable accommodations for these cities ranged from zero to a maximum of one per cent with an average well below one-half of one per cent. Proper protection of millions of our American families requires that effective rent and eviction control be extended beyond June 30, 1947, for a further period of one year, and I so recommend.

As for the agency of the Government to administer rent controls, it was my original recommendation that the Office of Temporary Controls be assigned this responsibility. However, recent legislation requires the liquidation of that agency, and a bill now under consideration by the Senate would transfer these functions to the Housing Expediter. I raise no objection to this proposal.

HARRY S. TRUMAN

NOTE: On June 30 the President approved a bill providing for an extension of rent controls (61 Stat. 193). For his special message to Congress upon signing the act, see Item 131.

66   Statement by the President on the Death of the King of Greece. *April 1, 1947*

I AM GRIEVED by the news of the death of George II, King of the Hellenes, who had so recently returned to his country to share with the Greek people the heavy tasks of reconstruction following the ravages of enemy occupation. It is a satisfaction to me that, only a few weeks before his unexpected death, I assured His Majesty and Greece of continuing American interest in the welfare of our gallant ally.

67   The President's News Conference of *April 3, 1947*

THE PRESIDENT. Gentlemen, I have no particular announcements to make—just having a press conference for your edification. If you want to ask me questions, I will try to answer them if I can.

[1.]   Q. Mr. President, in the case of the impending telephone strike, do you have the power to seize the telephone industry?

THE PRESIDENT. I don't think so. I don't know about it for sure. We are having it looked up now.

Q. You are having——

THE PRESIDENT. The Labor Department is handling that.

Q. Will you seize it if you have the power, Mr. President?

THE PRESIDENT. Let's wait to see if conditions warrant that situation, then we will see what we ought to do.

[2.]   Q. In view of the possible delay in getting the Greek-Turkish bill through, is there any interim plan?

THE PRESIDENT. No, there is not.

[3.]   Q. Mr. President, is Henry Grady going to be Ambassador to India?

THE PRESIDENT. I can't answer that question. I don't know.

Q. Have you offered the job to him, sir?

THE PRESIDENT. I have not.

[4.]   Q. Mr. President, have you any reactions from last week's request for price cuts?

THE PRESIDENT. No. No concrete reaction that I know of.

Q. Mr. President, have you had any indication when your Board of Economic Advisers will have their report on the price situation?

THE PRESIDENT. They are working on it now. I don't know when they will have it ready.

[5.] Q. Mr. President, do you think that Mr. Kennelly's victory in Chicago is the beginning of a trend?

THE PRESIDENT. I think so. Mr. Reece didn't seem to think so, although he made that statement before the vote was had, that it would be a trend. But it wasn't a trend the way he wanted it!

[6.] Q. Mr. President, are you planning to bring Robert Moses into the Government in any capacity?

THE PRESIDENT. No.

Q. Or any foreign assignment, sir?

THE PRESIDENT. No.

[7.] Q. Mr. President, the—Secretary Snyder said you were revising current budget estimates. Can you make any estimate of the surplus this year?

THE PRESIDENT. I'm not—I haven't the figures ready yet. Whenever they are ready I will make my prediction.

Q. Have you any approximation?

THE PRESIDENT. No, not at the present time, until I have all the figures.

[8.] Q. Mr. President, what do Democrats do at Think Councils?

THE PRESIDENT. Just what anyone else does at Think Councils. They look over the situation from a Democratic viewpoint.

Q. Who invented the name?

THE PRESIDENT. Well, I don't know.

Q. I think Mr. Sullivan[1] told us that these were Thought Councils when he came——

Q. ——Thought Clinics.

Q. ——Thought Clinics—yes, that was his——

THE PRESIDENT. Thought Clinics—well, that's a good name for them! [*Laughter*]

[9.] Q. Will your speech Saturday night be a political speech, Mr. President?

THE PRESIDENT. Well, the speech will speak for itself, Bert,[1] when it comes out. I think that's the best way to analyze it. I will let you have a copy just as quick as anybody else. [*Laughter*]

[10.] Q. Mr. President, former Governor Earle of Pennsylvania released the text of a letter which he said he received from you, in which he said you were not worried about the danger of the Communist "bugaboo." Is that your opinion today?

THE PRESIDENT. I am not worried about the Communist Party taking over the Government of the United States, but I am against a person, whose loyalty is not to the Government of the United States, holding a Government job. They are entirely different things. I am not worried about this country ever going Communist. We have too much sense for that.

[11.] Q. Mr. President, how is the program for aiding southern Korea going forward? We understood that there would be something coming up, following the Greek-Turkish——

THE PRESIDENT. I have no information on the subject at the present time.

[12.] Q. Mr. President, have you selected a man to head the—to supervise extension of American aid to Greece?

THE PRESIDENT. No I haven't, because I haven't the authority yet to appoint anyone.

Q. Certain aid will go forward, regardless of the $400 million program, sir. Certain Greek funds are included under the 350 million——

THE PRESIDENT. That's true. I haven't selected the man to handle the 350 million. And that, too, hasn't passed the Congress.

Q. Mr. President, do you approve of the

---

[1] Gael Sullivan, Executive Director, Democratic National Committee.

[1] Bert Andrews of the New York Herald Tribune.

amendment which the Senate committee wrote into the Greek-Turkish bill today?

THE PRESIDENT. I haven't seen it. I will let you know about it when the bill comes up here.

[13.] Q. Mr. President, is Mr. Myron Taylor returning to Rome?

THE PRESIDENT. Not at the present time. If it is necessary for him to go back, he will.

[14.] Q. Mr. President, do you have any comment on the John L. Lewis charges against Krug?

THE PRESIDENT. No comment. Mr. Krug will answer that.

Q. You have no intention of removing Mr. Krug from office?

THE PRESIDENT. I certainly have not. Mr. Krug is an efficient public official.

[15.] Q. Mr. President, have you given any thought to grocery prices? I have been trying to—I am thinking about the——

THE PRESIDENT. I have given it no thought. Only when I go to pay my bill. [*Laughter*]

Q. For the housewives it would make a good story, that's the reason I asked——

THE PRESIDENT. I haven't given it any special thought. It goes along with the statement I made last week on general prices.

Q. Has Mrs. Truman complained to you about the price of groceries?

THE PRESIDENT. Yes, she has. She realizes it just as the housewife has.

[16.] Q. Mr. President, are there any further plans for your Canadian trip?

THE PRESIDENT. None. I will announce the plans whenever they are ready.

Q. Do you think that the trip might come up before Congress adjourns?

THE PRESIDENT. I don't know when it will come up, Smitty.[1] I will let you know in plenty of time so that you can get ready!

[17.] Q. Mr. President, can you make any comment on the progress of the foreign ministers conference in Moscow?

THE PRESIDENT. No, I have no comment.

[18.] Q. Has Mrs. Truman developed any good shopping ideas, Mr. President?

THE PRESIDENT. She has always had good shopping ideas. [*Laughter*]

[19.] Q. Mr. President, is there any possibility that Secretary Marshall will be coming home soon from Moscow?

THE PRESIDENT. I have no comment on that.

Reporter: Thank you, Mr. President.

THE PRESIDENT. Entirely welcome.

NOTE: President Truman's one hundred and first news conference was held in his office at the White House at 4 o'clock on Thursday afternoon, April 3, 1947.

[1] Merriman Smith of the United Press Associations.

68   Address at the Jefferson Day Dinner.
April 5, 1947

Mr. Speaker—to me you will always be Mr. Speaker—fellow Democrats:

Our meeting together this evening carries forward an old party custom. In this annual tribute to the memory of Thomas Jefferson, we, who are members of the party he founded—the Democratic Party—take great pride and feel deep satisfaction.

We know that as long as we remain free, the spirit of Thomas Jefferson lives in America. His spirit is the spirit of freedom. We are heartened by the knowledge that the light he kindled a century and a half ago shines today, in the United States. It shines even more strongly and steadily than in his time. What was then an untried faith is now a living reality.

But we know that no class, no party, no

nation, has a monopoly on Jefferson's principles. Out of the silence of oppressed peoples, out of the despair of those who have lost freedom, there comes to us an expression of longing. Repeated again and again, in many tongues, from many directions, it is a plea of men, women, and children for the freedom that Thomas Jefferson proclaimed as an inalienable right.

When we hear the cry for freedom arising from the shores beyond our own, we can take heart from the words of Thomas Jefferson. In his letter to President Monroe, urging the adoption of what we now know as the Monroe Doctrine, he wrote:

"Nor is the occasion to be slighted which this proposition offers of declaring our protest against the atrocious violations of the rights of nations by the interference of any one in the internal affairs of another."

We, like Jefferson, have witnessed atrocious violations of the rights of nations.

We, too, have regarded them as occasions not to be slighted.

We, too, have declared our protest.

We must make that protest effective by aiding those peoples whose freedoms are endangered by foreign pressures.

We must take a positive stand. It is no longer enough merely to say "we don't want war." We must act in time—ahead of time—to stamp out the smoldering beginnings of any conflict that may threaten to spread over the world.

We know how the fire starts. We have seen it before—aggression by the strong against the weak, openly by the use of armed force and secretly by infiltration. We know how the fire spreads. And we know how it ends.

Let us not underestimate the task before us. The burden of our responsibility today is greater, even considering the size and resources of our expanded Nation, than it was in the time of Jefferson and Monroe. For the peril to man's freedom that existed then exists now on a much smaller earth—an earth whose broad oceans have shrunk and whose natural protections have been taken away by new weapons of destruction.

What is the responsibility that we must assume?

Our responsibility is to stand guard before the edifice of lasting peace which, after so long a time, is at last being built.

That edifice is the United Nations.

The function of the United Nations is to quench the flames wherever they may break out; to watch throughout the world and extinguish every spark that comes from a difference between governments; to do this, if possible, through the machinery of peaceful arbitration, but to do it in any case. This is so, even if armed conflict must be prevented by the use of an international police force.

We believe that formula is sound and workable. Our faith in it is strong and resolute. The United Nations is man's hope of putting out, and keeping out, the fires of war for all time. In supporting the United Nations we must, when necessary, supplement its activities. By aiding free nations to maintain their freedom we strengthen the United Nations in the performance of its functions.

The foreign policy of this country transcends in importance any other question confronting us. It would be fatal if it were to become the subject of narrow political consideration.

Our foreign policy must not be wrecked on the rocks of partisanship.

United support of a policy that serves the interests of the Nation as a whole must be our aim.

I wish to commend the efforts of those members of both parties who have worked, side by side, to achieve this goal.

To meet the responsibilities placed upon

us today this Nation must be strong. A strong United States means a country that maintains a military power commensurate with its responsibilities. It means a country of sound domestic economy. It means a country that holds its place in the forefront of industrial production and continues its leadership in creating the techniques of abundance. It means, most of all, a strong, united, confident people, clear in the knowledge of their country's destiny, unshaken and unshakable in their resolve to live in a world of free peoples at peace.

No matter how great our military potential may be, military potential alone is not enough. It is necessary that we maintain sufficient military strength to convince the world that we intend to meet our responsibilities.

Now, what of our domestic economy? How strong are we at home?

As we appraise our domestic scene—our mighty array of factories, mines, farms, producing at or near capacity, and with employment at an all time high—our doubts, if we had any, are put at rest. We are viewing a panorama of prosperity—such prosperity as no generation of Americans before us ever experienced.

You may recall hearing dire predictions, in the last year and a half—predictions that the United States was heading into an economic crackup, predictions of glutted markets, of a great deflationary plunge. It is significant that the most pessimistic cries of calamity came from men who had little confidence in our American system of free enterprise.

They were wrong in their predictions. They were wrong because they do not understand the strength of our system of free competitive enterprise. Under that system, each man is free to go where he likes, to follow the calling of his choice, and to be rewarded in proportion to the productivity of the effort or the property he contributes. Insofar as we insure that each individual has the opportunity and inducement to make the largest contribution he can to this country's total production, we not only strengthen our Nation against any possible encroachments, but we also set an example to all other peoples of the desirability of free government in the economic as well as the political sense.

Our country's financial stamina was tested in the recent war as it had never been tested before. But in spite of the tremendous cost of the war, we emerged with our financial leadership in the economic world greater than ever before. Beyond making our best effort to eliminate waste in the conduct of the war, the cost of the war was not a matter within our power to control. We emerged bearing a burden of debt, representing that cost, and what we do with that burden is a question of tremendous import, but fortunately it is a question that we have the power to decide for ourselves.

The first decision that we made was to reduce Federal Government spending as quickly as possible.

The extent of retrenchments by the Government is shown by the record.

In the fiscal year 1945 the Federal Government spent $100 billion. In 1946 we cut expenditures to $64 billion. In 1947 we have further reduced expenditures to an estimated figure of $42 billion. The budget for the next fiscal year, which I have sent to the Congress, totals $37.5 billion.

Not only have we greatly reduced expenditures, but we have made tremendous progress toward the elimination of deficits.

In the fiscal year 1945, the Federal Government had a deficit of over $53 billion. In the fiscal year 1946 it was in the red about $21 billion. But now we have worked our way into the black, and I am happy to be able to say tonight that for the present fiscal year 1947 we shall balance the budget and we shall have a surplus. That was done without any Republican help!

I am determined that stringent economy shall govern all peacetime operations of the Government.

When the several departments and agencies were called upon, a few months ago, to submit their requests for funds for the coming fiscal year, they were told of my determination.

They responded by eliminating many of their former activities. This was not enough. When the estimates were in, I went over them, making further substantial reductions. When I finished, these department estimates had been reduced by a total of some $7 billion under their original level.

I was warned by some that I was going too far. I was aware of the risk. But I was aware, too, of the greater risk of a weakened postwar financial structure. I knew that in the public interest, sacrifices of some Government services had to be made.

The result was a budget of $37.5 billion. That figure marked the borderline beyond which we could not reduce the activities of our Government without entering the area of false economy. In other words, further so-called "economies" would not have been economies at all. They would merely have meant curtailment of services that would cost our taxpayers—all taxpayers—more than the reduction in cost that appeared on the surface.

You, my fellow citizens, are properly cautious of false economy in your daily lives. If the foundation of your house needs repair, or if the roof leaks, you know that you are wasting money, not saving it, by failing to make that repair.

So with Government. If we abandon our work of reclamation, of soil conservation, of preserving our forests, of developing our water resources, we are wasting money, not saving it. If we cease our vigilance along the borders of our country and at our ports of entry, we are wasting money, not saving it. If we falsely economize by reducing the staff of men and women who audit tax returns, or who increase the country's productivity by settling labor disputes, we are wasting money, not saving it. If we cut down the effectiveness of our Armed Forces, we run the risk of wasting both money and lives.

Any substantial reduction of the 1948 Federal budget, as submitted to the Congress, must be clearly understood by the American people as a venture into false economy. To the extent that we countenance any such reduction, we shall weaken our own house by our refusal to keep it in basic repair. At best, this is poor judgment. At worst, it is an invitation to disaster.

The second decision we must make, affecting the strength and health of our economy, concerns the public debt. We must resolve to begin the long process of reducing that debt, which represents a large part of the cost of winning World War II. That debt amounts to almost $2,000 for every man, woman, and child in the United States.

In deciding whether we shall start substantial payment on the debt, or whether we shall reduce taxes instead, we are deciding a question which will affect the future of every one of us. Our decision will affect the number of jobs in the future, the wages men and women will earn, what those wages will buy, and how much our savings, our insurance, and our bonds will be worth.

We, as a Nation, are now having prosperous years. This is the time when we must start paying off the debt in earnest. When a man is earning good wages, and at the same time owes a lot of money, he is wise if he uses his excess income to pay off his debts.

He would be shortsighted if he cut his income just because he was not spending it all at the moment. When the people, through their Government, owe a lot of money—as we do today—it is the course of wisdom to make payment on our debt. It would be extremely shortsighted to cut down the Federal revenue without making a real effort toward debt reduction.

I recognize, frankly, that the present burden of taxation on our people is too heavy to be considered as permanent, and at a proper time I will support tax reduction and tax readjustment designed to reduce the burden and to adjust that burden to the needs of a peacetime economy.

In further evaluating the strength of our domestic economy, I must express to you my deep concern over the level of prices prevailing today. A system of free enterprise does not automatically work out its own adjustments without our giving thought to the process.

The main factor that can weaken our economy at this time is our own selfishness—the kind of selfishness which is now expressed in the form of unnecessarily high prices for many commodities and for many manufactured articles. These prices must be brought down if our entire economy is not to suffer.

With the exception of a very few items, all price controls have been removed. But freedom from such controls, like other freedoms, cannot be abused with impunity. A profound moral responsibility rests upon those citizens whose decisions have widespread effect on our markets—to put it simply, the responsibility of playing fair, of not going whole hog for profits. The alternative is inflation, industry priced out of the market and, eventually, men priced out of their jobs.

The world today looks to us for leadership.

The force of events makes it necessary that we assume that role.

This is a critical period of our national life. The process of adapting ourselves to the new concept of our world responsibility is naturally a difficult and painful one. The cost is necessarily great.

It is not our nature to shirk our obligations. We have a heritage that constitutes the greatest resource of this Nation. I call it the spirit and character of the American people.

We are the people who gave the world George Washington, Thomas Jefferson, Andrew Jackson, Abraham Lincoln, Woodrow Wilson, and Franklin D. Roosevelt.

We are a people who not only cherish freedom and defend it, if need be with our lives, but we also recognize the right of other men and other nations to share it.

While the struggle for the rights of man goes forward in other parts of the world, the free people of America cannot look on with easy detachment, with indifference to the outcome.

In our effort to make permanent the peace of the world, we have much to preserve—much to improve—and much to pioneer.

As we strive to reach the fulfillment of our quest we will do well to recall the words of Thomas Jefferson:

"I have sworn, upon the altar of God, eternal hostility against every form of tyranny over the mind of man."

NOTE: The President spoke at 10:30 a.m. at the Mayflower Hotel in Washington. His opening words "Mr. Speaker" referred to Representative Sam Rayburn of Texas, Minority Leader in the 80th Congress, who served as Speaker of the House of Representatives during the 76th, 77th, 78th, and 79th Congresses.

69 Statement by the President: The Diamond Anniversary of Arbor Day. *April 10, 1947*

SEVENTY-FIVE years ago the pioneer settlers of Nebraska dedicated a day to the planting of trees. That was the first Arbor Day. Since then the observance of Arbor Day has spread to every State in the Union and to many countries.

Arbor Day was established by Julius Sterling Morton, one-time United States Secretary of Agriculture, and lifelong advocate of tree planting. As its founder said, Arbor Day is a national observance that looks to the future rather than the past. The trees which start growing today, whether we plant them with our own hands or they are seeded by nature, are the trees that will provide the wood for industry, and beauty and recreation, for the next and succeeding generations.

The Diamond Anniversary of Arbor Day finds the Nation never more appreciative of the indispensable value of trees. There is evidence of this on every hand. Throughout the Nation the movement is spreading to keep America green, to prevent fires which needlessly and tragically destroy trees. Tree farming and tree growing by public and private agencies, and scientific management of our forests for permanent production, are gaining momentum. Only recently, in Washington, a great Forest Congress convened, the third such meeting in our history, bringing together representatives of agriculture, labor, industry, and government to consider the problems of our forests.

And we have today, without question, a very real forest problem. Once, when the Nation's vast forests seemed inexhaustible, we could afford to be lavish, even careless, with this great natural resource. Today, we are coming to think of trees as a crop which, with care and protection, can produce endless harvests of essential timber. The forests of the future will consist of trees we purposefully grow, rather than the trees we found here.

The products of the forests contributed mightily to building this Nation. They will be needed for our continued progress and prosperity. If this country is to be sure of an adequate supply of forest products, it must stop destructive cutting and unwise depletion, and build up timber growth.

The inspiration of Arbor Day is a challenge especially to those who have our forest lands under their stewardship—the farmers and other smaller woodland owners, who own, I am informed, 64 percent of our commercial forest lands, the forest industries who own 11 percent, and our Federal, State, and municipal governments which own 25 percent. To them all, the Nation looks for assurance that the productivity of our woodlands will reach an abundance adequate to our needs.

70 The President's News Conference of *April 10, 1947*

THE PRESIDENT. Gentlemen, I have no—and ladies—[*laughter*]—I have no special announcements to make to you this morning. If you have any questions you want to ask, I will try to answer them.

[1.] Q. Mr. President, can you tell us something about your economic survey with the Cabinet yesterday?

THE PRESIDENT. The meeting of the Cabinet on the quarterly review of the economic situation was a postponed meeting from the week before. There wasn't any special meeting for any special purpose. It was just simply a discussion of the situation, which is continuing.

[2.] Q. Mr. President, judging from your Saturday night speech,[1] you are concerned about higher prices still?

THE PRESIDENT. I have stated that emphatically here, I think—as emphatically as it can be said.

Q. Well, this reporter has been going around to some people who are a little afraid to reduce prices on their own as they want company against their competitors. After talking about the possibility of getting together a group of companies to reduce them, they are a little afraid of the antitrust laws, afraid they might be accused of combining for the purpose of reducing prices. Would the Department of Justice prosecute under the antitrust laws?

THE PRESIDENT. Yes, the Department of Justice could. But I think, if the Department of Justice is consulted about the meeting, that it wouldn't.

Q. Have you received any news from other companies that——

THE PRESIDENT. Yes. We have had telegrams from several companies, and I am very much gratified that they are making the attempt to reduce the high price structure.

[3.] Q. Mr. President, in that same speech you spoke about the budget being balanced this year.

THE PRESIDENT. That's right.

Q. What are your figures on that?

THE PRESIDENT. The figures are not—the total figures are not available. We know that there will be a surplus, and I will announce the amount just as soon as I have the exact figures.

[4.] Q. Mr. President, that question on

---

[1] Item 68.

the Department of Justice and the meeting, what you are suggesting, as I understand it, is that if a group came in and obtained consent from the Attorney General, they could then take combined action to reduce prices?

THE PRESIDENT. I think that can be done.

Q. Mr. President, on higher prices again, Mr. Nourse said before his meeting with you, that he considered the situation serious and that the administration so considered it. Do you contemplate taking any action in addition to appeals by—any executive action on prices?

THE PRESIDENT. We are surveying this situation, to see whether there is any action possible. You see, the price control law was repealed on the 30th day of last June, and an impossible price control bill was passed on the 25th of July which was not workable, and which came out just exactly as the veto message explained that it would come out. We have no real authority now, although we may—we are going to try to do everything we possibly can to meet the situation. That's what the discussion is for.

Q. Mr. President, still on prices, would you favor an increase in the ceiling on the veterans on-the-job training?

THE PRESIDENT. I haven't gone into that subject, but I think the veterans have been very liberally taken care of on that situation.

[5.] Q. Mr. President, what do you think of what John Hanes said yesterday, that there would be a surplus of 3 or 4 billion this fiscal year?

THE PRESIDENT. Is that the gentleman who had the center column in the New York Times this morning? [*Laughter*]

Q. I believe he was.

THE PRESIDENT. I wonder where he got his figures? It seems to me that he must have got his figures from the same place that Knutson got his $6 billion cut—I don't think from any reliable source.

[6.] Q. Mr. President, do you think that

the Joint Committee on the Economic Report has any responsibility for any of the tensions we now are coming up to?

THE PRESIDENT. I can't answer that question. I don't know.

[7.] Q. Mr. President, may I ask you a local question?

THE PRESIDENT. Sure.

Q. Would you care to say anything about the visit of Commissioner Young to your office yesterday morning?

THE PRESIDENT. He just came in to discuss administrative matters in the District, which he does once in a while. We had a very pleasant conversation on the situation in the District.

Q. He says you asked him to come up here on something that you wanted to tell him? It might make news.

THE PRESIDENT. I don't want to tell you anything about the conversation we had. It will come out later all right.

[8.] Q. Mr. President, have you a successor named yet to District Attorney Woll of Chicago?

THE PRESIDENT. No, not that I know of. I don't think it has been handed to me as yet.

[9.] Q. Mr. President, going back to the last question on the Economic Report, your Economic Report went to Congress and was rather well ignored, I thought. I am wondering whether you think it would be constructive if Congress would pay some attention to your Economic Report?

THE PRESIDENT. The reorganization bill in Congress was passed by it for that purpose.

[10.] Q. Mr. President, were you instructing the Department of Justice to entertain inquiries from American business on joint action cutting prices?

THE PRESIDENT. The matter is under discussion. I can give you an answer on that at a later date.

Q. Mr. President, what would be the safeguards against price fixing in that arrangement?

THE PRESIDENT. That is a matter that the smart legal boys will have to work out. There is one decision of the Supreme Court which places a restriction on a unanimous price cut, just the same as it does on a unanimous price rise, and that will have to be examined by the Attorney General before any decision can be made.

Q. Mr. President, did your economic experts find any evidence that prices are about to turn down?

THE PRESIDENT. They made some statements to the effect that some prices are likely to come down, and some have.

Q. Mr. President, are you in favor of reduction in the prices of foodstuffs as well as manufactured articles?

THE PRESIDENT. Certainly.

Q. Mr. President, are you in favor of a buyers' strike against high prices?

THE PRESIDENT. No I am not. I think a buyers' strike wouldn't help the situation at all.

Q. Mr. President, would you tell us why that is? That buyers' strike is something that is very popular with people. I would like to hear from you——

THE PRESIDENT. Well, the buyers' strike is just like any other sort of strike. It stops the economic machinery from working and that always throws a monkey wrench into the machinery. You know—none of these strikes that we had last year helped anybody—hurt the whole economy of the country.

Q. Mr. President, the Government buys enough materials—if it curtailed its purchases, would it affect the economy?

THE PRESIDENT. No, I don't think so. I think our purchases have been enormously curtailed. I know that is a fact.

Q. What about strikes this year, Mr. President?

THE PRESIDENT. Well, I hope the strikes this year will not have the same effect they did last year; and I am hoping for settlement of the proposed strikes this year.

Q. Mr. President, if high prices bring on an inability to buy, does——

THE PRESIDENT. That's a different thing.

Q. Does it have the same effect?

THE PRESIDENT. It would have the same effect as when a man can't sell his merchandise at his own price, he has to put them out at a price at which he can sell. That is supply and demand, if I know anything about free economy.

[11.] Q. Mr. President, going back to the question of the antitrust laws in group price reductions, do you think it is possible to make such reductions?

THE PRESIDENT. I hope it is possible. We are trying to find a way so that it will be possible. The Attorney General is working on it now.

Q. Would that have to be done by the manufacturers themselves, Mr. President?

THE PRESIDENT. I don't know anything about that. Have to go into the thing in detail. That is a matter for business itself to work out. Business wanted to be free of price control. They are free of price control. Now they will have to meet the situation.

Q. The Government itself, then, wouldn't have any machinery other than a moral request?

THE PRESIDENT. That's all. That's all.

[12.] Q. Mr. President, do you intend to make public the report of your Committee of Economic Advisers?

THE PRESIDENT. No. It isn't for publication.

[13.] Q. Mr. President, you specified receiving several telegrams from different companies. Would you care to specify what those companies were?

THE PRESIDENT. There were half a dozen

of them. Their names will be released later. I haven't them before me now.

[14.] Q. Mr. President, there has been some talk about you and Senator Taft going into a huddle on labor regulatory measures. Would you welcome such a conference?

THE PRESIDENT. I haven't been asked to go into such a conference.

[15.] Q. What about those telegrams? Are these from concerns that want to reduce prices? I didn't——

THE PRESIDENT. Yes. They were from concerns who have reduced prices as a result of the statement that was made here in the press conference last week and before.

Q. Mr. President, at the present moment, until this investigation is completed, you are pretty limited to moral persuasion, is that right?

THE PRESIDENT. That's right. That's right.

Q. What was that? We didn't hear.

THE PRESIDENT. He said I was limited to moral suasion on this thing. He is correct.

Q. Mr. President, in line with moral suasion, have you any intention of calling in any great business leaders, presenting the situation to them personally?

THE PRESIDENT. I have talked to a great many of them already.

Q. Personally?

THE PRESIDENT. Personally, yes.

Q. Whom have you talked to?

THE PRESIDENT. Well—that is my business. [*Laughter*]

Q. Mr. President, has any group of representative maufacturers proposed to the Government that the antitrust laws be so adjusted so that they——

THE PRESIDENT. I think some questions have been asked of the Attorney General.

Q. Mr. President, in the meantime, as I understand it, the responsibility is now on business?

THE PRESIDENT. What's that?

Q. Is the responsibility now on business?

THE PRESIDENT. Absolutely. Squarely on business. That is where they wanted it. They want free enterprise. They have got it. Now let's see if they will make it work.

Q. In your conversations with the business heads, did they make any request to cut prices, unless they have to stand wage boosts? Do they bring that into the——

THE PRESIDENT. No, that hasn't been brought into the subject——

Q. That is not tied up——

THE PRESIDENT. ——and the profits this year are, for the year 1947—have been very great.

Q. Mr. President, you made an interesting statement a moment ago, that responsibility is squarely on business. I wonder if we could put—have that read back and put it in quotes, sir?

THE PRESIDENT. I think you can handle it well enough without putting it in direct quotes. [*Laughter*] You ought to be able to handle that.

Q. Mr. President, you said 1947 profits. Do you mean 1947 or 1946?

THE PRESIDENT. 1946, and the first——

Q. And the first quarter of 1947?

THE PRESIDENT. ——the first quarter of 1947, and the whole of 1946, except the first quarter of 1946.

Q. How did you describe that—very large?

THE PRESIDENT. Very great profits.

Q. Mr. President, in view of these high profits and high prices, would that soon justify wage increases if they are not brought down?

THE PRESIDENT. Yes.

Q. Mr. President, how do you fit labor into the picture?

THE PRESIDENT. I have been trying to fit labor into the picture ever since 1945, when the war ended. You remember we called a labor-management conference to try to work these things out together. Didn't succeed very well. And we have been, ever since, trying to arrive at adjustments between labor and management so that everybody could have a fair deal. Everybody ought to have a fair deal on this situation. If we get a fair deal for everybody, why the country will be all right.

Q. Mr. President, did you say that wage increases—further wage increases would be justified if prices didn't come down?

THE PRESIDENT. Yes.

[16.] Q. Mr. President, your budget for the fiscal year 1948 would include an item of $160 million for keeping up the prices of foodstuffs on farm commodities?

THE PRESIDENT. That is correct. On a parity basis, that is.

Q. Is there any proposal to amend that?

THE PRESIDENT. It has been under consideration.

[17.] Q. Mr. President, are you also studying the matter of taxing away abnormal profits?

THE PRESIDENT. Well, if you remember, the excess profits tax was repealed, with the idea that it would help business, and it was repealed for that purpose. It did help business, and therefore I am inclined to think that business appreciates that help and will make every effort to meet this situation. At least, I hope so.

Q. I understand some show an increase up to 300 percent in profits.

THE PRESIDENT. I haven't seen the exact figures.

[18.] Q. Mr. President, can we take that to mean, sir, that you are suggesting you have under consideration amending the price support on agricultural commodities? Would that go to cotton, too, and wool?

THE PRESIDENT. The situation is being considered by the Congress. I don't know what action they are going to take on it, and I can't make any prophecies as to what action they will take. Your guess is as good as mine on that.

Q. Mr. President, would it be desirable for Congress to remove these supporting subsidies?

THE PRESIDENT. Well, we can't answer that. We can't answer that question until we find out what the world crop situation will be in the coming year. Depends altogether on what that situation is. If there are tremendous farm surpluses, we would be faced with the same conditions that we were in the past on that subject.

Q. Mr. President, wasn't the Government committed to support of farm prices for 2 years?

THE PRESIDENT. The Government is committed for 2 years after the war. That is, 2 years from the 31st day of last December.

Q. What you are talking about then now is, in answer to these questions, would it mean going back on that?

THE PRESIDENT. No. No. Can't go back on that commitment.

[19.] Q. Mr. President, a few weeks ago you said you didn't believe for a minute that there was going to be a recession. Do you still feel that way?

THE PRESIDENT. I feel that there is no necessity for a recession.

[20.] Q. Mr. President, all these questions show how concerned everybody is about high prices, and I wonder if——

THE PRESIDENT. That is true.

Q. ——there is any way you could say whether you, as President, have any concrete program——

THE PRESIDENT. The only concrete program I have has been put up to you right here. And we are surveying the situation now to find out just exactly what is in prospect, and then see what can be done about it. The repeal of price controls ended all control of the Government over prices.

Q. Mr. President, am I right to assume that you would like to restore price controls?

THE PRESIDENT. No. I have no desire to restore price controls. Not be feasible at the present time, because what we are trying to do now is get prices to come down to a reasonable point.

Q. Yes. If there was another way—somebody may rush forward with a price control act—proposal.

THE PRESIDENT. Well, I don't think—I don't think you would have——

Q. I was thinking, sir, that is what you were leading up to. Maybe I'm wrong.

THE PRESIDENT. No. No, no. I am not at all.

Q. How long would it take you to set up machinery, if you reinstituted price controls?

THE PRESIDENT. I don't think it is practicable to reinstitute price controls. I think people want to get away from controls. We want free enterprise in this country, but everybody has got to work at it, if we are going to have it.

[21.] Q. Mr. President, to get away from this subject for a moment, do you find the Senate's action on Lilienthal [1] very gratifying?

THE PRESIDENT. Yes indeed. I thought it was very satisfactory. I am sorry they delayed so long in taking it.

[22.] Q. Mr. President, if moral suasion doesn't work, then would you say that the Government will take some sort of action?

THE PRESIDENT. I am not ready to answer that question yet.

---

[1] On the previous day the Senate had confirmed David E. Lilienthal as Chairman of the Atomic Energy Commission.

Q. Mr. President, the Government has some fiscal controls they could exert, doesn't it?

THE PRESIDENT. Yes. We are investigating that situation now.

Q. Do you contemplate a message to Congress on this situation?

THE PRESIDENT. No, I do not, at the present time. Congress is getting plenty of messages from the general public, I think!

[23.] Q. Mr. President, I notice Senator Pepper was on the list last Saturday night. Would you care to comment on the status of Senator Pepper and Wallace as members in good standing of the Democratic Party?

THE PRESIDENT. Mr. Pepper was at the Democratic dinner the other night, and I received him very cordially. I have no desire to read anybody out of the Democratic Party.

Q. Does that go for Mr. Wallace too, Mr. President?

THE PRESIDENT. Certainly.

Q. Would you like to have him campaign on the Democratic ticket next year, Mr. President?

THE PRESIDENT. We will take care of that situation when it arises. I think they will probably campaign for the Democratic ticket.

[24.] Q. Any news, Mr. President, on Mr. Hannegan's possible retirement?

THE PRESIDENT. No.

Reporter: Thank you, Mr. President.

THE PRESIDENT. You're welcome.

NOTE: President Truman's one hundred and second news conference was held in his office at the White House at 10:30 a.m. on Thursday, April 10, 1947.

71   Remarks Broadcast as Part of a Franklin D. Roosevelt Memorial Program.   *April* 12, 1947

My fellow countrymen:

One year ago today I stood in silence beside a newly built tomb in the rose garden at Hyde Park. The tomb is a simple memorial of pure white marble. The inscription on it tells only that the man whose body lies there was born in 1882, and that he died in 1945.

But there is another and greater memorial to Franklin Delano Roosevelt which tells a fuller story. That story has been told to me a thousand times. I have seen it in the eyes, I have heard it in the words, and I have read it in the hearts of men and women all over the country. It has come to me from those whom I have met in my travels, on trains, on ships, and in the air; even in foreign countries. It is the natural human response of people everywhere to something in the character and personality of Franklin Roosevelt. It is a response to his understanding and his sympathy for suffering—an understanding and a sympathy that were deep and sincere because they were born of a tragic personal experience.

That experience made Franklin Roosevelt peculiarly sensitive not only to the sorrows and sufferings of others but also to their most cherished hopes and aspirations.

More impressive than marble monolith or anything printed on paper or carved in stone is the unending pilgrimage to that sheltered grave behind a high hemlock hedge above the Hudson. In the twelve months just passed a half million persons have stood where I stood a year ago today.

Time will confirm Franklin Roosevelt's outstanding place in history. It is not for me or for any of his contemporaries to attempt to measure his great stature or to estimate the impact of his words and his deeds upon the days of his years. Today, as I think back to my visit to his grave a year ago, it is uppermost in my mind that he was a great humanitarian—that he brought hope and courage to despairing hearts when fear was destroying the faith of the people—and that through the most terrible war in history he remained the symbol of fortitude, justice, and humanity.

Franklin Roosevelt rests in the spot he held dearest—his home. He died fighting for what he loved most—his country—its homes—its institutions—its people, sharing

their stubborn belief in freedom under a just God in whose Almighty beneficence rests the hope of the world this day.

His home and his grave are in the Nation's keeping. Let us bow together in a moment of silent tribute to his memory.

NOTE: The President spoke at 3:40 p.m. from his room in the Muehlebach Hotel in Kansas City, Mo., as part of a nationwide radio broadcast of the memorial service held at Hyde Park, N.Y. Mrs. Roosevelt and Henry Morgenthau, Jr., also participated from Hyde Park.

---

72 Special Message to the Congress on Control of Trade in Arms and Munitions of War.   *April 15, 1947*

To the Congress of the United States:

I transmit herewith a proposal for legislation to authorize supervision of the exportation of arms, ammunition, implements of war and related commodities, and the importation of arms, ammunition, and implements of war; to provide for the registration, under certain conditions, of manufacturers, exporters, importers, and certain dealers in munitions of war; and to provide for obtaining more adequate information concerning the international traffic in arms. The principal purpose of this proposal is to supersede the present provisions of law in Section 12 of the Neutrality Act of November 4, 1939. For the reasons outlined below it is believed that the Congress will agree that this section of the present law is particularly ineffective in dealing with current problems and that the Congress will wish to take prompt action to enact a new law along the lines proposed herein.

Section 12 of the Neutrality Act provides for: the establishment of a National Munitions Control Board; the administration of the provisions of that section by the Secretary of State; the registration of those engaged in the business of manufacturing, importing

or exporting arms, ammunition, and implements of war; the conditions under which export and import licenses may be issued; the reports which the National Munitions Control Board shall make to the Congress; and the determination by the President of what articles shall be considered arms, ammunition, and implements of war. Reports of the activities carried on by the Department of State pursuant to Section 12 for the years 1941 to 1946, inclusive, have been submitted to assist the Congress in its consideration of the legislation now suggested. Operations prior to 1941 are contained in the first to sixth Annual Reports of the National Munitions Control Board.

The proposed legislation contemplates continuing certain of the essential aspects of Section 12 of the Neutrality Act, particularly those pertaining to the administrative framework of the controls now exercised. However, it is different in its objective and it proposes a more flexible and efficient administration.

The present system of supervising this country's international traffic and trade in arms and munitions of war was conceived during a period of neutrality and with the view to remaining out of war. To achieve this end the successive Neutrality Acts of 1935, 1937, and 1939 were founded on the principle of impartiality toward all who would secure munitions from us regardless of their motives. As long as Section 12 of the Neutrality Act is in effect that requirement of impartiality is still the law and the Secretary of State must treat aggressor and aggrieved, peacemaker and troublemaker equally by granting every application for a license for the exportation of any arms, ammunition, or implements of war unless such action would be in violation of a treaty. Such a provision of law is no longer consistent with this country's commitments and requirements. We have committed ourselves to international cooperation through the United Nations. If this participation is to be fully effective this Government must have control over traffic in weapons which will permit us to act in accordance with our position in the United Nations and will be adaptable to changes in the international situation. Therefore, there must be new legal provisions enabling the exercise of discretion in the granting or rejecting of applications for export or import licenses for arms, ammunition, and implements of war and related items.

Weapons and implements of war are material weights in the balance of peace or war and we should not be legally bound to be indiscriminate in how they are placed in the scales. If war should ever again become imminent, it would be intolerable to find ourselves in our present position of being bound by our own legislation to give aid and support to any power which might later attack us. The proposed legislation is designed to permit in normal times of peace control over traffic in arms or other articles used to supply, directly or indirectly, a foreign military establishment, and in times of international crisis, to permit control over

any article the export of which would affect the security interests of the United States.

The exercise of discretion necessarily requires a revision of the administration of the controls presently in operation. The suggested legislation provides for the exercise of discretion in the types of licenses which may be used, and in determining the activities which may be subject to registration. The new proposal differs from Section 12 in as much as it permits the issuance of various types of licenses designed to take into account under what circumstances and in what quantities the export of the articles covered by the proposed bill should be subject to control. The purpose of this procedure is to permit freedom of trade in items of a purely commercial nature.

With regard to the registration requirements it should be noted that under the present law anyone engaged in manufacturing, exporting or importing any of the articles defined as arms, ammunition or implements of war must register with the Secretary of State, whether the item handled by that person is a battleship or merely a .38 caliber pistol. Under the new proposal the President upon recommendation of the National Munitions Control Board may determine when the manufacture, exportation or importation of any designated arms, ammunition, and implements of war shall require registration. This will mean that consideration may be given to the relative military significance of the item handled.

Another important change provides for obtaining fuller information which will be made available to the Congress in the reports of the National Munitions Control Board. With a number of agencies of this Government actively concerned with the disposal of arms and related items, the proposed legislation will allow for the amalgamation of all such information into one comprehensive report.

In addition to the foregoing, the proposed legislation differs from Section 12 of the Neutrality Act by providing export controls over two additional categories; namely, (1) articles especially designed for or customarily used only in the manufacture of arms, ammunition and implements of war and (2) articles exported for use, directly or indirectly, by a foreign military establishment.

With regard to item (1) it is certainly unsound to endeavor to regulate traffic in arms and ammunition and permit a free flow of the special machinery and tools used in the production of those arms and ammunition. In the absence of such a provision those countries from whom munitions are withheld would soon seek and obtain the equipment with which to supply themselves.

In the interest of world peace articles supplying a foreign military establishment cannot be left free from Government supervision so far as exports are concerned. Prior to the last war there were no provisions for controlling articles supplying foreign military establishments. This condition must not be allowed to recur. The proposed legislation is consistent with the international trade policies I outlined a short time ago at Waco, Texas. It is designed to protect the security interests and to carry out the foreign policy of the United States.

There is one other aspect of the suggested legislation which warrants comment. At present there is no provision for supervising the activities of those persons who do not manufacture, import or export arms, ammunition, and implements of war, but who, as free agents, buy or sell these items for export, or who obtain commissions or fees on contracts for manufacture or exportation of such items. These brokers assume none of the responsibilities of this important traffic, yet they promote it, often irresponsibly, and need only concern themselves with the profits to be found in the trade. It is scarcely fair to those who have the responsibility of carrying on what experience has shown to be a legitimate business, that such people should not be subject to regulation.

The international traffic in munitions and related items is a matter of major concern to us and to the other nations of the world. By such legislation as is now proposed for consideration by the Congress, the Government would be given powers essential for the safeguarding of its security interests in this international trade.

HARRY S. TRUMAN

NOTE: The draft bill, transmitted with the President's message, is printed in House Document 195 (80th Cong., 1st sess.).

73 Citations Accompanying Medal for Merit Awarded to Cordell Hull. *April 15, 1947*

CITATION TO ACCOMPANY THE AWARD OF

THE MEDAL FOR MERIT

TO

CORDELL HULL

CORDELL HULL, for exceptionally meritorious conduct in the performance of outstanding services to the United States as the Secretary of State from September 9,

1939 to December 6, 1941. With a high order of statesmanship based on deep loyalty to his country, Mr. Hull served with great distinction and selfless devotion during the years of crises and difficulties. He labored unceasingly through these years to create conditions for peace. At the same time, he endeavored to prepare the United States to meet the rising dangers from abroad. He contributed immensely to the Good Neighbor policy, which was to bear rich fruit in a tragic hour for the United States and the entire Western Hemisphere.

HARRY S. TRUMAN

CITATION TO ACCOMPANY THE AWARD OF

THE MEDAL FOR MERIT

TO

CORDELL HULL

CORDELL HULL, for exceptionally meritorious conduct in the performance of outstanding services to the United States as the Secretary of State from December 7, 1941

to November 30, 1944. After war came to the United States, Mr. Hull gave himself unsparingly to the war effort. He made diplomacy a powerful weapon in support of our armed strength. He made diplomacy also a potent instrument in laying the foundations of a stable and peaceful world order in the postwar era. As a tribute to his effective work in bringing about the establishment of an international organization, he is now known as the "Father of the United Nations."

HARRY S. TRUMAN

NOTE: The presentation was made by the President at 2:55 p.m. at the Naval Medical Center, Bethesda, Md., where Mr. Hull was a patient.

74   Remarks at a Meeting With the American Society of Newspaper Editors.   *April* 17, 1947

WELL, this looks just like a press conference! Remember last year? We had a meeting over in the East Room. I had hoped that today would be a bright and sunny one, for we were expecting to have it out here in the garden. Due to that fact, Mrs. Truman arranged to see about as many women as there are men here this afternoon. She is having two big teas over in the East Room, so we had to stay put. But it's so raw outside, I thought we would try to get everybody in here. A record for press conferences, I think, is about 314, and I think there's about that number here now.

Just not long ago I passed the hundredth press conference, and one of the lady reporters there—just about as scarce as the lady editors in here today—asked me what I thought of the press and my treatment. I was glad to tell her that I thought the press had been extremely kind to me, and that the young men who represent you gentlemen here had done a good job of reporting, in that they had conveyed the facts as nearly

and as truthfully as they could be conveyed under the circumstances, and that I was exceedingly happy that this country had a press that could say and do what it pleased under the law.

And it is a situation that does not prevail in very many countries. I don't know of any country where the head of a state is willing to submit himself to a gang of gentlemen—[*laughter*]—who ask him any sort of a question they please. I always try, so far as I am capable, to give a truthful answer, and as nearly as I can to state the facts.

Sometimes, due to things that are pending, it isn't possible to answer all the questions, and therefore the answer is a stilted one, it is "no comment." I don't have to use that very often, but whenever it is necessary, I do use it.

And then, sometimes, in some instances there are questions that are asked with the idea of political answers, which it hasn't been my policy to answer either. The political matters have to speak for themselves in actions, and they do, I think, most of the time.

But I am appreciative of the press this United States has, and of its present management. I think they have been as fair in stating the facts as it is possible for them to be. As I have said time and again here to the young men who represent you here in the White House, that I didn't care much what was said on the editorial page if I got the facts on the front page! And that has been the case. And that has been particularly true of this announcement of the foreign policy with regard to Greece and Turkey. I think the press has given the country a completely clear and fair statement of that situation, and the necessity for it.

I might say a word or two to you, off the record if I may, as to the development of that situation.

There has been a great deal of speculation as to the why and the wherefore, and how it came about—to quote one paper that I saw, "so suddenly." It didn't come about so suddenly.

Back about the 25th of April, if I remember correctly, in 1945, the Foreign Minister of Russia stopped by to make a courtesy call on me on his way to San Francisco, and he stated categorically what he expected to get out of San Francisco. And I told him, categorically, what he was going to get. And he made the statement when he went out of here that he had never been talked to in that manner by anybody before in his life. It did him good.

And I finally, if you remember, had to send Harry Hopkins to Moscow to get the final agreement on the Charter for the United Nations in a manner in which it would be fair to the whole world.

Then I had a trip to Potsdam a few months later, in July—if I remember correctly—and I had some very interesting experiences at that meeting of the so-called Big Three. Then Mr. Byrnes went to Paris—to Moscow and then to Paris, and Mr. Byrnes took along with him on that trip the Members of the Senate Foreign Relations Committee who had been assigned to be present at those negotiations—the Chairman, and the ranking members of the then minority.

And another thing I want to say to you gentlemen is that the fact that we have a bipartisan foreign policy is due to the fact that Cordell Hull, way back in the early part of his administration, began calling in the members of the Foreign Relations Committees of the House and the Senate and explaining to them the things that were before the country in foreign affairs; and he set out to them what the situation actually is.

That policy has been followed straight through ever since. And it is a very, very fine thing that it has, because it makes no difference how much we quarrel among ourselves here at home—that is a part of the game. Whenever a President is in office everybody has a right to throw mudballs at him if they want to, but if he can't dodge them it's too bad—[*laughter*]—but in the foreign policy it is necessary that this country present a solid front to the world on the policy which we want to pursue. The fact that these gentlemen had been to all these conferences gave them a viewpoint as to what we have to contend with in our negotiations.

It has been a most difficult 2 years in arriving at a solution of the problems with which the world is faced. I am sure that we are going to arrive at a proper solution of those problems, and we are going to live to see a long era of peace. I believe that as sincerely as I am standing here.

But the approach in our dealing—dealings with the Russian Government—I am being very frank with you—must be an approach that is right from our viewpoint, and we have got to stand for what we believe is right. And eventually they will come around and agree to it. They have, up to date. We tried going along with them as far as we possibly could, trying to please them. There is no way to please them. They deal from day to day, and what's done yesterday has no bearing on what's done today or tomorrow. We have to make up our mind what our policy is.

And after Mr. Byrnes came back from Moscow, we had a long conference with Mr. Byrnes and the members of the delegations who were with him. And we have made up our minds that we wanted only what is right. I stated frankly and candidly in Berlin, at the raising of the American flag over Berlin, that we had no desire for territory, we were not asking reparations, we only wanted peace, and a peace that would be continuing. We hoped that by getting a continuing peace and good will in the world, that our whole machine—which had been built as a result of the war and which had shown us what we could do—would, by that means, be a continuing—continuing in the process of operations so that our country could continue to be prosperous legally and helpfully to its neighbors. That is the only ambition or ideal that the country has had. We want world peace—a just peace for all concerned; and we want to see our home fires kept burning so we can meet the obligations created by this tremendous expenditure for war. And that is all we have in view.

Well, this situation continued in Paris and in the other conferences that we have had. And it has been a most difficult situation to meet. And finally, when Great Britain came to the point where she could no longer maintain the situation in Greece and Turkey, I called in the Foreign Relations Committees of the House and the Senate, and the leaders of both parties in the House and the Senate, and laid the facts before them.

And they agreed with me that we had reached a point where we had to state our position, and to meet the situation straight on—head on.

And that is how the situation developed. It wasn't a sudden proposition that happened in 5 minutes. It had been developing ever since the Germans surrendered. And it finally got to the point where we had to state our case to the world.

I tried to state it as clearly and fairly as I could to the Congress, and I say that you gentlemen presented the matter and the facts to the country in a manner which the country understood.

And I think the country is behind our foreign policy. And we must continue that bipartisan foreign policy for the welfare of ourselves and the welfare of the world, because our own welfare is mixed up in the welfare of the world as a whole. We no longer have all the distances, and the oceans, and things of that sort to guard us. I just had a gentleman in here this morning who had been around the world, I think it was in 78 hours elapsed time. I think the actual flying time was nearer a little over 68 hours.[1] Now Jules Verne was considered a very great liar when he said he could go round the world in 80 days. I think the time is coming when we will probably go round the world in 24 hours. And we have got to be prepared to meet that situation.

And you gentlemen can help us prepare to meet that situation. We must catch up morally and internationally with the machine age. We must catch up with it, and we must catch up with it in such a way as to create peace in the world, or it will destroy us and everybody else. And that we don't dare to contemplate.

---

[1] The President referred to Milton J. Reynolds who as navigator with Capt. William Odom, pilot, had completed a record-breaking, round-the-world flight on April 16.

Now I have been exceedingly frank with you gentlemen in stating the situation. I thought you were entitled to know what is in the mind of your President so far as foreign policy is concerned, and so far as the policy that has so-called suddenly developed—it hasn't suddenly developed, it has been developing over a period of years, in fact. And it is a policy that I think is for the welfare of this country. And the welfare of this country is wrapped up in the welfare of the whole world. And I—I appreciate highly, I can't tell you how much I do appreciate the fact that you have placed this matter before the country in a manner that they understood.

And I sincerely wish it were possible for me to hold a press conference with you, and answer a lot of questions, but we would be bootlegging on your hired men here. They don't like it! [*Laughter*]

[*At this point Wilbur Forrest, president of the Society, expressed appreciation to the President for the trouble and effort he had taken to meet with them. The President then resumed speaking.*]

I am very sorry because of the crowded conditions here, but as I explained to you, I didn't expect the weather to behave the way it did.

NOTE: The President spoke in his office at the White House at 3:45 p.m. The meeting is carried in the White House Official Reporter's records as the President's one hundred and third news conference.

75 Statement by the President on the Improved Budget Outlook. *April* 19, 1947

REVISED ESTIMATES now indicate that there will be a surplus of about $1.25 billion in the fiscal year 1947. This is a sharp improvement over the estimated deficit of $2.3 billion shown for fiscal 1947 in the Budget Document last January.

The improvement is due to two factors. First of all, we have been able to hold expenditures below our earlier expectations. While some items, such as refunds, terminal leave payments, and international payments will exceed the earlier estimates, these increases will be more than offset by reductions in the areas where economy is possible.

It is now estimated that expenditures will amount to about $41.25 billion in the fiscal year, or $1.25 billion lower than the estimate last January.

I have required the major departments of the Government to limit their expenditures to the fullest possible extent. Economies in the War and Navy Departments and in the Public Works expenditures of the Government have contributed substantially to the reduced estimate for expenditures.

The second factor accounting for the improved budgetary situation is that revenues have been running ahead of our earlier estimates. It now appears that receipts of the Government will amount to $42.5 billion in fiscal 1947—an increase of $2.3 billion above the January estimate. This has been due to the extraordinary high levels of economic activity that have been achieved—and also, I regret to say, to the sharp increase in prices that has taken place since the removal of controls. This has inflated the entire economic structure and currently is resulting in very sharply increased corporate profits.

Arrangements have been made to add a new section to the Daily Treasury Statement, effective immediately, comparing the budget estimates for this fiscal year with the actual figures to date each day. This comparison now shows a surplus for the fiscal year to April 15 of $2.6 billion, or more than $1 billion in excess of the new estimate for the entire fiscal year. This is because of an important concentration of expenditure in the last part of the fiscal year. For example, the heaviest payments of interest on the public debt are made in the month of June. Also, there will be large payments to the National Service Life Insurance Fund during the last part of the fiscal year. These and other items account for the difference between the surplus now shown in the Daily Treasury Statement and the expected surplus for the entire fiscal year.

I have stated on many occasions my firm resolve to balance the Budget and provide for reduction of the public debt. Now that we are achieving a balanced budget I want to emphasize the need for reducing the public debt to the fullest possible extent *now,* while times are good. A good start has been made on this objective by bringing the debt down from its alltime peak of almost $280 billion to the present level of $258 billion. The soundness of our policies in managing the debt is evident from the fact that almost all the reduction to date has occurred in the holdings of Federal securities by banks. But the most important thing we can do in debt management today is to continue to reduce the debt as rapidly as possible.

It is natural for taxpayers to wish to see taxes reduced. But to do this now would promote inflation, so that the benefits of any reduction would be largely dissipated.

76 Address in New York City at the Annual Luncheon of the Associated Press. *April* 21, 1947

Mr. President, ladies and gentlemen:

I appreciate most highly your cordial welcome. I appreciate the toast very much, and I thank you.

It is a very great pleasure for me to be here today, and I am going to make some statements which will affect the whole Nation, from this platform.

Freedom, in the American tradition, is always coupled with service. The American press—a free press—must never forget its obligation to the American people. Its treatment of the recent war and its discussion of our present foreign policy are examples of the finest effort of a free, responsible press. Without abandoning constructive criticism, the press, with rare exceptions, has carried the facts fully and fairly to the American people, so that they could be the judge.

We are now at a stage in our national economic life when the American press can render similar service.

The manner in which the American press makes clear to our citizens the problems that we face in maintaining our prosperity—and the reasons why it is essential to advance that prosperity—can help determine the future welfare of every family in the United States.

We all want continued and ever-increasing prosperity. It is a simple, normal, human desire to want to improve the standards of living of all our people. The desire for better living conditions is not the only reason, however, why continued prosperity in this country is essential.

We know that the freedom and integrity of the United States are safe only in a world of free peoples living at peace with their neighbors and engaging in free and friendly commerce. Hence, it is our policy to aid the free peoples of the world in their efforts to maintain their freedom.

Many of these peoples are confronted with the choice between totalitarianism and democracy. This decision has been forced upon them by the devastation of war which has so impoverished them that they are easy targets for external pressures and alien ideologies.

By providing economic assistance, by aiding in the tasks of reconstruction and rehabilitation, we can enable these countries to withstand the forces which so directly threaten their way of life and, ultimately, our own well-being. But we can provide the necessary assistance only if we ourselves remain prosperous.

And only if we maintain and increase our prosperity can we expect other countries to recognize the full merits of a free economy. We know that our system of private competitive enterprise has produced the highest standard of living the world has ever seen. By steadily raising this standard, we can demonstrate to all other nations the vitality and superiority of a free economy. Our system of private enterprise is now being tested before the world. If we can prove that it is more productive and more stable, more generous and more just than any other economic system, we shall have won the test.

But if we ignore the needs and shirk the responsibilities of our economy, we shall lose both our power to help others and our capacity to inspire others. Economic trouble in the United States would provide agitators with the opportunity they seek.

It is necessary that we develop a new realization of the size and strength of our economy. Our tremendous production during the war astounded the world. It was a phenomenon which no one thought could endure after hostilities ceased.

We are beginning to sense the fact, however, that our peacetime economy can not

only equal our wartime economy, but can surpass it.

The progress we have made is demonstrated by comparing the present time with the year 1929, which was the year of highest economic activity before the war.

The physical volume of industrial production is now 71 percent greater than it was in 1929. This is actual physical volume. It is not dollar value.

The physical volume of agricultural production is now 32 percent greater.

Civilian employment is now 10 million greater.

Our national income—including individuals and corporations—is now running at an annual rate of 176 billion, contrasted with only $83 billion in 1929.

Now, what have these great gains since 1929 meant to all of us?

In 1929 the average income of individuals in this country was $654, after taxes. Today it is $1,090, after taxes. Expressed in dollars of equal purchasing power, the increase has been from $825 in 1929 to $1,090 today. This means, on the average, for every man, woman, and child in the country, an increase of 32 percent in the power to buy goods and services with current income. This is the measure of the rise in our standard of living in less than one generation.

This is not a record of war production. It is an unparalleled record for peacetime goods and services, devoted to the needs and enjoyments of our people.

But I must say in all frankness that the economic skies are not entirely clear. One cloud is shadowing our economic future.

That cloud is caused by the sharp and rapid rise in prices.

Some say this cloud is certain to burst. They are sure of a recession or a depression. I do not share their belief that either of these is inevitable.

I believe that we, as a Nation, can prevent

this economic cloudburst. But it requires prompt, preventive steps.

Price increases have been felt by every American family. No one needs to tell them how much the cost of living has increased!

House furnishings, for example, have gone up 25 percent above the 1945 average.

Clothing has gone up 24 percent.

Food has risen 31 percent. Just before I came down here from the apartment upstairs, I was informed that the latest figures show that the food rise has been 36 percent!

Only rent, because it is under rent control, has remained practically stable.

Even more dangerous than the rise in retail prices is the sharp rise in wholesale prices since 1945. Here are examples:

Textiles—up 39 percent.

Farm products—up 40 percent.

Building materials—up 51 percent.

Food—up 53 percent.

Excessive wholesale prices are translated inevitably into higher retail prices. With higher and higher retail prices, families can buy less and less. Thus, excessive wholesale prices are hitting at the foundation of our prosperity, for we can be prosperous only when business activity is at its maximum.

There are some who say that prices are not too high, so long as buying stays at high levels.

From the human standpoint, I reject this argument.

It provides no answer to those living on fixed incomes, such as teachers, civil servants, and widows.

It provides no answer to those veterans who must pay substantially more for houses than they are able to afford.

It provides no answer to many millions of American families in every city, town, and rural area. Because of high prices, too many of these families are spending their meager savings and cashing their war bonds. They

are postponing necessary medical care. They have gone into debt in an amount 50 percent greater than a year ago. They are doing this, not through choice, but in order to make both ends meet. And most of these many millions have no one, except their Government, to speak for them.

In addition to this human aspect, it is a dangerous economic fallacy to say that prices are not too high, simply because people are still buying. A bridge designed to carry 10 tons is not safe with 15 tons on it even though it has not yet begun to cave in. The excess weight must be taken off the bridge in time. When it begins to crack, it is too late.

There is one sure formula for bringing on a recession or a depression: that is to maintain excessively high prices. Buying stops, production drops, unemployment sets in, prices collapse, profits vanish, businessmen fail.

That formula was tried after the First World War. And we paid for it. Between 1920 and 1921, annual national income fell by $18 billion. Industrial production dropped 23 percent. Unemployment increased by more than 4 million. Business failures more than doubled. Farm losses were appalling.

We must not choose that formula again.

If we are to avoid a recession we must act before it starts.

Prices must be brought down.

I speak first to those businessmen who have it within their power to reduce their prices.

Price reductions will bring more prosperity and profits in the long run. Lower prices will sustain further increase in the present high volume of sales and stimulate greater production. This Nation will grow only through increased productivity and more and more production. Higher prices for the same amount of goods will lead only to an artificially inflated economy, not a sound economy.

Present business conditions permit—in fact, they require—lower prices in many important fields.

Profits in the aggregate are breaking all records although profit margins vary greatly in individual cases. In 1946, corporate profits, after taxes, were 33 percent higher than in 1945. In the first quarter of 1947 they ran even higher. These figures are total figures and do not, of course, apply to every industry or every business.

I do not have to name the particular industries or the particular businesses. The men who run them know exactly which are included and which are not.

Our private enterprise system now has the responsibility for prices. During the war the Government shared that responsibility through the mechanism of price control. In the spring of 1946 I strongly recommended the continuation of price control so that we could attain an orderly withdrawal from control of prices as supply approached demand. A group saw fit to sabotage price control and represented to the public that prices would come down in a free market.

This has not taken place. On the contrary, prices rose sharply after controls were taken off and they have continued to rise. Private enterprise must display the leadership to make our free economy work by arresting this trend. Some price reductions have already shown that this leadership does exist. I commend what has been accomplished. I ask other business leaders to step forward in the same direction.

In the present economic situation, labor also has a responsibility.

I said, in January of this year, that excessive wage demands would threaten another inflationary wage-price spiral. I said also that some moderate wage increases were justified by economic or equitable considerations.

Since then, this counsel of moderation has generally been followed by wage earners and their leaders.

Some moderate wage adjustments have already been made this year—peacefully. Some others may be expected. Price adjustments and wage adjustments have been the traditional method of sustaining mass buying power and sharing the benefits of our increasing wealth. In our immensely productive economy, fair prices and good wages are the earmarks of American prosperity.

To wage earners and their leaders I repeat my counsel of moderation.

But it does not require much foresight to see that, if the cost of living does not come down, the size of wage demands might be magnified. Peaceful management-labor relations would be jeopardized. Bitterness and strife would become harder to avert.

This is another reason—and a most compelling one—for bringing prices and the cost of living down. This will help wage negotiations to proceed toward peaceful adjustments beneficial to all. Another important contribution in bringing about lower prices is increased productivity on the part of labor. Higher productivity results in greater production, which in turn leads to lower prices to the public.

After the war and postwar inflation it is difficult to find solutions fair to the consumer, fair to the worker, and fair to business. Employers and workers must both give to this task all their energies, good will, and understanding of their country's best interests.

In considering the high cost of living we must also examine prevailing food prices. The phenomenal world demand for farm products is maintaining farm prices at present levels. The unprecedented purchasing power of our own people and the needs of war-devastated countries abroad have combined to force farm products upward. The Government policy of supporting farm prices at 90 percent of parity is not the cause. Of the major food commodities potatoes are the only crop currently being given Government support. The support price of wheat, for example, is $1.82 a bushel, while wheat is currently selling at about $2.50 a bushel. The support price of hogs is $14.94 per hundred pounds. The recent price has been around $25.

Let me repeat: the Government policy of supporting farm prices is not the cause of prevailing high food prices.

Without the support program, farmers, mindful of the disastrous farm collapse shortly after World War I, would not have planted their tremendous recent crops. The consequence would have been smaller acreage, greater excess of demand over supply, and prices much higher than they are now. Because of the support program, the consumer is better off and the world food situation is more manageable.

With this sound bulwark against a repetition of the agricultural depression which started in 1920, farmers should continue their efforts to bring about maximum production.

I have been speaking about the role of businessmen, workers, and farmers in maintaining our present prosperity. The Government also has responsibilities. It is an axiom of good economics and good business that, in times of great inflationary pressures, taxes should not be reduced. Any surplus which the Treasury can secure should be applied to the reduction of the Federal debt. Reduction of the debt reduces the annual interest obligations of the Government and also tends to check inflationary forces. When we are over the hump of inflation, tax reduction will be feasible and proper. It should then be

extended first to those who need relief most.

Additional weapons which the Government possesses in its fight against inflation are rent control, export controls, and credit control.

Rent control is vitally necessary until construction costs are lower and the present acute housing shortage has been eased.

Export controls must be maintained to avoid price increases arising from uncontrolled foreign purchases in this country.

Credit control cannot be relaxed so long as prices are so high that many consumers must go into debt to make both ends meet. Making more money available on easier credit terms would only enable people to go into debt at a faster rate. Over-extension of credit to support over-extension of prices is fuel on the inflationary fires. It would help no one in the long run. It is in the tradition of "boom and bust." The Government should retain and use its measures for wise credit control.

The economic policies here discussed have not been devised hastily to meet a situation which has just appeared. I have been urging them for many months. The reiteration of these policies is made necessary by the acute situation existing today.

The responsibility of preserving our free enterprise system will continue to rest upon the joint efforts of business, labor, the farmers, and the Government.

There must be moderation on the part of business, forbearance on the part of labor, all-out effort on the part of the farmer, and wise guidance and action on the part of the Government.

There must be unity of effort and a willingness to cooperate in the achievement of our goal of a strong, stable economy.

The men and women here today, and the rest of the press of the Nation, have a great opportunity for service at this time. Not only must the facts be presented, but there must be brought home to our people the seriousness of the issue and the need for united effort for the good of all, rather than separate effort for the benefit of any single group.

I take comfort in the knowledge that the press of this country will accept this oppor-

tunity for service in the same high spirit which it has always served our Nation.

NOTE: The President spoke at 2 p.m. at the Waldorf-Astoria Hotel in New York City. His opening words "Mr. President" referred to Robert McLean, publisher of the Philadelphia Bulletin and president of the Associated Press, who served as chairman at the luncheon.

77   Veto of Resolution Limiting Application of Provisions of Law to Counsel of the Senate Committee To Investigate the National Defense Program.   *April 23, 1947*

[Released April 23, 1947.   Dated April 22, 1947]

To the Senate:

I am withholding my approval of the Resolution (S.J. Res. 97) "Limiting the application of provisions of Federal law to counsel employed under S. Res. 46."

S. Res. 46 created the Senate Special Committee to investigate the National Defense Program.

The purpose of the Resolution is to limit the application of certain provisions of existing law to counsel employed by the Special Committee. Mentioned specifically in the Resolution are sections 109 and 113 of the Criminal Code (18 U.S.C. 198 and 203). Section 109 of the Criminal Code forbids officers of the United States to aid or assist in the prosecution of claims against the United States. Section 113 forbids officers and employees of the United States to receive any compensation for services rendered in connection with any proceeding or other matter in which the United States is interested before any administrative body.

Exemptions similar to the foregoing have been contained in a number of previous statutes and are not unusual (55 Stat. 861; Public Laws 287 and 456, 78th Congress).

The Resolution, however, enumerates sections 361, 365, and 366 of the Revised

Statutes (5 U.S.C. 306, 314, 315). The inclusion of these sections in this type of legislation is novel. Section 361 provides that the officers of the Department of Justice, under the direction of the Attorney General, shall give all opinions and render all services requiring the skill of persons learned in the law necessary to enable the President and the heads of the various departments, and other officers, to discharge their respective duties; and shall, on behalf of the United States, procure the proper evidence for, and conduct, prosecute, or defend all suits and proceedings in the Supreme Court of the United States, and in the Court of Claims, in which the United States, or any officer thereof, is a party or may be interested. Section 365 provides that no compensation shall be allowed to any person, other than the United States attorneys and their assistants, for services as an attorney or counselor to the United States, except when specially authorized by law, and then only upon the certificate of the Attorney General to the effect that the services were actually rendered, and that they could not be performed by the officers of the Department of Justice, or the United States attorneys. Section 366 provides that every counselor or attorney specially retained, under the authority of the Department of Justice, to assist in the trial of any case in which the government is interested, shall receive a commission as a special assistant to the Attorney General, or to one of the United States attorneys, or as a special attorney, as the nature of the appointment may require; and shall take the oath required by law to be taken by the United States attorneys, and be subject to all liabilities imposed upon them by law.

The exemptions with respect to sections 361, 365, and 366 of the Revised Statutes do not appear to be necessary in order to carry out the intent of the Congress. Of more importance, however, is the fact that the inclusion of these sections in the Resolution might be interpreted as granting authority to the Committee counsel to initiate civil or criminal proceedings on behalf of the United States.

I am confident that this was not the intention of the Congress and it is for this reason that I am withholding my approval of the legislation.

HARRY S. TRUMAN

---

78 The President's News Conference of *April* 24, 1947

THE PRESIDENT. I have no special announcements to make. Most of them have been made. If you have any questions you would like to ask, I will try to answer them.

[1.] Q. Mr. President, I have been asked to ask you whether you plan to go to Warm Springs for a dedication?

THE PRESIDENT. It hasn't come up. I have not—I know nothing about it. I had made no such plan, that's the best way to put it.

[2.] Q. Are you going to Puerto Rico this year, or do you plan——

THE PRESIDENT. I had planned to go to Puerto Rico, as you know, but that plan was upset by the message which had to be sent to the Congress. I hope that it will be possible for me to go to Puerto Rico.

Q. This year?

THE PRESIDENT. This year.

Q. How about Alaska?

THE PRESIDENT. That has been on the agenda this year, but these things are only in contemplation. I can never know until the announcements are made creating the firm appointment that I will go.

[3.] Q. Mr. President, do you have any comment on Mr. Wallace's proposal that we lend 17 billion to Russia?

THE PRESIDENT. [*Very softly*] No comment—no comment.

Q. What was that answer, Mr. President?

THE PRESIDENT. [*Louder*] No comment! [*Laughter*]

Q. Three no comments, Mr. President?

THE PRESIDENT. No comment. [*More laughter*]

[4.] Q. Mr. President, Congressman Celler reported to the House, after a call on you, that from talking to you he could put two and two together and that you would veto the labor bill. Did you give him any basis——

THE PRESIDENT. We didn't discuss the labor bill. I don't want to cut the ground from under Congressman Celler. We probably discussed past messages, but we didn't discuss the labor bill. I do not discuss legislation until it's here for me to consider.

[5.] Q. Have you heard from Republican Senators who have been talking about asking a conference with you on what you would or would not veto?

THE PRESIDENT. No, I have not.

[6.] Q. Mr. President, you are reported as having received a letter from Mr. Baruch affecting a new loan to Britain.

THE PRESIDENT. I have received no such letter. It may be in the mail, but I haven't received it as yet.

[7.] Q. Mr. President, have you decided on your nomination for Federal Judgeship of the Western District of Texas?

THE PRESIDENT. Yes. That was announced. Robert Ewing Thomason was the name sent down this afternoon—Congressman from El Paso.

[8.] Q. Mr. President, what do you think of Chicago as a site for the Democratic National Convention?

THE PRESIDENT. That is a matter for the National Democratic Committee to decide.

[9.] Q. Mr. President, may I return to the labor bill and ask whether you would be friendly to consultation with the Republican leaders to see if an area of agreement on labor legislation could be worked out?

THE PRESIDENT. The Republican leaders or anyone else has a perfect right to come up and discuss any subject they choose with me. I don't think that there's any comment to be made on the matter in question.

[10.] Q. Mr. President, have you signed the copper tax suspension bill?

THE PRESIDENT. Yes, I signed that this morning, I think.

Q. I haven't seen it.

[11.] Q. Mr. President, there's a non-partisan bill introduced by Senators Barkley and Taft to control pollution in harbors and streams, and especially to protect the fishing industry, and is now before the Public Works Committee. Have you any comment on that?

THE PRESIDENT. When I was in the Senate, I voted for such a bill.

[12.] Q. Mr. President, would you approve of Senator Lucas's tax substitute bill?

THE PRESIDENT. I can't—I haven't read it—I can't make any comment on it, because I don't know.

[13.] Q. Mr. President, have you any plans on the telephone strike?

THE PRESIDENT. The telephone strike is being handled by the Department of Labor.

[14.] Q. Mr. President, have you solved that mystery about this veto [1] yesterday?

THE PRESIDENT. I have a memorandum from the Attorney General which I will be glad to read to you, if you like.

Q. We would like to hear it read. It wasn't a Russian that slipped in that veto, was it?

THE PRESIDENT. No. Here is the memorandum from the Attorney General, and you can get this outside later, if you want it.

[*Reading*] "With reference to your inquiry concerning your veto of Senate Joint Resolution 97, I beg to advise:

"The inclusion in the veto message, prepared in the Department, of language stating that 'this type of legislation is novel' is incorrect. Further investigation has disclosed that similar language has been included in previous resolutions.

"There is no question that sections 361, 365, and 366 of the revised statutes did not have to be included in the resolution to accomplish the objective of the sponsor of the resolution. These sections deal with the attorneys in the Department of Justice and those who represent the United States in litigation. In view of this fact, it was my thought that these three sections were inadvertently included in the resolution when it was originally drafted. Certainly this inclusion might be interpreted as an effort to grant authority to the committee counsel to initiate civil or criminal proceedings on

---

[1] Item 77.

behalf of the United States. This duty, as you know, has been placed in the Department of Justice by the Congress. I am sure that the Congress had no intention in this resolution to change this long established practice and the inclusion of these three sections certainly is subject to that interpretation.

"For these reasons, in my opinion, the resolution was properly vetoed."

That is signed by the Attorney General.

I want to make it perfectly clear that Senator Wheeler did not enter into this thing at all. I have no objection to Senator Wheeler representing that committee or any other committee that he sees fit. I have always been very fond of Senator Wheeler. He and I were the best of friends while I was in the Senate.

[15.] Q. Mr. President, have you received the resignation of Judge Kimbrough Stone of the 12th——

THE PRESIDENT. I am not ready to make an announcement on that. I may be able to make an announcement on it in another week.

[16.] Q. Mr. President, have you any comment to make on Mr. Bowles' suggestion that a special price commission——

THE PRESIDENT. No comment. No, I have no comment.

[17.] Q. Mr. President, has the price situation changed any, one way or another, since your speech Monday? [1]

THE PRESIDENT. All I know is what I see in the papers. Seems to be some action being taken in various parts of the country on the subject. I am very much pleased with the action of the merchants in Newburyport, Mass., and I notice there are several other instances of similar action which has been taken.

[1] See Item 76.

[18.] Mr. Ross [*to the President*]: Judge Latta says that the copper bill is not signed yet.

THE PRESIDENT. I see. On that question about that copper bill, Judge Latta says it has come to the White House, but has not been signed as yet.

I had a memorandum on it, I know, and I couldn't remember whether I had signed it or not. The Judge says I have not signed it.

Q. Mr. President, will you sign it, sir?

THE PRESIDENT. I will answer that when it comes to the final decision.

[19.] Q. Mr. President, does that veto affect Senator Wheeler's standing?

THE PRESIDENT. All I know is what I saw in the paper. I didn't know it was speculative.

Q. Mr. President, are you going to do anything to either recall—I understand you can't recall a veto——

THE PRESIDENT. Can't recall a veto. The proper thing, I imagine, is to pass the resolution without the objectionable sections in it.

[20.] Q. Have you given that Senate committee permission to get those Roosevelt letters on the oil?

THE PRESIDENT. I have informed the Senate committee that specific documents that they want from my files I shall always give to them.

Q. Have they named a specific document yet?

THE PRESIDENT. They have named the specific document that they want.

Q. One or several?

THE PRESIDENT. Being gotten for them. One.

[21.] Q. Mr. President, do you plan to do anything about Chester Bowles's price plan——

THE PRESIDENT. No comment on it.

[22.] Q. Would you favor a price board

composed of businessmen to discuss prices?

THE PRESIDENT. I don't know of any neces-sity for that. I have made all the discussion on prices that it was necessary to have made, in the speech that I made to the AP in New York. That covered the ground so far as I am concerned.

[23.] Q. Mr. President, do you have any comment on General Marshall's role in the foreign ministers conference in Moscow?

THE PRESIDENT. General Marshall will make the comment on that when he gets home.

Q. When do you expect that? When will that be?

Q. Mr. President, is he going to make a speech?

THE PRESIDENT. General Marshall will make a report, of course, when he returns home.

Q. When will that be, Mr. President?

THE PRESIDENT. I can't answer that.

Q. Monday or Tuesday night?

THE PRESIDENT. I can't answer that. I don't know.

[24.] Q. Mr. President, may I get clear—my thinking clear on this? The veto stands until they change the legislation?

THE PRESIDENT. That's right.

Q. You still object to the inclusion of the last sections?

THE PRESIDENT. The last three sections, yes sir. And the first—if you will study the history of the thing, you will find that the first bill of that sort, in which those three sections are included, was necessary. The other bills which have been subsequently brought up, with inclusion of the three sections, was not necessary, but they were in-cluded just as a matter of form.

Q. Well, Mr. President, I got the erroneous idea at the Capitol last night then. The way they understood it was a suggestion to repass the identical resolution again.

THE PRESIDENT. I have made no such sug-

gestion at all. I have talked to nobody about it except right here now.

Q. Mr. President, another set of words allowing the Senator to act, you would sign it, we take it, is that right?

THE PRESIDENT. If it complies with the sug-gestion of the Attorney General.

Q. It would have to be different from the one already passed?

THE PRESIDENT. If it complies with this memorandum of the Attorney General, I will sign it.

Q. Did the Attorney General prepare the original veto, sir?

THE PRESIDENT. It was sent to the Attorney General's office for consideration and ap-proval. It came from that office approved.

[25.] Q. Mr. President, are you in favor of Government support for any farm prod-ucts above the 90 percent parity formula?

THE PRESIDENT. No I am not, and there has been no such support.

Q. Mr. President, I don't think that is true as to wool, I think.

THE PRESIDENT. Well, if you—there has been special legislation on wool.

Q. Yes. I understand that. But——

THE PRESIDENT. Special legislation. I don't think it's good sense even for wool.

[26.] Q. Mr. President, one other thing, everybody has gotten out you are going to veto this tax cutting bill when it reaches you. You don't discuss legislation——

THE PRESIDENT. The best way to find that out is to wait and see.

Q. You think it would be a wrong inter-pretation from your speeches——

THE PRESIDENT. You can make any sort of an interpretation from my speeches you want, but so far as legislation is concerned I don't comment on it until it's here!

Reporter: Thank you, Mr. President.

NOTE: President Truman's one hundred and fourth news conference was held in his office at the White House at 4:15 p.m. on Thursday, April 24, 1947.

79 Remarks of Welcome to President Alemán of Mexico at the Washington National Airport. *April 29, 1947*

Mr. President, distinguished guests, and friends:

It is an especial pleasure for me to greet you here in Washington, Mr. President, as the guest of the Government and people of the United States. It gives me the deepest personal satisfaction to do this, and in extending a welcome to Your Excellency, I greet you not only as the President of the United Mexican States, but as a man whom I have come to know and value as a personal friend.

The people of this country followed closely each of the many acts of genuine hospitality that were extended to me as their Chief of State during my visit to Mexico a few weeks ago. They interpret your many kindnesses to me, not only as an example of the whole-hearted Mexican hospitality that thousands of our visitors to your country have experienced, but also as a symbol of the relationship between the friendly peoples of two neighboring countries.

The nations of this hemisphere are confronted today with problems of many kinds, some affecting the two American continents and serious in their import to the well-being and happiness of our Western World, and others that influence our actions as individual republics. We can all do much to raise the living standard of the hemisphere and of the world by increasing our production of food-stuffs and of raw materials needed by industry, and by improving the distribution of these products, in the spirit of our Inter-American Association.

We have, as a group of free nations, the moral strength, and moreover have the proved good will of our several countries, to find equitable and peaceful solutions to differences of any nature that arise among us who live in the New World. One can find no better testimony of this than the manner in which the peoples of Mexico and the United States are living side by side today.

The people of every State of the Union have asked, by means of letters and telegrams to me, to their Congressmen, to civic organizations, and to the press, that this Government endeavor to the best of its ability to reciprocate the most hospitable welcome that you and the Mexican people extended 6 weeks ago to me and through me to the people of the United States. My small part in carrying out this mandate will be one of the happiest events of my tour of office. We want to show you the full extent of our appreciation of your visit to our country and of our determination to perpetuate friendship with the great Mexican nation.

In welcoming you today to Washington, I express to Your Excellency and to the distinguished members of your party the sincere hospitality of the people of the United States.

NOTE: President Alemán's response (as translated) follows:

"*Mr. President:*

"I have followed with deep interest the kind words of Your Excellency welcoming me to the capital city of this great country. Your country is great not only by reason of its vast resources and the spirit of its people, but because of the overwhelming responsibilities that the moral rule of democracy impresses on all nations that are strong and prosperous.

"In a world where skepticism and discord still becloud peace, our confidence, the confidence of all the Americas, in the fitness of democracy, is one of the most valuable assets which we have inherited in our hemisphere. Therefore, I fervently wish to declare to you on this occasion that Mexico has absolute faith in democracy. The democratic ideals are bonds that bring my countrymen in closeness with the citizens of this Nation. Many thousands of Mexicans live here and we earnestly wish the same happiness in their homes and success in their undertakings that we desire for ourselves in Mexico.

"We have not forgotten, Mr. President, your visit to my country, gratifying for us, the nobility of your homage as a man and as a Chief Executive to the best loved heroes of our history, or your lucidity as a statesman and your genuineness as a friend.

"During your brief stay in Mexico you won the affection of my countrymen on your own merits, for what you are, a vigorous champion of good neighborliness in our hemisphere.

"Political relations between Mexico and the United States have nothing to hide or to dissemble. We deal together in broad light, without subterfuge or reservations. Their Chief Executives do not meet secretly to discuss agreements that cannot be openly avowed, but to reiterate out loud, in public, their sincere desire to live together in mutual respect and under law and to cooperate in strengthening the economy of their nations, increasing thereby their production and applying their resources to industry.

"It is our peoples, Mr. President, who in fact shape our diplomacy. And as leaders of our peoples, we ought to regard ourselves the trustees of

their hopes, the emissaries of their enthusiasm and the official interpreters of their devotion for the cause of justice.

"While in Mexico, Your Excellency had an opportunity to prove the manly natural cordiality of the Mexican people. Although just arrived in this capital city, I am pleased to perceive the same manly natural cordiality in the people of the United States.

"On the basis of a political awareness so alive in our peoples, I look forward with certainty to the growing affirmation of Mexican-American friendship every year, for the good of a world that is impatient for all men to understand, appreciate, and help one another.

"In gratefully acknowledging your welcome, I extend through Your Excellency greetings to the people of the United States of America. I earnestly wish the prosperity of your country and that the relations between our two republics may be constantly pointed out, in the future, as a clear example of self-respecting cooperation and of solidarity without loss of independence."

The text of President Truman's remarks and President Alemán's response was released in both English and Spanish.

80 Message to the Congress Transmitting Reorganization Plan 1 of 1947. *May 1, 1947*

To the Congress of the United States:

I am transmitting herewith Reorganization Plan No. 1 of 1947. The provisions of this Plan are designed to maintain organizational arrangements worked out under authority of Title I of the First War Powers Act. The Plan has a two-fold objective, to provide for more orderly transition from war to peacetime operation and to supplement my previous actions looking toward the termination of wartime legislation.

The First War Powers Act provides that Title I "shall remain in force during the continuance of the present war and for 6 months after the termination of the war, or until such earlier time as the Congress by concurrent resolution or the President may designate." Upon the termination of this Title all changes in the organization of activities and agencies effected under its authority expire and the functions revert to

their previous locations, unless otherwise provided by law.

Altogether, nearly 135 Executive orders have been issued in whole or in part under Title I of the First War Powers Act. The internal organization of the War and Navy Departments has been drastically overhauled under this authority. Most of the emergency agencies, which played so vital a role in the successful prosecution of the war, were based in whole or in part upon this Title. Without the ability, which these provisions afforded, to adjust the machinery of government to changing needs, it would not have been possible to develop the effective, hard-hitting organization which produced victory. The organization of war activities had to be worked out step by step as the war program unfolded and experience pointed the way. That was inevitable. The problems and the functions to be performed

222

were largely new. Conditions changed continually and often radically. Speed of action was essential. But with the aid of Title I of the First War Powers Act, it was possible to gear the administrative machinery of the Government to handle the enormous load thrust upon it by the rapidly evolving war program.

Since V-J Day this same authority has been used extensively in demobilizing war agencies and reconverting the governmental structure to peacetime needs. This process has been largely completed. The bulk of temporary activities have ceased and most of the continuing functions transferred during the war have already been placed in their appropriate peacetime locations.

The organizational adjustments which should be continued are essentially of two types. First, changes in the organization of permanent functions, which have demonstrated their advantage during the war years. Second, transfers of continuing activities which were vested by statute in temporary war agencies but have since been moved by Executive order upon the termination of these agencies.

In most cases, the action necessary to maintain organizational gains made under Title I of the First War Powers Act can best be taken by the simplified procedure afforded by the Reorganization Act of 1945, the first purpose of which was to facilitate the orderly transition from war to peace. All of the provisions of this Plan represent definite improvements in administration. Several are essential steps in demobilizing the war effort. The arrangements they provide for have been reviewed by the Congress in connection with appropriation requests. Since the Plan does not change existing organization, savings cannot be claimed for it. However, increased expense and disruption of operations would result if the present organization were terminated and the activities

reverted to their former locations.

In addition to the matters dealt with in this Reorganization Plan and in Reorganization Plan No. 2 of 1947, there are several other changes in organization made under Title I of the First War Powers Act on which action should be taken before the termination of the Title. The proposed legislation for a National Defense Establishment provides for continuing the internal organizational arrangements made in the Army and Navy pursuant to the First War Powers Act. I have on several occasions recommended the creation of a single agency for the administration of housing programs. Since Section 5(e) of the Reorganization Act of 1945 may cast some doubt on my authority to assign responsibility for the liquidation of the Smaller War Plants Corporation by reorganization plan, I recommend that the Reconstruction Finance Corporation be authorized by legislation to continue to liquidate the affairs relating to functions transferred to it from the Smaller War Plants Corporation.

It is imperative that Title I of the First War Powers Act remain effective until all of these matters have been dealt with. An earlier termination of the Title would destroy important advances in organization and impair the ability of the Executive Branch to administer effectively some of the major programs of the Government.

I have found, after investigation, that each reorganization contained in this Plan is necessary to accomplish one or more of the purposes set forth in Section 2(a) of the Reorganization Act of 1945. Each of these reorganizations is explained below.

FUNCTIONS OF THE ALIEN PROPERTY CUSTODIAN

The Reorganization Plan provides for the permanent location of the functions vested by statute in the Alien Property Custodian and the Office of Alien Property Custodian. In

1934 the functions of the Alien Property Custodian were transferred to the Department of Justice, where they remained until 1942. Because of the great volume of activity resulting from World War II, a separate Office of Alien Property Custodian was created by Executive Order No. 9095 of March 11, 1942. This Office was terminated by Executive Order No. 9788 of October 14, 1946, and the functions of the Office and of the Alien Property Custodian were transferred to the Attorney General except for those relating to Philippine property. The latter were transferred simultaneously to the Philippine Alien Property Administration established by Executive Order No. 9789.

While the Trading with the Enemy Act, as amended at the beginning of the war, authorized the President to designate the agency or person in which alien property should vest and to change such designations, subsequent legislation has lodged certain functions in the Alien Property Custodian and the Office of Alien Property Custodian. Similarly, though the Philippine Property Act vested in the President the then existing alien property functions as to Philippine property, certain functions affecting such property have since been established which have been assigned by statute to the Alien Property Custodian.

In order to maintain the existing arrangements for the administration of alien property and to avoid the confusion which otherwise would occur on the termination of Title I of the First War Powers Act, the Reorganization Plan transfers to the Attorney General all functions vested by law in the Alien Property Custodian and the Office of Alien Property Custodian except as to Philippine property. The functions relating to Philippine property are transferred to the President, to be performed by such officer or agency as he may designate, thus permitting

the continued administration of these functions through the Philippine Alien Property Administration.

APPROVAL OF AGRICULTURAL MARKETING ORDERS

Section 8c of the Agricultural Marketing Agreements Act of 1937 provides that marketing orders of the Secretary of Agriculture must in certain cases be approved by the President before issuance. In order to relieve the President of an unnecessary burden, the responsibility for approval was delegated to the Economic Stabilization Director during the war and was formally transferred to him by Executive Order No. 9705 of March 15, 1946. Since the Secretary of Agriculture is the principal adviser of the President in matters relating to agriculture and since final authority has been assigned to the Secretary by law in many matters of equal or greater importance, the requirement of Presidential approval of individual marketing orders may well be discontinued. Accordingly, the Plan abolishes the function of the President relative to the approval of such orders.

CONTRACT SETTLEMENT FUNCTIONS

The Office of Contract Settlement was established by law in 1944 and shortly thereafter was placed by statute in the Office of War Mobilization and Reconversion. The principal purposes of the Office of Contract Settlement have been to prescribe the policies, regulations, and procedures governing the settlement of war contracts, and to provide an Appeal Board to hear and decide appeals from the contracting agencies in the settlement of contracts. A remarkable record has been achieved for the rapid settlement of war contracts, but among those which remain are some of the largest and most complex. Considerable time may be required to complete these cases and dispose of the appeals.

Though the functions of the Office of Contract Settlement cannot yet be terminated, it is evident that they no longer warrant the maintenance of a separate office. For this reason, Executive Order No. 9809 of December 12, 1946, transferred the functions of the Director of Contract Settlement to the Secretary of the Treasury and those of the Office of Contract Settlement to the Department of the Treasury. As the central fiscal agency of the Executive Branch the Treasury Department is clearly the logical organization to carry to conclusion the overall activities of the contract settlement program. The Plan continues the present arrangement and abolishes the Office of Contract Settlement, thereby avoiding its reestablishment as a separate agency on the termination of Title I of the First War Powers Act.

NATIONAL PROHIBITION ACT FUNCTIONS

The Act of May 27, 1930 (46 Stat. 427) imposed upon the Attorney General certain duties respecting administration and enforcement of the National Prohibition Act. By Executive Order No. 6639 of March 10, 1934, all of the powers and duties of the Attorney General respecting that Act, except the power and authority to determine and to compromise liability for taxes and penalties, were transferred to the Commissioner of Internal Revenue. The excepted functions, however, were transferred subsequently to the Commissioner of Internal Revenue by Executive Order No. 9302 of February 9, 1943, issued under the authority of Title I of the First War Powers Act, 1941.

Since the functions of determining taxes and penalties under various statutes and of compromise of liability therefor prior to reference to the Attorney General for suit are well-established functions of the Commissioner of Internal Revenue, this minor function under the National Prohibition Act is more appropriately placed in the Bureau of Internal Revenue than in the Department of Justice.

AGRICULTURAL RESEARCH FUNCTIONS

By Executive Order No. 9069 of February 23, 1942, six research bureaus, the Office of Experiment Stations, and the Agricultural Research Center were consolidated into an Agricultural Research Administration to be administered by an officer designated by the Secretary of Agriculture. The constituent bureaus and agencies of the Administration have, in practice, retained their separate identity. This consolidation and certain transfers of functions between the constituent bureaus and agencies have all been recognized and provided for in the subsequent appropriation acts passed by the Congress.

By the Plan the functions of the eight research bureaus and agencies which are presently consolidated into the Agricultural Research Administration are transferred to the Secretary of Agriculture to be performed by him or under his direction and control by such officers or agencies of the Department of Agriculture as he may designate.

The benefits which have been derived from centralized review, coordination, and control of research projects and functions by the Agricultural Research Administrator have amply demonstrated the lasting value of this consolidation. By transferring the functions of the constituent bureaus and agencies to the Secretary of Agriculture, it will be possible to continue this consolidation and to make such further adjustments in the organization of agricultural research activities as future conditions may require. This assignment of functions to the Secretary is in accord with the sound and long-established practice of the Congress of vesting substantive functions in the Secretary of Agriculture rather than in subordinate officers or agencies of the Department.

CREDIT UNION FUNCTIONS

The Plan makes permanent the transfer of the administration of Federal functions with respect to credit unions to the Federal Deposit Insurance Corporation. These functions, originally placed in the Farm Credit Administration, were transferred to the Federal Deposit Insurance Corporation by Executive Order No. 9148 of April 27, 1942. Most credit unions are predominantly urban institutions, and the credit union program bears very little relation to the functions of the Farm Credit Administration. The supervision of credit unions fits in logically with the general bank supervisory functions of the Federal Deposit Insurance Corporation. The Federal Deposit Insurance Corporation since 1942 has successfully administered the credit union program, and the supervision of credit union examiners has been integrated into the field and departmental organization of the Corporation. In the interests of preserving an organizational arrangement which operates effectively and economically, the program should remain in its present location.

WAR ASSETS ADMINISTRATION

The present organization for the disposal of surplus property is the product of two and a half years of practical experience. Beginning with the Surplus Property Board in charge of general policy and a group of agencies designated by it to handle the disposal of particular types of property, the re-

sponsibility for most of the surplus disposal has gradually been drawn together in one agency—the War Assets Administration—headed by a single Administrator. Experience has demonstrated the desirability of centralized responsibility in administering this most difficult program.

The Reorganization Plan will continue the centralization of surplus disposal functions in a single agency headed by an Administrator. This is accomplished by transferring the functions, personnel, property, records, and funds of the War Assets Administration created by Executive order to the statutory Surplus Property Administration. In order to avoid confusion and to maintain the continuity of operations, the name of the Surplus Property Administration is changed to War Assets Administration.

Because the Plan combines in one agency, not only the policy functions now vested by statute in the Surplus Property Administrator, but also the immense disposal operations now concentrated in the temporary War Assets Administration, I have found it necessary to provide in the Plan for an Associate War Assets Administrator also appointed by the President with the approval of the Senate. It is essential that there be an officer who can assist the Administrator in the general management of the agency and who can take over the direction of its operations in case of the absence or disability of the Administrator or of a vacancy in his office.

HARRY S. TRUMAN

NOTE: Reorganization Plan 1 of 1947 is published in the U.S. Statutes at Large (61 Stat. 951) and in the 1943–1948 Compilation of title 3 of the Code of Federal Regulations (p. 1070). It became effective July 1, 1947.

81 Message to the Congress Transmitting Reorganization Plan 2 of 1947. *May 1, 1947*

To the Congress of the United States:

I am transmitting herewith Reorganization Plan No. 2 of 1947, prepared in accordance with the provisions of the Reorganization Act of 1945. The Plan permanently transfers to the Department of Labor the United States Employment Service, which is now in the Department by temporary transfer under authority of Title I of the First War Powers Act. In addition, the Plan effects two other changes in organization to improve the administration of labor functions.

I am deeply interested in the continued development of the Department of Labor. The critical national importance of effective governmental action on labor problems requires proper assignment of responsibility for the administration of Federal labor programs. Such programs should be under the general leadership of the Secretary of Labor, and he should have an adequate organization for this purpose. The provisions of this Plan are directed to this objective.

I have found, after investigation, that each reorganization contained in the Plan is necessary to accomplish one or more of the purposes set forth in section 2(a) of the Reorganization Act of 1945.

UNITED STATES EMPLOYMENT SERVICE

The United States Employment Service was established by the Wagner-Peyser Act in the Department of Labor. Later, by Reorganization Plan No. 1, effective July 1, 1939, it was transferred to the Social Security Board in the Federal Security Agency and administered in conjunction with the unemployment compensation program.

During the war the Employment Service was extensively reorganized. The critical nature of the labor supply problem greatly increased the importance of the Service and compelled the Federal Government to take over the administration of the entire employment office system on a temporary basis.

Soon after the creation of the War Manpower Commission the United States Employment Service was transferred to the Commission, by Executive Order No. 9247 of September 17, 1942, and became the backbone of the Commission's organization and program. When the Commission was terminated shortly after V-J Day, most of its activities, including the United States Employment Service, were shifted by Executive Order No. 9617 to the Department of Labor, the central agency for the performance of Federal labor functions under normal conditions. Both of these transfers were made under authority of Title I of the First War Powers Act. More recently, the Employment Service was returned to its prewar status as a joint Federal-State operation.

The provision of a system of public employment offices is directly related to the major purpose of the Department of Labor. Through the activities of the employment office system the Government has a wide and continuous relationship with workers and employers concerning the basic question of employment. To a rapidly increasing degree, the employment office system has become the central exchange for workers and jobs and the primary national source of information on labor market conditions. In the calendar year 1946, it filled 7,140,000 jobs, and millions of workers used its counsel on employment opportunities and on the choice of occupations.

The Labor Department obviously should continue to play a leading role in the development of the labor market and to participate in the most basic of all labor activities—assisting workers to get jobs and employers to obtain labor. Policies and operations of the Employment Service must be determined in relation to over-all labor standards, labor statistics, labor training and labor law—on all of which the Labor Department is the center of specialized knowledge in the Government. Accordingly, the Reorganization Plan transfers the United States Employment Service to the Department of Labor.

FUNCTIONS OF THE ADMINISTRATOR OF THE WAGE AND HOUR DIVISION

The Plan transfers the functions of the Administrator of the Wage and Hour Division to the Secretary of Labor to be performed subject to his direction and control. The Fair Labor Standards Bill was drafted on the assumption that the Wage and Hour Division would be made an independent establishment. As finally passed, however, the Act placed the Division in the Department of Labor but was entirely silent on the authority of the Secretary over it. As a result, the Secretary has lacked an adequate legal basis for supervising and directing the affairs of the Division, and it has had an ambiguous status in the Department. The transfer effected by the Plan will eliminate uncertainty as to the Secretary's control over the administration of the Wage and Hour Division and will enable him to tie it into the Department more effectively. This in turn will facilitate working out a sound combination of wage and hour, child labor, and related enforcement activities of the Department, and will

permit the Secretary to simplify and strengthen the organization of the Department.

COORDINATION OF ADMINISTRATION OF LABOR LAWS ON FEDERAL PUBLIC WORKS CONTRACTS

The Congress has enacted several laws regulating wages and hours of workers employed on Federal public works contracts. The oldest of these are the Eight-Hour Laws fixing a maximum eight-hour day for laborers and mechanics on such projects. More recently the Davis-Bacon Act established the prevailing wage rates for the corresponding classes of workers in the locality as the minimum rates for employees on certain Federal public works contracts and required the Secretary of Labor to determine the prevailing rates. Another measure, the Copeland Act, prohibited the exaction of rebates or "kick-backs" from workers on public works financed by the Federal Government and authorized the Secretary of Labor to prescribe regulations for contractors on such works.

The actual enforcement of these acts rests almost entirely with the Federal agencies entering into the contracts. This is proper since the engineers and inspectors of the contracting agencies are in close touch with the operation of the projects and, in the case of cost plus contracts, the payrolls and accounts of the contractors are examined by the auditors of these agencies.

The enforcement practices of the various contracting agencies, however, differ widely in character and effectiveness. Some agencies have instructed their inspectors thoroughly as to the acts and their enforcement and have adopted procedures for carefully checking the records of the contractors and the operation of the projects to determine compliance with Federal labor laws. On the other hand, some agencies have failed to institute effective enforcement procedures. As a result, enforcement has been very uneven and workers have not had the protection to which they were entitled. With the return to a normal peacetime labor market the danger of violations will be much greater than in recent years.

To correct this situation, the Plan authorizes the Secretary of Labor to coordinate the administration of the acts for the regulation of wages and hours on Federal public works by establishing such standards, regulations, and procedures to govern the enforcement efforts of the contracting agencies, and by

making such investigations, as may be necessary to assure consistent enforcement. The Plan does not transfer enforcement operations from the contracting agencies to the Department of Labor as the former can perform the work more economically than the Department because of their close contact with the projects. Rather it assures more uniform and effective action by the contracting agencies.

HARRY S. TRUMAN

NOTE: Reorganization Plan 2 of 1947 is printed in House Document 231 (80th Cong., 1st sess.). It did not become effective.

82   Remarks to a Special Group on the Role of the Press in Traffic Safety.   *May 1, 1947*

I AM HAPPY to learn of the splendid program the daily and weekly newspapers of the country have adopted for the summer months as their contribution to the effort all of us are making to reduce the shocking cost in lives and human injuries of traffic accidents on America's streets and highways. The accomplishment of this objective is one of the most important tasks with which we are confronted.

Last year there was a series of tragedies which caught the headlines of the press everywhere because of their dramatic nature. In Illinois 47 persons died in a railroad wreck; a half-dozen sensational hotel fires caused the death of some 250 persons; and during the Christmas holiday season a succession of airplane disasters throughout the world brought death to another 250.

These were appalling accidents, and newspapers everywhere gave them great prominence. Through such publicity the public determination to prevent their recurrence

was aroused. A fact that most of us overlooked, however, was that at the very same time many more persons were dying in traffic accidents on city streets and rural highways. Those first accidents were dramatic because we caught the impact of their cost in the aggregate, whereas the cost of traffic accidents usually receives little more than local attention because they are so widely scattered.

Therein is the nub of the problem before us. We must make the people understand that the aggregate of traffic accidents every year is a national tragedy. Once the people understand, they can be counted upon to apply the remedy that is within their own hands. The press of the country can make them so understand.

I have called the second President's Highway Safety Conference to convene in Washington on June 18, 19, and 20. Following the first conference last year traffic accidents decreased so sharply that some 6,600 lives were saved. I am asking the second conference to fix as its minimum goal the saving of 10,000 lives this year.

You gentlemen here today constitute a committee which speaks for most of the great press associations of the country, and through them for a majority of our newspapers. I am happy to welcome you to your meeting with General Fleming and I ask you to take this message to your own member publishers and your colleagues in the other States:

It is traditional in America for the people to look to the daily and weekly press not only as their source of information about current events but as their trusted guide in bettering the common welfare. The editors and publishers can perform no higher service than to guide their readers, those who walk as well as those who ride, to a complete understanding of the cost of traffic accidents in lives and injuries, and show them how simple it is to stop this tragic loss by merely practicing common sense safety.

NOTE: The President spoke to a delegation of managers of national and State press and publishers associations and to representatives of the President's Highway Safety Conference. The group was in Washington for a meeting with Maj. Gen. Philip B. Fleming, Administrator of the Federal Works Agency and Chairman of the Safety Conference.

83 Joint Statement Following Discussions With the President of Mexico. *May 1, 1947*

DURING the conversations that have taken place in Washington as a continuation of those begun in Mexico in March of this year, the Presidents of the United Mexican States and of the United States of America have had an opportunity to ratify in the friendliest spirit their common purpose to further develop, for the reciprocal benefit of their peoples, the cordial relations existing between the two Republics.

Recognizing that one of the most important and practical methods of strengthening the policy of solidarity of the two Nations is undoubtedly a program of cooperation to solve the complex economic problems of the present postwar period, both Chiefs of State have agreed that their respective administrations must exert all efforts to raise the standards of living in their countries by increasing productivity and, consequently, the purchasing power of their peoples.

To this end the Presidents of the United Mexican States and of the United States of America are pleased to announce that they concur in the desirability of signing a new agreement to stabilize the rate of exchange between the peso and the dollar.

In addition, the Export-Import Bank of Washington is prepared to approve additional credits to Mexico to assist in financing a number of projects laid before it by the Mexican Government—projects which are designed to make the greatest and earliest contribution to the economy of Mexico.

Other important aspects of the program of economic cooperation between the two Republics are under study.

In issuing this statement both Chiefs of State express their satisfaction with the great cordiality attained in the relations of the peoples they represent, and both, inspired by the ideals of Good Neighborliness and by mutual and full understanding of their problems, reaffirm their decision to strengthen the bonds of the inter-American community.

84   Citation Accompanying Legion of Merit Awarded to Miguel Alemán, President of Mexico.   *May 1, 1947*

CITATION TO ACCOMPANY THE AWARD OF
THE LEGION OF MERIT

DEGREE OF CHIEF COMMANDER

TO

MIGUEL ALEMÁN

HIS EXCELLENCY Miguel Alemán, President and Commander-in-Chief of the Armed Forces of Mexico, has displayed unswerving friendship to the United States and to the ideals of the Good Neighbor Policy, the success of which he has done so much to assure. His eagerness to enhance the bonds of friendship between Mexico and the United States and his strong backing of the progressive and liberal foreign policy of his government have established a shining pattern of the spirit which is making Pan Americanism the true brotherhood of the nations of America.

HARRY S. TRUMAN

NOTE: The presentation was made by the President at a dinner at the White House. The text of the citation was released in both English and Spanish.

85   Letter to the President, National Association of Wholesalers.   *May 3, 1947*

[Released May 3, 1947.   Dated May 2, 1947]

Dear Mr. Kolodny:

This is to acknowledge your letter of April 29, enclosing a copy of "Wholesaler," the official publication of your Association. I note with interest that you utilized the April issue of your publication to speak to your members on the subject of prices.

I was particularly impressed with your statements that the present price level is too high, that it is out of relationship with the income level of most wage earners, and that there is a responsibility on the part of the producer, the wholesaler, and the retailer to make an "honest contribution to the maintenance of a sound economy."

It is gratifying to see this fine response to the plea for price reduction. It is important that there be a continuing recognition of the price problem in all segments of our economy.

Very sincerely yours,

HARRY S. TRUMAN

[Mr. Joseph Kolodny, President, National Association of Wholesalers, Inc., 200 Fifth Avenue, New York 10, N.Y.]

NOTE: Mr. Kolodny's letter to the members of the Association, as printed in "Wholesaler," and his letter of transmittal dated April 29 were released with the President's reply.

86   Address at the Opening of the Conference on Fire Prevention.   *May 5, 1947*

Ladies and gentlemen:

It is a pleasure for me to have the privilege to come over here and discuss with you this morning some things in which I am intensely interested.

The Nation has been shocked by a long series of spectacular fires in the last few years—particularly in the last few months—which have resulted in such great loss of life and such widespread misery. Just the other day, the Texas City disaster drove home anew the lesson that we must find ways and means to combat the ever-present danger of fire and explosion. The great hotel fires of last year again showed that we cannot afford to entrust our citizens' lives to unsafe buildings.

But these fires which make headlines are only a small fraction of the total. Thousands of lives are lost annually and tens of thousands of people are injured in the many less spectacular fires which occur hour after hour, and day after day, throughout the year.

This conference brings together for the first time the highest officials of municipalities, States, the Federal Government, and national groups interested in fire prevention and in saving lives from fires. We are approaching the fire problem on a truly national basis.

Our first concern is for the lives of our people, especially those of young people. Fire strikes hardest at youth. Two thousand children, on the average, die every year from burns, and thousands of others are scarred and injured for life. This toll must be reduced.

Next in importance is the fact that we as a Nation cannot continue to ignore the staggering destruction of goods, natural resources, buildings, and other property by fire. During the last 12 months fires destroyed more than $560 million worth of our wealth. The loss for 1947 will be more than three-quarters of a billion dollars unless we can reduce the present fire rate.

No dollar value can ever be put on the irreplaceable things which fire destroys. Who can count the value of a human life destroyed by fire? Who can say what a fire costs when it destroys thousands of tons of food sorely needed here and abroad? What is the value of a house, the burning of which makes a family homeless during this housing shortage? Who can put a dollar value on a burning forest?

The fire loss, in lives and in property, which occurs annually in our forests and rural areas makes up a highly important part of the annual toll. Such destruction of our precious natural resources is of concern to each of us.

Who can say what fire costs the Nation when a single fire in one factory can result in lost jobs and lost wages for hundreds of workmen, reduced savings and reduced volume of trade throughout a community?

These are some of the tragic consequences of more than 830,000 fires that occur annually in the United States. It is for this conference to determine the causes of this destruction and map out a program of preventive action. We must use all our experience, knowledge, and organizational facilities to solve our fire problems.

Great advance has been made in the technical methods of prevention and protection. The concerted effort of all our people is needed in order to make effective the known methods of preventing fires and preventing large losses where fire occurs.

A contributing factor in our fire death toll is our legacy of old construction. Also, we have a complexity of building laws and codes in some communities, and too few in others. In many communities, these laws are outdated, and the responsibility for safety from fire is not clearly defined.

We have wide areas in the Nation with inadequate fire protection. Our forests need to be safeguarded against the thousands of fires—most of them set by human carelessness—that sweep over millions of acres annually. Our rural areas must have improved and better coordinated protection.

We also have entered upon a new era of scientific and industrial development, with the accompanying special hazards of new chemicals and industrial processes. Many of these hazards are not yet widely understood.

For the protection of our industrial plants, we must see that fire prevention keeps pace with scientific research.

The recent war showed that we had grave shortages of experienced fire fighters both in our Armed Forces and in our civilian life. The question of using some of the training methods developed during the war and the National Guard facilities for the training of firemen is certainly to be considered if we are to provide our cities and our Armed Forces with the skilled firemen we need.

I want to pay a tribute to our firemen. Were it not for their bravery and their willingness to sacrifice, our death toll would be much higher and our losses even more appalling than they are today. I hope that this conference will help to produce conditions that will make our firemen's dangerous work less necessary, and their services, when needed, of even greater effectiveness.

There is also to be considered the matter of personal responsibility for fires. This is not a new problem, for it is recorded in the Book of Exodus, more than three thousand years ago:

"If a fire break out, and catch in thorns, so that the stacks of corn, or the standing corn, or the field, be consumed therewith; he that kindled the fire shall surely make restitution."

The conference might well consider the strengthening of the present laws having to do with negligence.

These are but a few of the problems that face us. I know that you will try to find practical solutions that will save lives and resources.

Safety from fire should not be a topic for discussion during only 1 or 2 weeks of the year. It is definitely a year-round public responsibility. I believe that the highest State and municipal officials must assume greater responsibility for leadership in this field. We in the Federal Government can give aid within the framework of existing agencies. But the impetus must come from the States and from every community and every individual in the land.

Your public officials at home are going to need the expert help which you in attendance at this conference can give them. And you must provide part of the leadership in your own communities for any public support to be given to your local officials and fire departments.

Just a year ago I called a similar national conference to consider the shocking toll of highway traffic accidents and to work out an effective program to meet that problem. General Fleming was also chairman of that conference. Since then we have seen a reduction in deaths and injuries from traffic accidents that has more than justified all our efforts. We can fight the fire problem in exactly the same way.

I deeply appreciate your acceptance of my invitation to come here. In working out a plan which will reduce the fire menace and cut down the toll of death and destruction, you will be making a most valuable contribution to the welfare of our Nation. You have my pledge of help, during the period of this conference, and in the days to come.

[Additional remarks of the President which were not included in the prepared text follow:]

I would like to call your attention further to just a few things in which you should be vitally interested. We have an appalling situation in this country, brought about by neglect and carelessness for the most part.

There are 23 million people in this country who have been physically injured in some manner, either in automobile wrecks, or fires, in the home, or in other places, and most of these people were unnecessarily injured.

Now we are trying to start at the source to see if we can't cut down that immense toll which negligent accidents take from the citizens of this country. Imagine 23 million people with eyes out, arms off, legs off! It's terrible! We are rehabilitating our soldiers who were injured in the war. We are teaching those without legs how to walk; and we have legs invented that are almost equal to the natural article. Nothing is really equal to that, but these are, almost. And they have artificial arms for those men. But the 23 million are the cares of the local communities, they are the cares of their families.

You can help prevent that. You can help cure that awful situation.

As a result of the conference on automobile accidents last year, we estimate that we have saved six thousand lives in this past year. It was well worth the effort, but it still isn't enough—it still isn't enough. I sincerely hope that you will earnestly go to work on this other phase, this unnecessary loss of life by fire, and will make a contribution at least equal to the one that was made by the effort to stop automobile accidents.

Lots of these things are absolutely unnecessary, in fact most of them are. Most of them are due to carelessness. Most of them are due to the fact that people are ignorant on what to do in an emergency.

Let's teach them. Let's cure this situation. With this organization, and with the one which we have working on the automobile situation, and with others which we intend to call into being, I think we can cut that 23 million down, instead of increasing it.

I want to see all those people rehabilitated and given their places back in society. We can do that, too. And that is partly up to you.

I am immensely interested in the health and welfare of the people of this country. You will find that this all fits in a pattern which is covered in a health message which I sent to the Congress last year,[1] and which fits in with these meetings to prevent accidents which we have been having.

I appreciate very much, more than I can tell you, your interest and your help in trying to get this awful situation cured.

Thank you very much.

NOTE: The President spoke at 11 a.m. in the Departmental Auditorium.

---

[1] The President's message recommending a comprehensive health program was submitted to the Congress on November 19, 1945 (see 1945 volume, this series, p. 475).

87 Letter Appointing Members of Panel on Labor Problems in Government-Possessed Plants or Mines. *May 7, 1947*

Dear Mr. ———:

Executive Order 9809, signed on December 12, 1946, was issued for the purpose of consolidating certain wartime agencies and functions.

By the terms of that Order, the functions of Section 5 of the War Labor Disputes Act, relating to wages or other terms and conditions of employment in plants or mines in possession of the Government, are to be administered by a special board to be constituted as may be necessary by the Secretary of Labor from among members of a panel to be appointed by the President. You are hereby appointed as a member of this panel.

I hope you will find it possible to serve as a member of a special board if the Secretary of Labor finds it necessary to call upon you.

Very sincerely yours,

HARRY S. TRUMAN

NOTE: This is the text of identical letters addressed to the following appointees to the panel: Hon. Lloyd K. Garrison, Weiss, Whorton & Garrison, New York, N.Y.; Dr. Edwin E. Witte, University of Wisconsin, Madison, Wis.; Edward F. McGrady, Radio Corporation of America, New York, N.Y.; Hon. Walter P. Stacy, Chief Justice, State of North Carolina, Raleigh, N.C.; Dr. William M. Leiserson, Washington, D.C.; Dr. Frank P. Graham, University of North Carolina, Chapel Hill, N.C.; Prof. W. Willard Wirtz, Northwestern University, Evanston, Ill.; Dr. Harry Shulman, Yale University, New Haven, Conn.; Dr. Sumner H. Slichter, Harvard University, Cambridge, Mass.; Hon. Phillips L. Garman, University of Illinois, Urbana, Ill.; and Dr. Nathan P. Feinsinger, University of Wisconsin, Madison, Wis.

88 The President's News Conference of *May 8, 1947*

THE PRESIDENT. [1.] Well, I am glad to see you this morning. Just 2 years ago I called you in here at 8:30 in the morning and made an announcement that the Germans had surrendered officially, and read you two proclamations, I think, one calling for a day of prayer the following Sunday, and one outlining the necessity for continued work until the Japanese had surrenderd. There was a grand rush, after that announcement was made, and Merriman Smith broke his arm as he went out the door, and another fellow here[1] who broke his leg, almost but not quite.

Q. Not quite, Mr. President. [*Laughter*]

THE PRESIDENT. So I hope there won't be any occasion for such a tremendous rush this morning.

A great many things have happened during that period that have been interesting and we hope constructive. The outlook now, from my viewpoint, is much improved to what it was then. I am still an optimist that we will eventually get a peace which will be lasting, and that the United Nations will effectually carry out its Charter. I am as sure of that as I am standing here.

At that time, we were still working on the United Nations Charter. It was my privilege after that to go and speak to the windup of that conference on the writing of the United Nations Charter. A short time after that I went to Potsdam and spent several weeks there. A great many of you were with me on that trip.

And then on August 14th the Japanese folded up. Both the end of the war with Germany and the war with Japan were ahead of the anticipated schedule—left us with a great many problems, particularly some 12,800,000 men under arms, whose mothers and fathers immediately wanted them discharged the next day—which couldn't be done.

We got over that hump in very good shape, and I think successfully got over most of the others that we have had to meet. We still have a great many to meet, and we're still expecting to meet them successfully, for the welfare of the United States.

I didn't intend to make you a speech, but I thought you ought to be reminded that this is just the second birthday of the windup of the war with Germany, and still have 3 months to go for 2 years after the Japanese folded up.

Now I would be willing to answer any questions I can.

[2.] Q. Mr. President, how old do you feel today, in view of all that?

---

[1] Robert G. Nixon of the International News Service.

THE PRESIDENT. Oh, about the same as I did when I came to the Senate in 1935. [*Laughter*]

[3.] Q. Mr. President, regarding the price situation, is that one of the things you still have to get over?

THE PRESIDENT. I stated my position on the price situation in the speech to the Associated Press in New York.[1] I think it is pretty thoroughly covered in that.

[4.] Q. Mr. President, I have been asked to ask you whether you, being a Missourian, would comment on a Missouri bill to ban utility strikes?

THE PRESIDENT. I have no comment, because I know nothing about the bill, and I understand it isn't a law yet.

[5.] Q. Mr. President, do the Baltimore election results make you optimistic——

THE PRESIDENT. Make me very happy. Made me very happy, just as the Chicago election did. [*Laughter*]

[6.] Q. Mr. President, when do you expect your report on universal military training, sir?

THE PRESIDENT. At any time now. I am anticipating it in a very short time.

Q. Do you still expect to get UMT through this session of Congress?

THE PRESIDENT. I am going to try. What was the question back there?

[7.] Q. Have you had an opportunity to look over the portal-to-portal bill?

THE PRESIDENT. We are studying it now. I will give you an answer on that just as soon as I have all the facts.

[8.] Q. Mr. President, William C. Bullitt has been reported conferring with your Ambassador in Paris. Is Mr. Bullitt on any sort of mission for you?

THE PRESIDENT. No, he is not.

Q. There are also reports, sir, that he conferred with Admiral Leahy before his departure. Do you know whether that is true?

THE PRESIDENT. I know nothing about it.

[9.] Q. Mr. President, is Emmet O'Neal on your list to be the next Ambassador to Manila?

THE PRESIDENT. I have no comment to make on that. There is no vacancy yet in the Philippine ambassadorship.

[10.] Q. Have you received yet a recommendation from the Secretaries of War, Navy, and State on the standardization— military standardization program?

THE PRESIDENT. No I have not.

[11.] Q. Mr. President, you have been in office about a little over 2 years, and you are having another birthday. Has your philosophy of life changed any in those 2 years?

THE PRESIDENT. Not the slightest. Not the slightest. I think we have the greatest Government in the world. I think we have the greatest Government the world has ever seen. The more I become familiar with it, the better I like it, even if it does make a slave out of the President. [*Laughter*]

[12.] Q. Mr. President, the head of the Southern Baptist Convention[1] in St. Louis yesterday said that you had promised him last June that as soon as treaties were ready for the countries in Europe you would recall Mr. Taylor. They urge his immediate recall. Have you any comment on that?

THE PRESIDENT. I think I made the statement when the gentlemen were in to see me, that when peace was consummated we would consider the recall of Mr. Taylor. Peace is by no means consummated yet.

[13.] Q. Mr. President, there was a bill introduced last week which concerns an amendment barring Federal funds for sectarian schools. Would you favor such an amendment?

---

[1] Item 76.

[1] Dr. Louie Newton.

THE PRESIDENT. I have no comment on that. I know nothing about it.

[14.] Q. Mr. President, I hate to be persistent on prices——

THE PRESIDENT. Go ahead.

Q. ——but since you spoke last, sir, the idea has been fanfared forth by the United States Chamber of Commerce that a drive from the White House to use "moral suasion" to get prices down might cause the depression that it seeks to avert. Do you want to comment on that, sir?

THE PRESIDENT. No I do not. No comment.

Q. Mr. President, also on prices, your campaign seems to have had quite a reaction.

THE PRESIDENT. I have been very much pleased with the reaction.

Q. Do you think that we might be over the peak of inflation?

THE PRESIDENT. I never have thought that we were in inflation. What we have been trying to do is to prevent inflation.

Q. Do you think we are over the peak of high prices?

THE PRESIDENT. I can't answer that question. You will have to see what develops.

Reporter: Thank you, Mr. President.

NOTE: President Truman's one hundred and fifth news conference was held in his office at the White House at 10:35 a.m. on Thursday, May 8, 1947.

---

89   Letter to the Speaker of the House of Representatives Requesting Appropriations for the Employees Loyalty Program. *May 9, 1947*

Sir:

I have the honor to transmit herewith for the consideration of Congress supplemental estimates of appropriation for the fiscal year 1947 for the Civil Service Commission in the amount of $16,160,000, and for the Department of Justice, Federal Bureau of Investigation, in the amount of $8,740,000, in all $24,900,000.

The details of these estimates, the necessity therefor, and the reasons for their submission at this time are set forth in the letter of the Director of the Bureau of the Budget, transmitted herewith, in whose comments and observations thereon I concur.

Respectfully yours,

HARRY S. TRUMAN

[Honorable Joseph W. Martin, Jr., The Speaker, The House of Representatives, Washington, D.C.]

NOTE: The White House release announcing the President's action stated that the funds were needed to carry out the purposes of Executive Order 9835, prescribing procedures for the administration of the employees loyalty program (3 CFR, 1943–1948 Comp., p. 627). The release noted that the order was signed March 21 following a report to the President by his Temporary Commission on Employee Loyalty, appointed in November 1946.

The release also made public the greater part of the Budget Director's letter. It outlines the methods to be followed in the preliminary screening of both employees and applicants, together with the provision for a full field investigation in the event that derogatory information is uncovered or in the case of sensitive positions. This letter, except for the details of the appropriation estimates, is essentially a summary of the loyalty procedures set forth in the Executive order. The letter is printed in House Document 242 (80th Cong., 1st sess.).

90   The President's Special Conference With the Association of Radio News Analysts.   *May 13, 1947*

THE PRESIDENT. Well, it's good to have you here. As I told you all on several occasions, there is nothing much that I can tell you. You are always telling *me* what to do! Very frankly, I think every one of you has given me the right advice on Greece and Turkey, internal affairs and foreign affairs, and taxes, and this portal-to-portal, and the labor bill. If I don't get those things right, I can assure you gentlemen it won't be *your* fault. [*Laughter*]

H. V. Kaltenborn (President of the Association): Well, Mr. President, we try to give you advice. Not sure whether the advice is going to be taken.

THE PRESIDENT. Well, that is one of the privileges of the United States. You can do as you please.

[1.] Q. Perhaps we can tell, if you will allow us to ask one or two questions. On the Greco-Turkish relation, there are two approaches to it. One is direct military, the other is the direct economic one—one against aggression, the other the attempt to build up constructively. Which do you feel is the most important at the present moment?

THE PRESIDENT. I will make——

Q. May I interrupt, Mr. President? This is entirely off the record, is that——

THE PRESIDENT. Well, I will answer that, anyway, because it is an easy question. The internal construction and the restoration to a peacetime economy is what we principally are interested in, on a free basis. We are trying to—you know, there are differences in definition of the word "democracy." Our definition doesn't work all the way around the world. It is a much misused word, anyway, to begin with. Our Government is not a democracy, thank God. It's a republic. We elect men to use their best

judgment for the public interest, and if you get that sort of legislature and you get that sort of President, you have a republic that will work in the public interest. A democracy is a town meeting. There is only one place in the world where there is any democracy, and that is in a New England town meeting.

And the radio, I have always been afraid, would restore the Greek approach to the demagogue's ability to mislead the country. I hope it will never come about, the man with the sweet voice and the great personality, for he can do things to this country, if he controlled the air.

My idea is the restoration of a peacetime economy in these countries, with the hope that they will themselves inaugurate a free government that will be for the benefit of the people. That is the principal thing we have in view.

There isn't any difference in totalitarian states. I don't care what you call them—you call them Nazi, Communist or Fascist, or Franco, or anything else—they are all alike. That is not our intention, to tell any country what its internal business should be, how its internal business should be handled. We are hopeful that that internal business will be along lines of most benefit to the individual. I believe in the Bill of Rights. I think that is the most important part of our Constitution—the right of the individual to go where he pleases, to do what he pleases, say what he pleases, as long as he is not materially injuring his neighbors. That is the basis on which our Government is founded, and I think it is the greatest basis in the world for a government. Totalitarian governments do not work that way. The police state is a police state; I don't care what you call it.

I have tried my level best to get along with our friends the Russians, and I still want to get along with them. But when I make straight out and out agreements with a government, in the name of the United States of America, and not a single one of those agreements is carried out, I have got to use other methods. They understand one language, and that is the language they are going to get from me from this point.

I want peace in the world worse than any one thing on earth. I sit here studying that globe over there behind you, and think just what a grand place it could be made—the raw materials, its ability, and its room, and with everything else there for everybody in the world to have a decent standard of living. It could be, if we just stick together and work out the proper distribution of the things that we need today.

That is what is in the back of my mind. Does that answer your——

Q. It does, indeed. But you make a broader application of the Truman Doctrine than just confining it to Greece and Turkey.

THE PRESIDENT. All I am interested in is the doctrine of the Republic of the United States of America, to restore free government in the world, to make the United Nations work—in the same manner in which the Colonies made the Federal Government work. That is what we want to do. If we think that can be done in 15 minutes, or 6 months, or 5 years, or 10 years, you are just as mistaken as you can be. It took exactly 80 years before we got the Republic of the United States on a working basis, and we had to lick ourselves in order to get that done.

I am looking forward to the time when the United Nations will be a going concern, and I am doing everything I possibly can to make it a going concern, because that is the only hope for peace in the world. If we can get

an understanding with all our neighbors for the exchange of our ability to make things for their own materials, and set this thing up on the basis that the Colonies were set up as a government, which is now the greatest Government in the world, I think we can make that United Nations work, as it did in time of war. I wish you would study that Charter carefully. It has got some good things in it. But they are no good on paper.

Q. Mr. President, would you say——

THE PRESIDENT. I beg your pardon?

Q. I was going to say that the Constitution of the United States is no good on paper unless they make it work. Would you say that application of the principles you just set forth to Western Europe would be in order?

THE PRESIDENT. Exceedingly helpful— would be exceedingly helpful, and I think it will improve the situation in Eastern Europe.

I think you—eventually that the Russian people will come up with a free government. I am not saying that I want to see the present government overthrown. If they want that kind of government, that's their business. But I don't want them interfering with our own form of government—telling me what to do.

Q. Do you think it will have some effect?

THE PRESIDENT. Very decided effect.

[2.] Q. I have just come from the Senate, where they are working on the labor bill, some measures of which it is rumored you might disagree?

THE PRESIDENT. Well, I never analyze a bill or talk about it until it's on my desk for signature or for my veto. When that bill comes to me, I will tell you exactly what I think about it—but not now.

Q. Carl Hatch made a little talk last night for you, and he made a prediction.

THE PRESIDENT. Did he? Well, Carl Hatch is my friend, and I think very highly of him, but nobody is entitled to predict my attitude of mind on any piece of legislation; and I say that kindly.

Q. I don't think he pretended to say——

THE PRESIDENT. He was guessing as to what I would do, and he had the privilege of that.

Q. Probably obliging, Mr. President.

THE PRESIDENT. Which is all right. No, I can't—Congress has to create the legislation. I have a right to decide on what to sign or what not to sign, and I don't like to have a prophecy made as to what I am going to do until I have all the facts. Nobody knows what I am going to do until I know—make up my mind.

[3.] Q. Would you care to discuss the price problem?

THE PRESIDENT. Well, I discussed it as thoroughly and as completely as I could with the Associated Press in New York.[1] I gave each one of you a copy of that speech.

[4.] Q. What about Korea, Mr. President?

THE PRESIDENT. The Korean situation has all been published. We want a united Korea with a democratic form of government, and we are approaching it now, I think, more nearly to a point of agreement than we ever have been. General Marshall knows how to handle it. He has been over there.

[5.] Q. Have you seen any definite results from your Associated Press speech?

THE PRESIDENT. Yes, I have seen some definite results from it. I get reports on the—on the—what do you call it?

Q. Indices.

THE PRESIDENT. Indices, yes. Level of industry, and costs, and things of that sort. It has been going down a little bit. Of course, one of the reasons for the food situation is the fact that all the world—nearly all the world

has been fed from our production, and it creates a shortage here which naturally pushes the price up. I was very much pleased to see the report on the anticipated wheat crop for this year, which will be the greatest one we have ever had, if we have the weather. And that will have a good effect on the food prices.

We are in the situation now that is just exactly opposite to the situation in 1930. From 1930 until 1939 we were endeavoring to put a floor under wages to keep the prices of basic commodities at a point where they could be produced economically. We are at the other end of that thing now. We are trying to keep that thing from getting away, getting into a spiral. The roof is there, and the roof is here—[*indicating with his hands, up and down*]—and somewhere in between is where we belong.

[6.] Q. Have we taken a position on Palestine? Has it become one of our strategic considerations?

THE PRESIDENT. No. Palestine—everything that has been said about Palestine is still on the record, and still stands.

[7.] Q. Are you disturbed about the situation in Germany, Mr. President?

THE PRESIDENT. I am, yes. Very much disturbed about it. If the Potsdam agreement could be carried out, the situation would be very—[*inaudible words*]—situation in Japan has been handled because we had control of it. And I think that the situation in Germany, if it had been carried out, if we had got that economic unity which is necessary for the country—[*inaudible*]— Germany is the industrial heart of Europe, and all we can do is prevent that industrial situation from becoming—[*inaudible*]—so as to make it work as an individual whole. Italy also is—[*inaudible*]—if it has no chance to get coal, bread, and things of that sort, of which they are short, and until we can get those things all worked out as a unit,

---

[1] Item 76.

we are going to struggle through. That struggle will continue until its done. I don't know how long it is going to take. I hope it will be done inside 2 or 3 years. I started at Potsdam.

Q. Do you feel we should go ahead with the political implications?

THE PRESIDENT. Yes, I think so.

[8.] Q. Mr. President, in this program of reconstruction, do you perceive that we could reduce taxes in this country?

THE PRESIDENT. Not now. I don't think there's any possible chance to reduce taxes now, if we are going to maintain the economic stability of this country.

Two hundred and fifty-seven billion dollars in bonds are out in this country. This is off the record, because I am going to have a bill—going to have something on this later, and I don't want any question about it. Two hundred and fifty-seven billion dollars out in this country, in the hands of 80 million people. Forty percent of the assets of 60 million insurance policy-holders are based on that $250 billion in bonds of the Government of the United States. It is absolutely essential that that $257 billion be whittled down as far as we possibly can, so that there won't be any fluctuation in the price of the bonds and we can keep double the interest on those bonds. In order to do that, we have got to have a complete going concern in this country. And while that is a complete going concern here, we ought to scale that debt down, and not be all demagoguing about—talking about tax reduction. That is what it amounts to.

Q. Mr. President, at the price of great self-abnegation, some of us agree with you entirely on this matter of taxes. [*Laughter*]

THE PRESIDENT. Taxes, you know, are always the court of the demagogue. If you are—want to run for office, you are going to cut taxes and decrease appropriations. Never vote against an appropriation. Never vote against a tax reduction. They come together, sometimes.

Mr. Kaltenborn: We are very grateful to you, sir. We know you have a luncheon engagement waiting.

THE PRESIDENT. Nice to see you all.

NOTE: President Truman's special conference with the radio news analysts was held in his office at the White House at 12:45 p.m. on Tuesday, May 13, 1947. The White House Official Reporter noted that the following members of the Association, in addition to Mr. Kaltenborn, were present: Lowell Thomas, Cecil Brown, Ned Calmer, Charles Hodges, Larry Lesueur, John McVane, Cesar Saerchinger, Paul Schubert, Ernest Lindley, George Fielding Eliot, Albert Warner, George Hamilton Coombs, Leland Stowe, Robert Trout, Gregor Ziemer, Elmer Davis, Richard Harkness, Joseph C. Harsch, Bill Henry, William Hillman, Eric Sevareid, and Raymond Swing.

The meeting is listed in the Official Reporter's records as the President's one hundred and sixth news conference.

---

91   Exchange of Messages With President Alemán of Mexico. *May* 13, 1947

[Released May 13, 1947. Dated May 12, 1947]

I THANK YOU for your courteous message sent me upon your departure from the United States.

The visit which you and your distinguished companions have graciously paid to me and to the people of the United States has strengthened the already firm ties of friendship and understanding between our two countries. I share your confidence that our relations will grow ever stronger in the same cordial spirit that governed my recent visit to your great country and your visit to the United States.

May I express to you, Mr. President, my best wishes for your personal well-being and happiness.

HARRY S. TRUMAN

[His Excellency Miguel Alemán, President of the Mexican States, Mexico D.F. (Mexico)]

NOTE: President Alemán's message, dated May 8 and sent from Olmsted Field, Middleton, Pa., follows:

His Excellency Harry S. Truman:

Upon leaving the territory of the United States, I desire to express to you once again my deep gratitude for all the courtesies which you were so good as to extend to me during my stay in your great country, for whose happiness I express sincere wishes as President of a people which believes deeply in the democratic solidarity of liberty-loving men, governed by justice and associated in progress.

The spirit of complete and reciprocal understanding which guided all our conversations in Washington as well as in Mexico is an excellent guarantee of the cordiality of our Republics.

In view of your high qualities as a statesman and as a man which give value to your noble sincerity, that spirit of understanding has found in you a strong champion of inter-American cohesion.

Confident that the cordiality to which I refer will continue to be the best basis for strengthening and promoting the relations of our governments and our peoples, I repeat to you, Mr. President, the sentiments of my constant and steadfast friendship.

MIGUEL ALEMÁN

92   Statement by the President Concerning Final Burial of the Dead of World War II. *May 13, 1947*

THE WAR and Navy Departments recently began their inquiries to determine the wishes of the next of kin concerning the final burial of the men and women who gave their lives in our country's service during World War II. In compliance with the directions given by the Congress, the desires of the next of kin will be followed as promptly as is practicable.

It is possible that in making their decision some of the relatives of these brave men and women desire assurance that their dead shall rest in dignity and honor—a desire which would be satisfied by the prospect of visiting the burial places in our national cemeteries or in the local cemeteries near their homes. I feel sure, however, that if they could see for themselves the care which is devoted to the graves of those who died in the First World War, and to the temporary cemeteries in which their own dead lie buried today, many of the next of kin would prefer that their loved ones should rest forever in the countries where they fell.

I believe, therefore, that our Government should make possible a pilgrimage to the permanent cemeteries overseas. To this pilgrimage should be invited those of the next of kin who elect that their sons or husbands shall rest in permanent cemeteries overseas under the care of their Government. It should be organized after the permanent military cemeteries have been established and after the erection of headstones and memorial chapels has sufficiently advanced to give reassurance of the perpetual care which our country will devote to the resting places of our honored dead.

93   Special Message to the Congress Upon Signing the Portal-to-Portal Act.   *May 14, 1947*

To the Congress of the United States:

I have today signed H.R. 2157, the Portal-to-Portal Act of 1947. The primary purpose of this Act is to relieve employers and the Government from potential liability for billions of dollars in so-called "portal-to-portal" claims. These claims have emerged since judicial interpretation of the "Wage and Hour Law" raised the possibility that employers might be required to pay back wages for certain activities which in most industries had not previously been considered by either workers or employers to be compensable. I believe that, in the interest of the economic stability of our Nation, it is essential to clarify this matter by statute.

The Portal-to-Portal Act should end this uncertainty with respect to claims of still undetermined magnitude. Current wage negotiations can proceed more readily to a satisfactory conclusion, and businessmen will be able to plan with assurance for full production and price reductions. This will be of real value to labor and management in the maintenance of a continued high level of employment.

I am confident that the purpose of the main provisions of the Act is to eliminate the immense potential liabilities which have arisen as the result of the "portal-to-portal" claims. It is not the purpose of the Act to permit violation of our fundamental wage and hour standards, or to allow a lowering of these standards. This is evident from the findings of the Congress set forth in Section I of the Act as to the need for legislation.

Some doubts have been expressed to me, however, concerning the effects of this legislation upon our wage and hour standards.

Section 2 of the Act relates to existing claims. From my consideration of this Section, I understand it to be the intent of the Congress to meet the problem raised by portal-to-portal claims, but not to invalidate all other existing claims. The plain language of Section 2 of the Act preserves minimum wage and overtime compensation claims based upon activities which were compensable in any amount under contract, custom or practice. Various provisions of the Act such as Sections 3, 9, and 12, would be rendered absurd or unnecessary under any other interpretation. Moreover, a contrary interpretation would raise difficult and grave questions of constitutionality.

As to Section 4, relating to future claims, the legislative history of the Act shows that the Congress intends that the words "principal activities" are to be construed liberally to include any work of consequence performed for the employer, no matter when the work is performed. We should not lose sight of the important requirement under the Act that all "principal activities" must be paid for, regardless of contract, custom, or practice. I am sure the courts will not permit employers to use artificial devices such as the shifting of work to the beginning or the end of the day to avoid liability under the law.

I wish also to refer to the so-called "good faith" provisions of Sections 9 and 10 of the Act. It has been said that they make each employer his own judge of whether or not he has been guilty of a violation. It seems to me that this view fails to take into account the safeguards which are contained in these Sections. The employer must meet an objective test of actual conformity with an administrative ruling or policy. If the employer avails himself of the defense under these Sections, he must bear the burden of proof. He must show that there was affirmative action by an administrative agency and that he relied upon and conformed with such action. He must show further that he acted in good faith in relying upon that administrative action.

Section 11 of the Act gives the Court discretionary authority to waive liquidated damages. Under the language of the Section, however, it continues to be the duty of the court to award liquidated damages unless convinced that the employer has, in good faith, sought to comply with his obligations under the Act. I do not believe this Section will be used to permit employers to engage in violation of the law with impunity.

I am aware that this Act introduces new and possibly ambiguous language, the effects of which can be accurately measured only after interpretation by the Courts. I have therefore instructed the Secretary of Labor to keep me currently informed as to the effects of this Act upon the preservation of wage and hour standards. If those effects prove to be detrimental to the maintenance of fair labor standards for our workers, I shall request the Congress to take prompt remedial action.

The enactment of H.R. 2157 makes necessary additional appropriations for the administration and enforcement of the wage and hour laws. The two-year statute of limitations under this Act will in most cases substantially reduce the period of time within which workers' claims may be asserted under the wage and hour laws. It

will be necessary, therefore, to augment the Government's program of inspection and enforcement in order to detect violations early enough to protect workers from undue losses. Other provisions of the Act also place additional responsibilities upon the Department of Labor. I shall submit estimates to the Congress for the necessary appropriations.

Prior to its adjournment last year, the Congress had reached a large measure of agreement as to legislation to increase minimum wage standards. I trust that with the passage of the Portal-to-Portal Act, relieving the business community of a heavy burden of doubt, the Congress will now turn to a re-examination of minimum wage standards.

In enacting the Fair Labor Standards Act of 1938, the Congress declared it to be our national policy to eliminate labor conditions "detrimental to the maintenance of the minimum standard of living necessary for health, efficiency, and general well-being of workers." It has become increasingly evident that the minimum wage of 40 cents an hour established by that Act is far from adequate to meet that national policy. I am convinced that immediate amendment of the Act to provide a minimum of at least 65 cents an hour is necessary. In addition, minimum wage benefits should be extended to many persons not now protected by the law, as I have recommended in previous Messages to the Congress.

I recommend that the Congress take action upon these matters now.

HARRY S. TRUMAN

NOTE: The Portal-to-Portal Act of 1947 is Public Law 49, 80th Congress (61 Stat. 84).

94   Citation Accompanying Medal for Merit Awarded to John Wesley Snyder. *May 14, 1947*

CITATION TO ACCOMPANY THE AWARD OF

THE MEDAL FOR MERIT

TO

JOHN WESLEY SNYDER

JOHN WESLEY SNYDER, for exceptionally meritorious conduct in the performance of outstanding services to the United States from August, 1940 to August, 1943. Mr. Snyder, as Executive Vice President of the Defense Plant Corporation, effectively directed the detailed organization of the Corporation to provide for the financing and construction of facilities required for the successful prosecution of the war. As a result of his foresight, initiative, and great ability he played an outstanding part in providing American industry and the Armed Services with the machine tools and plants with which to forge the weapons for victory. Under his aggressive leadership and diligent efforts, aircraft plants were constructed and equipped in a minimum of time, and the productive capacity to support a modern air force was thus established. Mr. Snyder's achievements and patriotic devotion reflect the highest credit upon himself and the Government of the United States.

HARRY S. TRUMAN

NOTE: The presentation was made at the White House at 12:30 p.m.

95   The President's News Conference of *May 15, 1947*

THE PRESIDENT. [1.] I signed an important bill this morning, and it is usual to give the pen to those who contributed most to the passage, so I am going to make Joe Fox a present of the pillar bill pen—[*laughter*].

Joseph A. Fox, Washington Star: I knew my work would be recognized! Thank you, Mr. President! [*More laughter*]

Q. What was the bill?

THE PRESIDENT. Bill that took these pillars out of Executive Avenue—the pillar bill.

Q. The pillar bill.

THE PRESIDENT. Executive Avenue pillar bill.[1]

[2.] I also see that my good friend Tony[2] has turned columnist. He starts off by complaining that the reporters don't get sleep enough on their trips with me. Quite an interesting article, in some out-of-town papers. I don't think Tony knew I was going to get hold of that. [*Laughter*] I will try to give you a real merry-go-round next time. We really haven't had a strenuous trip yet, Tony. [*More laughter*]

Q. Mr. President, you are not solely responsible for that loss of sleep, are you, sir?

THE PRESIDENT. No sir. No sir, I get plenty. I didn't know why Tony didn't.

Q. Can we have that in quotes, Mr. President?

THE PRESIDENT. Better not. That might embarrass Tony at home. [*Laughter*]

Q. Do you think there will be any trips in 1948, Mr. President?

THE PRESIDENT. Well, I imagine that there will be. Be a trip home, at any rate.

---

[1] The so-called pillar bill authorized the removal of stone piers in West Executive Avenue between the White House grounds and the Department of State building (61 Stat. 95).

[2] Ernest B. Vaccaro of the Associated Press.

Q. Lot of prophecy there, isn't it, Mr. President?

THE PRESIDENT. Whether you want to hire a plane on that occasion and follow me or not remains to be seen.

Q. That would be 1949, wouldn't it?

THE PRESIDENT. Well, we will discuss that when it comes up. I never want to discuss it or think about it.

Now I am ready for questions, if you have any you think I can answer.

[3.] Q. Mr. President, do you believe some further labor legislation, in addition to the portal act, should be enacted this session?

THE PRESIDENT. I expressed my views on that in the message I sent to the Congress on the State of the Union.

Q. Do you stand on what you said then?

THE PRESIDENT. I do.

[4.] Q. Mr. President, French papers claim that you are going to send a new Ambassador to France?

THE PRESIDENT. I hadn't heard about it. Maybe they know my mind better than I do.

[5.] Q. Mr. President, do you intend to keep Mr. Messersmith in the Argentine indefinitely?

THE PRESIDENT. When Mr. Messersmith went to the Argentine, he made it a condition of his going that he was only going temporarily, but I don't know when that time will end. That is a matter that we will have to work out at the proper time. Mr. Messersmith has not been in good health, and he explained to me that when he was down there he was doing it as a favor to Mr. Byrnes and myself.

[6.] Q. Mr. President, could you tell us who is going to head the mission to Greece?

THE PRESIDENT. No, I can't.

Q. When will that appointment be made, sir?

THE PRESIDENT. Just as quickly as I can get the man I am interested in to take the job.

Q. Have you got such a man in mind?

THE PRESIDENT. Yes, I have.

Q. Is he reluctant to take the job, sir?

THE PRESIDENT. Yes sir. People are always reluctant to take a hard job. There's a difference, you know, between doing a patriotic duty in peacetime and doing a patriotic duty when the country is in a shooting war, when there is some sort of incentive that makes people more cooperative, more anxious to make sacrifices—and I can't blame them.

But the present period is just as important for the welfare of the country as actual shooting warfare would be. And I hope the patriots will bear that in mind: it is necessary to do things that you don't want to do—some good—for the welfare and benefit of your country.

I didn't intend to give you a lecture.

[7.] Q. Is there any change in sight regarding the ambassadorship in Chile?

THE PRESIDENT. No.

[8.] Q. Mr. President, I see Governor Wallgren here. Are you in complete accord with the mission that he came on?

THE PRESIDENT. I don't know what his mission is. He hasn't talked to me about it. He came to see me socially!

[9.] Q. Mr. President, have you ever lifted that freeze order on reclamation of funds that went out about January 10?

THE PRESIDENT. No, I have not. That freeze order was worked out on the basis of what we thought the Interior Department could spend, and I think you can get—I know you can get all the details in regard to it from the Budget. It is a complicated proposition, and I would advise you to talk to the Budget about it.

[10.] Q. Mr. President, are you preparing to ask Congress again to grant powers and supply armaments in Latin America, as advanced last year?

THE PRESIDENT. We have that matter under consideration in the State Department. I will answer it when it has reached the completion of it.

[11.] Q. Mr. President, is there any chance that there will be more than one administrator for the Greek-Turkey program?

THE PRESIDENT. I haven't gone into any detail.

[12.] Q. Mr. President, has Chester Bowles's group presented a price reduction plan to you?

THE PRESIDENT. I understand that there is one in the mails for me. I haven't read it yet—I haven't seen it, in fact.

[13.] Q. Mr. President, have you reached any decision yet on the Korean aid program?

THE PRESIDENT. No, I have not.

[14.] Q. Mr. President, there are some reports that you are being urged by various branches of the Government to visit Latin American countries next year. Is that correct?

THE PRESIDENT. No, it is not.

Q. I beg your pardon?

THE PRESIDENT. I said no, that I am not being urged by any branches of the Government.

[15.] Q. Mr. President, returning to Mr. Messersmith, would it be correct to say that Mr. Messersmith will return to this country when he has completed his mission?

THE PRESIDENT. Yes, that is perfectly correct.

Q. Would that go for Mr. Caffery too, Mr. President?

THE PRESIDENT. I have no comment on that. Mr. Caffery is not on the same sort of mission that Mr. Messersmith is.

[16.] Q. Mr. President, all of the "dopesters" around you are saying that this is just the first step, the Greek-Turkey plan, and that there will soon be other countries that will have to be bolstered against communism. Can you comment on that?

THE PRESIDENT. We will meet that situation should it arise.

[17.] Q. Mr. President, the Mexican Ambassador said this morning that he brought a personal message for you from President Alemán. Can you tell us anything about that?

THE PRESIDENT. It was a very cordial and friendly message about the treatment which the President received in the United States. A beautiful letter, one that I am going to frame and keep for my daughter.

[18.] Q. Mr. President, I understand the Army will soon deliver a new—make delivery of the new plane to succeed the *Sacred Cow*. Do you have any idea of what you might like to name the new plane?

THE PRESIDENT. Well, when that event takes place, I shall name the plane.

[19.] Q. Mr. President, would you comment on Senator Taft's giving every priority to the Taft-Ellender-Wagner housing bill?

THE PRESIDENT. I would like to see that bill have all the priority it could get.

[20.] Q. Mr. President, will you comment on a report published in Manila newspapers, that you would name Emmet O'Neal Ambassador to the Philippines this week?

THE PRESIDENT. I do not care to comment on that at this time.

[21.] Q. Mr. President, getting back to Chester Bowles—those recommendations he is sending over. He predicts quite a bust in 3 to 5 months. Have you any comment?

THE PRESIDENT. No comment. I haven't read Mr. Bowles's article yet. I don't like to comment on a piece of paper that I haven't seen or haven't read. I had better know what's in it before I make any comment.

[22.] Q. Mr. President, the subject of displaced persons is coming up again, it seems to be becoming more acute. I thought last year you urged admission of more people up to the limit of the laws——

THE PRESIDENT. That is true.

Q. ——and I wondered if you had any rough estimate of how many you thought we might be able to absorb now?

THE PRESIDENT. I have no estimate on the subject. I went into it in some detail at that time, and instructions have been given to the State Department. For myself, I have suggested using the unused quota of northern Europe for displaced persons. They have been working on that. The results have not been very satisfactory.

[23.] Q. Mr. President, with regard to Mr. Bowles's belief—that other people have and that you do not have yet, sir—do you think there is going to be a bust in 3 to 5 months?

THE PRESIDENT. I think I have told you time and again that I do not believe so. I think I made that statement categorically to you at least half-a-dozen times.

[24.] Q. Returning to the question of displaced persons for a moment, there is a bill in Congress which would admit, I think, 400,000 persons in the next 4 years. Do you have any plan to send a message to Congress on the general question of admission?

THE PRESIDENT. Not at the present time. Doing everything we possibly can to get the displaced persons situation worked out. It is an international problem, and it will have to be worked out on an international basis. We should do our share toward alleviating that situation, and I have said that from the beginning.

Q. Would legislation be required, sir?

THE PRESIDENT. I think it would.

[25.] Q. Mr. President, do you have any plans to ask for new funds, or additional funds, for the Export-Import Bank?

THE PRESIDENT. If it is necessary for the Export-Import Bank to have additional funds, of course they will be asked for.

Q. Have you had any indication that it is likely that they will have need for them?

THE PRESIDENT. No, I have not.

Q. Mr. President, I would like to know——

[26.] Q. Mr. President, has the Greek-Turkish bill come down to you yet?

THE PRESIDENT. No, it has not. What was your question?

[27.] Q. On this question of "bust," you said you don't think that it will be in 5 months—I mean, what is your affirmative attitude on the economic outlook for the future?

THE PRESIDENT. I don't think there is any necessity for ever having a bust. If we use good sense and follow just common—the rules of commonsense, don't let the greedy people get control of the country, we won't have any bust. We shouldn't have any boom. That is what we have been trying to prevent. Would like to keep a ceiling on prices, and things of that sort, so there wouldn't be any boom or bust. We have had not much cooperation either legislatively or publicly on that, except that there are a large number of people who have made every effort they can to cooperate with us in this price situation.

Q. Mr. President, do you think this pending tax bill would accentuate the boom?

THE PRESIDENT. I can't answer that because I don't know what's in it. I will tell you that when it comes up here.

Q. Mr. President, you had an "if" in your statement, that *if* we use commonsense, and it gave me the impression that you might think we are a trifle off the beam somewhere. Could you indicate that?

THE PRESIDENT. Well, I think prices are too high, particularly commodity prices.

Q. Is that the main——

THE PRESIDENT. That is the main ill.

[28.] Q. Mr. President, are you hopeful that the cuts made by the House Appropriations Committee in western reclamational and power projects will be restored by the Congress——

THE PRESIDENT. My Budget Message covered that situation completely. I set down in the budget exactly what I thought should be done, and I am sticking by that budget.

Reporter: Thank you, Mr. President.

NOTE: President Truman's one hundred and seventh news conference was held in his office at the White House at 4 o'clock on Thursday afternoon, May 15, 1947.

96 Letter to Senator Wherry Concerning the Moratorium on Reclamation Projects and Other Federal Construction. *May* 16, 1947

Dear Senator Wherry:

This refers to your letter dated May 2, 1947, requesting certain information concerning the 60-day moratorium and the expenditure ceilings which were placed on Reclamation projects and other Federal construction.

As you know, the moratorium and the expenditure ceilings did not provide for the cancellation of any projects authorized by the Congress. They were designed, rather, to guide the timing of construction and, as such, were an important aid to reconversion. The program was clearly authorized by Section 101(c) of the War Mobilization and Reconversion Act of 1944 which, among other things, authorizes the Director of War Mobilization and Reconversion, subject to the direction of the President, to formulate plans to meet the problems of reconversion and to require executive agencies to exercise their powers in a manner consistent with such plans; and such program was within the well-recognized authority of the President, acting directly or through the Bureau of the Budget, to exercise general supervision over the expenditures of the executive departments, in discharging his duties as Chief Executive and his responsibility for the proper execution of the laws.

The correct figures for current expenditure ceilings for the Bureau of Reclamation are set forth in your letter, namely, $130 million for the construction program for fiscal year 1947 and $177.4 million for expenditures for all purposes during the fiscal year 1948. The expenditure ceiling for fiscal year 1947 will, of course, terminate June 30, 1947, with the close of the current fiscal year. Any upward revision of the 1947 ceiling at this time would not result in expenditures in excess of the existing limitations for this fiscal year because of the lag inherent in heavy construction and the short time remaining in this fiscal year.

The limitation of $177.4 million for expenditures during fiscal year 1948 is the total included as an estimate of expenditures in the President's Budget and is based on the assumptions of that Budget, that is, that the carry-overs from fiscal year 1947 would agree with the estimates made for the Budget, and that the appropriations made by Congress for fiscal year 1948 would agree with the requests in the Budget. It is not possible to make a re-evaluation of these figures until it is known what sums Congress will appropriate for the agency.

I may add that at this time it is not anticipated that it will be necessary or desirable to place restrictions on the expenditure of funds available for fiscal year 1948.

Very sincerely yours,

HARRY S. TRUMAN

[The Honorable Kenneth S. Wherry, United States Senate]

97 Letter to Secretary Anderson Calling a Conference on Farm Real Estate Prices. *May 16, 1947*

My dear Mr. Secretary:

Recalling the distress among farmers which resulted from land inflation in the World War I period, I am deeply concerned about the recent rise in farm real estate prices. I understand the reports of your Department indicate that for the country as a whole farm real estate values have reached a level 92 percent above the 1935–39 average. I also understand that in 24 States real estate values are now above the inflationary peak of 1920 and that in many areas of the country farms are selling at prices which cannot be sustained by probable long-time farm earnings.

It is apparent that a united effort by all concerned is needed if we are to prevent further inflation in farm real estate prices and over-expansion of farm debts. While on the whole agriculture is in strong financial condition, the fact remains that there are a large number of farmers, including veterans, who are going heavily into debt to purchase farms at inflated prices. These farmers are likely to find themselves in difficulty when prices of farm products decline to lower levels.

I believe that the existing farm price situation presents a serious problem which should be given careful consideration by institutional lenders and others concerned. For this reason I suggest that at an early date you call a conference of representatives of the appropriate Government agencies and the general farm organizations for a consideration of the problem. Invitations to the conference should also be extended to representatives of life insurance companies currently making a large number of farm mortgage loans, the American Bankers Association and the Federal Reserve System. From this conference I hope there will develop a specific program of methods for discouraging further inflation in farm real estate prices and unwise expansion of farm debts.

Very sincerely yours,

HARRY S. TRUMAN

[The Honorable The Secretary of Agriculture, Washington, D.C.]

98 Special Message to the Congress on Health and Disability Insurance. *May 19, 1947*

To the Congress of the United States:

Healthy citizens constitute our greatest national resource. In time of peace, as in time of war, our ultimate strength stems from the vigor of our people. The welfare and security of our nation demand that the opportunity for good health be made available to all, regardless of residence, race or economic status.

At no time can we afford to lose the productive energies and capacities of millions of our citizens. Nor can we permit our children to grow up without a fair chance of survival and a fair chance for a healthy life. We must not permit our rural families to suffer for lack of physicians, dentists, nurses and hospitals. We must not reserve a chance for good health and a long productive life to the well-to-do alone. A great and free nation should bring good health care within the reach of all its people.

In my message to the Congress on November 19, 1945, I said that every American should have the right to adequate medical care and to adequate protection from the economic threat of sickness. To provide this care and protection is a challenging task, requiring action on a wide front.

I have previously outlined the long-range health program which I consider necessary to the national welfare and security. I say again that such a program must include:

1. Adequate public health services, including an expanded maternal and child health program.

2. Additional medical research and medical education.

3. More hospitals and more doctors—in all areas of the country where they are needed.

4. Insurance against the costs of medical care.

5. Protection against loss of earnings during illness.

I am pleased to observe that important advances were made by the last Congress toward realization of some of the goals which I set forth in my earlier message. But we must not rest until we have achieved all our objectives. I urge this Congress to enact additional legislation to authorize the program I have outlined, even though the fulfillment of some aspects of it may take time.

Our public health services—federal, state and local—provide our greatest and most successful defense against preventable diseases. But in many states, cities and counties in America, limited funds reduce the work of our public health services to a dangerously inadequate level. Public services related to maternal and child health were expanded by the 79th Congress, through amendments to the Social Security Act. This action was gratifying, but the long-range need for additional health services for children and expectant mothers, and for care of crippled or otherwise physically handicapped children,

should be carefully studied by the Congress.

The Nation's medical research programs must in the future be expanded so that we can learn more about the prevention and cure of disease. The Congress has already recognized this by providing for research into the causes of cancer and mental diseases and abnormalities. Further dividends will accrue to our Nation—and to our people— if research can point the way toward combatting and overcoming such major illnesses as arthritis and rheumatic fever, and diseases of the heart, kidneys and arteries.

We still face a shortage of hospitals, physicians, dentists and nurses. Those we have are unfairly distributed. The shortage of doctors, dentists and nurses can be met only through expanded educational opportunities. The shortage of hospitals will be met in part through the action of the last Congress which provided Federal aid for the construction of hospitals.

In the last analysis the patient's ability to pay for the services of physicians or dentists, or for hospital care, determines the distribution of doctors and the location of hospitals. Few doctors can be expected to practice today in sparsely settled areas or where prospective patients are unable to pay for their services. Doctors tend to concentrate in communities where hospitals and other facilities are best and where their incomes are most secure. The unequal distribution of doctors and hospitals will plague this nation until means are found to finance modern medical care for all of our people.

National health insurance is the most effective single way to meet the Nation's health needs. Because adequate treatment of many illnesses is expensive and its cost cannot be anticipated by the individual, many persons are forced to go without needed medical attention. Children do not receive adequate medical and dental care. Symptoms which should come early to the attention of a physician are often ignored until too late. The poor are not the only ones who cannot afford adequate medical care. The truth is that all except the rich may at some time be struck by illness which requires care and services they cannot afford. Countless families who are entirely self-supporting in every other respect cannot meet the expense of serious illness.

Although the individual or even small groups of individuals cannot successfully or economically plan to meet the cost of illness, large groups of people can do so. If the financial risk of illness is spread among all our people, no one person is overburdened. More important, if the cost is spread in this manner more persons can see their doctors, and will see them earlier. This goal can be reached only through a national medical insurance program, under which all people who are covered by an insurance fund are entitled to necessary medical, hospital and related services.

A national health insurance program is a logical extension of the present social-security system which is so firmly entrenched in our American democracy. Of the four basic risks to the security of working people and their families—unemployment, old age, death and sickness—we have provided some insurance protection against three. Protection against the fourth—sickness—is the major missing element in our national social insurance program.

An insurance plan is the American way of accomplishing our objective. It is consistent with our democratic principles. It is the only plan broad enough to meet the needs of all our people. It is—in the long run—far less costly and far more effective than public charity or a medical dole.

Under the program which I have proposed patients can and will be as free to select their own doctors as they are today. Doctors and hospitals can and will be free to participate or to reject participation. And a national health insurance plan can and should provide for administration through state and local agencies, subject only to reasonable national standards.

Finally, I should like to repeat to the Congress my earlier recommendation that the people of America be protected against loss of earnings due to illness or disability not connected with their work. Protection against temporary disability is already provided by two states and is being considered in others. Comprehensive disability insurance should exist throughout the Nation. It can and should be a part of our social insurance system.

The total health program which I have proposed is crucial to our national welfare. The heart of that program is national health insurance. Until it is a part of our national fabric, we shall be wasting our most precious national resource and shall be perpetuating unnecessary misery and human suffering.

I urge the Congress to give immediate attention to the development and enactment of national health and disability insurance programs.

HARRY S. TRUMAN

99 Special Message to the Congress Recommending Extension of the Second War Powers Act. *May 22, 1947*

To the Congress of the United States:

In March of this year the Congress passed and I approved a bill known as the First Decontrol Act of 1947, extending for three months a few of the powers originally granted in the Second War Powers Act.

This extension was authorized to enable the Congress to make a further review of the specific controls needed during the coming year.

Since the enactment of this law, the interested departments have reexamined the need for continuation of these powers. Their review shows that it is still essential to maintain certain limited materials controls, in order to prevent harm to our own economy and give concrete support to our foreign policy.

Since V–J Day, American industry, agriculture and labor have established notable production records. If production abroad had reached similar heights, no materials controls at all would be needed today. But the progress of world reconstruction has been necessarily difficult and slow. In a few respects the United States has been adversely affected by this delay, and therefore, in a few instances, controls over certain imported commodities are still needed. However, any adverse effects suffered by us are slight in comparison with the tragic conditions of life faced by most countries of the world today. It is primarily because of these conditions, with their enormously important political and social repercussions, that we must still retain a very limited portion of our wartime powers over materials.

The remaining powers which it is necessary to retain fall into two groups:

(1) Allocation and priority powers to maintain the stability of our economy.

(a) While our economy is still hampered by the lack of a number of imported materials, there are only a few in which the lack is so serious and the importance so great that continued controls are required. The need in these cases is well known. Specifically, it is necessary to continue the power to allocate the following imported materials: tin and tin products, manila and agave fibers and cordage, antimony, cinchona bark, qui-

nine and quinidine. Except in the case of tin products, where the allocation of tin plate is also essential to the solution of world food problems, the continuation of these controls is solely for the purpose of assisting our own industry and agriculture.

(b) As a corollary to the above, it is also necessary to continue the power to issue export priorities for materials needed to increase the production abroad of products that we urgently need in this country. This is a matter of direct and immediate self-interest.

(2) Allocation and priority powers needed to carry out our foreign policy and to assist in world reconstruction.

(a) FOODS. Our own food production has reached great heights, and our own food supplies are excellent. In contrast the food situation abroad continues to be desperate. For that reason we are actively participating in the International Emergency Food Council, which is a noteworthy example of practical international economic cooperation. Our participation in this activity conforms with our national ideals and interests. But participation is not merely a matter of words. We must be able to take the steps necessary to make certain that we do not add to the hunger of other peoples by importing more than our agreed share of scarce foods. I recommend, therefore, continued authority to maintain import controls on fats and oils, and rice and rice products.

(b) FERTILIZER. The world fertilizer situation is similar to, and is directly related to, the world food situation. While our own fertilizer production and consumption have risen spectacularly since the pre-war period, supplies available to foreign countries have fallen sharply. This has resulted in retarded agricultural recovery, loss of food production and consequent malnutrition over widespread areas. The lack of fertilizer is particularly acute in the case of nitrates. It is therefore essential that there be continued authority to restrict imports and to issue priorities for export of nitrogenous fertilizer materials.

(c) INDUSTRIAL MATERIALS. In general our supply of industrial products and materials has reached the point where delays in production and delivery are no longer crucial. The pipelines are full, or are filling up, and no general use of allocation powers is needed. But economic and political conditions in many other countries are so critical that it is necessary to continue the power to issue export priorities in special cases for key industrial items that are vitally required for reconstruction and rehabilitation. In most countries, supplies of industrial materials and products are still far short of minimum essential levels. Entirely apart from the use of priorities, the United States is furnishing substantial quantities of industrial equipment and supplies so urgently needed to reactivate the economies of these countries. However, great damage can be done by inability to obtain an occasional machine, or machine parts needed to complete a program or project. It is in such cases that priority assistance is needed. The Congress has already recognized the importance of supporting our foreign policy with financial assistance. Financial assistance alone, without occasional priority backing, may be useless in instances where speedy aid in concrete form is essential. The use of the priority powers that I am recommending would be limited to cases certified by the Secretary of State to be of high public importance and essential to the successful carrying out of the foreign policy of the United States.

In this message I have not considered it necessary to discuss certain powers originally derived from the Second War Powers Act but now covered by separate legislation, i.e., the Sugar Act, the Rubber Act and the Patman Act. I have also omitted reference to the great importance of continued authority to allocate the use of transportation equipment and facilities by rail carriers. This matter is covered by separate bills, H.R. 3152 and S. 1297, now pending before the Congress. Prompt action on these bills is urgently needed. Similarly, the Congress now has under consideration an extension of the Export Control Act. It, too, is essential in implementing our foreign policy. I also urge prompt action on this bill.

The further extension of the Second War Powers Act in the limited form described above is of direct interest to our own economy and is indispensable in supporting our international policy. The powers that I have outlined are the minimum needed to accomplish these ends. I therefore recommend that the Congress enact legislation to extend these powers for a period of one year.

HARRY S. TRUMAN

NOTE: On July 15 the President approved the Second Decontrol Act of 1947 providing for an extension until February 29, 1948, of certain emergency powers of the President. For his statement upon signing the act, see Item 143.

100 Statement by the President Upon Signing Bill Endorsing the Truman Doctrine. *May 22, 1947*

THE ACT authorizing United States assistance to Greece and Turkey, which I have just signed, is an important step in the building of the peace. Its passage by overwhelming majorities in both Houses of the Congress is proof that the United States earnestly desires peace and is willing to make a vigorous effort to help create conditions of peace.

The conditions of peace include, among other things, the ability of nations to maintain order and independence, and to support themselves economically. In extending the aid requested by two members of the United Nations for the purpose of maintaining these conditions, the United States is helping to further aims and purposes identical with those of the United Nations. Our aid in this instance is evidence not only that we pledge our support to the United Nations but that we *act* to support it.

With the passage and signature of this act, our Ambassadors to Greece and Turkey

are being instructed to enter into immediate negotiations for agreements which, in accordance with the terms of the act, will govern the application of our aid. We intend to make sure that the aid we extend will benefit all the peoples of Greece and Turkey, not any particular group or faction.

I wish to express my appreciation to the leaders and members of both parties in the Congress for their spendid support in obtaining the passage of this vital legislation.

NOTE: As enacted, the bill providing assistance to Greece and Turkey is Public Law 75, 80th Congress (61 Stat. 103).

On May 22 the President also issued Executive Order 9857 prescribing regulations for carrying out the provisions of the act (3 CFR, 1943–1948 Comp., p. 646).

101　Special Message to the Congress on Military Collaboration With Other American States. *May 26, 1947*

[Released May 26, 1947. Dated May 23, 1947]

To the Congress of the United States:

I submit herewith for the consideration of the Congress a bill to be entitled "The Inter-American Military Cooperation Act" authorizing a program of military collaboration with other American States including the training, organization, and equipment of the armed forces of those countries.

I submitted a similar bill to the 79th Congress and recommended at that time that the Congress give the bill favorable consideration and enact it. The Committee on Foreign Affairs of the House of Representatives reported the bill with amendments to the Committee of Whole House as H.R. 6326. This present draft agrees with H.R. 6326. World developments during the year that has passed give still greater importance to this legislation, and I again ask the Congress to give this bill favorable consideration and enact it.

As stated in my message to the 79th Congress our Army and Navy have maintained cordial relations of collaboration with the armed forces of other American republics within the framework of the good-neighbor policy. Under authorization of the Congress, military and naval training missions have been sent to various American republics. During the recent war, even prior to Pearl Harbor, this collaboration was intensively developed on the basis of inter-American undertakings for hemisphere defense. Training activities were expanded, and under the Lend-Lease Act limited amounts of military and naval equipment were made available to the other American republics as part of the hemisphere defense program. Forces from two of the American republics participated in combat overseas, and others joined in the defense of the shores and seas of the Americas at a time when the danger of invasion of our continents was all too great.

The American republics have assumed new responsibilities, for their mutual defense and for the maintenance of peace, in the Act of Chapultepec and the Charter of the United Nations. The close collaboration of the American republics provided for in the Act of Chapultepec, the proposed treaty to be based upon that act, and other basic inter-American documents, make it highly desirable to standardize military organization, training methods, and equipment as has been recommended by the Inter-American Defense Board.

I can find no better way to describe the intent and purpose of this bill than to repeat my message to the Congress of May 6, 1946.

Under the bill transmitted herewith, the Army and Navy acting in conjunction with the Department of State, would be permitted to continue in the future a general program of collaboration with the armed forces of our sister republics with a view to facilitating the adoption of similar technical standards. Certain additional training activities, not covered by existing legislation, would be permitted. The President would also be authorized to transfer military and naval equipment to the governments of other American states by sale or other method.

The collaboration authorized by the bill could be extended also to Canada, whose cooperation with the United States in matters affecting their common defense is of particular importance.

A special responsibility for leadership rests upon the United States in this matter because of the preponderant technical, economic, and military resources of this country. There is a reasonable and limited purpose for which arms and military equipment can rightfully be made available to the other American states. This Government will not, I am sure, in any way approve of, nor will it participate

in, the indiscriminate or unrestricted distribution of armaments, which would only contribute to a useless and burdensome armaments race. It does not desire that operations under this bill shall raise unnecessarily the quantitative level of armament in the American Republics. To this end the bill specifies that amounts of nonstandard material shall be sought in exchange for United States equipment.

It is my intention that any operations under this bill, which the Congress may authorize, shall be in every way consistent with the wording and spirit of the United Nations Charter. The bill has been drawn up primarily to enable the American nations to carry out their obligations to cooperate in the maintenance of inter-American peace and security under the charter and the Act of Chapultepec which is intended to be supplanted by a permanent Inter-American treaty.

It is incumbent upon this Government to see that military developments in which we have a part are guided toward the maintenance of peace and security and that military and naval establishments are not encouraged beyond what security considerations require. In this connection the bill provides that operations thereunder are subject to any international agreement for the regulation of armaments to which the United States may become a party. In addition, provision will be made for continuing coordination of the actual operations under the legislation with developing plans and policy in the field of armaments regulation.

In executing this program it will be borne in mind, moreover, that it is the policy of this Government to encourage the establishment of sound economic conditions in the other American Republics which will contribute to the improvement of living standards and the advancement of social and cultural welfare. Such conditions are a prerequisite to international peace and security. Operations under the proposed legislation will be conducted with full and constant awareness that no encouragement should be given to the imposition upon other people of any useless burden of armaments which would handicap the economic improvement which all countries so strongly desire. The execution of the program authorized by the bill will also be guided by a determination to guard against placing weapons of war in the hands of any groups who may use them to oppose the peaceful and democratic principles to which the United States and other American nations have so often subscribed.

In entering into agreements with other American states for the provision of training and equipment as authorized by the bill, the purposes of this program will be made clear to each of the other governments.

HARRY S. TRUMAN

NOTE: The draft bill, submitted with the President's message, is printed in House Document 271 (80th Cong., 1st sess.).

102 Special Message to the Congress Transmitting Reorganization Plan 3 of 1947. *May 27, 1947*

To the Congress of the United States:

I am transmitting herewith Reorganization Plan No. 3 of 1947, prepared in accordance with the Reorganization Act of 1945. This Plan deals solely with housing. It simplifies, and increases the efficiency of, the administrative organization of permanent housing functions and provides for the administration of certain emergency housing activities pending their liquidation. I have found, after investigation, that each reorganization contained in this Plan is necessary to accomplish one or more of the purposes set forth in section 2(a) of the Reorganization Act of 1945.

The provision of adequate housing will remain a major national objective throughout the next decade. The primary responsibility for meeting housing needs rests, and must continue to rest, with private industry, as I have stated on other occasions. The Federal Government, however, has an important role to play in stimulating and facilitating home construction.

Over the years, the Congress has provided for a number of permanent housing programs, each involving a special approach to the basic objective of more adequate housing for our citizens. The Congress first enacted a series of measures to facilitate home construction and home ownership by strengthening the savings and loan type of home financing institution. These measures established a credit reserve system for such agencies, authorized the chartering of Federal savings and loan associations to provide more adequate home financing facilities, and provided for the insurance of investments in savings and loan institutions in order to attract savings into this field. The Congress also created a system for the insurance of home loans and mortgages to stimulate the flow of capital into home mortgage lending and thereby facilitate home ownership and improvement and increase home construction. These measures were supplemented by legislation extending financial assistance to local communities for the clearance of slums and the provision of decent housing for families of low income who otherwise would be forced to live in the slums. It is significant that these programs were first established, and have been continued, by the Congress because of their special contributions to home construction and improvement.

In my Message of January 6 on the State of the Union, I recommended legislation establishing certain additional programs to help to alleviate the housing shortage and achieve our national objective of a decent home and a suitable living environment for every American family. No lesser objective is commensurate with the productive capacity and resources of the country or with the dignity which a true democracy accords the individual citizen. The Congress is now considering measures authorizing these programs. I again recommend the early enactment of this legislation.

But whatever may be the permanent housing functions of the Government, whether they be confined to the existing programs or supplemented as the Congress may determine, they are inevitably interrelated. They require coordination and supervision so that each will render its full contribution without conflict with the performance of other housing functions.

The Government, however, lacks an effective permanent organization to coordinate and supervise the administration of its principal housing programs. These programs and the machinery for their administration were established piecemeal over a period of years. The present consolidation of housing agencies and functions in the National Housing Agency is only temporary. After the termination of Title I of the First War Powers Act this Agency will dissolve and the agencies and functions now administered in it will revert to their former locations in the Government. When this occurs, the housing programs of the Government will be scattered among some 13 agencies in 7 departments and independent establishments.

I need hardly point out that such a scattering of these interrelated functions would not only be inefficient and wasteful but also would seriously impair their usefulness. It would leave the Government without effective machinery for the coordination and supervision of its housing activities and would thrust upon the Chief Executive an impossible burden of administrative supervision.

The grouping of housing functions in one establishment is essential to assure that the housing policies established by the Congress will be carried out with consistency of purpose and a minimum of friction, duplication, and overlapping. A single establishment will unquestionably make for greater efficiency and economy. Moreover, it will simplify the task of the Congress and the Chief Executive by enabling them to deal with one official and hold one person responsible for the general supervision of housing functions, whereas otherwise they will be forced to deal with a number of uncoordinated officers and agencies.

It is vital that a sound permanent organization of housing activities be established at the earliest possible date in order to insure that housing functions will not be scattered among numerous agencies, with consequent confusion and disruption. To avoid this danger and to accomplish the needed changes promptly, it is desirable to employ a reorganization plan under the Reorganization Act of 1945. No other area of Federal activity affords greater opportunity than housing for accomplishing the objectives of the Reorganization Act to group, consolidate, and coordinate functions, reduce the number of agencies, and promote efficiency and economy; and in no other area could the application of the Reorganization Act be more appropriate and necessary.

In brief, this Reorganization Plan groups nearly all of the permanent housing agencies and functions of the Government, and the remaining emergency housing activities, in a Housing and Home Finance Agency with the following constituent operating agencies: (a) A Home Loan Bank Board to administer the Federal Savings and Loan Insurance Corporation, the Home Owners' Loan Corporation, and the functions of the Federal Home Loan Bank Board and its members; (b) a Federal Housing Administration with the same functions as now provided by law for that agency; and (c) a Public Housing Administration to take over the functions of the United States Housing Authority and certain remaining emergency housing activities pending the completion of their liquidation. Each constituent agency will possess its individual identity and be responsible for the operation of its program.

By reason of the reorganizations made by the Plan, I have found it necessary to include therein provisions for the appointment of (1) an Administrator to head the Housing and Home Finance Agency, (2) the three members of the Home Loan Bank Board, and (3) two Commissioners to head the Federal Housing Administration and the Public Housing Administration, respectively. Each of these officers is to be appointed by the President by and with the advice and consent of the Senate.

The Plan places in the Housing and Home Finance Administrator the functions heretofore vested in the Federal Loan Administrator and the Federal Works Administrator with respect to the housing agencies and functions formerly administered within the Federal Loan and Federal Works Agencies, together with supervision and direction of certain emergency housing activities for the remainder of their existence.

Under the Plan, the Home Loan Bank Board and the Federal Housing Administration will have the same status in, and relation to, the Housing and Home Finance Agency and the Housing and Home Finance Administrator as the Federal Home Loan

Bank Board, and its related agencies, and the Federal Housing Administration formerly had to the Federal Loan Agency and the Federal Loan Administrator. Similarly, the Public Housing Administration will have the same status in, and relation to, the Housing and Home Finance Agency and the Administrator as the United States Housing Authority formerly had to the Federal Works Agency and the Federal Works Administrator.

Since there are a few housing activities which it is not feasible to place within the Housing and Home Finance Agency because they form integral parts of other broad programs or because of specific limitations in the Reorganization Act of 1945, the Plan also creates a National Housing Council on which the Housing and Home Finance Agency and its constituent agencies, and the other departments and agencies having important housing functions, are represented. In this way the Plan provides machinery for promoting the most effective use of all the housing functions of the Government, for obtaining consistency between these functions and the general economic and fiscal policies of the Government, and for avoiding duplication and overlapping of activities.

To avoid a hiatus in the administration of housing functions pending the confirmation by the Senate of the new officers provided for by the Plan, it permits the designation by the President of appropriate existing housing officials to perform temporarily the functions of these officers. This period should be brief, as I shall promptly submit nominations for the permanent officers.

Under the limitations contained in the Reorganization Act of 1945, the compensation of the Housing and Home Finance Administrator and the other officers provided for by the Plan, cannot be fixed at a rate in excess of $10,000 per annum. Both the temporary National Housing Administrator provided for by Executive Order No. 9070 and the Federal Housing Administrator have received salaries of $12,000 a year. I do not consider the salary of $10,000 provided in the Plan as compensation commensurate with the responsibilities of the Administrator, the members of the Home Loan Bank Board, and the Commissioners of the other constituent agencies, or consistent with a salary scale which must be paid if the Government is to attract and retain public servants of the requisite caliber. Accordingly, I recommend that the Congress act to increase the salary of the Housing and Home Finance Administrator to $15,000 per annum, and to increase the salaries of the members of the Home Loan Bank Board and the two Commissioners provided for by this Plan to $12,000 per annum.

The essential and important difference between the organization established by the Plan and the pre-war arrangement, to which housing agencies and functions would otherwise automatically revert on the termination of Title I of the First War Powers Act, is that under the old arrangement these agencies and functions were scattered among many different establishments primarily dealing with matters other than housing, whereas under the Plan the major permanent housing programs are placed in a single establishment concerned exclusively with housing. Thus, the Plan effectuates the basic objective enunciated by the Congress in the Reorganization Act of 1945 of grouping agencies and functions by major purpose, and provides the necessary framework for a more effective administration of Federal housing activities in the post-war period.

HARRY S. TRUMAN

NOTE: Reorganization Plan 3 of 1947 is published in the U.S. Statutes at Large (61 Stat. 954) and in the 1943–1948 Compilation of title 3 of the Code of Federal Regulations (p. 1071). It became effective July 27, 1947.

103 Statement by the President Upon Signing Orders Relating to Meritorious Awards for Wartime Services. *May 30, 1947*

BELIEVING that the period for which recognition should be given for wartime services considered adequate for the conferring of the Medal for Merit should conform insofar as possible with that for military decorations, I have signed an Executive order amending Executive Order 9637 of October 3, 1945, fixing December 31, 1946, as the terminal date for wartime services for which the Medal for Merit may be awarded, with the initiating recommendations to be submitted not later than June 30, 1947. This decision has been reached in view of the fact that I proclaimed the date of the termination of hostilities of World War II to be December 31, 1946, and because Public Law 444, approved June 26, 1946, states that an act or service justifying the award of certain military decorations shall end with the date of the termination of hostilities as proclaimed by the President or the Congress, and that initiating recommendations must be submitted not later than 6 months after the termination of hostilities.

I have also signed an Executive order, amending Executive Order 9734 of June 6, 1946, which fixes the same terminal date for services for which the President's Certificate of Merit may be awarded, as well as the date by which such proposals must be submitted.

This latter action terminates the President's Certificate of Merit, since the Executive order creating it expressly states that the award shall be given "to any civilian who . . . has performed a meritorious act or service which has aided the United States or any nation engaged with the United States in the prosecution of World War II."

NOTE: The President signed Executive Orders 9857A "Medal for Merit" and 9857B "Amendment of Executive Order 9734 of June 6, 1946, Establishing the President's Certificate of Merit" on May 27, 1947 (3 CFR, 1943–1948 Comp., pp. 646, 647).

104 Special Message to the Congress Transmitting Agreement Extending Interstate Compact To Conserve Oil and Gas. *June 2, 1947*

To the Congress of the United States:

I transmit herewith a certified photostatic copy of an agreement, executed by the States of Alabama, Arkansas, Colorado, Florida, Kansas, Louisiana, Montana, New Mexico, New York, Ohio, Oklahoma, Pennsylvania, Texas, West Virginia, Tennessee and Indiana, to extend for four years, commencing September 1, 1947, the Interstate Compact to Conserve Oil and Gas. The original of this agreement, in accordance with a provision contained therein, has been deposited in the archives of the Department of State.

The original compact between the States of Oklahoma, Texas, New Mexico, Illinois, Colorado and Kansas was first executed in February 1935 and received the consent of Congress in August 1935. Since that time the original compact, with the consent of Congress, has been thrice extended and renewed for two-year periods and once for a period of four years, the last extension period expiring September 1, 1947. It is of interest to observe that the original compact, first ratified by six States, has now been ratified by sixteen. The increasing membership in this compact is especially encouraging at this time, in view of the necessity for the conservation of our resources of oil and gas.

I hope that the Congress will, by appropriate legislation, approve this extension agreement in accordance with the provisions of Article 1, Section 10 of the Constitution of the United States.

HARRY S. TRUMAN

NOTE: On July 12 the President signed a joint resolution approving the extension agreement (61 Stat. 316).

105 Joint Statement Following Discussions With Ambassador Ivanissevich of Argentina. *June 3, 1947*

THE ARGENTINE Ambassador, who has just returned from Argentina, reviewed with the President and the Secretary of State the steps which his government has taken and is continuing to take in fulfillment of its commitments undertaken in the Final Act of the Inter-American Conference on Problems of War and Peace. He expressed the view of his government that no obstacle remained to discussions looking toward the treaty of mutual assistance contemplated by the Act of Chapultepec. The President indicated his willingness to renew the consultations with the governments of the other American Republics initiated by the United States memorandum of April 1, 1946, on this subject.

106 Letter to the President of the Senate and to the Speaker of the House Transmitting Report of the Advisory Commission on Universal Training. *June 4, 1947*

My dear Mr. ————:

On October 23, 1945, I recommended to the Congress the enactment of a system of universal training. From the extensive discussion which followed, it was obvious that there was great disparity of viewpoint on the subject.

In an effort to clarify the situation, I appointed, on November 20, 1946, an Advisory Commission on Universal Training. I asked the Commission to determine whether the security of this Nation and the preservation of world peace required the establishment of a system of universal training. I asked further, that if such a system were deemed necessary, how it should be carried out to give this country the largest measure of protection, make maximum allowance for the spiritual, mental and physical development of the young men in training, and keep costs at the lowest level consistent with attainment of its security goal.

The Commission has made an exhaustive investigation and has submitted an excellent report. It is significant to note that the members of the Commission, consisting of outstanding Americans in various fields of endeavor, unanimously recommend the adoption of universal training.

Copies of the Report of the Commission are transmitted herewith for the information of the Congress and I urge that the Congress give early consideration to the subject of universal training which is, in the words of the Commission, "an essential element in an integrated program of national security designed to protect the United States against possible aggression, to perpetuate the freedoms for which millions shed their blood, and to hasten the advent of universal disarmament and peace through the United Nations."

Very sincerely yours,

HARRY S. TRUMAN

NOTE: This is the text of identical letters addressed to the Honorable Arthur H. Vandenberg, President pro tempore of the Senate, and to the Honorable Joseph W. Martin, Jr., Speaker of the House of Representatives.

The report entitled "A Program for National Security" is dated May 29, 1947 (Government Printing Office, 453 pp.). A list of the members of the Commission is appended to the President's remarks at a meeting with them in December 1946 (see 1946 volume, this series, Item 268).

107 The President's News Conference of *June 5, 1947*

THE PRESIDENT. I have a couple of announcements to make this morning, and a statement to read to you.

[1.] Dwight Griswold, former Governor of Nebraska, and Director of Internal Affairs for General Clay, will be Chief of the United States Mission to Greece. And Richard F. Allen will be Field Administrator for Relief for the $350 million. In 1940 Mr. Allen became Delegate for Europe of the American Red Cross, and directed the relief program in Europe. He directed important relief programs in France before and after the Germans invaded France, and worked closely with Admiral Leahy, then Ambassador to France. We will furnish you all that detailed information after this conference is over.

Q. Will Governor Griswold be in charge, overall, of Greece and Turkey?

THE PRESIDENT. Just Greece.

Q. Just Greece?

THE PRESIDENT. We haven't decided on the Turkish situation as yet.

[2.] Now I have got a statement here that I want to read to you. It is mimeographed, and you will get copies of it. It is rather long.

[*Reading*] "Senator Taft is reported to have said that 'apparently the President and the administration are abandoning talk of keeping prices down in favor of heavy spending abroad that will keep them up.' The Senator said that loans to other countries for the purchase of goods here increase the competition on home markets and thus force prices up.

"The administration did not advocate the Greek-Turkish aid program for the purpose of bringing prices down. It advocated that program for two important reasons—first, to extend aid to starving millions and to help restore their economies so that the world may regain its prosperity in the long run; and second, to help those nations which want to preserve their freedoms and to set up a bulwark against totalitarian aggression. The administration fully recognized that these foreign aid programs would place some strain upon the American economy, particularly in the current inflationary situation caused by the high domestic demand and the shortages of some goods. But the fact that necessary foreign aid programs add to our economic problems at home makes it all the more important that we handle these domestic problems with vigor and commonsense.

"Price reductions, wherever they are possible, are made even more urgent because of the additional strain which the world situation inescapably places upon our economy.

To say that we should abandon our efforts directed toward enduring world peace and freedom because these efforts create economic problems is like saying that we should have abandoned our war effort because it created economic problems.

"During the war, the tremendous demand for goods would have forced prices to unfortunately high levels except for price control. With price control, we held prices at reasonable levels. Yet, because of the tremendous volume, business made fine profits even after taxes. We now have a tremendous peacetime demand, domestic and foreign, but we have no price control. In such a situation, it is up to those whose profits are high at the current inflated prices to reduce these prices voluntarily—in their own interest as well as the interest of the American economy and the world situation. The very heart of my request for voluntary price reductions is that business intelligence must now take the place of Government regulation if our economy is to operate in the interest of all the people.

"The economic implications of Senator Taft's arguments should be fully recognized. The Senator states that the only way to bring prices down is to reduce the demand for goods. If this were true of foreign demand, it would also be true of domestic demand. Let us see where this would lead us. If the Government were to abandon its vitally necessary loan and expenditure programs, if wages were reduced, if savings were exhausted, and if unemployment set in, then there would be less demand and prices would drop. Senator Taft would call this an adjustment. I would call it a tragic recession or a depression. There is nothing novel and nothing worthy about getting a price collapse through reducing demand. That is the typical road to depression.

"The problem facing the American people is to maintain full employment, full production, and high demand, and still keep prices at reasonable levels. This is the problem to which I have constantly addressed my efforts. Senator Taft's argument that high demand justifies or necessitates high prices is fallacious and dangerous. It is based upon the idea that prices should seek as high a level as the traffic will bear, rather than the lowest level that is consistent with fair profits. That kind of practice is indefensible, and in the long run it would destroy both prosperity and profits. The higher and more stable the demand, the more opportunities there are to sell goods—and with assured high volume operations there is less and less justification for wide margins of profit per unit.

"Senator Taft's economic philosophy follows the old idea of boom and bust. Under this economic philosophy, when demand is high, those who have it within their power to administer prices charge every penny that they can get. After a while, purchasing power is unable to keep up with the excessive price level. Then unemployment, business failures, cuts in production, and price reductions all follow in rapid succession.

"For my part, I utterly reject this defeatist economic philosophy, and I believe in maintaining a full employment and full production economy. This necessarily means a high demand economy. But a high demand economy should not be a high price economy. On the contrary, high demand makes it feasible to earn good profits at reasonable prices. The boom and bust approach could endanger our prosperity even at a time when underlying economic conditions are favorable.

"My interest in voluntary price reductions is undiminished. They are as important now as ever before—if not more important.

"The drive for voluntary price reductions, while it has not gone far enough, has already yielded substantial results. First, the peaceful wage adjustments in some of the major industries took place without corresponding price advances, and this helped to bring production and purchasing power into better balance. Second, in recent months, the trend toward extraordinary price increases which commenced with decontrol has been checked and moderate price declines have taken place. This is illustrated in the following table."

I won't read the whole table, but it shows that all commodities have decreased 2 points. Farm products have increased 5.8. Foods have increased 9.1. All others have decreased 0.1 of a point. You can analyze that table when you get your mimeographed sheet.

"Price reduction in many items of farm products and foods is as important as in the case of industrial products. As the table shows, these prices have been reduced recently. Further reductions may be anticipated. Neither the individual farmer, however, nor the trader, nor the Government can—in the absence of price control—determine agricultural prices. They depend largely on competitive market conditions.

"On the other hand, in the case of many industrial products deliberate voluntary price reduction is feasible, and in some cases, such as construction and construction materials, high prices impede activity of the highest economic and social importance. Yet, as the table shows, industrial prices have not come down as much as prices of farm products and food. They have been more resistant to desirable decreases. It is true that intensive foreign demand has kept some farm prices higher than they otherwise would be. But this is no reason for keeping industrial prices high where they could now be reduced for the longrun advantage of business and the country."

You will get a copy of that when you go out. Now I am ready for questions.

[3.] Q. Mr. President, across the country I have found that they blame not so much the purchasing of wheat for relief abroad but the method used by the Agriculture Department in failing to consult the users of grain in this country before they went into market.

THE PRESIDENT. I don't think that is true at all because those purchases remain after consultation with the very people you are talking about.

Q. They just claim not.

THE PRESIDENT. Of course they want something to hide behind.

[4.] Q. Can you give us an advance on what the President is going to do on the tax and labor bills?

THE PRESIDENT. No, I cannot. I will give you that when I get those bills and analyze them.

Q. Mr. President, can you tell us when you expect to act on the tax bill?

THE PRESIDENT. As soon as I get it officially.

Q. You haven't received the bill officially?

THE PRESIDENT. It came up officially yesterday afternoon, and I haven't seen it. As soon as I can, I will give you an announcement on it.

[5.] Q. Mr. President, so many people have criticized in this field, I wonder why you picked Senator Taft?

THE PRESIDENT. Senator Taft made a statement that wouldn't hold water the other day, and he had to be answered. He represents that sort of economy, and I think that's a thing I should comment on.

[6.] Q. What is your comment on the Kansas City vote fraud investigation?

THE PRESIDENT. The Kansas City vote fraud investigation should be carried through to its logical conclusion. No one wants to condone vote frauds. It is the worst thing that can happen in a democracy.

Q. Mr. President, does that mean a grand jury investigation of the primaries?

THE PRESIDENT. I can't answer that, sir.

The grand jury investigation of the primary has been made by State courts.

Q. Federal grand juries?

THE PRESIDENT. I don't know anything about that. I don't know what the laws are in regard to Federal powers in a primary investigation. You will have to look it up.

Q. Have you discussed the matter with Attorney General Clark?

THE PRESIDENT. No, I have not.

[7.] Q. Mr. President, a few weeks ago you said that Messersmith was on a temporary mission in Argentina. Has he finished that mission now, sir?

THE PRESIDENT. Yes, he has.

Q. Does that mean he is coming back right away?

THE PRESIDENT. I judge so.

Q. Have you selected a successor for him?

THE PRESIDENT. No I have not. He hasn't come back yet.

Q. Will he remain in the diplomatic service, Mr. President?

THE PRESIDENT. Well now, he will have to answer that question.

[8.] Q. Mr. President, do you want to say anything at all about this Hungarian situation? [1]

THE PRESIDENT. I think it's an outrage. The Hungarian situation is a terrible one. And we are having it looked into right now.

Q. May I go a little further on that?

THE PRESIDENT. Sure.

Q. I think the Star—Evening Star tells you what to do. [*Laughter*]

THE PRESIDENT. Do they? Nobody in the country can——

Q. Shake a fist, not a finger, something of that sort, which leads up to the question which I think you answered—you said it's an outrage and you don't intend to stand by——

---

[1] On May 30 in a coup d'état Hungarian Communists had installed a pro-Communist government, forcing the resignation of Premier Nagy.

THE PRESIDENT. Idly by. And that we are looking into the matter. The State Department is making a complete investigation.

Q. Will the State Department withdraw the loan to Hungary for the purchase of American cotton?

THE PRESIDENT. You will have to ask the State Department on that. I don't know what they have done—only what I see in the paper.

[9.] Q. Mr. President, going back to Argentina, I believe you answered the question, but I didn't hear. Can you say when Mr. Messersmith is coming back?

THE PRESIDENT. No, I can't.

[10.] Q. I want to ask you about Henry Savage [1] who is running for Congress in the Third District——

THE PRESIDENT. He is the nominee of the Democratic Party, and he will be supported by the National Democratic Committee. Is that what you want?

Q. Yes sir. [*Laughter*]

[11.] Q. Mr. President, isn't Governor Griswold a Republican?

THE PRESIDENT. He has been the Republican Governor of Nebraska for 6 years.

[12.] Q. On—with regard to Ambassador Messersmith, have you accepted his resignation?

THE PRESIDENT. No. I haven't received any resignation from him as yet.

---

[1] The reporter may have been referring to Charles R. Savage, Democratic candidate for U.S. Representative for the 3d District of the State of Washington. In a special election held on June 7, 1947, Mr. Savage was defeated by Russell V. Mack, a Republican.

Q. I would like to get this clear. Have you recalled him?

THE PRESIDENT. I have taken no action on it at all. That is up to the State Department. They will handle the matter. His mission is completed, and he went down there with the understanding that when his mission was completed he would want to come home.

Q. Do you regard his mission as successful, Mr. President?

THE PRESIDENT. Yes, I do.

[13.] Q. Mr. President, the Democratic pamphlet "Capital Comment" says, "Watch for further Democratic action soon on housing." Can you tell us anything about that action?

THE PRESIDENT. No comment.

[14.] Q. Mr. President, can you say specifically what the Messersmith mission was?

THE PRESIDENT. It is accomplished. We are on friendly terms with Argentina. That is what he went there for.

[15.] Q. Mr. President, was Senator Taft correct in saying that foreign loans and advances exert an inflationary influence on the domestic price level?

THE PRESIDENT. It will have some effect of that sort, but I don't think it is a dangerous effect. I have answered that in the statement which I just made.

Reporter: Thank you, Mr. President.

THE PRESIDENT. You're welcome.

NOTE: President Truman's one hundred and eighth news conference was held in his office at the White House at 10:30 a.m. on Thursday, June 5, 1947.

108   Statement by the President on Palestine.
June 5, 1947

THE GENERAL ASSEMBLY of the United Nations in special session on May 15, 1947, unanimously adopted the following resolution:

"The General Assembly calls upon all governments and peoples, and particularly on the inhabitants of Palestine, to refrain, pending action by the General Assembly on the report of the Special Committee on Palestine, from the threat or use of force or any other action which might create an atmosphere prejudicial to an early settlement of the question of Palestine."

The search for a fair and workable solution of the Palestine problem is one of the most difficult and important tasks confronting the United Nations. It is in the interest of the United States as well as of the United Nations that the efforts of the United Nations to solve this problem meet with success. Activities calculated further to inflame the passions of the inhabitants of Palestine, to undermine law and order in Palestine, or to

promote violence in that country are certain to create an atmosphere prejudicial to an early settlement of the Palestine problem and to render still more difficult the tasks which the United Nations has before it.

I therefore urge every citizen and resident of the United States, in the interests of this country, of world peace, and humanity, meticulously to refrain, while the United Nations is considering the problem of Palestine, from engaging in, or facilitating, any activities which tend further to inflame the passions of the inhabitants of Palestine, to undermine law and order in Palestine, or to promote violence in that country.

109 Statement by the President Upon Receiving the Attorney General's Report on Governmental Patent Practices and Policies. *June 7, 1947*

I HAVE today received from the Attorney General a comprehensive report on governmental patent practices and policies. The extensive study involved in its preparation was undertaken by the Claims Division of the Department of Justice. The report is being made public in order to obtain full and frank discussion by all individuals and organizations concerned, including private companies, educational institutions, and the interested Government departments and agencies.

The Attorney General's report is one of a series of studies relating to the wide range of problems created by the expanded role of the Federal Government in research and development. This group of inquiries, includ-

ing the report submitted by Dr. Vannevar Bush to President Roosevelt in 1945, the present report by Attorney General Clark, and the studies by the President's Scientific Research Board to be completed this summer, will comprise the most thorough examination ever made of the Government's role in support of scientific research. On the basis of careful study of all aspects of this complex problem, the Government will be enabled to formulate national policies in relation to scientific research and development.

NOTE: The report is entitled "Investigation of Government Patent Practices and Policies, 1947" (Government Printing Office, 3 vols.).

The Attorney General's letter dated June 5, transmitting the report, was released with the President's statement.

110 Address in Kansas City at the 35th Division Reunion
Memorial Service. *June 7, 1947*

Mr. President of the 35th Division; Admiral Leahy; General Eisenhower; distinguished guests; members of the 35th Division and their guests:

This has been a great convention of the veterans of two wars. I was deeply touched by the turnout of my World War I Battery D of the 129th Field Artillery. A man can have no higher honor paid to him. I appreciate it.

We are honored by the presence of our highest ranking naval officer, Admiral William D. Leahy, and our highest ranking Army officer, General Eisenhower. We are also very highly honored by the presence of His Excellency the Ambassador to the United States of America from the great Republic of France, and by the presence of his lovely wife, and by the presence also of His Honor the Mayor of St. Lo. Those are distinguished honors to us veterans, and we appreciate it.

We come together tonight to honor the memory of the men of the 35th Division who died in the defense of their country and, in honoring them, we pay tribute also to the memory of all those who have lost their lives in the wars in which our Nation has been engaged.

Men of the 35th Division have twice fulfilled the obligation of every American citizen to serve in the defense of his homeland. More than 300 years ago the first settlers of North American colonies established a tradition of military training and service. Service through defense of the new colonies was, to them, an essential and unquestioned duty of citizenship. We owe our existence as a Nation to the tradition of service by our citizens, for it was an army of citizen soldiers which George Washington led to victory in the American Revolution. At the end of that war, the Congress asked General Washington to give his views on what the military policy of the new nation should be. This is what Washington replied:

"It may be laid down as a primary position, and the basis of our system, that every Citizen who enjoys the protection of a free Government, owes not only a portion of his property, but even of his personal services to the defense of it . . ."

The responsibility, described by Washington, of the citizens of the new Nation to maintain the security of their homes has become, in our time, responsibility to serve in the cause of world security. The only security for the United States, or for any other nation, when the alternative to peace is death and destruction, lies in the abolition of war.

Our obligation, as citizens of the strongest nation in the world, is to lead the peoples of the earth toward the goal of lasting peace.

Our hopes for peace based on justice and international cooperation are embodied in the United Nations. We shall continue every effort to attain the ideal of a United Nations which can banish war for all time.

In supporting the United Nations, we must always sustain the principle on which world peace must rest. That principle is that all people should have the right to live free from fear of aggression under institutions of their own free choice. Our responsibility to lead the peoples of the world in the search for peace takes the form of helping less fortunate peoples who are earnestly striving to improve or reconstruct the institutions of free and independent nations.

We can fulfill our obligation of service in the cause of peace only by maintaining our strength.

The will for peace without the strength for peace is of no avail.

The disintegration of our military forces since the surrender of Germany and Japan is an encouragement to nations who regard weakness on the part of peace-loving nations as an invitation to aggression. And the countries whose people share our ideals, and who look to us for leadership, but who are weak in resources or manpower, lose faith in our ability to support the principles for which we stand.

Hitler's dream of controlling the world was spurred by his belief that the Western nations were weak and lacked the will to resist. Hitler's eagerness for war increased as his estimate of the strength of the democracies decreased. Unpreparedness on the part of his opponents precipitated his decision to march into Poland in 1939. Japan struck at Pearl Harbor because she thought the United States was too weak to fight back. What a mistake she made! And I can say that for any other nation that gets that notion.

We must maintain our Army, our Navy, and our Air Force in effective readiness for any emergency. They should be organized in an efficient single military establishment and they should be supported by reserves of well-trained citizens.

Maintaining strong military forces is not the only requirement that exists in the cause of peace. We must also have a sound and prosperous economy, thriving agriculture, natural resources wisely conserved and adequately developed, and vigorous citizens conscious of our duty and confident of our destiny.

A healthy citizenry is the most important element in our national strength. We must develop a national health program which will furnish adequate public health services, and ample medical care and facilities for all areas of the country and all groups of our people.

We must also raise the level of minimum wages, broaden our social security benefits, provide decent housing, equalize educational opportunities, and in every way insure that the welfare and standards of living of our citizens improve steadily. The strength that derives from a people confident of their personal security, and aware of world needs, is an overwhelming power for peace.

We must work earnestly to insure that our economy stays in high gear, that we have maximum production, maximum employment, and maximum purchasing power. We must have an economic system that provides opportunities for all men willing and able to work. This will take much effort. Some necessary steps are long overdue. Prudent fiscal and tax policies, certain price and wage adjustments, labor-management harmony, and a carefully planned program of essential public works will go far toward insuring that the present level of productivity—the highest in our history—will continue.

To a greater extent than ever before, our prosperity and security depend upon our natural resources. We are fast becoming a "have not" nation with respect to many important minerals. We are short of some basic materials essential to an economy of full production and full employment. We are short of copper, of steel, of lead, and of many other critical materials. We are faced with the danger of a shortage of petroleum products. The United States is now using more oil each day than the entire world used before the war. Shortages of fuel oil have already appeared in parts of the Middle West. A nation is only as strong as its productive capacity, and our capacity is now limited by our shortages.

We have laws designed to conserve and develop our natural resources and these laws, if wisely administered, would largely eliminate our shortages. However, we are now in grave danger that these protecting laws will be made ineffective by the failure of the Congress to provide the money necessary for their administration.

We have a longstanding policy that public power resources should be developed for the benefit of the people. As a result of this policy, our country had the means of rapidly expanding our supply of electric power in the early days of the war. These supplies of low-cost hydroelectric power, particularly in the Tennessee Valley and the Pacific Northwest, provided the means by which we were able speedily to increase our production of aluminum and other light metals and to supply the huge amounts of power required for our atomic energy plants.

Despite the wartime expansion, however, we face critical shortages in our national supply of power in the next few years. We need more and more electric power to expand old industries, to build new ones, extract minerals from low-grade ores, produce atomic materials for peacetime use, and to expand the electrification of our farms.

Our public power program must be carried forward. We must continue to build the multiple-purpose projects that conserve our precious resources and develop low-cost energy. We must build transmission lines and substations and bring power to markets. The hydroelectric power program is vital to the economic welfare of the Nation, and in some western States hydroelectric power is almost the sole resource of available energy. All the great industries of the West—lumbering, agriculture, mining—will be retarded for want of electric power. Nothing must

prevent the full development and use of public power in these areas where it is needed most.

The great dams which harness the power of our western rivers also store the water and make it available to reclaim lands that once were barren deserts.

Reclamation projects are providing the country with additional acreage to grow food which is needed at home and abroad in this time of world food shortages. The utilization of water resources of the West for power and reclamation is the key to the development of economic opportunities in this vast part of our country. It will ultimately provide the millions of jobs for our citizens in areas which are now sparsely settled.

Our veterans are hungry for these opportunities. They want land on which to settle so that they can become a constructive part of the Nation's economic life. We must provide our veterans with the land they need. It is my hope that the reclamation projects so essential to the development of this part of our economy will not be curtailed.

Money spent for water control, reclamation, and power projects cannot be regarded in the same light as expenses for other construction programs. Appropriations for reclamation and power are investments which are repaid by the water and power consumers. To curtail construction on projects already begun because construction costs are high is to waste vast amounts of public capital already invested by postponing the time when repayment begins.

Our national strength requires that we think in terms of our 1947 needs and responsibilities, and not in terms of the past. I earnestly hope that the Senate will not follow the House of Representatives in cutting our conservation, reclamation, and power programs back to the level of a decade ago. We must go forward with the development of the natural resources upon which depend our economic strength and our position of world leadership.

One of the great lessons of history is that no nation can be stronger than its agriculture. Hungry and ill-nourished people cannot practice the arts of democratic government and peaceful commerce. Peace cannot be built on a foundation of human want.

We in this country some years ago wisely adopted a national policy which declared that all of us must share with the farmer the responsibility for maintaining our agricultural resources. We said that the farmer must be protected against low prices and low income, against some of the hazards of weather, and against the danger of inadequate credit. We decided to keep reserves of basic crops from the fat years for use in the lean years.

Because we had adopted that policy, American agriculture was able to set new production records during every year of the war. Because of its reserves, in the granary and in the soil, because of its basic strength, agriculture increased its production fully one-third even though many people left farms to join the armed forces and to work in industry.

The most remarkable aspect of our production records was that the increases were in the crops for which the Government asked increases. We were able to supply our armed forces the kind of food they needed in the amount they needed. We had the best fed fighting forces the world has ever seen—and we supplied our allies with the kinds of food they especially required.

When the fighting ended, there was a worldwide food emergency. Grain was the most needed commodity. During the war the United States had not specialized in grain production. But as a result of our farm policy our agriculture was so adaptable that

we were able, almost at once, to set new world records in grain exports. We have saved millions of lives of persons abroad. Our grain shipments have helped us to meet the test as the world proponent of democracy, freedom, and peace.

We face a new challenge now. Our entire farm program is endangered by recent legislative action. I would be gravely concerned if any effort to undermine our farm policy were successful.

A year ago our Government made a pledge to our farmers to carry on the program of soil conservation which is so vital to prosperous, productive farming. The farmers have a right to expect that this pledge will be kept. We should guard against all efforts to destroy the program designed to carry out soil conservation practices on our farms.

The farmer-committee system, a basic part of the program for balanced farm production and soil conservation, has worked successfully. Under it, farmers elect committeemen from among their neighbors to run the agricultural conservation program, to handle commodity loans, to maintain the ever-normal granary, and to carry out emergency marketing programs in time of extreme surplus. The farmer-committee system should be continued.

We must always bear in mind the effect on our national strength and welfare of our people when restrictions or curtailments in our farm program are proposed. We cannot afford to deprive veterans and farm tenants of the opportunity to buy farms of their own.

If American agriculture is to continue its rapid progress, we must maintain our important research projects in natural science and economics, and we must continue with our work of rural electrification, forest protection, and aid to locally organized soil conservation districts.

I sincerely hope that on careful reflection and consideration, the Congress will provide the appropriations necessary for those projects and services which are designed to provide a better, fuller life for our people and a more stable, productive economy for our Nation.

By renewing the wellsprings of our strength, by enlarging our capacities for growth, we shall be able to fulfill the obligation of service which is our heritage.

I have commented at length on some of the facts that are necessary elements in our leadership toward the goal of enduring peace.

But more important than any of these is the need for divine guidance to direct our steps. When the peoples of the world shall accept the principle that it is the will of God that there be peace—there will be peace.

And it is our obligation to be strong and to have faith in order that we may do our share toward carrying out the will of God.

The inspiration which we receive from the heroic men whom we honor here tonight will make more resolute our determination to put into practice the teachings of the great Disciple of Peace.

NOTE: The President spoke at the Municipal Auditorium in Kansas City, Mo., at 9 p.m. During his remarks he referred to Fleet Adm. William D. Leahy, Chief of Staff to the Commander in Chief of the U.S. Army and Navy; General of the Army Dwight D. Eisenhower, Chief of Staff, U.S. Army; Ambassador Henri Bonnet and Madame Bonnet; and Mayor Georges Pierre Lavalley of St. Lo, France. The commander of the 35th Division in Europe during World War II, Maj. Gen. Paul W. Baade, also attended the reunion. The address was carried on a nationwide radio broadcast.

111 Address Before the Canadian Parliament in Ottawa. *June 11, 1947*

Mr. Prime Minister, Honorable Members of the Senate, and Members of the House of Commons of Canada:

This is my first visit to Canada as President of the United States, and I am happy that it affords me the opportunity to address this meeting of the members of both houses of the Canadian Parliament. Here is a body which exemplifies the self-government and freedom of the nations of the great British Commonwealth. The history of the Commonwealth proves that it is possible for many nations to work and live in harmony and for the common good.

I wish to acknowledge the many courtesies extended to me on this visit by the Governor General, Viscount Alexander, who paid me the honor of a visit in Washington a few months ago. His career as a soldier and as a statesman eminently qualifies him to follow his illustrious predecessors.

For the courtesy of appearing before you, as for other courtesies, I am sure I am largely indebted to my good friend, Prime Minister Mackenzie King. I was particularly happy to be present yesterday when he was honored in the rotunda of this Parliament building. It was a wonderful ceremony, and one which I think he richly deserved.

I also appreciate very highly his political advice which he gave me.

I have come to value and cherish his friendship and statesmanship. As our two nations have worked together in solving the difficult problems of the postwar period, I have developed greater and greater respect for his wisdom.

Americans who come to know Canada informally, such as our tourists, as well as those whose approach is more academic, learn that Canada is a broad land—broad in mind, broad in spirit, and broad in physical expanse. They find that the composition of your population and the evolution of your political institutions hold a lesson for the other nations of the earth. Canada has achieved internal unity and material strength, and has grown in stature in the world community, by solving problems that might have hopelessly divided and weakened a less gifted people.

Canada's eminent position today is a tribute to the patience, tolerance, and strength of character of her people, of both French and British strains. For Canada is enriched by the heritage of France as well as of Britain, and Quebec has imparted the vitality and spirit of France itself to Canada. Canada's notable achievement of national unity and progress through accommodation, moderation, and forbearance can be studied with profit by her sister nations.

Much the same qualities have been employed, with like success, in your relations with the United States. Perhaps I should say "your foreign relations with the United States." But the word "foreign" seems strangely out of place. Canada and the United States have reached the point where we no longer think of each other as "foreign" countries. We think of each other as friends, as peaceful and cooperative neighbors on a spacious and fruitful continent.

We must go back a long way, nearly a century and a half, to find a time when we were not on good terms. In the War of 1812 there was fighting across our frontier. But permanent good came of that brief campaign. It shocked Canadians and Americans into a realization that continued antagonism would be costly and perilous. The first result of that realization was the Rush-Bagot Agreement in 1817, which embodied a spirit and an attitude that have permeated our relations to this day. This agreement originally was intended to limit and to regulate the naval vessels of both countries on the Great Lakes. It has become one of the world's most effective disarmament agreements, and it is the basis for our much-hailed unfortified frontier.

I speak of that period of history to make the point that the friendship that has characterized Canadian-American relations for many years did not develop spontaneously. The example of accord provided by our two countries did not come about merely through the happy circumstance of geography. It is compounded of one part proximity and nine parts good will and commonsense.

We have had a number of problems, but they have all been settled by adjustment, by compromise, and by negotiations inspired by a spirit of mutual respect and a desire for justice on both sides. This is the peaceful way, the sensible way, and the fair way to settle problems, whether between two nations that are close neighbors or among many nations widely separated.

This way is open to all. We in Canada and the United States are justifiably proud of our joint record, but we claim no monopoly on that formula.

Canada and the United States will gladly share the formula, which rejects distrust and suspicion in favor of commonsense, mutual respect, and equal justice with their fellow members of the United Nations. One of the most effective contributions which our two countries can make to the cause of the United Nations is the patient and diligent effort to apply on a global scale the principles and practices which we have tested with success on this continent.

Relations between Canada and the United States have emphasized the spirit of cooperation rather than the letter of protocol. The Rush-Bagot Agreement was stated in less than 150 words. From time to time it has been revised by mutual agreement to meet changing conditions. It was amended as recently as last December.

The last war brought our countries into even closer collaboration. The Ogdensburg Agreement of 1940 provided for the creation of the Permanent Joint Board on Defense. It was followed by the Hyde Park Agreement of 1941, which enabled us to coordinate our economic resources with increased efficiency. Common interests, particularly after Pearl Harbor, required the creation of several joint agencies to coordinate our efforts in special fields. When victory ended the necessity for these agencies, they were quietly disbanded with a minimum of disturbance of the national economies of the two countries. Commonsense again.

The Permanent Joint Board on Defense will continue to function. I wish to emphasize, in addition to the word "permanent," the other two parts of the title. The Board is joint, being composed of representatives of each government. Canada and the United States participate on the basis of equality, and the sovereignty of each is carefully respected. This was true during the gravest dangers of the war, and it will continue to be true, in keeping with the nature of all our joint undertakings.

The Board was created, and will continue to exist, for the sole purpose of assuring the most effective defense for North America. The Board, as you know, has no executive powers and can only make recommendations for action. The record of the Board provides another example of the truly cooperative spirit that prevails between our two countries.

The spirit of common purpose and the impressive strength which we marshaled for action on all fronts are the surest safeguard of continental security in the future.

The people of the United States fully appreciate the magnificent contribution in men and resources that Canada made to the Allied war effort. The United States soldiers, sailors, and airmen in the heat of battle knew their Canadian comrades as valiant and daring warriors. We look back with pride on our association as stanch allies in two wars.

Today our two nations are called upon to make great contributions to world rehabilitation. This task requires broad vision and constant effort.

I am confident that we can overcome the difficulties involved, as we overcame the greater difficulties of the war. The national genius of our peoples finds its most satisfying expression in the creation of new values in peace.

The record proves that in peaceful commerce the combined efforts of our countries can produce outstanding results. Our trade with each other is far greater than that of any other two nations on earth.

Last year the flow of trade in both directions across the border reached the record peacetime total of $2¼ billion. We imported from Canada more than twice the value of goods we received from the United Kingdom, France, China, and Russia combined. The United States purchases from Canada were about 6 times our purchases from Great Britain, and nearly 10 times those from China, and 11 times those from France. We sold to Canada nearly as much as we sold to Britain and France together.

Gratifying as the volume of our trade now is, it is capable of even further expansion to our mutual benefit. Some of our greatest assets are still to be developed to the maximum. I am thinking of one particularly that holds tremendous possibilities, the magnificent St. Lawrence-Great Lakes System, which we share and which we must develop together.

The St. Lawrence project stirs the imagination long accustomed to majestic distances and epic undertakings. The proposal for taking electric power from the river and bringing ocean shipping 2,400 miles inland, to tap the fertile heart of our continent, is economically sound and strategically important.

When this program is carried out, the waterway that is part of our boundary will more than ever unite our two countries. It will stimulate our economies to new growth and will spread the flow of trade.

There have been times when shortsighted tariff policies on both sides threatened to raise almost insurmountable barriers. But the need to exchange goods was so imperative that trade flourished despite artificial obstacles. The Reciprocal Trade Agreements of 1936 and 1939 made possible a sensible reduction of tariff rates, and paved the way to our present phenomenal trade.

Something more than commercial agreements, however, is required to explain why Canada and the United States exchange more than $2 billion worth of goods yearly. Ambassador Atherton has aptly given the reason as not "free trade," but "the trade of free men." The record flow of goods and the high standard of living it indicates, on both sides of the border, provide a practical demonstration of the benefits of the democratic way of life and a free economy.

The benefits of our democratic governments and free economies operating side by side have spread beyond our countries to the advantage of the whole world. Both nations expanded their productivity enormously during the war and both escaped the physical damage that afflicted other countries. As a result, Canada and the United States emerged from the war as the only major sources of the industrial products and the food upon which much of the world depends for survival.

Canada has responded as nobly to the challenge of peace as she did to that of the war. Your wheat has fed millions who otherwise would have starved. Your loan strengthened Britain in her valiant battle for recovery.

The United States is particularly gratified to find Canada at our side in the effort to develop the International Trade Organization. We attach great importance to this undertaking, because we believe it will provide the key to the welfare and prosperity of the world in the years immediately ahead.

In sponsoring the International Trade Organization, the United States, with the cooperation of Canada and other countries, is making a determined effort to see that the inevitable adjustments in world trade as a result of the war will result in an expanding volume of business for all nations.

Our goal is a vast expansion of agriculture and industry throughout the world, with freer access to the raw materials and markets for all nations, and a wider distribution of the products of the earth's fields and factories among all peoples. Our hope is to multiply the fruitfulness of the earth and to diffuse its benefits among all mankind.

At this critical point in history, we of the United States are deeply conscious of our responsibilities to the world. We know that in this trying period, between a war that is over and a peace that is not yet secure, the destitute and the oppressed of the earth look chiefly to us for sustenance and support until they can again face life with self-confidence and self-reliance.

We are keenly aware that much depends upon the internal strength, the economic stability and the moral stamina of the United States. We face this challenge with determination and confidence.

Free men everywhere know that the purpose of the United States is to restore the world to health and to reestablish conditions under which the common people of the earth can work out their salvation by their own efforts.

We seek a peaceful world, a prosperous world, a free world, a world of good neighbors, living on terms of equality and mutual respect, as Canada and the United States have lived for generations.

We intend to expend our energies and invest our substance in promoting world recovery by assisting those who are able and willing to make their maximum contribution to the same cause.

We intend to support those who are determined to govern themselves in their own way, and who honor the right of others to do likewise.

We intend to aid those who seek to live at peace with their neighbors, without co-ercing or being coerced, without intimidating or being intimidated.

We intend to uphold those who respect the dignity of the individual, who guarantee to him equal treatment under the law, and who allow him the widest possible liberty to work out his own destiny and achieve success to the limit of his capacity.

We intend to cooperate actively and loyally with all who honestly seek, as we do, to build a better world in which mankind can live in peace and prosperity.

We count Canada in the forefront of those who share these objectives and ideals.

With such friends we face the future unafraid.

NOTE: The President spoke in the House of Commons chamber at 11:30 a.m. His opening words "Mr. Prime Minister" referred to W. L. Mackenzie King, Prime Minister of Canada.

112   The President's Special News Conference With Prime Minister Mackenzie King Near Ottawa. *June* 12, 1947

THE PRESIDENT. I want to say to you that this Canadian trip has been most interesting to me. I think it is an event in the history of the two countries. I think we understand each other better as a result of this visit, and I sincerely hope that the Canadians will pay us a visit. There isn't a chance in the world of our being able to give them the sort of reception that they have given me, but we do the best we can.

Our objective, of course, in the visit to Mexico and in the visit to Canada, is to solidify the friendship of the people who live on this continent. We want to do that for the whole Western Hemisphere, and then we want to do it for the whole world.

We have only one objective, and that is peace in the world for the benefit of all the peoples of the world. Unless we can do that, all the men who died in both our world wars died in vain. Unless we can do that, all the men who died in both the world wars died in vain. I repeat that. Because that is exactly what it means. The United States has but one objective in view, and that is peace in the world, and friendship with every nation in the world, and underline that *every*.

That's all I have to say, gentlemen.

Q. Thank you very much, sir.

THE PRESIDENT. Lovely place.

Q. Direct quotes?

THE PRESIDENT. You can say "the President said."

Q. No direct quotes, Mr. President?

THE PRESIDENT. I don't think you ought to make it direct quotes.

Q. Thank you so much for coming over.

THE PRIME MINISTER. I want to say, on behalf of the Canadian Government, that every sentiment that the President expressed is reechoed in the hearts of all of us who had the great pleasure of meeting him, seeing him, and talking to him on his delightful visit to our country.

THE PRESIDENT. I wasn't trying to put you on the record, but you went on record. [*Laughter*]

THE PRIME MINISTER. I am going to keep alongside you, as good neighbors.

Reporter: Thank you, Mr. President.

NOTE: President Truman's special news conference with Prime Minister Mackenzie King was held on the lawn of the Seignory Club at Monte-Bello, Ontario, at 3:50 p.m. The meeting is listed in the records of the White House Official Reporter as the President's one hundred and ninth news conference.

---

113   Statement by the President on the Treaty of Peace With Italy. *June* 14, 1947

WITH the ratification of the Treaty of Peace with Italy we bring to a close an unhappy chapter in Italian-American relations. At the same time we mark the beginning of a new era for Italy to which the Italian people can look with hope and confidence. Certain of the terms of the treaty are not in full accord with our desires. But the reestablishment of peace does provide a foundation for building anew a strong, free, and democratic Italy. And within the framework of the United Nations it should be possible to secure such changes in the treaty clauses as may be required in the light of future experience.

From the first days of the Allied liberation of Italy we found the Italian people as eager as we ourselves to destroy the tyrannies of fascism and nazism which had despoiled their country and destroyed their liberties. Marching by our side against the common foe, the Italian armed forces and the Italian people contributed mightily to the ultimate victory. This common sacrifice has strengthened the deep and lasting friendship between our two peoples. More than this, Americans have the satisfaction of standing at the side of Italy while her people, through adversity, are rebuilding with their own labors a new democracy and restoring their lost freedoms. During these most difficult years we have been able to do much to help the Italians to help themselves.

In order that their victory, and ours, may be preserved—in order that their freedoms and their reborn democracy may live and grow as Italy again takes her rightful place of honor and leadership among the free nations of the world—Americans will continue to stand by the side of their Italian friends, to work with them in our common efforts to rebuild and to restore a free world at peace.

NOTE: The treaty and related papers are published in the U.S. Statutes at Large (61 Stat. 1245). The treaty entered into force September 15, 1947.

---

114   Statement by the President on the Peace Treaties With Hungary, Rumania, and Bulgaria. *June* 14, 1947

AT THE TIME of ratification of the treaties establishing peace with Hungary, Rumania, and Bulgaria, I feel I must publicly express regret that the governments of those countries not only have disregarded the will of the majority of the people but have resorted to measures of oppression against them. Ever since the liberation of these countries from the Nazi yoke and the commitments undertaken by the three Allies at Yalta, I had hoped that governments truly representative of the people would be established there. Such governments do not exist today in those three countries.

It is, however, in the interests of the Hungarian, Rumanian, and Bulgarian peoples to terminate the state of war which has existed between their governments and the United States for over 5 years. The establishment of peace will mean that all occupation forces (not including Soviet units needed to maintain lines of communication to the Soviet zone of occupation in Austria) will be withdrawn from these countries and armistice Control Commissions terminated.

NOTE: The treaties and related papers are published in the U.S. Statutes at Large: Hungary (61 Stat. 2065), Rumania (61 Stat. 1757), Bulgaria (61 Stat. 1915). The treaties entered into force September 15, 1947.

115 Letter Appointing Members of a Special Board of Inquiry on Air Safety. *June 15, 1947*

Dear Mr. ————:

The development of our air transportation system has repeatedly been recognized as a matter of vital concern to our nation. One of the essential factors which can contribute greatly to the progress of our air transportation system, or can seriously hinder that progress, is the safety of our air transport operations. The public interest demands that every effort be made to obtain the highest degree of safety in those operations.

I am deeply concerned about this subject, especially in view of the recent accidents to aircraft of our certified domestic air carriers. I have, therefore, determined that the whole problem of air transport safety in the United, States should be carefully examined by a group of citizens representative of all those interests of our society to whom this safety is a matter of constant concern. Accordingly, I am appointing a special board of inquiry on air transport safety, and request you to serve as a member of that board.

This board should study the pertinent data and information relating to the program for safety in air transportation and the factors, both mechanical and human, which enter into safe operation. It should study, among other things, the recent series of accidents to determine how the findings in relation thereto can be utilized to advance air safety. It should consider also the way in which new equipment, already predictable, must be keyed to mechanical aids and human capabilities.

The board should in its discretion avail itself of all information and data in any Government Department or agency, and to the extent feasible in any private agency or group which may have an interest in or contribute to the solution of this problem. In conducting its study, the board is authorized to hold such public hearings as it may in its discretion determine to be desirable.

The board should present for my consideration, as soon as possible and from time to time, recommendations as to any action or measures which it would deem appropriate in order further to promote safety in air transportation. The board's findings will assist me in determining any further steps which should be taken by the Executive Branch of the Government to assure the highest degree of safety, and to formulate proposals to the Congress for any necessary legislation. Any executive departments and agencies concerned will of course give you every possible aid in this undertaking.

Very sincerely yours,

HARRY S. TRUMAN

NOTE: This is the text of identical letters addressed to the following appointees to the Special Board of Inquiry: Brig. Gen. Milton W. Arnold, Vice President for Operations and Engineering, Air Transport Association of America; Dr. Jerome C. Hunsaker, Chairman, National Advisory Committee for Aeronautics; James M. Landis, Chairman, Civil

Aeronautics Board; Theodore P. Wright, Civil Aeronautics Administrator; and H. B. Cox, member of the Air Line Pilots Association. Mr. Landis was designated Chairman of the Special Board, and Dr. Hunsaker, Vice Chairman.

The letter and list of appointees were part of a White House release announcing that the President had that day appointed the Special Board of Inquiry for Air Safety.

The Board's first interim report, relating mainly to problems of take-off, was released by the White House on June 28. Additional brief reports, dealing with such problems as approach and landing, terrain clearance, structural capacity, and accident survival, were released on July 2, July 7, August 1, August 16, and January 2, 1948.

116 Veto of Bill To Reduce Income Taxes.
June 16, 1947

To the House of Representatives:

I return herewith, without my approval, H.R. 1, entitled: "An Act to reduce individual income tax payments."

The right kind of tax reduction, at the right time, is an objective to which I am deeply committed. But I have reached the conclusion that this bill represents the wrong kind of tax reduction, at the wrong time. It offers dubious, ill-apportioned, and risky benefits at the expense of a sound tax policy and is, from the standpoint of Government finances, unsafe. Proposals for tax reduction must be examined in the light of sound and carefully-related fiscal and economic policies. Unless they are consistent with the demands of such policies, they should not be approved.

In my Budget Message of January 10, 1947, I said:

"As long as business, employment, and national income continue high, we should maintain tax revenues at levels that will not only meet current expenditures but also leave a surplus for retirement of the public debt. There is no justification now for tax reduction."

Developments since January do not warrant a change in that conclusion. Total employment in May increased by a million and a half over that in April, and the total number now employed is over 58 million. The number of unemployed is now less than 2 million, practically a peace-time minimum. Income payments to individuals are estimated to be at the record annual rate of $176 billion. Department store sales in May were up 6 percent over April, and equalled the all-time high in dollar volume. The number of houses begun by private enterprise in May was the largest in any month since V-J Day. Despite many gloomy predictions, there is no convincing evidence that a recession is imminent.

Ample evidence points to the continuation of inflationary pressures. Tax reduction now would increase them. If these pressures are long continued, and if essential readjustments within the price structure are long deferred, we are likely to induce the very recession we seek to avoid.

Reductions in income tax rates are not required now to permit necessary investment and business expansion. There is no shortage of funds for this purpose in any wide sector of our economy. As a matter of fact, the amount of liquid funds in the hands of corporations and individuals at the present time is nearly $200 billion. Under these circumstances, tax reduction is not now needed to provide additional funds for business expansion.

The argument is made that the funds added to consumer purchasing power through this tax reduction are needed to maintain employment and production at maximum levels.

It is true, as I have pointed out many times, that the purchasing power of large groups of our people has been seriously reduced. We must take every step possible to remedy the disparity between prices and the incomes of the rank and file of our people, so as not to put brakes on our continued prosperity and lead us toward a recession. Tax reduction as proposed in H.R. 1 is not the proper way to remedy the current price situation and its effect upon consumers and upon prospective employment. Necessary adjustments in incomes, production, and prices should be made by wise policies and improved practices of business and labor, not by hastily invoking the fiscal powers of Government on a broad scale.

The time for tax reduction will come when general inflationary pressures have ceased and the structure of prices is on a more stable basis than now prevails. How long it will take for this point to be reached is impossible to predict. Clearly, it has not been reached as yet. Tax reduction now would add to, rather than correct, maladjustments in the economic structure.

Sound fiscal policy also requires that existing tax rates be maintained for the present. I have always been keenly aware of the necessity for the utmost economy in government and of the need for a progressive reduction in government expenditures to the greatest extent possible consistent with our national interests. However, necessary expenditures for essential Government operations are still high. We are still meeting heavy obligations growing out of the war. We continue to be confronted with great responsibilities for international relief and rehabilitation that have an important bearing on our efforts to secure lasting peace. We are still in a transition period in which many uncertainties continue. In the face of these facts, common prudence demands a realistic and conservative management of the fiscal affairs of the Government.

A time of high employment and high prices, wages, and profits, such as the present, calls for a surplus in Government revenue over expenditures and the application of all or much of this surplus to the reduction of the public debt. Continuing public confidence in Government finances depends upon such a policy. If the Government does not reduce the public debt during the most active and inflationary periods, there is little prospect of material reduction at any time, and the country would, as a result, be in a poorer position to extend supports to the economy should a subsequent deflationary period develop.

With the present huge public debt, it is of first importance that every effort now be made to reduce the debt as much as possible. If H.R. 1 were to become law, the amount available for debt retirement would be entirely too low for this period of unparalleled high levels of peacetime income and employment.

The integrity of the public debt is the financial bedrock on which our national economy rests. More than half of the American people are direct owners of Government securities. A major portion of the assets of banks, insurance companies, and trust funds is invested in Government bonds. To maintain the integrity of the public debt, we must now reduce it by substantial amounts.

In addition to the fact that this is not the time for tax reduction, there is a fundamental objection to this particular bill. An adjustment of the tax system should provide fair and equitable relief for individuals from the present tax burden, but the reductions proposed in H.R. 1 are neither fair nor equitable. H.R. 1 reduces taxes in the high income brackets to a grossly disproportionate extent as compared to the reduction in the low income brackets. A good tax reduction bill would give a greater proportion of relief to the low income group.

H.R. 1 fails to give relief where it is needed most. Under H.R. 1, tax savings to the average family with an income of $2500 would be less than $30, while taxes on an income of $50,000 would be reduced by nearly $5000, and on an income of $500,000 by nearly $60,000.

Insofar as "take-home" pay is concerned under H.R. 1, the family earning $2500 would receive an increase of only 1.2 percent; the family with an income of $50,000 would receive an increase of 18.6 percent; and the family with an income of $500,000 would receive an increase of 62.3 percent.

If H.R. 1 were to become law, the inequity of its provisions would be frozen into the tax structure. The reduction in government receipts resulting from this bill would be such that the Government could ill afford to make fair tax reductions at the proper time in the form of a carefully-considered revision of our entire tax structure.

Now is the time to plan for a thoroughgoing revision of the tax system. We should consider not only individual income tax rates, but also the level of personal exemptions and many other adjustments in the personal income tax structure. We should also consider changes in excise tax laws, gift and estate taxes, corporation taxes, and, in fact, the entire field of tax revenues. Such a program of tax adjustment and tax reduction should be geared to the financial and economic needs of this country. It will be an important contribution to economic progress. The timing of such a program is highly important to achieve economic stability, to promote the investment of capital, and to maintain employment, purchasing power and high levels of production.

For the compelling reasons I have set forth, I return H.R. 1 without my approval.

HARRY S. TRUMAN

---

117 Commencement Address at Princeton University. *June* 17, 1947

President Dodds, distinguished guests, ladies and gentlemen:

The President of Princeton University spoke of crises a while ago. He should try sitting in my chair for about an hour and a half!

It is with a great deal of pleasure, and much pride, that I am now able to count myself as a member of the Princeton family.

Princeton University has conferred an honor upon me for which I am deeply grateful. I consider it a special privilege to have received the degree of Doctor of Laws at the Final Convocation of the Bicentennial Year in the presence of this distinguished company.

On an earlier occasion of equal significance in the history of this University, the

President of the United States, Grover Cleveland, spoke in 1896 at the Princeton Sesquicentennial Ceremonies. President Cleveland seized that opportunity to charge our colleges and universities with the task of supplying a "constant stream of thoughtful, educated men" to the body politic—men who were eager to perform public service for the benefit of the Nation. He chided our institutions of higher learning for their lack of interest in public affairs, and held them responsible for the disdain with which many of the best educated men of the day viewed politics and public affairs.

Happily for us, that attitude on the part of our universities vanished long ago. I am certain that no observer of the American scene in recent years has detected any reluctance on the part of our educators to enter the political arena when their services have been needed. And our schools have made much progress in supplying the "constant stream of thoughtful, educated men" for public service called for by President Cleveland half a century ago.

That task is more important today than at any previous time in our national history.

In our free society, knowledge and learning are endowed with a public purpose—a noble purpose, close to the heart of democracy. That purpose is to help men and women develop their talents for the benefit of their fellow citizens. Our advance in the natural sciences has led to almost miraculous achievements, but we have less reason to be proud of our progress in developing the capacity among men for cooperative living. In the present critical stage of world history, we need, more than ever before, to enlist all our native integrity and industry in the conduct of our common affairs.

The role of the United States is changing more rapidly than in any previous period of our history. We have had to assume worldwide responsibilities and commitments.

Our people have placed their trust in the Government as the guardian of our democratic ideals and the instrument through which we work for enduring peace.

The success of the Government's efforts in achieving these ends will depend upon the quality of citizenship of our people. It will also depend upon the extent to which our leaders in business, labor, the professions, agriculture, and every other field, appreciate the role of their Government and the greatness of its tasks.

Our schools must train future leaders in all fields to understand and concern themselves with the expanded role of the Government, and—equally important—to see the need for effective administration of the Government's business in the public interest.

I call your attention particularly to the problem of effective administration within the Government, where matters of unprecedented magnitude and complexity confront the public servant. If our national policies are to succeed, they must be administered by officials with broad experience, mature outlook, and sound judgment. There is, however, a critical shortage of such men—men who possess the capacity to deal with great affairs of state.

The Government has recruited from our academic institutions many members of its professional staffs—geologists, physicists, lawyers, economists, and others with specialized training. These men are essential to the conduct of the Government and to the welfare of the Nation. But we have been much less effective in obtaining persons with broad understanding and an aptitude for management. We need men who can turn a group of specialists into a working team and who can combine imagination and practicability with a sound public program.

All large organizations, public and private, depend on the teamwork of specialists. Coordination is achieved by administrators trained to assemble the fruits of specialized knowledge and to build on that foundation a sound final decision. Men trained for this kind of administrative and political leadership are rare indeed.

In the task of finding and training men and women who will add strength to the public service, universities have a particular responsibility. They should develop in their students the capacity for seeing and meeting social problems as a whole and for relating special knowledge to broad issues. They should study the needs of Government, and encourage men and women with exceptional interests and aptitudes along the necessary lines to enter the Government service.

The Woodrow Wilson School of Public and International Affairs of this university was established with this purpose in mind. It seeks to prepare students for public careers. It is significant that the school bears the name of a statesman whose concept of civic duty contributed so much to the Nation and to the world.

Of course, the Government cannot and does not expect to rely entirely upon our educational institutions for its administrators. It must bring into service from business and labor, and the professions, the best qualified persons to fill the posts at all levels.

The Government must take several steps to make its career service more attractive to the kind of men and women it needs.

Salary limitations prevent the Government, in many instances, from securing the kind of executives required to manage its vital activities. Capable administrators are too frequently drawn away from the Government to private positions with salaries many times what they could earn in the Government service. This situation can be remedied only by laws to bring salaries more nearly in line with the heavy responsibilities that executives carry at the higher levels in the public service.

The complexities of the tasks now facing our top officials force them to spend most of their time in studying matters of policy. These officials should be supported by a career group of administrators skilled in the various aspects of management. If capable men and women can look forward to holding such posts as a reward for able service, they will be more eager to accept Government employment.

Because of the difficult tasks of Government today, we should plan a program for the systematic training of civilian employees once they have entered the public service. It is not generally possible at the present time for the Federal Government to send its employees to universities for special short-term training programs. Nor is it permissible under existing law to spend Federal funds for Government schools to develop the knowledge and techniques required by officials in their work.

This is a problem that can be solved only by the joint efforts of the Government and the universities. Training programs can be formulated, both on the job and on the campus. The Government must make provision for its employees to participate. The universities will need to provide courses well adapted to increasing the effectiveness of the employee in his job. Such a plan is certain to pay substantial dividends.

I have been speaking about the important contribution which educational institutions can make to the service of the Nation through preparing men and women to administer our farflung public enterprises.

Another contribution which I regard as important at this time is support for a program of universal training. I consider such a program vital to the national welfare. Since universal training necessarily affects young men of college age, I believe that our educational institutions should be particularly aware of the need for such a program and what it can accomplish.

The recent war left in its wake a tremendous task of repair and reconstruction, of building a new and orderly world out of the economic and social chaos of the old. It is a task too great for us, or for any other nation, to undertake alone. Even though we are contributing generously and wholeheartedly, no single nation has the means to set the world aright. It is a job for all nations to do together. Unfortunately, however, generosity of impulse and abundant good will are not enough to insure the political stability essential to social and economic reconstruction. Peace-loving nations can make only slow progress toward the attainment of a stable world—in which all peoples are free to work out their own destinies in their own way—unless their moral leadership is supported by strength.

Weakness on our part would stir fear among the small or weakened nations that we were giving up our world leadership. It would seem to them that we lacked the will to fulfill our pledge to aid free and independent nations to maintain their freedoms, or our commitments to aid in restoring war-torn economies. In such an atmosphere of uncertainty, these nations might not be able to resist the encroachments of totalitarian pressures.

We must not let friendly nations go by default.

A few days ago, I sent to the Congress a report outlining a program designed to provide this country with the military strength required to support our foreign policy until such time as the growing authority of the United Nations will make such strength unnecessary.[1] That report was prepared by

an advisory commission of distinguished citizens. One of them was President Dodds. The Commission reported its belief that the United States should have small professional armed forces. These should be supported by a reserve of trained citizens, derived from a carefully planned program of universal training for young men. Without such training, in the opinion of the commission, we cannot maintain effective reserves. Hence the commission regards universal training as an essential element in a balanced program for security.

Universal training represents the most democratic, the most economical, and the most effective method of maintaining the military strength we need. It is the only way that such strength can be achieved without imposing a ruinous burden on our economy through the maintenance of a large standing armed force.

The justification for universal training is its military necessity. However, it is a matter of deep concern to me that the training program shall be carried out in a manner that will contribute materially to the health and character of our young men. I am certain that the kind of training recommended in the report of the advisory commission will not only make our youth better equipped to serve their country, but better mentally, morally, and physically. The experience of living together and fulfilling a common responsibility should strengthen the spirit of democracy. It will be an experience in democratic living, out of which should come in increased measure the unity so beneficial to the welfare of the Nation.

We must remember, above all, that these men would not be training in order to win a war, but in order to prevent one.

I am confident that our educational institutions understand the need for universal training and recognize it as a vital responsibility of citizenship in our day.

---

[1] See Item 106.

The obligations of our educational institutions which I have been discussing are great, but in the world today there is a still greater obligation. It is the obligation of service to all nations in the cause of lasting peace.

There can be no greater service to mankind, and no nobler mission, than devotion to world peace.

The course has been charted.

The Constitution of the United Nations Educational, Scientific and Cultural Organization states the basic truths by which we must be guided. That Constitution reads: "Since wars begin in the minds of men, it is in the minds of men that the defenses of peace must be constructed."

The construction of the defenses of peace in the minds of men is the supreme task which our educational institutions must set for themselves.

This convocation is a symbol of what our educational institutions can do in the cause of peace. It marks the end of a great series of conferences, attended by scholars from all over the world, who assembled here for free discussion of the most challenging problems facing men today.

The special significance of these meetings is that they restored bonds in many fields of learning between our own and other lands—bonds which had been impaired by the war. The resumption of meetings of scholars, businessmen, religious leaders and Government officials is evidence of our conviction that the peace must "be founded, if it is not to fail, upon the intellectual solidarity of mankind."

Free and inquiring minds, with unlimited access to the sources of knowledge, can be the architects of a peaceful and prosperous world.

As we gain increasing understanding of man, comparable to our increasing understanding of matter, we shall develop, with God's grace, the ability of nations to work together and live together in lasting peace.

NOTE: The President spoke at 12:30 p.m. from the steps of Nassau Hall at Princeton University after receiving an honorary degree. His opening words referred to Harold W. Dodds, president of the university.

118   Address Opening the President's Second Highway Safety Conference. *June 18, 1947*

IT IS a pleasure to welcome you to the second Highway Safety Conference. You are here to grapple with a problem of prime importance to every resident of our Nation. Please accept my hearty personal thanks for your attendance.

Automobiles — including trucks and buses—traveled nearly 350 billion vehicle-miles last year over the streets and highways of the United States. This tremendous volume of travel was the greatest in the history of our country. It exceeded that of 1941, the next highest year, by 4 percent.

In a very real sense, the increase in post-war highway travel is a measure of our re-turn to the happier peacetime pattern of life in America. There is one tragic aspect of that pattern, however, that no one wishes to see restored. I refer to the appalling destruction of life and property through highway accidents.

In 1941, accidents on the streets and highways cost 40,000 lives. In 1946, with travel 4 percent higher, an even greater loss would have been sustained if the prewar death rate had continued.

Fortunately, that did not happen. Beginning in May 1946, the highway fatality rate showed a sharp and gratifying decline. Last year, the rate was 9.8 deaths per 100 million vehicle-miles, compared with 12 in 1941. So far this year, the trend has continued definitely downward.

Measured against the black record of 1941, this means that at least 6,500 lives were saved last year. We have won a major victory in the campaign against carelessness. For that result, the major share of the credit must go to the efficient and devoted efforts which were set in motion at the first Highway Safety Conference here in Washington in May 1946.

This reduction in the accident rate offers heartening promise of what eventually can be achieved through the concerted effort of motorists and pedestrians, under the leadership of governmental agencies and with the support of organized groups of public-spirited citizens.

The job has been well started, but it is by no means done.

Last year, 33,500 men, women, and children died as a result of highway accidents, and well over a million were injured. That is a tribute to inefficiency this Nation cannot afford to pay.

If those deaths had occurred at the same time in a single community, the whole world would have been profoundly shocked. Every resource of the United States would have been mobilized immediately to prevent the recurrence of such an awful tragedy.

The challenge is no less urgent because it is less spectacular. We are dealing here with what amounts to a national disaster. The fact that most of the death and destruction could have been prevented only intensifies the tragic character of the problem.

The "Action Program" developed at the Highway Safety Conference of 1946 is a sound and workable program. It can and does get results. Now the task is to get more of that program applied by more of the States and more of the communities. I hope that your deliberations this week will direct principal attention to finding ways and means of achieving that goal.

The reports from the States indicate unusually good progress in the field of safety education, especially in the development of driver training courses by our high schools. More than 2 million young people reach the legal driving age each year in the United States. We certainly have an obligation to see that they receive the most adequate preparation possible for useful citizenship in a motor age.

Unfortunately, the driver license part of the program is not keeping pace. Since the 1946 safety conference, two additional States have enacted driver license laws, which leaves now only one State in the Union without such legislation. But uniformity is still lacking among the States. And in too many jurisdictions, as I have pointed out before, the licensing laws are nothing more than revenues measures and their administration a travesty on public safety.

Moreover, the States report little or no progress during the last year in raising standards of motor vehicle administration.

This situation obviously cannot be permitted to continue indefinitely. A licensing law is a basic weapon in the war on accidents. Properly administered, it eliminates the dangerously unfit and the dangerously irresponsible from our streets and highways. It is vital to the protection of the vast majority of law-abiding motorists and pedestrians.

Last year I said there was no desire on the part of the Federal Government to encroach upon State jurisdictions in this field, but that the Congress would not stand idly by in the face of a grievous national accident toll.

In the regulation of interstate commerce, in research and investigation, and in many other activities the Federal Government has direct concern with the problem of highway safety.

The Federal-Aid Highway Act of 1944, for example, provides for the development jointly with the States of modern traffic arteries, both rural and urban, which will incorporate maximum safety into their design and construction. Improvements of this kind in the highway plant will make a permanent and substantial contribution to accident prevention.

Since the "Action Program" was formulated last year, vigorous steps have been taken by nearly all the Federal agencies involved to carry it out in their own operations. Especially encouraging are the programs which have been undertaken for the intensive training of drivers.

Many shortcomings, of course, still exist. But I am happy to report that progress is highly satisfactory, and that plans have been made to intensify these activities in the months ahead. They are fully coordinated through a Federal Committee on Highway Safety in which 13 Federal agencies are now participating.

Three national committees were established in accordance with recommendations made by the 1946 conference. These committees suggested to me the desirability of calling this followup meeting, and I was most happy to act on their suggestion. The purpose of the meeting is to weigh the strength and the weakness of the current program, and to outline further steps which can be taken to speed the adoption of the "Action Program" by all jurisdictions.

I am confident that your work will be fruitful. I am confident that the American people will respond again, and wholeheartedly, to a renewed appeal from this Conference for greater care and courtesy on the roads and streets.

In opening your deliberations, I join with you this morning in making that appeal.

NOTE: The President spoke at 11:30 a.m. at the opening meeting of the conference. Maj. Gen. Philip B. Fleming, Federal Works Administrator, presided over the conference as general chairman.

119 Letter to the President of the Senate and to the Speaker of the House on the Administration of Guam, Samoa, and the Former Japanese Mandated Islands. *June 19, 1947*

My dear Mr. ————:

There is enclosed a copy of a report from the Secretary of State indicating a course of action which the Secretaries of State, War, Navy and Interior have agreed should be followed with respect to the administration of Guam, Samoa and the Pacific islands to be placed under United States trusteeship.

On October 20, 1945, I appointed a committee consisting of the Secretaries of these four departments to make recommendations concerning this matter. After preliminary consideration it seemed inadvisable to

formulate a final recommendation until a determination had been made of the status of certain islands formerly under Japanese control. In the meantime the departments represented on the committee continued to give study to the problems involved.

After the United Nations Security Council approved a trusteeship agreement designating the United States as the administering authority for the former Japanese mandated islands, I requested that the members of the committee again give joint consideration to problems relating to the administration of the Pacific islands. The enclosed report has been submitted pursuant to that request.

I am sure that the agreement reached by the four Secretaries will be of interest to the Congress in connection with its consideration of legislation to provide civilian government for these islands, and that the information obtained by the departments in studying this question will also be helpful in the consideration of such legislation.

It has long been my view that the inhabitants of Guam and Samoa should enjoy those fundamental human rights and that democratic form of government which are the rich heritage of the people of the United States. We have already extended those rights and that form of government to other possessions of the United States, such as Puerto Rico and the Virgin Islands, and with respect to the inhabitants of the trust territory have given solemn assurance to the United Nations of our intention to grant these inhabitants a full measure of individual rights and liberties.

I hope that the Congress will approve legislation for the purposes indicated in the enclosed report and that such legislation will provide for the full enjoyment of civil rights and for the greatest practicable measure of self government.

Very sincerely yours,

HARRY S. TRUMAN

NOTE: This is the text of identical letters addressed to the Honorable Arthur H. Vandenberg, Presi-

dent pro tempore of the Senate, and to the Honorable Joseph W. Martin, Jr., Speaker of the House of Representatives.

Secretary Marshall's report was also released by the White House. The report, in the form of a letter dated June 18, stated that pursuant to the President's request the Secretaries of State, War, Navy, and Interior had held several meetings and that they had agreed upon the following course of action:

"1. Separate organic legislation for Guam to provide civil government and to grant citizenship, a bill of rights, and legislative powers to Guamanians should be enacted this session. In recent hearings on such organic legislation, the Departments have recommended the transfer of administration from the Navy Department to a civilian agency designated by the President at the earliest practicable date, the exact date to be determined by the President.

"2. Organic legislation for American Samoa, providing civil government and granting citizenship, a bill of rights, and legislative powers, should be prepared by the Navy and Interior Departments and presented to the next session of Congress.

"3. Suggestions for organic legislation for those Pacific Islands placed under United States trusteeship are in preparation by the Department of State for presentation to Congress, provided favorable Congressional action is taken on the Trusteeship Agreement to be shortly presented for approval.

"4. The Navy Department should continue to have administrative responsibility for Guam and American Samoa on an interim basis pending the transfer to a civilian agency of the government at the earliest practicable date, such date to be determined by the President. With respect to the trust territory, a similar transfer should be effected by the President at the earliest practicable date.

"5. Provided Congress acts favorably on the Trusteeship Agreement, an Executive order should be issued when the Agreement enters into force, terminating military government in the Trust Territory and delegating civil administration to the Navy Department on an interim basis, subject to the conditions set forth in paragraph 4."

See also Items 137 and 151.

120 Veto of the Taft-Hartley Labor Bill.
June 20, 1947

To the House of Representatives:

I return herewith, without my approval, H.R. 3020, the "Labor Management Relations Act, 1947."

I am fully aware of the gravity which at-

taches to the exercise by the President of his constitutional power to withhold his approval from an enactment of the Congress.

I share with the Congress the conviction that legislation dealing with the relations between management and labor is necessary. I heartily condemn abuses on the part of unions and employers, and I have no patience with stubborn insistence on private advantage to the detriment of the public interest.

But this bill is far from a solution of those problems.

When one penetrates the complex, interwoven provisions of this omnibus bill, and understands the real meaning of its various parts, the result is startling.

The bill taken as a whole would reverse the basic direction of our national labor policy, inject the Government into private economic affairs on an unprecedented scale, and conflict with important principles of our democratic society. Its provisions would cause more strikes, not fewer. It would contribute neither to industrial peace nor to economic stability and progress. It would be a dangerous stride in the direction of a totally managed economy. It contains seeds of discord which would plague this Nation for years to come.

Because of the far-reaching import of this bill, I have weighed its probable effects against a series of fundamental considerations. In each case I find that the bill violates principles essential to our public welfare.

I. The first major test which I have applied to this bill is whether it would result in more or less Government intervention in our economic life.

Our basic national policy has always been to establish by law standards of fair dealing and then to leave the working of the economic system to the free choice of individuals. Under that policy of economic freedom we have built our nation's productive strength. Our people have deep faith in industrial self-government with freedom of contract and free collective bargaining.

I find that this bill is completely contrary to that national policy of economic freedom. It would require the Government, in effect, to become an unwanted participant at every bargaining table. It would establish by law limitations on the terms of every bargaining agreement, and nullify thousands of agreements mutually arrived at and satisfactory to the parties. It would inject the Government deeply into the process by which employers and workers reach agreement. It would superimpose bureaucratic procedures on the free decisions of local employers and employees.

At a time when we are determined to remove, as rapidly as practicable, Federal controls established during the war, this bill would involve the Government in the free processes of our economic system to a degree unprecedented in peacetime.

This is a long step toward the settlement of economic issues by government dictation. It is an indication that industrial relations are to be determined in the halls of Congress, and that political power is to supplant economic power as the critical factor in labor relations.

II. The second basic test against which I have measured this bill is whether it would improve human relations between employers and their employees.

Cooperation cannot be achieved by force of law. We cannot create mutual respect and confidence by legislative fiat.

I am convinced that this legislation overlooks the significance of these principles. It would encourage distrust, suspicion, and arbitrary attitudes.

I find that the National Labor Relations Act would be converted from an instrument with the major purpose of protecting the right of workers to organize and bargain collectively into a maze of pitfalls and complex procedures. As a result of these complexities employers and workers would find new barriers to mutual understanding.

The bill time and again would remove the

settlement of differences from the bargaining table to courts of law. Instead of learning to live together, employers and unions are invited to engage in costly, time-consuming litigation, inevitably embittering both parties.

The Congress has, I think, paid too much attention to the inevitable frictions and difficulties incident to the reconversion period. It has ignored the unmistakable evidence that those difficulties are receding and that labor-management cooperation is constantly improving. There is grave danger that this progress would be nullified through enactment of this legislation.

III. A third basic test is whether the bill is workable.

There is little point in putting laws on the books unless they can be executed. I have concluded that this bill would prove to be unworkable. The so-called "emergency procedure" for critical nation-wide strikes would require an immense amount of government effort but would result almost inevitably in failure. The National Labor Relations Board would be given many new tasks, and hobbled at every turn in attempting to carry them out. Unique restrictions on the Board's procedures would so greatly increase the backlog of unsettled cases that the parties might be driven to turn in despair from peaceful procedures to economic force.

IV. The fourth basic test by which I have measured this bill is the test of fairness.

The bill prescribes unequal penalties for the same offense. It would require the National Labor Relations Board to give priority to charges against workers over related charges against employers. It would discriminate against workers by arbitrarily penalizing them for all critical strikes.

Much has been made of the claim that the bill is intended simply to equalize the positions of labor and management. Careful analysis shows that this claim is unfounded.

Many of the provisions of the bill standing alone seem innocent but, considered in relation to each other, reveal a consistent pattern of inequality.

The failure of the bill to meet these fundamental tests is clearly demonstrated by a more detailed consideration of its defects.

1. The bill would substantially increase strikes.

(1) It would discourage the growing willingness of unions to include "no strike" provisions in bargaining agreements, since any labor organization signing such an agreement would expose itself to suit for contract violation if any of its members engaged in an unauthorized "wildcat" strike.

(2) It would encourage strikes by imposing highly complex and burdensome reporting requirements on labor organizations which wish to avail themselves of their rights under the National Labor Relations Act. In connection with these reporting requirements, the bill would penalize unions for any failure to comply, no matter how inconsequential, by denying them all rights under the Act. These provisions, which are irrelevant to the major purposes of the bill, seem peculiarly designed to place obstacles in the way of labor organizations which wish to appeal to the National Labor Relations Board for relief, and thus to impel them to strike or take other direct action.

(3) It would bring on strikes by depriving significant groups of workers of the right they now enjoy to organize and to bargain under the protection of law. For example, broad groups of employees who for purposes of the Act would be classed as supervisors would be removed from the protection of the Act. Such groups would be prevented from using peaceful machinery and would be left no option but the use of economic force.

(4) The bill would force unions to strike or to boycott if they wish to have a juris-

dictional dispute settled by the National Labor Relations Board. This peculiar situation results from the fact that the Board is given authority to determine jurisdictional disputes over assignment of work only after such disputes have been converted into strikes or boycotts.

In addition to these ways in which specific provisions of the bill would lead directly to strikes, the cumulative effect of many of its other provisions which disrupt established relationships would result in industrial strife and unrest.

2. The bill arbitrarily decides, against the workers, certain issues which are normally the subject of collective bargaining, and thus restricts the area of voluntary agreement.

(1) The bill would limit the freedom of employers and labor organizations to agree on methods of developing responsibility on the part of unions by establishing union security. While seeming to preserve the right to agree to the union shop, it would place such a multitude of obstacles in the way of such agreement that union security and responsibility would be largely cancelled.

In this respect, the bill disregards the voluntary developments in the field of industrial relations in the United States over the past 150 years. Today over eleven million workers are employed under some type of union security contract. The great majority of the plants which have such union security provisions have had few strikes. Employers in such plants are generally strong supporters of some type of union security, since it gives them a greater measure of stability in production.

(2) The bill would limit the freedom of employers and employees to establish and maintain welfare funds. It would prescribe arbitrary methods of administering them and rigidly limit the purposes for which they

may be used. This is an undesirable intrusion by the Government into an important matter which should be the subject of private agreement between employers and employees.

(3) The bill presents a danger that employers and employees might be prohibited from agreeing on safety provisions, rest-period rules, and many other legitimate practices, since such practices may fall under the language defining "feather-bedding."

3. The bill would expose employers to numerous hazards by which they could be annoyed and hampered.

(1) The bill would invite frequent disruption of continuous plant production by opening up immense possibilities for many more elections, and adding new types of elections. The bill would invite electioneering for changes in representatives and for union security. This would harass employers in their production efforts and would generate raiding and jurisdictional disputes. The National Labor Relations Board has been developing sound principles of stability on these matters. The bill would overturn these principles to the detriment of employers.

(2) The bill would complicate the collective bargaining process for employers by permitting—and in some cases requiring—the splitting up of stable patterns of representation. Employers would be harassed by having to deal with many small units. Labor organizations would be encouraged to engage in constant inter-union warfare, which could result only in confusion.

(3) The bill would invite unions to sue employers in the courts regarding the thousands of minor grievances which arise every day over the interpretation of bargaining agreements. Employers are likely to be besieged by a multiplicity of minor suits, since management necessarily must take the initiative in applying the terms of agree-

ments. In this respect, the bill ignores the fact that employers and unions are in wide agreement that the interpretation of the provisions of bargaining agreements should be submitted to the processes of negotiation ending in voluntary arbitration, under penalties prescribed in the agreement itself. This is one of the points on which the National Labor-Management Conference in November, 1945, placed special emphasis. In introducing damage suits as a possible substitute for grievance machinery, the bill rejects entirely the informed wisdom of those experienced in labor relations.

(4) The bill would prevent an employer from freely granting a union shop contract, even where he and virtually his entire working force were in agreement as to its desirability. He would be required to refrain from agreement until the National Labor Relations Board's workload permitted it to hold an election—in this case simply to ratify an unquestioned and legitimate agreement.

Employers, moreover, would suffer because the ability of unions to exercise responsibility under bargaining agreements would be diminished. Labor organizations whose disciplinary authority is weakened cannot carry their full share of maintaining stability of production.

4. The bill would deprive workers of vital protection which they now have under the law.

(1) The bill would make it easier for an employer to get rid of employees whom he wanted to discharge because they exercised their right of self-organization guaranteed by the Act. It would permit an employer to dismiss a man on the pretext of a slight infraction of shop rules, even though his real motive was to discriminate against this employee for union activity.

(2) The bill would also put a powerful new weapon in the hands of employers by permitting them to initiate elections at times strategically advantageous to them. It is significant that employees on economic strike who may have been replaced are denied a vote. An employer could easily thwart the will of his employees by raising a question of representation at a time when the union was striking over contract terms.

(3) It would give employers the means to engage in endless litigation, draining the energy and resources of unions in court actions, even though the particular charges were groundless.

(4) It would deprive workers of the power to meet the competition of goods produced under sweatshop conditions by permitting employers to halt every type of secondary boycott, not merely those for unjustifiable purposes.

(5) It would reduce the responsibility of employers for unfair labor practices committed in their behalf. The effect of the bill is to narrow unfairly employer liability for anti-union acts and statements made by persons who, in the eyes of the employees affected, act and speak for management, but who may not be "agents" in the strict legal sense of that term.

(6) At the same time it would expose unions to suits for acts of violence, wildcat strikes and other actions, none of which were authorized or ratified by them. By employing elaborate legal doctrine, the bill applies a superficially similar test of responsibility for employers and unions—each would be responsible for the acts of his "agents." But the power of an employer to control the acts of his subordinates is direct and final. This is radically different from the power of unions to control the acts of their members—who are, after all, members of a free association.

5. The bill abounds in provisions which would be unduly burdensome or actually unworkable.

(1) The bill would erect an unworkable administrative structure for carrying out the National Labor Relations Act. The bill would establish, in effect, an independent General Counsel and an independent Board. But it would place with the Board full responsibility for investigating and determining election cases—over 70 per cent of the present case load—and at the same time would remove from the Board the authority to direct and control the personnel engaged in carrying out this responsibility.

(2) It would invite conflict between the National Labor Relations Board and its General Counsel, since the General Counsel would decide, without any right of appeal by employers and employees, whether charges were to be heard by the Board, and whether orders of the Board were to be referred to the Court for enforcement. By virtue of this unlimited authority, a single administrative official might usurp the Board's responsibility for establishing policy under the Act.

(3) It would straitjacket the National Labor Relations Board's operations by a series of special restrictions unknown to any other quasi-judicial agency. After many years of study, the Congress adopted the Administrative Procedures Act of 1946 to govern the operation of all quasi-judicial agencies, including the National Labor Relations Board. This present bill disregards the Procedures Act and, in many respects, is directly contrary to the spirit and letter of that Act. Simple and time-saving procedures, already established and accepted as desirable by employers and employees, would be summarily scrapped. The Board itself, denied the power of delegation, would be required to hear all jurisdictional disputes over work tasks. This single duty might require a major portion of the Board's time. The review function within the Board, largely of a non-judicial character, would be

split up and assigned to separate staffs attached to each Board member. This would lead to extensive and costly duplication of work and records.

(4) The bill would require or invite government supervised elections in an endless variety of cases. Questions of the bargaining unit, of representatives, of union security, of bargaining offers, are subject to election after election, most of them completely unnecessary. The National Labor Relations Board has had difficulty conducting the number of elections required under present law. This bill would greatly multiply this load. It would in effect impose upon the Board a five-year backlog of election cases, if it handled them at its present rate.

(5) The bill would introduce a unique handicap, unknown in ordinary law, upon the use of statements as evidence of unfair labor practices. An anti-union statement by an employer, for example, could not be considered as evidence of motive, unless it contained an explicit threat of reprisal or force or promise of benefit. The bill would make it an unfair labor practice to "induce or encourage" certain types of strikes and boycotts—and then would forbid the National Labor Relations Board to consider as evidence "views, argument or opinion" by which such a charge could be proved.

(6) The bill would require the Board to "determine" jurisdictional disputes over work tasks, instead of using arbitration, the accepted and traditional method of settling such disputes. In order to get its case before the Board a union must indulge in a strike or a boycott and wait for some other party to allege that it had violated the law. If the Board's decision should favor the party thus forced to violate the law in order that its case might be heard, the Board would be without power over other parties to the dispute to whom the award might be unacceptable.

(7) The bill would require the Board to determine which employees on strike are "entitled to reinstatement" and hence would be eligible to vote in an election held during a strike. This would be an impossible task, since it would require the Board arbitrarily to decide which, if any, of the employees had been replaced and therefore should not be allowed to vote.

6. The bill would establish an ineffective and discriminatory emergency procedure for dealing with major strikes affecting the public health or safety.

This procedure would be certain to do more harm than good, and to increase rather than diminish widespread industrial disturbances. I am convinced that the country would be in for a bitter disappointment if these provisions of the bill became law.

The procedure laid down by the bill is elaborate. Its essential features are a Presidential board of inquiry, a waiting period of approximately 80 days (enforced by injunction) and a secret ballot vote of the workers on the question of whether or not to accept their employer's last offer.

At the outset a board of inquiry would be required to investigate the situation thoroughly, but would be specifically forbidden to offer its informed judgment concerning a reasonable basis for settlement of the dispute. Such inquiry therefore would serve merely as a sounding board to dramatize the respective positions of the parties.

A strike or lockout might occur before the board of inquiry could make its report, and perhaps even before the board could be appointed. The existence of such a strike or lockout would hamper the board in pursuing its inquiry. Experience has shown that fact-finding, if it is to be most effective as a device for settlement of labor disputes, should come before the men leave their

work, not afterwards. Furthermore an injunction issued after a strike has started would arouse bitter resentment which would not contribute to agreement.

If the dispute had not been settled after 60 days of the waiting period, the National Labor Relations Board would be required to hold a separate election for the employees of each employer to find out whether the workers wished to accept the employer's last offer, as stated by him. Our experience under the War Labor Disputes Act showed conclusively that such an election would almost inevitably result in a vote to reject the employer's offer, since such action amounts to a vote of confidence by the workers in their bargaining representatives. The union would then be reinforced by a dramatic demonstration, under Government auspices, of its strength for further negotiations.

After this elaborate procedure the injunction would then have to be dissolved, the parties would be free to fight out their dispute, and it would be mandatory for the President to transfer the whole problem to the Congress, even if it were not in session. Thus, major economic disputes between employers and their workers over contract terms might ultimately be thrown into the political arena for disposition. One could scarcely devise a less effective method for discouraging critical strikes.

This entire procedure is based upon the same erroneous assumptions as those which underlay the strike-vote provision of the War Labor Disputes Act, namely, that strikes are called in haste as the result of inflamed passions, and that union leaders do not represent the wishes of the workers. We have learned by experience, however, that strikes in the basic industries are not called in haste, but only after long periods of negotiation and serious deliberation; and that in the secret-ballot election the workers almost always vote to support their leaders.

Furthermore, a fundamental inequity runs through these provisions. The bill provides for injunctions to prohibit workers from striking, even against terms dictated by employers after contracts have expired. There is no provision assuring the protection of the rights of the employees during the period they are deprived of the right to protect themselves by economic action.

In summary, I find that the so-called "emergency procedure" would be ineffective. It would provide for clumsy and cumbersome government intervention; it would authorize inequitable injunctions; and it would probably culminate in a public confession of failure. I cannot conceive that this procedure would aid in the settlement of disputes.

7. The bill would discriminate against employees.

(1) It would impose discriminatory penalties upon employers and employees for the same offense, that of violating the requirement that existing agreements be maintained for 60 days without strike or lockout while a new agreement is being negotiated. Employers could only be required to restore the previous conditions of employment, but employees could be summarily dismissed by the employer.

(2) The bill would require the Board to seek a temporary restraining order when labor organizations had been charged with boycotts or certain kinds of jurisdictional strikes. It would invite employers to find any pretext for arguing that "an object" of the union's action was one of these practices, even though the primary object was fully legitimate. Moreover, since these cases would be taken directly into the courts, they

necessarily would be settled by the judiciary before the National Labor Relations Board had a chance to decide the issue. This would thwart the entire purpose of the National Labor Relations Act in establishing the Board, which purpose was to confer on the Board, rather than the courts, the power to decide complex questions of fact in a special field requiring expert knowledge. This provision of the bill is clearly a backward step toward the old abuses of the labor injunction. No similar provision directed against employers can be found in the bill.

(3) The bill would also require the Board to give priority in investigating charges of certain kinds of unfair labor practices against unions, even though such unfair labor practices might have been provoked by those of the employer. Thus the bill discriminates, in this regard, in the relief available to employers and unions.

(4) It would impose on labor organizations, but not on employers, burdensome reporting requirements which must be met before any rights would be available under the Act.

(5) In weakening the protections afforded to the right to organize, contrary to the basic purpose of the National Labor Relations Act, the bill would injure smaller unions far more than larger ones. Those least able to protect themselves would be the principal victims of the bill.

8. The bill would disregard in important respects the unanimous convictions of employer and labor representatives at the National Labor-Management Conference in November, 1945.

(1) One of the strongest convictions expressed during the Conference was that the Government should withdraw from the collective bargaining process, now that the war

emergency is over, and leave the determination of working conditions to the free agreement of the parties. This bill proceeds in exactly the opposite direction. In numerous ways the bill would unnecessarily intrude the Government into the process of reaching free decisions through bargaining. This intrusion is precisely what the representatives of management and labor resented.

(2) A unanimous recommendation of the Conference was that the Conciliation Service should be strengthened within the Department of Labor. But this bill removes the Conciliation Service from the Department of Labor. The new name for the Service would carry with it no new dignity or new functions. The evidence does not support the theory that the conciliation function would be better exercised and protected by an independent agency outside the Department of Labor. Indeed, the Service would lose the important day-to-day support of factual research in industrial relations available from other units of the Department. Furthermore, the removal of the Conciliation Service from the Department of Labor would be contrary to the praiseworthy policy of the Congress to centralize related governmental units within the major government departments.

9. The bill raises serious issues of public policy which transcend labor-management difficulties.

(1) In undertaking to restrict political contributions and expenditures, the bill would prohibit many legitimate activities on the part of unions and corporations. This provision would prevent the ordinary union newspaper from commenting favorably or unfavorably upon candidates or issues in national elections. I regard this as a dangerous intrusion on free speech, unwarranted by any demonstration of need, and quite foreign to the stated purposes of this bill.

Furthermore, this provision can be interpreted as going far beyond its apparent objectives, and as interfering with necessary business activities. It provides no exemption for corporations whose business is the publication of newspapers or the operation of radio stations. It makes no distinctions between expenditures made by such corporations for the purpose of influencing the results of an election, and other expenditures made by them in the normal course of their business "in connection with" an election. Thus it would raise a host of troublesome questions concerning the legality of many practices ordinarily engaged in by newspapers and radio stations.

(2) In addition, in one important area the bill expressly abandons the principle of uniform application of national policy under Federal law. The bill's stated policy of preserving some degree of union security would be abdicated in all States where more restrictive policies exist. In other respects the bill makes clear that Federal policy would govern insofar as activities affecting commerce are concerned. This is not only an invitation to the States to distort national policy as they see fit, but is a complete forsaking of a long-standing Constitutional principle.

(3) In regard to Communists in unions, I am convinced that the bill would have an effect exactly opposite to that intended by the Congress. Congress intended to assist labor organizations to rid themselves of Communist officers. With this objective I am in full accord. But the effect of this provision would be far different. The bill would deny the peaceful procedures of the National Labor Relations Act to a union unless all its officers declared under oath that they were not members of the Communist party and that they did not favor the forceful or unconstitutional overthrow of the Government. The mere refusal by a single

individual to sign the required affidavit would prevent an entire national labor union from being certified for purposes of collective bargaining. Such a union would have to win all its objectives by strike, rather than by orderly procedure under the law. The union and the affected industry would be disrupted for perhaps a long period of time while violent electioneering, charges and counter-charges split open the union ranks. The only result of this provision would be confusion and disorder, which is exactly the result the Communists desire.

This provision in the bill is an attempt to solve difficult problems of industrial democracy by recourse to oversimplified legal devices. I consider that this provision would increase, rather than decrease, disruptive effects of Communists in our labor movement.

The most fundamental test which I have applied to this bill is whether it would strengthen or weaken American democracy in the present critical hour. This bill is perhaps the most serious economic and social legislation of the past decade. Its effects—for good or ill—would be felt for decades to come.

I have concluded that the bill is a clear threat to the successful working of our democratic society.

One of the major lessons of recent world history is that free and vital trade unions are a strong bulwark against the growth of totalitarian movements. We must, therefore, be everlastingly alert that in striking at union abuses we do not destroy the contribution which unions make to our democratic strength.

This bill would go far toward weakening our trade union movement. And it would go far toward destroying our national unity. By raising barriers between labor and management and by injecting political considera-

tions into normal economic decisions, it would invite them to gain their ends through direct political action. I think it would be exceedingly dangerous to our country to develop a class basis for political action.

I cannot emphasize too strongly the transcendent importance of the United States in the world today as a force for freedom and peace. We cannot be strong internationally if our national unity and our productive strength are hindered at home. Anything which weakens our economy or weakens the unity of our people— as I am thoroughly convinced this bill would do—I cannot approve.

In my message on the State of the Union which I submitted to the Congress in January, 1947, I recommended a step-by-step approach to the subject of labor legislation. I specifically indicated the problems which we should treat immediately. I recommended that, before going on to other problems, a careful, thorough and nonpartisan investigation should be made, covering the entire field of labor-management relations.

The bill now before me reverses this procedure. It would make drastic changes in our national labor policy first, and would provide for investigation afterward.

There is still a genuine opportunity for the enactment of appropriate labor legislation this session. I still feel that the recommendations which I expressed in the State of the Union Message constitute an adequate basis for legislation which is moderate in spirit and which relates to known abuses.

For the compelling reasons I have set forth, I return H.R. 3020 without my approval.

HARRY S. TRUMAN

NOTE: On June 23 the Congress passed the bill over the President's veto. As enacted, H.R. 3020 is Public Law 101, 80th Congress (61 Stat. 136).

121   Radio Address to the American People on the Veto of the Taft-Hartley Bill.   *June* 20, 1947

[Broadcast from the White House at 10 p.m.]

My fellow countrymen:

At noon today I sent to Congress a message vetoing the Taft-Hartley labor bill. I vetoed this bill because I am convinced it is a bad bill. It is bad for labor, bad for management, and bad for the country.

I had hoped that the Congress would send me a labor bill I could sign.

I have said before, and I say it now, that we need legislation to correct abuses in the field of labor relations.

Last January I made specific recommendations to the Congress as to the kind of labor legislation we should have immediately. I urged that the Congress provide for a commission, to be made up of representatives of the Congress, the public, labor and management, to study the entire field of labor-management relations and to suggest what additional laws we should have.

I believe that my proposals were accepted by the great majority of our people as fair and just.

If the Congress had accepted those recommendations, we would have today the basis for improved labor-management relations. I would gladly have signed a labor bill if it had taken us in the right direction of stable, peaceful labor relations—even though it might not have been drawn up exactly as I wished.

I would have signed a bill with some doubtful features if, taken as a whole, it had been a good bill.

But the Taft-Hartley bill is a shocking piece of legislation.

It is unfair to the working people of this country. It clearly abuses the right, which millions of our citizens now enjoy, to join together and bargain with their employers for fair wages and fair working conditions.

Under no circumstances could I have signed *this* bill!

The restrictions that this bill places on our workers go far beyond what our people have been led to believe. This is no innocent bill.

It is interesting to note that on June 4, Congressman Hartley on the floor of the House of Representatives, made the following statement, and I quote: "You are going to find there is more in this bill than may meet the eye."

That is a revealing description of this bill by one of its authors.

There is so much more in it than the people have been led to believe, that I am sure that very few understand what the Taft-Hartley bill would do if it should become law.

That is why I am speaking to you tonight. I want you to know the real meaning of this bill.

We have all been told, by its proponents, that this is a "moderate" bill. We have been told that the bill was "harsh" and "drastic" when it was first passed by the House of Representatives, but that the Senate had persuaded the House to drop out the harsh provisions and that the final bill— the bill sent to me—was "mild" and "moderate."

But I found no truth in the claims that the bill sent to me was mild or moderate. I found that the basic purpose and much of the language of the original House of Representatives bill were still in the final bill. In fact, the final bill follows the provisions of the original House bill in at least 36 separate places.

We have all been told that the Taft-Hartley bill is favorable to the wage earners of this country. It has been claimed that workers need to be saved from their own folly and that this bill would provide the means of salvation. Some people have called this bill the "workers' bill of rights."

Let us see what this bill really would do to our workingmen.

The bill is deliberately designed to weaken labor unions. When the sponsors of the bill claim that by weakening unions, they are giving rights back to individual workingmen, they ignore the basic reason why unions are important in our democracy. Unions exist so that laboring men can bargain with their employers on a basis of equality. Because of unions, the living standards of our working people have increased steadily until they are today the highest in the world.

A bill which would weaken unions would undermine our national policy of collective bargaining. The Taft-Hartley bill would do just that. It would take us back in the direction of the old evils of individual bargaining. It would take the bargaining power away from the workers and give more power to management.

This bill would even take away from our workingmen some bargaining rights which they enjoyed before the Wagner Act was passed 12 years ago.

If we weaken our system of collective bargaining, we weaken the position of every workingman in the country.

This bill would again expose workers to the abuses of labor injunctions.

It would make unions liable for damage suits for actions which have long been considered lawful.

This bill would treat all unions alike. Unions which have fine records, with long years of peaceful relations with management, would be hurt by this bill just as much as the few troublemakers.

The country needs legislation which will get rid of abuses. We do not need—and

we do not want—legislation which will take fundamental rights away from our working people.

We have been told that the Taft-Hartley bill is a means by which the country can be protected from nationwide strikes in vital industries. The terms of the bill do not support this claim.

Many people are under the impression that this bill would prevent or settle a strike in the coal industry. I sincerely trust that the coal operators and the miners will soon come to an agreement on the terms of a contract and that there will be no interruption of coal mining. But if the miners and the operators do not reach agreement, and if this bill should become law, it is likely that the most that could be accomplished under the complicated procedures of the bill would be postponement of a strike from July until October.

Under this bill a work stoppage in the coal mines might be prevented for 80 days and then, if agreement had not been reached, the miners would be free to strike, and it would be mandatory for the President to refer the whole matter to Congress, even if Congress were not in session.

Postponing a strike in the coal industry until the approach of winter, when our need for coal is acute, is certainly not the way to protect the Nation against the dangers of a shortage of coal.

The bill would not aid fair and early settlements of disputes in vital industries.

We have been told, by the supporters of the Taft-Hartley bill, that it would reduce industrial strife.

On the contrary, I am convinced that it would increase industrial strife.

The bill would soon upset security clauses in thousands of existing agreements between labor and management. These agreements were mutually arrived at and furnish a satisfactory basis for relations between worker and employer. They provide stability in industry. With their present types of agreements outlawed by this bill, the parties would have to find a new basis for agreement. The restrictions in this bill would make the process of reaching new agreements a long and bitter one.

The bill would increase industrial strife because a number of its provisions deprive workers of legal protection of fundamental rights. They would then have no means of protecting these rights except by striking.

The bill would open up opportunities for endless law suits by employers against unions and by unions against employers. For example, it would make employers vulnerable to an immense number of law suits, since grievances, however minor, could be taken into court by dissatisfied workers.

Insofar as employers are concerned, I predict that if this bill should become law they would regret the day that it was conceived. It is loaded with provisions that would plague and hamper management. It is filled with hidden legal traps that would take labor relations out of the plant, where they belong, and place them in the courts.

Another defect is that in trying to correct labor abuses the Taft-Hartley bill goes so far that it would threaten fundamental democratic freedoms. One provision undertakes to prevent political contributions and expenditures by labor organizations and corporations. This provision would forbid a union newspaper from commenting on candidates in national elections. It might well prevent an incorporated radio network from spending any money in connection with the national convention of a political party. It might even prevent the League of Women Voters—which is incorporated—from using its funds to inform its members about the record of a political candidate.

I regard this provision of the Taft-Hartley bill as a dangerous challenge to free speech and our free press.

One of the basic errors of this bill is that it ignores the fact that over the years we have been making real progress in labor-management relations. We have been achieving slow but steady improvement in cooperation between employers and workers.

We must always remember that under our free economic system management and labor are associates. They work together for their own benefit and for the benefit of the public.

The Taft-Hartley bill fails to recognize these fundamental facts. Many provisions of the bill would have the result of changing employers and workers from members of the same team to opponents on contending teams.

I feel deep concern about what this would do to the steady progress we have made through the years.

I fear that this type of legislation would cause the people of our country to divide into opposing groups. If conflict is created, as this bill would create it—if the seeds of discord are sown, as this bill would sow them—our unity will suffer and our strength will be impaired.

This bill does not resemble the labor legislation which I have recommended to the Congress. The whole purpose of this bill is contrary to the sound growth of our national labor policy.

There is still time to enact progressive, constructive legislation during the present session. We need such legislation to correct abuses and to further our advance in labor-management relations.

We seek in this country today a formula which will treat all men fairly and justly, and which will give our people security in the necessities of life.

As our generous American spirit prompts us to aid the world to rebuild, we must, at the same time, construct a better America in which all can share equitably in the blessings of democracy.

The Taft-Hartley bill threatens the attainment of this goal.

For the sake of the future of this Nation, I hope that this bill will not become law.

122   Statement by the President on the Economic Effects of Foreign Aid. *June 22, 1947*

THE IMPACT upon our domestic economy of the assistance we are now furnishing or may furnish to foreign countries is a matter of grave concern to every American. I believe we are generally agreed that the recovery of production abroad is essential both to a vigorous democracy and to a peace founded on democracy and freedom. It is essential also to a world trade in which our businessmen, farmers, and workers may benefit from substantial exports and in which their customers may be able to pay for these goods. On the other hand, the extent to which we should continue aiding such recovery is less easy to ascertain, and merits most careful study.

Much attention has already been given to these questions by various agencies of the Government, as well as by a number of well-informed and public-spirited citizens. The results of current study and discussion have not, however, been brought together and objectively evaluated in a form suitable for guidance in the formulation of national policy.

Accordingly, I am creating immediately three committees to study and report to me within the shortest possible time on the relationship between any further aid which may be extended to foreign countries and the interests of our domestic economy. Two of these studies will be conducted within the Government; the third will be conducted by a nonpartisan committee of distinguished

citizens headed by the Secretary of Commerce.

Of the two studies to be conducted within the Government, one will deal with the state of our national resources, and will be made by a committee of specialists under the direction of the Secretary of the Interior. The other governmental study will deal with the impact on our national economy of aid to other countries, and will be conducted by the Council of Economic Advisers.

The nonpartisan committee will be requested to determine the facts with respect to the character and quantities of United States resources available for economic assistance to foreign countries, and to advise me, in the light of these facts, on the limits within which the United States may safely and wisely plan to extend such assistance and on the relation between this assistance and our domestic economy. This committee will be drawn from representatives of American business, finance, labor, agriculture, and educational and research institutions. In carrying out its work this committee will have the benefit of the studies which are to be made within the Government, as well as the materials already prepared by various Government agencies.

The names of those being asked to serve on the committe are as follows:

Hiland Batcheller, President, Allegheny-Ludlum Steel Corp., Pittsburgh, Pa.

Robert Earle Buchanan, Dean, Graduate

College, Iowa State College, Ames, Iowa.

W. Randolph Burgess, Vice Chairman, National City Bank of N.Y., New York, N.Y.

James B. Carey, Secretary-Treasurer, CIO, Washington, D.C.

John L. Collyer, President, B. F. Goodrich Co., Akron, Ohio.

Granville Conway, President, The Cosmopolitan Shipping Co., Inc., 42d and Broadway, New York, N.Y.

Melville F. Coolbaugh, 1700 Maple Street, Golden, Colo.

Chester C. Davis, President, Federal Reserve Bank, St. Louis, Mo.

R. R. Deupree, President, Procter & Gamble Co., Cincinnati, Ohio.

Paul G. Hoffman, President, The Studebaker Corp., South Bend, Ind.

Calvin B. Hoover, Dean, Graduate School, Duke University, Durham, N.C.

Robert Koenig, President, Ayrshire Colliers Co., Big Four Building, Indianapolis, Ind.

Robert M. La Follette, Jr., Barr Building, Washington, D.C.

Edward S. Mason, Dean, School of Public Administration, Harvard University, Cambridge, Mass.

George Meany, Secretary-Treasurer, American Federation of Labor, Washington, D.C.

Harold G. Moulton, President, The Brookings Institution, Jackson Place, Washington, D.C.

William I. Myers, Dean, College of Agriculture, Cornell University, Ithaca, N.Y.

Robert Gordon Sproul, President, University of California, Berkeley, Calif.

Owen D. Young, Honorary Chairman of the Board of Directors, General Electric Co., Van Hornesville, N.Y.

NOTE: Statements by the President making public the requested reports of the Secretary of the Interior, the Council of Economic Advisers, and the President's Committee on Foreign Aid appear below as Items 212, 217, and 219.

123 Special Message to the Senate Transmitting Conventions and Recommendations of the International Labor Conference. *June 23, 1947*

To the Senate of the United States:

In accordance with the obligations of the Government of the United States of America as a Member of the International Labor Organization, I transmit herewith authentic texts of nine Conventions and four Recommendations formulated at the Twenty-eighth (Maritime) Session of the International Labor Conference, held at Seattle, Washington, June 6 to 29, 1946.

I transmit also the report of the Secretary of State regarding these Conventions and

Recommendations, together with a copy of each of the communications with respect thereto addressed to the Department of State by the Secretary of Labor, the Acting Secretary of the Treasury, the Attorney General, the Secretary of Commerce, the Chairman of the United States Maritime Commission, the Federal Security Administrator, and the Assistant Secretary of Agriculture.

I ask that the Senate give its advice and consent, subject to appropriate definitions in certain cases as indicated in the enclosed communications, to ratification of the following Conventions:

Convention (No. 68) concerning food and catering for crews on board ship;

Convention (No. 69) concerning the certification of ships' cooks;

Convention (No. 70) concerning social security for seafarers;

Convention (No. 73) concerning the medical examination of seafarers;

Convention (No. 74) concerning the certification of able seamen;

Convention (No. 75) concerning crew accommodation on board ship; and

Convention (No. 76) concerning wages, hours of work on board ship and manning.

I request advice and consent to ratification of Convention (No. 72) concerning vacation holidays with pay for seafarers only in the event that the conditions explained in the accompanying report of the Secretary of State have been met.

In view of certain objections thereto, as explained more fully in the enclosed report and communications, I do not request at this time advice and consent to ratification of Convention (No. 71) concerning seafarers' pensions.

The Constitution of the International Labor Organization under Article 19, paragraph 5, requires that Recommendations be brought "before the authority or authorities within whose competence the matter lies, for the enactment of legislation or other action." Accordingly, I request consideration of the following Recommendations:

Recommendation (No. 75) concerning agreements relating to the social security of seafarers;

Recommendation (No. 76) concerning medical care for seafarers' dependents;

Recommendation (No. 77) concerning the

organization of training for sea service; and

Recommendation (No. 78) concerning the provision to crews by shipowners of bedding, mess utensils and other articles.

Many of the provisions of the enclosed Conventions and Recommendations fall short of standards already in effect in the American merchant marine. Some of the provisions are disappointing to those who had hoped through these instruments to raise substantially the level of standards in all Member Countries. It is believed, however, that general acceptance of the instruments by Member Countries will result in definite progress being made where that progress is most needed. Any such progress will benefit the competitive position of American seafarers and shipowners. At the same time, participation by the United States will necessitate relatively small change in the statutes or regulations of this Government.

Inasmuch as concurrent action by the Senate and House of Representatives would be necessary for the implementation of any of the enclosed Conventions or Recommendations, I am transmitting to the House of Representatives authentic copies of the Conventions and Recommendations, together with a copy of this message, a copy of the report by the Secretary of State, and a copy of each of the above-mentioned communications. I call attention particularly to the need for extending the provisions of any implementing legislation to the territories and insular possessions in accordance with Article 35 of the Constitution of the International Labor Organization.

Enclosures:

1. Authentic text of Conventions and Recommendations,
2. Report of Secretary of State,
3. From Secretary of Labor,

4. From Acting Secretary of the Treasury,
5. From Attorney General,
6. From Secretary of Commerce,
7. From Chairman of United States Maritime Commission,
8. From the Federal Security Administrator,
9. From Assistant Secretary of Agriculture,

10. Memorandum from Shipping Division, Department of State.

HARRY S. TRUMAN

NOTE: The text of the conventions and recommendations and related documents is printed in House Document 342 (80th Cong., 1st sess.).

Convention No. 74 was favorably considered by the Senate and after ratification entered into force with respect to the United States on April 9, 1954. It is published with related papers in the Treaties and Other International Agreements series (5 UST 605).

---

124 Special Message to the House of Representatives Transmitting Conventions and Recommendations of the International Labor Conference. *June 23, 1947*

To the House of Representatives of the United States:

In accordance with the obligations of the Government of the United States of America as a Member of the International Labor Organization, I transmit herewith the authentic texts of nine Conventions and four Recommendations with respect to maritime employment which were adopted at the Twenty-eighth (Maritime) Session of the International Labor Conference at Seattle, Washington, June 6 to 29, 1946.

The Constitution of the International Labor Organization provides in Article 19 thereof that each Member is obligated within a year after the closing of a session of the Conference to bring each Convention or Recommendation adopted at such session before the authority or authorities within whose competence the matter lies, for the enactment of legislation or other action. In the case of a Convention, the Member is obligated, upon obtaining the consent of the authority or authorities within whose competence the matter lies, to report the formal ratification and to take the necessary action to bring the provisions of such Convention into effect. The Member is obli-

gated, in the case of a Recommendation, to report the action taken. It is required under Article 35 of the Constitution of the International Labor Organization that subject to certain exceptions, Members will apply Conventions which they have ratified to their colonies, protectorates, and possessions which are not self-governing. In the case of a federal government, the power of which to enter into Conventions on labor matters is subject to limitations, Article 19 provides also that a Convention to which such limitations apply may be treated as a Recommendation.

It is indicated by established practice that submission to the legislative body is essential to the full observance of the obligations of membership. Under the present Constitution of the Organization, no further action is required "if on a recommendation no legislative or other action is taken to make a recommendation effective, or if the draft convention fails to obtain the consent of the authority or authorities within whose competence the matter lies."

Accordingly, I am also transmitting the authentic texts of the Conventions and Recommendations adopted at the Twenty-

304

eighth Session of the International Labor Conference to the Senate of the United States of America with a view to receiving the advice and consent of that body to ratification of certain of those Conventions and to obtaining legislative action by that body concurrently with the House of Representatives to give effect to certain of those Conventions and Recommendations.[1]

I ask that you consider legislative implementation of certain of those Conventions and Recommendations in the light of the comments contained in the report of the Secretary of State and the communications of the Secretary of Labor, the Acting Secretary of the Treasury, the Attorney General, the Secretary of Commerce, the Chairman of the United States Maritime Commission, the Federal Security Administrator, and the Assistant Secretary of Agriculture, copies of which are attached.

Enclosures:

1. Authentic text of Conventions and Recommendations,
2. Report of Secretary of State,
3. Message to the Senate,
4. From Secretary of Labor,
5. From Acting Secretary of the Treasury,
6. From the Attorney General,
7. From Secretary of Commerce,
8. From Chairman of the United States Maritime Commission,
9. From the Federal Security Administrator,
10. From Assistant Secretary of Agriculture,
11. Memorandum from Shipping Division, Department of State.

HARRY S. TRUMAN

---

[1] See Item 123 and note.

125   Letter to Senator Barkley on the Attempt To Override the Taft-Hartley Veto. *June 23, 1947*

Dear Senator Barkley:

I feel so strongly about the labor bill which the Senate will vote on this afternoon that I wish to reaffirm my sincere belief that it will do serious harm to our country.

This is a critical period in our history and any measure which will adversely affect our national unity will render a distinct disservice not only to this Nation but to the world.

I am convinced that such would be the result if the veto of this bill should be overridden.

I commend you and your associates who have fought so earnestly against this dangerous legislation.

I want you to know you have my unqualified support and it is my fervent hope, for the good of the country, that you and your colleagues will be successful in your efforts to keep this bill from becoming law.

Very sincerely yours,

HARRY S. TRUMAN

126 Special Message to the Senate Transmitting a Convention of the International Labor Conference. *June 24, 1947*

To the Senate of the United States:

With a view to receiving the advice and consent of the Senate to ratification, I transmit herewith an authentic text of the Final Articles Revision Convention, 1946 (No. 80), adopted at the Twenty-ninth Session of the International Labor Conference at Montreal on October 9, 1946. In my opinion this Convention is essential to bring the language of previously adopted Conventions into conformity with present conditions and specifically to recognize the present relationship of the International Labor Organization to the United Nations under Article 57 of the Charter of the United Nations.

This Convention was adopted unanimously by the Conference. On the part of the United States delegation, affirmative votes were cast by the two Government delegates, by the delegate representing employ-

ers, and by the delegate representing workers.

The purpose of the Convention is to make verbal changes in the texts of Conventions adopted at the previous twenty-eight sessions and to assign responsibility to the Director-General of the International Labor Office for certain of the chancery functions for which previously the Secretary-General of the League of Nations was responsible.

The effect of this Convention is described in more detail in the report of the Secretary of State, enclosed herewith, and in a communication from the Secretary of Labor, a copy of which is enclosed.

HARRY S. TRUMAN

NOTE: The convention was favorably considered by the Senate and after ratification entered into force with respect to the United States on June 24, 1948. It is published with related papers in the U.S. Statutes at Large (62 Stat. 1672).

127 The President's News Conference of *June 26, 1947*

THE PRESIDENT. [1.] I want to read you a statement, then you can ask questions.

"The Taft-Hartley labor bill has been passed by the Congress over the President's veto.

"I have expressed my objections to this legislation and my concern as to its effects. Nevertheless, it is now the law of the land. It has become law in accordance with the constitutional processes of our Government. We must all respect its provisions.

"For my part, I want to make it unmistakably clear that, insofar as it lies within my power as President, I shall see that this law is well and faithfully administered.

"I have already received the assurances of the present members of the National Labor Relations Board that they will seek to give the new act the fairest and most efficient administration within their power.

"The persons who are to be appointed to the new offices created under the act will be selected with the same objective. I regard it as of the utmost importance that persons be selected for these offices who have the confidence of management and labor, and who can be depended upon to deal fairly with both. Above all, they should understand the paramount interest of the Nation as a whole.

"Insofar as management and labor are concerned, there is a vital responsibilty upon them to comply with the law in a spirit of tolerance and fair play. Neither management nor labor will achieve any long-range benefit by seeking to use the provisions of this act to gain unfair advantage or to sustain arbitrary attitudes. It is in the interests of both to maintain steady production at fair wages while the effect of the new act is being tested by experience. At this time, as at all others, they will serve their mutual welfare best by working together with full recognition by each of the legitimate rights of the other.

"I call upon labor and management, therefore, to exercise patience and moderation in accommodating themselves to the changes made necessary by the act.

"Industrial strife at this critical time can result only in economic dislocation injurious to all of us. If it should reach serious proportions it would threaten the stability of our economy and endanger the peace of the world.

"We cannot afford such a result. It is our solemn duty to make every effort to maintain industrial peace under the provisions of the new law.

"We must all do our part."

That is the end of the statement. Copies of it will be handed to you as you go out.

[2.] Q. Mr. President, may I ask you about this new tax bill that Knutson has introduced, setting back the effective date until January 1, 1948? Would you still be opposed to that?

THE PRESIDENT. I will take care of that when it comes up here, as I usually do.

[3.] Q. Mr. President, with reference to the discussion now going on in Europe regarding rehabilitation, if the European nations agree on a plan of mutual self-help, is it proposed that the United States would make a contribution to that plan either in dollars or in goods and services?

THE PRESIDENT. General Marshall, I think, covered that very completely in his press conference yesterday, and General Marshall and I are in complete agreement.

Q. I asked the question, sir, because the Secretary of the Treasury's statement yesterday——

THE PRESIDENT. The Secretary of the Treasury and the Secretary of State and the President are in complete agreement.

[4.] Q. Mr. President, is former Senator La Follette being considered for one of these new labor-management——

THE PRESIDENT. No one is at present being considered for any of these jobs.

Q. Have you any idea, Mr. President, about when we could expect some nominations to be——

THE PRESIDENT. Well, I will let you know immediately as soon as I am ready to put it out.

[5.] Q. Mr. President, have you any statement on the spreading wildcat strikes in the coal mines?

THE PRESIDENT. No, I have no statement on it. No comment.

[6.] Q. Mr. President, have you had an appeal from Mayor Curley for action in his case?[1]

THE PRESIDENT. No, I have not.

Q. Do you plan any action in that case?

THE PRESIDENT. The case has not been put up to me.

[7.] Q. Sir, could you explain what was the reason for withdrawing Wakefield's nomination in sending up[2]——

THE PRESIDENT. I have no comment on that.

[8.] Your question is answered in the

---

[1] Mayor James M. Curley of Boston had been convicted and sentenced for mail fraud.

[2] On June 18 the President withdrew his nomination of Ray C. Wakefield for a new term as Federal Communications Commissioner.

statement that I have just made about this.

Q. As to what? Wildcat——

THE PRESIDENT. Yes.

[9.] Q. Mr. President, our Ambassador to Brazil, Mr. Pawley, is coming back. Would you tell us what that means?

THE PRESIDENT. That's news to me. I didn't know he was coming back.

Q. Will Secretary Marshall accompany you on your visit to Brazil?

THE PRESIDENT. There has been no definite arrangement made for a visit to Brazil. The Brazilian Ambassador invited me to come to Brazil, and I told him I would like very much to come, but I could not make any firm commitments on that situation until we found out what the further situation would develop.

Q. Mr. President, aside from a firm commitment on it, there are stories coming out of Brazil that they expect you down there in August. Do you think you can possibly arrange it that soon?

THE PRESIDENT. No. No. You know that we will be busy as we can be in August.

Q. It didn't look like it from here, but that is coming from down there.

THE PRESIDENT. The Brazilians are a very hospitable people. I know I would have a grand time if I could go down there.

[10.] Q. Mr. President, does your statement on the labor law imply that you will use it, if there is a coal strike this summer threatening the welfare of the Nation?

THE PRESIDENT. The statement speaks for itself. Read it very carefully.

[11.] Q. Referring to Brazil, Mr. President, have you given any thought to going at the time of the proposed Rio conference?

THE PRESIDENT. That was the objective in view, if the Rio conference is held.

Q. Mr. President, what will you be busy at in August?

THE PRESIDENT. Legislation. If the Congress——

Q. They will be about wound up then, I think. They fixed July 26.

THE PRESIDENT. Have they definitely passed a resolution for July 26?

Q. No.

THE PRESIDENT. They haven't passed any resolution. You see, I served 10 years in the Congress. [*Laughter*]

Q. Mr. President, does that—your previous reply respecting the conference indicate that you would not go if the conference were held in August?

THE PRESIDENT. Don't put me on the spot in such a manner as that. I don't want to be impolite to our neighbors. I would like to go to Brazil, conference or no conference, but I don't think I will be able to go at the time they are interested in having me come. If there is a conference, I hope I can attend the conference. Let's put it that way.

[12.] Q. Mr. President, could you tell us what you discussed with Ambassador Cooper of Peru yesterday?

THE PRESIDENT. Mr. Cooper was just making a report on conditions in Peru to me.

[13.] Q. Mr. President, does the premonition that Congress may not be able to adjourn before August indicate you may be sending them something else for them to do?

THE PRESIDENT. If it is necessary for me to send them things to do, I shall certainly do it. [*Laughter*]

[14.] Q. Do you still hope for universal military training?

THE PRESIDENT. I certainly do. I think it is absolutely necessary for the peace of the world and the welfare of this country.

[15.] Q. Mr. President, on these wildcat strikes again, has there been any indication that the coal—have you been given any reports that the coal stockpile situation is approaching critical——

THE PRESIDENT. No, I have had no reports on that subject.

Q. Mr. President, do you contemplate

any injunction against the United Mine Workers?

THE PRESIDENT. I don't contemplate anything against the United Mine Workers at the present time. The Attorney General is looking into the coal situation as it develops, and whatever action can be taken or is necessary to be taken will be taken if it becomes necessary. There is nothing before us at the present time.

[16.] Q. Mr. President, Senator Flanders suggested on the Hill today that you ask for some sort of voluntary meat rationing, in view of the foreign crop situation, to hold down prices, and so forth?

THE PRESIDENT. I made that request, I think, a little over a year ago. It was not complied with.

[17.] Q. Mr. President, do you desire to have the military cooperation bill passed at this session?

THE PRESIDENT. What's that?

Q. The military cooperation bill with the rest of the hemisphere?

THE PRESIDENT. Oh yes. That should be passed. General Marshall made the case for that, as did General Eisenhower, the Secretary of War, and the Secretary of the Navy, I think. We are all in agreement.

Reporter: Thank you, Mr. President.

THE PRESIDENT. You're welcome.

NOTE: President Truman's one hundred and tenth news conference was held in his office at the White House at 4 o'clock on Thursday afternoon, June 26, 1947.

128   Veto of the Wool Act.
June 26, 1947

To the Senate of the United States:

I return herewith, without my approval, S. 814, entitled "The Wool Act of 1947."

This Bill contains features which would have an adverse effect on our international relations and which are not necessary for the support of our domestic wool growers.

As originally passed by the Senate, the Bill directed the Commodity Credit Corporation to continue until the end of 1948 to support prices to domestic producers of wool at not less than 1946 levels. It further authorized the Commodity Credit Corporation to sell wool held by it at market prices. I have no objection to these provisions.

As passed by the House, the Bill carried an amendment intended to increase the tariff on wool through the imposition of import fees. This was done to provide a means of increasing the domestic market price for wool to approximately the support price, thus shifting the cost of the support from the

Treasury to the consumers of wool products. The prices of these products are already high.

The conferees of the two Houses agreed upon a measure closely following the House bill, but empowering me to impose import quotas as well as import fees.

The enactment of a law providing for additional barriers to the importation of wool at the very moment when this Government is taking the leading part in a United Nations Conference at Geneva called for the purpose of reducing trade barriers and of drafting a Charter for an International Trade Organization, in an effort to restore the world to economic peace, would be a tragic mistake. It would be a blow to our leadership in world affairs. It would be interpreted around the world as a first step on that same road to economic isolationism down which we and other countries traveled after the first World War with such disastrous consequences.

I cannot approve such an action.

The wool growers of this country are entitled to receive support. There is still ample time for this Congress to pass wool legislation consistent with our international responsibilities and the interests of our economy as a whole. I urge that the Congress do so promptly.

A bill based on the general principles and policy of the original Senate Bill would be acceptable to me, although I would prefer a more permanent wool program, as suggested in my memorandum which was made public on March 12, 1946.

For these reasons I am returning S. 814 without my approval.

HARRY S. TRUMAN

NOTE: On August 5 the President approved S. 1498 "An Act to provide support for wool, and for other purposes" (61 Stat. 769). For the President's memorandum made public on March 12, 1946, see 1946 volume, this series, p. 150.

129   Remarks Broadcast on the Second Anniversary of the United Nations. *June 26, 1947*

TODAY, on the second anniversary of the signing of the United Nations Charter, I am happy to speak for the Government and the people of the United States in saluting the Organization and the ideals of international cooperation which gave it life.

For the last 2 years, the Members of the United Nations have been exerting great effort to build and set in motion its machinery. This process of organization has gone forward in an atmosphere of disturbance and uncertainty, the aftermath of the Second World War. From the very first sessions of its principal components, the United Nations has been asked to contend with some highly controversial international political issues. It has found it necessary to chart new paths of economic and social cooperation in the complexities of a postwar world.

The effectiveness of the United Nations depends upon the Member States meeting all their obligations. Assurance that these obligations will be met depends in turn upon the will of the peoples of the Member States. The vigor of the United Nations stems therefore from a public opinion educated to understand its problems.

The existence of the United Nations obviously affords no guarantee that every international problem can be solved easily, or automatically, or immediately. It should not be a matter for surprise or disillusionment that many issues arising as a result of the war still remain unsettled. The strength of the United Nations rests in the recognition by the Member States that, despite all differences, they have a common interest in the preservation of international peace and in the attainment of international security.

The Member States are not only bound by the Charter, jointly and severally, to execute the decisions of the Organization; they are bound to conduct their day-to-day foreign relations in accordance with the principles of freedom and justice prescribed by the Charter.

During the last 2 years the Government and the people of the United States have demonstrated their support of the United Nations. They have attempted consistently and actively to achieve the purposes set forth in the United Nations Charter—to prevent war, to settle international disputes by peaceful means and in conformity with the principles of justice, to cooperate in securing economic and social advancement, to encourage respect for fundamental human rights and freedoms, and to build genuine security.

The Government and the people of the United States are aware that the realization of these objectives is not easy. They know that it is a continuing task. They will not be discouraged by temporary setback or delay.

The enterprise which was launched at San Francisco 2 years ago is the hope of the world for lasting peace. It provides mankind today with the best opportunity to unite for the preservation of civilization and for the continuation of human progress.

On behalf of the United States Government and its people, I renew the pledge of our utmost efforts to insure the success of the United Nations. We shall do our part.

NOTE: The remarks were recorded for broadcast at 12:30 p.m. on June 26 as part of a United Nations radio program.

130 Address Before the National Association for the Advancement of Colored People. *June* 29, 1947

Mr. Chairman, Mrs. Roosevelt, Senator Morse, distinguished guests, ladies and gentlemen:

I am happy to be present at the closing session of the 38th Annual Conference of the National Association for the Advancement of Colored People. The occasion of meeting with you here at the Lincoln Memorial affords me the opportunity to congratulate the association upon its effective work for the improvement of our democratic processes.

I should like to talk to you briefly about civil rights and human freedom. It is my deep conviction that we have reached a turning point in the long history of our country's efforts to guarantee freedom and equality to all our citizens. Recent events in the United States and abroad have made us realize that it is more important today than ever before to insure that all Americans enjoy these rights.

When I say all Americans I mean all Americans.

The civil rights laws written in the early years of our Republic, and the traditions which have been built upon them, are precious to us. Those laws were drawn up with the memory still fresh in men's minds of the tyranny of an absentee government. They were written to protect the citizen against any possible tyrannical act by the new government in this country.

But we cannot be content with a civil liberties program which emphasizes only the need of protection against the possibility of tyranny by the Government.

We cannot stop there.

We must keep moving forward, with new concepts of civil rights to safeguard our heritage. The extension of civil rights today means, not protection of the people *against* the Government, but protection of the people *by* the Government.

We must make the Federal Government a friendly, vigilant defender of the rights and equalities of all Americans. And again I mean all Americans.

As Americans, we believe that every man should be free to live his life as he wishes. He should be limited only by his responsibility to his fellow countrymen. If this freedom is to be more than a dream, each man must be guaranteed equality of opportunity. The only limit to an American's achievement should be his ability, his industry, and

311

his character. These rewards for his effort should be determined only by those truly relevant qualities.

Our immediate task is to remove the last remnants of the barriers which stand between millions of our citizens and their birthright. There is no justifiable reason for discrimination because of ancestry, or religion, or race, or color.

We must not tolerate such limitations on the freedom of any of our people and on their enjoyment of basic rights which every citizen in a truly democratic society must possess.

Every man should have the right to a decent home, the right to an education, the right to adequate medical care, the right to a worthwhile job, the right to an equal share in making the public decisions through the ballot, and the right to a fair trial in a fair court.

We must insure that these rights—on equal terms—are enjoyed by every citizen.

To these principles I pledge my full and continued support.

Many of our people still suffer the indignity of insult, the narrowing fear of intimidation, and, I regret to say, the threat of physical injury and mob violence. Prejudice and intolerance in which these evils are rooted still exist. The conscience of our Nation, and the legal machinery which enforces it, have not yet secured to each citizen full freedom from fear.

We cannot wait another decade or another generation to remedy these evils. We must work, as never before, to cure them now. The aftermath of war and the desire to keep faith with our Nation's historic principles make the need a pressing one.

The support of desperate populations of battle-ravaged countries must be won for the free way of life. We must have them as allies in our continuing struggle for the peaceful solution of the world's problems.

Freedom is not an easy lesson to teach, nor an easy cause to sell, to peoples beset by every kind of privation. They may surrender to the false security offered so temptingly by totalitarian regimes unless we can prove the superiority of democracy.

Our case for democracy should be as strong as we can make it. It should rest on practical evidence that we have been able to put our own house in order.

For these compelling reasons, we can no longer afford the luxury of a leisurely attack upon prejudice and discrimination. There is much that State and local governments can do in providing positive safeguards for civil rights. But we cannot, any longer, await the growth of a will to action in the slowest State or the most backward community.

Our National Government must show the way.

This is a difficult and complex undertaking. Federal laws and administrative machineries must be improved and expanded. We must provide the Government with better tools to do the job. As a first step, I appointed an Advisory Committee on Civil Rights last December. Its members, fifteen distinguished private citizens, have been surveying our civil rights difficulties and needs for several months. I am confident that the product of their work will be a sensible and vigorous program for action by all of us.

We must strive to advance civil rights wherever it lies within our power. For example, I have asked the Congress to pass legislation extending basic civil rights to the people of Guam and American Samoa so that these people can share our ideals of freedom and self-government. This step, with others which will follow, is evidence to the rest of the world of our confidence in the ability of all men to build free institutions.

The way ahead is not easy. We shall need

all the wisdom, imagination and courage we can muster. We must and shall guarantee the civil rights of all our citizens. Never before has the need been so urgent for skillful and vigorous action to bring us closer to our ideal.

We can reach the goal. When past difficulties faced our Nation we met the challenge with inspiring charters of human rights—the Declaration of Independence, the Constitution, the Bill of Rights, and the Emancipation Proclamation. Today our representatives, and those of other liberty-loving countries on the United Nations Commission on Human Rights, are preparing an International Bill of Rights. We can be confident that it will be a great landmark in man's long search for freedom since its members consist of such distinguished citizens of the world as Mrs. Franklin D. Roosevelt.

With these noble charters to guide us, and with faith in our hearts, we shall make our land a happier home for our people, a symbol of hope for all men, and a rock of security in a troubled world.

Abraham Lincoln understood so well the ideal which you and I seek today. As this conference closes we would do well to keep in mind his words, when he said,

". . . if it shall please the Divine Being who determines the destinies of nations, we shall remain a united people, and we will, humbly seeking the Divine Guidance, make their prolonged national existence a source of new benefits to themselves and their successors, and to all classes and conditions of mankind."

NOTE: The President spoke at the Lincoln Memorial at 4:30 p.m. In his opening words he referred to Walter F. White, Executive Secretary of the National Association for the Advancement of Colored People, who served as chairman of the conference, and to Mrs. Franklin D. Roosevelt and Senator Wayne Morse who also spoke. The address was carried on a nationwide radio broadcast.

---

131   Special Message to the Congress Upon Signing the Housing and Rent Act. *June 30, 1947*

To the Congress of the United States:

I have today signed H.R. 3203, the Housing and Rent Act of 1947, despite the fact that its rent control provisions are plainly inadequate and its housing provisions actually repeal parts of the Veterans' Emergency Housing Act which have been most helpful in meeting the housing needs of veterans.

Had I withheld my signature, national rent control would die tonight. It is clear that, insofar as the Congress is concerned, it is this bill or no rent control at all. I have chosen the lesser of two evils.

Without any rent control, millions of American families would face rapidly soaring rents and wholesale evictions. We are still suffering from a critical housing shortage. Many families are desperately seeking homes. In their desperation, they would have to submit to demands for exorbitant rent. Even this inadequate law presents fewer dangers than would the complete lack of rent control.

I have been confronted with a problem similar to the one which the Congress placed before me in the price control bill which it sent me on June 28, 1946. That bill was so damaging to price control that I vetoed it and addressed the country on the subject. Then, on July twenty-fifth, the Congress sent me a second price control bill, in some respects worse than the first. The time was so late that I had to sign that bill in order to

313

prevent the complete destruction of price control. But effective price control was impossible under the new law.

If I had vetoed H.R. 3203, rent controls would end, and the prospects of another bill being sent to me would be negligible. I had no choice but to sign.

It is clear that this legislation marks a step backward in our efforts to protect tenants against unjustified rent increases arising out of war conditions. For millions of families, it will result in substantial increases in rents which until now have been held at reasonable levels. The cost of living is already too high without this additional burden.

It is evident that the present high cost of living should not be increased further by a sharp increase in rents. We must get prices down, not devise means of getting the price of shelter up.

Since the end of price control, the consumer price index has risen 17 percent. Food has gone up 29 percent. During the second quarter of 1947, we have made real progress in checking these sharp price increases. On the whole, prices and the cost of living have leveled off. This progress—and the further progress we must make—would be nullified for millions of families by higher rents. Rents amount to 25 percent to 35 percent of many family budgets. Rent increases could revive the inflationary dangers which we have greatly reduced.

A basic weakness of the rent control provisions of the Act is the so-called "voluntary" increase of 15 percent in cases where the landlord and tenant enter into a lease that will continue until December 31, 1948. This is voluntary only so far as the landlord is concerned. Many tenants, however, will feel that there is no choice. The tenant will naturally fear that unless he enters into such a lease he will be subjected to even more exorbitant increases when rent control is ended. Whenever a vacancy occurs, the landlord can refuse to rent except under a lease providing for the rent increase. Many landlords will press for rent increases whether or not there is need for adjustment. Severe hardship will thus be imposed on many tenants. The hardship will be particularly acute in the case of veterans, who comprise such a large portion of those seeking rental housing accommodations.

The Act also weakens the protection against eviction which is necessary for effective rent control, and completely removes the protection of rent control in many cases where it is still badly needed. Administration of the law will be made more complex by the injection of new procedures and will be made less effective by the weakening of enforcement provisions.

All of this represents the abandonment of a system which has been both fair and effective. In its administration of rent control, the Federal Government has made every effort to give full protection to both landlords and tenants. The net rental income of landlords today is substantially higher than in the pre-war years of 1939 and 1940, or in the previous decade. Provisions for granting rent increases in meritorious cases have been liberalized and simplified. Over one million rent increases have been granted. Controls have been removed in cases where the need no longer appeared acute. These steps and many more have been taken to keep the administration of rent control simple, practicable, and fair to prevent hardship. This has been accomplished without permitting substantial increases in the general rent level.

Since Federal rent control is being irreparably weakened, I appeal to the Governors of the States—particularly those populous States where rental housing is more prevalent—to exert every effort to protect tenants from hardship, eviction or exploitation.

They can soften, although not avoid completely, the blow to rent control dealt by H.R. 3203.

The Housing and Rent Act of 1947 also marks a step backward in our efforts to solve the critical problem of providing sufficient additional housing for our citizens. It repeals almost all the emergency aids to housing provided in the Veterans' Emergency Housing Act of 1946.

In January 1946, I recommended the enactment of legislation to meet an immediate emergency in housing. I recommended that the Housing Expediter be given the necessary powers to expedite the production of building materials and the construction of houses.

The Congress responded to my recommendations by passing the Veterans' Emergency Housing Act of 1946. With the emergency measures provided by that Act, the supply of building materials has increased tremendously and the number of new homes built has increased at a rate surpassing our best pre-war achievements.

The Veterans' Emergency Housing Program was announced in February 1946. By the close of that year 670,500 permanent family housing units, in addition to over 300,000 units of other types, had been started. In the first five months of this year 280,300 new permanent family dwelling units were begun, and 300,000 were completed. Although this accomplishment is heartening, it is not enough.

H.R. 3203 will weaken rather than strengthen our means for greater achievement.

The most serious loss in housing aids under this Act is the virtual elimination of controls which have prevented the diversion of building materials from homes to nonessential and deferable construction. As the supply of building materials has increased, the Housing Expediter has eased and simpli-

fied controls over materials and construction. Those which were retained were necessary and important, however, and their removal by this Act may prove disastrous to home building.

The increased demand for materials and labor resulting from removal of these controls may delay a decline in building costs and may even result in further cost increases. Already many veterans are unable to pay for homes at present cost levels, and this will further aggravate their problems. Moreover, delays in the completion of veterans' hospitals and of other essential construction will result from the increased competition for materials and labor.

It is of deep concern to me that this most unsatisfactory law represents the only major action taken by the Congress at this session with regard to the housing problem which confronts the Nation. We should be taking steps to provide additional aids to housing, rather than eliminating the aids which have been in effect.

On many occasions I have placed housing high on the list of subjects calling for decisive Congressional action.

On September 6, 1945, in my message to the Congress, I called attention to the shortage of decent homes and the enforced widespread use of substandard housing and warned that the housing shortage would become more acute as veterans returned and began to look for places to live. I urgently recommended that the Congress enact comprehensive housing legislation to meet this problem. My proposals were directed especially to the needs of those families of low or moderate income who cannot buy or rent high priced houses. The overwhelming majority of veterans need such legislation for this reason.

On January 14, 1946, in the message on the State of the Union, I again emphasized that we faced a major post-war housing problem. I recommended that the Seventy-ninth Congress promptly enact general legislation for a comprehensive housing program along the lines of the Wagner-Ellender-Taft bill then under consideration. The Senate approved the bill, but the House of Representatives was denied the opportunity to vote by delaying tactics within one of its committees.

On January 6, 1947, in the Message on the State of the Union, I again recommended action by the Eightieth Congress on comprehensive housing legislation. Such legislation has been introduced and favorably reported to the Senate during this session, but has not yet been passed by either the Senate or the House of Representatives.

The obligation upon the Federal Government is one which cannot be ignored.

Again I urge the Congress to complete action upon legislation to accomplish the following objectives:

1. To provide public aid to localities for low rent housing for families in the lowest income group.

2. To encourage private investment in rental housing by Federal insurance.

3. To provide a more adequate program of farm housing.

4. To extend aid to our cities for the clearance of slums and blighted areas.

5. To perfect and supplement existing aids to home financing.

6. To provide a substantial program of housing research to assist industry in progressively reducing the cost of housing.

Means are at hand for the prompt enactment of legislation which will go far toward accomplishing these objectives. I refer to the Taft-Ellender-Wagner bill now before the Senate. This bill has been developed after long and careful consideration of our housing needs. These needs are known. Now is the time for action to set in motion a comprehensive program which will assure the greatest possible number of Americans a decent place to live, in a decent environment, at a cost they can afford.

In the face of our acute need for more effective aid for housing, it is unthinkable that the Congress would actually take steps to make more difficult or even impossible the efficient administration of the Government's present activities relating to housing and home finance. Yet, I fear that this may happen.

The House of Representatives has already indicated its disapproval of a Reorganization Plan which would preserve the grouping of our principal housing functions in a single establishment. The administration of these functions within a single establishment is essential if our housing policies are to be carried out with a consistency of purpose and a minimum of duplication. I strongly urge that this Plan be allowed to become effective.

Another danger threatening even the existing aids to housing and home financing arises from the action of the House of Representatives upon the appropriations for the National Housing Agency, including the Office of the Administrator and the constituent agencies. The drastic cuts made by the House of Representatives in these appropriations, if they are allowed to stand, will seriously handicap the efforts of both Government and private enterprise. The effectiveness of the National Housing Agency will be greatly impaired. If we are to have an effective housing program now and in the future, this agency must have adequate funds and personnel.

A continuing high volume of home-building activity is essential to provide decent housing for all the people. It is equally important because of its contribution to the maintenance of prosperity and full employment. Home-building should provide continuous employment to several million workers, directly or indirectly, and be a strong support to the rest of the economy when postwar restocking is over and when the extraordinary foreign demand for American products has leveled off. In the past, this major industry has been an unstable element in the national economy, fluctuating between boom conditions and almost complete stagnation. Without effective action, it cannot contribute its full share to the maintenance of high levels of production and employment.

To be successful, an attack on the housing problem will require vigorous action by Federal, State and local authorities, in cooperation with representatives of industry and labor. It will require simultaneous action in many fields, including an expanded program of research—both public and private—on housing materials and techniques and joint action to standardize and simplify construction items. It will require far-sighted action by industry and labor to eliminate restrictive practices. It will require revisions of zoning ordinances and local building codes to remove archaic and obsolete provisions. Finally, it will require a good measure of the genius for which American business is famous to improve home-building methods and to apply mass production methods to the manufacture of houses and housing components.

One of the most stubborn obstacles in the way of any constructive housing program has been the opposition of the real estate lobby. Its members have exerted pressure at every point against every proposal for making the housing program more effective. They have constantly sought to weaken rent control and to do away with necessary aids to housing. They are openly proud of their success in blocking a comprehensive housing program.

This group has sought to achieve financial gains without regard to the damage done to others. It has displayed a ruthless disregard of the public welfare.

It is intolerable that this lobby should be permitted by its brazen operations to block programs so essential to the needs of our citizens. Nothing could be more clearly subversive of representative government. I urge the Congress to make a full investigation of the activities of this selfish and short-sighted group. When the truth is known I am confident that this obstacle to constructive housing legislation will be removed.

The lack of adequate housing marks a glaring gap in our achievements toward fulfilling the promise of democracy. The American people today are better fed than ever before. They have more clothes and more goods of almost all sorts. In the few cases where war-induced scarcities still exist, American industry is catching up with demand at great speed. But this is not true of housing.

The progress in housing has not kept pace with progress in other fields. Private industry has not done and cannot do the whole job without Government aid. Much has been achieved with the measures heretofore authorized by the Congress. But they are far from adequate. In no part of our national life is there more urgent need for constructive legislation at this time.

I sincerely trust that the Congress will not end this session without meeting the problem squarely.

HARRY S. TRUMAN

NOTE: The Housing and Rent Act of 1947 is Public Law 129, 80th Congress (61 Stat. 193).

The Taft-Ellender-Wagner housing bill (S. 866) passed the Senate on April 22, 1948, but was not concurred in by the House of Representatives.

After reconsideration by the House of Representatives, Reorganization Plan 3 of 1947, providing for a consolidation of certain designated agencies to form the Housing and Home Finance Agency, became effective on July 27, 1947. It is published in the U.S. Statutes at Large (61 Stat. 954) and in the 1943–1948 Compilation of title 3 of the Code of Federal Regulations (p. 1071).

132   Citation Accompanying Medal for Merit Awarded to Dean Acheson. *June 30, 1947*

CITATION TO ACCOMPANY THE AWARD OF

THE MEDAL FOR MERIT

TO

DEAN ACHESON

DEAN ACHESON, for exceptionally meritorious conduct in the performance of outstanding services to the United States from 1940 to December 31, 1946. Mr. Acheson, as a private citizen in 1940, was among those who first saw clearly the Fascist threat to our national existence. He exerted his distinguished advocacy to rally his fellow citizens in favor of the delivery of American destroyers to beleaguered Britain. As Assistant Secretary of State from February 1, 1941 to

August 16, 1945, and as Under Secretary of State until today, he has been one of the architects of victory and of the struggle for peace. In his relations with the Congress, Mr. Acheson fostered a responsive relationship between the Executive and Legislative Branches of the Government in the field of foreign affairs; and he brought to the councils of government a long view and a genius for bold design typified by the Acheson-Lilienthal plan for international control of atomic energy.

HARRY S. TRUMAN

NOTE: The presentation was made at a ceremony at the White House at 12:15 p.m.

133   Statement by the President Upon Signing Resolution Authorizing Him To Accept Membership in the International Refugee Organization. *July 1, 1947*

I HAVE just signed the joint resolution authorizing the President to accept membership in the International Refugee Organization. Pursuant to this authorization I have also signed, on behalf of the United States, the necessary instrument of acceptance, which will be deposited promptly with the Secretary General of the United Nations by our Representative, the Honorable Warren R. Austin.

This action constitutes an important step toward the creation of an operating special-

ized agency established by the United Nations. I am confident that, through the International Refugee Organization, we shall give the world new reason to believe that no problem is too difficult if the nations firmly resolve to cooperate in solving it.

I am happy to accept membership in the International Refugee Organization on behalf of the United States.

NOTE: As enacted, the joint resolution providing for membership and participation by the United States in the International Refugee Organization is Public Law 146, 80th Congress (61 Stat. 214).

134   Letter to the President of the Senate and to the Speaker of
      the House Transmitting Bill Providing Benefits to
      Philippine Army Veterans. *July 1, 1947*

My dear Mr. —————:

I am transmitting a draft of a bill "To provide a more satisfactory program of benefits relating to active service in the armed forces of the Commonwealth of the Philippines during World War II, and for other purposes." I request the early consideration of this measure by the Congress.

The proposed legislation would enlarge veterans' benefits available to Philippine Army veterans who were called and ordered into the service of the armed forces of the United States pursuant to the military order of the President dated July 26, 1941. Under the provisions of the First Supplemental Surplus Appropriations Rescission Act, 1946, all veterans' benefits were taken from this group except those providing compensation for service-connected disabilities or death (which are paid on the basis of one Philippine peso for each dollar authorized) and benefits of the National Service Life Insurance Act of 1940, as amended, under contracts entered into prior to February 18, 1946.

The draft submitted would revise the compensation benefits on a practicable basis and would restore the following classes of benefits which were taken away by the Rescission Act: (1) educational, (2) hospitalization for service-connected disability, and (3) burial and funeral allowance. Existing benefits under the National Service Life Insurance Act would not be altered except to extend for two years the time within which eligible persons may apply for gratuitous insurance benefits after the death of a veteran who was deemed to have been issued such insurance under the law. This extension would not be limited to cases involving Philippine Army veterans, but would be of general applicability. However, it is designed primarily to afford relief to the dependents of Philippine Army veterans who were unable to make the necessary applications for benefits by reason of the extended occupation of the Philippines by the enemy. The proposal also contains general administrative and penal provisions which are deemed necessary to carry out its provisions. Further details of the proposed legislation are set forth in the enclosed section by section analysis.

You will recall that upon approving the Rescission Act I took exception to that portion of the Act which limited veterans' benefits available to Philippine Army veterans. I stated, among other thing, that enactment of that legislation did not release the United States from its moral obligation to provide for the heroic Philippine Army veterans who sacrificed so much for the common cause during the war. Practical difficulties in administering benefits to such veterans were recognized and, accordingly, I referred the matter to the Secretary of War, the Administrator of Veterans' Affairs, and the United States High Commissioner to the Philippines to prepare for me a plan to meet these difficulties.

On May 18, 1946, I submitted to the Congress the plan evolved by these officials.[1] In my communication I stated in part:

"The record of the Philippine soldiers for bravery and loyalty is second to none. Their assignments were as bloody and difficult as any in which our American soldiers engaged. Under desperate circumstances they acquitted themselves nobly.

---

[1] See 1946 volume, this series, p. 272.

"There can be no question that the Philippine veteran is entitled to benefits bearing a reasonable relation to those received by the American veteran, with whom he fought side by side. From a practical point of view, however, it must be acknowledged that certain benefits granted by the 'G.I. Bill of Rights' cannot be applied in the case of the Philippine veterans. * * * [Enactment of the proposed legislation] will clearly indicate to the Filipinos that it is the purpose of the United States Government to do justice to their veterans. More important, it will provide the help so direly needed by many Filipinos who served our cause with unwavering devotion in the face of bitter hardship and wanton cruelty."

Those statements are equally applicable at this time.

The legislation proposed last year was passed by the Senate but failed of enactment in the closing days of the Seventy-ninth Congress.

This year I requested an Interdepartmental Committee, consisting of the Secretary of State, the Secretary of War, the Administrator of Veterans' Affairs, and the United States Ambassador to the Philippines, to reconsider the problem and submit its recommendations. After extended study the Committee recommended enactment of the enclosed draft of a bill and the legislation which is pending before the Congress to restore the benefits of the Missing Persons Act to Philippine Army veterans. In its latest report, with which was submitted the enclosed draft of a bill, the Committee stated:

"It is the view of the Committee that, if the proposal submitted with this report and the mentioned legislation pending before the Congress are enacted into law, the discrimination against Philippine Army veterans brought about by the First Supplemental Surplus Appropriation Rescission Act, 1946, will, so far as possible, be removed and that substantial justice will have been done such veterans."

I concur in these views of the Committee and, accordingly, urge upon the Congress the early enactment of the proposals in question.

Very sincerely yours,

HARRY S. TRUMAN

NOTE: This is the text of identical letters addressed to the Honorable Arthur H. Vandenberg, President pro tempore of the Senate, and to the Honorable Joseph W. Martin, Jr., Speaker of the House of Representatives.

On July 25, 1947, the President signed a bill providing for the extension of benefits of the Missing Persons Act to certain members of the military forces of the Philippines (61 Stat. 455).

135 Statement by the President on the Reduction in Appropriations for the Bureau of Internal Revenue. *July 1, 1947*

I HAVE today approved H.R. 2436, providing appropriations for the Treasury and Post Office Departments for the fiscal year ending June 30, 1948, because it provides for continuing in part the essential activities of these Departments. However, I would be remiss in my duty if I failed to bring to the attention of the Congress and the people the gross inadequacy of the funds made available for the collection of our revenue.

The administration of the taxing statutes should never be influenced by political considerations. People of all political faiths are called upon to support their Government through the payment of taxes and are entitled to adequate administrative controls to insure that the dishonest do not shift their share to the honest.

The employees who have been trained in the technical work of tax administration and who have done and are now doing an excellent job are civil service employees. The training of this personnel has been paid for by the Government at great cost and this investment should not now be dissipated. Once these people are released it is not reasonable to suppose that they will be available for reemployment should additional funds be provided later. It will take years to restore the damage done by the failure of the Congress to support the current efforts of our tax collecting agency.

I am advised by the Secretary of the Treasury and the Commissioner of Internal Revenue that the reduction of $20 million in the appropriation for the Bureau of Internal Revenue will mean a reduction in personnel of 4,000 to 5,000 employees and will result in a direct loss of revenue of not less than $400 million in the fiscal year 1948. There is at the present time, with present personnel, a backlog of 30,000 "leads" on tax evasions awaiting investigation.

The vast majority of our taxpayers are scrupulously honest in tax matters. Taxpayer moral is now generally high, but it will remain so only if the odds remain strong that the would-be tax evader will be detected and punished.

It is a fallacy to assume that the reduction can be absorbed without weakening the enforcement activities of the Bureau, because it is not possible to decrease materially the now inadequate number of employees necessary for the routine tasks of tax collection. Tax returns must be recorded and funds deposited even though the returns are never investigated.

It is another fallacy that the workload of the Bureau of Internal Revenue has decreased since the close of hostilities. From a tax collection standpoint the present period resembles in many respects the period immediately following World War I. At that time the Congress appreciated the needs of the Bureau in the matter of meeting its accumulated load of wartime tax cases and provided increased funds commensurate with such burden. This policy was followed for almost 6 years after that war in order that the Bureau might be able to dispose adequately of such cases.

The action which the Congress has just taken fails to recognize the much greater task of tax collection resulting from World War II.

NOTE: As enacted, H.R. 2436 is Public Law 147, 80th Congress (61 Stat. 216).

136 Special Message to the Congress on the Control and Administration of the United Nations Headquarters in New York City. *July 2, 1947*

To the Congress of the United States:

I transmit herewith for the consideration of the Congress an agreement between the United States and the United Nations concerning the control and administration of the Headquarters of the United Nations in the City of New York. I also enclose a letter from the Secretary of State regarding this Agreement.

As you will recall, on December 10 and 11, 1945 the Congress by concurrent resolution unanimously invited the United Nations to locate its permanent headquarters in the United States. After long and careful study, the General Assembly of the United Nations decided during its session last winter to make its permanent home in New York City.

The United States has been signally honored in the location of the headquarters of the United Nations within our country. Naturally the United States wishes to make all appropriate arrangements so that the Organization can fully and effectively perform the functions for which it was created and upon the successful accomplishment of which so much depends.

This Agreement is the product of months of negotiations between representatives of this Government and the United Nations. Representatives of the City and State of New York participated in these negotiations. The Agreement carefully balances the interests of the United States as a Member of the United Nations and the interests of the United Nations as an international organization.

I urge the Congress to give early consideration to the enclosed Agreement and to authorize this Government by joint resolution, to give effect to its provisions.

When the General Assembly of the United Nations meets in New York City this fall it would be most appropriate if this Government were ready for its part to bring the Agreement into effect.

HARRY S. TRUMAN

NOTE: On August 4 the President approved a joint resolution authorizing him to bring into effect an agreement between the United States and the United Nations for the purpose of establishing the permanent headquarters of the United Nations in the United States (61 Stat. 756). The agreement became effective November 21, 1947, through an exchange of notes on that date between Warren R. Austin, Permanent Representative of the United States at the United Nations, and Trygve Lie, Secretary General of the United Nations.

Secretary Marshall's letter, dated June 30, 1947, is printed in House Document 376 (80th Cong., 1st sess.).

---

137 Special Message to the Congress on the Trusteeship Agreement for the Territory of the Pacific Islands. *July 3, 1947*

To the Congress of the United States:

I wish to recommend to the Congress action enabling this Government to approve the Trusteeship Agreement for the Territory of the Pacific Islands which was approved unanimously by the Security Council of the United Nations on April 2, 1947. There is attached a letter from the Secretary of State enclosing a copy of the Trusteeship Agreement and a memorandum with reference to its negotiation in the Security Council.

The Trusteeship Agreement was proposed by the United States to the Security Council and approved by the Council with certain changes which were acceptable to the United

States Government. Its terms are in conformity with the policy of this Government and with its obligations under the Charter of the United Nations. The terms of the Agreement make ample provision for the political, economic, social, and educational development of the inhabitants of the Trust Territory, and at the same time fully protect the security interests of the United States.

The United States has taken an active role from the beginning in the establishment of the trusteeship system of the United Nations. I believe, therefore, that it would be only fitting, as well as in the interest of the inhabitants of the islands, that the Trusteeship Agreement should be brought into force as soon as possible.

I have given special consideration to whether the attached Trusteeship Agreement should be submitted to the Congress for action by a joint resolution or by the treaty process. I am satisfied that either method is constitutionally permissible and that the agreement resulting will be of the same effect internationally and under the supremacy clause of the Constitution whether advised and consented to by the Senate or whether approval is authorized by a joint resolution. The interest of both

Houses of Congress in the execution of this Agreement is such, however, that I think it would be appropriate for the Congress, in this instance, to take action by a joint resolution in authorizing this Government to bring the Agreement into effect.

I hope that the Congress may give early consideration to this matter.

HARRY S. TRUMAN

NOTE: The text of the trusteeship agreement and related documents is printed in House Document 378 (80th Cong., 1st sess.).

For the President's statement upon signing a bill authorizing approval of the agreement, see Item 151.

---

138 Independence Day Address Delivered at the Home of Thomas Jefferson. *July 4, 1947*

Governor Tuck, Mr. Houston, distinguished guests, fellow countrymen:

I certainly appreciate that warm welcome extended to me by the Governor of Virginia most highly, and I appreciate the courtesies which have been extended to me since I have been here. Virginia is always courteous to her guests.

It is fitting that we should come to Monticello to celebrate the anniversary of our independence. Here lived Thomas Jefferson, author of the Declaration of Independence. Here Thomas Jefferson died on July 4, 1826, 50 years from the day the Declaration was adopted by the Continental Congress and proclaimed to the world.

The Declaration of Independence was an expression of democratic philosophy that sustained American patriots during the Revolution and has ever since inspired men to fight to the death for their "unalienable Rights."

The standard phrase used by writers of Jefferson's day to describe man's essential rights was "life, liberty and property." But to Jefferson, human rights were more im-

portant than property rights, and the phrase, as he wrote it in the Declaration of Independence, became "Life, Liberty and the pursuit of Happiness."

The laws and the traditions of the colonies in 1776 were designed to support a monarchial system rather than a democratic society. To Thomas Jefferson the American Revolution was far more than a struggle for independence. It was a struggle for democracy.

Within a few weeks after independence had been proclaimed at Philadelphia, Jefferson resigned his seat in the Continental Congress and returned to his place in the Virginia Legislature. There he began his monumental work of laying the foundation of an independent democracy.

Within a few years the Virginia Legislature, under Jefferson's leadership, instituted full religious freedom, abolished the laws which had permitted great estates to pass undivided from generation to generation, prohibited the importation of slaves, revised the civil and criminal code of laws, and estab-

323

lished a general system of public education. These acts, according to Jefferson, eradicated every fiber of the ancient and future aristocracy. These acts formed the basis for a truly democratic government.

Jefferson knew it was necessary to provide in law the requisites for the survival of an independent democracy. He knew that it was not enough merely to set forth a Declaration of Independence.

Two years ago the United States and 50 other nations joined in signing a great Declaration of Interdependence known as the Charter of the United Nations. We did so because we had learned, at staggering cost, that the nations of the world cannot live in peace and prosperity if, at the same time, they try to live in isolation. We have learned that nations are interdependent, and that recognition of our dependence upon one another is essential to life, liberty, and the pursuit of happiness of all mankind.

It is now the duty of all nations to converge their policies toward common goals of peace. Of course, we cannot expect all nations, with different histories, institutions, and economic conditions, to agree at once upon common ideals and policies. But it is not too much to expect that all nations should create, each within its own borders, the requisites for the growth of worldwide harmony.

The first requisite of peace among nations is common adherence to the principle that governments derive their just powers from the consent of the governed. There must be genuine effort to translate that principle into reality.

The respective constitutions of virtually all the members of the United Nations subscribe to the proposition that governments derive their just powers from the consent of the governed. In many countries, however, progress toward that goal is extremely slow. In other countries, progress in that direction is nonexistent. And in still others, the course of government is in the opposite direction.

It is necessary, if we are to have peace, that the peoples of the earth know each other, that they trade with each other and trust each other, and that they move toward common ideals. And yet, when governments do not derive their powers from the consent of the governed, these requirements are usually denied, and the peoples are kept in isolation.

The stronger the voice of a people in the formulation of national policies, the less the danger of aggression. When all governments derive their just powers from the consent of the governed, there will be enduring peace.

A second requisite of peace among nations is common respect for basic human rights. Jefferson knew the relationship between respect for these rights and peaceful democracy. We see today with equal clarity the relationship between respect for human rights and the maintenance of world peace. So long as the basic rights of men are denied in any substantial portion of the earth, men everywhere must live in fear of their own rights and their own security.

We have learned much in the last 15 years from Germany, Italy, and Japan about the intimate relationship of dictatorship, aggression, and the loss of human rights. The problem of protecting human rights has been recognized in the Charter of the United Nations, and a Commission is studying the subject at this time.

No country has yet reached the absolute in protecting human rights. In all countries, certainly including our own, there is much to be accomplished. The maintenance of peace will depend to an important degree upon the progress that is made within nations and by the United Nations in protecting human rights.

The third requisite of peace is the free and

full exchange of knowledge, ideas, and information among the peoples of the earth, and maximum freedom in international travel and communication.

Jefferson well understood this principle. On one occasion he said, "If a nation expects to be ignorant and free in a state of peace, it expects what never was and never will be." Today, we can paraphrase these words in international terms as follows: "If the nations of the world expect to live in ignorance and suspicion of each other in a state of peace, they expect what never was and never will be."

Many members of the United Nations have jointly created and now support the United Nations Educational, Scientific and Cultural Organization for the purpose of promoting the free exchange of ideas and information among the peoples of the earth. In the preamble to the Constitution of this Organization the member nations have declared that "the wide diffusion of culture and the education of humanity for justice and liberty and peace . . . constitute a sacred duty which all the nations must fulfill."

The United States has taken a leading role in furthering this ideal. We believe that it is essential to a peaceful and prosperous world. We believe that common knowledge and understanding among men can be greatly expanded in the years to come. We have the mechanical facilities—the radio, television, airplanes—for the creation of a worldwide culture. We have only to set them to work for international good.

Unfortunately, a number of countries maintain barriers against the flow of information and ideas into, or out of, their territories. Many of them restrict international travel. Some of them, behind barriers of their own creation, present to their citizens carefully selected or distorted versions of the facts about other countries. They teach and broadcast distrust and scorn of their neighbors.

These activities of organized mistrust lead the people away from peace and unity. They are a far cry from contributing to the full and free exchange of knowledge and ideas which we need if we are to have a peaceful world.

The first step to end ignorance and suspicion would be to stop propaganda attacks upon other nations. The second step would be to let down the barriers to information, ideas, and travel. The final step would be to cooperate with other nations who are so earnestly endeavoring to increase friendly understanding among men.

Here at the home of Thomas Jefferson, who dedicated his life to liberty, education, and intellectual freedom, I appeal to all nations and to all peoples to break down the artificial barriers which separate them. I appeal for tolerance and restraint in the mutual relations of nations and peoples. And I appeal for a free flow of knowledge and ideas that alone can lead to a harmonious world.

The fourth requisite of peace is that nations shall devise their economic and financial policies to support a world economy rather than separate nationalistic economies.

It is important to recognize that the United States has heavy responsibilities here. The United States is the greatest industrial nation of the world, the leading exporter of agricultural products, and the greatest creditor nation. Europe and Asia, on the other hand, have been devastated by war, and with insufficient funds and materials are struggling desperately with mountainous problems of reconstruction. In this situation the economic and financial policies maintained by the United States are of crucial importance.

We have contributed nearly $20 billion since the war to world relief, reconstruction, and stabilization. We have taken the lead in the establishment of the World Bank and the World Stabilization Fund. We have cooperated fully in the work of the Economic and Social Council of the United Nations. We have authorized aid to Greece and Turkey. We have made generous loans through our Export-Import Bank. And we have suggested to European nations that further requests for American aid should be on the basis of a sound plan for European reconstruction.

Our representatives are in Geneva negotiating a series of tariff-reducing trade agreements. They are seeking agreement with other nations on the charter of an International Trade Organization designed to bring fairness and a spirit of cooperation into the trade relations of nations.

I believe that the United States is living up to its responsibilities for creating the economic conditions of the peace. We must realize that these responsibilities are continuous. Even the emergency aspects of the job are not yet behind us.

It is not enough, however, for one nation to live up to its responsibilities for aiding reconstruction and for cooperating in the production and exchange of goods. The cooperation of all nations is necessary if the job is to be done. To the extent that any nation falls behind, to that extent will urgent needs for food, clothing, and shelter remain unfilled.

Yet, certain nations today are withholding their support of reconstruction plans on the ground that this would mean interference by some nations in the internal affairs of others. This is as fallacious as the refusal of a man to enter a profitable business partnership on the ground that it would involve interference in his private affairs.

Surely after two world wars, nations should have learned the folly of a nationalism so extreme as to block cooperative economic planning among nations for peaceful reconstruction.

The life of Thomas Jefferson demonstrates, to a remarkable degree, the strength and power of truth.

He believed, with deep conviction, that in this young Nation the survival of freedom depended upon the survival of truth.

So it is with the world.

As the spirit of freedom and the spirit of truth spread throughout the world, so shall there be understanding and justice among men.

This is the foundation for peace—a peace which is not merely the absence of war, but a deep, lasting peace built upon mutual respect and tolerance.

Our goal must be—not peace in our time—but peace for all time.

NOTE: The President spoke at 1:30 p.m. from the east portico of Monticello near Charlottesville, Va. His opening words referred to William M. Tuck, Governor of Virginia, and Frank Houston, President of the Thomas Jefferson Memorial Foundation. The address was carried on a nationwide radio broadcast.

139   Statement by the President on the Report of the Cabinet Committee on World Food Programs. *July 5, 1947*

THE CABINET Committee on World Food Programs, which I appointed last September to coordinate the activities of the United States in shipping food abroad, has submitted a report that should gratify every American.

To meet urgent human needs abroad, nearly 18½ million long tons of grain and other food were exported by the United States in the year ending June 30, 1947. This is the largest total of food ever shipped from one country in a single year.

Our country was blessed last year with the most bountiful harvest in our history. Our farmers worked hard to produce record crops. The food industries, the railroads, the shipping companies, and the Government agencies cooperated to make possible the movement of food on schedule from American farms to foreign ports.

But we must not lose sight of the fact that even the great efforts of this and other exporting countries fell short of meeting the world's urgent postwar needs for food. Many millions of people are still desperately hungry.

The Cabinet Committee reports that crop prospects abroad have been reduced by the severe winter in Northern Europe, and that in the months ahead substantial shipments of food—especially wheat—must be continued.

Within our ability to share our resources, we will continue to do our part to relieve human suffering and to help other countries to help themselves. It is the course we must follow.

The arrangements under which it was possible for us to ship such large quantities of food abroad are, therefore, being continued. I have asked the Cabinet Committee and the Coordinator of Emergency Export Programs to carry on for the coming year. The Assistant to the President will, as in the past, take all possible steps to help expedite this program.

NOTE: The report in the form of a 4-page letter dated July 1, together with a 3-page attachment summarizing the more important commodity export programs and a table giving preliminary estimates of all food shipments for the year, was released with the President's statement. The report was signed by Clinton P. Anderson, Secretary of Agriculture, who served as Chairman of the Committee, George C. Marshall, Secretary of State, and W. Averell Harriman, Secretary of Commerce.

140   Special Message to the Congress on Admission of Displaced Persons. *July 7, 1947*

To the Congress of the United States:

On several occasions I have advocated legislation to enable a substantial number of displaced persons to enter the United States as immigrants. I stated this view in opening the Second Session of the General Assembly of the United Nations. In the Message on the State of the Union on January 6, 1947, I said:

". . . The fact is that the executive agencies are now doing all that is reasonably possible under the limitation of existing law and established quotas. Congressional assistance in the form of new legislation is needed. I urge the Congress to turn its attention to this world problem, in an effort to

find ways whereby we can fulfill our responsibilities to these thousands of homeless and suffering refugees of all faiths."

I express appreciation to the Congress for the attention already being given to this problem, an appreciation which appears to be generously shared by the public with increasing understanding of the facts and of our responsibilities.

Because of the urgency of this subject I should like again to call attention to some of its fundamental aspects. We are dealing here solely with an emergency problem growing out of the war—the disposition of a specific group of individuals, victims of war, who have come into the hands of our own and the other Western Allied Armies of Occupation in Europe.

We should not forget how their destiny came into our hands. The Nazi armies, as they swept over Europe, uprooted many millions of men, women, and children from their homes and forced them to work for the German war economy. The Nazis annihilated millions by hardship and persecution. Survivors were taken under the care of the Western Allied Armies, as these Armies liberated them during the conquest of the enemy. Since the end of hostilities, the Armies of Occupation have been able to return to their homes some 7,000,000 of these people. But there still remain, in the Western Zones of Germany and Austria and in Italy, close to a million survivors who are unwilling by reason of political opinion and fear of persecution to return to the areas where they once had homes. The great majority come from the northern Baltic areas, Poland, the Russian Ukraine and Yugoslavia.

The new International Refugee Organization, supported by the contributions of this and other countries, will aid in the care and resettlement of these displaced persons. But, as I have pointed out before, the International Refugee Organization is only a service organization. It cannot impose its will on member countries. Continuance of this Organization and our financial support of its work will be required as long as the problem of these homeless people remains unsolved.

It is unthinkable that they should be left indefinitely in camps in Europe. We cannot turn them out in Germany into the community of the very people who persecuted them. Moreover, the German economy, so devastated by war and so badly overcrowded with the return of people of German origin from neighboring countries, is approaching an economic suffocation which in itself is one of our major problems. Turning these displaced persons into such chaos would be disastrous for them and would seriously aggravate our problems there.

This Government has been firm in resisting any proposal to send these people back to their former homes by force, where it is evident that their unwillingness to return is based upon political considerations or fear of persecution. In this policy I am confident I have your support.

These victims of war and oppression look hopefully to the democratic countries to help them rebuild their lives and provide for the future of their children. We must not destroy their hope. The only civilized course is to enable these people to take new roots in friendly soil. Already certain countries of Western Europe and Latin America have opened their doors to substantial numbers of these displaced persons. Plans for making homes for more of them in other countries are under consideration. But our plain duty requires that we join with other nations in solving this tragic problem.

We ourselves should admit a substantial number as immigrants. We have not yet been able to do this because our present statutory quotas applicable to the Eastern European areas from which most of these people come are wholly inadequate for this purpose. Special legislation limited to this particular emergency will therefore be necessary if we are to share with other nations in this enterprise of offering an opportunity for a new life to these people.

I wish to emphasize that there is no proposal for a general revision of our immigration policy as now enunciated in our immigration statutes. There is no proposal to waive or lower our present prescribed standards for testing the fitness for admission of every immigrant, including these displaced persons. Those permitted to enter would still have to meet the admission requirements of our existing immigration laws. These laws provide adequate guarantees against the entry of those who are criminals or subversives, those likely to become public charges, and those who are otherwise undesirable.

These displaced persons are hardy and resourceful or they would not have survived. A survey of the occupational backgrounds of those in our Assembly Centers shows a wide variety of professions, crafts, and skills. These are people who oppose totalitarian rule, and who because of their burning faith in the principles of freedom and democracy have suffered untold privation and hardship. Because they are not communists and are opposed to communism, they have stanchly resisted all efforts to induce them to return to communist-controlled areas. In addition, they were our individual allies in the war.

In the light of the vast numbers of people of all countries that we have usefully assimilated into our national life, it is clear that we could readily absorb the relatively small number of these displaced persons who would be admitted. We should not forget that our Nation was founded by immigrants many of whom fled oppression and persecution. We have thrived on the energy and diversity of many peoples. It is a source of our strength that we number among our people all the major religions, races and national origins.

Most of the individuals in the displaced persons centers already have strong roots in this country—by kinship, religion or national origin. Their occupational background clearly indicates that they can quickly become useful members of our American communities. Their kinsmen, already in the United States, have been vital factors in farm and workshop for generations. They have made lasting contributions to our arts and sciences and political life. They have been numbered among our honored dead on every battlefield of war.

We are dealing with a human problem, a world tragedy. Let us remember that these are fellow human beings now living under conditions which frustrate hope; which make it impossible for them to take any steps, unaided, to build for themselves or their children the foundations of a new life. They live in corroding uncertainty of their future. Their fate is in our hands and must now be decided. Let us join in giving them a chance at decent and self-supporting lives.

I urge the Congress to press forward with its consideration of this subject and to pass suitable legislation as speedily as possible.

HARRY S. TRUMAN

NOTE: On June 25, 1948, the President approved the Displaced Persons Act of 1948 which authorized for a limited period of time the admission of certain European displaced persons for permanent residence (62 Stat. 1009).

141   The President's News Conference of *July* 10, 1947

THE PRESIDENT. I have no special announcements to make this morning. I thought maybe you might have some questions you might like to ask me.

[1.]   Q. Mr. President, Senator Barkley, on his way out a moment ago, said you would veto the new tax bill. Would you——

THE PRESIDENT. I told Senator Barkley that I didn't see any reason why my attitude should change if they sent me the same bill they did before.

[2.] Q. Mr. President, you conferred this week with Gordon Clapp and Generals Pick and Wheeler. Could you tell us what plans you have for controlling the Ohio River in the Missouri Valley?

THE PRESIDENT. Well, I have told you, I think, on numerous occasions, that the Missouri Valley Authority is the best way to control the Missouri Valley, but that doesn't affect the flood situation on the Des Moines River, or the Mississippi River or the Ohio River. We are trying to work out a comprehensive flood control program for the whole Mississippi Valley.

Q. For the whole valley? You said you are for the Missouri Valley Authority plan?

THE PRESIDENT. I think I have said it a dozen times. You want me to put it down in writing and hand it to you? [*Laughter*]

Q. You haven't actively supported it, have you?

THE PRESIDENT. Why not? That is the only bill that is pending on the subject. Murray[1] was in here and had a conference with me just the other day, and I told him to push the bill.

Q. You will actively support it?

THE PRESIDENT. Why of course. I have always actively supported it.

Q. They don't think so out in Missouri.

THE PRESIDENT. Who doesn't think so?

Q. Most of that Missouri Valley crowd.

THE PRESIDENT. Uh huh.

Q. You will support the Missouri——

THE PRESIDENT. I shall support the comprehensive flood control program. That is the emergency at the present time, not the Missouri Valley Authority.

[3.] Q. Have you decided yet when you can accept the Brazilian invitation to go to Rio?

THE PRESIDENT. No. That is still in contemplation.

[4.] Q. Mr. President, are you considering J. Copeland Gray for one of these new places on the National Labor Relations?

THE PRESIDENT. Not that I know of. Nobody put him up to me that I know of.

Q. Anything—are any of those appointments nearing announcement?

THE PRESIDENT. We hope to be able to make announcements in a short time. As soon as I am able to make the announcements, I will let you know right away.

Q. Have you decided on a successor to Judge Collet?

THE PRESIDENT. The successor to Judge Collet will be announced just as soon as I am ready to send it up.[1]

[5.] Q. Mr. President, do you favor equalization of taxes between community property States and the other States?

THE PRESIDENT. Well, that is a matter for the Congress to decide. When it comes up to me I will act on it. Congress has control on taxation and the collection of revenue.

Q. The Treasury sent a voluminous report to the Congress without any recommendations. I thought you might have some ideas——

THE PRESIDENT. No. The Congress has to decide on that.

[6.] Q. Mr. President, have you a meeting Monday with the congressional leaders?

THE PRESIDENT. Yes.

Q. Is that to discuss the Marshall plan?

THE PRESIDENT. No. That is—it may— the Marshall plan may come up, but it is particularly to discuss the displaced persons situation—the message which I sent.[2]

[7.] Q. Any comment on Congress coming back here in the fall, as it has been reported?

THE PRESIDENT. I had no thoughts on the matter. Of course, if it is necessary for the

---

[1] Senator James E. Murray.

[1] See Item 174.
[2] See Item 140.

Congress to be called back, it will be called. I don't anticipate that there will be any necessity for it.

[8.]   Q. Mr. President, have you seen any flying saucers?

THE PRESIDENT. Only in the newspapers. [*Laughter*]

Q. Any explanations of them from over here?

THE PRESIDENT. Only the explanations I have seen in the newspapers. Did you ever hear of the moon hoax?

[9.]   Q. Mr. President, do you have any comment on the contract signed by the United Mine Workers and the owners of the coal mines?

THE PRESIDENT. No comment. That is a contract strictly between the owners and the miners. I have no comment on it.[1]

Q. Is there a study being conducted within the Government, sir, as to the effect that might have on the general level of prices?

THE PRESIDENT. None that I know of. Mark Sullivan probably can tell you. [*Laughter*]

[10.]   Q. Mr. President, what are the prospects for a trip west this fall?

THE PRESIDENT. None.

Q. Next spring, Mr. President?

THE PRESIDENT. None.

Q. Mr. President, have you decided anything about this trip across the country this fall with party leaders?

THE PRESIDENT. I was just saying that no plans were made for any trip anywhere.

[11.]   Q. Mr. President, there was a story broke yesterday about this disappearance of the atomic energy secret papers. There are still persistent rumors this morning that the—in some publications—that the White Sands—rather Los Alamos was not the only one. Have you had any——

THE PRESIDENT. I think Senator Hickenlooper very clearly explained the situation in his statement to the Senate. He is chairman of that committee, and I am perfectly willing to accept his statement on the matter. They have been investigating it.[1]

[12.]   Q. Mr. President, what is your attitude toward the political arrests in Greece?

THE PRESIDENT. I have no attitude.

[13.]   Q. Mr. President, have you heard about Roger Slaughter's speech saying that there would be a scandal breaking on this administration?

THE PRESIDENT. All I know about it is the memorandum that *you* sent in to me, Tony.[2] [*Laughter*]

Q. That's below the belt!

THE PRESIDENT. I consider the source of the remarks which you said were made in the speech by Mr. Slaughter, so it doesn't worry me any.

[14.]   Q. Mr. President, Congress and congressional leaders are attempting to get away the 26th of July. Do you see any reason why they shouldn't?

THE PRESIDENT. No, I don't see any reason why they shouldn't. Congress understands it much better than I do.

Q. There has been discussion as to whether they should recess or adjourn.

THE PRESIDENT. Well, that is up to the Congress. That is none of my business. I don't intend to adjourn them myself. [*Laughter*]

[15.]   Q. Mr. President, on this special session this fall, with the Marshall plan being discussed and probably some plan to evolve out of Europe, wouldn't that more or less necessitate some sort of action——

THE PRESIDENT. The—if the necessity arises we certainly will take whatever steps are necessary.

---

[1] See Item 142.

[1] See Congressional Record (vol. 93, p. 8494).
[2] Ernest B. Vaccaro of the Associated Press.

Q. I was trying to get a little clarification on this, that you didn't think that the necessity would arise?

THE PRESIDENT. I don't see any necessity in the immediate future now, but of course if the necessity arises we will do whatever is necessary to meet the situation.

Q. Mr. President, is there any possibility of a message going up during this session only, to communicate to Congress your present plans on the Marshall plan and what would be required?

THE PRESIDENT. No.

Q. No recommendations on the way?

THE PRESIDENT. I can't make any recommendations on that situation until we find out how the Paris conference goes.

[16.] Q. Mr. President, there has been some printed speculation that Dr. Steelman

might leave your personal staff and head the new Federal Conciliation Service. Would you care to comment on that?

THE PRESIDENT. I hadn't heard about it, and I don't think Dr. Steelman has, either. I think he is pretty well satisfied working 24 hours a day for me. [*Laughter*] How about it, John?

Dr. Steelman: About right.

[17.] Q. Have you any comment to make, sir, on the refusal of the eastern European countries to join the Paris conference on the Marshall plan?

THE PRESIDENT. No comment.

Reporter: Thank you, Mr. President.

THE PRESIDENT. You're welcome.

NOTE: President Truman's one hundred and eleventh news conference was held in his office at the White House at 10:30 a.m. on Thursday, July 10, 1947.

142   Statement by the President on the Wage Increase of the Coal Miners. *July 14, 1947*

DEEP CONCERN is being expressed in many quarters over possible results of the recent settlement between the miners and the coal operators. It is widely feared that this settlement may lead to a substantial increase in the price of coal, which is an important factor on the cost sheets of American industry, and that this would in turn induce an increase in commodity prices and renew the inflationary spiral which we had much reason to hope had been halted.

This would be a serious blow to our economy and to the continuance of the present high level of production and employment. But such a blow need not fall upon us.

The effect of the wage settlement is badly misrepresented by the bare statement that it amounts to an increase of about 45 cents per hour in the wages of miners. It is unfortunate that the public does not yet fully understand, through the complicated details of

the agreement, what is the actual impact of this settlement upon the cost of producing coal.

The major features of the wage settlement are these: The miners receive a daily wage of $13.05 instead of $11.85, this being the $1.20 increase recently awarded in other major industries. The working day becomes 8 hours at straight rates instead of 9 hours, of which 7 hours have been at straight time rates and 2 hours have been at overtime premium rates. Overtime is paid for Saturday work only if it has been preceded by 5 days of work in that week, and the employers will no longer find their schedules disorganized by the inclination of some miners to work on the overtime Saturday and to lay off on some other day. The employers also pay an additional five cents per ton into the welfare fund.

When the most important coal operators

and steel producers in the country made this settlement, they asserted that it would be of great benefit to the country by making it possible to continue full production and employment for a long period. We can all agree that a coal strike would have seriously endangered our prosperity. But whether this settlement does permit that prosperity to continue depends in very large degree upon the decisions of these business managers themselves as to how they will deal with their costs and prices in the light of this settlement.

In their explanation to the public and to their stockholders of the reasons which led them to make this contract, these business leaders have emphasized the desirability of certain provisions and conditions which they assert will increase productivity and offset a considerable part of the increase in money wage rates. It is quite impossible for them, they say, to make any estimate of the savings in costs which will accrue from the regularized workday and workweek, from the increased effort of workers who enjoy better wages and greater security, and from the improvement in plant efficiency which it is always the duty of management to create and in the present situation is even more emphatically the obligation of these managers to secure.

In view of the uncertainty as to whether or how much mine costs of coal may be raised, the people of the country have the right to demand that their prosperity shall not be imperiled by immediate increases in the price of coal and in the price of steel. It is only reasonable to ask coal and steel producers to wait until a fair test has been made of the actual effects of the wage advances under conditions of maximum production. If prices are raised at once and a wave of increases in related prices upsets our economy, we never will know what would have happened if the coal and steel managers had been willing to wait.

The risk involved by continuing present prices of coal and steel long enough to learn what the increased costs of production will actually be under the new wage agreement is not serious, especially in view of the fact that such action will greatly reduce the hazards of renewed inflation. The producers of coal and steel have been enjoying their full share of the high profits which are flowing to industry today in our present prosperous economy. I am sure that they, as responsible leaders of industry, will want to invest a portion of those profits in the maintenance of business stability and prosperity for all our people.

143 Statement by the President Upon Signing the Second Decontrol Act. *July 15, 1947*

I HAVE today approved H.R. 3647, extending until March 1, 1948, the authority of the Government to regulate the export of commodities which are in critically short supply here and abroad; to control the importation and domestic use of a small group of essential commodities which we must obtain from sources of supply abroad; to allocate transportation equipment of rail carriers; and to

direct the delivery abroad of goods required for the production in foreign countries of commodities urgently needed in the United States, or required for carrying out our foreign policy.

The bill differs only in detail from that requested in my message to the Congress on this subject. Thus, we have again demonstrated to the world our unanimity on mat-

333

ters affecting our international relations. This is particularly significant and timely at this moment when so much attention is focused abroad on our desire to assist nations willing to cooperate in the common objective of reconstruction.

I wish it had not been necessary to request a continuation of these controls. But world shortages have by no means been dispelled and the threat of inflation has not been dissipated. The haphazard distribution of our produce throughout the world could only lead to higher prices at home and suffering for the neediest of our friends abroad.

Our objective continues to be the removal of interferences with world trade. We shall, accordingly, use these controls sparingly and dispense with them as soon as conditions permit. I should be less than candid, however, were I not to say that I believe the need for some supervision of our foreign trade will continue beyond next February.

Under this legislation, it will be the duty of the Secretary of Commerce to watch the effect upon the domestic economy of the exercise of these powers. This responsibility ties in closely with the work I requested him to undertake when, on June 22, I appointed a representative, nonpartisan public committee headed by him to consider the effect upon our domestic economy of the exports we are now shipping abroad or may furnish as economic assistance to foreign countries. It is imperative that these programs of assistance be conceived and executed so as to be of maximum benefit to such foreign countries, without having an unduly adverse effect upon our domestic economy.

I am gratified that the Congress has again demonstrated its willingness to support the achievement of our foreign policy objectives. Despite the aversion of our people to controls, I am confident that under these circumstances they will approve of their continuance.

NOTE: The Second Decontrol Act of 1947 is Public Law 188, 80th Congress (61 Stat. 321).

144 Special Message to the Congress on Flood Control in the Mississippi River Basin. *July 16, 1947*

To the Congress of the United States:

The major opportunity of our generation to increase the wealth of the Nation lies in the development of our great river systems. I urged in the State of the Union message on January 6, 1947, that the program for improvement of our rivers be pushed with full vigor.

Since that time, the urgency of one phase of our water resources control program has been demonstrated forcefully and tragically. Vast areas of the most productive sections of the Missouri and Upper Mississippi River Valleys have been subjected to a series of the most destructive floods in our history. Too frequently within our memory, as well as in earlier years, the Mississippi River Basin has been similarly stricken. This continued threat and the recurring and accumulative damage to the national economy and well-being call strongly for the prompt use of more effective counter-measures. Prudence requires that adequate measures be taken for protection against these devastating floods.

Measures for flood control should be integrated with plans for the use and conservation of water resources for other purposes. This will insure maximum control of floods at the least cost and will permit the full utilization of water resources in the development of this vast region.

The drainage basin of the Mississippi River and its tributaries comprises nearly half of the Nation in area and population. It is a rich central core from which stem goods and services vital to the entire country. A large proportion of the people in this great central basin, their homes and businesses, their fertile farm lands and their transportation and communication systems are concentrated in the flood plains and low lands immediately adjacent to the rivers. Nature also requires the use of these flood plains for drainage. Consequently, we must pay the price for occupancy of these lands, either in the form of continued flood damage or in preventive measures.

The economy of controlling floods as compared with the cost of continuing under the handicap of their disruptive force has been amply demonstrated.

In the short 10-year period from 1937 through 1946 a total of more than a billion dollars in flood damage has been suffered in the Mississippi Basin. The real cost to the Nation, of course, has been much greater. Dollars are not adequate to measure the toll in the hundreds of lives lost and the suffering of millions of persons affected. The cost of rehabilitation and repair of flood damage, though staggering, is but the initial burden. Extended effects, both in distance and time, are reflected throughout the Nation as a result of the disruption of lives and activities in the flood zone. These more remote inroads on our health and prosperity are not so obvious, but they may total many times the more apparent losses in the flood area.

In the light of the accumulative burden of our flood problem in the decade just past, the impact of this year's floods in the Missouri and Upper Mississippi Valleys is even more appalling. Again, unprecedented flood stages have been experienced at many points on these rivers, and the total damages will approach and may exceed the half billion dollar loss suffered in 1937. Again thousands of our people have been forced to leave their homes and their normal pursuits. All or a large part of the year's income has been ruthlessly taken from thousands of farmers. The loss of their crops is not only a personal calamity to these farmers but is a staggering blow to the Nation and to other countries where many additional thousands will be deprived of essential foods.

The recurrent floods in the Mississippi Basin constitute a national problem which demands immediate attention. The means for solution are available to us and will permit us, at the same time, to prevent destruction and waste of productive soils, to improve the utility of the rivers for transportation, to conserve water that would otherwise be wasted with destructive force and to use this water constructively for domestic purposes, for irrigation, for development of needed electric power, for the abatement of pollution and for the enjoyment of recreational activities.

After the destructive floods of 1927 in the Lower Valley of the Mississippi, the Congress charged the Corps of Engineers of the War Department with the preparation of plans for control of floods in that valley, and with the making of surveys of tributary rivers for their development for flood control and allied purposes. Since that time, surveys, studies and preparation of plans have gone forward hand in hand with urgently needed construction. As a result we now have available comprehensive and detailed plans for most of the work needed to eliminate destructive floods and provide for the beneficial use of water in the Mississippi River Basin.

The Congress has also provided legislative authority to proceed with these plans.

The Flood Control Act of May 15, 1928, authorized a plan for the protection of the Lower Mississippi Valley. Subsequent legislation has permitted the extension and development of that plan to a high degree of completion. The Flood Control Act of 1938 approved comprehensive flood control plans for each of the five major tributary basins of the Mississippi River and authorized the expenditure of funds for the initiation and partial accomplishment of those plans. Subsequent general flood control acts have authorized expenditure of additional sums to continue this work. These acts provided that Federal investigations and improvements for flood control and allied purposes should be prosecuted by the War Department, under the direction of the Secretary of War and the supervision of the Chief of Engineers.

The Flood Control Act of 1936 provided for Federal investigation of watersheds and for measures of run-off and water-flow retardation and soil erosion prevention on watersheds, to be prosecuted by the Department of Agriculture. The Reclamation Laws authorize irrigation programs and the prosecution of such programs by the Bureau of Reclamation of the Department of the Interior, in coordination with plans for flood control. The Federal Water Power Acts and appropriate parts of the flood control acts provide for participation of the Federal Power Commission when hydroelectric power is involved in these programs.

A comprehensive program for flood control in the entire Mississippi River Basin is essential. The Lower Mississippi River, as it flows through its alluvial valley, must carry the flood discharge from every tributary river basin from the Appalachians to the Rocky Mountains. Fortunately we have never had a simultaneous occurrence of major floods on all the great tributaries: the Missouri, Ohio, Upper Mississippi, Arkansas, and Red Rivers. Such a coincidence of flood crests is highly improbable, but if it did occur under present conditions, the floods would overflow the entire Lower Mississippi Valley from Cairo, Illinois, to the Gulf of Mexico and would cause untold damage to one of the richest areas in the world. It would not be feasible to build levees high enough and floodways wide enough to pass such a flood safely to the Gulf. Therefore, it is necessary to prevent the concurrence of tributary floods by a coordinated system of storage reservoirs in the major tributary basins. In these same tributary basins, levees, floodwalls and diversion channels are necessary to protect cities, towns and farms. Farther up on the headwater tributaries of each major basin, and throughout their watersheds, soil conservation measures are needed to retard the flow and run-off and reduce the loss of topsoil which is impoverishing our farm lands and clogging our reservoirs and river channels.

Corollary to the control of floods is the harnessing of flood waters for productive uses which will return to the Government a large share of the initial investment. Fortunately the means available to us for control of floods in many cases furnish the opportunity for use of water for irrigation, navigation, and development of hydroelectric power. Multiple-use reservoirs produce these and other benefits, including the improvement of municipal and industrial water supplies, new recreational areas and opportunities, the preservation of fish and wildlife, and the abatement of pollution.

The problem confronting us is of prime importance in our national life. During the war it was unavoidably necessary to defer in large part works of this character. In the immediate post-war period conflicting needs for other Government programs caused further deferment. These conflicting needs are now diminishing, and the experience of the past few months has presented convincing evidence that we must press forward vigorously toward a solution of this problem.

In the execution of a comprehensive program for the development of the Mississippi River Basin, protection from floods is of such urgency that it should be given first attention. We already have plans for the projects which will largely provide this protection. The construction agencies of the Departments of War, Interior, and Agriculture are ready to proceed with these projects when funds are provided.

I therefore urge that this Congress undertake a program which will provide for the substantial completion within ten years of the flood control projects necessary for the protection of the Mississippi River Basin. Most of these necessary projects have already been authorized by the Congress. This ten-year program should also contain a smaller group of projects which have not yet been authorized by the Congress but are now being planned and investigated. As rapidly as the plans are completed, these projects will be submitted for approval by the Congress in accordance with present law and procedure.

An orderly program of appropriations for prosecution of this work on a sustained and comprehensive basis is essential. Any plan of this magnitude can be accomplished in an efficient manner only if the planning and constructing agencies have advance knowledge of the funds that they may expect over a period of years. If construction schedules and contracts are extended over long periods because of limited and varying appropriations, excessive costs to the Federal Government are the result. An orderly program of appropriations will get the job done efficiently and economically.

I recommend that this ten-year program be initiated during this fiscal year. The appropriations required for the first year (in addition to appropriations heretofore made or considered for the fiscal year 1948) will be approximately as follows:

War Department, Corps of Engineers	$237,000,000
Department of the Interior, Bureau of Reclamation...	10,000,000
Department of Agriculture, Soil Conservation Service.	3,000,000
Total	$250,000,000

The formal estimate of supplemental appropriations for the fiscal year 1948 to finance this proposal will be transmitted to the Congress promptly.

The projects for which these appropriations are recommended are essential to any program for flood control and the development of the water resources of the Mississippi River Basin. A prompt start on the ten-year program proposed in this message will be consistent with whatever type of administrative authority may be determined to be best suited to meet regional and national needs.

This plan does not change the desirability of the ultimate establishment of valley authorities, but the urgency of the flood problem is such that we must take necessary steps to expedite this program without awaiting determination of the administrative pattern for the various regional valley development programs.

In addition to the program aimed primarily at flood control, there are many valuable projects for navigation, irrigation, hydroelectric power development and other utilization of water resources which are essential to a complete and well rounded valley development program. These projects will be included in their proper place in the regular annual budget program and consequently are not specifically within the scope of this message.

We must never forget that the conservation of our natural resources and their wise use are essential to our very existence as a nation. The choice is ours. We can sit idly by—or almost as bad, resort to the false economy of feeble and inadequate measures—while these precious assets waste away. On the other hand, we can, if we act in time, put into effect a realistic and practical plan which will preserve these basic essentials of our national economy and make this a better and a richer land.

In the development of our river valleys, first things must come first. The most pressing problem is that of flood control. It is a problem of desperate urgency. What we need to do is to take immediate advantage of the Mississippi Basin authorizations—totalling almost six billion dollars—which the Congress has already voted for flood control and related purposes. Of this amount,

from three and a half to four billion dollars is either directly or closely related to flood control. Let us through the next ten years accelerate our program and put this money to work, together with such additional moneys as may be required and as our economy from year to year shall permit. In that way we shall save ourselves untold billions and pave the way for the wealth production that surely will flow from the integrated development of our valleys.

HARRY S. TRUMAN

NOTE: On July 31 the President approved appropriations bills including provisions for flood control work on the Mississippi River and tributaries (61 Stat. 686, 695).

145   The President's News Conference of *July* 17, 1947

THE PRESIDENT. I have a couple of announcements to make to you.

[1.] I am going to appoint the Honorable James Forrestal, the Secretary of the Navy; the Honorable Arthur S. Flemming, Civil Service Commissioner; the Honorable Dean Acheson of Washington, D.C.; and the Honorable George H. Mead, Dayton, Ohio, on the Commission on the Organization of the Executive Branch of the Government. There will be a mimeographed copy of the letter which went to each one of them for you when you go out.

[2.] Now I am reappointing the three members presently on the National Labor Relations Board, Mr. Paul Herzog whose term expires in 1950, Mr. John Houston whose term expires in 1948, Mr. James Reynolds whose term expires in 1951, and J. Copeland Gray, Buffalo, N.Y., for a term of 2 years, Abe Murdock of Utah for a term of 5 years; and I am nominating as General Counsel, Mr. Robert N. Denham of Mary-

land for a term of 4 years.

Q. Is that D-e——

THE PRESIDENT. D-e-n-h-a-m.

I am designating Paul Herzog as Chairman of the new Board. We will have autographs — autobiography — a biography of each one of them when you go out.

Q. Will that include Denham's biography?

THE PRESIDENT. Yes.

Q. Mr. President, does that take care of the Counsel?

THE PRESIDENT. The Counsel is Denham.

Q. Denham, you said? Of Maryland.

THE PRESIDENT. He lives in Maryland.

Q. What's he been doing?

Q. What's he been doing, Mr. President?

THE PRESIDENT. One at a time, please. [*Laughter*]

Q. Autobiography contain their—what their politics are— their biographies?

THE PRESIDENT. Well, I don't know. I suppose it will. I suppose it will. Gray is a Republican. Murdock is a Democrat.

And Denham's a Republican, if that will be of any help to you.

Q. Just helping out the Republicans!

THE PRESIDENT. Oh, you are helping them out? [*Laughter*]

Q. Was it legally necessary for you to reappoint the present members?

THE PRESIDENT. I think it was.

[3.] Q. Mr. President, is there a nomination for the Mediation Conciliation Service?

THE PRESIDENT. No, not yet. I will announce that.

[4.] Q. Can you tell us anything more about Mr. Denham, Mr. President?

THE PRESIDENT. He is the General Counsel for the Board. A Maryland Republican.

Q. What's he been doing lately, Mr. President?

THE PRESIDENT. He has been one of the assistant counselors to the Board.

Mr. Ross: The background is fully given on that.

THE PRESIDENT. You will have the background when you get outside.

[5.] Q. Mr. President, in view of the fact that I asked you about Mr. Gray the other day, when you said his name hadn't been presented to you——

THE PRESIDENT. It hadn't.

Q. Can you tell us now how it happened to be presented, or who presented it?

THE PRESIDENT. No, I can't.

Q. I asked you about him the other day.

THE PRESIDENT. I couldn't answer you then because his name hadn't been presented to me at that time. It was presented and I thought he filled the bill, so I appointed him.

[6.] Q. These people are more or less in sympathy with the new act?

THE PRESIDENT. They certainly are. They have to be.

Q. I just wanted to bring it up.

THE PRESIDENT. They have to be.

[7.] Q. Mr. President, are you going to Kentucky about the first of August?

THE PRESIDENT. I don't think so. I have no engagements from now until next Christmas that I know of. [*Laughter*]

[8.] Q. Mr. President, I understand your shipping commissioners met yesterday with Dr. Steelman. I imagine their recommendations concerned additional passenger ships—construction?

THE PRESIDENT. I haven't discussed the matter with Dr. Steelman.

Q. Mr. President, has anything in particular been done to revive coastwise shipping, which is pretty dormant now?

THE PRESIDENT. I imagine that's what the conference was about yesterday, but I haven't discussed the matter with Dr. Steelman or anybody else.

[9.] Q. Mr. President, I have noticed some stories and some editorials to the effect that more gas and oil were consumed last year than in the peak of the wartime period, and that within 25 years our supplies here would be exhausted. Is that being taken up on your level at all?

THE PRESIDENT. Yes, it is being studied.

Q. Is there anything you can give us?

THE PRESIDENT. I can give you nothing in regard to it, because that is a part of the economic survey which is being made for the country now.

Q. What was that answer?

THE PRESIDENT. That is a part of the economic survey being made—being made now for the country.

Q. Is that the one you will send to Congress Monday?

THE PRESIDENT. No—no, no. This is the one that has to do with implementation of the Marshall plan.

[10.] Q. Mr. President, will your veto message on the tax bill indicate what you think is the right way and the right time to reduce taxes?

THE PRESIDENT. I think the best thing for you to do is to wait and read the veto message which will be out soon. You only have about 9 hours to wait. [*Laughter*]

[11.] Q. Mr. President, you spoke just now of the implementation of the Marshall plan. That's what the point of your economic message will be?

THE PRESIDENT. No, no, we have appointed a large commission to make a survey of the resources of the United States. That will take in oil and everything else.

[12.] Q. Mr. President, many European countries have interpreted the fact that there will be no special session of Congress in the fall to mean that they can't look forward to any aid from us until some time next spring when the Congress would act. Is that a correct interpretation?

THE PRESIDENT. I can't answer that for you. I don't know anything about what the interpretations are.

[13.] Q. Mr. President, the oil—National Coal Association, rather, issued a statement yesterday regarding a letter they had sent to you. Is that letter—which indicates that they can't hold down prices—going to affect your message to Congress Monday?

THE PRESIDENT. I haven't seen the letter and it wouldn't affect the message.

[14.] Q. Mr. President, are you prepared to grow a beard or pay a fine, in connection with that question that Earl Godwin asked you a while ago?[1]

THE PRESIDENT. I just now heard about it, but I haven't been officially notified as yet. But I will be fined. I will wait and see what happens. I don't expect to grow a beard. [*Laughter*]

---

[1] The White House Official Reporter noted that prior to the opening of the news conference Earl Godwin of the American Broadcasting Company told the President of an Associated Press item which stated that the President was going to be fined $3.25 for not growing a beard for the celebration marking the 125th anniversary of the opening of the Santa Fe Trail.

[15.] Q. Mr. President, are you going to appoint—I am asked to ask you this——

THE PRESIDENT. Sure.

Q. ——an emergency board in the Southern Pacific Railway case? You know they have a strike call for Monday.

THE PRESIDENT. I imagine that they will follow the usual procedure of the Railway Labor Act.

[16.] Q. Mr. President, is the Ambassador to Mexico coming home soon?

THE PRESIDENT. Not that I know of.

Q. There has been some talk about it.

THE PRESIDENT. I haven't heard it.

[17.] Q. Mr. President, are you going to touch on the GI terminal leave bonds—the bill is pending in Congress—on Monday in your Economic Report?

THE PRESIDENT. Well now, the Economic Report is just like the veto message. It will speak for itself. You will have it this Saturday, so you will have plenty of time to study it for Monday. That will answer your question.

[18.] Q. Mr. President—what is your opinion, Mr. President, on the very cool reception given to your message on flood control by the majority group in the——

THE PRESIDENT. Did it have a cool reception? I didn't know that.

Q. Mr. Taber received it——

THE PRESIDENT. Oh, that's to be expected. He criticizes everything. [*Laughter*] I don't think that's a barometer as to what the Congress may do.

Q. Are you hopeful then, sir, that they will appropriate $250 million at this session?

THE PRESIDENT. Of course I am. That's the reason I asked for it. I am sending down the budget on the subject immediately.

Q. This session?

THE PRESIDENT. In fact they have it, I think, now.

Q. When did you say you were sending down the budget?

THE PRESIDENT. I think it went today.

I am sure I signed the request today.

[19.] Q. Mr. President, last week you were asked what your stand might be on the community property states and the non-community property states being put on the same basis of taxation. You said that was up for the Congress to decide.

THE PRESIDENT. That's right.

Q. Does that mean, though, that you would sign a bill that the Congress gave you that had such provisions?

THE PRESIDENT. Well now, I will have to decide that when the bill comes before me.

[20.] Q. Mr. President, is there any possibility of your attending the opening of the Rio de Janeiro conference?

THE PRESIDENT. I don't think so.

Q. Mr. President, will Senator Vandenberg be named a member of the United States delegation to the Rio conference?

THE PRESIDENT. Well, I will answer that when the appointments are made.

[21.] Q. Mr. President, is there anything you can say on this report that Mr. Forrestal is to be the head of all the armed services?

THE PRESIDENT. I have no comment on that. I will take care of that when it comes up. The bill hasn't even been passed yet. When it comes to me, I will let you know just as soon as I have made up my mind.

[22.] Q. Mr. President, back to this question of your trip to Brazil, is there any possibility that you will go down there in August?

THE PRESIDENT. I can't answer that, Smitty.[1] I have been contemplating a trip to Brazil, but no arrangements have been made for the trip, and I don't know what the situation will be. When I get ready to go to Brazil, I will let you know in plenty of time so you can get ready, Smitty. [*Laughter*]

[23.] Q. Mr. President, have you reached a decision about where the USES should be, either in the Labor Department——

THE PRESIDENT. I have always held that it should be in the Labor Department. My position hasn't changed on that at all.

[24.] Q. Mr. President, what is your reaction to the fact that coal prices seem to be going right up?

THE PRESIDENT. I have no comment on that because I don't know what's going to happen. I will answer that at a later date.

Reporter: Thank you, Mr. President.

THE PRESIDENT. You're welcome.

NOTE: President Truman's one hundred and twelfth news conference was held in his office at the White House at 4 o'clock on Thursday afternoon, July 17, 1947.

[1] Merriman Smith of the United Press.

---

146 Letter to Members of the Commission on Organization of the Executive Branch. *July 17, 1947*

My dear Mr. —————:

I am glad to know that you will serve as a member of the Commission on Organization of the Executive Branch of the Government.

The Act establishing this Commission provides for a cooperative approach by the Legislative and Executive Branches of the Gov-

ernment to the improvement of the effectiveness of the organization and operations of the Executive Branch. The method of appointing the twelve members of the Commission is significant. One-third of the members are appointed by the President Pro Tempore of the Senate; one-third by the Speaker of the House of Representatives;

and one-third by the President. Each group of appointees must be equally divided as between the two major political parties, and as between those in Government and in private life. This arrangement should be conducive to a well-balanced Commission.

The role conferred upon the Commission affords an opportunity to attack basic problems of government. That role is to study and investigate the present organization, methods, and operations of all executive agencies in order to determine what changes are necessary to promote economy and efficiency, and to improve service in the transaction of the public business.

The proposed study should prove of great value. The proper organization and administration of executive agencies is a continuing problem, requiring frequent evaluation in order to adapt their structure to current conditions. The present organization of the Executive Branch has a long history, and many and varied factors have shaped its growth. Manageability and facility of administration have not always received sufficient emphasis in this shaping.

I feel certain that your presence on the Commission will be of great assistance in making sure that the problem is attacked with vigor. A bold, comprehensive and fundamental review of all aspects of the organization and operation of the Executive Branch is required if our government is to be adequately equipped to meet the challenges it must face in a modern world.

Sincerely yours,

HARRY S. TRUMAN

NOTE: This is the text of identical letters addressed to the following appointees to the Commission: James Forrestal, Secretary of the Navy; Arthur S. Flemming, Commissioner, Civil Service Commission; Dean Acheson, Under Secretary of State; and George H. Mead, member of the Price Decontrol Board.

147 Veto of Second Bill To Reduce Income Taxes. *July 18, 1947*

To the House of Representatives:

I return herewith, without my approval, H.R. 3950, entitled "An Act to reduce individual income tax payments."

The provisions of this bill are identical with those of H.R. 1 except that this bill would not become effective until January 1, 1948, whereas H.R. 1 would have become effective on July 1, 1947.

I returned H.R. 1 to the House of Representatives on June 16, 1947, without my approval, stating that it represented the wrong kind of tax reduction at the wrong time.

This is still the wrong kind of tax reduction and this is still the wrong time to provide for tax reduction.

The present bill is not consistent with sound fiscal policy. As I have stated to the Congress on previous occasions, while business, employment, and national income continue high, we should maintain tax revenues at levels that will meet current expenditures and also leave a surplus for retirement of the public debt. No other course is consistent with realistic and conservative management of the fiscal affairs of the Government.

Since H.R. 1 was disapproved, there has been no lessening of the need to make substantial payments on the public debt. Maintaining the integrity of this debt is one of the primary obligations of the Government. I repeat that, if we do not reduce the public debt by substantial amounts during a prosperous period such as the present, there is little prospect of material reduction at any time.

I also pointed out in my message on H.R. 1 that necessary Government expenditures are still high. We are meeting tremendous obligations growing out of the war. The national defense establishment still requires large sums. Our responsibilities for international rehabilitation have an important bearing on our efforts to secure lasting peace. The recent refusal of certain nations to join in common endeavors to establish conditions of world stability increases the difficulty of our task and exposes us to greater risk. Until we are better able to estimate the cost of our investment in world peace and collective security, it is unwise to make so large a cut in our Government's future income that our ability to meet our needs would be impaired.

As far as can be determined at present, it is not likely that expenditures in the fiscal year 1948 will be substantially less than I estimated in the January budget message. A careful appraisal of the outlook for both receipts and expenditures indicates that it is not possible, under present conditions, to make a major tax reduction and an adequate payment on the public debt at the same time.

Not only does this bill represent an unsound fiscal policy, but it would also contribute to inflationary pressures which we have made progress in combatting but have by no means overcome. As stated in the message on H.R. 1, there is no justification for tax reduction so long as price stability at sound levels has not been secured and business, employment, and national income continue at peak levels.

Since the veto of H.R. 1, income payments to individuals have continued to rise, and the general level of business activity is establishing new high records. The total number of civilians gainfully employed has also continued to rise. Total employment in June increased by 1,725,000 over May, and the total number now employed is over 60,000,000—the highest in our history. There is still no convincing evidence that a recession is imminent.

Tax reduction now would delay the readjustments of prices and wages necessary to maintain this high prosperity. It would lead to an even higher level of prices for consumer goods. It would increase the danger of a recession.

For all these reasons, which are more compelling now than they were one month ago, I regard the present bill as unsound and unsafe.

I also regard it as unfair.

In my message of disapproval of June 16, I pointed out that H.R. 1 was inequitable in that it would reduce taxes in the high income brackets to a grossly disproportionate extent as compared with the reduction in the low income brackets. I stated that a good tax reduction bill should give a greater proportion of relief to low income groups.

Since the present bill is identical except as to its effective date, it is, of course, subject to the same criticism.

It is important to remember that, during the war, Federal income taxes were extended to millions of low-income families who had never before paid them, and taxes on moderate incomes were increased by a far greater proportion than those in higher incomes. The amount by which present income taxes exceed those payable under the Revenue Act of 1940 represents a special wartime tax burden.

When the time comes to lessen this wartime tax burden, it is only fair that we should follow a pattern which is the reverse of that under which the burden was imposed. That is to say, this wartime tax burden should be reduced on a basis that is fair to low income groups as well as to high income groups.

The failure of H.R. 3950 to follow this equitable principle is strikingly demonstrated by the following examples:

The bill would remove 21 per cent of this wartime tax burden for a married couple with an income of $2,500.

The bill would remove 64 per cent of this wartime tax burden for a couple with an income of $100,000.

The bill would remove 85 per cent of this wartime tax burden for a couple with an income of $1,000,000.

I am unequivocally committed to the right kind of tax reduction at the right time. The right kind of tax reduction must be based upon a careful consideration of all elements of our tax structure.

A premature and faulty tax reduction bill such as H.R. 3950 would inject into our tax system inequities which would greatly increase the difficulty of making desirable revisions.

A fair and proper revision of our tax structure should result in an equitable distribution of tax reductions. It should be designed, also, to assure a balanced budget, adequate debt retirement, and an adequate reserve for meeting our international commitments and carrying out our foreign policy. It should be designed to provide stability rather than instability in our economy, and should be properly timed for that purpose.

Because H.R. 3950 is at complete variance with the fundamental requirements of a good tax bill, I am compelled to return it without my approval.

HARRY S. TRUMAN

NOTE: For the President's veto message of June 16, see Item 116.

148   Letter Appointing Members to the Air Policy Commission. *July* 18, 1947

Dear Mr. ————:

The rapid development of aviation in recent years has made many of our former concepts out of date. At the same time, there exists a danger that our national security may be jeopardized and our economic welfare diminished through a lowered aircraft production and a failure of the aircraft industry to keep abreast of modern methods, with consequent retarding of the development of air transportation. There is an urgent need at this time for an evaluation of the course which the United States should follow in order to obtain, for itself and the world, the greatest possible benefits from aviation.

It is for these reasons that, upon the recommendation of the Secretaries of State, War, Navy, and Commerce and of the Air Co-ordinating Committee, I am creating a temporary Air Policy Commission to make an objective inquiry into national aviation policies and problems, and to assist me in formulating an integrated national aviation policy. Because of your knowledge of our national needs and our industrial capabilities, as well as your public-spirited concern for the national welfare, I ask you to serve on this Commission.

The Air Policy Commission should study, among other pertinent aspects of the problem, such questions as the current and future needs of American aviation, including commercial air transportation and the utilization of aircraft by the armed services; the nature, type, and extent of aircraft and air transportation industries that are desirable or essential to our national security and welfare;

methods of encouraging needed developments in the aviation and air transportation industry; and improved organization and procedures of the Government that will assist it in handling aviation matters efficiently and in the public interest.

The final recommendations of the Commission must, however, go beyond the limits of any one phase of aviation. They should be so broad in scope and purpose that they will assist in revising old policies and in framing new ones, and will serve as a guide for formulating a carefully considered national air policy.

Because of the urgency of the problem, I request the Commission to complete its studies in time to submit its final recommendations to me by January 1, 1948. In its work the Commission will have the full cooperation of all agencies of the Government, including the Air Coordinating Committee, which has been making detailed studies of aviation policies and problems.

Although the Commission will organize its own regular staff and secretariat, the Secretary of Commerce will provide any special staff assistance which may be needed, as well as office headquarters and routine administrative services.

Sincerely yours,

HARRY S. TRUMAN

NOTE: This is the text of identical letters addressed to the following appointees to the Commission: Thomas K. Finletter, New York, N.Y., to serve as chairman; George P. Baker, Cambridge, Mass., to serve as vice chairman; Palmer Hoyt, Denver, Colo.; Henry Ford II, Detroit, Mich.; and Arthur D. Whiteside, New York, N.Y.

On December 30 the Commission transmitted to the President its report "Survival in the Air Age," dated January 1, 1948 (Government Printing Office, 166 pp.).

149 Letter to the Chairman of the Air Coordinating Committee. *July 18, 1947*

Dear Mr. Norton:

I have read with great interest your letter of June 16, 1947, discussing the present condition of the aircraft manufacturing industry and recommending that I appoint a board of disinterested citizens to study the relationship of this industry to the national security and welfare.

Your recommendation seems to me well taken. I have, therefore, appointed an Air Policy Commission with the request that it make an objective inquiry into our aviation policy in its broadest aspects.

In a letter from the Air Coordinating Committee to me dated December 26, 1946, it was stated that the Committee was undertaking a comprehensive survey of aviation policy from the Governmental standpoint. The background and experience which the Committee has in this field would be of material assistance to the Commission, and I am, therefore, requesting that you send me your report for its use.

I am deeply appreciative of the fine work which your Committee has done in calling to my attention the present condition of the aircraft industry and in carrying forward the compilation of Government aviation policy.

Sincerely yours,

HARRY S. TRUMAN

[Hon. Garrison Norton, Chairman, Air Coordinating Committee, Department of State]

NOTE: The Committee's report entitled "A Statement of Certain Policies of the Executive Branch of the Government in the General Field of Aviation" is dated August 1, 1947 (Government Printing Office, 17 pp.).

For letter appointing members to the Air Policy Commission, see Item 148.

150 Letter Accepting Resignation of Robert P. Patterson as Secretary of War. *July 18, 1947*

Dear Bob:

Your letter of this date leaves me no choice but to accept your resignation as Secretary of War, effective at the close of business July twenty-fourth. Never have I accepted a resignation from the Government service with more poignant regret. I yield to your desire only because I can no longer in good conscience ask you to stay on.

It is hard for me to find the proper words with which to describe the character of your service to our country. It has been magnificent. It has been utterly selfless. I saw a great deal of your work when I was head of the Senate Committee to Investigate the National Defense Program and you were Under Secretary of War. You then had charge of the procurement of supplies for our Army. How well you acquitted yourself in that vital task is attested by the results. When Secretary Stimson resigned I was comfortable in the knowledge that the admin-istration of the War Department would be carried on with the same zeal and efficiency that he had demonstrated. Again, the results prove the truth of this conviction.

I want to add, Bob, that I value, more than words can tell, the friendship that has grown up between us. The official loss of your services is also to me a deep personal loss.

I want to feel free to call on you from time to time for counsel.

With every good wish, believe me, as always

Very sincerely yours,

HARRY S. TRUMAN

[The Honorable Robert P. Patterson, Secretary of War, Washington 25, D.C.]

NOTE: Mr. Patterson served as Under Secretary from December 19, 1940, to September 26, 1945, and as Secretary through July 24, 1947. His letter of resignation, dated July 18, was released with the President's reply.

151 Statement by the President Upon Signing Resolution Authorizing Approval of Trusteeship Agreement for the Trust Territory of the Pacific Islands. *July 19, 1947*

I HAVE SIGNED the joint resolution authorizing approval by this Government of the Trusteeship Agreement for the Trust Territory of the Pacific Islands and have instructed the Secretary of State to notify the appropriate organs of the United Nations that this agreement, having been duly approved by the Security Council and by this Government, enters into force as of this date. It is the intention of this Government to carry out in full the obligations toward the people of the trust territory and toward the United Nations, as specified in the terms of the Trusteeship Agreement and Chapters XI, XII, and XIII of the Charter of the United Nations.

Under Article 12 of the Trusteeship Agreement, the United States is obligated to enact such legislation as may be necessary to place the provisions of this agreement in effect in the trust territory. This is a responsibility which falls primarily upon the Congress of the United States. In order to assist the Congress in this task, I have asked the Department of State to prepare, in consultation with other interested departments, suggestions for organic legislation for the trust territory. It is expected that these suggestions will be ready for presentation to the Congress at its next session.

With my letter of June 19, 1947, to the President pro tempore of the Senate and the Speaker of the House of Representatives, I enclosed a letter addressed to me from the Secretary of State. This letter set forth recommendations which were agreed upon by the Secretaries of State, War, Navy, and Interior with respect to the future administration of Guam, American Samoa, and the trust territory, and which I have approved.

Accordingly, I have issued an Executive order terminating military government in the trust territory and delegating responsibility for civil administration on an interim basis to the Navy Department, pending transfer to a civilian department or agency of the Government at the earliest practicable date.

NOTE: The joint resolution, approved by the President on July 18, 1947, is Public Law 204, 80th Congress (61 Stat. 397). The text of the agreement is printed in House Document 378 (80th Cong., 1st sess.).

For the President's letter of June 19, 1947, see Item 119.

Executive Order 9875 "Providing an Interim Administration for the Trust Territory of the Pacific Islands" was issued July 18, 1947 (3 CFR, 1943–1948 Comp., p. 658).

152 Excerpts from Special Message: The President's Midyear Economic Report to the Congress. *July 21, 1947*

To the Congress of the United States:

When my first Economic Report was presented to the Congress on January 8, 1947, the Nation was turning from the economic controls of wartime to a free economy. Now, 6 months later, it is appropriate that we consider carefully what success we have had in meeting the problems of that process, what difficulties lie ahead, and what action should now be taken. It is for this reason that I transmit to the Congress this Midyear Economic Report.

I. FOREWORD AND SUMMARY

Americans today live in a richer and more productive economy, and are enjoying its benefits more equitably, than ever before in peacetime history.

At midpoint in the year 1947, we have surpassed previous high records of civilian production, and are now producing goods and services at a rate of 225 billion dollars annually. Month by month there has been talk of recession; month by month recession has failed to materialize. In June we reached a level of 60 million civilian jobs, regarded by many as impossible of attainment. Our standard of livng is exceptionally high, and purchasing power has thus far been adequate to absorb completely the enormous production of American farms, mines, and factories. Farm income has attained a record level. The financial position of business is strong. A healthy slowing down in inventory accumulation has taken place. Business investment in plants and equipment has increased this year, even above the record highs of last year. Management and labor have cooperated in maintaining industrial peace, and a wide range of important collective-bargaining agreements have been signed without widespread strikes. With a slight reduction in the workweek, productivity is on the increase.

The credit for this magnificent record is shared by American farmers, who exerted great efforts to plant and reap bumper crops;

347

by workers, who stayed on the job and increased their productivity; by businessmen, who overcame many shortages and established new records in the production of more and better goods; and by leaders of industry and labor who strove for industrial peace in the face of serious difficulties.

The unprecedented prosperity of our Nation must not be a cause for idle self-congratulation. We must remember that full employment at a high price level is being sustained at present by the reconversion demands of business and the backlog demands of consumers, by extensive use of savings and credit, and by an extraordinary excess of exports over imports. These are temporary props to our economic system. As they weaken, we shall need to make many basic readjustments to complete the transition to a permanently stable and maximum-level peacetime economy.

These adjustments take time to accomplish in our free, enormous, and complex economic system. They must be made before the lack of them produces serious unemployment and business decline. Adjustment through recession or depression is tragic, costly, and wasteful. Moderate adjustments, made in time, can accomplish more than drastic measures in a crisis produced by delay or neglect.

Price and income adjustments stand foremost in need of attention.

Industrial and agricultural prices.—Prices increased sharply in the second half of 1946, increased more slowly in the first quarter of 1947, and then leveled off in the second quarter. This leveling off reflected some catching up of supply with immediate demand, an increase of consumer resistance, and the encouraging response of many businessmen to the Government's price advice, which they recognized to be in their own long-range interest.

This improvement in the price situation should not blind us to further need for price reductions in some cases. In other cases, there is need to hold the price line in the face of recent developments which revive some fears of another upswing of inflation.

There are many areas where price reductions still are necessary to check current or prospective declines in demand and to provide outlets for increased production. In the numerous instances where profit margins permit, or where future profits would be better protected by assuring larger volume through lower prices, business should make these adjustments now.

At the beginning of this year, the prospect for abundant crops gave promise that the price increases in farm and food products would be checked. Although there was a leveling off in food prices in the second quarter of this year, bad weather, extensive floods, and unexpectedly urgent foreign need have caused some further price increase in food and farm products in recent weeks. There are fears of a short corn crop, but no general or present scarcity of farm and food products as a whole.

Although most farmers cannot voluntarily reduce their prices because they do not make price decisions, we are not entirely without recourse in the farm situation. We may still obtain a total agricultural output as large as last year. But in view of the existing uncertainty in the farm outlook, it is the duty of food growers, processors, and the Government to keep the public currently informed of the real facts concerning our food supply. Unfounded fear of food shortages should not be allowed to lead to speculation, hoarding, and unnecessary buying. We should all realize, too, that any slight inconveniences or momentary shortages that may develop are the consequence primarily of the high incomes and standard of living most of us are enjoying today.

Wages and salaries.—Although the moderate and peaceful wage adjustments during the first half of the year improved the position of many wage earners, the majority of consumers were not directly benefited. Because of increases in the cost of living, the purchasing power of total consumers' incomes is no higher than at the beginning of the year.

In some cases wage increases are still needed to attain workable relations in the wage and salary structure, and to alleviate hardship due to wages which are substandard or which have risen substantially less than the increase in the cost of living.

Except for such special circumstances, wage increases should be related to general trends in productivity and not made on a basis which forces price increases or prevents price reductions needed to assure sale of increasing supplies.

With the wage adjustments already made and those still needed in special wage areas, it follows that the patterns of workable price relations ultimately arrived at will be on a somewhat higher price level than would otherwise have come about. However, this is not a justification for pyramiding wage-price increases or failing to make price reductions whenever and wherever possible.

In the interest of those whose income has remained substandard, it is imperative that legislation be enacted to extend the coverage of the Fair Labor Standards Act, to increase the minimum wage level to at least 65 cents an hour, and to enlarge social-security benefit payments in view of the higher cost of living.

Under the recent wage settlement in the coal mining industry, the wages of coal miners occupy a place near the top of the wage structure. The earnings of the coal miners under the new contract must be judged in the light of the character of their work and the labor needs of the industry. There has been exaggeration of the size of this adjustment compared with the adjustments previously made in many other industries. Every effort should be made to absorb the cost increases in the coal mining industry and the industries indirectly affected, through increased productivity and through reduction in profit margins.

The increases that have already been made in coal prices are contributing to inflationary pressures. We have a right to expect that, as operating adjustments toward maximum efficiency are made and present shortages are overcome, the price of coal will be restored to a lower level, thus easing the cost situation for industrial, railway, and domestic users. Meanwhile, pyramiding of price advances by coal distributors is wholly unjustified.

Similarly, increases in the price of steel would have a widespread inflationary effect. Steel companies should exercise extraordinary caution at this stage of our reconversion effort to see that increases in coal prices or other costs are offset as fully as possible through the savings of continuous and high-level operation. Recent favorable earnings should permit the absorption of an extraordinary cost over a short period in order to stabilize prosperity for the longer run.

In no case should the particular wage increases in the mining industry be made the basis for wage demands in other fields governed by different circumstances.

It is in the interest of steady expansion of the economy that, with the aid of collective bargaining, prices and wages be brought in line with general productivity trends.

Housing and other construction.—Although housing construction has been higher in 1947 than in 1946, it lags far behind the real needs of our people for homes. A much

349

higher volume of housing output will be needed to help sustain maximum employment when temporarily sustaining forces—such as the huge net export balance, high investments in reconversion, and an abnormal rate of inventory accumulation—begin to decline or decline further.

The needed stimulus to more housing construction, and also to industrial and commercial construction, depends largely upon lower prices. Housing costs can and should be substantially lowered through the efforts of material suppliers, builders, and workers.

Of utmost importance is immediate enactment of the comprehensive housing program which I have previously recommended to the present Congress. Without such a law, housing is seriously handicapped.

Public construction for the time being should be held to moderate amounts consistent with essential needs.

The foreign aid program.—The United States has indicated its readiness to consider further aid toward reconstruction in Europe if the foreign countries themselves present a plan that makes such help truly effective. We must continue to help other countries help themselves, until the reconstruction of their own economies reaches the point where they are able to pay their way by exchange of goods and services. The possibility of additional foreign aid programs makes it all the more necessary to appraise the impact of exports on the domestic economy during the last 6 months. A large excess of exports over imports occurring at a time of inflationary pressure has created some strain on the economy. But this strain is of moderate proportions and will be of temporary duration. Our exports have not necessitated undue denial at home, where our standards of living are much higher than before the war.

These exports for the aid of other countries are directed toward the winning of the peace—they are at the core of this Nation's foreign policy.

The responsibilities of government.—Economic adjustment to changing conditions is, in a free enterprise economy, accomplished largely through a multitude of voluntary decisions by business management, farmers, and labor. Wise and farsighted policy by these groups is necessary to assure the satisfactory operation of our economic system. Government must, however, at all times exert its complementary influence.

Legislative action on minimum wages, on social security and on housing, as already indicated, forms part of the immediate responsibility of government.

In addition, the recent uncertainties arising in four fields—uncertainties as to the effect of the crop situation upon food prices, the effect of the coal mine settlement upon industrial prices, the trend of housing costs and house production, and the whole matter of foreign economic policy—have a vital bearing upon the immediate fiscal policies of the Government. The developments in these areas mean that the inflationary factors in the economy may become stronger.

Tax reduction now would add to inflationary pressures and would also prevent the debt reduction which should be carried out in prosperous times to strengthen the Nation's financial position against future contingencies. A policy of restraint at the present time will enable the Government to use fiscal measures effectively should the time come when they might be needed to lend support to the economy.

The sound financial policies that the Government has been following have been vindicated by every test of experience. These policies should not be abandoned nor weakened.

———

The Employment Act of 1946 contemplated that prompt attention would be given to the maintenance of maximum prosperity in all its phases—employment, production, and purchasing power.

This midyear report, unlike the first Economic Report in January, deals only with problems requiring immediate attention. It is a check-up on the extent to which we have thus far achieved the goals we set in January.

Many of the short-range recommendations made in January have not yet been adopted—especially those requiring legislation. The fact that this delay has not yet produced bad results is no reason for further delay. Waiting until bad results appear means that action is too late to be fully effective.

Long-range economic programs will also be required. They embrace resource and regional development, health and welfare, antimonopoly programs, stabilization devices, and many other undertakings essential to the full realization of our superb economic potential. The first Economic Report indicated the range of these programs, and studies are now under way to make them ready for presentation by next year.

We must adjust our minds to the fact that we are living in a 225 billion dollar economy; that our free system has become today, and tomorrow must continue to be, the richest and most powerful productive machine ever devised by the minds and hands of man. Our task is to create for the functioning of this great productive force an environment in which it can operate smoothly at capacity. Thus far we have avoided the economic misfortunes which followed World War I and then culminated in a disastrous depression in 1929. Today we are wiser, more experienced, infinitely more blessed with material riches, more united as a people, stronger as a nation. If, calmly and realistically, we assess our strong points and our weaknesses and boldly take necessary steps in time, we can place the high production and the high employment that we have today

on a firm foundation of enduring prosperity and peace.

II. FROM WAR TO PEACE

LESSONS FROM 1919–21

At the end of World War I, the traditional reluctance of the American people to accept restraints by Government on their business decisions and their personal choices brought about the immediate abandonment of wartime controls. Production, employment, and national income, after a brief lag, bounded forward, but with such faulty internal adjustments that prosperity was short-lived. In less than 2 years a sharp recession ensued. Although industry recovered promptly from this recession, agriculture was seriously depressed and was by no means securely adjusted when industry again suffered collapse in 1929.

The failure of the prosperity of 1919–20 to continue was due to maladjustments growing out of an unrestrained market. Credit was freed of wartime controls, resulting in a surging demand from business, eager to exploit the glittering profit opportunities of the day. Also consumers, who had been unable to buy many articles during the war, had incomes of unexampled size further bolstered by wartime savings, creating a demand for many types of goods far greater than the markets could supply. There was an intensive foreign demand, resulting in a temporary increase in the value of exports.

Prices in this free market skyrocketed far above wartime levels, which, under the limited price controls of that period, were already very high. Between the armistice in 1918 and May 1920 wholesale commodity prices rose about 23 percent to a point 148 percent above the prewar level. Retail prices outstripped the increase in consumers' incomes so far that consumer buying fell sharply, labor controversies increased, inventories became financial nightmares, orders were canceled, and the price structure collapsed. Then came a sharp drop in production and employment.

The factors which during World War I led to the difficult conditions of postwar transition were present in aggravated degree in World War II. Diversion of national productive power to war uses was much greater. Expansion of money and credit was severalfold larger. War incomes went to a larger proportion of the people and over a period more than twice as long. Requirements for new industrial equipment were far greater. A much more effective control of prices established a relatively low level from which postwar inflation could spring. The problem of changing from the controlled economy of wartime to the traditional American economy of free enterprise, which the Nation did not solve successfully after World War I, was far more serious when World War II came to a close in a devastated world.

THE APPROACH TO POSTWAR READJUSTMENT

We were, however, determined to effect both physical and economic reconversion with less waste and on a better stabilized basis than the record shows for the 1920's and the 1930's. This determination was reflected not merely in the words and actions of individuals and organizations but also in Government policies and programs. It was registered with clarity and force in the Employment Act of 1946. As we looked forward toward making that act effective in realizing the high purposes which it set forth, we had occasion to be much gratified by the proofs afforded since V-J day of the great productive power and financial resources of our economy. The shift from war produc-

tion to the production of civilian goods and services was carried through so rapidly that prompt employment was given to the labor force, rapidly expanded by the return of millions of veterans. Unemployment never approached the magnitude that many experts were predicting.

Economic phases of reconversion, however, presented greater difficulties than the physical or technological ones. The American people were united in their determination to return to free enterprise and to discontinue wartime controls as rapidly as possible, but there was no clear and certain standard or formula by which timing and method could be determined. Many economic controls were progressively discarded in the year following the Japanese surrender. Price control was materially reduced and in the fall of 1946 was finally discontinued except for a few commodities and rents.

Claims made by the advocates of early decontrol, that OPA prices had retarded production and that it would promptly catch up with demand after the removal of the controls, were not fully borne out by developments. Production, with important exceptions, did not increase as rapidly in the first few months after decontrol as in the last few months before decontrol.

In the face of this failure of production to respond more sensitively to the freeing of market demand, the abundant purchasing power of both consumers and business buyers met a sharp response in soaring prices. The price index of food products at wholesale jumped 28 percent in a single week in October when price control was ended on meats, fats and oils, and other foods. Though it reacted promptly, it has not since then approached the previous level. Wholesale prices of goods other than farm and food products, which had risen about 5 percent during the first half of 1946, climbed by the end of the year to 24 percent above the level of 12 months earlier. Retail prices, though their changes are ordinarily more sluggish, moved upward almost as much as wholesale prices. The index of consumers' prices of goods and services rose 15 percent between June and December, even though rents, which were kept under control, remained stable.

Personal incomes increased at a much slower rate. In the last quarter of 1946 these incomes were at a rate about 9 percent above that of 6 months earlier. The real purchasing power of consumers' current incomes had steadily declined, notwithstanding high employment and rising wage rates.

THE FIRST ECONOMIC REPORT

This was the situation at the time of my first Economic Report last January. In many respects the economic situation was good. Employment was at a very high level, and the labor-management controversies which caused many work stoppages in 1946 had quieted down. Profits of business were high, and new business investment was proceeding at a record rate. National credit was unimpaired, and we were showing our ability to manage the huge national debt. The banking structure and the monetary system were not under strain. There was no speculative color to the securities markets. The state of credit was good, although there was a rapid increase in consumers' credit. The export balance of foreign trade appeared too great to continue indefinitely, but it was evident that for the immediate future foreign demand for our goods would remain large.

At the same time it was clear that inflationary elements continued strong. Many prices were still rising under the influence of shortages and extraordinary backlog demands for consumer goods and capital goods

not available during the war. Yet there was danger that deflationary forces might develop during the year. For example, it was clear that the exceptional rate of inventory accumulation would not long continue, that the backlog demands would be filled sooner or later, and that many consumers were using up past savings or resorting to credit in order to keep up with the cost of living. If prices should continue to move ahead of the current buying power of consumers and business, it was evident that trouble would develop in the economy.

Under the Employment Act of 1946 it was the obligation of the President, with the assistance of the Council of Economic Advisers, to propose policies to sustain a high level of production and employment. To that end, among the policies recommended in the first Economic Report, adjustments were urged to bring prices and current incomes of our people into better balance. The main approach to attain this balance, it was said, was to reduce prices rather than to increase incomes. Price reductions automatically benefit all buyers of goods for consumption or business purposes. Increases in incomes cannot be spread evenly in a free economy, and many incomes are increased slowly or not at all. The standard of living of large numbers of our people had already become seriously threatened by the price advances which had taken effect, while their incomes had not increased in step with those of others. Among them were millions of workers, people dependent upon fixed incomes, and teachers and other public servants.

It was recognized, of course, that here, as in all aspects of our involved and dynamic economy, there are many complications. The price reductions which benefit buyers of goods likewise reduce the incomes of producers of these goods. Price reduction was necessary, but it needed to be made with discrimination to avoid placing an inequitable share of the burden upon certain groups of producers and to preserve a level of business profit and farm returns adequate to sustain a high level of business investment and a healthy agriculture. Our economic problems are never simple; they are not subject to solution by a pat formula.

The positive method to determine prices is by Government mandate, but it involves complicated determinations and irritating restraints which Americans have tolerated only under stress of war. In response to an insistent demand by business, with wide public support, positive control of the prices of most goods was ended late in 1946. In the free economy, prices are made by the forces of the market place and the action of business management. The initial responsibility for many prices is that of the businessman who decides at what figure he will sell. In the first Economic Report each businessman was urged to take a broad view of the long-run problem and, in the interest of sustaining large markets, to reduce his prices insofar as costs permitted.

Labor, in turn, was advised to bear in mind the greater benefit of sustained employment as a result of prices in balance with workers' incomes, as compared with the immediate advantage of such wage increases at particular points as would distort the wage and price structure, stimulate inflation, and lead to business maladjustment and unemployment. It was noted, however, that increase in the money incomes of many workers was desirable where it would not contribute to further price advances. For many workers in the lagging parts of the wage structure, moreover, it would be appropriate to increase their incomes even though to do so would in some instances increase prices. Both workers and farmers were urged to contribute vigorously to larger production, the best preventive of price inflation.

Specific action by the Government itself, as proposed in the first Economic Report, was designed to continue, and skillfully to extend, lines of action already adopted. The major short-range recommendations for immediate Government action included:

1. The continuance of existing taxes upon business and individual incomes.

2. The reduction of the public debt as promptly as Treasury surplus funds became available.

3. The continuance of rent control and the enactment of a comprehensive housing program.

4. The raising of minimum wage rates and the extension of coverage.

5. Increases in social security benefits in view of the higher cost of living.

The Nation-wide reception to the first Economic Report was encouraging, although neither in the area of private adjustment nor congressional legislation have its recommendations met with adequate response. It is because further adjustments by the people and further governmental action both are needed that this review of the economic situation at midyear is being presented. It undertakes to evaluate developments which have taken place since January, to identify the major problems with which we are now confronted, and to project forward the lines along which preventive or corrective efforts should proceed. Ever-increasing benefits should flow from improvement in our means of measuring economic causes and results and through constant retesting of our means of dealing with these situations. These periodic reviews should promote increasing appreciation by the people and their Government of the value of the economic stabilization undertaking embodied in the Employment Act of 1946.

*   *   *   *   *

HARRY S. TRUMAN

NOTE: The balance of this message is similar in content and language to the annual economic reviews

by the Council of Economic Advisers which were separated from the President's messages beginning in 1949.

The complete message is printed in "Midyear Economic Report of the President to the Congress, July 21, 1947" (Government Printing Office, 1947, 82 pp.).

---

153 Statement by the President: The Jewish New Year.
July 22, 1947

UPON this memorable anniversary, I extend to my fellow citizens of the Jewish faith sincere greetings for the New Year.

Let us all, of whatever religious faith, strive together in good works to the end that a just peace, based on the essential rights of man, shall reign throughout the world.

---

154 Letter to the President of the Senate and to the Speaker of the House Concerning a Proposed Statue of Commodore John Barry. *July 23, 1947*

Dear Mr. ————:

Public Law 109, Seventy-seventh Congress, approved June 10, 1941, authorized and directed the President of the United States to present to Eire a statue of Commodore John Barry in honor of the bicentenary of his birth in 1945. The act authorized an appropriation not to exceed $20,000 and provided for the selection of a sculptor by a committee of three members appointed by the President.

Before action could be taken, the United States was at war. Because of the shortage of bronze it became necessary to defer the project until after the end of the war. During the past year alternative plans for carrying out Public Law 109 have been investigated, and it has been ascertained by the Commission of Fine Arts that a sum of not less than $30,000 now will be needed to procure a suitable statue of John Barry. In view of this fact, it seems to me proper that the entire matter should be presented to the Congress for consideration as to the desirability of enacting legislation which will provide sufficient funds to enable the President to make the presentation to Eire.

HARRY S. TRUMAN

NOTE: This is the text of identical letters addressed to the Honorable Arthur H. Vandenberg, President pro tempore of the Senate, and to the Honorable Joseph W. Martin, Jr., Speaker of the House of Representatives.

155 The President's News Conference of July 24, 1947

THE PRESIDENT. I have no special announcements to make this morning. I thought maybe you might have some questions you might like to ask me and I will try to answer them.

[1.] Q. Mr. President, can you now tell us the date of your Rio trip?

THE PRESIDENT. No I can't. As soon as I can tell you, I will let you know, so you will have plenty of time to get ready. [*Laughter*]

[2.] Q. Mr. President, is there anything to the report that former Senator Mead may succeed Mr. Hannegan as Chairman of the Democratic National Committee?

THE PRESIDENT. I haven't heard anything about it.

[3.] Q. Mr. President, there have been consistent reports that Secretary Forrestal is going to head defense. How about that?

THE PRESIDENT. I haven't heard anything about that, either.

Q. You will, if you read the papers.

THE PRESIDENT. I will announce that when the time comes so you won't be in suspense for very long.

Q. You mean you will announce Mr. Forrestal's name?

THE PRESIDENT. No. I will announce who is the head of it. [*Laughter*]

[4.] Q. Mr. President, is there any administrative action you could take on displaced persons, in the absence of the—legislative action?

THE PRESIDENT. No, there is not. If there were any such action possible, I would have taken it long ago.

[5.] Q. Mr. President, some months ago you made a statement appealing for cooperation between the Executive and Congress. Do you think that the desire and purpose has in any large degree been realized? Would

you care to comment on that?

THE PRESIDENT. I think it has been realized to some extent. I wouldn't say just how far.

[6.] Q. Mr. President, sometime ago you said that if Congress did not take affirmative action on credit controls, particularly consumer controls, you would take action and remove them. And Congress—the House has repealed them in one form and the other has taken some action, but no final action has been taken.

THE PRESIDENT. Well, they haven't yet reached the completeness of what they are going to do. I can't tell you anything about it until I know what they are going to do.

Q. Your statement that you would take affirmative action—that you would take action——

THE PRESIDENT. I will—I didn't say I would remove, I said I would take action. That is an entirely different thing.

Q. What action could you take, Mr. President?

THE PRESIDENT. Well, you will have to wait and see. I can't tell you until Congress has decided what it wants to do. Then I will let you know what I am going to—what I can do.

Q. Mr. President, didn't you say that you would vacate those controls?

THE PRESIDENT. No, I don't think I ever made such a statement as that.

Q. Would you ask Mr. Dickson to supply us with the original question?

Q. Mr. President, that is in your——

THE PRESIDENT. Wait now—just a minute—one at a time. [*Laughter*]

Q. Would you ask Mr. Dickson to supply us with the original question as we leave?

THE PRESIDENT. I will be glad to do that.

Q. That is in your message to Congress?

THE PRESIDENT. I don't remember any such statement as that in any message I ever sent to Congress.

Q. Mr. President, in your Economic Message you said you—there might be some necessity for controls over grains. Is anything doing on that?

THE PRESIDENT. On what?

Q. Grains. Wheat and corn.

THE PRESIDENT. Well, I think that was in the manner of export controls and transportation.

Q. Rather than—no idea of any domestic——

THE PRESIDENT. No, no. That was for export controls and transportation controls so that it would be possible to get the export—the seashore for embarkation.

[7.] Q. Mr. President, have you given much consideration to Secretary Anderson's proposal for a world trade organization, whereby the Government would do their purchasing for grain and supplies for the Marshall plan?

THE PRESIDENT. That is under consideration.

Q. Has it advanced very far?

THE PRESIDENT. I say it is under consideration. That is as far as I can go.

[*Pause*]

Reporter: Well, thank you, Mr. President.

THE PRESIDENT. Kind of a "dry hole" this morning.

NOTE: President Truman's one hundred and thirteenth news conference was held in his office at the White House at 10:30 a.m. on Thursday, July 24, 1947.

156 Statement by the President Upon Signing Resolution Terminating Additional Emergency Powers. *July 25, 1947*

I HAVE today approved Senate Joint Resolution 123, providing for the repeal of certain temporary emergency and war statutes and for discontinuing operations under various permanent statutes which are effective only in time of war or national emergency. Under the terms of the new Act, certain wartime powers are ended immediately and others will terminate at stated times within a period of one year. Some 175 statutory provisions are affected.

This resolution is the result of joint studies made by the Attorney General and the Committee on the Judiciary of each House of the Congress, with the cooperation of the executive departments and agencies. It is part of a sound and systematic program for removing emergency and wartime powers of the Government, and is in accord with recommendations which I have previously made to the Congress on this subject.

The proclamation declaring the cessation of hostilities of World War II, issued on December 31, 1946, had the effect, under the law, of terminating operations under a large number of wartime statutes. The present bill makes suitable provision with respect to a number of additional statutes, the need for which has now ceased or will cease at a foreseeable future date.

The emergencies declared by the President on September 8, 1939, and May 27, 1941, and the state of war continue to exist, however, and it is not possible at this time to provide for terminating all war and emergency powers.

I have asked the Attorney General to continue his study of the problems involved in the termination of the remaining wartime and emergency legislation, as well as the other problems involved in declaring the end of the war and the end of the existing emergencies. We should complete the orderly reconversion of the machinery and operations of the Government to a peacetime basis as rapidly as practicable.

NOTE: As enacted, the joint resolution is Public Law 239, 80th Congress (61 Stat. 449).

157 Statement by the President on the Dangers of Explosive-Type War Souvenirs. *July 25, 1947*

IT HAS BEEN brought to my attention that the War, Navy, and Treasury Departments and the National Rifle Association have joined in a campaign of instruction to prevent the loss of life and destruction of property resulting from the possession of explosive-type war souvenirs. One need but scan the papers to see that such a safety program is badly needed.

The problem is primarily one of education. It is regrettable that a step of this kind was not taken after past wars. This neglect has cost us thousands of lives and millions of dollars.

Three Government agencies and a nonprofit sportsmen's organization have banded together in a public service. I trust the public will hear them—and heed.

158 Statement by the President Upon Signing Bill Authorizing Redemption of Veterans' Terminal Leave Bonds. *July 26, 1947*

I HAVE today signed H.R. 4017, an act amending the Armed Forces Leave Act of 1946. The amendment provides that terminal leave bonds now held by veterans may be redeemed for cash any time after next September 1st. For the convenience of bondholders, the Treasury Department is making arrangements with banks and other financial institutions in order that bonds may be cashed in local communities without cost to veterans.

I wish to emphasize strongly that it is to the veterans' best interest that they keep their bonds if they do not absolutely need to cash them now. Almost $2 billion of bonds are outstanding. If a sizable propor-

tion of these bonds should be redeemed in the near future, general inflationary pressures, which we have been endeavoring to control, would receive a substantial boost. Several hundred million new dollars poured into the spending stream would exert a strong upward pressure on prices. If, on the other hand, veterans choose the wise course, hold their bonds and continue to draw 2½ percent interest, their dollars will buy more when they cash their bonds after inflationary conditions have eased. I urge veterans not to cash their bonds unless they are in urgent need of the money now.

NOTE: As enacted, H.R. 4017 is Public Law 254, 80th Congress (61 Stat. 510).

159   Executive Order 9877: Functions of the Armed Forces.
July 26, 1947

BY VIRTUE of the authority vested in me by the Constitution and laws of the United States, and as President of the United States and Commander in Chief of the Armed Forces of the United States, I hereby prescribe the following assignment of primary functions and responsibilities to the three armed services.

Section I—The Common Missions of the Armed Forces of the United States are:

1. To support and defend the Constitution of the United States against all enemies, foreign or domestic.

2. To maintain, by timely and effective military action, the security of the United States, its possessions and areas vital to its interest.

3. To uphold and advance the national policies and interests of the United States.

4. To safeguard the internal security of the United States as directed by higher authority.

5. To conduct integrated operations on the land, on the sea, and in the air necessary for these purposes.

In order to facilitate the accomplishment of the foregoing missions the armed forces shall formulate integrated plans and make coordinated preparations. Each service shall observe the general principles and fulfill the specific functions outlined below, and shall make use of the personnel, equipment and facilities of the other services in all cases where economy and effectiveness will thereby be increased.

Section II—Functions of the United States Army

General

The United States Army includes land combat and service forces and such aviation and water transport as may be organic therein. It is organized, trained and equipped primarily for prompt and sustained combat incident to operations on land. The Army is responsible for the preparation of land forces necessary for the effective prosecution of war, and, in accordance with integrated joint mobilization plans, for the expansion of peacetime components of the Army to meet the needs of war.

The specific functions of the United States Army are:

1. To organize, train and equip land forces for:

a. Operations on land, including joint operations.

b. The seizure or defense of land areas, including airborne and joint amphibious operations.

c. The occupation of land areas.

2. To develop weapons, tactics, technique, organization and equipment of Army combat and service elements, coordinating with the Navy and the Air Force in all aspects of joint concern, including those which pertain to amphibious and airborne operations.

3. To provide, as directed by proper authority, such missions and detachments for service in foreign countries as may be required to support the national policies and interests of the United States.

4. To assist the Navy and Air Forces in the accomplishment of their missions, including the provision of common services and supplies as determined by proper authority.

Section III—Functions of the United States Navy

General

The United States Navy includes naval combat and service forces, naval aviation, and the United States Marine Corps. It is organized, trained and equipped primarily for prompt and sustained combat at sea. The Navy is responsible for the preparation of naval forces necessary for the effective prosecution of war, and in accordance with integrated joint mobilization plans, for the expansion of the peacetime components of the Navy to meet the needs of war.

The specific functions of the United States Navy are:

1. To organize, train and equip naval forces for:

a. Operations at sea, including joint operations.

b. The control of vital sea areas, the protection of vital sea lanes, and the suppression of enemy sea commerce.

c. The support of occupation forces as required.

d. The seizure of minor enemy shore positions capable of reduction by such landing forces as may be comprised within the fleet organization.

e. Naval reconnaissance, antisubmarine warfare, and protection of shipping. The air aspects of those functions shall be coordinated with the Air Force, including the development and procurement of aircraft, and air installations located on shore, and use shall be made of Air Force personnel, equipment and facilities in all cases where economy and effectiveness will thereby be increased. Subject to the above provision, the Navy will not be restricted as to types of aircraft maintained and operated for these purposes.

f. The air transport necessary for essential internal administration and for air transport over routes of sole interest to naval forces where the requirements cannot be met by normal air transport facilities.

2. To develop weapons, tactics, technique, organization and equipment of naval combat and service elements, coordinating with the Army and the Air Force in all aspects of joint concern, including those which pertain to amphibious operations.

3. To provide, as directed by proper authority, such missions and detachments for service in foreign countries as may be required to support the national policies and interests of the United States.

4. To maintain the U.S. Marine Corps whose specific functions are:

a. To provide Marine Forces together with supporting air components, for service with the Fleet in the seizure or defense of advanced naval bases and for the conduct of limited land operations in connection therewith.

b. To develop, in coordination with the Army and the Air Force those phases of amphibious operations which pertain to the tactics, technique and equipment employed by landing forces.

c. To provide detachments and organizations for service on armed vessels of the Navy.

d. To provide security detachments for protection of naval property at naval stations and bases.

e. To provide, as directed by proper authority, such missions and detachments for service in foreign countries as may be required to support the national policies and interests of the United States.

5. To assist the Army and the Air Force in the accomplishment of their missions, including the provision of common services and supplies as determined by proper authority.

Section IV—Functions of the United States Air Force

General

The United States Air Force includes all military aviation forces, both combat and service, not otherwise specifically assigned. It is organized, trained, and equipped primarily for prompt and sustained air offensive and defensive operations. The Air Force is responsible for the preparation of the air forces necessary for the effective prosecution of war except as otherwise assigned and, in accordance with integrated joint mobilization plans, for the expansion of the peacetime components of the Air Force to meet the needs of war.

The specific functions of the United States Air Force are:

1. To organize, train and equip air forces for:

a. Air operations including joint operations.

b. Gaining and maintaining general air supremacy.

c. Establishing local air superiority where and as required.

d. The strategic air force of the United States and strategic air reconnaissance.

e. Air lift and support for airborne operations.

f. Air support to land forces and naval forces, including support of occupation forces.

g. Air transport for the armed forces, except as provided by the Navy in accordance with paragraph 1 f, of Section III .

2. To develop weapons, tactics, technique, organization and equipment of Air Force combat and service elements, coordinating with the Army and Navy on all aspects of joint concern, including those which pertain to amphibious and airborne operations.

3. To provide, as directed by proper authority, such missions and detachments for service in foreign countries as may be required to support the national policies and interests of the United States.

4. To provide the means for coordination of air defense among all services.

5. To assist the Army and Navy in accomplishment of their missions, including the provision of common services and supplies as determined by proper authority.

HARRY S. TRUMAN

NOTE: The Executive order was issued following the President's signing, on the same day, of the act providing for a National Military Establishment (61 Stat. 495).

---

160   Memorandum of Disapproval of Bill To Amend the Interstate Commerce Act. *July 30, 1947*

I AM withholding my approval from the enrolled bill (H.R. 2331) "To amend section 20a of the Interstate Commerce Act."

Section 1 of this bill would amend the definition of "carrier" in section 20a of the Interstate Commerce Act, as amended, so as to include sleeping-car companies among the carriers whose financing is subject to approval by the Interstate Commerce Commission. There appears to be no reason why sleeping-car companies, which are common carriers subject to the Interstate Commerce Act, should not be regulated by the Commis-

sion in respect of their financing, and I find no objection to this section.

Section 2 of the bill, however, is highly objectionable in that it would facilitate banker control of railroads and would sanction a departure from the long-established policy against interlocking directorates.

Paragraph 12 of section 20a of the Interstate Commerce Act, as amended, now prohibits an officer or director of any carrier to receive for his own benefit, directly or indirectly, any money or thing of value in respect of the negotiation, hypothecation, or sale of any securities issued by such carrier, or to share in any of the proceeds thereof.

Section 2 of the bill here under consideration would provide an exception to this prohibition in regard to dealings in securities with another corporation, firm, partnership, or association, when the carrier shall have as officer or director any person who is at the same time a director, member, manager, or purchasing or selling officer of, or who has any substantial interest in, such other corporation, firm, partnership, or association, if such dealings shall be with the bidder whose bid is the most favorable to such carrier, to be ascertained by competitive bidding under regulations prescribed by rule or otherwise by the Interstate Commerce Commission, and if such participation is due solely to such officer's or director's relationship with such other corporation, firm, partnership, or association, and not to his relationship with such carrier.

It has been stated that one of the results of the existing law was to make it difficult or impossible for a railroad to award prospective security issues to banking or investment concerns with which some of its directors were connected and that since regulations now require that railroad securities be marketed as a general rule through competitive bidding, the restriction is unnecessary. It was the express purpose of existing law to make it difficult or impossible for railroads to deal with banking or investment companies with interlocking directorates and the requirement of competitive bidding is established, not by statute but by a recent Commission decision and is, therefore, subject to change at any time. Moreover, this bill would facilitate and encourage the banker control of railroads, which is the subject of complaint in an important government antitrust suit now pending against the railroads. The eradication of such control is sufficiently difficult, without the enactment of new legislation, to facilitate the establishment of such control. The evil of the kind of transactions here involved has long been recognized. It is merely one species of the general principle, recognized in the law governing the conduct of fiduciaries, that dealings in which both parties to the transaction are under common control, should be avoided. The companies on both sides of the transaction are entitled to arm's-length dealing by independent managements.

It is for the foregoing reasons that I am withholding my approval from the bill.

HARRY S. TRUMAN

---

161   Statement by the President Upon Approving Resolution Providing for Congressional Study of Aviation Problems. *July 30, 1947*

I HAVE today approved House Resolution 3587, providing for a study of United States aviation problems by the Congress. The act establishes a temporary Congressional Aviation Policy Board. This 10-man board, to be composed of 5 members of each House, will study such questions as the current and future needs of American aviation, including commercial air transportation and the utilization of aircraft by the armed services, and the nature, type, and extent of aircraft and air transportation industries that are desirable or essential to the national security and welfare.

The Congressional Board will also seek to find methods of encouraging needed developments in the aviation and air transportation industry, and will suggest improved organization and procedures of the Government designed to assist it in handling aviation matters efficiently and in the public interest.

I welcome the attention given by the Congress to our aviation problems, as evidenced by this act. A similar study was recently authorized by the executive branch, when I established a temporary Air Policy Commission, composed of private citizens, to assist me in formulating a national policy on aviation. The findings of the Air Policy Commission, which has been requested to submit its final recommendations by January 1, 1948, will be made available to the Congressional Aviation Policy Board, which will report to the Congress on March 1.

NOTE: As enacted, the House resolution is Public Law 287, 80th Congress (61 Stat. 676).

162   Memorandum of Disapproval of Bill Authorizing Commemorative Coins. *July 31, 1947*

I AM withholding my approval of H.R. 1180, "To authorize the coinage of 50-cent pieces in commemoration of the one-hundredth anniversary of the admission of Wisconsin into the Union as a State".

The proposed legislation would authorize the coinage of not to exceed five hundred thousand silver 50-cent pieces in commemoration of the one-hundredth anniversary of the admission of Wisconsin into the Union.

A year ago when I approved the legislation authorizing special coins honoring the late Booker T. Washington and the one-hundredth anniversary of the admission of Iowa into the Union, I stated that I would have preferred to approve legislation providing for commemorative medals and that in the future I would look with disfavor upon legislation authorizing the issuance of commemorative coins. My stand in this matter and the compelling reasons therefor were reiterated in a letter to the House Banking and Currency Committee on February 26, 1947.

I am well aware of the great accomplishments of the State of Wisconsin and its splendid citizens. My failure to approve the bill, H.R. 1180, should not be construed as a lack of appreciation of their contributions to the welfare of the United States. In withholding my approval of this bill, I am continuing the wise policy adopted by my predecessors, former President Hoover and the late President Franklin D. Roosevelt. This policy was given legislative sanction by the Congress when it enacted the Act of August 5, 1939, prohibiting the coinage of or the issuance of special commemorative coins authorized prior to March 1, 1939.

There are pending before the Congress 18 bills commemorating 12 events of importance in the history of our great country, all of which are well deserving of commemoration. In such a situation, it is evident that it is impossible to enact one bill and ignore all the others. Thus, the Senate has, at the session just closed, passed eight additional bills providing for commemorative coins.

Former President Hoover, in a message to the Congress vetoing a bill which would have authorized coins in commemoration of the 75th anniversary of the Gadsden Purchase, expressed very precisely the dilemma which confronts the Congress and the Chief Executive with reference to commemorative coin legislation. He said:

"There are a great many historical events

which it is not only highly proper but desirable to commemorate in a suitable way, but the longer use of our coins for this purpose is unsuitable and unwise. This would seem to be clear from the very number of events to be commemorated, and past experience indicates how difficult it is to draw the line and how such a practice, once it is recognized, tends constantly to grow. If this bill is to become law, it is not apparent on what grounds similar measures, no matter how numerous, may be rejected. Yet their enactment in such numbers must bring further confusion to our monetary system."

I have pointed out before that the multiplicity of designs on United States coins resulting from the coinage of commemorative coins tends to create confusion, to increase the possibility of counterfeiting, to encourage traffic in commemorative coins for private profit, and, in general, to detract from the fundamental purpose for which money is issued, namely, to provide a medium of exchange.

I take this opportunity to call attention again to my request of February 26, 1947, for the enactment of commemorative medal legislation. Such legislation was reported by the Senate Committee on Banking and Currency on March 10, 1947, and is still pending in the Senate. It is my hope that the Congress will enact such legislation at its next session in order to prevent abuses to, and to preserve the integrity of, the coinage system of the United States.

I regret the necessity of withholding my approval of H.R. 1180, and I take this action only because of the compelling reasons indicated above.

HARRY S. TRUMAN

163 Memorandum of Disapproval of Bill Relating to Refund of Taxes Illegally Paid by Indian Citizens. *July 31, 1947*

[Released July 31, 1947. Dated July 30, 1947]

I HAVE withheld my approval of H.R. 981, a bill "To amend section 2 of the Act of January 29, 1942 (56 Stat. 21), relating to the refund of taxes illegally paid by Indian citizens."

H.R. 981 would amend section 2 of the Act of January 29, 1942 (56 Stat. 21), to direct the refund of certain income taxes to Indians falling within designated classes who filed claims for refunds under that Act but whose claims were rejected. All claims for refund properly filed under the Act of January 29, 1942, relating to taxes illegally assessed upon the income of the Indians concerned, have been paid. The rejected claims which H.R. 981 would allow, related to legally collected taxes paid on income received during the taxable years from 1913

to April 26, 1931, the termination date for all restrictions on alienability and taxability of lands belonging to the affected Indians.

It has been clearly established by the courts that the Indians in question were fully taxable upon the income involved. Accordingly, the effect of H.R. 981 is to set up retroactively a period of exemption prior to 1931 when it is clear that the Indians concerned were taxable during that period. There appears to be no satisfactory reason why a particular group on whom taxes were legally assessed should be classified with other groups from whom taxes were collected illegally.

Another objectionable feature of the bill is the provision for the payment of interest at 4 per centum per annum for the years before and since 1931 when these persons had no claim, legal or equitable, to refund of the taxes paid. The amount of interest payable under the bill would almost equal the taxes. It would be unsound policy and an inadvisable precedent to provide for the payment of interest on these refunds of taxes which were legally and properly collected.

For these reasons, I have withheld my approval of the bill.

HARRY S. TRUMAN

164 Remarks to Reporters Following the Death of the President's Mother. *August 1, 1947*

THE PRESIDENT. I merely wanted to make a few remarks to you this morning. I couldn't hold a press conference this week, but I wanted to say to you personally a thing or two that I couldn't very well say any other way, so I asked Charlie[1] to ask you to come in.

I wanted to express to you all, and to your editors and your publishers, appreciation for the kindness to me during the last week.

I was particularly anxious to tell the photographers how nice they were to me, and to the family, and I didn't know any other way to do it but just call you in and tell you.

I had no news to give you, or anything else to say to you, except just that, and I felt like I owed it to you.

You have been exceedingly nice to me all during the whole business, and I hope you will believe it when I say to you that it is from the heart when I tell you that.

Q. Thank you, Mr. President.

NOTE: The President spoke in his office at the White House at 11:30 a.m. The meeting is carried in the White House Official Reporter's records as the President's one hundred and fourteenth news conference.

[1] Charles G. Ross, Secretary to the President.

165 Memorandum of Disapproval of Bill Reimbursing the District of Columbia for Expenses of U.S. Park Police. *August 5, 1947*

[Released August 5, 1947. Dated August 4, 1947]

I AM withholding my approval from H. R. 2471, an act "To provide for periodical reimbursement of the general fund of the District of Columbia for certain expenditures made for the compensation, uniforms, equipment, and other expenses of the United States Park Police force."

The purpose of the enrolled enactment is to require, beginning with the current fiscal year, the Director of the National Park Service, from sums appropriated from the general fund of the Treasury, for such purpose, to deposit in the general fund of the District of Columbia, within 30 days after the end of each quarter, an amount equal to the total amount expended during such quarter from sums appropriated from the general fund of the District of Columbia for the compensation, uniforms, equipment, and other expenses of the United States Park Police force.

In other words, the enrolled enactment contemplates two appropriations: one out of the general fund of the District of Columbia for the purpose of compensating, uniforming, and equipping the United States Park Police, and another out of the general fund of the Treasury for quarterly reimbursement to the general fund of the District, of the amount expended for this purpose from the District appropriation.

The Department of the Interior, in reporting to me upon this measure, expressed the view that the procedure set forth in the bill represents an unnecessary duplication of appropriations for expenditure for the purposes indicated, and thereby increases accounting and other costs.

Moreover, the provisions of the bill, in calling for quarterly reimbursement to the general fund of the District of Columbia from appropriations out of the general fund of the Treasury, would be ineffectual for the first one or two quarters of the fiscal year 1948, since no such appropriations have been made, and cannot be made until such time as the Congress shall have again assembled.

It seems to me that this is a matter to which the Congress might well and profitably give further consideration, including in its study the question of whether, in view of the Federal contribution to the District of Columbia, which has been increased for the present year from 8 to 12 million dollars, all or any part of the expenses of operating and maintaining the parks in the city of Washington should be paid from the general fund of the Treasury instead of, as at present, from the general fund of the District.

Under the circumstances, I feel constrained to withhold my approval of the bill.

HARRY S. TRUMAN

166 Letter to Governor Piñero of Puerto Rico Upon Signing Bill Providing for an Elected Governor. *August* 5, 1947

My dear Governor Piñero:

I have today signed the bill which will make the governorship of Puerto Rico an elected office, beginning in 1948. I consider it a great step toward complete self-government and I sincerely hope that the action of the Congress will meet with the approval of the people of Puerto Rico.

It is unfortunate, in my opinion, that the Congress did not enact the House version of the bill, which would have permitted the Governor to appoint the members of the Supreme Court of Puerto Rico. However, when the bill passed the Senate, the time of adjournment was so near that there was no opportunity for a conference. If the Senate amendment had not been accepted by the House of Representatives, no Puerto Rican bill would have been enacted at this session.

I am sure the people of Puerto Rico will prefer the bill as enacted to no bill at all. The essence of the bill, the provision for an elected governor, has been retained. Now that this momentous step forward has been taken, I am confident that it will be possible to secure a further amendment to the Organic Act at an early date, to empower the Governor to appoint the members of the Supreme Court.

Puerto Rico will be the first of the territorial areas under the jurisdiction of the United States whose chief executive and whose legislature are responsible to the electorate. Many years ago the Congress gave the Legislature of Puerto Rico legislative powers virtually as broad as those of the States, extending to almost all subjects of local legislation. Now the people of Puerto Rico, like the people of the States, will have a voice in the selection, not only of the men who make their laws, but also of the men who administer them. They will, more than ever before in their history, be managing their own affairs.

I send to the people of Puerto Rico my good wishes as they advance further along the road to self-government. I am certain that they will prove themselves worthy of the trust the Congress has placed in them.

Very sincerely yours,

HARRY S. TRUMAN

[The Honorable Jesús T. Piñero, Governor of Puerto Rico]

NOTE: The act providing for the governorship of Puerto Rico by election is Public Law 382, 80th Congress (61 Stat. 770).

---

167   Memorandum of Disapproval of Bill Repealing the Ship Warrants Act. *August* 6, 1947

I AM withholding my approval from the bill (H.R. 673) "To repeal certain provisions authorizing the establishing of priorities in transportation by merchant vessels."

The purpose of the bill is to repeal the Act of July 14, 1941 entitled "An Act to provide for priorites in transportation by merchant vessels in the interests of national defense, and for other purposes," as amended and extended (55 Stat. 591; 56 Stat. 371).

The Act in question, which was known as the Ship Warrants Act, authorized the War Shipping Administration to establish a system of ship warrants which became effective upon arrival by President Roosevelt on January 4, 1943. On June 6, 1946 the ship warrant rules and regulations were revoked and on July 25, 1947, the Act was repealed by Public Law No. 239.

Accordingly, this legislation is not necessary.

HARRY S. TRUMAN

---

168   Memorandum of Disapproval of Bill To Permit Part-Time Referees in Bankruptcy To Act for Claimants Against the United States. *August* 6, 1947

[Released August 6, 1947. Dated August 5, 1947]

I RETURN herewith, without my approval, the enrolled bill (H.R. 1810) "To amend the Criminal Code and certain other legislation to permit part-time referees in bankruptcy to act as agents or attorneys for claimants against the United States."

The bill, inter alia, exempts part-time referees in bankruptcy from the provisions of sections 109 and 113 of the Criminal Code (18 U.S.C. 198, 203).

Section 109 of the Criminal Code provides that whoever, being an officer of the United States, or a person holding any place of trust or profit, or discharging any official function under, or in connection with any executive department of the Government of the United States, or under the Senate or House of Representatives, shall act as an agent or attorney for prosecuting any claim against the United States, or receive any gratuity in consideration of having aided or assisted in the prosecution of such a claim, shall be fined not more than $5,000, or imprisoned not more than one year, or both.

Section 113 of the Criminal Code provides that any officer or employee of the United States who receives any compensation for representing a person before any governmental department or bureau shall be fined not more than $10,000 and imprisoned not more than two years, and shall thereafter be barred from holding any office of honor, trust, or profit under the Government of the United States.

Although it is believed that there would be relatively few, if any, officials who would intentionally abuse the privileges and powers of their positions, the foregoing provisions of the Criminal Code have been considered desirable as a deterrent to those few who might carelessly or through temptation besmirch the integrity of, and consequently undermine the public's respect for and confidence in, the Government. They also serve to discourage any undue influence which a government officer or employee might exert, intentionally or not, in representing a client before any of the various government departments, regardless of how remotely such representation may relate to the official duties of the officer or employee. In summary, the provisions are an assurance

that the Government will not sanction either the practice or the appearance of officials' or employees' taking improper advantage of their positions in the situations encompassed thereby.

It does not appear that sections 109 and 113 of the Criminal Code were intended to apply to any particular group or class of government personnel, but to all officers and employees in general who come within their provisions. There are doubtless many government officials and employees who would feel justified in seeking exemption from these provisions of law, on grounds as substantial as those which may be advanced by part-time referees in bankruptcy. If, however, the scope of the sections is narrowed by amendments to the point where there is an inference that only certain designated groups of officials are above error or reproach while others are not, the statutes may become less effective, as well as discriminatory and embarrassing.

It is for the foregoing reasons that I am constrained to withhold my approval from the bill.

HARRY S. TRUMAN

169   Memorandum of Disapproval of the National Science Foundation Bill.   *August 6, 1947*

I AM withholding my approval of S. 526, the National Science Foundation Bill.

I take this action with deep regret. On several occasions, I have urged the Congress to enact legislation to establish a National Science Foundation. Our national security and welfare require that we give direct support to basic scientific research and take steps to increase the number of trained scientists. I had hoped earnestly that the Congress would enact a bill to establish a suitable agency to stimulate and correlate

the activities of the Government directed toward these ends.

However, this bill contains provisions which represent such a marked departure from sound principles for the administration of public affairs that I cannot give it my approval. It would, in effect, vest the determination of vital national policies, the expenditure of large public funds, and the administration of important governmental functions in a group of individuals who would be essentially private citizens. The proposed National Science Foundation would be divorced from control by the people to an extent that implies a distinct lack of faith in democratic processes.

Moreover, the organization prescribed in the bill is so complex and unwieldy that there is grave danger that it would impede rather than promote the Government's efforts to encourage scientific research. The Government's expenditures for scientific research and development activities currently amount to hundreds of millions of dollars a year. Under present world conditions, this work is vital to our national welfare and security. We cannot afford to jeopardize it by imposing upon it an organization so likely to prove unworkable.

Under S. 526, the powers of the proposed Foundation would be vested in 24 members, appointed by the President by and with the advice and consent of the Senate. These members would be part time officials, required to meet only once each year. This group would, in turn, select biennially from among its 24 members an executive committee of 9 members and would exercise its powers through the executive committee. This 9 member executive committee would also be a part time body required to meet only six times a year.

The Foundation would have a chief executive officer, known as the Director. He would be appointed by the 9 member executive committee unless the 24 member body itself chose to appoint him. The power and duties of the Director would be prescribed by the executive committee and exercised under its supervision.

There would be within the Foundation a number of divisions, each exercising such duties and performing such functions as the Foundation prescribed. There would be no limit upon the number of divisions which the Foundation could establish. For each division there would be a divisional commit-

tee. In the case of the Committee for the Division of National Defense, there would be a limit of 36 members, half of whom would be appointed by the Foundation and half of whom would be representatives of the armed services. In other cases, there would be no limit upon the number of members of each divisional committee and all of the members would be appointed by the Foundation. Not only would these part time committees furnish advice and make recommendations concerning the Government's scientific research program, but each divisional committee would also "exercise and perform the powers and duties of its division".

The Foundation would also be empowered to appoint commissions in various fields of research. Three such commissions are specified in the bill, and the Foundation could appoint as many additional special commissions as it saw fit. Each such commission would consist of 6 eminent scientists and 5 members from the general public. After making a survey of public and private research already being carried on, each of these commissions would recommend a research program within its field and constantly review the manner in which such program was being carried out.

Apart from the conflicts and confusion which would result from this complex organization, the bill would violate basic principles which make for responsible government.

The Constitution places upon the President the responsibility for seeing that the laws are faithfully executed. In the administration of this law, however, he would be deprived of effective means for discharging his constitutional responsibility.

Full governmental authority and responsibility would be placed in 24 part time officers whom the President could not effectively hold responsible for proper administration. Neither could the Director be held responsible by the President, for he would be the appointee of the Foundation and would be insulated from the President by two layers of part time boards. In the case of the divisions and special commissions, the lack of accountability would be even more aggravated.

The members of the Foundation would also be authorized to appoint the full time administrative head of an important agency in the executive branch of the Government, as well as more than 70 additional part time officials in whom important governmental powers would be vested. This represents a substantial denial of the President's appointing power, as well as an impairment of his ability to see that the laws are faithfully executed.

The ability of the President to meet his constitutional responsibility would be further impaired by the provisions of the bill which would establish an Interdepartmental Committee on Science. The members of this committee would be representatives of departments and agencies who are responsible to the President, but its chairman would be the Director of the Foundation. It would be the duty of this committee to correlate data on all Federal scientific research activities and to make recommendations to the President, to the Foundation, and to the other departments and agencies of the Government concerning the performance of their functions in this field. Thus, an officer who is not appointed by the President, and not responsible to him, would be the man primarily charged with the performance of functions which are peculiarly within the scope of the President's duties—that is, the coordination of the work of executive agencies. This is especially unwise when the activities concerned are so intimately related to the national welfare and security.

There are other compelling reasons why control over the administration of this law should not be vested in the part time members of the Foundation. The Foundation would make grants of Federal funds to support scientific research. The recipients of these grants would be determined in the discretion of the Foundation. The qualifications prescribed in the bill for members of the Foundation would insure that most of them would be individuals employed by institutions or organizations eligible for the grants. Thus, there is created a conflict of interests which would inevitably give rise to suspicions of favoritism, regardless of the complete integrity of the members of the Foundation.

It is unfair to individuals asked to accept public office that they should be put in such a vulnerable position. Moreover, colleges and universities and other organizations seeking aid for scientific research deserve the assurance that the manner and extent of their participation in a national program will be determined on a completely impartial and objective basis.

Adherence to the principle that responsibility for the administration of the law should be vested in full time officers who can be held accountable will not prevent the Government from utilizing with great advantage the services of eminent scientists who are available only for part time duty. We have ample evidence of the patriotic and unselfish contributions which such citizens can make to the success of governmental programs. The role to be played by such part time participation, however, is more appropriately one of an advisory nature rather than of full responsibility. In other governmental programs of vast national importance, this method is used to obtain advice and recommendations from impartial experts as well as from parties in interest. There is no reason why such a system cannot be incorporated in legislation establishing a National Science Foundation.

For the reasons I have indicated, I believe that this bill raises basic issues of public policy. There would be no means for insuring responsible administration of the law. If the principles of this bill were extended throughout the Government, the result would be utter chaos. There is no justification in this case for casting aside sound principles for normal governmental operations. I cannot agree that our traditional, democratic form of government is incapable of properly administering a program for encouraging scientific research and education.

It is unfortunate that this legislation cannot be approved in its present form. The withholding of my signature at this time, however, will not prevent the Government from engaging in the support of scientific research. Research activities are carried on extensively by various executive agencies under existing laws, and would continue to be carried on whether or not this bill be-

came law. The only funds made available by the Congress for expenditure by the Foundation are funds which might be transferred from other agencies, thereby reducing the amounts which those other agencies could spend for similar purposes. No funds were made available for the scholarships and fellowships authorized in the bill. Thus, there would be no immediate gains which would justify accepting the risks involved in the approval of this legislation.

I am convinced that the long-range interests of scientific research and education will be best served by continuing our efforts to obtain a Science Foundation free from the vital defects of this bill. These defects in the structure of the proposed Foundation are so fundamental that it would not be practicable to permit its establishment in this form with the hope that the defects might be corrected at a later date. We must start with a law which is basically sound.

I hope that the Congress will reconsider this question and enact such a law early in its next session.

HARRY S. TRUMAN

---

170   Memorandum of Disapproval of Bill To Exclude Newspaper and Magazine Vendors From the Social Security System.
August 6, 1947

I AM withholding my approval of H.R. 3997, a bill "To exclude certain vendors of newspapers or magazines from certain provisions of the Social Security Act and Internal Revenue Code".

This bill proceeds in a direction which is exactly opposed to the one our Nation should pursue. It restricts and narrows coverage under our social security law, while our objective should be to enlarge that coverage. The strength, security and welfare of the entire Nation, as well as that of the groups

now excluded, demand an expanded social security system.

H.R. 3997 would remove social security protection from news vendors who make a full-time job of selling papers and who are dependent on that job for their livelihood. They and their families are exposed to the same risks of loss of income from old age, premature death, or unemployment as are factory hands or day laborers. They unquestionably fall in the group for whose protection our social security laws were devised.

Many, perhaps most, street vendors of newspapers are excluded even at present from coverage under the Social Security Act because they are independent contractors rather than employees of the publishers whose papers they sell. But some vendors work under arrangements which make them bona-fide employees of the publishers and, consequently, are entitled to the benefits of the Social Security Act. The standards used for determining whether or not the employer–employee relationship exists are the same in the newspaper business as they are in other enterprises. There is no justification for changing these standards so as to discriminate against employees in this particular industry.

It is said that the publishers have difficulty in keeping the necessary records and in collecting the employee contributions required by the social security system. In those cases where the vendors are so closely associated with the paper as to be its employees, the difficulties are no greater than those confronting many other employers of outside salesmen, or indeed employers of other kinds of labor. Certainly, it has not been shown that these difficulties are so formidable as to warrant a special rule of exclusion and the consequent destruction of benefit rights of insured persons and their dependents.

H.R. 3997 would invite other employers to seek exemptions whenever they can allege that the law is inconvenient or difficult for them to comply with. It would establish a precedent for special exemption, and the exclusion of one group would lead to efforts to remove social security protection from workers in other activities. Demands for further special legislation would be inevitable.

We must not open our social security structure to piece-meal attack and to slow undermining. We must, instead, devote our energies to expanding and strengthening that system.

HARRY S. TRUMAN

---

171   Memorandum of Disapproval of Bill Relating to Garbage Originating Outside the Continental United States. *August 7, 1947*

I HAVE withheld my approval from HR 597, "To protect American agriculture, horticulture, livestock, and the public health by prohibiting the unauthorized importation into, or the depositing in the territorial waters of, the United States of garbage derived from products originating outside of the continental United States, and for other purposes", for the following reasons:

1. In section 1(6) it is provided that the term "United States" when not limited by the adjective "continental", includes all territories and possessions of the United States, "with the exception of the Philippine Islands and the Canal Zone". The reference to the Philippine Islands as a territory or possession of the United States, however inadvertently used, would be seriously embarrassing to this Government in its relations with the Republic of the Philippines, which became a sovereign nation on July 4, 1946.

2. In section 2(a) it is prohibited and made unlawful to throw, discharge, or deposit garbage, or to cause, suffer or procure garbage to be thrown, discharged, or deposited, from any vessel, railway car, air-

craft, or other vehicle entering the United States into any territorial waters of the United States *"unless such garbage has been reduced to fluid form"*. This provision seems inadequate to prevent the placing in our territorial waters of garbage which is infected with human or animal diseases. It is necessary in addition to require that such garbage shall be disinfected prior to its discharge into our territorial waters. This requirement is of importance on account of the situation existing in the Canadian boundary waters, especially in the Great Lakes region, since such waters are used for human consumption. Under dates of April 1 and October 3, 1946, Canada and the United States submitted joint references to the International Joint Commission—United States and Canada, to consider measures for the suppression of the pollution of boundary waters consisting of the St. Marys River, St. Clair River, Lake St. Clair and the Detroit River. In connection with this investigation, it has been reported to me that measures may be taken to prevent the dumping of garbage from ships in the vicinity of the intakes of water systems. Such proceedings might be taken under the provision of section 13 of the Act of March 3, 1899 (30 Stat. 1152; 33 U.S.C. 407).

3. By section 9 of the proposed legislation it is provided that nothing contained in section 13 of the Act of March 3, 1899 shall be construed as forbidding the discharge of fluid garbage into the territorial waters of the United States. This provision would remove the legislation whereby proceedings could be instituted against persons dumping infected garbage into Canadian boundary waters although it had been reduced to a fluid state.

HARRY S. TRUMAN

172   Memorandum of Disapproval of Bill for the Construction of a Bridge Across the St. Lawrence River. *August 7*, 1947

I HAVE withheld my approval from H.R. 3332, a bill entitled "An Act creating the Saint Lawrence Bridge Commission and authorizing said Commission and its successors to construct, maintain, and operate a bridge across the Saint Lawrence River at or near Ogdensburg, New York."

A very similar bill was passed during the 73rd Congress and approved June 14, 1933 (48 Stat. 141), which created the Saint Lawrence Bridge Commission with authority to construct, maintain, and operate a bridge across the Saint Lawrence River at or near Ogdensburg. Section 4 of that Act contained, among other provisions, the following:

"The bridge constructed under the authority of this Act shall be deemed to be an instrumentality for international commerce authorized by the Government of the United States, and said bridge and ferry or ferries and the bonds issued in connection therewith and the income derived therefrom shall be exempt from all Federal, State, municipal, and local taxation."

The bridge has not been constructed under the authority granted by said Act, but during the years subsequent to 1933 acts were passed by the Congress and approved to extend the times for commencing and completing its construction, the last such act having been approved October 16, 1945. In the meantime, however, the policy was adopted by the Executive and Legislative Branches of the Government that legislation of this nature should contain no provision exempting the facilities constructed pursuant thereto or the obligations created to meet the cost thereof or the revenues derived therefrom from taxation. It was recognized that the matter of exempting such facilities and obligations created to defray the cost of their construction from State taxation should be a matter for determination by the States in which the facilities might be located, and not by the Federal Government. It was further recognized that the Federal Government should not provide exemption from Federal taxes to facilities of this class and to income derived from their operation and from obligations issued and outstanding to cover the cost of constructing such facilities any more than it should provide such exemption to other classes of facilities. Pursuant to this policy, a number of bills enacted by the Congress with tax exemption provisions therein were vetoed by the President, and when in 1940 a bill (H.R. 9411) was enacted and approved June 8, 1940 (54 Stat. 259), to further extend the times for commencing and completing the proposed bridge at Ogdensburg it provided for repeal of the above quoted provision from section 4 of the Act of June 14, 1933, and inserted in lieu thereof the following:

"The bridge hereby authorized or the income therefrom shall be subject to Federal, State, municipal, or local taxation only to the extent that a like structure or the income therefrom owned and operated by public authority or public agency of the State of New York shall be subject to taxation. The bonds or obligations of the Commission, from time to time outstanding, and the income derived therefrom shall be subject to taxation in the hands of the holders thereof."

The effect of the bill now before me, except for certain changes to which no objection is made, would be to reenact as new legislation the Act as originally approved June 14, 1933, including the objectionable tax exemption provision. I, therefore, do not feel that I can give it my approval. However, I am not otherwise opposed to legislation to authorize the construction of a bridge across the Saint Lawrence River at Ogdensburg.

HARRY S. TRUMAN

---

173 Statement by the President on the New Housing and Home Finance Agency. *August 7, 1947*

REORGANIZATION PLAN No. 3 of 1947, recently approved by the Senate, groups all the principal permanent housing agencies and functions of the Government, and the remaining emergency housing activities, in a Housing and Home Finance Agency. Under this new overall agency, as constituent parts of it, are the following: A Home Loan Bank Board to administer the Federal Savings and Loan Insurance Corporation, the Home Owners' Loan Corporation, and the functions of the Federal Home Loan Bank Board and its members; a Federal Housing Administration with the same functions as now provided by law for that agency; and a Public Housing Administration to take over the functions of the United States Housing Authority and certain remaining emergency housing activities that are being liquidated. Each constituent agency will have its own identity and be responsible for the operation of its program. There is also included a National Housing Council made up of representatives of agencies that are not direct constituents.

I have today made the following recess appointments in accordance with provisions of Reorganization Plan No. 3:

Administrator, Housing and Home Finance Agency—Raymond M. Foley of Michigan.

Commissioner, Federal Housing Administration—Franklin D. Richards of Utah.

Commissioner, Public Housing Administration—Dillon S. Myer of Ohio.

Chairman of the Home Loan Bank Board (term ending June 30, 1949)—John H. Fahey of Massachusetts.

Member of the Home Loan Bank Board (term ending June 30, 1951)—Nathaniel Dyke, Jr. of Arkansas (Democrat).

Member of the Home Loan Bank Board (term ending June 30, 1950)—J. Alston Adams of New Jersey (Republican).

I have said on numerous occasions that the primary responsibility for meeting the Nation's housing needs rests, and must continue to rest, with private industry. But the Federal Government also has the responsibility of assisting and stimulating the efforts of private industry to provide much-needed homes.

The building of sufficient low-cost homes to house our citizens adequately must be one of our most important objectives during the coming 10 years. It is a national problem, and can be solved only through a nationally integrated plan. It is for this reason that I drafted a plan which provided for the integration of the housing functions of the Federal Government into one agency. For the same reason, I have appointed to head the Housing and Home Finance Agency and its constituent agencies, as promptly as possible after approval of the Reorganization Plan, men of imagination, experience, and proved ability in the housing field.

The Federal Government now has a permanent and an effective housing organization to coordinate and supervise the administration of its major housing programs. If the Congress early in its next session enacts the nonpartisan housing program which it has long been considering, the Nation will be well equipped to meet and solve its pressing problem of providing decent homes at low cost for the majority of the American people.

174   The President's News Conference of *August 7, 1947*

THE PRESIDENT. [1.] I have a few announcements to make. I appointed Roy W. Harper of Missouri to be United States District Judge for the Eastern and Western Districts of Missouri today, in the place of Caskie Collet.

I appointed as Director of the Federal Mediation and Conciliation Service, Cyrus S. Ching of New York, who is widely recognized as an authority on labor relations.

The Housing Reorganization Plan No. 3 Administrator, Housing and Home Finance Agency: Raymond M. Foley of Michigan.

Commissioner of Federal Housing Administration: Franklin D. Richards of Utah.

Commissioner of Public Housing Administration: Dillon S. Myer of Ohio.

Chairman of the Home Loan Bank Board, term ending June 30, 1949: John H. Fahey of Massachusetts.

Member of the Home Loan Bank Board, term ending June 30, 1951: Nathaniel Dyke, Jr., of Arkansas, Democrat.

Member of the Home Loan Bank Board, term ending June 30, 1950: J. Alston Adams of New Jersey, Republican.

Q. I hope all those are mimeographed!

THE PRESIDENT. It's all mimeographed and tells the life history of each one of them, and a statement on the whole situation, which will be handed to you as you go out, and will answer all your questions in regard to the Home Loan Bank situation.

[2.] Q. Mr. President, what is your estimate of the savings effected by the last Congress?

THE PRESIDENT. Well, I asked the Budget Director for—to prepare me an outline of the situation, and here is the situation as it is now. I will read you it, then you will get the mimeographed copies too:

"In fairness to all concerned, I do not intend to make any hasty predictions on the amount of so-called 'savings' effected by the Congress in the 1948 budget until all the facts are in.

"A great many complex factors have to be taken into consideration before a complete, accurate, and understandable report can be made. In some cases, Congress has substituted contract authority for direct appropriations; in others, appropriations originally requested for the fiscal year 1947 were not enacted until 1948 and so must be considered as part of this fiscal year.

"In addition, Congress has provided funds for certain agencies, such as the Post Office and the National Labor Relations Board, on a 'part year' basis and instructed agencies to request deficiencies, if necessary, to complete the fiscal year.

"Among the other facts to be determined is the actual effect of rescissions upon expenditures during this fiscal year, since a large part of the rescissions made by Congress were in funds which would not have been spent anyway.

"What is most important, however, is the fact that none of the predictions I have seen have properly related congressional changes

in appropriations to estimated expenditures for 1948. In the last analysis, the American people are more interested in how much their Government will actually spend during this fiscal year than they are in shifts and changes in the appropriation structure.

"For these reasons, I have ordered a detailed and exhaustive study of all the facts. When this is completed, I shall issue a review and analysis, supported by detailed tables and summaries, which will bring up to date revised estimates of receipts and expenditures for this fiscal year."

And I will have no further comment to make on the budget until I have all the facts before me so I can understand them, and so you can understand them.

[3.] Q. Mr. President, what happens to Judge Collet?

THE PRESIDENT. Judge Collet is on the Court of Appeals.

Q. He is going to stay there then?

THE PRESIDENT. He was appointed. He was appointed to that job. That is the reason for the vacancy.

Q. He was confirmed, wasn't he?

THE PRESIDENT. He was confirmed.

Q. Eighth Circuit——

Q. Mr. President, isn't Ching director of labor relations for U. S. Rubber?

THE PRESIDENT. Yes.

Q. Thank you.

THE PRESIDENT. You'll have all the facts on it when you get to your mimeographed copies.

[4.] Q. Mr. President, do you have any more details on the Rio trip?

THE PRESIDENT. No. I have said all I had to say when that statement was given out. When further details are out, I will keep you informed.

[5.] Q. Mr. President, will the nomination of Harper be sent to the Senate again?

THE PRESIDENT. It will.

Q. That is an interim appointment, isn't it?

Q. Will he serve until——

THE PRESIDENT. Interim appointment. I beg your pardon?

Q. The Harper nomination again, will he serve until confirmed? Is it a recess appointment?

THE PRESIDENT. It is a recess appointment. He will serve until he is confirmed.

Q. That is a roving judgeship isn't it—commonly known—serve the big——

THE PRESIDENT. He can serve in either end of the State, in either one of the Eastern or Western Districts of the State of Missouri.

[6.] Q. Mr. President, what comment do you have on the British financial and political crisis?

THE PRESIDENT. None whatever.

[7.] Q. Mr. President, in connection with this Rio trip, are you considering any trip here in the United States—by train—across the——

THE PRESIDENT. No, I am not. None has ever been under consideration.

Q. This year or next year?

THE PRESIDENT. This year. [*Laughter*]

Q. Do you have any weekend travel plans?

THE PRESIDENT. Well, they will come up as is necessary. Whenever I feel like going anywhere over a weekend I shall go, and when I go I will let you know so some of you fellows can go along, if you want to. [*Laughter*]

Q. Mr. President, can you—can you say at this time whether or not the plan is for you to address the conference at Rio on your trip there?

THE PRESIDENT. No I can't. I am—just as soon as I know all the details I will inform you right away.

Q. Do you expect your family to go with you?

THE PRESIDENT. I hope they will go. They have been asked to go.

[8.] Q. Mr. President, do you have any comment on what your old committee is doing up on Capitol Hill?

THE PRESIDENT. No comment whatever.

Q. What was that question, Mr. President?

THE PRESIDENT. He wanted to know if I have had any—heard anything from my old committee.

[9.] Q. What did Mayor O'Dwyer have on his mind this morning, Mr. President?

THE PRESIDENT. He wanted to discuss with me that—the tunnel situation between the Battery and Brooklyn. There is some financial situation in which the Reconstruction Finance Corporation is interested, and he is talking to the Reconstruction Finance Corporation this afternoon.

[10.] Q. Mr. President, the British foreign minister—the Egyptian foreign minister said last week, after he spoke to you, that you had been rather sympathetic to his conference with you, concerning his plea before the United Nations to withdraw the British from Egypt.

THE PRESIDENT. I have no comment. No comment.

Reporter: Thank you, Mr. President.

THE PRESIDENT. You're welcome.

NOTE: President Truman's one hundred and fifteenth news conference was held in his office at the White House at 4:02 p.m. on Thursday, August 7, 1947.

175 Memorandum of Disapproval of Bill To Continue Certain Mining Subsidies. *August 8*, 1947

I AM withholding approval of H.R. 1602, a bill "To stimulate exploration, development, and production from domestic mines by private enterprise, and for other purposes".

I am taking this action only after the most careful consideration of its effect upon the mining industries directly concerned and its relation to the general interests of the public.

This bill would require the Reconstruction Finance Corporation to continue to make premium payments to subsidize high-cost production of copper, lead and zinc and would provide new subsidies for domestic manganese production. Payments of $70,-000,000 would be authorized for the two-year period ending June 30, 1949, with not to exceed $35,000,000 of this available in the fiscal year 1948.

The premium price plan was initiated early in the war. It was effective in stimulating production of non-ferrous metals for war purposes, while maintaining price ceilings at prewar levels. Two years ago in signing Public Law 88 of the 79th Congress, authorizing continuance of these and other wartime subsidies, I urged that these programs be reduced or discontinued as rapidly as feasible whenever such payments became no longer necessary for war purposes.[1] With the end of hostilities and the decontrol of prices, almost all other wartime subsidy programs have been discontinued. No adequate reason is apparent for continuing to subsidize the output of copper, lead and zinc; and even less reason exists for adding to the list of subsidized commodities.

Continuance of the present plan would contribute very little, if at all, to production of the metals now in shortest supply. Since the removal of price ceilings, prices of all these metals have risen sharply. The market prices of copper and lead, the two scarcest of these metals, have been high enough in the last six months so that only a negligible share of the total output has been eligible for subsidy payments. With the minor exception of payments for exploration and development work, therefore, continuance of the present plan could not materially increase the supply of these metals. If the plan were restored, the great bulk of the subsidy payments, in fact, would continue to go for high-cost production of zinc, the supply of which is becoming relatively ample. Similarly, the industrial demand for manganese does not now justify subsidy payments to make available a relatively minor increase in low-grade domestic ore.

Even if there were sufficient justification for continuing to subsidize production of these metals, the plan provided in this bill would be too inflexible to meet present needs. Since it was specifically designed to meet wartime needs, the largest amounts of subsidies were authorized for production of zinc and copper, the metals then in shortest supply. Now, lead is the scarcest of these three metals and zinc is in relatively adequate supply. Yet this bill would not permit any major revisions in payments to shift the emphasis from zinc to copper and lead production. If it were to become law, the taxpayer would be subsidizing primarily zinc production, and the benefits to lead and copper production would be of minor significance.

Most important, continuation of this wartime subsidy program would conflict with our long-run peacetime objective of conserv-

---

[1] See 1945 volume, this series, Item 65.

ing domestic mineral resources. While the provisions of the bill would encourage exploration and development of new ore bodies, other more efficient methods would be preferable—methods which do not inevitably involve the premature exhaustion of the newly discovered reserves. It is particularly shortsighted in time of peace to continue to encourage extraction of metal from previously produced dumps and tailings instead of allowing these to remain available for future emergencies.

H.R. 1602 would authorize $35,000,000 in subsidy payments in both the present fiscal year and the fiscal year 1949. The bill, however, would provide subsidy payments at rates which would probably require even larger amounts than those authorized, especially in the event of a decline in market prices of any one or more of these metals. Accordingly, supplemental authorizations might well be necessary to carry out the provisions of the bill. In the present fiscal situation, neither the expenditures specifically authorized by the bill nor such possible additional expenditures appear justified.

I am not unmindful of the dislocations in the mining industry which are caused by the expiration of the premium price plan. We must all agree, however, that we cannot regard this plan as a permanent part of our economy. It is clear that the changes in employment and other adjustments which are necessary at the time of the plan's termination, whenever it occurs, can be made more readily and with less hardship in a period of high employment and business activity, such as the present, than at any other time. Consequently, this seems to be the best time for making this inevitable postwar adjustment.

HARRY S. TRUMAN

176 Statement by the President Upon Approving Resolution Continuing Regulation of Consumer Credit. *August* 8, 1947

I HAVE today approved the joint resolution of Congress (S.J. Res. 148) authorizing continuation of regulation of consumer installment credit until November 1, 1947. I regret that the Congress did not see fit to follow the recommendation of the Federal Reserve Board and of the Council of Economic Advisers, in which I fully concurred, by enacting legislation to provide for continuing as long as necessary regulation of consumer credit as a means of helping to promote economic stability. It is unfortunate that the Congress did not provide for restraints on overexpansion of installment credit in order to diminish inflationary pressures arising from this source.

Continuation for the next 3 months of present controls, as now provided under Regulation W of the Federal Reserve Board, has, however, been permitted and implied by the Congress and this is preferable to immediate abandonment of these restraints. For that reason I have signed the joint resolution.

Not only during the next 3 months while the controls remain in full force and effect but for an indefinite period thereafter, it will be in the public interest for every merchant and financial agency extending installment credit to avoid undue relaxation of terms. It will be far better to reduce prices rather than to relax terms in seeking new customers. Self-restraint on the part of those who use credit as well as upon the part of those who extend it will reduce the danger of an overexpansion of installment credit

which would inevitably be followed by severe contraction, thereby contributing to unemployment and to reduced production.

NOTE: As enacted, S.J. Res. 148 is Public Law 386,
80th Congress (61 Stat. 921). For Regulation W
see 12 CFR, 1947 Supp., Part 222.

177 The President's News Conference of August 14, 1947

THE PRESIDENT. I have no announcements to
make this morning, but I thought maybe
you might have some questions you might
want to ask me, and I would let you come
in and do it.

[1.] Q. Mr. President, have you expressed yourself to the Democratic Committee on the site for the Democratic
convention?

THE PRESIDENT. No I haven't. That is a
matter for the Democratic Committee to
decide.

Q. Mr. President, have you expressed
yourself on the Chairmanship?

THE PRESIDENT. No I haven't. That is
still another matter for the Committee to
decide.

[2.] Q. Has Senator Mead been in with
any new postage stamp designs? [*Laughter*]

THE PRESIDENT. No, not that I know of.

[3.] Q. Mr. President, do you favor the
St. Lawrence waterway development?

THE PRESIDENT. Did you read my message
to Congress?

Q. I just wanted to see if you had some
new comment on it?

THE PRESIDENT. No new comment, no.
The message speaks for itself.[1] Of course
I favor it. I have been in favor of it for
14 years, that is, since I came to the Senate.

[4.] Q. Mr. President, particularly in
view of the British-American loan conferences next Monday, will you comment on
the British economic situation?

[1] See 1945 volume, this series, Item 155.

THE PRESIDENT. I have no comment about
it.

[5.] Q. Mr. President, when will Secretary Forrestal take the oath as your——

THE PRESIDENT. As soon as he gets through
with the—winds up the situation in the
Navy. That is—I suppose some time soon.
Whenever he is ready to—he is going to take
the oath. I will let you know whenever the
matter takes place.

Q. That actually puts unification into
effect?

THE PRESIDENT. That's right—that's right.
I may have some announcements to make to
you on those at the next press conference.
I can't make any today.

Q. That is relative to appointments, Mr.
President?

THE PRESIDENT. Yes.

[6.] Q. Mr. President, in view of the
poor crop outlook of corn, is there anything
under study to cut the export program, or
to meet that situation?

THE PRESIDENT. The Food Committee of
the Cabinet has had that in line and is
working on it now.

[7.] Q. Mr. President, have you anything to add to the high-price investigation——

THE PRESIDENT. No, I have nothing to add
to it. I hope it will obtain some results,
and I think probably it will. I am wholeheartedly in favor of it.

Q. Mr. President, may I ask you to have
him read that question again?

THE PRESIDENT. On what?

Q. Investigation of high prices?

Mr. Romagna: "Mr. President, have you anything to add to the high-price investigation"——

Q. Oh yes.

THE PRESIDENT. That's the investigation of high prices, not the high-price investigation! [*Laughter*]

Q. Mr. President, do you think that the Attorney General's investigation can actually check the rise of prices, or will it merely point the finger as to who is responsible for it?

THE PRESIDENT. I think the second part of your question is probably what would happen.

Q. That that in itself would probably not check——

THE PRESIDENT. Have to wait and see what the results would be.

Q. Mr. President, do you believe that it's the violations of the Sherman Anti-Trust law that are responsible for high prices?

THE PRESIDENT. I can't answer that until the investigation has found the answer. That is what the investigation is for.

[8.] Q. Mr. President, have you any comment on the state of the world 2 years after V–J Day?

THE PRESIDENT. Well, I was thinking when the press conference was called that it was—accidentally happened to be on the anniversary of the surrender of the Japanese. I think the announcement was made to you, as I remember, about 7 o'clock in the afternoon, and I had anticipated at that time that we would have arrived at a peaceful settlement of affairs in the world. I regret to say that we have not arrived at that situation. I am still hopeful that we will have peace in the world that will be for the benefit of all the peoples of the world, as I stated, I think, in my V–J Day announcement.

[9.] Q. Mr. President, there has been a lot of afterthinking, and recently Colonel Fellers, who was a brigadier general under MacArthur out there, had a piece in which he insisted that the dropping of the atomic bomb was unnecessary, that the war had been won before that time.

THE PRESIDENT. When I was going to school we were discussing the battle of Gettysburg, and a very bright young man got up and stated the maneuvers that should have been made by General Lee and those that should have been made by General Meade, in order to make a complete victory at that point. And the old professor made the statement that any schoolboy's afterthought is worth more than all the generals' forethought. And that is true in the case you state. [*Laughter*]

Q. So far as you are concerned, you have never had any doubt that it was necessary?

THE PRESIDENT. I have never had any doubt that it was necessary, and I didn't have any doubt at the time. I hated very much to have to make that decision. Anybody would. But I thought that decision was made in the interest of saving about 250,000 American boys from getting killed, and I still think that was true.

[10.] Q. Mr. President, would you be in favor of Secretary Anderson for Democratic National Chairman, if Mr. Hannegan doesn't stay on?

THE PRESIDENT. Well now, Tony,[1] I can't answer a question like that. [*Laughter*] The next time the Democratic Committee meets, they will probably decide on a chairman. I think very highly of Secretary Anderson, of course, but I am not naming him as Chairman of the Committee, Tony. A trick question like that! [*More laughter*]

Q. I just wanted to clarify my thinking.

THE PRESIDENT. That's all right, Tony. [*To another reporter*] Go ahead.

Q. Could I ask this? Mr. President, there has been a report that if Mr. Anderson does

---

[1] Ernest B. Vaccaro of the Associated Press.

make that move, you are going to appoint Roy Thompson as Secretary of Agriculture. Any idea——

THE PRESIDENT. That's the first I've heard of that. There is no vacancy in the Department of Agriculture yet.

[11.] Q. Mr. President, can you comment on the British political and financial situation?

THE PRESIDENT. I have no comment.

Q. How about these conferees coming on Monday?

THE PRESIDENT. I have no comment.

[12.] Q. Mr. President, do you have any comment on the CIO request that you call a conference of management and labor and industry to discuss rolling back prices?

THE PRESIDENT. I have no comment on that. I made an attempt at that in November 1945. It was not successful.

[13.] Q. Mr. President, do you foresee success of the Rio conference which opens tomorrow?

THE PRESIDENT. I certainly do. I made that statement, I think, to General Marshall yesterday.

[14.] Q. Mr. President, do you see any circumstances between now and, say, Christmas such as to change your opinion that a special session might not be necessary?

THE PRESIDENT. Nothing on the horizon at the present time.

[15.] Q. Any further details on the Rio trip, Mr. President?

THE PRESIDENT. No, I can't give you any details yet. As soon as I can, why I will furnish you with all the details.

Q. Learning any Portuguese or Spanish?

THE PRESIDENT. I don't know either Portuguese or Spanish, so it won't be necessary, any such comment as that.

Q. Mr. President, when you go to Brazil, is there any plan for you to meet the Presidents of any other countries except the President of Brazil?

THE PRESIDENT. No.

[16.] Q. Mr. President, are you giving any consideration to possible transfer of the Unemployment Compensation Division to the Labor Department?

THE PRESIDENT. Yes, I have been giving it a lot of consideration right along.

Q. Get the USES and the Unemployment Compensation Division together in one place?

THE PRESIDENT. They should be in one place, undoubtedly.

Q. To rebuild the Labor Department?

THE PRESIDENT. Well, we will rebuild the Labor Department, don't worry about that. It can't be torn—permanently torn up any more than any other Department can.

Q. Do you think it is sort of torn up at the moment?

THE PRESIDENT. Yes I do. Yes I do. I think that is one of the accomplishments of the last Congress. [*Laughter*]

Q. Mr. President, I notice that one of the 1944 Republican platforms was to take all the—put under the Secretary of Labor once again, they said, all the labor and independent agencies. That is correct?

THE PRESIDENT. That's the Republican platform. I can give you the chapter and verse, if you want it.

Q. Have you any comment on that?

THE PRESIDENT. None. None whatever. It speaks for itself.

[17.] Q. Mr. President, would you favor a west coast city for the National Convention?

THE PRESIDENT. I will be in favor of any city that the National Democratic Committee decides upon.

[18.] Q. Mr. President, have you got those supplemental budget estimates in view of the Congress appropriations?

THE PRESIDENT. I will have that information ready for you, I hope, inside of the next 10 or 15 days, and I will furnish it to you.

It isn't ready yet.

Q. Will you announce it, or the Budget Director?

THE PRESIDENT. The Budget Director, in all probability, will make his report to me, and I will announce it to you.

Q. Mr. President—what was that, Mr. President? We were a little bit behind.

THE PRESIDENT. On the budget figures, as to estimates. I made the statement sometime—I think at the last press conference or the one before that, that as soon as we could get the figures together, I would tell you exactly what happened so you could understand and so I could understand them.

Q. Mr. President, in that connection, the Budget Director is reported to have sent a message to the departments saying that the—referring to the 1949 estimates in terms of rigid economy. I wonder if that was done on your direction?

THE PRESIDENT. Yes, those are the same instructions that were given the departments last year. Just a repeat.

[19.] Q. I hate to ask you to repeat again that little description you had about the afterthought. What was it that the teacher said to you?

THE PRESIDENT. The teacher said to me that any schoolboy's afterthought is worth more than all the greatest generals' forethought.

Q. I see. Thank you.

[20.] Q. Mr. President, in connection with your statement on the failure of peace 2 years after the end of the war, I wonder if you would care to elaborate on what is holding up peace, what might be done about it?

THE PRESIDENT. I don't think I should elaborate on that, because we are trying to get the peace, and I don't think any comment I made at this time would be helpful in that direction.

[21.] Q. Mr. President, do you have any comment on the present status of the old Truman committee? [*Laughter*]

THE PRESIDENT. No, I have not. The Truman committee passed out when I resigned. It's another committee.

[22.] Q. Mr. President, will you have any budget figures in the next 10 or 15 days for some estimates on potential outlays under the so-called Marshall plan?

THE PRESIDENT. No, no, we can't figure any potential estimates of that until we have finished the surveys which are now being needed for that purpose. The Paris conference will have one side of it, and our own economic setup which they—which I sent up for the purpose will give us the other. Then I will give you the facts and figures as soon as I have them.

Q. Then would those—would that midyear revision then have to be revised some time later in the year on the basis of whatever outlays will have to be made for Europe?

THE PRESIDENT. I don't understand your question. You will have to make it a little clearer.

Q. Well, the midyear estimates usually mean a pretty firm set of figures for the balance of the year. If the Marshall plan figures can't be included, will there be a real set of figures to show an overall picture of the effect of the European part of it on our budget?

THE PRESIDENT. Well, when the Marshall plan figures are ready, of course they will have an effect on the budget, but I don't think there is any midyear estimate that is contemplated to be made now.

Q. In that connection, Mr. President, does the United States—is the United States taking any notice of the clamor on the part of Western Hemisphere nations for a Marshall plan, as it were, of their own?

THE PRESIDENT. Well, I think there has always been a Marshall plan in effect for the

Western Hemisphere. The foreign policy of the United States in that direction has been set for one hundred years, known as the Monroe Doctrine.

[23.] Q. Mr. President, is it true that you really laid the law down to the new members of the NLRB, and made it clear to them that they are members of the executive department rather than——

THE PRESIDENT. We discussed the situation, and I find that—I found that they were

in the same frame of mind that I am, that they are a branch of the executive department of the Government. We have no argument on the subject, and I didn't have to lay any law down.

Reporter: Thank you, Mr. President.

THE PRESIDENT. You're welcome.

NOTE: President Truman's one hundred and sixteenth news conference was held in his office at the White House at 10:30 a.m. on Thursday, August 14, 1947.

---

178 Statement by the President on Myron C. Taylor's Mission to the Vatican. *August 15, 1947*

AT MY REQUEST the Honorable Myron C. Taylor is proceeding to Rome as my personal representative for further exchanges of views with His Holiness Pope Pius XII, on problems relative to the establishment of peace under a moral world order and to the alleviation of the human suffering still continuing in many parts of the world. Mr. Taylor has also been asked to hold conversations with other leaders on similar problems while he is in Europe.

The purpose of these further conversations, as on earlier occasions, is to gather for my guidance and assistance various views and impressions concerning existing conditions affecting peace and the relief of distress, and to obtain the energetic cooperation of all men and women of good will, whether

in religion, in government, or in other activities of life, in the interest of progress toward solution of these problems.

I am seeking by this means a greater clarification of the nature of the vital tasks that confront each of the nations that have pledged themselves to cooperate in the establishment and maintenance of international peace and security and to promote economic and social advancement. I wish to have the benefit of the constructive views and suggestions of leaders everywhere, to the end that the thought and action of the United States as to world affairs may contribute to that moral world order of peace and security and well-being for which we and the other United Nations struggled to victory in World War II.

---

179 Citation Accompanying Medal for Merit Awarded to David K. Niles. *August 20, 1947*

CITATION TO ACCOMPANY THE AWARD OF

THE MEDAL FOR MERIT

TO

DAVID K. NILES

DAVID K. NILES, for exceptionally meritorious conduct in the performance of out-

standing services to the United States. Mr. Niles, as Adviser on labor problems to the War Production Board, with his immediate perception and keen insight into the complex labor-management problems which were created by a wartime economy, aided immeasurably in uniting both labor and management in the collaborative production of the weapons of war. In this task he won the full confidence and high regard of all those with whom he dealt by the display of an essential fairness and desire to understand and reconcile the problems of worker and employer, and by communicating to them his own zeal in the American principle of democratic action. His numerous contributions in this important field strengthened and vitalized the spirit of war workers and

their employers on the home front in forging the bond with the fighting front which made victory possible. He gave unstintingly of his time and efforts, and handled all of his assignments with finesse and dexterity. Mr. Niles worked assiduously, and rendered invaluable services to his country.

HARRY S. TRUMAN

NOTE: The presentation was made by the President in a ceremony in the Rose Garden at the White House at 12:30 p.m.

180 The President's News Conference on the Review of the Budget. *August* 20, 1947

THE PRESIDENT. I want to make a preliminary statement before I read this statement which you have in your hands.[1]

[1.] In the budget for 1945, that is, from June 30, 1945, to June 30, 1946—that would be the 1946 budget—the budget was for $103 billion. Sixty-three billion dollars was spent that year, and rescissions were made in the neighborhood of $55 billion of outstanding appropriations.

The estimated budget for 1947, that is, the 1946–47 budget, was for expenditures of 41.5. Expenditures finally wound up by being 42.5.

The estimated budget for this year, that is, for 1948—beginning June 30 this year and ending June 30 next year—was 37.5. Actual budget estimates for the period were about 31—between 31 and 32 billions. So you will see that the actual expenditure of funds in spite of the windup of the war has been cut more than a third since the war ended—more than two-thirds since the war ended. And if you will examine the figures

very carefully, you will find that these budgets have been made with extreme care and caution.

Now I will read the statement:

"In any analysis of the Federal budget, we must always keep in mind the fact that about three-fourths of our expenditures relate directly to war, the effects of war, or our efforts to prevent a future war. Thus, as finally approved by the Congress, 28 percent of our expenditures for 1948 are for national defense, 20 percent for our veterans' service and benefits, and 14 percent for interest on our national debt (which is largely a result of war), and of almost 12 percent to support our international programs and activities for world peace. This leaves 27 percent for all other Government programs, of which the share of 'general Government' is only 4 percent."[1]

---

[1] In addition to the statement which the President was about to read, the reporters had copies of a more detailed statement (see Item 181) to which frequent references are made throughout the news conference.

[1] The following paragraph, which appears at this point in the text of the White House release of the same day, was omitted in the reading of the statement:

"From another point of view, 40 percent of the civilian employees of the Government are engaged in national defense activities, 10 percent in the conduct of our veterans programs, and 22 percent in the postal service. This leaves only 28 percent to carry out all other Federal activities."

And I have heard it said they were going to take $9 billion out of that, and there's only 7.6 in it.

[Continuing reading] "We cannot disregard these facts if we are to reduce our expenditures intelligently and without crippling those public services to which we are by law committed.

"When I transmitted the 1948 budget to the Congress last January, I said that it was a realistic budget and as complete as I knew how to make it. I added that in its preparation we had been forced to make drastic reductions in the requests for a number of worthwhile programs because of the urgent need to cut expenditures.

"Now after 8 months we can look back on many events which were then hidden in the uncertainties of the future, and on new conditions which could not then be anticipated. Nevertheless, the fundamental fiscal policy on which the budget was based has proved sound. Furthermore, the searching review of the budget by the Congress and the country must convince everyone willing to look squarely at the facts that it was a tight budget. It was, in fact, a hard-boiled budget predicated on an efficient and economical administration of the programs established by the Congress.

"The budget included in detail for the first time all Government corporations and war agencies. This enabled both the Congress and the people to get a better perspective and a clearer understanding of the necessarily complex ramifications of the programs of the Federal Government. These programs are all authorized by the Congress in response to the needs or demands of the various segments of our democracy. They are carried out only so long as the Congress continues its authorization and supports them through appropriations. Hence, it is essential that all citizens and the Congress

continuously weigh the need for these services against the costs if we are to strike a just balance between the two.

[2.] "The actual reduction in expenditures of 528 million dollars for the fiscal year 1948, as indicated in the budget review, reflects this balancing of needs against costs by the Senators and Representatives in the Congress, as they came to grips with the problem during its session just ended. The indicated surplus of $4.7 billion applied to reducing the national debt, will be an important bulwark against the severe inflationary pressures to which the country is now subjected. The international situation has also made it imperative that we plan for a surplus, both in view of the problem of promoting world recovery and of the need for a reserve against emergencies, whether at home or abroad. Elementary prudence requires that we be prepared to face the unforeseeable as well as the foreseeable. This, we are now in a much stronger financial position to do than we were last year."

I want to add to that, too, that—don't let anybody fool you about how the surplus for 1947 came about. It was by cutting expenditures a billion, 500 million dollars by the executive, and in no other way was that $700 million surplus arrived at. Expenditures were cut a billion and a half by the executive, and that's how we came to have the $734 million surplus.

All right now, fire away.

[3.] Q. Mr. President, does your remark about the—this necessity for elementary prudence and your other remarks in regard to the surplus mean that you are opposed to any tax reduction next year?

THE PRESIDENT. I will answer that question when next year comes around. We will see what the situation is then. I can tell you more about it when I know a little more about what the situation will be next year. I won't hesitate to announce it when the time comes.

Q. Then we will be unwise to interpret this as meaning that you are definitely against—will definitely oppose reduction?

THE PRESIDENT. Well, I will tell you about that when the time comes to make a statement. When the 1949 budget is prepared and we know to some extent exactly where we stand as to what our foreign commitments are going to be, then I can tell you more about tax reduction.

[4.] Q. Mr. President, when you mention the international situation there and the need for surplus, do you have in mind the Marshall plan?

THE PRESIDENT. Yes.

[5.] Q. Mr. President, will the surplus that you have actually show a reduction of the Treasury statement on the public debt?

THE PRESIDENT. What's that?

Q. Will the surplus that you show in the budget estimates also be reflected in the Treasury statement and the reduction of the public debt?

THE PRESIDENT. Yes. Whenever the surplus accumulates it will show in the budget because that is where it is going to be used.

Q. No transfer immediately?

THE PRESIDENT. No. You can't transfer it until you get it. This budget is for 1948, which year ends on June 30th.

[6.] Q. Could you tell us what sort of national income level you expect to see throughout the year?

THE PRESIDENT. Well, that is a hard conclusion to arrive at. We are basing this budget on the changes in this budget, and the increased tax income on the increased national income—a very much increased national income. I can't tell you the exact figures.

Q. Mr. President, don't you sort of suggest that it would be continued at the present

level and that you base it on the present level?

THE PRESIDENT. Certainly. That's right.

Q. Is that correct, then, that you did base it on the present level and you expect——

THE PRESIDENT. We based it on the experience of the last 6 months—continuing present level, of course. That has to be based on the experience that we have had now. We based the budget in January on the experience we had up to that time. The present national income has increased to an extent where we changed our figures in the estimate of a larger surplus than we thought we would have in January.

Q. This does not, then, represent a projection of an increased national income?

THE PRESIDENT. No, it does not. No, it does not.

Q. Does it mean that you don't contemplate any appreciable reduction in prices to bring this down?

THE PRESIDENT. I can't answer that. I have been anticipating about the leveling off of the price situation ever since the debacle of 1946 when the price control situation was all "balled up," but it hasn't come about. Your guess on that would be as good as mine.

Q. This estimate doesn't include anything like that?

THE PRESIDENT. No. Based on the present setup.

[7.] Q. Mr. President, you said that the surplus of this past fiscal year was due to the saving of a billion and a half by the executive departments?

THE PRESIDENT. That is correct.

Q. As an actual fact, the receipts were larger than you originally estimated, some hundreds of millions, was it not?

THE PRESIDENT. A billion, a hundred million. The Secretary of the Treasury calls my attention to the fact that if we had not cut off the expenditures, even with the increased income, there would have been no appreciable surplus.

Q. Well, you can't say, though, that all of the surplus is due solely, then, to the Executive action?

THE PRESIDENT. Well, when you take into consideration—of course it was. There would have been—there would have been a deficit deficiency, the difference between $101 billion and whatever the surplus is. Couldn't have helped it. Hadn't made the cut, there wouldn't have been any surplus.

Q. Mr. President, I would like to look at the question against the background of Republican claims of savings—savings ranging anywhere from 2 billion to, I think, 7 billion or 9 billion. The thing you emphasize in your statement is the figure of the actual reduction in expenditures of $528 million. Then in the—in another—in this larger statement here you credit Congress with cuts amounting to a billion and a half, I think, approximately.

THE PRESIDENT. Yes, that's right—a billion, 540 I think it is.

[8.] Q. I was just wondering if there was some simple way, Mr. President, to account for the difference between the figure you mention, that half billion, and that——

THE PRESIDENT. Yes, yes. It's easy. Just as easy as it can be. Take things like atomic energy, where the appropriation was made on only a part-year basis, and there are several other reasons exactly like it, and this tax refund situation where they cut off funds for tax refund. If a man has a refund coming, he is entitled to know just the same as if he had money in the bank. That appropriation will have to be made. That's how the difference comes.

Director Webb: Greek relief.

[9.] Q. Mr. President, table 1 (p. 397),[1] you say—two items there—"reductions in authorizations which may be regarded as final." That figure is a billion, 843 million. Then you have "reductions in authorizations which will require offsets by deficiency appropriations." That is 929. The total of those figures is 2 billion, 770. Now, isn't the atomic energy appropriation and the tax refund included in that 929?

THE PRESIDENT. No. Go up in the table to get your 645 million and your 403 million, then you will know where you are going.

[10.] Q. Then the Executive has increased the $375 million figure submitted in January?

THE PRESIDENT. Yes. Yes, the Greek-Turkish loan, and several other things that had to be done. It's all set out in details in the folder which you have.

Q. I would like to get at the same question in a slightly different way. Could any of your experts reconcile the figures used in the final edition of the Congressional Record?[2]

THE PRESIDENT. Yes, they are all reconciled. In anticipation of that question, we have reconciled them for you right here.[3]

Q. Taber, Taft, Barkley——

THE PRESIDENT. Yes, they are all reconciled—Taber, Taft, Barkley—I have got them reconciled to show them exactly, that they come out almost to the letter—with a difference of a few million dollars of exactly what we have here. It's a long, complicated table. We will furnish it to you.

---

[1] Page references in parentheses, throughout this news conference, indicate where the subjects referred to may be found in the Statement on the Review of the Budget as published herein (Item 181).

[2] Congressional Record for July 26, 1947 (vol. 93, Appendix).

[3] The President was referring to a table which was not released.

Director Webb: I suggest they call the Budget and go over it, because it is a very complex thing.

THE PRESIDENT. If you will—the Budget Director says if you will get in touch with him, he will explain it in detail so you won't get it all mixed up.

Q. There isn't any easy way of explaining it?

THE PRESIDENT. No, there isn't. No, there isn't. You would have to ask the Budget, and you would have to understand the budget as the Budget Bureau does.

Director Webb: The extension which you may call is 201 at the Budget. Executive 3300, extension 201. They will be glad to furnish you all the details.

Q. Do you have any copies of it?

THE PRESIDENT. There will be copies of it available.

Director Webb: I am not sure, Mr. President, that we can distribute that statement, but we can answer the questions that should be legitimately answered.

THE PRESIDENT. I don't see why you can't distribute the statement. It sets out in detail exactly what the difference is. It makes a lot of difference. That budget is built on exactly the same basis as the budget in January. The figures are comparable.

[11.] Q. Mr. President, in the January budget you estimated that the surplus for the current fiscal year would be $202 million.

THE PRESIDENT. That's right.

Q. And now 4 billion and 7 for the surplus in this year. Could you justify that estimate for us, please sir?

THE PRESIDENT. Yes. You will find—it is justified for you right there—[*indicating*]— and shows the exact situation, what the result of it was.

Q. On what basis they reached the conclusion?

Q. Mr. President, on page 12 (p. 402), there's a reference to reduction——

THE PRESIDENT. Joe,[1] let me answer this other question first, will you?

Q. I beg your pardon. I thought that had been answered. [*Laughter*]

THE PRESIDENT. The increase in the income is the principal reason for the increase in the surplus, and it has increased to such an extent that the Treasury revised their figures on income, and then there was a $538 million cut which makes the difference. Those figures are all available in these tables that you have. As soon as I can find it, I will read it to you.

Joe, what was your question?

[12.] Q. It dealt with the second paragraph, page 12 (p. 402), with reference to making expenditures for airways, a reduction will delay improvement of many airports. I was just wondering if you would amplify that?

THE PRESIDENT. Expenditures on the— reduction of expenditures for the Commerce Department. Improvement of new airports was cut down—safety devices, flags for safe landings—and that is really dangerous. I will read you those figures in just a minute. That revenue question—if you will turn to table 3 (p. 410) on the back there, your question will be answered by that table. Now, Joe, I will give you your answer here as soon as I find the figures. I have got the figures on this airport thing right here. The Congress enacted only $65 million requested for Federal airport aid appropriations. As a result, the improvement of many existing airports and the construction of new ones will be delayed by a year or longer. Then the Congress provided less than a third of the funds requested for the establishment of

---

[1] Joseph A. Fox of the Washington Evening Star.

air navigation facilities. As a result, the program for a modernized airway system will be delayed. The landing aid program to permit safe and expeditious operation in unfavorable weather will be particularly affected by that cut. That is in the Commerce Department.

[13.] Q. Mr. President, as I understand it, you propose to use all of this $4.7 billion surplus on debt reduction, is that right?

THE PRESIDENT. Yes.

Q. Can you give us some idea when you expect to find the money for——

THE PRESIDENT. Of course, the whole net surplus will be used for debt retirement.

Q. Including the cash surplus?

Secretary Snyder: No, it does not include the cash surplus.

THE PRESIDENT. Yes, if you will turn back—the actual cash surplus.

Q. The question I was getting at, sir, is where in the budget can you give us some idea of this? Do you expect to be able to find money for the expenditures under the Marshall plan?

THE PRESIDENT. Well, if expenditures have to be made under the present plan, it will reduce the surplus by that much, and the debt reduction will be reduced by whatever that amounts to. It is the net surplus that we are talking about, of course.

Q. Mr. President, actually there is no debt reduction at the end of the fiscal year?

THE PRESIDENT. The Secretary of the Treasury will answer that question.

Secretary Snyder: We reduce the debt immediately out of our working cash. We keep a certain amount of cash for current operations, and as our monthly maturities or quarterly maturities come due, we pay those off and reduce the amount. Sometimes it's even beyond the surplus that we actually have. We are using all our cash to cut down costs of servicing the debt. It may be, of

course, we have to raise that back up as our cash runs down. Is that clear?

Q. In that event, I am still puzzled on where you get the money all of a sudden?

Secretary Snyder: It comes out of revenues as they are paid in through tax collections. We collect daily, you know, on that, and we watch our Treasury balance and keep it at working level to meet current expenses, and the balance of it we use to pay off the monthly accruals of maturities.

Q. Do you plan to build up any reserve for these foreign commitments or possible foreign commitments?

THE PRESIDENT. We have to find out whether we are going to have any or not.

Secretary Snyder: We cover it with our regular monthly financing, with bills and certificates and with our regular bond sales.

THE PRESIDENT. I want to go back to that Net Budget receipts that was referred to. If you will turn to page 18 (p. 406) you will see it set out very carefully. [*Reading*] "In my Budget Message, I requested that the war excise tax rates be continued throughout the fiscal year 1948. The Congress continued them without an expiration date. This added more than $1.1 billion to the estimate of receipts, thus raising it to $38.9 billion. Higher levels of national income account for the greater part of the further increase of $2.8 billion in the present estimate of Budget receipts over the January estimate." That answers your question that you asked me a while ago. I think you will find nearly every one of these set out, but I will be glad to tell you about it.

[14.] Q. I have one question on the budget, while we are on that subject. You say that it is going to be decreased throughout the year, yet I notice in the Budget Revision, under the heading of Interest on the Public Debt, interest on the public debt goes up 100 million. I wonder if Secretary Snyder—could you explain that to me, please?

THE PRESIDENT. Answer that.

Secretary Snyder: Yes, that is easily explained. On our savings bond program, the service charges are accumulating every day as those bonds grow older. There is an interest accrual that is built up so unless we materially reduce our total debt why there will be an interest charge increase from that—from that area also. As we go into longer maturities, switch from the longer to the short maturities, the interest rate is higher. As you know, the bill rate is pretty low, and the certificate a little higher, and the notes a little higher, and long-term bonds are around 2½ percent. Well now, if we move out of short-term obligations into the long-term obligations to stabilize the debt, the interest rate will naturally creep up, even though we may be reducing the actual dollars on the principal of the debt. So it takes a material reduction in the principal on the debt in order to hold down that service charge to keep it somewhere around the figure that we have here in the budget. Is that clear?

Q. Yes sir. Thank you.

Q. Mr. President, I also would like to ask the Secretary on that point, does he contemplate overall any really material increase in the cost of carrying the public debt?

Secretary Snyder: That is one of our definite aims, to try to prevent any material increase in the cost of servicing the debt.

Q. Will that be a tendency—I mean, if you take out that increment you mentioned on the savings bonds, the net and other categories, that will not be very great, will it?

Secretary Snyder: I beg your pardon?

Q. Most of that 100 million will be accounted for by the savings bonds, will it not?

Secretary Snyder: I think the greatest part of it, this particular year, would be, yes, because we haven't moved a great deal into the long-term area yet.

[15.] Q. Mr. President, on page 20 (p. 407) of the statement, on foreign commitments, you figure 4.3. The table on page 3—table 3 (p. 410) has it 3.6. Is that because the Army's special relief fund is included in your figure and not under the table figure?

THE PRESIDENT. Well, I will answer that in just a minute, as soon as I find the table. It isn't on that same page that you mentioned, in my book.

Q. It's next to the very last paragraph of the statement, Mr. President.

THE PRESIDENT. Oh.

Director Webb: What is the table you refer to?

Q. Table 3 (p. 410), under International Affairs and Finance.

Director Webb: Which figure?

Q. Total 3.617.

Director Webb: 3.617 as against 4.3?

Q. I don't see any figure there for the Army expenditures in occupied areas which came to around 600 million, I think.

THE PRESIDENT. The difference is that the figure in table 3 includes only general and special accounts. You have some additional expenditures which belong in corporate accounts.

Q. Well, we will make it 4.3 then?

THE PRESIDENT. 4.3; 4.3 is the figure I got.

[16.] Q. Mr. President, if you go back to the question of taxes for a moment, do I understand this to be the administration's position, that you hold out no promise of tax reduction for the simple reason that you can't until you know where you stand later on, until you know what international commitments face the country?

THE PRESIDENT. That's right—that's right. Until we know whether this continued high income is going to be maintained.

Q. Doesn't this exclude it, at least for the fiscal year 1948, by saying you are over surplus for debt reduction?

THE PRESIDENT. I think I have made that perfectly plain in the veto message.[1]

Q. 1949?

THE PRESIDENT. 1949. Can't come to a conclusion until we know more about it.

[17.] Q. Isn't there a main divergence between those figures and those by the various Republican leaders on rescissions?

THE PRESIDENT. Rescissions that were already made; 400 million rescissions already made. Between rescissions already made. That money never would have been spent. That was the tail end of the rescissions that we made in the past, and appropriations that would automatically have expired or were eliminated.

Q. Executive rescissions?

THE PRESIDENT. Executive rescissions. They were the big ones. Fifty-five billion dollars worth.

Q. I mean in this—in figuring——

THE PRESIDENT. The order that I issued December 30, terminating hostilities, terminated these appropriations on the 30th of June.

Q. Four billion rescissions, that's all that it mentions here.

THE PRESIDENT. These 4 billions in rescissions are the ones that I refer to. Automatically they were war expenditures that never would have been spent, most of them. The Budget Director says that the rescissions that were made by Congress—most of the rescissions made by Congress or recommended by us, they asked us not to recommend, because they would automatically

expire. Yet they are counting those that would automatically expire in their savings.

Q. I think there were 4 billion some odd in rescissions—came after the end of the war—hostilities were ended?

THE PRESIDENT. Yes—oh yes.

Q. Were they Executive rescissions or congressional rescissions?

THE PRESIDENT. They were effected by the termination of hostilities which took place on the basis of the order which was issued in December.

Secretary Snyder: They would automatically expire June 30th by the cessation of hostilities. That was the limit placed on them, 6 months after hostilities ended, so they would automatically expire then, the authorization on them, for June 30th.

Q. How did they get in the 1948 Budget, in the first place?

THE PRESIDENT. They weren't. They weren't. Actually I think the congressional figures have related to action taken in the session of Congress rather than specifically to the 1948 Budget. I think that is one thing that has caused confusion.

Q. There is a $4 billion figure that has been mentioned both in this message now and by some of the people on the Hill. In this message it says these rescissions were— amounted to money that wouldn't have been spent anyhow.

THE PRESIDENT. That is correct.

Director Webb: Go to page 14 (p. 403), second paragraph, you will see that of 4 billion, 100 million the President recommended rescissions of 565, and Congress took action on it. The rest of it would have automatically expired by operation of law. Therefore, the President made no recommendation about that. I might say that we were requested not to send those up by the Appropriations Committee, since it would automatically expire.

---

[1] Item 147.

Q. Then these congressional figures which count in these $4 billion worth of rescissions——

THE PRESIDENT. Just off $4 billion.

Q. ——are misleading?

THE PRESIDENT. I say they are just off $4 billion. You can figure it any way you want to, they are off $4 billion.

[18.]   Q. Mr. President, do you have any minimum goal on debt reduction, including the Marshall plan?

THE PRESIDENT. I can't have a minimum goal of debt reduction until I know what the surplus is going to be. Whatever the surplus is, the debt reduction is going to be.

[19.]   Q. Mr. President, getting back once again to the possibility of tax reduction, on page 2 (p. 396), second paragraph—page 2 of the statement—you describe the policy for this year by saying, the surplus "will be devoted to the retirement of the public debt." In the very next sentence you say, "The same prudent policy of planning for a surplus and for debt retirement will be followed in preparing the Budget for 1949."

THE PRESIDENT. That's right.

Q. Wouldn't that more or less give us reason to think that debt—tax reduction next year too will get a pretty rough going over?

THE PRESIDENT. Well, I can assure you on that all right. It will get a rough going over. [*Laughter*]

Q. The question in my mind—the question in my mind is how far to go on that point, because just to read it you would almost think that you had committed yourself to no tax reduction.

THE PRESIDENT. Well, I can't say that, because as I told you before, the 1949 Budget is not made yet, and we don't know what commitments we will be saddled with. Certainly I don't want to run into deficit financing again if we can help it. If the income situation in this country continues, now is the time to pay our debts while we have got the money.

Q. What would you call minimum debt reduction?

THE PRESIDENT. I can't answer that, either. We will have to see how this interpretation of the Secretary of the Treasury works out.

Q. I just—I wondered if it would be $4 billion, six? It would be necessarily over that, would it not, sir?

THE PRESIDENT. I can't answer that question.

Q. In that connection, Mr. President, I have a question which probably should be addressed to the Secretary of the Treasury. I think the record will show that in the last 2 years the Treasury has consistently underestimated tax receipts by a considerable percentage. Now I would like to propound this question. At the current level of business, assuming it continues, shouldn't tax receipts be more than the estimate in this budget? In other words, aren't they still running more than in the previous fiscal year?

Secretary Snyder: There was no possible way—we don't intend to be—as you know, we have never had any pretense in the Treasury of being occult. In trying to estimate the receipts, we have to take certain measurements, and when they finally turned out, why there was a very small percentage of difference in the actual receipts than those estimated in January. But there was a lot of things happened in our economy that there was no way for us to know about, about the increase in prices and the increased profits that came about, which in turn increased the revenues. We have measured as carefully as we can by all standards, and certainly the revenues from my point of view should always be on the conservative side rather than on the extravagant side, because if we are on the extravagant side and depend on revenues being a certain amount and they fall down on us, we are in a difficult position. If we are conservative, we have always got some way that we can use the excess. So it may well be that our estimates for the balance of this fiscal year are conservative. On the other hand, it could be, with the changing economic conditions, that they are pretty close to right or maybe a little bit optimistic, but we try to arrive at a figure that we feel comfortable in reporting to the President to measure against his expenditure budget.

Q. In that connection, Mr. President, had you had any reports—have you heard any rumors that a number of large taxpayers filed their returns last March in anticipation of the 20-percent tax reduction?

Secretary Snyder: I haven't had any real information on it, but I think you will take some comfort in the Treasury estimates when you compare them with some of them that were made before the committees up in Congress by the outside experts. I think that ours came near the end result by several million—several billions of dollars than some of the expert testimony from the outside.

[20.] Q. Is it possible, Mr. President, in that connection, to have a figure as to the anticipated average national income through-out the year on which your revenue estimate was predicated?

THE PRESIDENT. We haven't got it, no. I might be able to find it for you.

Director Webb: Close to the present level.

Secretary Snyder: Somewhat near the present level.

THE PRESIDENT. The Secretary of the Treasury tells me that it is a figure some-where near to the present level.

Q. What would that be?

Director Webb: We will obtain that from the Treasury and it will be available at this extension.

Q. What is that extension again?

Director Webb: 320—201.

[21.] Q. Mr. President, could I ask you this question? Do you believe that high taxes are inflationary or deflationary? [*Laughter*]

THE PRESIDENT. Well now, you will have to talk to the experts on that. In my opinion, of course, with conditions and prices and everything as they are, the more money in the pockets of the people to spend the more inflationary it is, and the Government should take its cut for the debt while things are prosperous. Don't know whether that an-swers your question or not, but that is the way I feel about it.

Q. Do you feel that the high taxes figure is an inflationary figure?

THE PRESIDENT. No, I do not.

[22.] Q. Mr. President, with the foreign commitments not going before Congress until—at least until next January, and with Congress going through its usual system of 2 or 3 months to get something out, there couldn't be a very great nick out of the 4.7 surplus in the next fiscal year?

THE PRESIDENT. Your guess is as good as mine as to what Congress will do and how they will handle it.

Q. Never very fast.

THE PRESIDENT. Well, I say your guess is as good as mine.

[23.] Q. Do you believe that Govern-ment spending on projects at this time con-tributes to the inflation of prices?

THE PRESIDENT. If you will notice, the Government's public works program is way down. That is the answer to your question.

Reporter: Thank you, Mr. President!

THE PRESIDENT. Thank *you* very much.

NOTE: President Truman's one hundred and seventeenth news conference was held in the Movie Projection Room in the East Wing of the White House at 3 o'clock on Wednesday afternoon, August 20, 1947. The President was assisted in presenting information on the budget by John W. Snyder, Secretary of the Treasury, and James E. Webb, Director of the Bureau of the Budget.

181   Statement by the President on the Review of the 1948 Budget.
August 20, 1947

CONTINUING the practice of former years, I submit at this time my annual mid-year review of the Budget. Since the 1948 Budget has aroused unusual public interest, I am presenting this year a detailed analysis of how the changes in it came about.

The revisions in this statement bring up to date the initial Budget estimates for the fiscal year 1948 which were transmitted to the Congress in January. They take account of Budget amendments submitted to the Congress, the action of the Congress on appropriations and other legislation, and numerous developments which have affected the outlook for Government programs.

1. *Summary: Budget Totals and Major Revisions*

The expenditures of the Federal Government during the fiscal year ending June 30, 1948, are now estimated at 37.0 billion dollars and net receipts at 41.7 billion dollars. On the basis of these estimates, a Budget surplus of 4.7 billion dollars is indicated.

Expenditures—When I transmitted the Budget last January, expenditures during this fiscal year were estimated at 37.5 billion dollars. The present Budget estimate is 37.0 billion dollars. The difference is the result of many changes. Some have tended to increase and others to reduce the total. A reduction of 1,520 million dollars is the result of congressional action. On the other hand, revisions and amendments which I have found necessary have added 638 million

dollars. Changes listed later under other headings have added 354 million dollars.

In preparing this review, it has not been possible to estimate the ultimate effect on the Budget of the emergency situation overseas. The amount that may be required to enable the United States to bear its proper share in world recovery cannot be determined until a later stage in the studies of the international situation now under way. The present uncertainties must be taken into consideration in deciding our Budget policy. They emphasize the need to maintain a balanced Budget with sufficient surplus to meet emergencies.

Receipts—The new estimate of net Budget receipts is 4.0 billion dollars above the estimate of 37.7 billion dollars included in the Budget in January. Of this increase, 1.1 billion dollars results from the continuation of war excise tax rates, which I recommended in the January Budget. But the greater part of this increase is due to the rise in prices and national income above the levels anticipated in January.

Surplus—In the fiscal year 1947 the Budget was balanced for the first time in seventeen years and a surplus was achieved—which in the long run is the only way to retire debt. As long as our total postwar commitments are still uncertain and as long as we are under strong inflationary pressures, it would be reckless not to include a reasonable surplus in the Budget. In the light of present conditions, the estimated surplus of 4.7 billion dollars for the fiscal year 1948 is essential to sound fiscal policy. The surplus, together with part of the present cash balance, will be devoted to retirement of the public debt.

The same prudent policy of planning for a surplus and for further debt retirement will be followed in preparing the Budget for 1949. The strictest economy consistent with the Government's obligation is imperative. I have already instructed the Executive departments and agencies to hold their 1949 Budget requests below the 1948 total. In a number of cases I have established certain definite limitations.

Appropriations and contract authorizations—In the Budget transmitted to the Congress last January, I recommended appropriations of 31.3 billion dollars and contract authorizations of 1.5 billion dollars to finance Government operations during the current fiscal year. Subsequent amendments to the Budget through July, and 1947 appropriations delayed to 1948 have raised the totals thus far recommended to the Congress to 32.3 billion dollars for appropriations and to 1.6 billion dollars for contract authorizations.[1] The 80th Congress at its first session enacted for the fiscal year 1948 appropriations and reappropriations of 29.8 billion dollars and contract authorizations of 2.0 billion dollars.[2]

I anticipate that at its second session it will be necessary for the 80th Congress to provide supplemental appropriations of 1.3 billion dollars and additional contract authorizations of more than 300 million dollars. The Congress itself has recognized that some of its reductions, such as those for tax refunds and the Atomic Energy Commission, will have to be restored. The estimates for

supplemental appropriations include 848 million dollars to restore such reductions made by the Congress. The remaining 403 million dollars of appropriations and 317 million dollars of contract authorizations relate for the most part to items on which the Congress has deferred consideration.[1] Thus, present indications are that the final total of appropriations and reappropriations will be about 200 million dollars lower than I recommended last January and the final total of contract authorizations, about 750 million dollars higher.

Rescissions—The Congress also rescinded wartime appropriations and other authorizations of 4.1 billion dollars. Most of this would not have been spent. The resulting reduction in expenditures during fiscal 1948 is estimated at 153 million dollars.

Major changes since January—Let us now review the three principal ways in which the January Budget estimates have been altered. Necessary amendments and revisions of my original recommendations have added 3 percent to the total of appropriations, 27 percent to contract authorizations, and less than 2 percent to expenditures. Revisions due to delays and transfers between fiscal years add 1 percent to appropriations and less than 1 percent to expenditures. Congressional action—following a vigorous and searching review of the Budget—has reduced appropriations 5 percent, increased contract authorizations 21 percent, and reduced expenditures 4 percent. In total, all these changes have reduced the expenditures side of the January Budget by 1.4 percent.

On the receipts side, there is an increase of 10.4 percent.

Table 1 shows the dollar changes since January in totals of appropriations, contract authorizations, and estimated expenditures.

---

[1] See Table 1, line for January Budget plus lines A–1 and B–1.
[2] See Table 2, part B.

[1] See Table 1, lines A–2 and C–2–b.

TABLE 1.   CHANGES IN THE 1948 BUDGET, JANUARY–AUGUST 1947

[Millions]

Type of change	Authorizations		
	Appropria- tions [1]	New contract authorizations	Estimated expenditures
January Budget..	$31,292	$1,542	$37,528
A. Revisions due to changes in recommendations:			
1. Amendments to the Budget through July (net)...........	645	101	300
2. Anticipated supplemental recommendations to be considered at next session of Congress..........................	403	317	338
Subtotal...	1,048	418	638
B. Revisions due to changes between fiscal years and in program outlook:			
1. 1947 appropriations delayed to 1948.....................	362	....	48
2. Transfers of expenditures between fiscal years.............	....	....	293
3. Changes in estimates of outlook for Government programs and revisions of related permanent appropriations.......	—15	....	13
Subtotal...	347	....	354
C. Revisions due to Congressional action:			
1. Reductions in authorizations which may be regarded as final.	—1,843	—3	—1,275
2. a. Reductions in authorizations which will require offsets by deficiency appropriations...........................	—929	....	—888
b. Estimated offsets by deficiency appropriations..........	848	....	832
3. Reductions in Government corporation expenditures.......	....	....	—345
4. Rescissions of authorizations of earlier years..............	....	....	—153
5. Substitution of contract authorizations for appropriations..	....	181	....
6. Increases initiated by Congress.........................	346	149	309
Subtotal...	—1,578	327	—1,520
Total, August Review...............................	31,109	2,287	37,000

[1] Includes appropriations to liquidate contract authorizations and reappropriations.

2. Appropriations and Expenditures

When we come to consider the changes in the expenditure side of the Budget in detail, we must consider the differences between expenditures in a given fiscal year and the authority to incur obligations which result in expenditures. Appropriations and expenditures are by no means the same thing.

The Congress, by enacting appropriations and contract authorizations, empowers Government agencies to incur obligations. The appropriations permit expenditure of money in payment of these obligations. In the case of the contract authorizations, an "appropriation to liquidate" is required before expenditures can be made to pay off the obligations.

Expenditures occur when obligations are paid off. Thus, appropriations to permit obligations this year may not affect expenditures until next year or the year after. On the other hand, this year's expenditures in part pay off obligations incurred under earlier appropriations. In the case of Government corporations, moreover, only a small part of the expenditures is made from appropriated funds, and the receipts of the corporations are generally treated as offsets against their expenditures. For these reasons, we can expect no precise correspondence between appropriations and Budget expenditures in any one fiscal year.

The following explanatory text is arranged under headings which correspond to the lines in Table 1.

A. *Revisions due to changes in recommendations*

(1) *Amendments to the Budget*—The requirements of the fiscal year 1948 made it necessary for me to recommend increases in certain programs after the Budget was transmitted. But in some instances our needs have fallen below the tentative figures used in January, and the difference has been deducted in computing the revised Budget total. Recommendations anticipated in January but not yet transmitted to the Congress have also been deducted, since a separate heading is used to cover supplemental recommendations for items to be considered at the next session of the Congress.

These increases and decreases together make up the amendments to the Budget. The net effect of such amendments has been to add 645 million dollars to recommended appropriations and 101 million dollars to recommended contract authorizations. These amendments, if adopted in full, would have increased expenditures by 300 million dollars during fiscal 1948.

The major new requirements have been as follows:

The situation in Europe made it imperative that we extend aid to Greece and Turkey. The recommended appropriation of 400 million dollars was approved and will add 320 million dollars to expenditures during fiscal 1948.

As a result of recent disastrous floods, I recommended to the Congress shortly before it adjourned a flood control program with supplemental appropriations of 250 million dollars for fiscal 1948. This included 237 million dollars for the Corps of Engineers, 10 million dollars for the Bureau of Reclamation, and 3 million dollars for the Department of Agriculture. Added expenditures during the current fiscal year would have amounted to an estimated 136 million dollars but for cuts shown under revisions due to Congressional action.

To permit the strategic stockpiling program to go forward, I recommended an additional appropriation of 150 million dollars and a contract authorization of 50 million dollars. I also requested 104 million dollars in new contract authorizations for the Army aircraft procurement program to make up for increases in costs since the January estimate. These recommendations contemplated an increase of 91 million dollars in expenditures for national defense during fiscal 1948.

Since January the requirements for the veterans' program have become clearer. Expenditures for pensions, loan guaranty programs, and construction of hospitals have been running lower than originally estimated. However, these savings have been more than offset by increases in outlays for education and training benefits and for medical care. To meet the changed needs, net increases of 75 million dollars in appropriations and 38 million dollars in contract authorizations were requested with an expenditure increase of 94 million dollars.

A supplemental appropriation of 36 million dollars was requested to pay the increased costs incident to completion of the veterans' re-use housing program. The estimated increase in expenditures during 1948 is 33 million dollars.

The outbreak of foot and mouth disease in Mexico made immediate action necessary to prevent the spread of this disease to our own herds. I therefore recommended an appropriation of 64 million dollars for this purpose. The estimated increase in expenditures during 1948 for this program will be 50 million dollars.

A supplemental appropriation of 39 million dollars and a reappropriation of 17 million dollars were recommended for the Department of Commerce, primarily to accelerate improvement of the Federal airway system and to permit greater flexibility in the grant-in-aid program for airport construction. A supplemental request of 22 million dollars was required because of an expected increase in the Post Office deficit due to a rise in the volume of mail. These and several smaller items added 92 million dollars to recommended appropriations for transportation and communication for the current fiscal year. If they had been allowed in full by the Congress, they would have added about 17 million dollars to expenditures this year.

Several large reductions have been included under the heading of amendments to the Budget. The January total included tentative estimates of anticipated supplemental appropriations of 262 million dollars and contract authorizations of 91 million dollars for military and naval public works which have not yet been transmitted to the Congress. They also included 123 million dollars in an indefinite appropriation for tax refunds which would have been payable if the Congress had not accepted my recommendation to continue war excise taxes beyond June 30, 1947. In addition, a supplemental appropriation of 74 million dollars was anticipated on the assumption that new permanent legislation to correct inequalities in State public assistance payments would be enacted, as recommended in the Budget. Deduction of these major items from the January totals reduces the expenditure estimate by 366 million dollars.

(2) *Anticipated supplemental recommendations*—At the next session of the Congress, in addition to supplementals to cover deficiencies in items on which the Congress has acted, it will be necessary to submit supplemental requests for items which the Congress has not yet considered. Excluding any new programs of international aid, these requests will add about 403 million dollars to appropriations and 317 million dollars to contract authorizations. This will mean 338 million dollars of expenditures in fiscal 1948.

The main new supplemental items that I now anticipate are as follows:

Supplemental requests for 60 million dollars in appropriations and 282 million dollars in contract authorizations for military and naval public works will be sent to the Congress as soon as the necessary basic legislation is passed. The delay that has already occurred will reduce expenditures in fiscal 1948 from 169 million dollars to 19 million dollars.

Refunds of internal revenue and of customs are now estimated 129 million dollars higher than in January, apart from the war excise tax refunds then included. A supplemental appropriation will be required.

Appropriations and expenditures of 115 million dollars will be required by recently enacted legislation extending present temporary increases in matching grants to the States for public assistance. This supersedes the anticipated supplemental appropriation of 74 million dollars which was included in the January Budget for the same program. The difference in these estimates reflects higher rates of benefit payments by the States, as well as heavier case loads.

399

In summary, revisions due to changes in recommendations increase appropriations by 1,048 million dollars, contract authorizations by 418 million dollars, and estimated expenditures by 638 million dollars.

B. *Revisions due to changes between fiscal years and in program outlook*

Three types of changes in the Budget are grouped under this heading:

(1) *1947 appropriations delayed to 1948*—A few appropriation items, chiefly the 350 million dollars for post-UNRRA relief, were recommended as supplementals for 1947 but were enacted by the Congress as appropriations for 1948. On the other hand, an appropriation of 20 million dollars recommended for fiscal 1948 was enacted as a 1947 supplemental. Shifts of this kind have increased appropriations for 1948 by 362 million dollars and expenditures in this year by 48 million dollars.

(2) *Transfers of expenditures between fiscal years*—Transfers to the Railroad Retirement trust account during fiscal 1947 were expected in earlier estimates to include 204 million dollars which was to have been available for transfer immediately upon passage of the appropriation for 1948. Delay in enactment of the appropriation postponed this transfer until fiscal 1948. Similarly, transfer of 81 million dollars to the veterans' life insurance trust funds, originally scheduled for fiscal 1947, has been delayed until 1948. On the other hand, only 25 million dollars of the Smaller War Plants Corporation capital stock, rather than the 100 million dollars estimated in January, will be retired by the Reconstruction Finance Corporation in the current fiscal year, since the major retirement has already been made.

These and other items will mean a net shift in expenditures of 293 million dollars from fiscal 1947 to 1948.

(3) *Changes in the estimates of program outlook and related revisions of permanent appropriations*—The expenditure estimates for several important programs have changed materially since last January because of factors other than revised recommendations or Congressional action. The estimates for some programs have increased; for others they have decreased. It is now estimated that the total of expenditures during fiscal 1948 will be increased for these reasons 13 million dollars above the January estimates. A net reduction of 15 million dollars in permanent indefinite appropriations is associated with these revisions.

The main items involved are as follows:

Expenditures for national defense will be 258 million dollars lower than was anticipated in January, quite apart from changes attributable to Congressional action. This drop is due mainly to difficulties in recruiting and to lower estimates for the supply and operating services in line with recent expenditure experience.

A 500-million-dollar increase in estimated withdrawals on account of the loan to the United Kingdom is the major change accounting for an increase under this heading of 495 million dollars above the January estimate of expenditures for international affairs and finance. Net expenditures of the U.S. Commercial Company are now estimated 74 million dollars higher; those of the Export-Import Bank, 80 million dollars lower. Other smaller program changes offset each other.

For agriculture and agricultural resources the expenditure estimate now is 341 million dollars lower than in January because of program changes. This is mainly due to increased receipts of the Commodity Credit Corporation in this fiscal year from the sale of Cuban sugar which was purchased last

June. These receipts will more than offset the expenditures of the Corporation during this year.

Estimated expenditures for natural resources programs will be 97 million dollars higher than was estimated in January, almost entirely because of a revised estimate for the Atomic Energy Commission.

A reduction of 160 million dollars in estimated expenditures for transportation and communication is accounted for by a slower rate of expenditures for Federal-aid highway grants than was estimated last January and a more rapid rate of repayments to the Reconstruction Finance Corporation on prewar railroad loans.

Program changes under general government since January have added 99 million dollars to estimated expenditures. More than half of this is in the War Department program for the return of our war dead.

Most of the 75-million-dollar increase in interest payments on the public debt under this heading arises from relaxation of wartime controls over short-term interest rates. Federal Reserve banks now hold most of the securities benefiting from these higher rates. Consequently, most of the added payments will come back to the Treasury through transfers of excess earnings of the Federal Reserve banks.

This increase in the permanent indefinite appropriation for interest is more than offset by reductions of 90 million dollars in the permanent indefinite appropriation (and 85 million dollars in expenditures) for transfers of receipts from the rental and sale of war housing. The reductions result from revisions in accounting procedures.

In summary, changes in timing and program outlook have increased appropriations for 1948 by 347 million dollars and expenditures by 354 million dollars.

C. *Revisions due to Congressional action*

Congressional action has affected the Budget in a variety of ways.

(1) *Reductions which may be regarded as final*—Authorizations of some departments and agencies have been cut and their activities must be reduced. Cuts under this heading amount to 1,843 million dollars in appropriations for 1948, 3 million dollars in contract authorizations, and an estimated 1,275 million dollars in expenditures during the fiscal year.

The main reductions are as follows:

National defense appropriations were reduced by 566 million dollars (including 515 million dollars for the War and Navy Departments and 50 million dollars for stockpiling). The cut in expenditures is 453 million dollars. These decreases will mean substantial cuts in the number of military personnel and considerable contractions in the supply services. They are partly offset by increases totaling 234 million dollars in appropriations and in contract authorizations, which are discussed under other headings below.

Appropriations for veterans' services and benefits for 1948 were cut by 113 million dollars. The expenditure reduction due to action by the Congress is 88 million dollars during the current year. This includes a reduction of 50 million dollars in the estimate for veterans' pensions and of 17 million dollars in construction of educational facilities because of a cut in the 1947 supplemental appropriation.

The Congress has cut appropriations for international affairs and finance by 208 million dollars. This means a cut of 66 million dollars in expenditures during the current year. The largest reduction in appropriations is 125 million dollars for War Department activities in governing the occupied areas. This cut, however, does not affect expenditures during this fiscal year. The cut of 45 million dollars in the appropriations requested for the State Department includes 19 million dollars in the foreign information and cultural program—a reduction which impairs our efforts to give other peoples accurate information about the United States.

Appropriations for agriculture and agricultural resources for 1948 were cut by 198 million dollars. These changes in appropriations, together with elimination by the Congress of 100 million dollars in transfers to the conservation and use program, mean a cut of 184 million dollars in expenditures during fiscal 1948. The largest reduction in appropriations is a 73-million-dollar decrease for the Farmers' Home Administration. This will mean a 63-million-dollar reduction in expenditures, mostly for production loans and other financial aid to low-income farmers. Expenditures for the conservation and land-use program in fiscal 1948 are reduced by 74 million dollars and for other programs by smaller amounts.

Appropriations for natural resources programs were cut 225 million dollars by the Congress—excluding cuts likely to be offset by deficiency appropriations, which are discussed in the following section. The corresponding expenditure cut is 127 million dollars. Appropriations for flood control work of the Corps of Engineers were reduced by 118 million dollars and expenditures during this fiscal year by 68 million dollars. Appropriations for the natural resource programs of the Department of the Interior were cut by 90 million dollars, with a 50-million-dollar reduction in expenditures during this fiscal year—mainly in the Bureau of Reclamation.

Appropriations for transportation and communication were cut 220 million dollars by the Congress. Expenditures during the fiscal year are reduced 133 million dollars on this account. The largest of these appropriation cuts is 71 million dollars for the Civil Aeronautics Administration. This will retard improvement of the Federal airways system, particularly the installation of instrument landing aids, and will delay improvement of many airports. The other major cuts in appropriations for 1948 are 49 million dollars for the Post Office Department, 46 million dollars for the Coast Guard, and 36 million dollars for Federal-aid highway grants.

The appropriation for the Labor Department has been reduced by 24 million dollars. Consequently the Department will be restricted in enforcing the minimum wage laws, in providing information desired by business and labor, and in aiding the development of fully effective State employment services.

A reduction of 145 million dollars was made in the appropriations for general government programs. The Congress made a 50-million-dollar cut in the recommended appropriation for the disposition of surplus war material by the War Assets Administration. In the Treasury Department the appropriation for the Bureau of Internal Revenue was cut 20 million dollars which, as I have previously pointed out, will make it more difficult for the Bureau to enforce the tax laws.

Many other small but nonetheless useful activities of the Government have been curtailed or eliminated.

(2) *Reductions which will require offsets*—In some instances, the Congress has conceded that its reductions may prove excessive by admitting that more money may have to be appropriated later in the fiscal year. A fair appraisal of Congressional action, therefore, requires that we deduct from the cuts originally made the amount of the estimated supplemental appropriations re-

quired to cover the deficiencies. Appropriation cuts of this type amounted to 929 million dollars, but it now appears that it will be necessary to restore 848 million dollars. The effect of Congressional action of this kind, therefore, will be to reduce appropriations by 81 million dollars and expenditures by 56 million dollars.

Following are the major items under this heading:

The recommended appropriations for refunds of receipts were reduced by 688 million dollars (in addition to the cut of 123 million dollars resulting from extension of war excise tax rates as requested in the Budget Message). However, it is now estimated that 680 million dollars of the 688-million-dollar cut must be restored, in addition to a new authorization of 129 million dollars referred to above.

The Congress cut the appropriation for the Post Office by 102 million dollars. The part of this cut which can be considered as not requiring restoration is included in the preceding section. However, it is anticipated that an increased volume of mail, together with higher costs, will require a supplemental appropriation for the Post Office of about 53 million dollars.

The 250-million-dollar appropriation recommended for the Atomic Energy Commission was reduced by the Congress to 175 million dollars. This action was expected to provide for part of the fiscal year until the Congress should have an opportunity to secure additional information as a basis for a full-year appropriation. I anticipate that the Atomic Energy Commission will need a supplemental appropriation of at least 25 million dollars to carry on its operations.

The Congress reduced the recommended appropriation for control of foot and mouth disease by 59 million dollars, but permitted borrowing from other funds in anticipation of a later appropriation. The required supplemental appropriation is now estimated at 55 million dollars.

The Congress has also indicated its willingness to consider deficiency appropriations to restore any necessary part of the cuts of 7 million dollars made in the appropriations for the National Labor Relations Board and the Federal Mediation and Conciliation Service. A substantial part of this may have to be restored.

(3) *Reductions in Government corporation expenditures*—Except for expenditures to meet earlier commitments, the Congress has revoked the authority of the Reconstruction Finance Corporation to support the market for home loans guaranteed by the Veterans Administration and to make direct real estate loans. The effect of this action is to reduce estimated net expenditures by 325 million dollars. In addition, the Congress reduced the limitations for administrative expenses of the RFC and other Government corporations by about 20 million dollars.

(4) *Rescissions*—Since January the Congress has rescinded appropriations and other authorizations for years prior to 1948 of 4.1 billion dollars. Of the 4.1 billion dollars rescinded, 565 million dollars was pursuant to recommendations which I submitted last January after a review, at the request of the Congress, of the unexpended balances of appropriations legally available for obligation beyond the end of the fiscal year 1947 and the unexpended balances of temporary war agencies. At that time I also indicated that through administrative action there was being carried to the Treasury surplus account over 1 billion dollars, primarily lend-lease appropriations and amounts in War Department replacing accounts.

In July I recommended that an estimated 325 million dollars in revolving funds held by the Maritime Commission for ship operation be carried to the Treasury surplus fund. In the process of changing the Maritime

Commission financing from a revolving fund to an annual basis, the Congress rescinded these and other unexpended balances estimated at 550 million dollars, but provided a new appropriation of not to exceed 200 million dollars to the Secretary of the Treasury to liquidate outstanding obligations.

The Congress has rescinded nearly 3 billion dollars of additional unexpended balances, mainly military and naval appropriations. Most of these additional funds rescinded were excess wartime appropriations which had ceased to be available for obligation on June 30, 1946, or earlier, and would never have been spent.

The total actual saving in expenditures due to rescissions is 153 million dollars, all except 5 million dollars in the Navy Department.

(5) *Substitution of contract authorizations*—For some programs, the Congress substituted a total of 181 million dollars in contract authorizations for recommended appropriations in cases in which the money was to be expended later than fiscal 1948. Under the action taken by the Congress, appropriations will be required, mostly in later years, to pay off the obligations incurred under the contract authority. Expenditures in fiscal 1948 probably will not be affected by this Congressional action.

Contract authorizations of 81 million dollars for veterans' hospital construction were enacted to replace an equal amount of requested and rescinded appropriations. Similarly, for the grant-in-aid hospital construction program of the Public Health Service the Congress voted 75 million dollars in new contract authorizations in lieu of 50 million dollars of the recommended appropriation. In the case of stockpiling for national defense, the Congress offset half of the 50-million-dollar cut in appropriations for new procurement by a 25-million-dollar increase in contract authorizations.

(6) *Increases initiated by the Congress*—The Congress, on its own initiative, has increased some appropriations and expenditure requirements in fiscal 1948. Through such action, appropriations have been increased by 346 million dollars and contract authorizations by 149 million dollars. This means an estimated increase of 309 million dollars in expenditures during fiscal 1948.

The main items involved here are:

The cuts in national defense previously discussed are partly offset by increases in certain segments of the program. Thus Congress provided an additional 61 million dollars in appropriations to the War Department and 148 million dollars in contract authorizations for the War and Navy Departments. The added amounts for the War Department include 51 million dollars in appropriations and authorizations for the civilian reserves. The increases in contract authorizations include 124 million dollars for Army and Navy aircraft procurement. Expenditures will be increased by 47 million dollars during 1948 and by greater amounts in later years as the contract authorizations flow into expenditures.

The Congress has changed the arrangements for handling the finances of certain operations of the Maritime Commission and the liquidation of the former War Shipping Administration. These changes, together with the temporary extension of authority to operate ships, result in an increase in appropriations and reappropriations now estimated at about 160 million dollars. Expenditures in fiscal 1948 will be increased by 177 million dollars, but this will in the main be offset by increases in miscellaneous receipts.

The legislation to permit veterans to cash 2 billion dollars of terminal leave bonds will not directly affect Budget expenditures because the face value of these bonds was charged as an expenditure when issued. However, an estimated 50 million dollars of accrued interest will have to be paid on the bonds cashed during the fiscal year.

Pensions for the veterans of the Civil, Indian, and Spanish-American wars and their dependents have been increased by 20 percent. This and other increases for veterans' programs mean 26 million dollars of additional expenditures, to be covered by corresponding supplemental appropriations.

Increases in other types of authorizations—In addition to appropriations and contract authorizations, the Congress has authorized the cancellation by the Treasury Department of 944 million dollars of notes of the Reconstruction Finance Corporation, and has provided authorizations for expenditures of 225 million dollars treated as public debt transactions. The authorizations to cancel the Reconstruction Finance Corporation notes will permit the transfer of certain assets from the Corporation to the Treasury Department. The cancellation of notes will be payment for these assets. Thus, they cause expenditures in one set of accounts and receipts in another. The 225-million-dollar authorization treated as a public debt transaction represents merely a shift in the method of financing new loans of the Rural Electrification Administration. S i n c e neither of these actions affects total Budget expenditures, they are omitted from Table 1.

In summary, the total effect of revisions due to Congressional action—aside from reductions which will require offsets by deficiency appropriations—is to reduce 1948 appropriations by 1,578 million dollars, to increase contract authorizations by 327 million dollars, and to reduce expenditures by 1,520 million dollars.

Recapitulation by functions

The effect of the various changes upon expenditures during the current fiscal year

for each of the major functions of the Government (see Table 2) may be summarized briefly as follows:

National defense expenditures are now estimated at 855 million dollars less than in January. About two-thirds of this change is due to Congressional cuts. The remainder is due to changes in timing and a slower rate of operations.

The estimate of expenditures for veterans' programs has increased by 126 million dollars, largely as the result of increases in education and training benefits which are partly offset by decreases in pensions and other programs.

Expenditures for international affairs and finance are now estimated 791 million dollars higher than in January, without allowing for possible additional aid programs. This is due chiefly to greater withdrawals under the British loan and to the addition of aid to Greece and Turkey.

For social welfare, health, and security, the expenditure estimate is now 299 million dollars higher than in January. Most of this increase reflects transfers of expenditures between fiscal years, but 54 million dollars represents increases in programs.

Housing expenditures are expected to be 375 million dollars below the January estimate. This results chiefly from the elimination by the Congress of the authority of the Reconstruction Finance Corporation to purchase veterans' housing mortgages and to make real estate loans.

The estimate for agriculture and agricultural resources has been reduced by 442 million dollars since January. This is due chiefly to increased receipts of the Commodity Credit Corporation (which offset its expenditures) and to reductions made by the Congress in the program of the Farmers' Home Administration and in the conservation and land-use program.

The expenditure estimate for natural resources programs has been raised by 59 million dollars. Additions largely on account of accelerated flood control work have been offset in part by Congressional reductions in other resource programs.

For transportation and communication, the expenditure estimate has been cut by 95 million dollars since January. This is largely due to the changed outlook for the public roads program and to Congressional action on the airport and air facility programs.

Estimated expenditures for finance, commerce, and industry have been reduced by 129 million dollars, chiefly because of retirement of most of the stock of the Smaller War Plants Corporation in fiscal 1947 rather than 1948.

Interest payments will be about 125 million dollars higher than was estimated in January—due to higher short-term interest rates and payment of accrued interest on terminal leave bonds cashed by veterans.

These are the chief changes in the totals for the larger functions of the Government. As we have seen, many internal changes have occurred which the changes in the totals do not show. Some important services have been reduced or eliminated. On the other hand, some constructive readjustments of the Budget have been made and the Congress has accepted many of my recommendations on urgent domestic and international programs.

3. *Revenue, Borrowing, and the Public Debt*

Net Budget receipts are now estimated at 41.7 billion dollars for fiscal year 1948. The January estimate was 37.7 billion dollars without including extension of the war excise tax rates. (See Table 3.)

In my Budget Message, I requested that the war excise tax rates be continued throughout the fiscal year 1948. The Congress continued them without an expiration date. This added more than 1.1 billion dollars to the estimate of receipts, thus raising it to 38.9 billion dollars. Higher levels of national income account for the greater part of the further increase of 2.8 billion dollars in the present estimate of Budget receipts over the January estimate. The revised estimates are based on a continuance of employment, prices, and incomes close to their present levels throughout the fiscal year.

The direct taxes on individuals, principally the individual income tax, which are most affected by the level of national income, are now estimated at 21.2 billion dollars. This is an increase of 2.1 billion dollars over the January estimate. Miscellaneous receipts now are estimated about 500 million dollars higher than in January, largely because certain surplus property and other receipts which previously went to Government corporations or the Maritime Commission will now be paid into miscellaneous receipts.

Employment taxes now are estimated about 400 million dollars lower than in January. The January Budget had assumed that the Social Security old-age payroll tax would rise to 2½ percent each on employer and employee as then scheduled by law. However, as in past years, the Congress froze the rate at the present 1 percent on each. This change does not affect net receipts, since the amount transferred to the Old-Age and Survivors Insurance Trust Fund will be reduced by the same amount.

As in the case of appropriations and expenditures, the revised estimate of net receipts reflects three types of change since the January estimate. Of the estimated total increase of 3,937 million dollars, 1,130 million dollars is due to amendment of the January Budget to reflect my recommendation for continuation of war excise taxes. Changes in estimates and shifts of receipts between fiscal years account for 2,656 million dollars. The remaining 151 million dollars represents an increase arising from Congressional action to revise the financing of the Maritime Commission.

Without allowing for the contingency of additional expenditures for international aid, the Budget surplus for fiscal 1948 is estimated at 4.7 billion dollars. The surplus, together with part of the present cash balance, will be devoted to retirement of the public debt. On this basis, the debt would decline from 258 billion dollars on July 1, 1947, to 253 billion dollars at the end of the fiscal year. (See Table 6.)

4. Receipts from and Payments to the Public

Receipts from the public during the fiscal year 1948 are now estimated at 44.7 billion dollars and payments to the public, excluding additional international aid, at 39.2 billion dollars. The excess of receipts thus is 5.5 billion dollars. These totals exclude all transactions among Government agencies, Government corporations, and trust funds. They include only the actual flow of money between the Federal Government and the public. (See Table 7.)

The revised estimate of receipts from the public is 4 billion dollars higher than the January estimate, largely because of the increase in the estimate of net Budget receipts. The revised estimate of payments to the public is nearly 1.5 billion dollars higher than the January estimate, despite the lower estimate of Budget expenditures. Most of the increase in payments arises from redemption of an estimated 1.4 billion dollars of terminal leave bonds, which involves a payment to the public but no Budget expenditure—except for payment of accrued interest.

The excess of receipts from the public, apart from any additional expenditures for international aid, is now estimated 2.5 billion dollars higher than in January, but 1.2 bil-

lion dollars lower than the actual excess of receipts for the fiscal year 1947. The excess, as well as a small portion of the cash balance, will be available to repay money previously borrowed from the public. Present estimates indicate that 6.2 billion dollars of such borrowing will be repaid in the fiscal year 1948. This figure, relating to that part of the debt which is held by the public, should not be confused with the estimate for budgetary debt retirement.

Last January in my message to the Congress I pointed out that five items in the Budget—interest on the public debt, refunds of receipts, national defense, international affairs, and the veterans' programs—would require expenditures during this fiscal year of 29.2 billion dollars, or nearly four-fifths of the entire Budget.

Expenditures for these items are now estimated at 29.4 billion dollars or 79 percent of the Budget.

Expenditures for national defense, totalling 10.4 billion dollars, account for 28 percent of the Budget.

Interest on the national debt will be 5.1 billion dollars and refunds due under tax laws 2.1 billion dollars. These two items total 7.2 billion dollars, or nearly 20 percent of total expenditures.

Expenditures for veterans' services and benefits are estimated at 7.5 billion dollars, or 20 percent of the Budget.

Finally, our efforts to achieve a stable world through a program of international affairs and finance will cost 4.3 billion dollars, or nearly 12 percent of our Budget. This does not allow for possible additional international aid.

This leaves—to carry out all the remaining programs and activities of the Government—7.6 billion dollars, or 21 percent of all the money which the Federal Government will spend this year.

TABLE 2.[1] BUDGET RÉSUMÉ BASED ON EXISTING AND PROPOSED LEGISLATION
FOR THE FISCAL YEARS 1947 AND 1948

[In millions]

PART A.   BUDGET RECEIPTS AND EXPENDITURES

Description	1947 actual	1948 estimated Budget document January 1947	1948 estimated Revision August 1947
Budget receipts....................................	$43,259	[2] $37,730	$41,667
Budget expenditures:			
National defense.................................	14,451	11,256	10,401
Veterans' services and benefits......................	7,373	7,343	7,469
International affairs and finance.....................	6,669	3,510	4,301
Social welfare, health, and security.................	1,356	1,654	1,953
Housing and community facilities....................	385	539	164
Education and general research......................	71	88	72
Agriculture and agricultural resources................	1,331	1,381	939
Natural resources not primarily agricultural..........	578	1,101	1,160
Transportation and communication..................	861	1,530	1,435
Finance, commerce, and industry....................	237	426	297
Labor..	121	118	102
General government...............................	1,375	1,492	1,494
Interest on the public debt..........................	4,957	5,000	5,125
Refunds of receipts................................	3,056	[2] 2,065	2,063
Reserve for contingencies...........................	....	25	25
Adjustment to daily Treasury statement basis.........	—316	....	....
Total Budget expenditures......................	42,505	37,528	37,000
General and special accounts........................	42,819	36,699	37,193
Corporation checking accounts......................	—314	829	—193
Total Budget expenditures......................	42,505	37,528	37,000
Excess of Budget receipts over expenditures.......	754	202	4,667

[1] This table is a revision of the Budget Résumé, p. M63, of the 1948 Budget.

[2] On the basis of the law then in effect, the January estimates assumed that the war excise tax rates would terminate on June 30, 1947. However, these higher wartime rates were continued by subsequent legislation as recommended in the January Budget Message, and are reflected in the August estimates. If the continuation of the higher rates had been assumed in the January estimates, the estimated receipts from excise taxes would have been $1,130 million more and the estimated expenditures for refunds of taxes would have been $123 million less.

TABLE 2. BUDGET RÉSUMÉ BASED ON EXISTING AND PROPOSED LEGISLATION
FOR THE FISCAL YEARS 1947 AND 1948—Continued

PART B.   APPROPRIATIONS AND OTHER AUTHORIZATIONS [3]

[General and special accounts]

Description	1947 enacted	1948 recommended		
		Budget document January 1947	Revision August 1947	1948 enacted or anticipated
Appropriations....................................	$36,907	$31,276	$32,304	$29,696
Deduct: Appropriations to liquidate contract authorizations...	—530	—342	—306	—267
Anticipated supplemental appropriations (estimated):				
To cover Congressional reductions which were made with recognition that additional appropriations might be required...	....	....	....	833
To cover items to be considered at next session of Congress...	....	....	429	429
New contract authorizations..........................	—401	1,542	1,643	1,970
Anticipated supplemental contract authorizations (estimated)..	....	....	317	317
Authorizations treated as public debt transactions........	....	....	....	225
Authorizations to borrow from Reconstruction Finance Corp..	370	225	225	....
Reappropriations....................................	350	16	37	136
Total appropriations and other authorizations [3]......	36,696	32,717	34,649	33,339

[3] Excludes cancellation of corporation notes, which do not affect Budget expenditures; see "memorandum" at end of Table 4.

409

TABLE 3.[1]   Budget Receipts and Expenditures by Function for the Fiscal Years 1947 and 1948

[In millions]

Description	1947 actual	1948 estimated	
		Budget document January 1947	Revision August 1947
Budget receipts:			
General and special accounts:			
Direct taxes on individuals.........................	$20,408	$19,120	$21,195
Direct taxes on corporations......................	9,678	8,270	8,499
Excise taxes.......................................	7,269	[2] 6,118	[2] 7,246
Employment taxes...............................	2,039	[3] 2,694	[3] 2,271
Customs..	494	517	463
Miscellaneous receipts...........................	4,815	2,998	3,519
Deduct: Net appropriation to Federal old-age and survivors' insurance trust fund..................	—1,444	—1,987	—1,526
Net Budget receipts............................	43,259	37,730	41,667
Budget expenditures:			
General and special accounts:			
National defense:			
War Department..............................	7,087	6,658	6,061
Navy Department..............................	5,016	4,415	4,037
Terminal leave for enlisted military personnel.....	1,992	250	191
Stockpiling of strategic materials................	11	243	397
Other..	372	21	90
Total national defense.......................	14,478	11,587	10,776
Veterans' services and benefits:			
Pensions......................................	1,932	2,492	2,235
Insurance......................................	840	73	150
Readjustment benefits...........................	3,637	3,463	3,979
Hospitals, other services, and administration......	964	1,315	1,105
Total veterans' services and benefits...........	7,373	7,343	7,469
International affairs and finance:			
Treasury loan to United Kingdom..............	2,050	1,200	1,700
Subscription to International Bank and Fund......	1,426	....	....
Subscription to capital stock of Export-Import Bank..	325	....	....
Greek-Turkish aid.............................	....	....	320
Foreign relief.................................	1,529	1,197	1,168
Other..	692	423	429
Total international affairs and finance..........	6,022	2,820	3,617

See footnotes at end of table.

TABLE 3.[1]   BUDGET RECEIPTS AND EXPENDITURES BY FUNCTION FOR THE FISCAL YEARS 1947 AND 1948—Con.

[In millions]

Description	1947 actual	1948 estimated	
		Budget document January 1947	Revision August 1947
Budget expenditures—Continued			
Social welfare, health, and security..............	1,356	1,654	1,953
Housing and community facilities.................	520	225	312
Education and general research...................	71	88	72
Agriculture and agricultural resources.............	2,209	1,603	1,517
Natural resources not primarily agricultural.......	583	1,099	1,154
Transportation and communication...............	890	1,533	1,518
Finance, commerce, and industry.................	164	112	61
Labor..	121	118	102
General government............................	1,303	1,427	1,429
Interest on the public debt.......................	4,957	5,000	5,125
Refunds of receipts............................	3,056	[2] 2,065	[2] 2,063
Reserve for contingencies.......................	....	25	25
Adjustment to daily Treasury statement basis.......	—284	....	....
Total expenditures, general and special accounts..	42,819	36,699	37,193
Checking accounts of wholly owned Government corporations and credit agencies with U.S. Treasury (net):[4]			
National defense:			
Reconstruction Finance Corporation.............	—27	—331	—375
International affairs and finance...................	647	690	684
Housing and community facilities.................	—135	314	—148
Agriculture and agricultural resources.............	—878	—222	—578
Natural resources not primarily agricultural.......	—5	2	6
Transportation and communication...............	—29	—3	—83
Finance, commerce, and industry.................	73	314	236
General government............................	72	65	65
Adjustment to daily Treasury statement basis.......	—32	....	....
Net expenditures, corporation checking accounts [4]...............................	—314	829	—193
Total Budget expenditures...................	42,505	37,528	37,000
Excess of Budget receipts over expenditures.....	754	202	4,667

[1] This table is a revision of Table 1, p. A4, of the 1948 Budget.

[2] On the basis of the law then in effect, the January estimates assumed that the war excise tax rates would terminate on June 30, 1947. However, these higher wartime rates were continued by subsequent legislation as recommended in the January Budget Message, and are reflected in the August estimates. If the continuation of the higher rates had been assumed in the January estimates, the estimated receipts from excise taxes would have been $1,130 million more and the estimated expenditures for refunds of taxes would have been $123 million less.

[3] On the basis of the law then in effect, the January estimates assumed that the social security old-age tax rate would rise to 2½% each on employers and employees on January 1, 1948. Because of later legislation, the August estimates are based on continuation of the 1% rate on each.

[4] Sales and redemptions of obligations of Government corporations and credit agencies are shown in Table 5.

TABLE 4.[1] GENERAL AND SPECIAL ACCOUNT APPROPRIATIONS AND AUTHORIZATIONS BY FUNCTION, FOR THE FISCAL YEARS 1947 AND 1948

[In millions]

Description	1947 enacted	1948 recommended		1948 enacted or anticipated
		Budget document January, 1947	Revision August, 1947	
Appropriations:				
National defense:				
War Department...............................	$7,308	$5,942	$5,717	$5,508
Navy Department [2]............................	4,140	3,541	3,512	3,268
Terminal leave for enlisted military personnel.......	2,432	....	....	....
Stockpiling of strategic materials..................	100	....	150	100
Other.......................................	32	10	7	5
Total national defense..........................	14,012	9,493	9,386	8,881
Veterans' services and benefits:				
Pensions......................................	2,147	2,492	2,222	2,172
Insurance.....................................	711	73	73	73
Readjustment benefits...........................	4,365	3,484	3,806	3,806
Hospitals, other services, and administration........	1,209	960	983	920
Total veterans' services and benefits.............	8,432	7,009	7,084	6,971
International affairs and finance:				
Greek-Turkish aid..............................	....	....	400	400
Foreign relief.................................	725	725	1,075	932
Other..	190	444	440	375
Total international affairs and finance...........	915	1,169	1,915	1,707
Social welfare, health, and security.................	1,287	1,877	1,824	1,746
Housing and community facilities....................	82	179	114	106
Education and general research......................	66	85	100	67
Agriculture and agricultural resources................	695	824	882	652
Natural resources not primarily agricultural..........	538	779	1,015	719
Transportation and communication...................	1,012	1,196	1,279	1,073
Finance, commerce, and industry....................	168	116	90	59
Labor..	119	118	127	96
General government.............................	1,500	1,341	1,421	1,240
Interest on the public debt........................	4,957	5,000	5,125	5,125
Refunds of receipts..............................	3,124	2,065	1,942	1,254
Reserve for contingencies..........................	....	25	....	....
Total appropriations............................	36,907	31,276	32,304	29,696

See footnotes at end of table.

TABLE 4.[1] GENERAL AND SPECIAL ACCOUNT APPROPRIATIONS AND AUTHORIZATIONS BY FUNCTION, FOR THE
FISCAL YEARS 1947 AND 1948—Continued

[In millions]

Description	1947 enacted	1948 recommended		
		Budget document January, 1947	Revision August, 1947	1948 enacted or anticipated
Deduct appropriations to liquidate contract authorizations:				
National defense................................	250	37	....	....
International affairs and finance....................	4	8	8	8
Education and general research.....................	....	....	2	2
Natural resources not primarily agricultural..........	5	2	2	....
Transportation and communication..................	268	292	292	256
General government.............................	3	3	2	1
Total appropriations to liquidate contract authorizations...................................	530	342	306	267
Total appropriations, excluding appropriations to liquidate contract authorizations..............	36,377	30,934	31,998	29,429
Anticipated supplemental appropriations (estimated):				
To cover Congressional reductions which were made with recognition that additional appropriations might be required:				
Refunds of receipts.............................	....	....	....	680
Post Office Department (general fund).............	....	....	....	53
Atomic Energy Commission.......................	....	....	....	25
Department of Agriculture........................	....	....	....	55
Other..	....	....	....	[3] 20
Total to cover Congressional reductions which were made with recognition that additional appropriations might be required.............	....	....	....	[3] 833
To cover items not yet considered by Congress:				
Refunds of receipts.............................	....	....	129	129
Army and Navy public works programs..............	....	....	60	60
Grants to States for increased public assistance.......	....	....	115	115
Veterans' pensions..............................	....	....	26	26
Other..	....	....	74	74
Reserve for contingencies.........................	....	....	25	25
Total to cover items not yet considered by Congress....................................	....	....	429	429
Total anticipated supplemental appropriations (estimated).................................	....	....	429	[3] 1,262

See footnotes at end of table.

TABLE 4.[1] GENERAL AND SPECIAL ACCOUNT APPROPRIATIONS AND AUTHORIZATIONS BY FUNCTION, FOR THE
FISCAL YEARS 1947 AND 1948—Continued

[In millions]

		1948 recommended		
Description	1947 enacted	Budget document January, 1947	Revision August, 1947	1948 enacted or anticipated
New contract authorizations:				
National defense...................................	[4] —1,352	541	603	777
Veterans' services and benefits........................	441	219	258	338
Social welfare, health, and security....................	....	....	....	75
Housing and community facilities......................	....	2	....	....
Education and general research........................	....	5	5	4
Natural resources not primarily agricultural...........	....	256	256	257
Transportation and communication....................	510	517	519	519
General government...................................	....	2	2	....
Total new contract authorizations................	—401	1,542	1,643	1,970
Anticipated supplemental contract authorizations (estimated):				
Army and Navy public works programs................	....	....	283	283
Other..	....	....	34	34
Total anticipated supplemental contract authorizations (estimated)............................	....	....	317	317
Authorizations treated as public debt transactions:				
Rural Electrification Administration...................	....	....	....	225
Authorizations to borrow from Reconstruction Finance Corp.:				
Rural Electrification Administration..................	250	225	225	....
Farmers' Home Administration........................	120	....	....	....
Total authorizations to borrow from Reconstruction Finance Corporation...........................	370	225	225	....
Reappropriations:				
National defense.....................................	193	....	....	....
Social welfare, health, and security...................	2	1	1	....
Housing and community facilities......................	4	....	1	1
Education and general research........................	7	....	....	....
Agriculture and agricultural resources.................	115	....	....	....
Natural resources not primarily agricultural...........	11	14	18	18
Transportation and communication....................	18	1	17	117
General government...................................	....	....	....	....
Total reappropriations............................	350	16	37	136
Total appropriations and other authorizations.....	36,696	32,717	34,649	33,339

See footnotes on following page.

Table 4.[1] General and Special Account Appropriations and Authorizations by Function, for the Fiscal Years 1947 and 1948—Continued

FOOTNOTES

[1] This table is a revision of Table 2, p. A5, of the 1948 Budget.

[2] Excludes funds made available by transfer from unexpended prior year appropriations as follows: 1947, Enacted, $500 million; 1948, Recommended, Budget Document, January 1947, $180 million; 1948, Recommended, Revision, August 1947, $180 million; and 1948, Enacted or Anticipated, $100 million.

[3] Net of anticipated supplemental appropriations of $15 million to liquidate contract authorizations for the Public Health Service, hospital construction program.

[4] Represents rescissions of prior-year contract authorizations and reductions in the estimated cost of uncompleted tonnage authorized in prior authorizations.

MEMORANDUM

[In millions]

	1947 enacted	Budget document January, 1947	Revision August, 1947	1948 enacted or anticipated
			1948 recommended	
Cancellation of notes payable to the United States Treasury:				
Commodity Credit Corporation:				
Restoration of capital impairment..................	1,563	830	....	....
Reconstruction Finance Corporation:				
Reimbursement for strategic materials transferred to military stockpile..............................	....	210	260	260
Reimbursement for loans to Rural Electrification Administration..	....	....	....	511
Reimbursement to Secretary of Agriculture for farm tenancy loans....................................	....	....	....	40
Reimbursement for capital stock of Federal home loan banks..	....	....	....	123
Reimbursement for transfer of office buildings........	....	....	....	10
Total cancellations of notes payable to United States Treasury...........................	1,563	1,040	260	944

NOTE: The cancellations of notes listed above (authorized by appropriation acts) represent bookkeeping adjustments which do not affect the current Budget programs.

TABLE 5.[1]   TRUST ACCOUNT RECEIPTS, EXPENDITURES, AND INVESTMENTS, FOR THE FISCAL YEARS 1947 AND 1948

[In millions]

Description	1947 actual	1948 estimated Budget document January 1947	Revision August 1947
Trust account receipts:			
Unemployment trust fund:			
Deposits by States...............................	$1,006	$1,124	$1,124
Deposits by Railroad Retirement Board...........	128	115	122
Transfers from general and special accounts........	9	9	10
Interest on investments...........................	147	166	164
Federal old-age and survivors insurance trust fund:			
Net appropriation from general account receipts....	1,444	1,987	1,526
Interest on investments...........................	163	190	184
Veterans' life insurance funds:			
Premiums, etc....................................	570	406	561
Transfers from general and special accounts.........	817	53	143
Interest and profits on investments................	251	234	240
Federal employees' retirement funds:			
Deductions from employees' salaries..............	259	182	204
Transfers from general and special accounts.........	223	246	246
District of Columbia share.......................	1	2	2
Interest and profits on investments................	95	106	102
Railroad retirement account:			
Transfers from general and special accounts.........	298	481	728
Interest on investments..........................	24	37	40
Other trust accounts:			
Transfers from general and special accounts........	8	9	13
Miscellaneous trust receipts.....................	785	240	400
Total receipts, trust accounts..................	6,228	5,587	5,809

See footnotes at end of table.

TABLE 5.[1]   TRUST ACCOUNT RECEIPTS, EXPENDITURES, AND INVESTMENTS, FOR THE FISCAL YEARS 1947 AND 1948—Continued

[In millions]

Description	1947 actual	1948 estimated Budget document January 1947	Revision August 1947
Trust account expenditures:			
Unemployment trust fund: Withdrawals by States and other expenditures..............................	869	749	874
Federal old-age and survivors insurance trust fund: Benefit payments...............................	426	543	543
Veterans' life insurance funds: Insurance losses and refunds.......................................	349	359	370
Federal employees' retirement funds: Annuities and refunds.......................................	323	167	302
Railroad retirement account: Benefit payments........	173	270	228
Other trust accounts: Miscellaneous trust expenditures.	1,098	411	600
Special deposit accounts (net):			
Government corporations (partially owned)........	8	247	72
Other special deposit accounts....................	364	250	200
Sales and redemptions of obligations of Government corporations and credit agencies in the market (net).	359	[2] 216	[2] 100
Total expenditures, trust accounts..............	3,969	2,780	3,089
Net accumulations in trust accounts...........	2,259	2,807	2,720
Trust account investments:			
Unemployment trust fund.........................	443	665	546
Federal old-age and survivors insurance trust fund.....	1,194	1,604	1,137
Veterans' life insurance funds......................	1,294	334	574
Federal employees' retirement funds.................	282	369	252
Railroad retirement account.......................	149	250	540
Other trust accounts.............................	([3])	[2] 1	[2] 1
Total investments, trust accounts..............	3,362	3,221	3,048
Total expenditures and investments, trust accounts.	7,331	6,001	6,137
Clearing account for outstanding checks................	—555	....	....
Adjusted total expenditures and investments, trust accounts..................................	6,776	6,001	6,137

[1] This table is a revision of Table 4, p. A7, of the 1948 Budget.
[2] Excess of redemptions, deduct.
[3] Less than $500,000.

TABLE 6.[1] EFFECT OF FINANCIAL OPERATIONS ON THE PUBLIC DEBT FOR THE FISCAL YEARS 1947 AND 1948

[In millions]

Description	1947 actual	1948 estimated Budget document January 1947	1948 estimated Revision August 1947
Public debt at beginning of year......................	$269,422	$260,400	$258,286
Change in public debt during the year:			
Net Budget receipts..............................	43,259	37,730	41,667
Budget expenditures:			
General and special accounts......................	42,819	36,699	37,193
Checking accounts of wholly owned Government corporations and credit agencies with U.S. Treasurer (net)......................................	—314	829	—193
Total Budget expenditures......................	42,505	37,528	37,000
Excess of Budget receipts over expenditures.......	754	202	4,667
Trust account receipts.............................	6,228	5,587	5,809
Trust account expenditures..........................	3,969	2,780	3,089
Net accumulations in trust accounts...............	2,259	2,807	2,720
Trust account investments in United States securities....	3,362	3,221	3,048
Clearing account for outstanding checks..............	—555	....	....
Excess of trust account expenditures and investments over receipts...................................	548	414	328
Treasury cash balance at beginning of year............	14,238	2,515	3,308
Treasury cash balance at end of year.................	3,308	2,104	2,561
Change in Treasury cash balance during year..........	—10,930	—412	—747
Total change in public debt during the year.......	—11,136	—200	—5,086
Public debt at end of year...........................	258,286	260,200	253,200

[1] This table is a revision of Table 5, p. A8, of the 1948 Budget.

TABLE 7.[1] RECEIPTS FROM AND PAYMENTS TO THE PUBLIC, EXCLUDING MAJOR INTRAGOVERNMENTAL AND NONCASH TRANSACTIONS, FOR THE FISCAL YEARS 1947 AND 1948

[In millions]

Description	1947 actual	1948 estimated Budget document January 1947	1948 estimated Revision August 1947
RECEIPTS FROM THE PUBLIC			
General and special accounts:			
Direct taxes on individuals.........................	$20,408	$19,120	$21,195
Direct taxes on corporations........................	9,678	8,270	8,499
Employment taxes [2]...............................	595	707	745
Excise taxes and customs...........................	7,763	6,635	7,709
Miscellaneous receipts.............................	4,502	2,127	2,804
Trust accounts [2].................................	3,697	3,874	3,731
Total receipts from the public.................	46,643	40,733	44,683
PAYMENTS TO THE PUBLIC			
General and special accounts, and checking accounts of wholly owned Government corporations and credit agencies with U.S. Treasurer (net):			
National defense.................................	12,605	11,054	11,710
Veterans' services and benefits......................	6,564	7,295	7,331
International affairs and finance.....................	5,301	3,962	5,198
Social welfare, health, and security.................	1,044	1,160	1,211
Housing and community facilities....................	296	434	121
Education and general research.....................	71	88	72
Agriculture and agricultural resources...............	1,327	1,377	934
Natural resources not primarily agricultural.........	567	1,092	1,151
Transportation and communication.................	861	1,530	1,435
Finance, commerce, and industry...................	101	116	62
Labor..	121	118	102
General government..............................	1,054	1,152	1,142
Interest on the public debt.........................	3,812	3,705	3,863
Refunds of receipts...............................	3,095	2,080	2,075
Reserve for contingencies..........................	....	25	25
Trust accounts...................................	3,270	2,772	3,001
Exchange stabilization fund........................	1,026	....	....
Deductions from Federal employees' salaries for retirement fund..	−259	−182	−207
Clearing account for outstanding checks..............	−555	....	....
Adjustment to daily Treasury statement basis..........	−316	....	....
Total payments to the public...................	39,985	37,778	39,226
Excess of payments to the public......................	....	....	....
Excess of receipts from the public....................	6,658	2,955	5,457
BORROWING FROM AND REPAYMENT OF DEBT TO THE PUBLIC			
Excess of receipts from the public....................	6,658	2,955	5,457
Decrease in stabilization fund balance................	1,800	....	....
Decrease in Treasury cash balance....................	10,930	412	747
Repayment of debt to the public (net)................	19,388	3,367	6,204

[1] This table is a revision of Table 18, p. A128, of the 1948 Budget.

[2] Net appropriation to Federal old age and survivors insurance trust fund is excluded from employment taxes, but included as trust account receipt.

182   The President's News Conference of
August 21, 1947

THE PRESIDENT. [1.] I just have one announcement to make, and that is that Kenneth C. Royall will be the Secretary for the Army, and the Honorable John L. Sullivan, the present Under Secretary of the Navy, will be Secretary for the Navy; and Stuart Symington will be Secretary for Air.

The other appointments, under the new bill, are not ready to be announced yet. They will be announced later.

And Mr. Ross has gotten up a picture of the setup for you, which will be handed to you as you go out, along with the life and background of these gentlemen whose appointments are being announced today.

That's all the announcements I have to make.

Q. Mr. President, in that connection, is it necessary to reappoint all members of the Munitions Board on the old Army and Navy—

THE PRESIDENT. Well, the law, I think, provides that civilian—civilians under the present War Department Act automatically go under this one. We are having it thoroughly looked up, so in case it is necessary to reappoint them, why they will be appointed.

Q. Mr. President, when can we look for this to become effective? In other words, when——

THE PRESIDENT. About the middle of September—sometime around then.

Q. That will be when Mr. Forrestal takes his oath of office?

THE PRESIDENT. That will be when Mr. Forrestal takes his oath of office.

Q. About the middle, not the first?

THE PRESIDENT. About the middle of September.

[2.] Q. Mr. President, have you any comment on the death of Senator Bilbo?

THE PRESIDENT. Of course I was sorry to hear of Senator Bilbo's death. I was there for 10 years in the Senate. Used to sit right behind him. Knew him very well. Sending the usual condolences to his family.

[3.] Q. Mr. President, have you decided as yet to accept the American Legion Convention invitation?

THE PRESIDENT. No I haven't. I have announced that I wouldn't be able to be present.

[4.] Q. Mr. President, who will take over the Conciliation and Mediation Service since the——

THE PRESIDENT. I just named the man. Judge, what's his name?

Judge Latta: Colvin.

THE PRESIDENT. Colvin. Couldn't think of it. Colvin will temporarily take over that job.

Q. Mr. President, will your appointments to the labor-management panel under the Taft-Hartley Act be ready soon?

THE PRESIDENT. I hope so. I hope they will be ready by the time the act goes into effect—I hope.

Q. Mr. President, most major portions of the act become effective tomorrow.

THE PRESIDENT. That is true.

Q. Any comment on them at this time?

THE PRESIDENT. No comment. No comment. I made all the comment I could on it.

Q. You don't feel the same way——

THE PRESIDENT. Both before and after. [*Laughter*]

[5.] Q. Is it true, Mr. President, that you talked to Mr. Denham recently about the relationship between him and the joint legislative committee?

THE PRESIDENT. I had a conference with the whole board in here, and we discussed the difference between the legislative and

420

the executive branches of the Government. The Board and the Council were all in agreement with my viewpoint.

[6.] Q. Mr. President, Representative Merrow is reported to have sent you a wire urging a special session in view of all the crises overseas.

THE PRESIDENT. I haven't received any such wire as yet. My position in the matter hasn't changed. If it is ever—becomes a necessity for a special session, I won't hesitate to call it. I don't think there is any necessity at this time to be calling any special session.

[7.] Q. Mr. President, have you had any report from Mr. Clayton on the progress of the ITO in Geneva?

THE PRESIDENT. No, I have not.

Q. Is that supposed to be over and completed by this time, sir?

THE PRESIDENT. I don't know whether there was any time set on it or not. I think the idea was to arrive at an agreement as soon as they could. They are still working at it.

[8.] Q. Mr. President, did you see a Mr. Tom Connors today from Scranton, Pa.?

THE PRESIDENT. Yes.

Q. Former newspaperman?

THE PRESIDENT. Yes.

Q. Do you know what he is doing in town?

THE PRESIDENT. No, I don't. You will have to ask him. He just came in here to pay his respects to me.

Q. Somebody told me he was trying to buy a paper and wanted to talk with you about it.

THE PRESIDENT. No, he didn't discuss his business with me. I think maybe he will tell you probably what he was in for, if you would ask him.

Q. This was just a handshake?

THE PRESIDENT. We just had a friendly visit. I have known him a long time ago, when I went up to Scranton for Frank Walker way back yonder when I was a Senator, and I made a speech for them on St. Patrick's Day; and Mr. Connors was one of my hosts at that time and he was running a paper in Scranton. And he told me this morning that he was the first man that suggested me for Vice President of the United States in 1944. I did not thank him.

Q. When didn't you thank him?

THE PRESIDENT. This morning, or then, either. [*Laughter*]

[9.] Q. Mr. President, has Commissioner Lowell Mason spoken to you about any desire to resign from FTC?

THE PRESIDENT. No, I am sure he doesn't care about resigning. He is doing a good job over there.

[10.] Q. Mr. President, do you plan any new approaches to the displaced persons?

THE PRESIDENT. No. Still making the effort, and those appointments the other day were all interested in getting some concrete action on that subject. I am very much interested in it. I think it is up to us to do our share along that line. I don't think any of our people have any right to quarrel with doing the right thing, for the simple reason that all of them are descendants of displaced persons—everybody in this country.

Q. You intend to propose legislation when Congress returns?

THE PRESIDENT. Well, I proposed it at the last session, and I proposed it at the session before that, and I shall probably propose it to this session.

[11.] Q. Sir, can you say what was discussed with former Senator Huffman yesterday?

THE PRESIDENT. Oh, he just came in to talk over politics. I had a very nice meeting with him.

Q. Did he say you do all right in Ohio?

THE PRESIDENT. That's what he told me.

Q. You will be a candidate then, sir?

[*Laughter*]

THE PRESIDENT. I didn't say that. No—I am making no announcement.

Reporter: Well, thank you, Mr. President.

THE PRESIDENT. Entirely welcome.

NOTE: President Truman's one hundred and eighteenth news conference was held in his office at the White House at 4:03 p.m. on Thursday, August 21, 1947.

183   Statement by the President Upon Receiving Report of His Scientific Research Board.   *August 27, 1947*

THE CHAIRMAN of the President's Scientific Research Board, whom I directed last October to study the scientific research and development of this country, has made his first report to me.

Mr. Steelman's report, entitled "Science and Public Policy: A Program for the Nation," makes a comprehensive survey of the present position of the United States in the field of science. It outlines a broad program over the next 10 years that should greatly advance the Nation's position in scientific research and development. This program places a heavier emphasis upon basic research and upon medical research, indicates effective methods of increasing our supply of highly trained scientists, and suggests the goal by 1957 of a total expenditure by industry, the universities, and the Government of an amount equal to at least 1 percent of our national income.

The report confirms a belief previously expressed by me that the national welfare requires support by the Federal Government of basic research in universities and non-profit research institutions, through creation by the Congress of a National Science Foundation. This Foundation should be set up from the outset in accordance with sound principles of administration and with the recognized democratic controls that should characterize all our public institutions.

The report is also concerned with strengthening and improving the Federal Government's own research and development program, which represents a substantial part of the national total of research. In order to assist in the coordinating of the Federal Government's scientific programs and in studying the special problems involved in research administration, I shall shortly name a permanent committee of Government officials most concerned with scientific research, as recommended in the report.

The position of world leadership this Nation occupies is due in large part to the fact that in a few generations we transferred our pioneering way of life into a modern industrial economy resting on the principle of scientific and human progress. We must constantly enlarge the boundaries of scientific knowledge in order to continue to provide the benefits of full production and full employment, and in order to protect our democracy from the dangers it faces in an uneasy world. The fact that only a thin trickle of scientific knowledge is today reaching us from other countries constitutes an emergency and a challenge. To meet this challenge, we must promote the rapid growth of basic research, the cross-fertilization of ideas among our scientists, and the maturing of a new generation of scientists who will think boldly and daringly.

We must concentrate on training young men and women who not only can handle technological devices, machinery and equipment, but who understand the laws by which these devices function. We must educate young people who will be able not only to apply known scientific principles to the peaceful development of new techniques in industry, agriculture, and medicine, but who will have the creative ability and the scientific training to discover new basic principles themselves.

These are matters that should be carefully considered by scientists, educators, industrialists, and legislators, as well as by private citizens. I hope this report will be read thoughtfully by all those who take seriously their responsibilities as Americans for the future growth, prosperity, and security of our country.

NOTE: The report, first in a series prepared by the President's Scientific Research Board, is dated August 27, 1947 (Government Printing Office, 73 pp.). The Board was established by Executive Order 9791 on October 17, 1946 (3 CFR, 1943–1948 Comp., p. 578). For subsequent reports of the President's Scientific Research Board, see Items 194, 201, 206, 211.

The President established a permanent Committee on Scientific Research and Development on December 24 (see Item 241).

184   Letter to Secretary Schwellenbach on Employment of the Physically Handicapped.   *August 27, 1947*

My dear Mr. Secretary:

I have today issued the attached proclamation calling upon the people of the United States to observe the week of October 5–11, 1947, as National Employ the Physically Handicapped Week. In that proclamation I asked the heads of all government agencies to make every effort to enlist public support for a sustained program aimed at the employment and full use of the capacities of physically handicapped workers.

Because of your responsibilities in the Federal Government's contribution to the efficient employment of the Nation's working force, I am relying upon you to take a vigorous part in the observance of National Employ the Physically Handicapped Week. You may wish to consult with the Federal Security Administrator and the Administrator of Veterans Affairs who are also especially concerned with the effectiveness of this campaign.

Sincerely yours,

HARRY S. TRUMAN

[The Honorable The Secretary of Labor, Washington, D.C.]

NOTE: The letter was part of a White House release announcing that the President had that day proclaimed the first week in October as a week of observance for the employment of the physically handicapped. The release stated that identical letters had also been sent to Oscar R. Ewing, Administrator, Federal Security Agency, and Gen. Omar N. Bradley, Administrator of Veterans Affairs.

Proclamation 2745 "National Employ the Physically Handicapped Week, 1947" is printed in title 3 of the Code of Federal Regulations (3 CFR, 1943–1948 Comp., p. 128).

185   Exchange of Messages With Pope Pius XII. *August 28, 1947*

[Released August 28, 1947. Dated August 6, 1947]

Your Holiness:

In continuance of the exchanges of views undertaken from time to time since their beginning, on December 23, 1939, for the purpose of facilitating parallel endeavors for peace and the alleviation of human suffering, I am requesting Mr. Taylor to return to Rome and to resume audiences with Your Holiness at such times as may be found appropriate. These exchanges have already contributed profoundly toward a sound and lasting peace and to the strengthening of the impelling convictions pursued by the peoples of the world in their quest for a moral world order firmly established in the life of nations.

I desire to do everything in my power to support and to contribute to a concert of all the forces striving for a moral world. Those forces are in the homes of peaceful and law-abiding citizens in every part of the world who are exemplifying in their own lives the principles of the good neighbor: the Golden Rule itself. They are on the farms, in the factories, mines, and little shops in all parts of the world where the principles of free cooperation and voluntary association in self-government are honored. These moral aspirations are in the hearts of good men the world over. They are in all churches, and in schools. The war demonstrated that all persons, regardless of divergent religious allegiances, can unite their efforts for the preservation and support of the principles of freedom and morality and justice. They must unite their efforts in the cause of enduring peace if they are not one by one to be weakened and rendered impotent at the times of their great need. They have, individually and together, the duty to vindicate, by their thoughts and deeds, the great hopes for which men fought in World War II and the hopes which today all serious-thinking men and women throughout the world know must be attained.

The tasks now confronting us are formidable. The conditions for meeting the heavy problems of war settlement and of new problems still unsolved are accompanied by multiplied discouragements. Unless the moral forces of the world now join their strength, discouragement must inevitably deepen, and the strength and effectiveness which thereby would be lost by these moral forces would be gained by those forces which oppose and seek to destroy them. The hopes and ideals of mankind have often been jeopardized by force. They will be jeopardized today by any division of the moral forces of the world or, by any refusal to support and strengthen the hopes and ideals of all mankind.

As the chosen leader of the people of the United States I am privileged to pledge full faith to you once again to work with Your Holiness and with every agency of good the world over for an enduring peace. An enduring peace can be built only upon Christian principles. To such a consummation we dedicate all our resources, both spiritual and material, remembering always that except the Lord build the house, they labor in vain who build it.

Your Holiness, this is a Christian Nation. More than a half century ago that declaration was written into the decrees of the highest court in this land. It is not without significance that the valiant pioneers who left Europe to establish settlements here, at the very beginning of their colonial enterprises, declared their faith in the Christian religion and made ample provision for its practice and for its support. The story of the Christian missionaries who in earliest days endured perils, hardship—even death itself in carrying the message of Jesus Christ to untutored savages is one that still moves the hearts of men.

As a Christian Nation our earnest desire is to work with men of good will everywhere to banish war and the causes of war from the world whose Creator desired that men of every race and in every clime should live together in peace, good will and mutual trust. Freedom of conscience, ordained by the Fathers of our Constitution to all who live under the flag of the United States, has been a bulwark of national strength, a source of happiness, from the establishment of our Nation to this day.

I believe that the greatest need of the world today, fundamental to all else, is a renewal of faith. I seek to encourage renewed faith in the dignity and worth of the human person in all lands, to the end that the individual's sacred rights, inherent in his relationship to God and his fellows, will be respected in every land. We must have faith in the inevitable triumph of truth and decency; faith that mankind shall live in freedom, not in the chains of untruth nor in the chains of a collectivist organization of their lives; faith of such fullness that it will energize men and women everywhere to build with tenacity, the better social world order under self-rule. The times demand faith that is strong enough to struggle if need be for the right, that is able to endure troubles and hardships, attack and even contempt from forces of evil—and able to arise reborn and revitalized from the daily struggle. Faith leads to hope, to determination, to trust in the truth and the good, and to sustained effort to create the kind of peace and well-being sought by humble men and women in all lands and which will ultimately prevail between all nations. Through faith, the purposes of God shall be carried out in the hearts and deeds of Man. I believe with heartfelt conviction that those who do not recognize their responsibility to Almighty God cannot meet their full duty toward their fellow men.

I have asked Mr. Taylor to convey these views and to say that I seek to cooperate with the efforts of Your Holiness and the efforts of every leader of the world's moral forces. Our common goal is to arouse and invigorate the faith of men to attain eternal values in our own generation—no matter what obstacles exist or may arise in the path.

Faithfully yours,

HARRY S. TRUMAN

NOTE: The Pope's reply, dated August 26 at Castel Gandolfo, follows:

Your Excellency:

We have just received from the hands of your Personal Representative, Mr. Myron Taylor, Your Excellency's letter of August 6 and we hasten to express our satisfaction and thanks for this latest testimony to the desire and determination of a great and free people to dedicate themselves with their characteristic confidence and generosity to the noble task of strengthening the foundations of that peace for which all peoples of the earth are longing. As their chosen leader Your Excellency seeks to enlist and cement the cooperation of every force and power which can help to accomplish this task. No one more than we will hope for its success and for the happy achievement of the goal. We pledge our resources and earnestly beg God's assistance.

What is proposed is to ensure the foundations of a lasting peace among nations. It were indeed futile to promise long life to any building erected on shifting sands or a cracked and crumbling base. The foundations, we know, of such a peace (the truth finds expression once again in the letter of Your Excellency) can be secure only if they rest on bedrock faith in the one true God, the Creator of all men. It was He who of necessity assigned man's purpose in life. It is from Him, with consequent necessity, that man derives personal imprescriptible rights to pursue that purpose and to be unhindered in the attainment of it. Civic society is also of Divine origin and indicated by nature itself but it is subsequent to man and meant to be a means to defend him and to help him in the legitimate exercise of his God-given rights. Once the state to the exclusion of God makes itself the source of the rights of the human person, man is forthwith reduced to the condition of a slave or a mere civic commodity to be exploited for the selfish aims of a group that happens to have power. The order of God is overturned and history surely makes it clear to those who wish to read that the inevitable result in the subversion of order between peoples is war. The task then before the friends of peace is clear.

Is Your Excellency oversanguine in hoping to find men throughout the world ready to cooperate for such a worthy enterprise? We think not. Truth has lost none of its power to rally to its cause the most enlightened minds and noblest spirits. Their ardour is fed by the flame of righteous freedom struggling to break through injustice and lying. But those who possess the truth must be conscientious to define it clearly when its foes cleverly distort it; bold to defend it and generous enough to set the course of their lives both national and personal by its dictates. This will require moreover correcting not a few aberrations. Social injustices, racial injustices and religious animosities exist today among men and groups who boast of Christian civilization. And they are a very useful and often effective weapon in the hands of those who are bent on destroying all the good which that civilization has brought to men. It is for all sincere lovers of the great human family to unite in wresting those weapons from hostile hands. With that union will come hope that the enemies of God and free men will not prevail.

Certainly Your Excellency and all defenders of the rights of the human person will find wholehearted cooperation from God's Church, faithful custodian of eternal truth and loving mother of all. From her foundation almost two thousand years ago she has championed the individual against despotic rule, the labouring man against oppression, religion against persecution. Her divinely-given mission often brings her into conflict with the powers of evil whose sole strength is in their physical force and brutalized spirit and her leaders are sent into exile or cast into prison or die under torture. This is history of today but the Church is unafraid. She cannot compromise with an avowed enemy of God. She must continue to teach the first and greatest Commandment incumbent on every man: "Thou shalt love the Lord thy God with thy whole heart, with thy whole soul, with all thy strength." And the second like unto the first: "Thou shalt love thy neighbor as thyself." It is her changeless message that man's first duty is to God, then to his fellowman, that that man serves his country best who serves his God most faithfully, that the country that would shackle the Word of God, given to men through Jesus Christ, helps not at all the lasting peace of the world. In striving with all the resources at her power to bring men and nations to a clear realization of their duty to God, the Church will go on, as she has always done, to offer the most effective contribution to the world's peace and man's eternal salvation.

We are pleased that the letter of Your Excellency has given us the opportunity of saying a word of encouragement for all those who are gravely intent on buttressing the fragile structure of peace until its foundations can be more firmly and wisely established. The munificent charity shown by the American people to the suffering and oppressed in every part of the world, truly worthy of the finest Christian traditions, is a fair token of their sincere desire for universal peace and prosperity. The vast majority of the peoples of the world, we feel sure, share that desire, even in countries where free expression is smothered. God grant their forces may be united towards its realization. There is no room for discouragement or for relaxing of their efforts under the gracious and merciful providence of God, the Father of all that is good and holy, and justice will in the end prevail.

Let us assure Your Excellency of our cordial welcome to Mr. Taylor, your Personal Representative, on his return to Rome; and we are happy to renew the expression of our good wishes for the people of the United States, for the members of their Government, and in particular for its esteemed Chief Executive.

PIUS XII

---

186   Letter to Secretary Krug on the Forthcoming International Conference on Natural Resources. *August 29, 1947*

[Released August 29, 1947. Dated August 27, 1947]

My dear Mr. Secretary:

The Economic and Social Council of the United Nations is undertaking to set up a preparatory commission to plan the International Scientific Conference on the Conservation and Utilization of Natural Resources. As this conference will be held in the United States and because it was initiated at my suggestion, I am especially eager to give the fullest possible cooperation to its planning and preparation.

The subject matter of this conference falls largely in the area of the work of the Department of the Interior. I, therefore, ask that you undertake to set up and give direction to a technical committee to assist representatives of the United Nations' preparatory commission in this work. The scope of the conference will, of course, include the interests of other Departments of the Government, especially State, Agriculture and Commerce, so that representatives of these De-

426

partments and other interested agencies should be included on your technical committee. I believe that you will need a full-time assistant to work with this group and to provide a liaison with the preparatory commission.

American participation in this conference should be based upon the broadest possible representation of scientific, educational, industrial and labor groups, as well as governmental agencies. I, therefore, ask that you also set up an advisory committee of members of these interested groups to assist the technical committee in the task of assuring the success of this important undertaking.

Sincerely yours,

HARRY S. TRUMAN

[The Honorable The Secretary of the Interior]

187 Statement by the President: Labor Day. *August* 30, 1947

LABOR DAY offers us a yearly opportunity to pay tribute to the contribution the free working men and women of the United States have made to their country's progress, prosperity, and world leadership. This Labor Day of 1947, 2 years after we defeated our enemies in battle, is an appropriate moment for us to evaluate our accomplishments during war and reconversion, and to plan for the peace we still must win. Labor Day, therefore, should be a holiday not alone for celebration of past accomplishments, but for dedication to the future, and to the hope which that future holds for mankind.

The organized labor movement of America has rewarded working men and women with higher wages, shorter hours, and improved working and living conditions. But these rewards have been possible only because, as unions grew stronger, they developed increasing responsibility for helping the wheels of industry to turn. Wherever a responsible labor movement flourishes, there industry prospers, production increases, and the living standards of the community, State, or region improve.

The right to join a union of one's own choice is unquestioned today, and is sanctioned and protected by law. The bargaining table at which labor and management sit to work out their common problems is indispensable to our democracy, and must be safeguarded against any attempts by misguided or ill-intentioned groups or individuals to weaken or replace it.

Good labor relations, however, cannot be brought about by legislation. They are created by the men and women concerned, cooperating sincerely and earnestly within the framework of a minimum amount of regulatory law. I believe that enlightened labor and enlightened management, working together, can accomplish far more by peaceful bargaining than is possible through legislation. Cooperation by labor and management, in a spirit of honest concern for the welfare of all the people, will speed the day when strikes and lockouts are discarded, and will safeguard labor's freedom to solve its problems without restrictive Government regulation.

Government, also, has a responsibility for promoting the welfare of all the people by pointing out and eliminating injustice and inequity. In order to enable the Government to discharge its constitutional and legal duties, the Department of Labor must be adequately staffed, and be given jurisdiction over those governmental functions which are an appropriate part of a department created to foster, promote, and develop the welfare of the wage earners of the United States.

427

Millions of our unorganized workers are living, in this day of high national income and high profits, on substandard wages. A prompt increase in the minimum wage rates is needed. Our social security system can and must be broadened by extending its benefits to a greater number. Nor can we long delay, without incalculable loss to the Nation, the establishment of an adequate system of health insurance. All these prob-

lems deserve the attention of the Congress early in its next session.

It is fitting that on Labor Day we should acknowledge the debt this country owes to its workers of hand and mind, and that at the same time we should solemnly recognize our common responsibility to preserve and strengthen the democratic principles which have made labor and the Nation strong.

188   Address Before the Rio de Janeiro Inter-American Conference for the Maintenance of Continental Peace and Security. *September 2, 1947*

Mr. President, delegates to the Inter-American Conference for the Maintenance of Continental Peace and Security, ladies and gentlemen:

It is a distinguished privilege to address the final session of this historic conference. You are assembled here as the representatives of the nations of this hemisphere which have been banded together for over a half century in the Inter-American System. You have successfully accomplished the task of putting into permanent form the commitments made in the Act of Chapultepec. You have made it clear to any possible aggressor that the American Republics are determined to support one another against attacks. Our nations have provided an example of good neighborliness and international amity to the rest of the world, and in our association together we have strengthened the fabric of the United Nations. You can be justly proud of the achievements of this conference and I commend the noble spirit which has inspired your efforts.

The cordial and gracious invitation of President Dutra to visit this beautiful land has allowed me to fulfill a desire I have long cherished. I consider it most fortunate that

I am enabled also to meet with the Foreign Ministers and other leaders of the American Republics. Thus, in a sense, I am visiting not only Brazil, but I am visiting all your countries, since each of you carries his country in his heart.

While we are assembled here together, I wish to discuss with you the responsibilities which our nations share as a result of the recent war. For our part, the United States is deeply conscious of its position in world affairs. We recognize that we have an obligation and that we share this obligation with the other nations of the Western Hemisphere. Therefore, I take this occasion to give you a frank picture of our view of our responsibility and how we are trying to meet it.

The people of the United States engaged in the recent war in the deep faith that we were opening the way to a free world, and that out of the terrible suffering caused by the war something better would emerge than the world had known before.

The postwar era, however, has brought us bitter disappointment and deep concern.

We find that a number of nations are still subjected to a type of foreign domination

428

which we fought to overcome. Many of the remaining peoples of Europe and Asia live under the shadow of armed aggression.

No agreement has been reached among the allies to maintain the outlines of a peace settlement. In consequence, we are obliged to contemplate a prolonged military occupation of enemy territories. This is profoundly distasteful to our people.

Almost everywhere in Europe, economic recovery has lagged. Great urban and industrial areas have been left in a state of dependence on our economy which is as painful to us as it is to them. Much of this economic distress is due to the paralysis of political fear and uncertainty in addition to the devastation caused by war.

This situation has impeded the return to normal economic conditions everywhere in the world and has hampered seriously our efforts to develop useful forms of economic collaboration with our friends in other areas.

We did not fully anticipate these developments. Our people did not conceive, when we were fighting the war, that we would be faced with a situation of this nature when hostilities ceased. Our planning for peace presupposed a community of nations sobered and brought together by frightful suffering and staggering losses, more than ever appreciative of the need for mutual tolerance and consideration, and dedicated to the task of peaceful reconstruction.

In view of the unfortunate conditions which now prevail, we have faced some difficult problems of adjustment in our foreign policy. I would not say that we have made no mistakes. But I think that the elements of the policy we have evolved thus far are sound and justifiable.

The fundamental basis of the policy of the United States is the desire for permanent world peace.

We are determined that, in the company of our friends, we shall achieve that peace.

We are determined because of the belief of our people in the principle that there are basic human rights which all men everywhere should enjoy. Men can enjoy these rights—the right to life itself, the right to share fully in the bounties of modern civilization—only when the threat of war has been ended forever.

The attainment of worldwide respect for essential human rights is synonymous with the attainment of world peace. The peoples of the earth want a peaceful world, a prosperous world, and a free world, and when the basic rights of men everywhere are observed and respected, there will be such a world.

We know that in the hearts of common people everywhere there is a deep longing for stability and for settled conditions in which men can attain personal security and a decent livelihood for themselves and their children. We know that there are aspirations for a better and a finer life which are common to all humanity. We know—and the world knows—that these aspirations have never been promoted by policies of aggression.

We shall pursue the quest for peace with no less persistence and no less determination than we applied to the quest for military victory.

There are certain important elements in our policy which are vital to our search for permanent peace.

We intend to do our best to provide economic help for those who are prepared to help themselves and each other. But our resources are not unlimited. We must apply them where they can serve the most effectively to bring production, freedom, and confidence back to the world. We undertook to do this on an individual basis in the case of Greece and Turkey, where we were confronted with specific problems of limited scope and peculiar urgency. But it

429

was evident, at the time that the decision was made early this year, that this precedent could not be applied generally to the problems of other European countries. The demands elsewhere were of far greater dimensions. It was clear that we would not be able to meet them all. It was equally clear that the peoples of Europe would have to get together and work out a solution of their common economic problems. In this way they would be able to make the most of their resources and of such help as they might receive from others.

The representatives of 16 nations are now meeting in Paris in an effort to get to the root of Europe's continued economic difficulties and to chart a program of European recovery based on helping themselves and each other. They will then make known their needs in carrying this program to completion. Unquestionably it is in the interest of our country and of the Western Hemisphere in general that we should receive this appeal with sympathy and good will, prepared to do everything we can, within safe limits, that will be helpful and effective.

Our own troubles—and we have many— are small in contrast with the struggle for life itself that engrosses the peoples of Europe. The nations of free Europe will soon make known their needs. I hope that the nations of free America will be prepared, each according to its ability and in its own manner, to contribute to lasting peace for the benefit of mankind.

Another important element of our policy vital to our search for peace, is fidelity to the United Nations. We recognize that the United Nations has been subjected to a strain which it was never designed to bear. Its role is to maintain the peace and not to make the peace. It has been embroiled from its infancy in almost continuous conflict. We must be careful not to prejudge it by this un-

fair test. We must cherish the seedling in the hope of a mighty oak. We shall not forget our obligations under the Charter, for we shall not permit others to forget theirs!

In carrying out our policy we are determined to remain strong. This is in no way a threat. The record of the past speaks for us. No great nation has been more reluctant than ours to use armed force. We do not believe that the present international differences will have to be resolved by armed conflict. The world may depend upon it that we shall continue to go far out of our way to avoid anything that would increase the tensions of international life.

But we are determined that there shall be no misunderstanding in these matters. Our aversion to violence must not be misread as a lack of determination on our part to live up to the obligations of the United Nations Charter or as an invitation to others to take liberties with the foundations of international peace. Our military strength will be retained as evidence of the seriousness with which we view our obligations.

This is the course which our country is endeavoring to follow. I need not tell you how important it is to our success that we have your understanding, support, and counsel. The problem is in the deepest sense a common one for this hemisphere. There is no important aspect of it which does not affect all of us. No solution of it can be fully successful in which we do not all cooperate.

I have already mentioned our collective responsibility for economic assistance. By the grace of God and by our united armed efforts our countries have been saved from the destruction of war. Our economies are intact, our productive powers undiminished, our resources not even yet fully explored. In consequence, our collective importance in the affairs of a distressed world has become immense.

The Western Hemisphere cannot alone assure world peace, but without the Western Hemisphere no peace is possible. The Western Hemisphere cannot alone provide world prosperity, but without the Western Hemisphere no world prosperity is possible.

Insofar as the economic problems common to the nations of North and South America are concerned, we have long been aware that much remains to be done. In reaching a solution there are many subjects which will have to be discussed among us. We have been obliged, in considering these questions, to differentiate between the urgent need for rehabilitation of war-shattered areas and the problems of development elsewhere. The problems of countries in this hemisphere are different in nature and cannot be relieved by the same means and the same approaches which are in contemplation for Europe. Here the need is for long-term economic collaboration. This is a type of collaboration in which a much greater role falls to private citizens and groups than is the case in a program designed to aid European countries to recover from the destruction of war. You have my solemn assurance that we in Washington are not oblivious to the needs of increased economic collaboration within the family of American nations and that these problems will be approached by us with the utmost good faith and with increased vigor in the coming period.

If acceptable solutions to these economic problems can be found, and if we can continue to work with mutual confidence and courage at the building of the great edifice of political security to which this Conference has made so signal a contribution, then I believe that we can look with high hopes on the further development of our community life in this hemisphere.

I have no desire to overlook the difficulties that have been encountered in the past and will continue to be encountered in the future.

All of us are young and vigorous nations. At times we have been impetuous in our relations with one another. There has been a natural tendency for us to exhibit the same exuberance in our differences and our criticisms as in our friendships. Wide differences of background and tradition have had to be overcome.

But I believe that we may view with sober satisfaction the general history of our hemisphere. There has been steady progress in the development of mutual respect and of understanding among us. As the United States acquires greater maturity, as its experience becomes deeper and richer, our people gain in appreciation of the distinguished cultural traditions which flourish among our neighbors in the Western Hemisphere. I hope that as your acquaintance with us broadens, you will appreciate our fundamental good will and will understand that we are trying to bear with dignity and decency the responsibility of an economic power unique in human history.

There are many concrete problems ahead of us on the path to inter-American relations. They will not be solved with generalities or with sentimentality. They will call for the utmost we can give in practical ingenuity, in patience, and good will. But their solution will be easier if we are able to set our sights above the troubles of the moment and to bear in mind the great truths upon which our common prosperity and our common destiny must rest.

This Western Hemisphere of ours is usually referred to as the New World. That it is the New World is clearer today than ever before. The Old World is exhausted, its civilization imperiled. Its people are suffering. They are confused and filled with fears for the future. Their hope must lie in this New World of ours.

The sick and the hungry cannot build a peaceful world. They must have the support of the strong and the free. We cannot depend upon those who are weaker than we to achieve a peace for us to enjoy.

The benefits of peace, like the crops in the field, come to those who have sown the seeds of peace.

It is for us, the young and the strong, to erect the bulwarks which will protect mankind from the horrors of war—forever.

The United States seeks world peace—a peace of free men. I know that you stand with us. United, we can constitute the greatest single force in the world for the good of humanity.

We approach our task with resolution and courage, firm in the faith of our Lord, whose will it is that there shall be Peace on Earth.

We cannot be dissuaded, and we shall not be diverted, from our efforts to achieve His will.

NOTE: The President spoke at 10:30 a.m. at the Quitandinha Hotel in Petropolis. His opening words "Mr. President" referred to Eurico Gaspar Dutra, President of Brazil.

189   Address in Rio de Janeiro Before a Joint Session of the Congress of Brazil.   *September 5, 1947*

President Dutra, Mr. President of the Congress, Senators and Deputies:

Thank you very, very much. You overwhelm me.

I am deeply grateful for the invitation to appear before the Congress of this great nation whose history is so entwined with that of the United States.

Speaking as one who has come to executive position from legislative halls, I am all the more appreciative of the honor you have extended to me. The legislature of a democratic country is identified with the people themselves. This must be so if responsible self-government is to be accomplished. Brazil is justly proud of a history of government by free men. I salute the Congress of this great Brazilian nation, and I extend my best wishes to the noble people which it represents.

The ties between the United States and Brazil have always been close. It is not too much to describe our relations as those of "lifelong friendship." Your declaration of independence was brief, but just as challenging as ours. The Cry of Independence, uttered on that famous September 7, 1822, told the world that the time had come when Brazil was to be governed by its own people and for their own welfare. I am happy to recall that the United States was the first of the nations of the world to recognize the new independent state. We were not troubled by the fact that it took the form of an empire, for the foundations of the empire were democratic. The Constitution which was adopted 2 years later was the expression of the ideals of free government, not those of an absolute monarchy.

The history of Brazil in many respects parallels that of the United States. Both are nations which have carved civilizations out of the wilderness. Both have been endowed with great natural resources and both have been developed by people whose dominant motive is freedom.

If I am happy that the United States was the first to recognize the new nation of Brazil, I am equally happy that it was to the United States that Brazil turned for support in its struggle for independence. The alliance which Brazil proposed to us was a singular mark of confidence. It was the beginning of our historical friendship which I have described as "lifelong."

The long reign of the great Dom Pedro II

put Brazil among the leading democratic nations. Americans of today know him well, for you have engraved his noble features upon a postage stamp which comes to the United States with every mail from Brazil. We recall with pleasure that he was the first monarch to visit the United States, when he came to the exposition at Philadelphia in 1876 which marked the centenary of our independence.

Then in 1889, when Brazil felt that the form of a republic fitted better its national aspirations, the Congress of the United States of America adopted a joint resolution congratulating the country upon its new form of government. It is interesting to note also that Brazil adopted a Constitution modeled closely upon that of the Federal system of the United States.

Why are these ties so close? The distance between our countries is great and until of recent years communications were slow and difficult. But it is not physical proximity alone that makes friends and neighbors. It is rather the fact that we have common interests, common principles, and common ideals.

We look upon the state as the agent of the people for the attainment of the general welfare. We have the same belief in the fundamental rights of man. We have the same respect for the dignity of the individual. We look upon international relations as governed by the same moral standards of conduct by which individuals are governed.

In short, the declarations of September 7th and July 4th demonstrate that we have the same concept of freedom and democracy.

One of your great statesmen, Ruy Barbosa—whose name has left an imperishable memory—once said that the nations of the world constituted a single society and that the principles which formed the basis of stability and justice within each state should be applied equally to nations. He felt that

this was the only hope of maintaining civilized relations between them. The idea was not new. It was part of Brazil's inheritance, as it is a part of the inheritance of every other Christian nation. But Ruy Barbosa's eloquence has made it a living principle of the foreign policy of Brazil. His declaration that there can be no neutrality between right and wrong will remain forever a part of the moral traditions of your country.

In a recent exchange of correspondence with Pope Pius XII, I said that I desired to do everything in my power to support and to contribute to a concert of all the forces striving for a moral world.[1] I believe, in making that statement, I expressed the thought not only of my own country but of Brazil as well.

The United States has been fortunate in having Brazilian friends who have been wise counselors when joint action was called for. The name of Ambassador Joaquim Nabuco—who served in the spirit of your great Foreign Minister, Rio Branco—will always be associated with the maintenance of the Monroe Doctrine within its proper limitations. He is but one of a long line of your distinguished countrymen who have contributed so greatly to the understanding that exists between us. Through the years we have learned that because there is agreement between us upon the fundamental principles of justice and equity, we can face our common problems with an assurance of agreement upon the ways and means of solving those problems.

The recent war again gave convincing proof of our friendship. The mutual trust and confidence that exists between us manifested itself at an early date in the immediate response of your Government to our need for air bases and for supplies and strategic materials. And we are here to say to you

---

[1] Item 185.

433

that we are not people who forget our friends, when those friends are friends in need. When both our countries were attacked, our people fought side by side until victory was attained.

The bravery of your fighting men, against an experienced and resourceful enemy, cemented our comradeship and gave us another reason to feel a deep sense of pride in our friendship.

The memory of those days of struggle and sacrifice together will always be a sacred bond between us.

But today, the problems of peace still lie ahead of us. They are more difficult than we could have anticipated. They will require the closest collaboration between us. But I am confident that we can solve them with mutual good will and forbearance. The one essential is that we maintain our common ideals and our common principles of morality and justice. With these to guide us we can go forward together, and we shall not permit any minor differences to divert us from the pursuit of our common objectives.

We are in a period in which Brazil and the United States must continue to cooperate with their sister nations of the Western Hemisphere in the development of a strong and concerted force for the good of mankind. One of the great lessons we have learned in recent generations is that we do not dwell alone. Destruction, suffering, and confusion in other parts of the world confront us now as never before. Our nations made great sacrifices throughout the war, but we have been spared the wanton destruction and dislocation suffered by many. I am confident that Brazil and the United States will be faithful to a great trust on which depend the lives and liberty of so many millions of disillusioned and discouraged people.

The people of the United States followed with keen interest and high hopes the prog-

ress of the Inter-American Conference which has just ended. The splendid result attained brings to us a sense of deep satisfaction. We in this hemisphere have demonstrated to the world that right-thinking men can submerge their individual prejudices and their individual aims in the accomplishment of an agreement that will bring great benefit to the world.

The Conference of Rio de Janeiro will go down in history as a tremendously important milestone in our progress toward the outlawing of force in international relations and the establishment of the rule of law and order.

In some quarters today one hears expressions of disappointment in the accomplishments thus far of the United Nations. This must not deter us in our constant effort to build the organization that the world needs so badly. Furthermore, we must keep ever in mind that the United Nations was not intended to settle the problems arising immediately out of the war, but to provide the means for maintaining international peace after just settlements have been made.

The United Nations was not born fully developed by the signing of its charter at San Francisco. It will take steadfastness of purpose, unremitting toil, and infinite patience to achieve our goal.

The United Nations is not a temporary expedient. It is a permanent partnership—a partnership among the peoples of the world for their common peace and their common well-being.

The difficulties that we have encountered in this early phase in the life of the United Nations have not discouraged us.

On the contrary, they have increased our determination that it shall succeed.

The United States is resolved to support the United Nations with all the resources at our command.

Brazil and the United States have ad-

434

vanced side by side in developing progressive concepts of the democratic way of life. We have proved to ourselves that policies founded firmly on belief in the dignity of man and in his possession of certain inalienable rights inspire us to greater endeavor and lead us to new heights of achievement. I shall leave Brazil with the conviction that here flourishes a people dedicated to the firm ideals upon which my countrymen and I were nurtured.

It is difficult for me to tell you how deeply I appreciate the wonderful reception I have been accorded in your country. Because this Congress consists of the chosen representatives of the people, and because you men, through the operation of the democratic process, are so closely identified with the people, I wish to express my heartfelt thanks, through you, to all the people of Brazil.

As I passed through your beautiful capital city on the day of my arrival, the warm expressions of friendship on the faces of hundreds of thousands of your people deeply moved me and left me with an impression that I shall never forget.

When the time comes for me to depart I shall carry away in my heart strengthened confidence in the enduring friendship of our two countries and in the goodness and generosity of the people of Brazil.

NOTE: The President spoke at 4 p.m. at the Tiradentes Palace. His opening words referred to Eurico Gaspar Dutra, President of Brazil, and Mello Viana, President of the Brazilian Congress.

190 Letter to the President, National Federation of Federal Employees. *September* 17, 1947

[Released September 17, 1947. Dated August 28, 1947]

My dear Mr. Steward:

I wish to express my regret at being unable to accept your kind invitation to join with you in celebrating the thirtieth anniversary of the founding of the National Federation of Federal Employees, as it would be most pleasant to be with you on that occasion.

Over this period of thirty years you have made an outstanding contribution to the cause of good government. You have taken the lead many times in urging action on the part of both the legislative and executive branches of the government which, when taken, has proved to be sound from every point of view. Above all, you have so conducted the affairs of your organization that today your advice and counsel is welcomed by leaders in both the legislative and executive branches of the government.

The type of constructive leadership which has been reflected in your work over the years is needed today more than ever before. For the past two years the executive branch has been in the process of being converted from a wartime to a peacetime basis. During this period, the number of civilian employees on the federal pay roll has been reduced from 3,770,000 to approximately 2,088,000. Never before in the history of this or any other country has a single employer, within such a short period of time, been called upon to discharge 1,680,000 persons.

And yet, on the whole, the program has been carried forward in a fair and orderly manner. The fact that it has been done in this way is a tribute to thousands of civilian employees who have been called upon to plan large reductions in force and to see to it that they were carried out in accordance with the applicable laws and regulations.

This sharp reduction has, however, left

435

problems in its wake. In some instances men and women who over a period of years have been serving as career employees in the Federal service have been separated while temporary and war-service employees remain. In this connection I believe it to be the responsibility of the Federal government to see that those who choose to make its service a career are protected in their right to useful and efficient employment as long as there are positions for which their qualifications are suited occupied by temporary or war-service employees. To this end it is the policy of the Federal government to return to duty in the Federal service as soon as possible separated career employees whose work has been satisfactory and whose services are needed. When they cannot be placed in vacancies, war-service and temporary employees must be separated from jobs the career employees are qualified to fill.

As we look to the future, however, we must not only think in terms of protecting the career service, but we must also think in terms of strengthening it so that it will be

in a position to render an increasingly effective service to the people of this nation. There are many things which still need to be done, such as the modernizing of salary structures, the introduction of effective programs for promoting employees in the departments and agencies, the handling of grievances, and increasing the competence of those who occupy supervisory positions. I invite and solicit your cooperation in solving these and other related problems.

I know that the many constructive accomplishments of the past thirty years, as far as your organization is concerned, will serve to spur you on to even more constructive activity in the years which lie immediately ahead.

You have my continued best wishes for success and for a most enjoyable anniversary meeting.

> Sincerely yours,
>
> HARRY S. TRUMAN

[Mr. Luther C. Steward, President, National Federation of Federal Employees, 10 Independence Avenue, S.W., Washington 4, D.C.]

191 The President's News Conference of
    September 25, 1947

THE PRESIDENT. I have some rather lengthy statements to make to you this morning, and I have just asked Mr. Merriman Smith not to say "Thank you, Mr. President," too quickly. I didn't want anyone to think that I want to avoid any questions you want to ask.

[1.] The first announcement I have to make is Arthur S. Barrows of Illinois to be Under Secretary for Air. Eugene M. Zuckert of Connecticut and Cornelius Vanderbilt Whitney of New York to be Assistant Secretaries for Air. Gen. Carl Spaatz will be Chief of Staff.

Dr. Vannevar Bush has been appointed Chairman of the Research and Development Board. And there is a letter—mimeographed letter from me that will be available for you when you go out.

[2.] I am calling a meeting of the Commission on Organization of the Executive Branch of the Government for 11 o'clock on Monday the 29th.

[3.] And now I have got a couple of rather long statements here, which I hope you will bear with me while I read them: one on food and one on the Marshall plan.

Q. Mimeographed, sir?

THE PRESIDENT. All mimeographed. Everything is available in mimeographed form so that you can get it all written down, but I want you to hear it because it's right important.

[*Reading*]. "I am making public today a report from the Cabinet Committee on World Food Programs which emphasizes a critical situation calling for immediate action by every American.[1] The report stresses the extremely grave food situation abroad and the relationship between our ability to help meet urgent foreign food needs and the price situation in the United States.

"The Committee states that adverse crop developments, including those of recent weeks, both in North America and in Europe, make apparent a food shortage even worse than a year ago. The losses from heavy frosts in northwestern Europe last winter have been increased by a general European drought this spring and summer. Any significant cut in the already low rations in those countries will have most serious consequences for their rehabilitation.

"In the face of this situation, the report shows that, without further action, we would be able to carry through a large export program; but, as a result of sharply reduced corn production and continued high domestic demand for grain, exports would not equal last year's total shipments—even though world needs are greater.

"The United States cannot rest on this export prospect. To ship more abroad without adjustments in domestic demand, however, would aggravate our own price situation.

"In presenting their report, the Cabinet Committee stressed the urgency of doing everything possible to meet the problem at home and abroad. It recommended further emphasis on shipments of food other than grain in rounding out our export program, and on arrangements for the fullest participation by other nations in the combined effort to increase available supplies and to channel them to points of greatest need.

"The Committee made it clear, however, that definite steps to conserve on use of foodstuffs at home and reduce the feeding of grain to livestock will be essential if we are to make our fullest contribution towards meeting minimum foreign needs and at the same time relieve the upward pressure on prices at home.

"As a primary step, I am therefore appointing a Citizens Food Committee to advise on ways and means of carrying out the necessary conservation effort. Charles Luckman of Cambridge, Mass., will serve as chairman of this nonpartisan committee. I am asking the Citizens Food Committee to meet at the earliest possible moment to develop plans for bringing the vital problem of food conservation to the attention of every American for action.[1]

"At the same time, I am establishing a working organization which will mobilize the resources of the Government in support of the overall program. I will also confer with the congressional leaders of both parties regarding legislative action which may be necessary.

"While waiting for detailed recommendations from the Citizens Committee, there is one immediate and personal thing each of us can do. We can start now to conserve by being more selective in foods we buy, particularly livestock products whose production requires large quantities of grain. Such

---

[1] The 5-page mimeographed report dated September 22, with letter of transmittal of the same date, was released by the White House later in the day. Also released was the text of a letter, dated September 24, summarizing the Committee's recommendations.

[1] The President's telegram to those invited to serve on the Committee announced that the first meeting would be held at the White House on October 1 at 10 a.m. (see Item 198). The telegram, dated September 25, was released by the White House on September 26.

action on our part will do two things. We will save on our family budget and we will help others who are in desperate need. I am confident that the American people, realizing the extreme seriousness of the situation, will fully cooperate."

Here is a list of the committee:

Charles Luckman, President of Lever Brothers, Cambridge, Mass., is chairman. These other people have been asked to serve. Mr. Luckman has accepted, and the others, I am sure, will accept as soon as the word reaches them.

Mrs. J. L. Blair-Buck, President, General Federation of Women's Clubs, Richmond, Va.

Harry A. Bullis, President, General Mills, Inc., Minneapolis, Minn.

Chester C. Davis, President, Federal Reserve Bank of St. Louis, St. Louis, Mo.

Albert S. Goss, Master of the National Grange, Washington, D.C.

Lester B. Granger, Executive Secretary, National Urban League of New York City.

William Green, President, American Federation of Labor.

James S. Knowlson, Chairman of the Board and President, Stewart-Warner Corporation of Chicago.

Herbert H. Lehman, Lehman Brothers, New York.

G. R. LeSauvage, National Restaurant Advisory Committee of New York City.

John A. Logan, President, National Association of Food Chains, Washington.

John Holmes, President of Swift and Company, Chicago.

James H. McGraw, Jr., McGraw-Hill Publishing Co., Inc., New York.

Eugene Meyer, Washington Post, Washington, D.C.

Justin Miller, President, National Association of Broadcasters, Pacific Palisades, Calif.

Philip Murray, President, Congress of Industrial Organizations.

Dr. William I. Myers, Dean of Agriculture, Cornell University, Ithaca, N.Y.

Edward A. O'Neal, President, American Farm Bureau Federation, Chicago.

James G. Patton, President, Farmers Union, Denver.

T. S. Repplier, President, Advertising Council, Washington.

Quentin Reynolds, President, National Council of Farmer Cooperatives, West Springfield, Mass.

Spyros Skouras, President, 20th Century Fox Film Corporation, New York.

A. E. Staley, Jr., President, A. E. Staley Manufacturing Co., Decatur, Ill.

Miss Anna Lord Strauss, President, League of Women Voters, Washington.

Paul S. Willis, Executive Secretary, Grocery Manufacturers of America, Inc., New York.

And Harry W. Zinsmaster, Chairman, American Bakers Association, Duluth, Minn.

[4.] [*Reading*]. "The Secretary of State has transmitted to me the official report of the Committee of European Economic Cooperation"—that's it right there [*indicating on his desk*] for anybody who wants to read it—"prepared by the representatives of the 16 nations who have been meeting in Paris since early July.[1] At my request, Secretary Marshall is sending a message to the Chairman of the Committee, Foreign Minister Bevin, acknowledging receipt of the report by the United States Government.

"As the document itself states, it is an 'initial report,' and is subject to review and revision. Nonetheless, it reflects an unprecedented effort at economic cooperation by the 16 countries participating in the Paris Conference. In the light of the political

---

[1] The report dated September 21, 1947, is printed in two volumes "General Report," 138 pp., and "Technical Reports," 552 pp. (Government Printing Office).

tensions and the economic instability in Europe, it is an important and encouraging first step that these nations had the initiative and the determination to meet together and produce this report.

"The problem to which this report is addressed not only underlies the political and economic well-being of Europe but is also of key importance to a stable peace in the world. The people of the United States recognize, as do the people of the European nations, that the earliest practicable achievement of economic health, and consequent political stability in Europe, is of utmost importance for the peace and well-being of the world.

"I note that the program presented in the report is based on the 4 following lines of action by the 16 European nations: (1) a strong productive effort on their part; (2) creation of internal financial stability; (3) maximum cooperation among the participating countries; and (4) a solution to the trading deficit with the American Continent, particularly by exports. These are sound principles and will appeal to the common-sense of the American people. Their effective translation into practice is vital both to European recovery and to worldwide economic health.

"While the 16-nation committee has been meeting in Paris, the United States Government has been proceeding with complementary studies on this side of the Atlantic.

"Last June I appointed three committees to study the relationship between aid which may be extended to foreign countries and the interests of our domestic economy. One of these, headed by the Secretary of the Interior, has been making a study of the state of our natural resources. Another of these studies, relating to the impact on our national economy of aid to other countries, is being conducted by the Council of Economic Advisers. The third group, a nonpartisan

committee of distinguished citizens under the chairmanship of the Secretary of Commerce, was requested to determine the character and quantities of United States resources available for assistance to foreign countries and to advise the President on the limits within which the United States may safely and wisely plan to extend such assistance."

Each one of these agencies will receive a copy of the European Report.

"Other agencies of the executive branch of the Government have also been considering the role which should be played by the United States in European recovery.

"The great interest of the Congress in this subject has been demonstrated by the number of its Members whom it has sent abroad to study prevailing conditions at first hand.

"We shall need to consult with representatives of the European Committee to obtain clarification and amplification of the initial report and to obtain further information, as it becomes available, as to the specific measures to be adopted by the participating countries in carrying out the principles set forth in the report.

"I am requesting the special committees which I appointed and other Government agencies to appraise the information received from the European Committee in the light of the studies they have conducted. The results of this appraisal will be made available to the appropriate congressional committees.

"On the basis of these studies, which will go forward without delay, the facts will be presented and recommendations will be formulated so that the American people through their representatives in Congress can determine to what extent and in what manner the resources of the United States may be brought to the support of the renewed European efforts to achieve sustained economic recovery. When the American people are satisfied as to the scope of the necessary program and the sufficiency of measures of self-help and mutual help being taken by the European countries, and when we can determine what resources we should and can wisely make available, I am sure that we shall respond as quickly as possible.

"Meanwhile, certain problems have arisen in connection with the economic situation in Europe that are of such an urgent nature that their solution cannot await the careful study required for the overall decisions which will be based on the reports. These problems are of an emergency nature which demand immediate attention.

"It is for this reason that I have requested a group of congressional leaders to meet with me on Monday, September 29th, to discuss plans for determining the action to be taken by the United States to aid in preserving the stability and promoting the recovery of the nations which participated in the Paris Conference."

I am sorry that those things have to be so long, and that they had to be read, too, but they had to be specifically—state specifically what is meant. Those statements tell exactly what they mean, and the copies I have got show.

Now if you want to ask any questions, I will try to answer them.

[5.] Q. Mr. President, on your food statement, do we understand it correctly that you are asking the American people to eat less for the time being?

THE PRESIDENT. I am asking the American people to waste less for the time being. I was informed by one of the biggest restaurant men in the United States, just the other night, that one slice of bread would meet this wheat shortage.

Q. Mr. President, have you had any special offer of cooperation from the baking industry?

THE PRESIDENT. We expect to get it. They have promised it.

Q. Mr. President, is there any prospect of a return to so-called gray bread?

THE PRESIDENT. I don't know. That is what I have called this committee in for, to find out just how we stand to meet the situation.

Q. Is there any prospect of a return to rationing or price control?

THE PRESIDENT. Well now, you had better ask the Congress that. I can't answer that question.

[6.] Q. Does this plan of yours—what you said there—does that throw out the window a special or extra session of Congress, or reconvening of Congress?

THE PRESIDENT. The question was whether this threw out the possibility of an extra session of Congress. The meeting with the congressional leaders on Monday morning is to discuss the situation. Then I will make the announcement after we have had the conversations with them.

[7.] Q. Mr. President, you said one slice of bread would lick the wheat problem. Do you mean if everyone in the country would eat one slice less?

THE PRESIDENT. If they would save the bread that they throw away—this is what this restaurant man told me—we would have, I think, 70 million more bushels of wheat available for food.

Q. 70 million, did you say?

THE PRESIDENT. That's what the head of the packing mill industry told me, also.

Q. 17 or 70?

THE PRESIDENT. 70.

[8.] Q. Mr. President, does this stopgap relief you are talking about fall in the same category as more permanent relief?

THE PRESIDENT. No it does not.

Q. In other words, you might conceivably

work it out without a special session of Congress?

THE PRESIDENT. That is exactly what we are trying to do. I don't know whether we can or not. That is the reason I have called this committee in, to see just exactly what we can do.

Q. Do you know how many millions of dollars are involved in this stopgap relief?

THE PRESIDENT. I can't say. I can't say.

Q. But you said you are trying to work out the stopgap relief problem without a special session?

THE PRESIDENT. Yes. That's right.

Q. Have you had any indication yet as to about how many congressional leaders will be able to come on Monday?

THE PRESIDENT. The customary number. The ones that have always been asked—the Big Six and the heads of the minorities and the ranking members of the Appropriations and the Foreign Relations Committees.

I will give you the list of those that have accepted as soon as we have heard from them.

Q. Mr. President, would that stopgap aid be on the Marshall plan or the food situation?

THE PRESIDENT. It is the food situation. It is the food situation. There are certain countries in Europe that are scraping the bottom of the barrel on food and fuel. And nobody is going to let people starve to death or freeze to death, if we can possibly stop that from happening.

Q. Mr. President, you said rationing was up to Congress. Will you recommend rationing?

THE PRESIDENT. I will wait and see whether it is necessary or not. I have to get the stuff myself yet. That is what I called this committee in for.

[9.] Q. Mr. President, have you any reflections on where the responsibility or origination of the present high cost of living lies?

THE PRESIDENT. Well, I am not going to get into controversial questions this morning. I will answer that when I make any political speeches, which won't be very soon. You can work that out just as well as I can. [*Laughter*]

[10.] Q. Mr. President, do you have any inclination yourself, one way or the other, regarding a special session of Congress?

THE PRESIDENT. No I haven't. As I told you before this, I can be convinced if it is necessary—open mind on the subject.

[11.] Q. Mr. President, what is the nature of the legislative action you refer to in your statement on food?

THE PRESIDENT. The money that is necessary to get it with.

Q. Is there any consideration of reenactment of wartime controls which permit you to set aside——

THE PRESIDENT. That is a matter that we are going to discuss. I don't think there is any possibility of its being done, but it may be necessary. I don't know.

What is Mr. Wright's question? You have been trying to ask me a question for a half hour.

James L. Wright, Buffalo Evening News: Yes, and now I have forgotten what it was. [*Laughter*]

THE PRESIDENT. I'm sorry.

[12.] Q. Mr. President, there is the suggestion that there be two meatless days a week, something of that sort. Have you any recommendations on that?

THE PRESIDENT. That is a matter I am going to discuss with this special committee that I am calling, for the purpose of looking into the whole situation, to see what is necessary to be done. What is necessary to be done I will tell you about it frankly.

Q. In our house we are already having two meatless days.

THE PRESIDENT. I appreciate it.

[13.] Q. Mr. President, you specifically said that this immediate critical problem is one of food and fuel.

THE PRESIDENT. That's right.

Q. The dollar shortage is not concerned in any way?

THE PRESIDENT. Of course the dollar shortage has caused the shortage of food and fuel. They haven't got the money to buy it with.

Q. Then have you any estimate, sir, on how much——

THE PRESIDENT. I have not.

[14.] Mr. Wright: Mr. President, my inquiry comes back to me.

Q. On the Latin American contribution——

THE PRESIDENT. I am going to get Mr. Wright's question, and then I will answer yours.

Mr. Wright: All right. There has been quite a bit of point made by various Republicans—Martin, for example, and Vandenberg, to a certain extent—that they haven't the information that convinces you that this is an emergency proposition.

THE PRESIDENT. I am giving them the information just as quickly as I get it myself. I began receiving administrative—the reports on the battleship *Missouri,* and it was finally handed to me last Saturday, Monday, Tuesday, and up to now. And this—[*indicating reports before him*]—is the last thing in connection with it, which just came in this morning. I haven't had a chance to read it yet. As soon as all that information is coordinated, every one of those fellows will be informed, just the same as I am.

Q. I see.

THE PRESIDENT. That is what the Secretary of State is getting up for me now.

Q. The Speaker made the point that private sources of information were that there is not a desperate situation now, that they can wait over until the first of January.

THE PRESIDENT. I remember Senator Borah made a speech like that once.

What was your question there?

[15.] Q. I wonder if you could comment on the Latin American contribution of approximately——

THE PRESIDENT. We hope the Latin American countries will come in. It is necessary that they do come in, if we are going to meet this situation as it should be met.

Q. Would this program rule out the possibility of tax reduction next year?

THE PRESIDENT. I will answer that the first of January in the Message on the State of the Union.

[16.] Q. Yesterday, sir, Senator Flanders telegraphed you asking that you use your administrative powers to curb grain speculation.

THE PRESIDENT. I only saw the telegram in the paper. I haven't received any such telegram.

What was your question?

[17.] Q. Would you care to comment on the trend of events in U.N., specifically the trend indicated by Mr. Vishinsky's speech?

THE PRESIDENT. Mr. Vishinsky's speech speaks for itself, and I have no comment to make on it.

[18.] Q. Mr. President, is any conference planned with the Latin American countries regarding what part they can take in the Marshall plan?

THE PRESIDENT. There will be.

Q. There will be?

THE PRESIDENT. Yes.

[19.] Q. Mr. President, does the Spaatz announcement infer that Bradley will go back to the Veterans Bureau?

THE PRESIDENT. I will answer that question a little later.

[20.] Q. Mr. President, pardon me, sir, is it—is this conference already scheduled with the Latin American countries regarding——

THE PRESIDENT. No, but they will be consulted right along with the rest of the world. Everybody that has anything that is surplus, that will feed and keep people from starving, we are going to try to get it.

Q. You don't mean a formal conference like Rio or——

THE PRESIDENT. No, no. No. Consultation is what it amounts to.

[21.]   Q. Stopgap relief be in addition to the Marshall plan?

THE PRESIDENT. Yes.

[22.]   Q. Mr. President, you didn't mean Spaatz is going to be Chief of Staff of the Army?

THE PRESIDENT. No. Air Force.

[23.]   Q. Mr. President, are you going to the world series?

THE PRESIDENT. I am not.

Q. You are not.

THE PRESIDENT. I would like very much to go, but I have got too much to do right here on this desk. I have got to stay here whether I want to or not.

Q. Watch it by television, Mr. President.

THE PRESIDENT. I will, if they do have television over here, try to see one or two of the games, if it doesn't take me too long away from the desk.

[24.]   Q. If the program means voluntary rationing, doesn't that mean that people with money and without conscience get all the food?

THE PRESIDENT. I don't know, I hope that that isn't the case. I certainly hope that that isn't the case. I don't like to think that there are Americans with all the money who would want to see people starve for their benefit. I don't believe there are any such people in this country.

Q. We had a black market here during rationing.

THE PRESIDENT. I know that, but that was a very small minority. I think I have told you before that I think at least 95 percent of the people want to do the right thing, and all our troubles are caused by the 5 percent. That is true here, too! [*Laughter*]

Q. Mr. President, do you conclude that you have proposed a program of voluntary rationing?

THE PRESIDENT. I will answer that question when I have had the meeting with the committee.

Q. Your proposal this morning——

THE PRESIDENT. The proposal is to waste less, and see if we can't meet this situation. That is the beginning of the problem. Then we are going to work it out on a practical basis, which will be handled right here from this office.

Reporter: Thank you, Mr. President.

NOTE: President Truman's one hundred and nineteenth news conference was held in his office at the White House at 10:35 a.m. on Thursday, September 25, 1947.

192   Letter to Dr. Vannevar Bush Upon His Appointment as Chairman, Research and Development Board. *September 25, 1947*

My dear Dr. Bush:

I am happy to know that you are willing to continue in the public service as Chairman of the Research and Development Board created by the National Security Act of 1947.

Your work as chairman of the Office of Scientific Research and Development was of great importance to the armed services in the prosecution of World War II. Since V–J Day you have continued to render valuable service as chairman of the Joint Research and Development Board set up by the Secretaries of War and Navy.

The coordination of our scientific effort is one of the most important objectives of the National Security Act. It is a fortunate circumstance that, in carrying out these ob-

jectives, the Research and Development Board will have the benefit of your guidance.

Sincerely yours,

HARRY S. TRUMAN

[Dr. Vannevar Bush, Chairman, Joint Research and Development Board, Washington, D.C.]

193   Radio Address Opening the Community Chest Campaign. *September 26, 1947*

[Delivered from the White House at 10:53 p.m.]

My fellow citizens:

I am very proud to be numbered among the great company of volunteers who from coast to coast all during the month of October will be working for and giving to their Community Chests.

These volunteers differ in race, in religion, in politics, in income. However, they hold one deep conviction in common. That is the conviction that the first responsibility of a good citizen is to pitch in and help make his community a good and wholesome place in which to live. No governmental agency, no legislation, no miracle of science can do this thing. It is strictly a job for home town citizens to tackle together.

The American people long ago created the Community Chest as a new expression of a fine old American tradition—the tradition of neighborliness. We are a neighborly people at heart. We have the impulse to help each other. The Community Chest gathers together all our generous impulses, unites them and directs them into fruitful channels.

There is another aspect of our Community Chest activities which makes a special appeal to me. Through this helping hand all Americans are given an opportunity to exemplify one of the most fundamental Christian principles—the principle of Chris-

tian charity. In this modern world of science and sociology human values are sometimes overlooked.

That we must avoid at all costs. Let us always remember that we are dealing with human beings. In our generous impulses we should follow the admonition set forth in St. Matthew's Gospel. Our Lord, bidding us to aid and comfort our stricken neighbor, whoever he may be, spoke words as true today as when he uttered them more than nineteen hundred years ago: "Inasmuch as ye have done it unto one of the least of these my brethren, ye have done it unto me."

The "Red Feather Services" supported by our gifts to the Community Chest, benefit not one group of people—they benefit all of us. For the plain truth is that what is good for some people in a community is good for all. What harms some, harms all.

The ills of society spread like a contagion and no one is safe. But we may take hope in the fact that the good in society is also contagious. That is why the Community Chest volunteers are willing to work so hard.

These volunteers are businessmen, housewives, company officials, shop foremen and workers in our vast network of industries, professions, and trades. They are responding to a call to be good neighbors. I suspect that most of the unselfish, the truly noble actions of men and women are a response to an inner compulsion to be good neighbors.

So I salute proudly the volunteers of the Community Chests of America. And I urge you, their fellow citizens, to meet them half way. When one of them calls on you, pledge generously.

Your pledge to the Community Chest helps to solve the myriad of human problems which are the common lot of everybody. And when you give that pledge warmly and generously, everybody benefits.

---

194 Statement by the President Making Public a Report "The Federal Research Program." *September 27, 1947*

THE SECOND volume of his report on Science and Public Policy has been submitted today by John R. Steelman, Chairman of the President's Scientific Research Board. This volume, "The Federal Research Program," for the first time gives the American people an accounting of the scientific work of their Government, which last year expended $625 million for thousands of scientific projects.

Mr. Steelman's report reveals that Government research in the physical and biological sciences covers a multitude of widely varied programs which cannot profitably be undertaken by private industry or agriculture. The scope of Federal research extends from the development of guided missiles, rockets, and other military devices to the control of soil erosion and the development of disease-resistant plants. It affects the health and comfort and security of every citizen in countless ways.

The report consists of a description of the scientific research program of 16 Federal departments and agencies and includes an analysis of the money and manpower devoted to all major research. It should be studied carefully by everyone who wishes to understand the vast scope of our Federal program and the great benefits which result from it.

NOTE: The report, second in a series prepared by the President's Scientific Research Board, is dated September 27, 1947 (Government Printing Office, 318 pp.). For other reports of the Board, see Items 183, 201, 206, 211.

---

195 The President's News Conference Following a Meeting With Congressional Leaders. *September 29, 1947*

THE PRESIDENT. The conference this morning requested me to make a statement to you as to what happened. It was a very harmonious and a very good conference. Everybody had everything he wanted to say, and he had a chance to say it—had a chance to get it off his chest. And the whole meeting was very constructive, I think.

Now I am going to read you the statement, which will be available to you in mimeographed form by the time you get out of here.

[*Reading, not literally*] "I conferred at length with the congressional leaders, with reference to the critical economic situation which exists in Western Europe. I am writing the chairmen of the Senate Committee on Foreign Relations, the House Committee on Foreign Affairs, the Senate Committee on Appropriations, and the House Committee on Appropriations, requesting that they call their committees together to consider the urgent need for aid to Western Europe.

"I know that some of the members of these committees are now in Europe investigating conditions at first hand. It is my earnest hope that as soon as the members of the various committees have returned to this country, they will meet.

"The question of calling a special session of Congress was discussed at length with the congressional leaders. Whatever decision may be reached on this subject at a later date, it was the opinion of all that the committees should begin to consider the present emergency at the earliest possible date that members are available.

"Recent events have brought about increasingly critical economic conditions in some of the countries of Western Europe. Unusually bad European harvests, together with rising costs and lessened supplies of American food, have upset recovery plans and endangered the progress already made. In particular, France and Italy are without adequate fuel and food supplies for the fall and winter, and do not have the resources with which to buy them.

"The prospect of a general recovery program for Western Europe, aided by the United States, has raised their hopes for eventual recovery and has strengthened democratic forces. But, if this recovery program is to have a chance of success, means must be found for aiding France and Italy to survive this critical winter as free and independent nations.

"A searching examination has already been conducted of all possible ways in which France and Italy might be aided without additional action by the Congress. Action by the various agencies of the executive branch under existing authority may meet the most urgent needs of the next few weeks, but funds available from executive sources are inadequate to provide assistance beyond December. Assistance this winter, in sums much larger than the executive branch can provide with funds now at its disposal, is essential. That assistance can come only from the Congress.

"The early convening of the congressional committees referred to is the necessary first step in meeting the problems that confront us."

Q. Mr. President, were you able to determine the sentiment of the majority leaders on the question of giving stopgap aid?

THE PRESIDENT. I didn't attempt to make any survey of that sort. I was merely putting the problem up to them. I think most of them were of the opinion that it should be met.

Q. Mr. President, did you propose a special session eventually, after the committees have completed their work?

THE PRESIDENT. That remains to be seen. I am in the same position, in the same frame of mind, I have always been. If it becomes necessary to call that special session, I will call it.

Q. How much money do you need, Mr. President?

THE PRESIDENT. It runs about $580 million.

Q. That is from now until December?

THE PRESIDENT. No. That will run to the 31st of March.

Q. Mr. President, how much of that can you provide by executive action?

THE PRESIDENT. I can't provide any of it.

Q. Is that for France and Italy only, Mr. President?

THE PRESIDENT. No, that is for the whole situation.

Q. Mr. President, is there an additional

fund which could be made available without congressional action before the $580 million is made available?

THE PRESIDENT. No. The sums that are available now will carry until December. Then the pipeline will become empty unless it is filled up again, and that is the necessity for the additional cost.

Q. Carry *through* December, or *to* December?

THE PRESIDENT. It is estimated that would carry *to* December.

Q. To December 1st.

THE PRESIDENT. I can't set a date like that. It will carry just as far as we can.

Q. In other words, Mr. President, there is enough money now to meet these European relief needs from now until December?

THE PRESIDENT. There isn't enough, but there is enough to meet them on a starvation basis. That is the situation.

Q. Mr. President, is that 580 million in addition to the aid from now to December?

THE PRESIDENT. Yes.

Q. And beyond that starvation basis you need congressional action?

THE PRESIDENT. That's right.

Q. Mr. President, what funds are—can relief money be drawn at this time up to December 1st?

THE PRESIDENT. The Congress appropriated $342 million to carry on the program left by UNRRA, and then, of course, the $400 million for Greece and Turkey is specifically appropriated for that purpose.

Q. How much of the 342, sir, is now left?

THE PRESIDENT. I can't answer that question.

Q. Are there additional funds needed for the occupied German——

THE PRESIDENT. Yes, there will be additional funds needed for the occupied countries.

Q. How much would that bring the total to?

THE PRESIDENT. That is something aside from the 580 million.

Q. But this 580 covers everything?

THE PRESIDENT. That covers the starvation situation.

Q. Those countries are France——

THE PRESIDENT. Yes—keep people from freezing and starving to death this winter, just as it was last winter—almost the same situation.

Q. France and Italy, Mr. President?

THE PRESIDENT. France and Italy, Austria and Germany.

Q. Mr. President, isn't the appropriation for Germany carried on for the fiscal year?

THE PRESIDENT. That goes in the War Department appropriation. That is a separate program entirely. That is in the occupied countries program.

Q. Mr. President, the 580 million would be applied to the four countries you just named, France, Italy, Germany, and Austria?

THE PRESIDENT. France, Italy, Germany, and Austria—France and Italy—no—France, Italy, and Austria.

Q. Three countries, then, under that 580 million?

THE PRESIDENT. Yes.

Q. How about England?

THE PRESIDENT. England is not in any serious situation at the present time.

Q. Mr. President, without the special session, there would still be a month's period of time during which there would be no aid available, there would be no way to fill up the pipeline?

THE PRESIDENT. That is the situation.

Q. Mr. President, was there any discussion of the Marshall plan as such, in addition to the food program?

THE PRESIDENT. It was mentioned incidentally, but it was not discussed. We only discussed the emergency plan—emergency situation this morning, which is entirely separate—entirely separate. The situation that we are faced with. It has come upon us rather suddenly.

Q. Mr. President, do you have any idea when you could make a decision on the special session?

THE PRESIDENT. No I haven't.

Q. Do you have any idea when these committees will be able to meet?

THE PRESIDENT. No I haven't.

Q. Mr. President, the Senate Appropriations Committee is due back about the middle of November. I wonder if you were asking them to come earlier?

THE PRESIDENT. I am writing letters to the chairmen of all these committees, asking them to meet as soon as convenient.

Q. Mr. President, can you say what additional facts you might need before making a decision on a special session?

THE PRESIDENT. Well, it depends on the attitude of the committees of the Congress, as to whether the special session will be necessary or not. If they are wholeheartedly in favor of the program, of course then there would be no difficulty about calling a special session. If they were not in favor of doing anything, there would be no necessity for the special session.

Q. Mr. President, what about the funds in the Export-Import Bank, do you regard them——

THE PRESIDENT. They are not available.

Q. Not?

THE PRESIDENT. Not available. Prohibited from use for that purpose.

Q. The same applies to Commodity Credit Corporation?

THE PRESIDENT. Same applies to the Commodity Credit Corporation.

Q. Mr. President, we understand indirectly that part of the Turkish-Greek money could be used——

THE PRESIDENT. No, it cannot be used—only for what it is specifically appropriated for, and that is Greece and Turkey.

Q. Mr. President, I did not understand your use of the term starvation basis. We understood you to say that what money did exist will be sufficient to continue them on a starvation basis?

THE PRESIDENT. That is correct.

Q. Up to——

THE PRESIDENT. Up to December, we hope. France has already had to cut their bread ration from 250 to 200 grams. You are getting near starvation. You should see the weekly ration that is handed out to those people over there. It wouldn't make a good meal for us over here, but they have to live on it a week.

Q. Mr. President, you mentioned France, Italy, and Austria. What about Belgium and the Low Countries, are they continuing to——

THE PRESIDENT. Well, we have been—we have been furnishing grain to Belgium and the Low Countries, but they have been paying for their shipments, and I think they are still in the position to do that.

Q. Mr. President, could you notice the feeling of great urgency this morning among your conferees?

THE PRESIDENT. Oh yes. Everybody understands the urgency of the situation.

Q. Did you make a specific proposal for a special session, Mr. President?

THE PRESIDENT. I did not.

Reporter: Thank you, Mr. President.

THE PRESIDENT. You're welcome.

NOTE: President Truman's one hundred and twentieth news conference was held in his office at the White House at 3:25 p.m. on Monday, September 29, 1947.

196   The President's Special Conference With Editors of
      Business and Trade Papers.   *September 30, 1947*

THE PRESIDENT [*replying to a question as to what business-paper editors can do to assist the new Citizens Food Committee*]. Well, there are a lot of things you can do. I called the board of directors of that food committee together this morning—that is the Citizens Food Committee—and Mr. Luckman, who is the chairman of the organization, was there—and believe it or not, since Thursday he has arranged a system of ads that would knock your eyes off that covers the situation.

Now cooperation with Mr. Luckman in that line of approach—I think you can do more that way than any other way that I know of. And it is astonishing the situation with which we are faced, in connection with that program; and it will also be astonishing as to what you can accomplish if we go at it in the right way.

I have had an opportunity to interview several people who are vitally interested in this program, because it is simply another program to keep people from starving and freezing to death this winter. It is the same proposition almost exactly as we had last winter, only in a different location.

I met the other night the head of the managers of all restaurant associations in the country, and he informed me that they serve about 60 million meals a day, and he also informs me that one slice of bread from those meals would feed all these hungry people every day. And the head of the hotel organization told me that the garbage cans of all the hotels in the United States would leave a decided surplus of the necessities that we find it necessary to send to Europe, if we could save what went into the garbage cans.

What we are trying to do is get a situation of balance between prices and what we have to do to feed these people. Every time the Government makes an approach to purchase food and grains, and things of that sort, it causes a flurry in the market, although actually Government purchases in the market are less than 8 percent of the total crops in any one food grain. In fact, it is less than 8 percent of all of them. On the Chicago Board of Trade, however, 8 billion bushels of wheat have been bought and sold since 3 months ago. Now there is something "screwy" about a situation of that sort. And you can talk about prices and the effect of Government purchases on prices, but I know something about gambling on the Board of Trade, because I was an office boy for a grain firm there at one time, and I know how they do it and what they do. They are not fooling me. [*Laughter*]

What was the other question?

Paul Wooton (President of the Conference): Mr. President, the other question is, instead of accepting notes of debt, would it not be wise to trade our goods in Europe for their strategic materials for our stockpile for national security?

THE PRESIDENT. Surely it would. If we could get the material out of the ground. The only way we can trade with them now is to buy it out of the ground. And we have had that under consideration. I am in agreement with the suggestion that has been made there. We have had it under consideration for more than a year, but getting that material to the point of contact where we can get hold of it is the proposition we are up against. And we can't do something until some of these countries are rehabilitated. But there are certain strategic materials of which we are short that can be obtained on the programs such as you suggest. We hope that will work out in the long run.

But you must bear in mind that—I am going to talk to you very frankly now, and this is entirely off the record—I can't afford to be quoted on it, but there is something that you should know.

Mr. Wooton: That applies to everything you have said, Mr. President. They like to use the thoughts behind it, but not for attribution.

THE PRESIDENT. I understand that, but then this is a strategic situation. France and Italy are scraping the bottom of the barrel for food and fuel right now, which is the reason for the calling of the congressional leaders yesterday, and the discussions which we had. The situation in Italy is exceedingly grave. In northern Italy, where there are 46 million people in the Italian peninsula, about 26 million of them are in the Po Valley—northern part of Italy, in the industrial part of Italy; but the other 20 million are south of the Po Valley and down to Sicily, where they do not raise enough food in Italy to feed themselves. They always have exports to overcome that. Italy has made rather a remarkable comeback and is exporting $20 million worth of goods a month. France is only exporting 10. That situation should be reversed.

But the situation in northern Italy is anything but—well, it is dangerous at the present time. Should anything happen that Italy would go and the Jugoslavs should move in, France would go, and we have the Iron Curtain at the Atlantic Ocean. There would be nothing for us to do then but move out completely and prepare for war. That we don't want to do.

I have been, ever since this thing ended on the 14th of August of 1945, trying to arrive at a peace. I went to Potsdam for the purpose of trying to get a peace in the world. I have every kindly feeling in the world for the people who are causing us all the trouble now. And we made certain specific agreements, none of which have been carried out by the other party. And that is the cause of the present situation. They are hoping that we are going to blow up. There is no opportunity for us to blow up, at the present time, in the manner in which they think that is going to take place. But we must have complete and wholehearted cooperation in meeting these situations if we ever expect to get peace in the world.

I think we will eventually get it. General Marshall told me the other day that the situation was improving to a very great extent in the United Nations Assembly, and that there were countries behind the Iron Curtain now trying very—very earnestly to be friendly to us. And I think that is true. And I think you will find that our motives are open and aboveboard. We haven't tried to do anything but to make a peaceful and happy world. And that's all we are interested in. We didn't ask for reparations. We didn't ask for territory. But we are faced with a condition and not a theory, as Mr. Creedon says.

I thought you might be interested in knowing just exactly with what we are faced. You can throw all the bricks at the President you want to, on domestic and local affairs. I am used to that, and there's nothing you can do or say about me that hasn't been done or said. [*Laughter*]

In this international situation we must be a unit. That is the point I want to drive home to you.

Mr. Wooton: Mr. President, you have been so good to us. I want to thank you so much for giving us the opportunity to get your views. You have been very helpful indeed. Thank you so much.

NOTE: The President spoke in his office at the White House at 11:35 a.m. The conference is carried in the White House Official Reporter's records as the President's one hundred and twenty-first news conference.

197 Letter to Committee Chairmen on the Situation in Western Europe. *October* 1, 1947

[Released October 1, 1947. Dated September 30, 1947]

My dear Mr. Chairman:

The situation in western Europe has, in the last few months, become critical. This is especially true in the cases of France and Italy, where slow recovery of productivity, particularly of goods for export, combined with the increasing drain on their dollar resources, has produced acute distress.

The unusually bad harvests in western Europe, together with rising costs of imports, the unfortunate results of the temporary cessation of sterling convertibility and the near exhaustion of gold and dollar reserves, have placed these two countries in a position where they are without adequate food and fuel supplies for the fall and winter, and without sufficient dollars with which to purchase these essentials. They cannot, by their own efforts, meet this major crisis which is already upon them.

Political groups that hope to profit by unrest and distress are now attempting to capitalize on the grave fears of the French and Italian people that they will not have enough food and fuel to survive the coming winter.

The prospect of a successful general economic recovery program for Europe is one of the major hopes for peace and economic security in the world. The Congress will soon be called upon to consider the part which the United States should play in aiding this program. But the program will have no chance of success if economic collapse occurs in Europe before the program can be put into operation. Prompt and effective aid to meet the urgent needs of the present is essential, lest the strains become too great and result in an expanding economic depression which would engulf western Europe and, eventually, spread over much of the rest of the world.

I have examined with great care the means now available to the executive branch of the Government to provide the necessary assistance. They may meet the urgent needs of the next few weeks, but it is clear that they cannot provide the necessary assistance beyond December, if as long as that. Requirements beyond that time can be met only if further authority is granted by the Congress.

The problems arising out of these circumstances are of such importance that they should be considered by the Congress at the earliest practicable time. The early convening of your committee, together with other appropriate Congressional committees, is a necessary first step in this consideration.

I am requesting, therefore, that you call your committee together at the earliest possible date to consider these problems. I appreciate the fact that some of the members of your committee are investigating, or are planning to investigate, conditions in Europe at first hand. Time is of critical importance in this matter, however, and I earnestly hope that arrangements can be made for convening your committee at an early date.

The appropriate departments and agencies of the executive branch of the Government are prepared to provide information and make recommendations to your committee when its meetings begin.

Very sincerely yours,

HARRY S. TRUMAN

NOTE: This is the text of identical letters addressed to the Honorable Arthur H. Vandenberg, Chairman of the Senate Committee on Foreign Relations; the Honorable Charles A. Eaton, Chairman of the House Committee on Foreign Affairs; the Honorable Styles Bridges, Chairman of the Senate Committee on Appropriations; and the Honorable John Taber, Chairman of the House Committee on Appropriations.

198 Remarks to Members of the Citizens Food Committee. *October 1, 1947*

Members of the Citizens Food Committee:

This group of distinguished citizens has met to consider the grave food problem facing the world today. You are here because millions of people in many countries are hungry and look to the United States for help. You are here because the United States, in addition to being a granary of bread, is even more a granary of hope.

I have asked you to serve on the Citizens Food Committee, with Mr. Luckman as chairman, because I believe strongly that making our food serve the best possible use in these critical times is a matter for action not by the Government alone, but by all the people of the United States. Each of you possesses a special talent and long experience in some phase of this problem. I know that you have accepted membership on the Committee in the full knowledge that you will be called upon to devote to the situation we face a generous amount of work and much conscientious thinking, as well as a deep concern for the common welfare.

As is well known, this year's harvest has been poor in many parts of the world. All through Western Europe, cold and floods and drought have sharply reduced grain production. The result is that in the coming months these countries will have to cut their rations below the danger point unless they get more help, in the form of larger grain shipments, from the United States and other exporting countries.

It is extremely important to the United States that any serious reduction in the rations of hungry people be prevented. Apart from humanitarian considerations, if rations are significantly cut this winter, economic rehabilitation will come to a stop. This, in turn, would increase the degree and dura-

tion of dependence by other nations on special assistance by the United States. Most important, if we turn our backs upon these people they will turn from hunger to despair and from despair to chaos in areas where stability is essential to the peace and economic security of the world.

In the face of this situation, the amount of grain which the United States can export is limited. All estimates indicate that about 470 million bushels of grain are the most we can plan to export under present conditions. At the same time, there is strong evidence that we will have to export at least 100 million bushels more than this, if we are to do our share in meeting the absolute minimum needs of distressed people in other countries.

This 100 million bushels must be saved by the American people. This is our minimum goal. We know that only part of that saving can come from serving fewer slices of bread. The greater part of the saving must come out of what we feed our livestock. We must also save out of what we waste, and out of what we use in a score of ways for human food.

This saving must be achieved, not by increasing prices so that the brunt of the sacrifice will be borne by those least able to buy food, but through an equitable sharing by all of our citizens. There will be more than enough food in the United States to go around, provided it is fairly distributed. Excessive prices, however, result in unfair distribution. Already, increasing prices are bringing hardship to millions of Americans of low or moderate income. Failure to check price increases promptly will not only lower the American living standard, but would impair the confidence of business, and thus jeopardize the spendid record we have achieved in the maintenance of high employment, high production, and general prosperity. We must get prices down and help hungry people in other countries at the same time.

It has been estimated that we waste about 10 percent of all the food we buy. Just think of that! We waste 10 percent of all the food we buy. Clearly, by wasting less, American families can help significantly in feeding hungry families abroad. In addition to cutting down waste, Americans can save by being more selective in the foods they buy.

In our free enterprise system, we place major reliance on the voluntary actions of businessmen, farmers, workers, and consumers. It is in accordance with this principle that I have consistently set forth a program for voluntary action in all parts of the economy.

The appointment of the Citizens Food Committee is a further step in this direction. The conservation practices which this Committee works out, by reducing the demand for certain foods, should bring down some food prices, and hence reduce the cost of living.

As representatives of all segments of our population, the Citizens Food Committee can help us plan where, how much, and what kinds of food we should save. It can enlist the aid of those who should support the program—consumers, retailers, food distributors and processors, and farmers. It can also develop the best ways of informing the public on what steps Americans, as individuals and groups, can take.

We must deal with the problem quickly and decisively. Much depends, therefore, upon the voluntary conservation measures

which the Citizens Food Committee will propose. Much depends upon the speed and thoroughness with which the American people will put these voluntary measures into effect.

The saving asked of each individual is actually very, very small. One bushel of grain saved by every person in America in the next few months will do the job.

And it seems to me that we are all in the frame of mind to do the job, and I know you can get it done. I appreciate very much your being here for that purpose.

NOTE: The President spoke at 10 a.m. at the Committee's first meeting, held in the Moving Picture Theater in the East Wing of the White House.

On the same day the White House released the following statement by Secretary of State George C. Marshall:

"Every humane, economic, and world political interest of the United States dictates that we, the American people, should do everything within our power to help feed the people of Europe this winter.

"The many reasons for the grave shortage of food, particularly in Western Europe, have been explained to the country by the President. The urgency of the problem has developed with alarming rapidity. It has now reached the stage where only the immediate and concerted action of our people as a whole can avoid the possible disaster resulting from further cuts in pitifully low rations throughout Western Europe. Every American, I am sure, will gladly share his bounty with the hungry men, women and children of Europe. Food is the very basis of all reconstruction.

"Hunger and insecurity are the worst enemies of peace. For recovery and political stability, Europe needs many things, but the most elemental, indispensable need is food.

"Europe needs more food than she received from us last winter and this country has smaller quantity available to send her. This may seem to be an impossible situation but it is not so if the American people really wish to find the answer.

"The Citizens Food Committee has laid down the challenge: 'Buy wisely, eat sensibly, waste nothing.' In short, all of us must 'declare war on waste' in this country in order to win the 'war against hunger' in Europe, and its menace to world stability."

199 Citation Accompanying Medal for Merit Awarded to Louis Johnson. *October 1, 1947*

CITATION TO ACCOMPANY THE AWARD OF

THE MEDAL FOR MERIT

TO

LOUIS JOHNSON

LOUIS JOHNSON, for exceptionally meritorious conduct in the performance of outstanding services to the United States during the recent war period. Mr. Johnson, as Assistant Secretary of War from September, 1939 to July, 1940 reviewed and presented industrial mobilization plans and made recommendations for increasing their effectiveness; initiated a program to start the placing of educational orders with industry in order to build up munitions production capacity; obtained appropriations for constructing munitions plants of various types; supported a policy of stockpiling critical materials for use in emergency; and was instrumental in the establishment of the basic munitions program on which America mobilized for war. His services in the assurance of adequate provision for the mobilization of materials and industrial organizations essential to wartime needs, which continued throughout the war, was a major factor in the success of the allied war effort.

HARRY S. TRUMAN

NOTE: The presentation was made by the President in a ceremony at the White House at 12:45 p.m.

200 Citation Accompanying Medal for Merit Awarded to Fred M. Vinson. *October 3, 1947*

CITATION TO ACCOMPANY THE AWARD OF

THE MEDAL FOR MERIT

TO

FRED M. VINSON

FRED M. VINSON, for exceptionally meritorious conduct in the performance of outstanding services to the United States from May 1943, to June, 1946. Mr. Vinson demonstrated the peculiarly exacting qualities of statesmanship needed in a global war whose economics and organizational complexities created problems of a scope hitherto unknown to history. To the people he was a human symbol of the strength of American leadership, and to the two commanders-in-chief he served, he was one of the Nation's greatest contributors to victory in the war and to the successful reconversion to peace afterwards. In personality, in speech, in the tone and justice of wartime decisions whose wisdom have since been amply proved, he displayed solid knowledge of detail governed by a true perspective and a shrewd eye to the over-all needs of the Nation. His outstanding qualities as administrator, negotiator and conciliator were rooted deep in American character, and his words and acts, determining some of the greatest decisions of the war and postwar period, had their base in the principles that go back to the founding fathers. As the Director of the Office of Economic Stabilization he kept America's war economy pointed to victory without the concomitant chaos that had been the major disease of production in past wars. Few Americans contributed so much to the check of inflation during the war as this economist, financial expert and lawyer with the judicial mind, the broad-gauge imagination and the simple American talent for practical judgment. His policies as Director of the Office of War Mobilization and Reconversion lubricated the Nation's transition from the overwhelmingly strenuous war effort in the two-front war to the reduced pace required after Germany's capitulation and before Japan's surrender. He directed the liquidation of the Nation's nervous strain finally from total war to total peace so that the change created a pattern of economic smoothness and harmony unparalleled in previous postwar periods and hardly anticipated in this one. As Secretary of the Treasury, he maintained the same high level of statesmanship, carrying his talents into the international field. The job he had done before as a leader in America's war and reconversion economy he now repeated on an international plane in the effort to rehabilitate world economy. Here, and in every post to which his President and his country assigned him, Mr. Vinson sustained the reputation that he had securely established as one of the foremost Americans of his generation.

HARRY S. TRUMAN

NOTE: The presentation was made by the President in a ceremony at the White House at 11 a.m.

201 Statement by the President Making Public a Report "Administration for Research." *October 4, 1947*

I HAVE received today the third volume of the report on Science and Public Policy, submitted by John R. Steelman in accordance with Executive Order 9791. This volume, entitled "Administration for Research" analyzes the management of research by the Federal Government, points out key problems and recommends ways of improving the administration of the vast research and development program conducted by the Government.

I am directing the Federal departments and agencies which have important research and development functions to give careful consideration to the analysis and recommendations made in this report. The report also merits careful study by scientists outside the Government.

NOTE: The report, third in a series prepared by the President's Scientific Research Board, is dated October 4, 1947 (Government Printing Office, 324 pp.).

A summary was released with the President's statement.

The report emphasizes the need for strengthening the administration and organization of research by Government agencies. Specific recommendations include (1) establishment of an Interdepartmental Committee on Scientific Research and Development, (2) creation of a unit in the Bureau of the Budget to review Federal scientific and research programs in relation to total Government activity, (3) designation of a member of the White House staff for scientific liaison both inside and outside the Government, and (4) establishment of a National Science Foundation.

The report further suggests that each agency establish a policy and program evaluation committee composed of its leading scientists and outside experts; that adequate staff be provided to relieve scientists of the burden of administrative detail; and that appropriation for research be provided for broad rather than specific programs and cover periods of from 3 to 5 years.

In conclusion the report makes 19 recommendations with respect to personnel problems among scientists in Government and cites the use of contracts as an outstanding development of World War II.

For other reports of the Board, see Items 183, 194, 206, 211.

202   Radio and Television Address Concluding a Program by the Citizens Food Committee.   *October 5, 1947*

[Delivered from the White House at 10:50 p.m.]

My fellow citizens:

The food-saving program which has just been presented to you has my wholehearted support. I am confident that it will have the support of every American.

The situation in Europe is grim and forbidding as winter approaches. Despite the vigorous efforts of the European people, their crops have suffered so badly from droughts, floods, and cold that the tragedy of hunger is a stark reality.

The nations of Western Europe will soon be scraping the bottom of the food barrel. They cannot get through the coming winter and spring without help—generous help— from the United States and from other countries which have food to spare.

I know every American feels in his heart that we must help to prevent starvation and distress among our fellow men in other countries.

But more than this, the food-saving program announced tonight offers an opportunity to each of you to make a contribution to the peace. We have dedicated ourselves to the task of securing a just and a lasting peace. No matter how long and hard the way, we cannot turn aside from that goal. An essential requirement of lasting peace is the restoration of the countries of Western Europe as free self-supporting democracies. There is reason to believe that those countries will accomplish that task if we aid them through this critical winter and help them get back on their feet during the next few years. They must do most of the job themselves. They cannot do it if thousands of their people starve. We believe they can— and will—do the job if we extend to them

that measure of friendly aid which marks the difference between success and failure.

Their most urgent need is food. If the peace should be lost because we failed to share our food with hungry people there would be no more tragic example in all history of a peace needlessly lost.

Another reason for conserving food is to aid in controlling inflationary spirals and in preventing undue price burdens for our people at home. Already many of our families with moderate or low incomes are being forced by high prices to lower their standard of living. Exports have some effect upon domestic prices of grain, but they do not exercise a controlling influence on food prices. Most of the upward pressure on prices is a result of competition among Americans for scarce goods. The success of our food-saving program will help to reduce these inflationary pressures.

Another factor that contributes to the high prices of food is gambling in grain. Grain prices naturally respond to the law of supply and demand, but they should not be subject to the greed of speculators who gamble on what may lie ahead in our commodity markets.

There is a place for legitimate trading in futures and for hedging transactions. But 90 percent of all accounts in a recent corn futures market were found to be speculative. Trading in wheat futures grew 75 percent in September compared with August. Normal trading in wheat at Chicago should amount to 3 or 4 million bushels a day. In this past September, however, trading averaged almost 30 million bushels a day. In a single month, on one exchange, almost half the year's crop was traded—bought and sold—just plain gambling.

I am instructing the Commodity Exchange Commission, which consists of the Attorney General and the Secretaries of Agriculture and Commerce, to demand of the grain exchanges that they increase their margin requirements to at least 33⅓ percent. If the grain exchanges refuse, the Government may find it necessary to limit the amount of trading.

I say this because the cost of living in this country must not be a football to be kicked about by gamblers in grain.

The food conservation program proposed by the Citizens Food Committee will be supported by every department of the Federal Government.

Mrs. Truman has today directed that the White House follow all the measures proposed by the Citizens Food Committee. In Government restaurants and cafeterias, throughout the country, these same measures will be followed. As Commander in Chief, I have ordered that the Army, the Navy, and the Air Force shall also comply with this program.

All segments of our population must make their contribution toward saving grain.

Farmers must cooperate by reducing the amount of grain now used to feed their livestock and poultry.

Industry must reduce the volume of grain used so as to make the greatest possible saving. The distillers in this country have on hand huge stocks of distilled spirits, and it will be no hardship on them to shut down for a 60-day period. This action alone will feed millions of hungry people.

Quite apart from the responsibilities of farmers and of industry, you and I—as individual Americans—have our responsibility. You have all heard Mr. Luckman give the immediate consumer program for the people of the United States. It has my complete approval and my full support.

It is simple and straightforward. It can be understood by all. Learn it—memorize it—keep it always in mind. Here it is:

One: Use no meat on Tuesdays.

Two: Use no poultry or eggs on Thursdays.

Three: Save a slice of bread every day.

Four: Public eating places will serve bread and butter only on request.

I realize that many millions of American housewives have already begun strict conservation measures. I say to those housewives, "keep up the good work" and save even more when and where you can. On the other hand, there are also many Americans who are overeating and wasting food. Unless these people cut their consumption in the ways required, they will be taking more than a fair share of the supplies available. They will be personally contributing to increased inflation at home and to the desperate scarcity of food overseas.

The battle to save food in the United States is the battle to save our own prosperity and to save the free countries of Western Europe. Our self-denial will serve us well in the years to come.

The voluntary program is the best way for us to do the job. We believe that self-control is the best control. From now on, we shall be testing at every meal the degree to which each of us is willing to exercise self-control for the good of all.

The program which has been presented to you tonight, if faithfully carried out, will save all the grain we need.

Hungry people in other countries look to the United States for help. I know that they will be strengthened and encouraged by this evidence of our friendship.

I know that they will be waiting with hope in their hearts and a fervent prayer on their lips for the response of our people to this program.

We must not fail them.

NOTE: The President's address, part of a special broadcast on the food conservation program, was the first of its kind ever televised from the White House. Other speakers on the program were George C. Marshall, Secretary of State; Clinton P. Anderson, Secretary of Agriculture; W. Averell Harriman, Secretary of Commerce; and Charles Luckman, Chairman of the Citizens Food Committee. The text of the remarks of the Secretaries and of Mr. Luckman was made public by the White House.

On October 6 the Citizens Food Committee announced the menus that would be served at the White House on the first two days of self-denial, as follows:

Tuesday, luncheon—grapefruit, cheese soufflé, buttered peas, grilled tomatoes, chocolate pudding; dinner—clear chicken soup, broiled salmon steak, scalloped potatoes, string beans, sautéed eggplant, perfection salad, sliced peaches.

Thursday, luncheon—corn soup, peppers stuffed with rice and mushrooms, lima beans, glazed carrots, baked apples; dinner—melon balls, baked ham, baked sweet potatoes, asparagus, cauliflower, green salad, coffee mallow.

203 Citation Accompanying the Legion of Merit Awarded to the Shah of Iran.   *October 7, 1947*

CITATION TO ACCOMPANY THE AWARD OF

THE LEGION OF MERIT

DEGREE OF CHIEF COMMANDER

TO

MOHAMMAD REZA SHAH PAHLAVI

HIS IMPERIAL MAJESTY Mohammad Reza Shah Pahlavi, Shah-en-Shah of Iran and Commander in Chief of the Imperial Armed Forces of Iran, mobilized the loyalties, efforts and resources of the Iranian nation in support of the Allied cause during the course of the recent war. By his loyal and steadfast devotion to the principles which united the Allies in war and in victory, he has contributed to the success of the war and peace efforts of the United Nations.

HARRY S. TRUMAN

NOTE: The President presented the Legion of Merit medal and the citation to Princess Ashraf Pahlavi of Iran for her brother, the Shah, at 12:30 p.m. at the White House. The Princess, who had been visiting in the United States for 6 weeks, was making a farewell call on the President before returning to Iran.

204 Address Broadcast to the Women of the United States.   *October 8, 1947*

[Delivered from the White House at 1:30 p.m.]

I SPEAK to you today—the women of the United States—in order to emphasize the need for greater participation by women in the affairs of our country. Our Nation, at this time, must have responsible citizens, thoughtful citizens, earnest citizens, who will work to solve the difficult problems confronting us.

The women of this country, by recognizing their responsibility to take an active part in the determination of the grave issues of the day, can furnish this type of citizenship.

Women can provide immediate leadership in dealing with one of these great issues. Women can make an invaluable contribution to the welfare of our Nation—and of the world—by lending their wholehearted support to our food-saving program. Indeed, the responsibility for the success of that program rests very largely with the American housewife. She is an indispensable fighter in our war against hunger. The American housewife has never failed her country when she has been called upon to sacrifice in its interest. I know that she will not fail in the great task before us now.

I know, too, that if the women of our Nation exert the tremendous moral force for good which they possess, we shall make greater and more lasting progress in overcoming the other difficulties that concern us and the world.

As a Nation we stand now on the threshold of a wonderful opportunity, unique in history. We are a thriving country. The facts of our high employment and our great farm and industrial production speak for themselves. We are a strong and peace-loving Nation.

The United States, more than any other nation, is in a position to give reality to the Four Freedoms. The United States should and can be the first nation in which the people—all the people—are free from want, free from fear, free to speak and to write as their hearts dictate, and free to worship as they will.

This is no idle dream. It is a goal well within the power of this mighty Nation of ours to achieve.

The actions of our Government to improve social security, public health, and education, and to develop and conserve our national resources, must not be allowed to lag behind the needs of the people. Nor can we falter in our unceasing quest for a just, permanent peace in the world. The need is for us, the people, to summon the will to achieve these goals, and to translate that will into positive action.

In this undertaking, the women of the United States have a great opportunity and a great responsibility to play a decisive part. Women in this country won the right to vote only after a long, hard struggle. Now, over one million more women than men are eligible to vote in the United States. Thus, the power lies in the hands of the American women—in your hands—to shape the destiny of America. And yet when the time comes to register and the opportunity comes to vote, many of our women neglect this responsibility of citizenship.

Foreign nations are deeply interested in the size of our vote. The reason is clear. The United States is the foremost example of democratic government in the world. Men and women of other lands are comparing the operation of our democratic system with other forms of government. We do not want them to conclude that we are not interested in the vigor of our Government, or that we are indifferent to the issues before us! We must prove to them that we take our democracy seriously. They must understand that we accept the responsibilities of our form of democracy as well as its privileges.

When you, the women of America, make your will felt at the polls, you make an invaluable contribution to this democratic system. The moral force of women has always had a wholesome influence upon the character of our civilization. They are deeply responsive to the fundamental human values. Women care more for people than for dollars, more for healthy children than fat dividends. Women want a society in which we build schools instead of prisons. Women want a world in which we sow and harvest the seeds of a good life instead of the seeds of war.

You now have a great opportunity to make this wholesome influence increasingly effective by the full use of your power at the ballot box.

Your vote is your insurance that the American people will always be free members of a democratic society; your insurance that we shall continue to live in a democracy where men can worship God in their own fashion, can speak and write as they please, and have equal justice under the law.

Your vote is your investment in the future of the United States, your investment to insure a country where your children will have opportunities for decent homes, good health, good jobs, and adequate education.

Your vote is a downpayment on the kind of world in which nations respect one another, a world in which nations are good neighbors because they know that good neighborliness offers the only hope of lasting peace.

Your vote is your best way of getting the kind of country—and the kind of world—you want.

NOTE: The President's address was part of a nation-wide broadcast arranged by the Women's Division of the Democratic National Committee to commemorate Democratic Women's Day. Other speakers on the program were Mrs. Philip L. Crowlie, South Dakota housewife; Mrs. David M. Levy of New York City; and Mrs. John Boettiger, daughter of President Franklin D. Roosevelt.

205 The President's News Conference of October 9, 1947

THE PRESIDENT. [1.] I have no particular announcements to make today, except that we found some interesting receipts and documents signed by President Lincoln and Mrs. Lincoln in reference to some of the White House furniture about which there had been controversy. So anybody who is interested in those controversies will be welcome to take a look at these papers.

All I am open to now is questions.

[2.] Q. Mr. President, this statement was made today—and we would like your comment—it was made by Secretary of Agriculture Anderson in a press conference——

THE PRESIDENT. I have no comment.

Q. You know what the statement was?

THE PRESIDENT. No, I do not. I have heard about it, but I have no comment on it because I haven't read the statement, so I can't possibly make a comment on it. If you want to ask me any specific questions on it, I might answer from my own viewpoint, but I can't comment on Anderson.

[3.] Q. Mr. President, do you consider meatless days of no importance in themselves but merely reminders?

THE PRESIDENT. The meatless days and the eggless days are for the purpose of saving grain, which is of vital importance, because it is expensive to feed grain to poultry and livestock; and when you save meat and save poultry products you save grain, and grain is what is necessary to meet the hunger situation in Europe. It is the most economical way to meet it.

[4.] Q. Mr. President, did you and Mr. Blythe[1] discuss the next year's election today?

THE PRESIDENT. We did not. He just paid me a courtesy call.

[5.] Q. Is it correct, sir, that General Spaatz is being considered for Chief of Staff to succeed General Eisenhower?

THE PRESIDENT. I have no comment to make on that. I never comment on people I am considering for a job. I will let you know when I make the appointment.

Q. Does that mean you are considering it?

THE PRESIDENT. I have no comment. I don't like questions like that, either.

Q. I'm sorry.

---

[1] Joe Blythe, National Democratic Committeeman from North Carolina.

[6.] Q. Mr. President, since your return from South America, have you had a chance to do anything about the fight among the California Democrats?

THE PRESIDENT. No, I have not. That fight was going on before I left, and I have never taken any part in it. I am not interested in Democrats fighting. I want harmony in the Democratic Party.

[7.] Q. Mr. President, would you say what importance you attach to the rebirth of the Comintern?

THE PRESIDENT. I think that was amply commented on yesterday by Secretary Lovett. And I want to reiterate again my viewpoint, that all this country has ever wanted is a lasting peace in the world, and prosperity in the world for the benefit of all the countries in the world. We have no—we have never asked for territory. We are not interested in the economic control of any country or any continent.

Q. Mr. President, how do you feel about the recent Russian propaganda, like in the newspapers——

THE PRESIDENT. That is just like the propaganda here at home. I am used to it. [*Laughter*] They got most of their information out of the papers here at home that have been in the political campaigns.

[8.] Q. Mr. President, the Housing Administrator today approved a 5-percent rent increase in Louisville, the first in the country. Have you any comment on that?

THE PRESIDENT. The only information I have on that is that the law provides—and I think I sent out a statement when it was signed—that these rent committees are locally appointed by the Governor of the State in which they operate, and that the Housing Expediter has no discretion except to accept their recommendations.

[9.] Q. Mr. President, it has been reported that the White House has issued orders for a resurvey of possible stopgap aid—sources of money——

THE PRESIDENT. Well, that—it's a resurvey that has been going on ever since this proposition came up. We are still making an effort to find every dollar we can to meet the situation. My viewpoint on the subject hasn't changed a bit from that last answer I gave you on the subject, that I didn't think it would last beyond December 1st.

Q. Has that search met with any great success so far?

THE PRESIDENT. I can't answer the question. I am in the same frame of mind when I talked to you before.

[10.] Q. Mr. President, some fear has been expressed by labor unions that this action of the Louisville rent advisory board is going to set a pattern for rent increases all over the country.

THE PRESIDENT. I can't comment. I can't comment on that. I am telling you what the law provides. If you get out the law and read it, you will see exactly where the Expediter stands and where the administration stands. I would advise you to read my comment on the law when it was signed.[1]

[11.] Q. Mr. President, do you approve the wearing of these new Truman buttons we see around?

THE PRESIDENT. I haven't seen any of them.

Q. We understood that some of the guests at the broadcast yesterday were wearing them?

THE PRESIDENT. I don't remember whether they were or not.

Q. We can't hear you.

THE PRESIDENT. I don't remember whether there were or not. There may have been. I saw the picture in the News this afternoon.

Q. What about the Truman earrings?

---

[1] See Item 131.

THE PRESIDENT. I saw that picture in the paper this afternoon. I have no comment to make on it.

Q. You don't disapprove of those earrings, do you?

THE PRESIDENT. Well, I don't think it's my province to disapprove of any sort of wearing apparel that anybody chooses to wear, as long as they want to. [*Laughter*]

Q. You mean you don't take a position on long skirts?

THE PRESIDENT. I don't think it's necessary for me to take that position.

[12.] Q. Mr. President, on that stuff you referred to there, about the Lincoln furniture, what is there to that? Are there now any historic pieces or any authentic pieces?

THE PRESIDENT. Oh yes. There is a rosewood bed over there, known as the Lincoln bed, and two dressers and a desk, and four Cabinet chairs, which are authentic, and are proven to be authentic by these bills which I have just run across in the file of the General Accounting Office. They are right interesting to anyone who is interested in that.

Q. Is there anything else you can tell us about them of an interesting nature?

THE PRESIDENT. There are a lot of dishes over in the showroom over there that are marked as Lincoln pieces, and they are all specifically described in here, and it makes them all authentic.

Q. What are those bills?

THE PRESIDENT. Bills approved by President Lincoln and Mrs. Lincoln for those purchases.

Q. What did the Lincoln bed cost, Mr. President?

THE PRESIDENT. Three hundred and seventy-five dollars. About the fourth item from the top.

Q. Had you been searching for these documents, Mr. President?

THE PRESIDENT. No, no. I am interested in everything of that sort, if it has anything to do with the White House, of course; and we accidentally ran across these Cabinet chairs which we had reupholstered and brought over to the House. And they are just exactly like the ones in the Brady picture of the Lincoln Cabinet, so I am sure that they are authentic.

Q. Mr. President, was there any indication that Mr. Lincoln said that $375 was too much for a bed?

THE PRESIDENT. No. He OK'd a bill for some $2600 there. Paid for a lot of other things, including draperies and things of that sort—curtains for the bed, and one thing and another.

[13.] Q. Mr. President, have you taken any steps to aid France in this present situation, in which they are asking for help between now and the stopgap aid?

THE PRESIDENT. We have been taking steps on that ever since the matter came up, of course. Done everything we possibly can.

Q. Is there any way in which you can get money now?

THE PRESIDENT. I can't answer the question. We haven't found any way as yet.

[14.] Q. Mr. President, someone has claimed that about 100,000 people would be put out of jobs by a shutdown of the distilling industry for 60 days, claiming another 30,000 would be out of work——

THE PRESIDENT. I can't answer the question. I don't know. What I am after is 10 million bushels of grain, to feed hungry people, from the distilleries.

[15.] Q. Mr. President, do you feel, on the basis of the recent Russian revival of the Comintern, that American aid to Western Europe assumes that much more of the character of urgency?

THE PRESIDENT. Well, it has always been urgent. I don't think it's any more urgent, no matter what anybody did. It's just as urgent now as it was in the beginning.

[16.] Q. Mr. President, do you have any comment on Representative Thomas'[1] idea of a federation of Western nations to oppose the new Comintern?

THE PRESIDENT. No, I haven't any comment on it.

[17.] Q. Mr. President, if we might get back on this rent control subject just a moment, your statement at the time pointed out the shortcomings of that rent bill.

THE PRESIDENT. That's right.

Q. And it seems to me you said that there should be public hearings before these local boards recommending rent increases.

THE PRESIDENT. I think that is correct. I can't quote that statement exactly, but I am sure that was in it, and that the local people themselves would have to be careful to look after their recommendations and see that people went on that board that were not prejudiced one way or the other.

Q. Yes sir. Well, in the Louisville case there was no public gathering, and Mr. Creedon OK'd that rent increase.

THE PRESIDENT. I don't think Mr. Creedon had any discretion in the matter, if you read the law.

Q. Well, one of the reports said Mr.

---

[1] Representative J. Parnell Thomas of New Jersey.

Creedon has decided to not permit any publicity on the recommendations—for the recommendations from the rent control board, which seems to me would interfere with the people making their——

THE PRESIDENT. You will have to question Mr. Creedon on that. I am not making recommendations for him.

[18.] Q. Mr. President, should the distillers as a whole refuse to cut down, is there any means that the Government might use——

THE PRESIDENT. I don't think they will refuse.

[19.] Q. Mr. President, back to the importance of meatless and poultryless days, do you mind if we quote two words "vital importance"?

THE PRESIDENT. No. Vital importance.

Q. May we quote them, sir?

THE PRESIDENT. Yes, you can quote that.

Q. Just those two words, sir, is that correct? Vitally important.

THE PRESIDENT. The answer to the question I think you can quote, if you feel like it. It's a statement of the facts.

Reporter: Thank you, Mr. President.

THE PRESIDENT. You're welcome.

NOTE: President Truman's one hundred and twenty-second news conference was held in his office at the White House at 4:10 p.m. on Thursday, October 9, 1947.

---

206 Statement by the President Making Public a Report "Manpower for Research." *October 11, 1947*

I HAVE received today the fourth volume of the report on Science and Public Policy, submitted by John R. Steelman in accordance with Executive Order 9791. This volume, entitled "Manpower for Research," deals with the shortage of scientists and scientist-teachers, the implications of that shortage, and the remedial steps that must be taken.

The shortage of highly trained scientists both for teaching and for research is the basic factor which sets the limits of the Nation's scientific progress. The remedial program suggested in the report calls for financial support to colleges and universities and to deserving students. Specific ways for accomplishing these objectives are now being studied by the President's Commission on Higher Education.

NOTE: The fourth of the series of reports prepared by the President's Scientific Research Board is dated October 11, 1947 (Government Printing Office, 166 pp.). A summary was released with the President's statement.

The report proposes three programs to meet the problems causing the shortage referred to by the President:

1. Development of sources of financial support for educational institutions to permit expansion of faculties and increases in instructional staff and salaries—all as a part of a general program for improving higher education.

2. Development of a broad program in support of basic research in the universities to insure a foundation for applied and developmental science and a training ground for experts. To carry out such a program, a National Science Foundation should be employed to strengthen the weaker but promising institutions.

3. Establishment of a national system of scholarships and fellowships in all fields of knowledge, as the benefits under the Servicemen's Readjustment Act expire.

For other reports of the Board see Items 183, 194, 201, 211.

207 Telegram to State Governors Urging Cooperation With the Citizens Food Committee. *October* 13, 1947

THE DESPERATE NEED of hungry people in other countries makes the success of our voluntary food-saving program an urgent necessity. I am therefore requesting that the Governor of each of the States designate an individual or a group to work with the Citizens Food Committee to organize the activity in his State to insure the success of this war on hunger. If you have already set up a food conservation organization in your State, that organization might appropriately be designated for this purpose.

Wholehearted cooperation among these State organizations, the Citizens Food Committee, and the groups appointed by the mayors of our cities will insure the success of the voluntary plan of conservation and will show the hard-pressed nations of the world an example of democracy in action that will strengthen and encourage them in their struggle for peace and security.

HARRY S. TRUMAN

NOTE: This is the text of identical telegrams addressed to the Governors of each of the 48 States.

208 Statement by the President Concerning Payment of Procurement Obligations to France. *October* 15, 1947

THE FRENCH GOVERNMENT has informed this Government that a sum in excess of $80 million remains to be paid by the United States to France on account of procurement obligations incurred by the United States Army in France and North Africa after September 2, 1945. The auditing of the basic records, which is now in process, is being pressed forward so that settlements can be reached as promptly as possible.

In the interim, in order to help the French Government meet its immediate dollar requirements for essential imports, I have today authorized the Secretary of the Army to purchase from the French Government francs in the equivalent of $50 million, such francs to be used in payment of procurement obligations or for other expenditures of the United States Government.

209 The President's News Conference of
      October 16, 1947

THE PRESIDENT. I have no special announcements to make this morning, but I thought maybe you might want to ask me some questions and I will answer them if I can.

[1.] Q. Mr. President, when the White House announced yesterday that you and Mrs. Truman had decided to cancel state dinners in order to conserve food, is there any attempt to have that as a national example, your action?

THE PRESIDENT. No, not necessarily. It was a voluntary procedure on our part. We will have the receptions as usual. The idea was that we could probably save a good deal of food by canceling the state dinners for this season, as we did during the war, but that doesn't make it incumbent upon anybody else to make any cancellations unless they desire to do so. I know what you are interested in—you are interested in that photographers' dinner that you have been getting ready for some time. [*Laughter*] As long as they comply with the rules of food conservation, I see no reason why they shouldn't go ahead with the dinner, if they want to.

[2.] Q. Mr. President, Governor Blue of Iowa sent a message to you on the food situation, in reply to your message to all the Governors. I have been asked to inquire whether you have any comment on it?

THE PRESIDENT. Well, I have had replies from 23 or 24 Governors. They have been coming in right straight along, and I haven't had a chance to read all of them as yet. I remember, though, that the Governor's message was one of them and that it was cooperative. All of them have been cooperative, which makes me believe that the food program is well on the way to success.

Q. Mr. President, I have been trying to rationalize this food thing, especially this morning at breakfast without any egg, but I wondered are you going to have the chickens not eat any grain the seventh day of the week? How are you going to save that grain? That is going to mean more grain unless you cut down the flocks.

THE PRESIDENT. The Citizens Food Committee is in conference now with the poultrymen and with the feedmen. What we are after is grain. We are trying to raise 100 million bushels of grain to feed starving people over the next 6 months.

Q. I understand that.

THE PRESIDENT. That is what we are after. We are trying to find a practical way to do it. Now we have to make this program—it was an emergency with which we were faced, and under ordinary conditions we would have worked out the program more deliberately and have consulted these people in advance. As it was, we had to work out the program and then find out where the "bugs" were and remedy that if it is necessary. What we are after is grain for the hungry people, and I know it is a—sometimes we feel like we have been imposed upon, but this is an attempt to get this free enterprise Nation to do voluntarily what other nations have to do by police state methods, and that we don't want to do.

Q. Well then, trying to reason this out, it seemed to me that what you would do is decrease the market for chickens and eggs to the point where you would lower the number in the flocks.

THE PRESIDENT. Well, what we are trying to do is, over a certain period of time, is save a certain amount of grain. Now we have got the distillers and the bakery people, and everybody else—the restaurant people and everybody—trying to help us do that job. Now if they will tell us some way to save grain, I have no objection to any method

465

that will save the grain to get to these hungry people. I am trying to keep people from starving to death this winter, that's all.

Q. Mr. President, if you ate more poultry, wouldn't you have fewer chickens to eat the grain?

THE PRESIDENT. Now that's like which came first, the chicken or the egg. Can't answer a question like that. Can't answer that question.

What I am trying to do is prevent grain, that should go to feed hungry people, from being fed to chickens and livestock for a certain period of time. If we can get that 100 million bushels of grain, then we can go on almost as usual.

Q. I should assume by this statement that if you find out that there are some deviations in this program which will do better, you wouldn't object to changing the program?

THE PRESIDENT. Well now, that's a matter that I am letting the Citizens Food Committee work out the best way that they know how. We have got some very able people on that committee, and they are holding conferences every day. Certain other people are trying to get this thing to work—some way to get the grain. That is what we are after. We are interested in grain to feed hungry people.

[3.] Q. Mr. President, have you, after these various food conservation measures and also reports of several financial plans—do you believe now that this stopgap aid for Europe can be provided without a special session of Congress?

THE PRESIDENT. I can't answer that question now. We are still working on it. We are still trying to find the funds for the stopgap aid, but that doesn't necessarily mean that there won't have to be a special session if it becomes necessary, as I have always told you. Not hesitate to call one.

Q. Have you had any success in finding

those funds, Mr. President?

THE PRESIDENT. Yes, we have had considerable success in finding funds. We have got the Export-Import Bank to release some of its regulations on this last 93 or 98 million dollars, whatever it was, that France still had coming on their loan; and we found this $50 million that was owing to them—France says we owe them—bought francs—so that France would have the dollars to spend. We are making every effort in other directions, which I will report to you as they come along.

Q. There is still a possibility of a special session coming along?

THE PRESIDENT. Of course there is.

[4.] Q. Do you intend to make public General Wedemeyer's report on China?

THE PRESIDENT. General Marshall will have a statement to make on that in a few days. The report was made to General Marshall.

[5.] Q. Mr. President, after a test run of this food conservation campaign, and if it fails, will you have other measures like restoring controls?

THE PRESIDENT. That matter—we will cross that bridge when we come to it.

[6.] Q. Mr. President, what do you think about Mr. Wallace's speech, on Cabinet being Wall Street men?

THE PRESIDENT. I have no comment to make on that.

[7.] Q. Mr. President, are you prepared yet to name the advisory panel in the Federal Mediation Service?

THE PRESIDENT. I will be prepared in a few days to name that panel. I will announce it to you just as soon as it is ready.

[8.] Q. Mr. President, I want to ask you a question as former Chairman of the Truman Investigating Committee. We have a situation in Washington which involves the death of a man[1]—a very unfortunate

---

[1] John Forrest Bunch.

466

prisoner—who died as a result of injuries from police custody. There are charges of police negligence. The chairman of the Senate District Committee intimates that he may have an investigation by that committee. Do you have any comment on a situation like that, or do you think that the District of Columbia authorities should wait for an investigation by the Senate in a case involving——

THE PRESIDENT. I have no comment. That is a local municipal matter, which should be handled in the proper way by the proper authorities. I have no comment on that.

[9.] Q. Mr. President, what about the Krug report, which has been over here about 10 days?

THE PRESIDENT. The Krug report will be released in a few days, as soon as we are ready. I want to read it carefully myself before I release it.[1]

[10.] Q. Mr. President, have you read Mr. Byrnes's new book? [2]

THE PRESIDENT. Not entirely, no. I have read some of it—extracts from it—but I haven't read it carefully.

Q. What do you think of what you have read, Mr. President?

THE PRESIDENT. I have no comment.

[11.] Q. Mr. President, in counterposing voluntary methods of saving food to police state methods—a few minutes ago—do you mean to suggest that consumer rationing would be a police state method?

THE PRESIDENT. Why necessarily. Anything that you have to enforce by police methods is a police state method. I remember all the argument about taking off price controls, and voluntary saving, and all that sort of thing, that prices wouldn't go up. Don't you remember all that conversation

[1] See Item 212.
[2] James F. Byrnes, "Speaking Frankly," New York: Harper and Brothers, 1947.

about what would happen when we got rid of price controls? Most interesting history, if you want to go back a little into it.

Q. The Star had a very interesting table on that last night, showing that prices had risen from 8 to 80 percent on meat.

THE PRESIDENT. That's right. I have some very interesting figures on that myself. I try to keep up with these things. There is a graph—[*taking one out of his desk and indicating*]—right there that shows the situation. Most interesting.

Q. Mr. President, if everybody is for this export relief of food abroad, you wouldn't have such high prices, would you?

THE PRESIDENT. Yes, it would be just the same high prices. The export—that is a piece of misinformation. The effect, of course, of large purchases in any market has a tendency to raise that price a small amount. But it is a very small percentage of the grain crop in this country that goes for exports. There has been a tremendous amount of gambling on those commodity exchanges, both in food and fiber. That is what causes high prices principally in the food products.

Q. Mr. President, this wheat crop is 1,400 million bushels——

THE PRESIDENT. Yes, it has been—it has been——

Q. ——over a third——

THE PRESIDENT. ——that wheat crop has been traded in about 8 or 9 times—8 or 9 billion bushels have been traded in on the Chicago Board of Trade alone. Now you can put that down for what it's worth, because about exports—the exports are not out of line with what it has always been. We have always exported a third or more of our wheat crop.

Q. Mr. President, since the higher margins were put on the grain exchanges, prices have continued to go up. Do you think they should be still higher than they are?

THE PRESIDENT. I don't know. We will have to wait and see how they are going. They haven't had a chance to work completely yet. Haven't been in force long enough.

[12.] Q. Is there any intention in the administrative side of the Government to investigate this gambling on the food exchanges?

THE PRESIDENT. Yes, we are having it looked into.

Q. By whom?

THE PRESIDENT. By the Attorney General.

Q. Mr. President, on this gambling in fiber also, are there investigations into cotton and wool trading too?

THE PRESIDENT. No, there hasn't been, so far.

Q. Well, that is on the—the Attorney General's investigation is in food and fiber?

THE PRESIDENT. Food and fiber, yes. This thing covers the whole ground.

Q. The grand jury that has now been in session in Chicago, or is it a separate investigation into the grain exchange?

THE PRESIDENT. You would have to ask the Attorney General about that, because I don't run the details. You ask the Attorney General.

Q. Mr. President, what I was getting at is whether you had requested a specific investigation of the grain exchanges?

THE PRESIDENT. No, the Attorney General took it up on his own initiative, which was right in his department, and should have been done.

Q. Deals with what you have called gambling on the exchanges?

THE PRESIDENT. That's right.

Q. Does livestock come in on that, sir? I think a few of these questions included something about meat.

THE PRESIDENT. No. No, these—they don't come in on that. You don't have commodity exchanges in livestock. The prices of livestock usually are set in the five market centers—in Chicago, St. Paul, Omaha, Fort Worth, and Kansas City.

Q. Mr. President, there has already been a grand jury investigation of the meat packers in Chicago?

THE PRESIDENT. That's right.

[13.] Q. Mr. President, has the decision been made yet whether the United States will take over the British Zone of operations in Germany?

THE PRESIDENT. No. No decision has been made on that.

[14.] Q. Mr. President, can we get back a minute to this business of consumer rationing and the police state? Did I understand you correctly, sir, to say that you thought that consumer rationing and price controls were methods of a police state?

THE PRESIDENT. Yes, they are. Anything you have to enforce and punish people for infringing is a police state approach.

Q. That is true of the Office of Price Administration, then—is it?

THE PRESIDENT. Yes, it had to be. It was the only way you could make it work. Under the emergency we have to assume those controls. But I was told, I think very vociferously, that this is a free country, that we wouldn't suffer from any of the things that we are now suffering from, if we took price controls off right away.

Q. But you don't consider you will have to reimpose them at this point?

THE PRESIDENT. I can't answer that. You will have to see how the situation works.

Q. That was true of rent controls, too, was it?

THE PRESIDENT. Yes.

[15.] Q. The other day the Vice Chairman of the Commodity Credit Corporation was in here. Can you tell us whether any decision has been reached on using the CCC funds?

THE PRESIDENT. No, I can't answer that now. I will make an announcement on it whenever we can.

[16.] Q. Mr. President, did you say that there was—I didn't hear very clearly—did you say that there was a grand jury investigation of this gambling on the exchange?

THE PRESIDENT. Yes.

Q. Just the Attorney General?

THE PRESIDENT. The Attorney General is making the investigation. I don't know how he is doing it. You will have to ask him.

[17.] Q. To clear up one thing that was asked, would that likewise apply to direct controls——

THE PRESIDENT. Any control enforced by the state is a police method of getting the job done. And of course it has to be done in any emergency, and everybody agrees to do it. But in a free country like this it wants to be done under the agreement of all the people, and not at the behest of just one man.

Q. In other words, both methods have their application according to the times, is that right, Mr. President?

THE PRESIDENT. That's right. It depends on the emergency.

Reporter: Thank you, Mr. President.

NOTE: President Truman's one hundred and twenty-third news conference was held in his office at the White House at 10:05 a.m. on Thursday, October 16, 1947.

---

210   Remarks and Question and Answer Period With the National Conference of Editorial Writers. *October* 17, 1947

THE PRESIDENT. I notice Mr. Mencken told you that you were no use—[*laughter*]—and that's not the first time I have disagreed with Mr. Mencken.

I make it a point to read a great many editorials. They are, most of them, thoughtful and well written, and are exceedingly useful to the welfare of the country. I can't say that for all of them, but that is true in any business, there are people who are outside the pale. And you have that to contend with, just as I do in politics.

[1.] I know that you are interested somewhat in the policy that the United States is pursuing. You have a right to be interested in it, because it is your policy. It is a policy that we have been interested in from time immemorial—and that is world peace. We have never wanted anything but

peace, peace in the world that is a peace that will work for the welfare of all the citizens in all the countries of the world.

The war ended suddenly. The German war ended just about 3 weeks after I sat down at this desk. All the prophets said that it would last 6 months longer. The Japanese war ended about 3 months afterwards, the 14th of August, and all the prophets said that it would last a year after the Germans had folded up. In that year we had appropriated $105 billion for war expenses. In October of that year, I made an order of rescission for $55 billion of that war expenditure, because it was no longer necessary to buy tanks and planes and guns and ammunition after the Axis powers had folded up.

This policy which we are endeavoring to

pursue is one in which we will be asked to make expenditures in the interests of peace. The Marshall report calls for an expenditure over a 4-year period of some 16 to 22 billions of dollars, about one third of the rescission which I made in October for 6 months of war.

The idea of the rehabilitation of the wartorn countries is to put them on a self-supporting basis, which is entirely to our selfish interest. There is only one other alternative to that.

There are two ideologies in the world now. We have, under our Constitution, a Bill of Rights. The right of the individual is the foremost thing in the formation of our form of government. The other ideology believes that the individual is the slave of the state, to be sent where they tell him, to do what they tell him, to act as they tell him to act.

In July of 1945 I made a trip to Potsdam to see if we could implement the preliminaries of a peace in the world. We made some progress, and made certain specific agreements in relation to what was to come afterwards to a peace that would affect the whole world.

Before that time—some time before that time, there had been a worsening of our relationships with one of our great allies, the one that has come out of the war apparently in better shape than any of those who went into it. Those relationships continue to grow worse, and we found by trial and error—I hope not too many errors—that we had to assume a position of firmness in our effort to get a workable peace in the world.

We have never wanted anything but peace. We didn't ask for territory, we didn't ask for reparations. All we asked for is a restoration of those principles for which we stand on, based on a just peace that will affect every country in the world to its welfare and benefit. We don't want to tell any country

how to run its internal affairs, or what to do in regard to its domestic policy. We do want the United Nations to become a going concern. And that, I think, is our only hope for a lasting peace.

We have only one other alternative, which is to go back into our shell. We may have to go back to that $105 billion a year expenditure, which nobody with any sense in his head wants to do.

We have established a going policy. You are a part of that policy. It is a bipartisan foreign policy of the United States of America, not the President's policy, or the policy of the Secretary of State. It is the policy of this country, of the United States, and you are just as much in it as I am.

I want to bring that home to you, so that when you write your editorials, try and get all the facts in relation to the foreign policy before you make up your mind. I have been sitting here for 2½ years, trying to get all the facts, and I haven't got them all yet! So you know it must be a rather difficult problem. But we are here, trying to give you as much information as is possible for us to give you, and to give you the facts as they are.

You have a tremendous influence on the welfare of this country. You can either make it or break it. I say that advisedly, although I would much rather have a good headline writer than a good editorial writer, any day. [*Laughter*]

If you have any questions that you want to ask, I will do my best to answer them. I am used to that.

[2.] Q. Mr. President, this may seem trivial, but I think it would interest us. You say you read a great many editorials. Could you tell us a little about how they are screened, whether they come to you, what method——

THE PRESIDENT. No sir, I take the papers themselves, and I read at least a dozen daily papers every day. Then there are a great many instances where editorials are mailed to me from out of town. But I spend—you see, I get up before daylight every morning—I have the reveille habit—and I spend a good part of that time going over all the Washington papers and the New York papers, Baltimore Sun, Philadelphia Bulletin, and any others that I have time to read. But I read them myself because I like to read them. And I find out lots of things about myself that I never heard of. [*Laughter*]

Q. Ever read any from beyond the Alleghenies regularly?

THE PRESIDENT. Yes, I get the St. Louis Post-Dispatch, sometimes the Pittsburgh papers, and the Kansas City Star. On occasion I get some west coast papers. That is, editorially they are—of course, by the time they get here the news is stale, but I usually read the editorial pages of these papers. The Morning Register I read sometimes, and Chicago papers—always very fond of the little afternoon Chicago daily[1] consolidated with the Chicago Sun. I never thought much of the rest of the Chicago papers. [*Laughter*]

[3.] Q. Mr. President, can you offer us any suggestions on how we can help the food-saving campaign?

THE PRESIDENT. Yes I can. The idea and object of the food-saving campaign is just one thing, that is, to keep people from starving to death this winter. We have an immense wheat crop this year, but our corn crop is short. What we are hoping to do is getting the people who feed livestock and poultry, and things of that kind—and the distillers and brewers to make a little less alcohol, leaving a little less grain to be put out to livestock and poultry, and see if we can't get enough additional grain so as not to allow people to starve to death.

---

[1] Chicago Times.

Of course, after the Napoleonic war, immense numbers of people in Europe starved to death. There wasn't any United States in existence at that time large enough to contribute to the starving people. They simply starved. We don't want to see that. It's a food-saving program to see if we can't keep these people from starving. When they tell you that exports of grain are principally because of the present market situation, that is a mistake, for the simple reason that we have always exported, anyway, anywhere from 25 percent to 40 percent of our wheat crop, and it is not unusual to export 570 million bushels of wheat out of a 1,400 million bushel crop. That is not out of line at all. That has been the average for the last 30 years.

Then, too, so many of our people have become able to eat more and to live so much better than they have lived in the past, that they scramble for food grains, and for meat, and things of that kind. It has become immense.

And there is also some connection with—I shouldn't bring in politics—but the price control situation, if you want to read the history on that, you will find that our present difficulties now result from that, just as it was prophesied by the President of the United States. But we are faced with a condition and not a theory. We must find a way to feed these people.

Q. Mr. President, many of the farmers of our section are holding their grain over because of income taxes. Has there been any effort to give them—sell them——

THE PRESIDENT. Yes. Well, I don't know about that tax thing. I don't think there is anything you can do on the tax thing, but an effort is being made by the Department of Agriculture to approach the problem on the ground and see if we can't get the farmers to sell to us directly, for the purpose for which we are going to use this, as we did last year. We had a difficult last year, if you remember, on account of the crop failure in the Southern Hemisphere. This year we are going to try the same plan we tried last year: to sell his grain directly to the Department of Agriculture for shipment abroad, so that will not make it cost quite so much, and I think will help the farmers, too; but I can't answer yet. In the history of a great many years, the farmer has been worried about this, and I am glad he is worried about it.

[4.] Q. Can you tell us anything more about the present outlook for a special session?

THE PRESIDENT. No, I can't give you any information on that, for I haven't all the facts together, as yet. As soon as I have all the facts on my desk, I will be able to see the situation as it is. I had the Ambassador from Great Britain in here yesterday—our Ambassador, Mr. Douglas; and General Clay, and Mr. Murphy from Germany in here this morning—I receive Bedell Smith tomorrow.[1] And then the Department of Agriculture and the Department of Commerce, the Secretary of State, are in conference with the Food Committee. And as soon as I get all those facts together, then I will tell you whether there will be a special session or not, but I can't tell you now. I can't operate on "by guess or by God." [*Laughter*]

[5.] Q. Mr. President, when do you expect the Harriman report on our resources?

THE PRESIDENT. It will be ready, I think, within the next 2 weeks.[2]

Mr. Ross: The Krug report is out now.

THE PRESIDENT. Has it been released?

Mr. Ross: It will be released for Sunday morning.

THE PRESIDENT. It will be released Saturday evening.[1] And that Krug report is necessary, and the information is necessary for the Food Committee and for Harriman's committee before they can finally come to a conclusion on what they will report.

[6.] Q. Mr. President, is there immediate danger of a march of events in such countries as Greece, Italy, and possibly France, getting ahead of the mechanics of help to those countries?

THE PRESIDENT. Yes there is. Yes there is. That is one of the worries that the President has to go through with. But our system of government requires a rather slow-motion approach to the thing. We have to proceed in the regular way, or we can't get anything done. It takes time. It takes a lot of effort and a lot of work in order to get these things coordinated so that they will work. I hope it will be in time, on France and Italy.

Q. How about Greece? Do you think we are——

THE PRESIDENT. I think we are possibly on time in the Greece situation. If France and Italy blow up, Greece is gone too, so there you are.

Q. Mr. President, what is your reaction as to those statements that the European peoples are not using enough effort on their own?

THE PRESIDENT. That may have some basis in truth. But I would like to make a statement on that situation, from this viewpoint. The cream of the crop of young men in Great Britain, in France, in Germany, and in Italy, has been wiped out—in two generations. Two generations of young men have been wiped out. France was under the heel of the conqueror for nearly 4 years. Nearly every other counrty in Europe was

---

[1] The President referred to Lewis W. Douglas, U.S. Ambassador to Great Britain; Lt. Gen. Lucius D. Clay, U.S. Deputy Military Governor in Germany; Robert D. Murphy, U.S. political adviser in Berlin; and Lt. Gen. Walter Bedell Smith, U.S. Ambassador to the Soviet Union.

[2] See Item 219.

[1] See Item 212.

overrun in exactly the same way by the ruthless Nazi machine. Those people are discouraged and tired, and they haven't enough to eat.

Suppose you had to live on a meal for a week that I saw presented to me the other day by a fellow who came back here from England. You wouldn't feel like working much yourself, if you were in that condition. The thing that we have got to do is to revive the spirit of those people, keep them from starving to death so that we can get them in a mood to work. I can't blame them, seriously, for being that way.

Q. Do you contemplate sending them some agricultural implements?

THE PRESIDENT. Doing that right now. Doing that right now. That is our principal export to Greece—agricultural implements and mules, and things of that kind.

Q. Is there anything you can pass on to us from the gentlemen who have just returned from Germany? Some of us are much interested in that.

THE PRESIDENT. No, I don't think there is anything I can say to you now that would be of use to you, until I get ready to make this final report on the whole thing. Then I will give it to you. I can't talk about Germany without putting the whole picture on the table, and I am not ready to do that

yet, because I haven't got it all.

Leslie Moore (Chairman of the National Conference): Thank you very much, Mr. President. We don't want to take any more of your time. We are grateful for this. These men could ask questions all day long, you know.

THE PRESIDENT. I will do my best to answer them. I don't know whether I can give you the answers you want.

[7.] Q. Mr. President, are we going to get any credit in the United States for sending all this stuff to Europe? It has frequently been said we don't—that they don't understand.

THE PRESIDENT. You know, we have no propaganda machine in the United States, and the little one we had the Congress abolished; but I am not doing this for credit. I am doing it because it's right, I am doing it because it's necessary to be done, if we are going to survive ourselves. That's the best answer I can give you.

NOTE: The President spoke in his office at the White House at 12:40 p.m. The meeting is carried in the White House Official Reporter's records as the President's one hundred and twenty-fourth news conference. The Official Reporter noted that permission was granted at the close of the conference for direct quotation of the following statement, based on the reply to the final question: "We are not doing this for credit; we are doing it because it's right and because it's necessary."

211 Statement by the President Making Public a Report "The Nation's Medical Research." *October 18, 1947*

THE FIFTH volume of the report on Science and Public Policy by John R. Steelman, Chairman of the President's Scientific Research Board, has been transmitted to me today. This volume, "The Nation's Medical Research," deals with the promotion and extension of scientific knowledge in medicine and related fields.

The health of our people is a matter of great national importance. Yet our rich and productive Nation invests only about $110 million annually for research in the medical sciences. This sum, which includes both public and private expenditures, amounts to less than 10 cents of each dollar spent for all types of scientific research. Mr. Steelman's report recommends that as soon as possible national expenditures should be tripled, and that the public share especially should be increased. In this expansion, Federal funds should supplement and not replace funds spent by industry and nonprofit institutions.

Another serious obstacle to obtaining a higher standard of health for all our citizens is the shortage of skilled medical investigators. In the field of medicine, as elsewhere in science, skilled manpower is in short supply. We need more trained medical scientists—not only doctors of medicine, but highly trained specialists in biology, chemistry, physics, and related fields.

Increasing research expenditures and the training of more scientists will not improve the health of our citizens unless the results of medical research are made available to them. I have previously emphasized that our national welfare demands a health program which will bring medical care within the reach of all of our people. Only a national health insurance system will meet that need. Such a system together with an expanded and well balanced research program, and an increased supply of medical scientists and doctors will strengthen our Nation and reduce unnecessary human suffering.

Publication of "The Nation's Medical Research," which is the fifth and final volume of Mr. Steelman's report on Science and Public Policy marks the completion of the tasks assigned to the Chairman and members of the President's Scientific Research Board, established by Executive Order 9791. The full report is a comprehensive and farsighted attack upon the complex problems of the Nation's scientific research. It deserves thoughtful study by all who are concerned with the role of science in the development and security of our Nation.

NOTE: The 118-page report, dated October 18, was published by the Government Printing Office.

For other reports of the President's Scientific Research Board, see Items 183, 194, 201, 206.

212 Statement by the President on Receiving Secretary Krug's Report "National Resources and Foreign Aid." *October* 18, 1947

I HAVE received a report from the Secretary of the Interior on national resources and foreign aid.

This report is the first in a series of three reports being prepared by special committees which I appointed in June to study the relationship between the interests of our domestic economy and the extent to which the United States can aid friendly foreign countries in programs of self-rehabilitation and reconstruction.

The task assigned Secretary Krug's committee was to explore the state of our resources and report upon their adequacy to contribute to foreign reconstruction. This report covers the physical aspects of the subject, with only such reference to economic and fiscal aspects as is necessary to define the problem of resource use.

Secretary Krug reports that on the whole our national resources are physically sufficient to preserve the national security and the American standard of living, and at the same time to support a considerable foreign aid program. The report emphasizes that intelligent utilization of our natural resources calls for an expanded program to conserve them from waste, and more intensive efforts to discover and develop new sources of supply for many of our basic raw materials.

The fact that our natural resources are adequate to permit sharing is heartening. But other vitally important factors must be weighed before we can determine the extent to which these resources can be shared.

The Council of Economic Advisers will shortly report on a related aspect of the problem. The task assigned the Council is to appraise the economic impact on the United States of aid to other countries. The basic data and analyses have been made available to the nonpartisan committee under the chairmanship of the Secretary of Commerce. Secretary Harriman's committee will report on the character and quantities of our resources which may be safely and wisely utilized in a program of foreign assistance.

The studies by the three groups are interrelated. The facts and conclusions of Secretary Krug's report are already being used by the other two communities. Aided by these three studies, and by information assembled by the State Department concerning the needs of other countries and the measures of self-help and mutual help being taken by these countries, I shall prepare recommendations to the Congress on the nature and extent of a balanced foreign aid program.

The remaining two reports will also be made public as soon as they are completed. I hope they will receive full discussion by Members of the Congress and by business, labor, agriculture, and the general public.

NOTE: The report is dated October 9, 1947 (Government Printing Office, 97 pp.).

For the President's statements upon making public the reports of the Council of Economic Advisers and of Secretary Harriman's committee, see Items 217 and 219.

213   The President's News Conference Announcing the Calling of a Special Session of Congress.   *October 23, 1947*

THE PRESIDENT. Gentlemen, I have a statement to read to you.

[*Reading, not literally*] "I have met this afternoon with a group of congressional leaders. I presented to them detailed information concerning the alarming and continuing increase in prices in this country and the situation regarding the need for emergency foreign aid. I informed them that I had concluded it was necessary to convene the Congress on Monday, November 17th.

"By that date the members of Congress who are now abroad obtaining firsthand information will have returned to the United States.

"There are two compelling reasons for convening Congress at an early date.

"It is urgently necessary for the Congress to take legislative action designed to put an end to the continued rise in prices, which is causing hardship to millions of American families and endangering the prosperity and welfare of the entire Nation. When the Congress meets, I shall recommend to it suitable measures for dealing with inflation, high prices, and the high cost of living.

"It is also necessary for this Government to take adequate steps to meet the crisis in Western Europe, where certain countries have exhausted their financial resources and are unable to purchase the food and fuel which are essential if their people are to survive the coming winter.

"It now appears that the minimum needs of France can be met with present funds only until about the end of December, and that it will enter the new year without funds to pay for essential imports. Italy's needs are even more immediate, for Italy will require substantial assistance before the end of this year. Moreover, it appears that additional funds will be needed to maintain our position in occupied areas. It is clear, therefore, that congressional action cannot be delayed until January.

"The convening of the Congress in November will also furnish an opportunity for it to speed up its consideration of the part to be played by the United States in the long-range European recovery program.

"I have just signed a proclamation [1] convening the Congress at 12 o'clock noon on Monday, November 17th.

---

[1] Proclamation 2751 "Convening the Congress" (Oct. 23, 1947, 3 CFR, 1943–1948 Comp., p. 132).

"Tomorrow evening, over all the network, I shall make a radio address [1] to the American people describing the present situation in detail and explaining why action by the Congress is necessary prior to the regularly scheduled session in January."

That's all, gentlemen.

Q. Will you give us the time you will go on the air, Mr. President?

THE PRESIDENT. Ten o'clock. Ten o'clock tomorrow night I will answer all questions.

Reporter: Thank you, Mr. President.

NOTE: President Truman's one hundred and twenty-fifth news conference was held in his office at the White House at 3:35 p.m. on Thursday, October 23, 1947.

---

[1] See Item 214.

214 Radio Address to the American People on the Special Session of Congress. *October* 24, 1947

[Broadcast from the White House at 10 p.m.]

My fellow countrymen:

I have called the Congress to meet on November 17th to consider the problems of high prices at home and emergency aid abroad. These are questions of vital importance to all of us. I want to talk to you frankly tonight about both of these problems.

Since V-J Day we have moved steadfastly toward two goals. We have sought peace and prosperity—prosperity for all our people, peace for all the world.

As we measure our progress toward these goals and chart the course ahead, we find that recent events have raised new and dangerous obstacles in our path. Our domestic prosperity is endangered by the threat of inflation. The peace of the world is endangered by hunger and cold in other lands.

These obstacles must be overcome by prompt and courageous action. Legislation

by the Congress is essential. The need is too pressing—the results of delay too grave—for congressional action to wait until the next regular session in January.

Let me speak first about our domestic prosperity.

In many ways we are now more prosperous than we have ever been. More workers have jobs—and at better wages—than at any time in the past. Farmers are receiving a greater share of our national income than they have in many years. Manufacturers and retailers are enjoying record business and record earnings. We are producing more goods for civilian use than ever before in history.

But these signs of prosperity do not tell the whole story. Although production is high, prices are shooting up. Although nearly everyone is employed, many people cannot afford essential items. Although national income has reached a new high, the buying power of many people is shrinking.

A few figures—and they are startling figures—show how the cost of living is going up.

Since the middle of 1946, this is what has happened: clothing prices have gone up 18 percent; household furnishings have gone up 18 percent; food has gone up 40 percent. The average for all items is up 23 percent.

And the cost of living is still climbing. In the last 3 months it has climbed at a rate of over 16 percent a year.

Wholesale prices are also increasing. Since the middle of 1946, textiles have gone up 30 percent; metals, up 35 percent; and building materials, up 41 percent. These increases in wholesale prices affect every industry and trade and they will eventually be reflected in retail prices.

For some of our people the increased cost of living has been offset by increased income. But for most of our people, increases in income are falling behind increases in the cost of living.

Millions of families of low or moderate income are already victims of inflation. These families are using up savings. They are mortgaging their future by going into debt. They are doing without things they should have.

I know the worries of the breadwinner whose earnings cannot keep up with the high cost of living. I know of the difficulties of the housewife who tries to stretch the family income to pay for groceries and clothes and rent. I know how hard it is to skimp, and save, and do without.

When so many people are not sharing fairly in prosperity, the road is being paved for a recession or a depression.

None of us can afford to overlook this danger. Farmers will remember how they suffered after 1920 because price inflation was followed by a collapse. Businessmen

and bankers will recall how they suffered after 1929 because wild speculation was followed by the depression. Even those who are prosperous today are prospective victims of inflation tomorrow.

Inflation must be stopped before it is too late.

It is within our power to stop it. Our economy is basically sound. It has been immensely strengthened in recent years. The average buying power of our people today is 40 percent higher than it was in 1929. But we are losing some of this gain as rising prices pull away from incomes. We can prevent further loss, and can even go on to new gains, if we use our economic strength wisely.

The major cause of high prices in this country is the great demand among our own people for available goods. An attempt has been made to place the blame upon our foreign aid program, but this is not borne out by the facts. During the war, we learned that we could improve our standard of living with less than 60 percent of our output available for civilian use. At present, even with current exports to all countries, a far greater percent of our production is available for civilian use. With sound policies, we can protect our own standard of living and carry on a substantial foreign aid program at the same time.

We now have—and will continue to have—enough food and clothing and other goods in the United States to meet our needs. But excessively high prices mean that these goods are not being distributed wisely and fairly. High prices ration the essentials of life by squeezing out the less fortunate of our citizens. We can meet this problem only by bringing prices into line with the incomes of our people.

In our free enterprise system, we place major reliance upon voluntary action by businessmen, farmers, workers, and consumers. That is why I have repeatedly urged voluntary price reductions.

But the responsibility of Government extends beyond aiding voluntary action. The Government must respond to the needs of the people.

The American people now have a compelling need for protection from the dangers of price inflation and the rising cost of living. They recognize this need and are asking for the protection to which they are entitled. The Government must assume a larger share of the responsibility for putting an end to excessive prices and the hardships and dangers which accompany them. For this purpose, prompt enactment by the Congress of comprehensive legislation is necessary.

This, then, is one reason why I am calling the Congress into session on November 17th. When it meets, I shall recommend a program for dealing with inflation, high prices, and the high cost of living. Adequate measures—enacted in time—are necessary to correct the present situation.

Let me turn now to the other reason for calling the Congress into session. This is the problem of hunger and cold and human suffering abroad. It is the problem of men and women and children who look to us for help at this critical time.

We are following a definite and clear foreign policy. That policy has been, is now, and shall be to assist free men and free nations to recover from the devastation of war, to stand on their own feet, to help one another, and to contribute their full share to a stable and lasting peace. We follow that policy for the purpose of securing the peace and well-being of the world. It is sheer nonsense to say that we seek dominance over any other nation. We believe in freedom, and we are doing all we can to support free men and free governments throughout the world.

In furtherance of this foreign policy, we now have under consideration the part which the United States shall play in aiding a long-range recovery program for Western Europe. This plan presents great hope for economic security and peace in that vital part of the world. It will take some time to complete the consideration of this plan and to make all the important decisions required for putting it into effect.

However, a period of crisis is now at hand. The perils of hunger and cold in Europe make this winter a decisive time in history. All the progress of reconstruction and all the promise of future plans are endangered. If European nations are to continue their recovery, they must get through this winter without being crippled by economic paralysis and resulting chaos.

In advance of our long-range European recovery plan, we must help some nations through this immediate crisis. The most imminent danger exists in France and in Italy. If the economies of these countries collapse and the people succumb to totalitarian pressures, there will be no opportunity for them or for us to look forward to their recovery so essential to world peace.

Their first need is food. Exceedingly bad weather this year has caused the worst crops in Western Europe in a generation. Crop failures in France—the worst in 100 years—and in Italy make it necessary for those countries to import half the grain they need to live on during the coming months.

The other major shortage is fuel. Fuel supplies were depleted by last year's severe winter. War damage to railroads, and the reduced efficiency of miners laboring on an inadequate diet, have prevented the rebuilding of fuel stocks.

The financial reserves of France and Italy have been nearly exhausted by the cost of their imports since the end of the war.

Rising prices in the United States and in other countries where they must buy have further reduced the purchasing power of their remaining funds. They now face the coming winter without sufficient resources to pay for essential food and fuel.

The figures tell the story.

France can meet her minimum needs, with present funds, until the end of December, but she will enter the new year without funds to pay for essential imports. The French will need $357 million to carry them until March 31, 1948.

Italy will not be able even to get through the rest of this year. Italy must have $142 million to carry her until December 31 and an additional sum of 143 million to get through the first quarter of 1948.

Serious difficulties have also been encountered in the occupied areas—Germany, Japan, and Korea. Additional funds will have to be appropriated this year in order for us to maintain our position in those areas.

It can readily be seen that congressional action to meet these needs cannot be delayed until January.

My action in convening the Congress on November 17th in no way reduces the necessity for pressing forward with our voluntary food saving program. Dollars appropriated by the Congress cannot feed hungry people if there is no food for the dollars to buy. There will not be enough food unless we— the people of the United States—save vast quantities of grain. I am deeply gratified at the splendid response of the American people to our national food saving program. It is an earnest effort to meet the needs of humanity.

Even with the proposed aid from this country, the people of Europe this winter will be on short rations. They will be cold, and they will be without many necessities. But our emergency aid will be definite assurance of the continuing support of this Nation for the free peoples of Europe.

The two problems I have been discussing with you tonight—high prices at home and hunger and cold abroad—present a challenge to the American people.

We could choose the course of inaction. We could wait until depression caught up with us, until our living standards sank, and our people tramped the streets looking for jobs. Other democratic nations would lose hope, and become easy victims of totalitarian aggression. That would be the course of defeatism and cowardice.

Our other course is to take timely and forthright action. If we do this, we can halt the spiral of inflation at home, relieve hunger and cold abroad, and help our friendly neighbors become self-supporting once again.

I know that it is the heartfelt wish of the American people that action be taken which will overcome the obstacles to peace and prosperity confronting this Nation.

It is within our power to lead the world to peace and plenty.

With resolution and united effort we shall achieve our goal.

215   Statement by the President Making Public a Report
      by the Civil Rights Committee.   *October 29, 1947*

THE PRESIDENT'S Civil Rights Committee has just submitted its report. I am going to read and study this report with great care and I recommend to all my countrymen that they do the same thing.

I created this Committee with a feeling of

urgency. No sooner were we finished with the war than racial and religious intolerance began to appear and threaten the very things we had just fought for.

In times past, when our American freedoms were threatened, groups of our citizens banded together and set out on paper the principles they felt would preserve freedom and the kinds of action that would defend freedom.

The Declaration of Independence was that kind of document, and I notice that the title of this report is taken from the Declaration of Independence. I hope this Committee has given us as broad a document as that—an American charter of human freedom in our time.

The need for such a charter was never greater than at this moment. Men of good will everywhere are striving, under great difficulties, to create a worldwide moral order, firmly established in the life of nations. For us here in America, a new charter of human freedom will be a guide for action; and in the eyes of the world, it will be a declaration of our renewed faith in the American goal—the integrity of the individual human being, sustained by the moral consensus of the whole Nation, protected by a Government based on equal freedom under just laws.

The members of this Committee are busy men and women. We all owe them a debt of gratitude. I feel I am speaking for all Americans when I thank them for their unselfish, devoted service.

NOTE: The Committee's report is entitled "To Secure These Rights" (Government Printing Office, 1947, 178 pp.).

216   Statement by the President on the General Agreement on Tariffs and Trade.   *October 29, 1947*

THE ANNOUNCEMENT today of the completion, among 23 nations at Geneva, of a General Agreement on Tariffs and Trade is a landmark in the history of international economic relations. Never before have so many nations combined in such a sustained effort to lower barriers to trade. Never before have nations agreed upon action, on tariffs and preferences, so extensive in its coverage and so far-reaching in its effects. In a world economic situation characterized until now by progressive deterioration, this agreement is heartening indeed. Viewed against the background of other plans for economic reconstruction, it confirms the general acceptance of an expanding multilateral trading system as the goal of national policies. By demonstrating the willingness of nations to attack their common difficulties in a spirit of cooperation, it gives ground for confidence that we shall succeed in solving the problems that are still ahead.

NOTE: The text of the General Agreement on Tariffs and Trade is printed in the U.S. Statutes at Large (61 Stat. A3).

On December 16, 1947, the President issued Proclamation 2761A "Carrying Out General Agreement on Tariffs and Trade Concluded at Geneva, October 30, 1947," making the agreement effective, provisionally, for the United States on January 1, 1948 (61 Stat. 1103; 3 CFR, 1943–1948 Comp., p. 139).

217   Statement by the President Making Public a Report
      "The Impact of the Foreign Aid Program Upon the
      Domestic Economy."   *November 1, 1947*

TWO WEEKS ago I made public the report on "National Resources and Foreign Aid," prepared under the direction of the Secretary of the Interior. At that time I noted that a second report in the series on foreign aid would soon be made by the Council of Economic Advisers. This report has now been completed and submitted to me under the title, "The Impact of the Foreign Aid Program upon the Domestic Economy."

Secretary Krug reported that on the whole our national resources, if intelligently utilized, are physically sufficient to support a considerable foreign aid program, while preserving the national security and the American standard of living. The report of the Council of Economic Advisers moves on from this point to present an economic analysis of the effect that a foreign aid program of substantial size would have on agricultural and industrial production in the United States, on domestic consumption and prices, and on Government finance and the tax structure.

The Council of Economic Advisers reaches the conclusion that the American economy can sustain the general impact of a new foreign aid program, and that there is no question of our general financial capacity to support such a program. At the same time, the Council stresses the fact that we must deal promptly and effectively with problems raised by key commodities—wheat, steel, certain items of industrial and agricultural machinery, coal, and fertilizer.

The materials contained in both Secretary Krug's report and the Council's report have been made available in advance to the committee of 19 private citizens working under the chairmanship of the Secretary of Commerce. That committee, after studying these analyses of domestic effects and the Paris Conference's presentation of European needs, will submit its conclusions and recommendations as to the limits within which we may wisely and safely extend assistance to foreign countries. Aided by these reports and other pertinent material, I shall make recommendations to the Congress concerning a program of foreign assistance.

NOTE: The report of the Council of Economic Advisers (112 pp., processed) is dated October 1947.

For the President's statements on receiving the reports of the Secretary of the Interior and of the Secretary of Commerce, see Items 212 and 219.

218   The President's News Conference of
      November 6, 1947

THE PRESIDENT. Ladies and gentlemen of the press, I have no particular announcements to make this morning, but I thought since we had to miss last week I had better let you in and you might have some questions on your mind.

[1.] Q. Mr. President, have you had a chance to analyze the election returns? Do you see a trend, perhaps?

THE PRESIDENT. I haven't analyzed the election returns. One thing I was happy to see, though, was the large turnout at the various elections. It shows the people are learning their responsibilities as citizens, and that their interest in free government rests in the ballot box. It was a big turnout in nearly all these elections. I haven't analyzed the situation for trends. Of course, I was very happy over the Kentucky election![1]

Q. Mr. President, do you believe a large turnout will help the Democrats next year?

THE PRESIDENT. I think it will help those who like free government.

[2.] Q. Mr. President, the American Society of Newspaper Editors sent you a resolution objecting to proposals of using military information secrecy procedures in civilian departments. Have you taken any action on that at all?

THE PRESIDENT. I have no reason to take any action, for no such thing has ever been put up to me. I think it is a very bad habit to get hold of fragments of preliminary reports which are likely to come up to the President, and then set up a strawman and knock him down. I have to pass on that thing if it ever comes to me. It never has yet.

[3.] Q. Mr. President, have you had a chance, or have you seen that report of Representative Auchincloss on the form of government——

THE PRESIDENT. Only what I saw in the paper. I haven't seen the report.

Q. You wouldn't like to say anything about it?

THE PRESIDENT. I can't comment on it, because I am not well enough informed.

[4.] Q. May I ask you another question? What happens to the big report of the civil rights? Does it stay here, or do you send that to Congress?

---

[1] Gubernatorial election in which the Democratic candidate, Representative Earle C. Clements, defeated the Attorney General of Kentucky, Eldon S. Dummit.

THE PRESIDENT. That report is made to me, and that report can be used as a basis for a part of the Message on the State of the Union, which of course in the long run will be sent to the Congress.

Q. In other words, you will use it as a part of your message?

THE PRESIDENT. I didn't say that. I said it could be used as a foundation for part of the message—some of it, maybe. I haven't read it carefully yet.

Q. Aside from that, what do you think of it, Mr. President?

THE PRESIDENT. I think it's a good report. I have already made that comment.

Q. I believe the last statement we had was just at the time you received the report.

THE PRESIDENT. That's right, but I hadn't read it even then.

[5.] Q. Mr. President, Congressman Doughton has been quoted that you will veto the tax bill this session. Is he correct in that?

THE PRESIDENT. I will take care of that situation when it comes up to me.

Q. Do you intend to propose any sort of tax changes——

THE PRESIDENT. I will let you know about that when I send down the Message on the State of the Union.

Q. You are referring to this special session message, Mr. President?

THE PRESIDENT. No I am not. The special session is called for two specific purposes, which has been very clear up to date. As far as my message is concerned, it will be confined to those two specific things.

Q. This is as far as your message is concerned?

THE PRESIDENT. The special session. It will be confined to the two things that I have already announced that the session is called for.

Q. Can you tell us anything more concrete as to what you might recommend on inflation?

THE PRESIDENT. No I can't. I will let you have that when I send the message down. I don't want to read that message to you here now, it wouldn't do the Congress any good. [*Laughter*]

[6.] Q. Mr. President, what do you think of the wheat price-fixing plan that Tom Campbell said he put up to you yesterday?

THE PRESIDENT. Oh, we just discussed it incidentally. He said that the only way to get wheat to market would be to put a ceiling on the price of wheat, then the farmers would all turn it loose. That was his opinion, and he expressed it to me.

Q. A ceiling of 50 cents a bushel above the present market price——

THE PRESIDENT. He didn't tell me what price he had in view.

Q. He told us $3.50, Mr. President. Did he tell you?

THE PRESIDENT. He did not discuss prices with me.

Q. Did he tell you, Mr. President, that he was holding back 100,000 bushels?

THE PRESIDENT. Oh yes, he said he had 600,000 bushels, and like every farmer he wanted to get as much for it as he could. I don't blame him for that.

Q. Mr. President, the Agriculture Department has estimated that about all the hundred million bushels of grain that Mr. Luckman was asked to conserve may now have been saved, because of less feeding to cattle than expected. In view of that, do you anticipate Mr. Luckman's resignation fairly soon?

THE PRESIDENT. No, I do not. Mr. Luckman made a report to me just recently, and I think when you read that report [1] you will

---

[1] The "Interim Report to the President From the Citizens Food Committee" is dated October 31, 1947 (37 pp., processed).

be very happy. I was very happy over the success that he has been having with this effort. He did a good job.

[7.] Q. Mr. President, another of the poll checks show that a lot of voters, average citizens, don't understand the form of the reconstruction problem too well. I wonder if, after your message to Congress, if you would have a radio talk to them?

THE PRESIDENT. Well, we have been working on a plan to get the matter before the country in as simple a manner as possible so that everybody can understand it. It has been a tremendous job to get that report ready. It required the meeting of the 16 nations in Europe. It required the Krug survey of our own resources. It required the Harriman survey, which has not yet reached me, but will tomorrow, I imagine. And it required the report of the Economic Advisers, and all those things have to be coordinated and put to work. It is a tremendous job. And we must be patient. We must not take a single report and say that that is the Marshall plan. When we get that worked out and coordinated, it will be sent up to Congress in the form of a message, and it will be explained specifically in all its ramifications as clearly as we can possibly explain it.

Q. That will be a separate message on the Marshall plan to the Congress?

THE PRESIDENT. Well, I hope—I have that under consideration.

Q. Mr. President, do you anticipate any meeting with Secretary Marshall the latter part of this week, or over the weekend, on this problem?

THE PRESIDENT. I meet with Secretary Marshall three times a week all the time, when he is here. We discuss all subjects in which he is interested and in which I am interested.

Q. Mr. President, would this message on

the Marshall plan go to the regular session of the Congress?

THE PRESIDENT. Well, I will have to tell you more about that when we get together. Not in shape yet even to write the message on. Whenever we get all those things coordinated, when we get the message ready, I will send it to the Congress—as soon as I can get it ready. I don't know whether that will be to the regular session or the special session.

[8.]   Q. Mr. President, has the Chairman of the CAB, Mr. Landis, offered you his resignation?

THE PRESIDENT. Not that I know of. He hasn't offered it to me.

[9.]   Q. Mr. President, could you indicate whether you consider inflation or foreign aid to be the priority subject of the special session?

THE PRESIDENT. They run side by side.

[10.]   Q. Mr. President, do you plan to nominate the FCC Chairman before the special session is over?

THE PRESIDENT. I hadn't thought about it. We have given that matter some consideration. Trying to find the proper man. Whenever we get him, I will announce him to you.

[11.]   Q. Mr. President, would you care to comment on the reports that the former opposition Polish leader, Mr. Mikolajczyk, is coming to the United States?

THE PRESIDENT. All I know about that is what I have seen in the paper. And I noticed this morning that it had been announced that he has no visa to come to this country. All I know is what I got out of the paper.

[12.]   Q. I don't want to ask you a leading question, but have you a choice of running mate yet?

THE PRESIDENT. What's that?

Q. Have you a choice of running mate yet?

THE PRESIDENT. Tony,[1] that's a leading question, and I have no comment! [*Laughter*]

Q. Mr. President, knowing—I know this may be a leading question——

THE PRESIDENT. All right.

Q. —— but most of your recent callers who have come in to invite you to things next September and October, have come out looking pretty dismayed, saying that you told them that you would be very busy at that period?

THE PRESIDENT. Well, I don't think I have ever been here in the White House when I haven't been as busy as I could be. Even on the so-called vacations, I work just as hard as if I were sitting at this desk.

[13.]   Q. Mr. President, which do you expect Congress to act on first, the interim proposal or anti-inflation?

THE PRESIDENT. I haven't got a crystal ball. [*Laughter*] You will have to talk to Congress about that. I want them to act on interim aid first. They will be told that very plainly in the message. As I say, I can't prophesy what the Congress will do. I am sure, though, that they will do the right thing.

[14.]   Q. Do you plan to resubmit any nominations that have been made to the National Labor Relations Board at the special session?

THE PRESIDENT. I don't—I didn't understand the question?

Q. Mr. Denham, Mr. Gray, Mr. Murdock—do you plan to resubmit their names to the Senate?

THE PRESIDENT. I don't know. Were they approved the last time or not? I can't remember.

Q. They were recess appointments.

THE PRESIDENT. Were they recess appointments? We have that under consideration.

---

[1] Ernest B. Vaccaro of the Associated Press.

Whenever we arrive at the proper conclusion on that, we will take action on it.

Q. That is the study of the situation on law and precedents, I believe, that Charlie[1] told us about the other day. That has not been completed yet?

THE PRESIDENT. That study hasn't been completed yet.

[15.] Q. Mr. President, does your answer to those previous questions mean that the special message to Congress will be concerned primarily with the interim aid program and not with the so-called Marshall plan as a whole?

THE PRESIDENT. It will be—the Congress was called for the purpose of going into the interim aid plan and for the control of prices and inflation in this country. They go side by side.

[16.] Q. Mr. President, would you care to comment on the request of the grain exchanges for an investigation?

THE PRESIDENT. No. I have no comment.

[17.] Q. Mr. President, have you seen any good movies lately?

THE PRESIDENT. Well, I never get a chance to see a movie unless they bring one to the White House, and about the only thing I see are news reels. I try to go when I am not in them. [*Laughter*]

[18.] Q. Mr. President, I want to clear up this impression I have got, possibly, that you are not going to submit anything on the long-range Marshall plan——

THE PRESIDENT. No, I didn't say that. I said whenever we are ready we would submit it. It takes a lot of time to get it ready.

Q. But that will be separate——

THE PRESIDENT. That is a separate proposition entirely, and the committees will commence meeting on this thing on the 10th, and they will begin hearings on the interim aid program on the 10th of November; and they will ask me—be at liberty to ask any questions they want, and we will try to give them all the information we have.

Q. Mr. President, does your comment that these things go side by side mean that you are——

THE PRESIDENT. I think they are equally important. I want to make it perfectly plain that I think they are equally important. One depends on the other, unless—no use making appropriations of money for a hundred million bushels of wheat if it won't buy more than 25 million bushels.

[19.] Q. Mr. President, have you any comment on the hearings of the House Committee on Un-American Activities?

THE PRESIDENT. No comment.

Q. Any comment on its actions when you were a member of the committee when it was being investigated?

THE PRESIDENT. No comment. I think that will take care of itself.

Reporter: Thank you, Mr. President.

NOTE: President Truman's one hundred and twenty-sixth news conference was held in his office at the White House at 10:35 a.m. on Thursday, November 6, 1947.

---

[1] Charles G. Ross, Secretary to the President.

219   Statement by the President Making Public a Report "European Recovery and American Aid." *November 8, 1947*

LAST JUNE I appointed a committee of 19 distinguished private citizens to determine the facts concerning the kinds and amounts of our resources available for economic assistance to foreign countries, and to advise me on the limits within which, in the opinion of the committee, the United States might safely and wisely plan to extend such aid. I asked the Secretary of Commerce to serve as chairman of the committee. The members of the committee were drawn from the ranks of American business, finance, labor, agriculture, and educational and research institutions.

During the intervening months, the members of this committee of private citizens have been diligently studying the many aspects of this complicated problem, particularly as it relates to Western Europe. They have carefully examined the analysis, by a committee of Government officials under the direction of the Secretary of the Interior, of the adequacy of our national resources to support a foreign aid program; the analysis by the Council of Economic Advisers of the impact of a substantial aid program upon our national economy; the report of the representatives of the 16 nations who met in Paris, and other data available from various sources.

This committee has now submitted to me its report, "European Recovery and American Aid." The report contains a careful discussion of the problem of European recovery and our interest therein: the requirements of the countries involved; the

supplies available; the size of an effective aid program and the feasibility of its being met; the problems of finance and administration; and the effects of a foreign aid program on our own economy. In addition, the committee's report contains detailed discussions of problems presented by specific commodities, food, raw materials, and manufactured goods that are needed.

The members of the committee have fulfilled their task without partisanship, and with no other purpose than to further the best interest of their country, and to aid in securing the peace and well-being of the world. I am deeply grateful to each member of the committee for putting aside so many other pressing duties in order to bring this difficult assignment to completion in so short a period. The committee's report should prove of great help in the prompt formulation of a program of sound assistance to Western Europe. I commend this report to the careful attention of Members of the Congress, officials of the executive branch, and all citizens concerned for our country's welfare.

NOTE: The report of the President's Committee on Foreign Aid is dated November 7, 1947 (Government Printing Office, 286 pp.).

---

220   Special Message to the Congress Transmitting Report on Assistance to Greece and Turkey.   *November* 10, 1947

[Released November 10, 1947. Dated November 7, 1947]

To the Honorable the President of the Senate pro tempore and the Honorable the Speaker of the House of Representatives:

Last May the Congress enacted Public Law 75 enabling the United States to render financial, technical, and material aid to the Governments of Greece and Turkey. This was done in response to urgent appeals by

those governments, which found that as a result of conditions arising out of the war their respective economies were unable to bear alone the financial burdens of reconstruction, of providing supplies for the civil population, even on a subsistence level, and of supporting the armed forces essential for the maintenance of security.

By Executive Order 9857, dated May 22, 1947, primary responsibility for the program's execution was delegated by me to the Secretary of State. The Department of State enjoys full cooperation of all other departments and agencies of the Government which can help in the implementation of the act.

Pursuant to the provisions of the act, I am submitting this, the first quarterly report on the activities and expenditure of funds under the authority of the act.

The economic situation in Greece has not basically improved since I addressed the Congress last spring about the need for American assistance. Athough economic collapse, which might otherwise have resulted, has so far been averted through the extension of our aid, underlying causes of economic and political unrest remain of grave concern.

This first period of administration of the act has been largely one of preparation. Missions have been assembled and sent to Greece and to Turkey and are now working with the respective governments of those countries to assure effective and proper use of American aid funds. While many operational steps of major importance have been taken, such as the letting of contracts and the ordering and delivery of supplies, the effects of many of these actions will not be discernible until later in the fiscal year. The enclosed report reveals in some detail the action that has been taken thus far and some of the problems which have yet to be solved.

Since the time when the amount of assistance needed was determined, there have been several unfavorable developments which materially affect both programs but most seriously that for Greece. The Greek cereals harvest has been reduced by the general European drought, and by guerrilla activity, to a point where the expenditure of foreign exchange for food imports will be a great deal more than originally estimated if hunger and starvation are to be avoided. Intensification of military operations in that country has necessitated a transfer of funds from the economic to the military program. Rising prices in the United States and elsewhere have reduced the buying power of foreign exchange available to the Greek Government, with the effect that greater sums than were anticipated must be spent for minimum basic essentials. An added factor in Greece is that exports have not, because of internal economic and security conditions, reached as high a level as might reasonably have been expected some months ago.

The difficulties which hamper the success of this program must be overcome. Continuation of marginal subsistence only in Greece, without real progress toward recovery, will provide fertile ground for totalitarian ideologies.

Our Missions in both countries are striving to achieve one main objective—that of helping free peoples in their effort to maintain the form and composition of their governments in accordance with the wishes of the majority. If this end is attained, every dollar that we have or will put into Greece and Turkey will have been fully justified. The United States, in accordance with its obligations under the United Nations Charter, will have served all peace-loving nations of the world in contributing to the security and well-being of a vital area, which, under circumstances of economic collapse and disorder, would threaten peace and tranquillity throughout the world.

HARRY S. TRUMAN

NOTE: The report, covering the quarter ending September 30, 1947, was published by the Department of State as Publication 2957, Near Eastern Series 11 (Government Printing Office, 53 pp.). A summary was released by the White House.

221   The President's News Conference of *November 13, 1947*

THE PRESIDENT. [1.] I have one announcement to make. Adm. Louis E. Denfeld will be Chief of Naval Operations—I have two announcements to make. The other one is the appointment by Executive order [1] of the National Security Resources Board, which is made up as follows: of the Secretary of the Treasury, Secretary of Defense, Secretary of the Interior—Agriculture—Commerce—and Labor; and you will receive a mimeographed sheet on that as you go out.

That's all the announcements I have, gentlemen.

Q. What's Admiral Denfeld's present assignment?

THE PRESIDENT. He is the Commanding Officer—in command of the Pacific Fleet, and I don't know when he will take office. I think Admiral Nimitz wants to get away as soon as possible.

[2.] Q. Mr. President, eggs and eggless Thursdays. What about eggs for eggnogs at Christmas? That is not a facetious question at all——

THE PRESIDENT. Is that so? Well, I think you will have to have eggs for eggnogs at Christmas. [*Laughter*]

[3.] Q. Mr. President, has Budget Director Webb said he is resigning?

THE PRESIDENT. The Budget Director has never said anything about resigning and has never discussed it, and he is not going to resign; and that's positive and final.

[4.] Q. Mr. President, do you think there is any possiblity you may go down to the Bogotá conference [2] next January?

THE PRESIDENT. No, there is not. I do not have that under consideration at all.

[5.] Q. Mr. President, have you discussed with Senator Lucas the possibility of his running for Governor of Illinois?

THE PRESIDENT. No, I haven't. I would be glad to discuss it with him if he decided he wanted to talk to me about it.

Q. What would you say?

THE PRESIDENT. I will say that to him. [*Laughter*]

[6.] Q. Mr. President, are you preparing to announce your nominations to the labor-management advisory committee to the Mediation Service?

THE PRESIDENT. No I am not. Whenever we are ready I will make that announcement.

[7.] Q. How about the Chief of Staff for the Army, Mr. President?

THE PRESIDENT. I will make that announcement at a later date.

[8.] Q. Mr. President, do you think of recommending lowering the tax on margarine because of the high price of butter?

THE PRESIDENT. I hadn't thought about it, but we may think about it at a later date. Not now.

[9.] Q. Mr. President, your former Ambassador to Greece, Paul Porter,[1] thinks that several men who happen to be his clients have gotten something of a raw deal in the State Department because they were fired without being told what the charges were against them. Do you have any comment, sir?

THE PRESIDENT. No comment.

[10.] Q. Mr. President, people down in Florida are rather upset about the—are you or do you think there is any chance of

---

[1] Executive Order 9905 "Designating the membership of the National Security Resources Board and defining the functions, duties, and authority of the Chairman of the Board" (Nov. 13, 1947; 3 CFR, 1943–1948 Comp., p. 673).

[2] Ninth International Conference of American States.

[1] In December 1946 the President sent Paul A. Porter to Greece as head of an economic mission. At the time Mr. Porter was Price Administrator.

your going to the Everglades for the dedication——

THE PRESIDENT. I would like to go, but I can make no firm appointments now, because of this special session coming on next Monday.

Q. It isn't entirely out of the picture then?

THE PRESIDENT. I say I wish I could go, but I can make no appointments.

[11.] Q. Mr. President, are you planning to do anything about the lapse in title VI of the National Housing Act? That is the act under which they are insured up to 90 percent of private housing—the loans in private housing. It's expired.

THE PRESIDENT. Well, that undoubtedly will be put up to me when we begin preparing the Message on the State of the Union. I haven't given it any consideration. All I know is what I read in the paper.

[12.] Q. Mr. President, is a loan to Argentina under consideration?

THE PRESIDENT. I hadn't heard about it. But they are good. They have got plenty of money.

Q. Do you regard them as a good risk?

THE PRESIDENT. I do. I didn't think they would need to borrow any money. I remember one time they had 600 million in gold on deposit in the Federal Reserve Bank in New York. I don't know whether they have still got it or not.

Q. It's supposed to be running out rapidly.

[13.] Q. Mr. President, have you picked a new Marine com——

THE PRESIDENT. No. It's under consideration. No decision has been arrived at as yet.

[14.] Q. Mr. President, the Harriman committee recommended taking all expenses for the Marshall plan out of taxes. Do you favor that?

THE PRESIDENT. Of course. That's what you have to do.

[15.] Q. Mr. President, do you favor reimposition of the excess profits tax?

THE PRESIDENT. I will answer that question in the Message on the State of the Union. I am not ready to answer it at the present time.

[16.] Q. Mr. President, are you planning a new policy statement regarding China?

THE PRESIDENT. Not immediately, no.

Q. Mr. President, Senator Taft said that sending the amount of aid to Europe as Secretary Marshall proposed, would be backing up Russia's charges that it is American imperialism. Have you any comment on that?

THE PRESIDENT. No comment. I think the Evening Star has a cartoon that comments very favorably on that.

Reporter: Thank you, Mr. President.

THE PRESIDENT. You're welcome.

NOTE: President Truman's one hundred and twenty-seventh news conference was held in his office at the White House at 4 o'clock on Thursday afternoon, November 13, 1947.

222   Statement by the President on the Government's Employee Loyalty Program. *November* 14, 1947

I DEEPLY appreciate the willingness of the members of the Loyalty Review Board, established within the Civil Service Commission, to give of their service to that Board. Their acceptance involves real personal sacrifice. At the same time, they will have the satisfaction of knowing that they are contributing to the solution of one of the most difficult problems confronting our Government today.

I believe I speak for all the people of the United States when I say that disloyal and subversive elements must be removed from the employ of the Government. We must not, however, permit employees of the Federal Government to be labeled as disloyal or potentially disloyal to their Government when no valid basis exists for arriving at such a conclusion. The overwhelming majority of Federal employees are loyal citizens who are giving conscientiously of their energy and skills to the United States. I do not want them to fear they are the objects of any "witch hunt." They are not being spied upon; they are not being restricted in their activities. They have nothing to fear from the loyalty program, since every effort has been made to guarantee full protection to those who are suspected of disloyalty. Rumor, gossip, or suspicion will not be sufficient to lead to the dismissal of an employee for disloyalty.

Any person suspected of disloyalty must be served with a written notice of the charges against him in sufficient detail to enable him to prepare his defense. In some unusual situations security considerations may not allow full disclosure.

It would have been possible for the Government to remove disloyal persons merely by serving them with the charges against them and giving them an opportunity to answer those charges. I realize fully, however, the stigma attached to a removal for disloyalty. Accordingly, I have ordered the agencies of the Government, except where a few agencies find it necessary to exercise extraordinary powers granted to them by the Congress, to give hearings to persons who are charged with disloyalty.

Loyalty boards are being set up in each agency for this purpose. They are definitely not "kangaroo" courts. The personnel of these boards is being carefully selected by the head of each agency to make sure that they are judicious in temperament and fairminded. Hearings before the boards will be conducted so as to establish all pertinent facts and to accord the suspected employee every possible opportunity to present his defense. The employee is to be given the right to be accompanied by counsel or a representative of his own choosing.

After the hearing has been completed the loyalty board in each department can recommend the retention or the dismissal of an employee. But the matter does not rest there. The employee may appeal the findings of the loyalty board to the head of the department, who can either approve or disapprove the board's recommendations.

If the head of the department orders the dismissal of the employee, he has still another avenue of appeal: namely, to the Loyalty Review Board within the Civil Service Commission. This Board is composed of outstanding citizens of the United States. These citizens have no ax to grind. They will not be concerned with personalities. Their judgment will be as detached as is humanly possible.

I expect the Civil Service Commission to function in a very real sense as a staff agency of the President for the purpose of doing everything it can to help him see to it that all aspects of this program are carried forward in an expeditious and satisfactory manner.

I am looking to the Federal Bureau of Investigation for the conduct of all loyalty investigations which may be necessary in connection with the operation of the program.

I am looking to the Loyalty Review Board to develop standards for the conduct of hearings and the consideration of cases within the various departments and agencies. With the cooperation of the staff of the Civil Service Commission, the Board should make sure that there is complete understanding of and adherence to these standards in all the departments and agencies.

The question of standards is of deep concern to me. Under the Executive order inaugurating this program, provision has been made, for example, for furnishing to the Loyalty Review Board by the Attorney General the name of each foreign or domestic organization, association, movement, group, or combination of persons which he, after appropriate investigation and determination, has designated as totalitarian, fascist, communist, or subversive. The Executive order in turn provides that the Loyalty Review Board shall disseminate such information to all departments and agencies.

This provision of the order has been interpreted by some to mean that any person who at any time happened to belong to one of these organizations would automatically be dismissed from the employ of the Federal Government.

This interpretation completely overlooks the fact that, under the provisions of the Executive order, "the standard for the refusal of employment or the removal from employment in an executive department or agency on grounds relating to loyalty shall be that, on all the evidence, reasonable grounds exist for belief that the person involved is disloyal to the government of the United States."

Membership in an organization is simply one piece of evidence which may or may not be helpful in arriving at a conclusion as to the action which is to be taken in a particular case.

The Government has a great stake in these loyalty proceedings. The Government, as the largest employer in the United States, must be the model of a fair employer. It must guarantee that the civil rights of all employees of the Government shall be protected properly and adequately. It is in this spirit that the loyalty program will be enforced.

NOTE: In his statement the President referred to Executive Order 9835 "Prescribing Procedures for the Administration of an Employees Loyalty Program in the Executive Branch of the Government" (March 21, 1947; 3 CFR, 1943–1948 Comp., p. 627).

223 Statement by the President Making Public the Report of the Advisory Committee on the Merchant Marine. *November* 15, 1947

EARLY this year, it became apparent that the Nation was faced with the serious problem of deciding how an adequate fleet of freight and passenger vessels should be maintained. Only a few cargo vessels, and no passenger liners, were scheduled to be built in American shipyards in the immediate future, and all existing contracts for such construction were to be completed by early 1948. Many war-built vessels were ill adapted for peacetime operation, and others, though suitable for commercial trade, were rapidly growing obsolete.

This situation called for a careful examination of the present condition and the future development of our merchant fleet which traditionally has played so important a part in the Nation's well-being and security. The problem had many aspects: the nature and extent of a sound ship construction program; the maintenance of American shipbuilding skills and techniques through a program of ship replacement; the incorporation of technological developments into future vessels; the training and welfare of merchant ship officers and men; the fiscal and administrative decisions that should be made if the United States were to build and maintain a strong merchant fleet.

With these considerations in mind, last March I named an Advisory Committee on the Merchant Marine, consisting of a group of private citizens, to examine the problem of our merchant marine and to present to me its recommendations for a stable, long-range program. After several months spent in hearing the views of representatives of executive departments of the Government, the shipping and shipbuilding industries, trade and labor organizations, and others interested, and in studying pertinent statistical reports and data, the Committee has submitted its report.

The Committee concludes that a modern, efficient American merchant fleet and a progressive shipbuilding industry are indispens-

able to our national security, and that these are sufficiently essential to our peacetime economy, as well, to justify the Government financial aid that is necessary to maintain them. In its recommendations, the Committee sets forth a series of specific measures which in its opinion would result in a well-balanced, modern merchant fleet.

The report is being made public, in the hope that it will prove helpful not only to Members of the Congress and heads of executive agencies who have long been dealing with the problem, but also to the many private citizens who are sincerely concerned with this important phase of the Nation's security and prosperity. I am truly grateful to Mr. Keller and the other members of the Committee for the time and effort they so unselfishly expended in the preparation of this careful and thorough study.

NOTE: For the President's letter naming the members of the Committee, see Item 55. In the last paragraph of the statement the President referred to K. T. Keller, Committee Chairman.

The "Report of the President's Advisory Committee on the Merchant Marine" is dated November 1947 (Government Printing Office, 69 pp.).

---

224 Special Message to the Congress on the First Day of the Special Session. *November* 17, 1947

[As delivered in person before a joint session]

Mr. President, Mr. Speaker, Members of the 80th Congress:

The Congress has been convened to consider two problems of major concern to the citizens of the United States and to the peoples of the world. The future of the free nations of Europe hangs in the balance. The future of our own economy is in jeopardy. The action which you take will be written large in the history of this Nation and of the world.

The Secretary of State and other representatives of the executive branch have appeared before the committees of Congress during the past week to present the facts regarding the necessity for immediate assistance by the United States to certain European countries. Austria, France, and Italy have nearly exhausted their financial resources. They must be helped if their peoples are to survive the coming winter, and if their political and economic systems are not to disintegrate. Exceedingly bad weather has brought on crop failures and fuel shortages, and has caused intense suffering. The food and fuel stocks of these countries are now near the vanishing point. Their peoples are in a dangerously weakened condition, due to years of short rations. Additional medical supplies and facilities are urgently necessary.

Austria needs $42 million, Italy needs $227 million, and France needs $328 million to buy food, fuel, and other essential goods during the next 4½ months. Detailed information has been presented to your committees concerning these needs and the purposes for which the funds to be appropriated by the Congress would be spent.

Additional funds will also be required to maintain our position in occupied countries.

Emergency assistance by itself will not solve the European problems. Emergency aid is no substitute for a long-range recovery program, but it is a vital prerequisite to such a program. If the Western European nations should collapse this winter, as a result of our failure to bridge the gap between their resources and their needs, there would be no chance for them—or for us—to look forward to their economic recovery. The providing of interim aid will give us time to plan our part in an economic recovery program and it will give the peoples of Europe the strength to hold out until such a program begins.

I will shortly submit to the Congress recommendations concerning the long-range European Recovery Program. This program is the result of the combined efforts of thoughtful men of two continents whose concern has been the most effective manner in which 16 European nations, Western Germany, and the United States can work together for European recovery, world prosperity, and lasting peace.

It is a tribute to the strength of our democracy that we are able to make so great a contribution to the freedom and welfare of other nations and other peoples. This Nation is strong both in material resources and in the spirit of its people. Our economic strength, born of our system of free institutions, has contributed to raising the standard of living the world over. Our moral strength, resulting from our faith in human rights, is the inspiration of free men everywhere.

I refer to the strength of this Nation with humility, for it is an awe-inspiring truth that the manner in which we exert our strength now, and in the future, will have a decisive effect upon the course of civilization.

There is a truth whose significance grows with the experience of each passing day. The American people are becoming more and more deeply aware of their world position. They are learning that great responsibility goes with great power.

Our people know that our influence in the world gives us an opportunity—unmatched in history—to conduct ourselves in such a manner that men and women of all the world can move out of the shadows of fear and war and into the light of freedom and peace.

We must make the most of that opportunity.

For we have learned, by the costly lesson of two world wars, that what happens beyond our shores determines how we live our own lives. We have learned that, if we want to live in freedom and security, we must work with all the world for freedom and security.

Human misery and chaos lead to strife and conquest.

Hunger and poverty tempt the strong to prey upon the weak.

Twice within this generation we have had to take up arms against nations whose leaders, misled by the hope of easy conquest, sought to dominate the world.

We are convinced that the best way to prevent future wars is to work for the independence and well-being of all nations. This conviction guides our present efforts, and will guide our future decisions. We have participated fully and gladly in the growth of the United Nations and we seek now to strengthen and improve it. We are assisting free nations who have sought our aid in maintaining their independence. We have contributed large sums to help rebuild countries devastated by war. We have taken the lead in breaking down barriers to world trade.

In our efforts, however, to achieve the conditions of peace for all the world, we have encountered unforeseen and most unwelcome obstacles.

We have found that not all nations seem to share our aims or approve our methods. We regret the differences which have arisen and the criticisms so loudly expressed. Yet we cannot afford, and we do not intend, to let current differences with some nations deter our efforts to cooperate in friendly fashion and to assist other nations who, like us, cherish freedom and seek to promote the peace and stability of the world.

The actions of this Government must be of a stature to match the dignity and influence of the United States in world affairs. The prompt provision by the Congress for interim aid will be convincing proof to all nations of our sincere determination to support the freedom-loving countries of Western Europe in their endeavors to remain free and to become fully self-supporting once again.

If that action is followed by the enactment of the long-range European Recovery Pro-gram, this Congress will have written a noble page in the world annals.

I have spoken of the economic and moral strength of the United States and of the way in which we must use that strength if we are to build a world community of free, strong, and independent nations.

The strength of the United States is not due to chance. It is due to the wise decisions and bold actions taken by free and courageous men throughout the history of our democracy.

The time is at hand for new decisions and new actions of equal wisdom.

On several occasions during the past year I have reported to the Congress and to the Nation on our general economic situation. These reports have told of new high levels of production and employment. Farmers are producing 37 percent more than in 1929. Industry is producing 65 percent more. In terms of actual purchasing power, the average income of individuals, after taxes, has risen 39 percent. The rapid growth of our postwar economic activity has exceeded expectations and has revealed anew the potentialities of our economy.

In each of my reports, however, I have had to warn of dangers which lay ahead.

Today, inflation stands as an ominous threat to the prosperity we have achieved. We can no longer treat inflation—with spiraling prices and living costs—as some vague condition we may encounter in the future. We already have an alarming degree of inflation. And even more alarming, it is getting worse.

Since the middle of 1946, fuel has gone up 13 percent; clothing prices have gone up 19 percent; retail food prices have gone up 40 percent. The average for all cost of living items has risen 23 percent.

The housewife who goes to buy food today must spend $10 to buy what $7 bought a year and a half ago. She must spend $10 to buy what $7 would have bought a year and a half ago!

The cost of living is still climbing. In the past 4 months it has risen at a rate of 16 percent a year.

Wholesale prices are rising, too. They affect every industry and trade, and they are soon translated into retail prices.

Since the middle of 1946, wholesale textile prices have gone up 32 percent; metals have gone up 36 percent; building materials have gone up 42 percent. Wholesale prices on the average have gone up 40 percent.

The harsh effects of price inflation are clear. They are felt by wage earners, farmers, and businessmen. Wage earners are finding that bigger pay checks this year buy less than smaller pay checks bought last year. Despite generalities about high farm prices, the income of many farm families cannot keep up with the rising costs of the things they buy. Small business men are being squeezed by rising costs. Even those who are well off are asking, "How long can it last? When is the break coming?"

In addition, price inflation threatens our entire program of foreign aid. We cannot abandon foreign aid, nor can we abandon our own people to the ravages of unchecked inflation.

We cannot allow the strength of this Nation to be wasted and our people's confidence in our free institutions to be shaken by an economic castastrophe. We shall be inviting that catastrophe unless we take steps now to halt runaway prices.

Our immediate approach to the problems of high prices and inflation should consist of three types of measures: one, to relieve monetary pressures; two, to channel scarce goods into the most essential uses; three, to deal directly with specific high prices.

The way to reduce monetary pressure is by restraining the excessive use of credit. At a time when the economy is already producing at capacity, a further expansion of credit simply gives people more dollars to use in bidding up the prices of goods.

Consumer credit is increasing at a disturbing rate. The amount outstanding has risen from $6½ billion in 1945 to more than $11 billion today. Even more rapid expansion is under way now, because the controls on consumer credit exercised by the Federal Reserve System expired November 1. These credit controls should be restored. Also, some restraint should be placed on inflationary bank credit.

Legislation is required, moreover, to prevent excessive speculation on the commodity exchanges.

Another effective weapon against inflation is increased savings by the public. Every dollar that is saved instead of spent is a dollar fighting against inflation. In order to encourage additional savings, the Government should intensify its vigorous efforts to sell savings bonds.

The second part of the program to curb inflation is to secure the most efficient use of scarce goods and otherwise channel their flow so as to relieve inflationary pressures. Grain, for example, is too badly needed to permit wasteful feeding to livestock. Steel, as another example, is too scarce to be used for nonessential purposes.

Legislation is required to authorize the allocation of scarce commodities which basically affect the cost of living, or basically affect industrial production. In these limited areas inventory control powers are also needed.

Authority to allocate transportation services should be extended.

In addition, existing export controls should be continued and strengthened. Goods that we cannot wisely export must be kept here, and the shipments we make must go where they are needed most. Profiteering in exports must be prevented.

The measures which I have already discussed will, when taken together, aid substantially in relieving inflationary pressures. For large segments of the economy, they should be adequate to meet the requirements of the present situation. However, there are limited areas of acute danger in which these measures cannot be regarded as guaranteeing adequate protection.

For example, present forecasts indicate that we are likely to have less grain and meat next year than we have this year. The pressure on the prices of these foods would then become increasingly great. If these pressures are permitted to bring further sharp increases in food prices, they may well set off a chain reaction that would spread throughout the economy. It is surely better to take timely action to check adverse forces at particular trouble spots than to wait until general inflation has become so serious as to require drastic controls over the whole economic life.

Therefore, we need a third group of measures to combat inflation. Legislation should be enacted, authorizing the Government to impose price ceilings on vital commodities in short supply that basically affect the cost of living. Basic elements in the cost of living are food, clothing, fuel, and rent. In addition, the legislation should be broad enough to authorize price ceilings on those vital commodities in short supply that basically affect industrial production. This will enable us to stamp out profiteering and speculation in these important areas.

This does not mean that price ceilings should be imposed on all items within the classes I have mentioned. For example, price ceilings would not be necessary for staple food and clothing items not in short supply or for any delicacies or luxuries. The same principle of selective treatment would apply to industrial items. This selective treatment of a relatively few danger spots is very different from overall wartime price controls.

Even should the shortages of a few commodities at the consumer level remain serious for a time, I believe that the fair distribution of such commodities can be largely accomplished without consumer rationing. But no one can foretell exactly how serious some shortages may become next year. With serious shortages, a free market works cruel hardships on countless families and puts an unbearable pressure on prices. I therefore recommend that authority be granted, as a preparedness measure, to ration basic cost of living items on a highly selective basis.

Adequate protection from high prices and unfair distribution can be assured only by establishing authority for price ceilings and rationing in the fields of critical importance. It takes several months to set up an organization and make the administrative arrangements necessary to put price control and rationing into effect. Thus, the only prudent course is to establish the authority at this time so the necessary preparations can be started. If we fail to prepare and disaster results from our unpreparedness, we shall have gambled with our national safety—and lost.

If the Government imposes price ceilings covering a specific area of production, it should in all fairness have the authority, in that same area, to prevent wage increases which will make it impossible to maintain price ceilings. This authority should be granted, although I believe that there would be few occasions for its use.

496

I am confident that, if the cost of living can be brought and held in reasonable relationship to the incomes of the people, wage adjustments through collective bargaining will be consistent with productivity and will avoid an inflationary round of wage increases.

Next to food, the most important element in the cost of living is rent. Under the modified rent control law, rents are rising at the rate of about 1 percent a month. A 12-percent annual increase in rents imposes an intolerable strain upon the family budget. The rent control law should be extended and the weaknesses in the present law should be corrected.

I am well aware that some of my proposals are drastic measures. No one regrets more than I the necessity for considering their use. But if we face the facts squarely, it is apparent that no other methods can safely be counted upon to protect our people from the dangers of excessively high prices and ruinous inflation.

The American people want adequate protection from these dangers and they are entitled to it. It should not be denied them. Nor should they be misled with half measures.

Even with the authority to impose price ceilings, the Government will intensify its efforts to obtain voluntary action. Wherever voluntary action will do the job there will be no necessity to impose the Government's authority. But the very existence of these powers should have a salutary effect. They will demonstrate to each of our citizens the importance of carefully weighing each step that might lead to higher prices. They will support expanded and more specific efforts to obtain voluntary action by businessmen, labor leaders, farmers, and consumers to hold prices down.

All the actions I have described are essential to a fair and effective anti-inflation program. I look upon them as shortrun insurance against the impairment of our prosperity and the threat to our future development.

We should all ponder the following questions:

What would it avail the farmer, in the long run, if farm prices should go substantially higher only to be followed by a disaster such as occurred after the first World War?

What would it avail the worker, in the long run, to obtain inflationary wage increases, if they were followed by a repetition of the bitter experience when 15 million workers were out of jobs?

What would it avail the businessman to have record breaking profits soar even higher, if they were followed by a depression which would imperil our whole system of enterprise?

The program which I have outlined is one designed to meet the existing emergencies of inflation and exorbitant price levels. It is an emergency program which should be adopted to protect our standard of living for the immediate present and to make possible economic security in the future.

But a program designed to meet a crisis cannot by itself be a program designed to build for the future. We must also make plans to prevent future difficulty of the same nature.

Our long-range programs must stress ever-increasing production.

To accomplish this for agriculture, we need a comprehensive farm program. We shall need programs to increase the use of farm products by industry and the consumers in this country when other countries become more nearly self-sufficient. Long-range national measures will be needed to protect the farm population against ruinous deflation in farm production and prices.

To expand industrial output, we need a long-range program to overcome basic shortages in capacity and equipment. To provide markets for increased output of farm and factory, we shall need long-range programs to raise the standard of living, particularly for families of low income.

But the first step toward this progress in the future is to deal with the critical present. We must win the battle against inflation, so that our long-range efforts may start from high levels of prosperity and not from the depths of a depression.

In summary, the immediate anti-inflation program that I recommend calls for the following legislative action:

1. To restore consumer credit controls and to restrain the creation of inflationary bank credit.

2. To authorize the regulation of speculative trading on the commodity exchanges.

3. To extend and strengthen export controls.

4. To extend authority to allocate transportation facilities and equipment.

5. To authorize measures which will induce the marketing of livestock and poultry at weights and grades that represent the most efficient utilization of grain.

6. To enable the Department of Agriculture to expand its program of encouraging conservation practices in this country, and to authorize measures designed to increase the production of foods in foreign countries.

7. To authorize allocation and inventory control of scarce commodities which basically affect the cost of living or industrial production.

8. To extend and strengthen rent control.

9. To authorize consumer rationing on products in short supply which basically affect the cost of living.

10. To authorize price ceilings on products in short supply which basically affect the cost of living or industrial production, and to authorize such wage ceilings as are essential to maintain the necessary price ceilings.

If we neglect our economic ills at home, if we fail to halt the march of inflation, we may bring on a depression from which our economic system, as we know it, might not recover. And if we turn our backs on nations still struggling to recover from the agony of war, not yet able to stand on their own feet, we may lose for all time the chance to obtain a world of free peoples that can live in enduring peace.

The freedom that we cherish in our own economy and the freedom that we enjoy in the world today are both at stake.

I have recommended interim aid for certain Western European countries and a program to curb inflation in the United States. I regard the measures which I have presented to you as vital and essential to the welfare of this Nation.

When the American people have faced decisions of such magnitude in the past, they have taken the right course.

I am confident that the Congress, guided by the will of the people, will take the right course on this occasion.

NOTE: The President spoke at 1:30 p.m. His address was carried on a nationwide radio broadcast.

On December 17 the President approved an act authorizing emergency aid as recommended in the message (61 Stat. 934); and on December 23 he signed a bill appropriating funds for carrying out the provisions of the act (61 Stat. 941).

On December 30 he signed a joint resolution "to aid in the stabilization of commodity prices, to aid in further stabilizing the economy of the United States, and for other purposes" (61 Stat. 945). For the President's statement upon signing the resolution, see Item 242.

225   Letter to the Chairman, Citizens Food Committee, on the Need for Continuing Conservation Efforts.   *November* 20, 1947

Dear Mr. Luckman:

Less than two months ago I appointed the Citizens Food Committee, with you as Chairman, to advise on ways and means of carrying out the necessary conservation effort. At that time I asked your Committee "to develop plans for bringing the vital problem of food conservation to the attention of every American for action."

In this very short period of time, the Citizens Food Committee has not only performed the planning task I set for it, but has, under your vigorous leadership, translated its plans into immediate and effective action. As a result, you now inform me that the grain conservation programs set in motion by the Committee, in cooperation with the Cabinet Food Committee, should result in a saving of considerably more than 100 million bushels of grain.

In order to bring about this result in so short a time, you and your staff have worked unceasingly, without regard to the clock or to your private business responsibilities. You have obtained the unstinting support of agriculture, business, labor and consumer organizations, and of the public, in furtherance of what has now become America's food conservation campaign. These are splendid achievements.

This food conservation campaign must continue. It must in fact be intensified, if we are to continue to save the utmost possible amount of grain that can be spared for the needs of hungry people overseas. I have told the Congress that the Government will intensify its efforts to obtain voluntary action, in order to enable us to extend aid to friendly nations and at the same time

protect our own living standards. The voluntary efforts inaugurated by your Committee will continue to be necessary to supplement the program which I have asked the Congress to authorize. Consequently, the programs planned and put into effect by the Citizens Food Committee must be pushed forward throughout the coming winter and at least through the first half of next year.

I call on the American people, the state and local committees, and all the organizations and groups, to continue their vigorous efforts in carrying out this program. To insure the continued success of the programs, I ask you and the Citizens Food Committee to continue on an advisory basis to give such counsel and assistance as may be necessary.

Please convey to the members of the Citizens Food Committee, and to its staff, my deep appreciation of the excellent job that has been done. To you, personally, I express my sincere thanks for the unselfish and untiring devotion with which you have so ably performed a most difficult assignment. I ask that you continue as Chairman of the Citizens Food Advisory Committee so that your services will be available to me on call for so long a period as may be necessary.

Very sincerely yours,

HARRY S. TRUMAN

[Honorable Charles Luckman, Chairman, Citizens Food Committee, Washington, D.C.]

NOTE: The President's letter was in reply to one from Mr. Luckman summarizing the work of the Committee and suggesting that the Citizens Food Committee be reconstituted as the Citizens Food Advisory Committee. Mr. Luckman's letter, dated November 20, 1947, was also released.

226 The President's News Conference of
November 21, 1947

THE PRESIDENT. [1.] I have some announcements for you this time.

General Bradley will go back to the War Department on the 1st of December, and Carl R. Gray, Jr., the vice president of the Chicago, North Western Railway Company, will take over the Veterans Administration on January 1st.

General Littlejohn will send in his resignation, and it will be accepted, the 28th of November. And Gen. C. B. Cates, who is now in the War College, will be Commandant of the Marine Corps.

[2.] And I want to make it plain that at this year's Army and Navy game I am going to be the guest of the Army, and sit on that side all the time. Next year I am going to sit with the Navy, when they will be the hosts. I like to enjoy a ball game just as well as anybody else, and don't want to be the show myself.

Q. Will that be after election day, Mr. President?

THE PRESIDENT. Yes, it will be after election day. The President's term doesn't expire until the 20th of January. [*Laughter*]

Q. Mr. President, is the Department of the Air Force going to have a team too, now?

THE PRESIDENT. I haven't gone into that. They have no school as yet, you see. They go to school both at Annapolis and at West Point, and I haven't heard of their organizing a team.

[3.] Q. Mr. President, just to clarify this thing a little bit to me, General Bradley is going back to the War Department presumably as Chief of Staff?

THE PRESIDENT. He will be Chief of Staff as soon as General Eisenhower goes to the Columbia University.

Q. When is that, Mr. President?

THE PRESIDENT. I can't answer that. That is up to General Eisenhower.

Q. It has been mentioned—mentioning April 1.

THE PRESIDENT. Well, you will have to talk to General Eisenhower. I can't give you that.

Q. Mr. President, when is General Littlejohn's resignation effective? I didn't get that.

THE PRESIDENT. The 28th of November—28th of November.

Q. Mr. President, what will General Bradley's duties be in the War Department between December 1st and the time he takes over?

THE PRESIDENT. General Bradley has certain accumulated leave coming, and he wants to make a survey of the War Department at the various headquarters around the country before he becomes Chief of Staff. He will have plenty to do. He made this request himself, and we are complying with what he wants.

Q. Mr. President, are you prepared at this time, sir, to name General Littlejohn's successor to War Assets?

THE PRESIDENT. The Deputy Administrator over there will take over.

Q. What is his name, sir?

Q. Deputy or acting?

THE PRESIDENT. Acting. Larson is his name.

Q. Mr. President, I understand Mr. Littlejohn is going to the Philippines to advise President Roxas on the war surplus situation?

THE PRESIDENT. I don't know what General Littlejohn is going to do. I know he is going to quit on the 28th. I don't know anything about his movements after that.

He handed me a check—photostatic copy of the biggest check I ever saw, for $143 million that we sold that pipeline for.

Q. He will start liquidating War Assets before very long, won't he?

THE PRESIDENT. War Assets is supposed to be liquidated by next June, and that is due to the efforts of General Littlejohn. He has done a most successful and a wonderful job. He was just tough enough to do it, and that's what it took.

Now you will have a letter from him and one from me handed to you as you go out, and you will also have the background of these appointments I made handed to you in mimeograph form.

[4.] Q. Mr. President, the other thing is: Dillon Myer announced yesterday that you are going to transfer him to another job. Could you tell us at this time what that job is?

THE PRESIDENT. No. Dillon hasn't made up his mind which one he wants. As soon as he does, I will make the transfer.

[5.] Q. Mr. President, do you have any comment on the Canadian Government's action prohibiting exports?

THE PRESIDENT. No, I have not.

[6.] Q. Mr. President, a few hours after you delivered the message to Congress here the other day, Senator Taft went on the air and called the proposal you made totalitarian. Will you comment on that, sir?

THE PRESIDENT. No comment. The speech speaks for itself. If you don't understand it, read it again.

Q. Your speech or his speech?

THE PRESIDENT. Both of them. [*Laughter*]

Q. Mr. President, are you satisfied—what comment can you make on the reception of your speech by the public?

THE PRESIDENT. It has been very satisfactory.

[7.] Q. Any indication when you might have to use consumer rations and price controls if authority is granted?

THE PRESIDENT. We will have to discuss that after we get the authority. Can't do it now.

[8.] Q. Mr. President, when will you be prepared to submit the Marshall plan to Congress?

THE PRESIDENT. In about 10 days.

[9.] Q. Mr. President, Republicans including Senator Taft say that you have export controls which you have not used.

THE PRESIDENT. I think that that probably is correct. We never make complete use of every power that we have. We use it where it will do the most good. The export controls will expire. We are asking for their extension.

[10.] Q. Mr. President, is there anything you can say about the particular point that we are shipping a lot of heavy machinery to Russia—allowed to go?

THE PRESIDENT. Russia has a purchasing mission in this country. They have been allowed to purchase those things that are necessary for the rehabilitation of Russia's electric dams that were destroyed by the Germans, and some farm machinery.

Q. Do you favor continuing that purchasing program, Mr. President?

THE PRESIDENT. I see no reason to stop it now.

[11.] Q. To return to the export controls a moment, sir, your message to Congress called for strengthening as well as extending them. Can you tell us in what way——

THE PRESIDENT. That is correct.

Q. —— you would strengthen them?

THE PRESIDENT. That speaks for itself. And the details will be given to the committee when they want to have a hearing. I don't want to have that hearing here.

[12.] Q. Mr. President, is Gray in Minneapolis now?

THE PRESIDENT. He lives in St. Paul, I think. Either Minneapolis or St. Paul.

[13.] Q. Mr. President, what do you propose—how do you propose to control the grain exchanges?

THE PRESIDENT. In the same manner that the New York Stock Exchange is controlled.

Q. You would apply the same margins there?

THE PRESIDENT. Well, along the same line. I can't go into details because it will have to be worked out before the committee. But we ought to have the same authority we have over the New York Stock Exchange and the Federal Reserve Bank.

[14.] Q. Well, Mr. President, have you considered block purchasing of crops for distribution?

THE PRESIDENT. Everything of that sort has been and is being considered. That will be given to the committees when hearings are held. You will have all that information at that time.

[15.] Q. Mr. President, would you extend this commodity control exchange to the cotton exchange, and to the wool exchange?

THE PRESIDENT. Is cotton a commodity? Is wool a commodity?

Q. Generally considered so.

THE PRESIDENT. All right. All right—that answers your question.

Reporter: Thank you, Mr. President.

NOTE: President Truman's one hundred and twenty-eighth news conference was held in his office at the White House at 9 o'clock on Friday morning, November 21, 1947.

227 Letter Accepting Resignation of Robert E. Hannegan as Postmaster General. *November 25, 1947*

Dear Bob:

It would not be possible for me to overstate the feeling of personal regret with which I have read your letter of yesterday advising me of your determination to return to private life.

The sense of regret is deepened because of the close friendship which has obtained between us for so long and because the country is losing the services of a most efficient public servant.

You have given the government more than five years of devoted service. My lamented predecessor trusted and admired you. Now for more than two years you have justified my own faith through your admirable administration of the office of Postmaster General, whose duties are onerous as well as complex.

I know that your influence and your talents will always be dedicated to the cause of progress at home and justice and a permanent peace among the nations of the world.

With every assurance that I heartily reciprocate your warm personal sentiments, I accept, with reluctance, your resignation as Postmaster General, effective at the close of business on December first.

Very sincerely yours,

HARRY S. TRUMAN

[Honorable Robert E. Hannegan, The Postmaster General, Washington, D.C.]

NOTE: Mr. Hannegan served as Postmaster General from May 8, 1945, to December 1, 1947. His letter of resignation, dated November 24, was released with the President's reply.

228   Special Message to the Congress on Extending the Maritime
       Commission's Authority To Operate, Sell, and Charter
       Vessels.   *December 1, 1947*

To the Congress of the United States:

The present authority of the United States Maritime Commission to operate, sell, and charter Government-owned vessels which were built during the war will expire on February 29, 1948.

It is now clearly apparent that this authority must be continued beyond that date in order to prevent a breakdown in vital shipping services.

Over 1200 dry-cargo vessels are now chartered to American citizens by the Commission. The bulk of this fleet is devoted to carrying vital relief cargo, chiefly coal and grain exports. Its continued operation will be essential in furnishing aid to foreign countries during this winter. Other portions of this chartered fleet are devoted to essential coastwise and intercoastal services.

Under its authority to operate vessels, the Maritime Commission, through general agents, is now operating emergency passenger vessels and tankers. It is necessary to continue the authority for the operation of these passenger vessels if we are to meet essential needs for which no other passenger service is available. While the number of tankers operated by the Commission is being steadily reduced as tankers are sold under the Ship Sales Act, those which re-

main unsold must be kept in operation to assist in averting a serious world-wide shortage of petroleum.

In order to avoid needless disruption of the vital services now being provided with Government-owned ships, the present authority of the Maritime Commission should be renewed well in advance of its expiration date. I recommend, therefore, that the Congress give consideration to this matter during its present session.

There are other questions concerning the maritime industry which will require consideration of new legislation in the near future. These questions relate to the shipping requirements of the European Recovery Program and the long-range requirements of our own merchant marine. Our most immediate need, however, is to assure the maintenance of essential shipping services by continuing in effect the present provisions of law which make possible the use of Government-owned ships.

Accordingly, I recommend that these provisions of law be extended until June 30, 1949.

HARRY S. TRUMAN

NOTE: On February 27, 1948, the President approved a joint resolution providing for continuation of the authority of the Maritime Commission until March 1, 1949 (62 Stat. 38).

229   Statement by the President Making Public a Report on the
       Needs of the Navajo Indians.   *December 2, 1947*

RECENTLY I requested the Secretary of the Interior to report to me on the emergency situation facing the Navajo Indians in Arizona and New Mexico this winter. Secretary Krug has submitted the attached

report, which describes the reasons why the Navajos are threatened with hunger and cold this winter and the steps which have been taken by the Federal Government, under the leadership of the Bureau of Indian Affairs of the Department of the Interior, to prevent suffering.

In addition to the funds for relief regularly appropriated by the Congress last summer, substantial amounts of surplus food, clothing, and equipment have been made available to the Navajos by the Government. At Secretary Krug's suggestion I have asked the Secretary of Defense, the Secretary of Agriculture, and the War Assets Administrator to continue the steps they are taking to alleviate suffering and to forestall a serious collapse in the Navajo community life. It is fortunate that the Government has available these resources which can help meet the immediate problem. The tribe itself has also made available a substantial amount of its limited funds for relief of its members. It seems, nevertheless, that additional relief appropriations by the Congress will prove necessary later in the winter.

The Secretary's report makes clear that the problems of the Navajos will not be solved merely by providing relief for them this winter. Long-range problems of health, education, and productive employment must be earnestly considered by the Federal Government, the States concerned, and the Indians themselves. I expect to submit to the next regular session of the Congress my recommendations for the Federal Government's part in a long-range program of rehabilitation for the Navajos.

Our basic purpose is to assist the Navajos—and other Indians—to become healthy, enlightened, and self-supporting citizens, able to enjoy the full fruits of our democracy and to contribute their share to the prosperity of our country. We must give our full support to the achievement of this goal. Only by so doing can we meet the obligation of our democracy to this group of our citizens.

NOTE: The "Report to the President on Conditions of the Navajo Indians," released with the President's statement, is dated December 2, 1947 (mimeographed, 8 pp.).

The report noted that the critical conditions facing the Navajo Tribe resulted from a combination of long- and short-term factors—the failure to develop a resource base capable of keeping up with the 600-percent increase in the population during the preceding 80 years; the livestock reduction program initiated to prevent the overgrazing of range lands; the loss of income from dependency allotments and war workers' wages; and the severe drought of the summer of 1947. The report also noted that there was, in addition, a serious shortage of most of the public services commonly enjoyed by other American citizens, such as health facilities, education, welfare, agricultural assistance and credit, soil conservation, domestic and institutional water supply, and road construction.

"It is my belief," the Secretary of the Interior reported, "that it is the responsibility of the Federal Government, the States concerned, and the Indians, working together, to develop those new sources of livelihood that will assure an American standard of living to this group of American citizens."

On December 19 the President approved a bill authorizing an appropriation for the immediate relief of the Navajo and Hopi Indians (61 Stat. 940).

---

230 Special Message to the Senate Transmitting the Inter-American Treaty of Reciprocal Assistance. *December 4, 1947*

[Released December 4, 1947. Dated December 1, 1947]

To the Senate of the United States:

With a view to receiving the advice and consent of the Senate to ratification, I transmit herewith a certified copy of the inter-American treaty of reciprocal assistance, formulated at the Inter-American Conference for the Maintenance of Continental Peace and Security and signed at Rio de Janeiro, Brazil, in the English, French, Portuguese, and Spanish languages on September 2, 1947, by the plenipotentiaries of the United States of America and by the plenipotentiaries of other American republics.

I transmit also, for the information of the Senate, the report which the Acting Secretary of State has addressed to me in regard to the treaty above-mentioned.

The principles, purposes and provisions of the treaty have my complete and wholehearted approval and I am happy to recommend the treaty to the favorable consideration of the Senate.

HARRY S. TRUMAN

NOTE: The treaty was favorably considered by the Senate on December 8, 1947, and after ratification entered into force on December 3, 1948. It was proclaimed by the President on December 9, 1948.

The text of the treaty is printed in the Department of State Bulletin (vol. 17, p. 565), and in the U.S. Statutes at Large (62 Stat. 1681). The report of Acting Secretary of State Robert A. Lovett is also printed in the Department of State Bulletin (vol. 17, p. 1188).

231   Address on Conservation at the Dedication of Everglades National Park.   *December 6, 1947*

Mr. Chairman Pennekamp, Mr. Secretary of the Interior, Governor Caldwell, Senator Holland, Senator Pepper, distinguished guests, and ladies and gentlemen:

I can't tell you what a great pleasure it is to me to be with you today. You know, I have a White House down in Key West. It is very conveniently located for this occasion.

Not often in these demanding days are we able to lay aside the problems of the times, and turn to a project whose great value lies in the enrichment of the human spirit. Today we mark the achievement of another great conservation victory. We have permanently safeguarded an irreplaceable primitive area. We have assembled to dedicate to the use of all the people for all time, the Everglades National Park.

Here in Everglades City we have the atmosphere of this beautiful tropical area. Southeast of us lies the coast of the Everglades Park, cut by islands and estuaries of the Gulf of Mexico. Here are deep rivers, giant groves of colorful trees, prairie marshes, and a great many lakes and streams.

In this park we shall preserve tarpon and trout, pompano, bear, deer, crocodiles and alligators—and rare birds of great beauty. We shall protect hundreds of all kinds of wildlife which might otherwise soon be extinct.

The benefits our Nation will derive from this dedication will outlast the youngest of us. They will increase with the passage of the years. Few actions could make a more lasting contribution to the enjoyment of the American people than the establishment of the Everglades National Park.

Our national park system is a clear expression of the idealism of the American people. Without regard for sectional rivalries or for party politics, the Nation has advanced constantly in the last 75 years in the protection of its natural beauties and wonders.

The success of our efforts to conserve the scenery and wildlife of the country can be measured in popular use. The national park system covers but a fraction of 1 percent of the area of the United States, but over 25 million of our fellow countrymen have visited our national parks within the last year. Each citizen returned to his home with a refreshed spirit and a greater appreciation of the majesty and beauty of our country.

These are the people's parks, owned by young and old, by those in the cities and

505

those on the farms. Most of them are ours today because there were Americans many years ago who exercised vision, patience, and unselfish devotion in the battle for conservation.

Each national park possesses qualities distinctive enough to make its preservation a matter of concern to the whole Nation. Certainly, this Everglades area has more than its share of features unique to these United States. Here are no lofty peaks seeking the sky, no mighty glaciers or rushing streams wearing away the uplifted land. Here is land, tranquil in its quiet beauty, serving not as the source of water but as the last receiver of it. To its natural abundance we owe the spectacular plant and animal life that distinguishes this place from all others in the country.

Our park system also embraces such national shrines as Jamestown Island, the Statue of Liberty, and the battlefields of Yorktown and Gettysburg. These historic places—as much as the scenic areas—also need to be protected with all the devotion at our command in these days when we are learning again the importance of an understanding loyalty to our national heritage.

Our parks are but one part of the national effort to conserve our natural resources. Upon these resources our life as a nation depends. Our high level of employment and our extraordinary production are being limited by scarcities in some items of our natural wealth. This is the time to develop and replenish our basic resources.

Conservation has been practiced for many decades and preached for many more, yet only in recent years has it become plain that we cannot afford to conserve in a haphazard or piecemeal manner. No part of our conservation program can be slighted if we want to make full use of our resources and have full protection against future emergencies.

If we waste our minerals by careless mining and processing, we shall not be able to build the machinery to till the land. If we waste the forests by careless lumbering, we shall lack housing and construction materials for factory, farm, and mine. If we waste the water through failure to build hydroelectric plants, we shall burn our reserves of coal and oil needlessly. If we waste our soil through erosion and failure to replenish our fields, we shall destroy the source of our people's food.

Each conservation need is dependent upon the others. A slashed and burned forest brings erosion of the uplands and fills downstream reservoirs with silt so that water power is lessened and irrigated farms lose their water supplies. Eroded farmlands contribute to devastating floods. Uncontrolled rivers means lost electricity, farms without water, and perennial, increasing flood danger.

To maintain our natural wealth we must engage in full and complete conservation of all our resources.

Full conservation of our energy resources can be accomplished by continued construction of dams, hydroelectric plants, and transmission lines; by greater use of natural gas, by research for more efficient methods of extraction of coal and oil, and by exploration for new reserves.

In forests, conservation can be achieved by adhering to the principle of sustained yield and forest management so that timber is harvested each year just as other crops are. This should be true for both privately owned and publicly owned forest lands.

In farmland, conservation can be achieved by expanding and intensifying the many soil conservation practices developed by our agricultural technicians to sustain productivity. The area of irrigated land can be expanded materially by new reclamation projects.

Range lands in the West can be protected by the control of erosion and by the enforcement of safe limits on the number of grazing stock.

In minerals, we can come closer to the proper balance with increased efficiency in extraction and with scientific exploration of new reserves. When ores contain several minerals, we should extract all the useful products and waste none. Despite a bounteous nature, this country has never been self sufficient in all minerals. We have always imported minerals to meet these deficiencies and we must continue to do so.

In water, we need to prevent further dropping of the water table, which in many areas is dangerously low. Surface water must be stored, and ground water used in such a way as to cause the least depletion. Although the water level is high now here in the Everglades, there has been damage from a lowered fresh-water table, and, during the war, fires raged through the glades—fires fed by dry grass which should have been covered by water.

The battle for conservation cannot be limited to the winning of new conquests. Like liberty itself, conservation must be fought for unceasingly to protect earlier victories. There are always plenty of hogs who are trying to get natural resources for their own personal benefit!

Public lands and parks, our forests and our mineral reserves, are subject to many destructive influences. We have to remain constantly vigilant to prevent raids by those who would selfishly exploit our common heritage for their private gain. Such raids on our natural resources are not examples of enterprise and initiative. They are attempts to take from all the people just for the benefit of a few.

As always in the past when the people's property has been threatened, men and women whose primary concern has been their country's welfare have risen to oppose these selfish attacks. We can be thankful for their efforts, as we can be grateful for the efforts of citizens, private groups, local governments, and the State of Florida which, joined in the common purpose, have made possible the establishment of the Everglades National Park.

The establishment of this park is an object lesson and an example to the entire Nation that sound conservation depends upon the joint endeavors of the people and their several governments. Responsibility is shared by town and State and the Federal Government, by societies and legislatures and all lovers of nature.

No man can know every element that makes a nation great. Certainly the lofty spirit of its people, the daily cooperation, the helpfulness of one citizen to another are elements. A nation's ability to provide a good living for its people in industry, in business, and on the farm is another. Intelligent recognition by its citizens of a nation's responsibility for world order, world peace, and world recovery is still another.

Wise use of our natural resources is the foundation of our effectiveness in all these efforts.

The problems of peace, like those of war, require courage and sustained effort. If we wish this Nation to remain prosperous, if we wish it still to be "the home of the free," we can have it so. But, if we fail to heed the lesson of other nations which have permitted their natural resources to be wasted and destroyed, then we shall reap a sorry harvest.

For conservation of the human spirit, we need places such as Everglades National Park where we may be more keenly aware of our Creator's infinitely varied, infinitely beautiful, and infinitely bountiful handiwork. Here we may draw strength and peace of mind from our surroundings.

Here we can truly understand what that great Israelitist Psalmist meant when he sang: "He maketh me to lie down in green pastures, He leadeth me beside still waters; He restoreth my soul."

NOTE: The President spoke at 2:30 p.m. in Everglades City, Fla. His opening words referred to John Pennekamp, chairman of the dedication ceremonies; Julius A. Krug, Secretary of the Interior; Millard Caldwell, Governor of Florida; and Spessard L. Holland and Claude Pepper, United States Senators from Florida. The address was carried on a nationwide radio broadcast.

232 The President's News Conference of December 11, 1947

THE PRESIDENT. I have no special announcements to make this morning. I thought maybe you might like to ask me some questions that I might be able to answer.

[1.] Q. Mr. President, last August, sometime during the summer, you were asked about the transfer of the Unemployment Service and the Unemployment Compensation Service to the Labor Department, and you said you had been thinking about it, but hadn't made up your mind. I wonder have you made up your mind?

THE PRESIDENT. I have made up my mind, and I am going to suggest in the reorganization plan after the first of the year, that both be transferred to the Department of Labor.

Q. After the first of the year?

THE PRESIDENT. Yes.

[2.] Q. Mr. President, we keep hearing reports that Secretary Forrestal may resign soon. Is there anything to that?

THE PRESIDENT. No. That is a categorical answer.

[3.] Q. Mr. President, do you intend to do anything about Mr. Stassen's charges that insiders in the administration have been speculating in the commodity market?

THE PRESIDENT. I know nothing about it. I have no comment to make on it.

Q. You haven't seen the story this morning?

THE PRESIDENT. No I haven't. Sorry to say I didn't read Stassen's speech. I read the paper, but I didn't read the speech.

[4.] Q. Mr. President, getting back to the switch of those two units of the Government, you mentioned the reorganization plan. How extensive is that reorganization plan going to be?

THE PRESIDENT. It is going to be rather extensive, but I can't give you the details until it is ready.

Q. Sir, is that the plan former President Hoover is connected with?

THE PRESIDENT. No. This is inside the Government. This has nothing to do with the reorganization of the departments. These things will be inside the departments—just transfers. It will not affect the Hoover committee at all.

[5.] Q. Mr. President, what is the administration's policy on Federal Reserve Chairman Eccles' proposal for special reserve requirements of banks? Secretary Snyder says——

THE PRESIDENT. I think, if you will read the message which I sent to Congress, it explains fully and carefully exactly what I meant, and I have no further comment to make on the subject.

[6.] Q. Mr. President, referring to your message, no legislation has gone in yet on price control or wage control which you asked for. Do you know if anything will go in this session?

THE PRESIDENT. Yes, I can say positively that it will go in, in a couple of days. Everything in that message will be covered by legislation proposed by the administration.

Q. All the 10 points will be covered?

THE PRESIDENT. Yes, all 10 points will be covered.

Q. What do you think of the Republican substitute?

THE PRESIDENT. I haven't given it any thought. In fact, I haven't seen the Republican substitute. The message is what I want, and I want it carried out to the letter. I think anything short of that will be inadequate to do the job.

Q. Mr. President, with regard to the wage and price controls, would there be any possibility of an administration bill proposing temporary suspension of the antitrust laws, to apply voluntarily——

THE PRESIDENT. No. The antitrust laws will be enforced to the limit, as long as I am President.

Q. Mr. President, will those price controls cover clothing?

THE PRESIDENT. They will cover everything that is necessary to be covered. I can't say positively item for item what it will be, but whatever is necessary to do to make the cost of living come down, that will be included.

Q. Cover basic commodities also?

THE PRESIDENT. Yes.

[7.] Q. Mr. President, have you chosen a successor to Mr. Dillon Myer yet?

THE PRESIDENT. No. No successor has been chosen. I will announce it as soon as he is chosen.

[8.] Q. Mr. President, if you—about a month ago, you characterized the OPA as a police state method. Would you care to say

whether current proposals have any of that aspect?

THE PRESIDENT. The police state methods are only when they are carried out by a dictator. If the Congress authorizes the carrying out of price controls, and the President is authorized by Congress to carry them out, that is the free government approach to the thing.

[9.] Q. Mr. President, can you tell us when the European Recovery Program will go up?

THE PRESIDENT. Just as soon as it is ready.

Q. Will that be——

THE PRESIDENT. In a short time. I can't give you the exact date.

Q. ——this week, Mr. President?

THE PRESIDENT. No. It will not go up this week. But I will give you the date. Just as quickly as it is ready, I will give you a copy.

[10.] Q. Mr. President, in connection with the enforcement of the antitrust laws, there is some sentiment in New England, in connection with the oil shortage up there, that there might be a relaxation of the laws so that oil companies could pool their resources and information, in order to meet spot shortages in certain areas.

THE PRESIDENT. There will be no relaxation of the antitrust laws as long as I am President—if I can help it.

[11.] Q. Mr. President, will you deliver your European aid message in person, or transmit it?

THE PRESIDENT. I will come to that conclusion when I get it ready. I think probably it will be transmitted. It will be too long to read. The Congress wouldn't want to listen to me for a couple of hours, although they listen to each other, sometimes! [*Laughter*]

Q. What was your longest speech in the Senate?

THE PRESIDENT. Oh, about 35 minutes.

Q. Was it really?

THE PRESIDENT. I never did any filibustering in the Senate.

Q. Are you opposed to the general policy of filibustering?

THE PRESIDENT. As a general policy, I am opposed to it.

Reporter: Thank you, Mr. President.

NOTE: President Truman's one hundred and twenty-ninth news conference was held in his office at the White House at 10:30 a.m. on Thursday, December 11, 1947.

---

233   Citation Accompanying the Distinguished Service Medal Presented to Fleet Admiral Chester W. Nimitz. *December 11, 1947*

THE PRESIDENT of the United States takes pleasure in presenting the Gold Star in lieu of the Fourth Distinguished Service Medal to

FLEET ADMIRAL CHESTER WILLIAM NIMITZ,

UNITED STATES NAVY

for service as set forth in the following CITATION:

For exceptionally meritorious service to the Government of the United States in duties of great responsibility as Commander-in-Chief, United States Pacific Fleet and Pacific Ocean Areas, from August 1945, and as Chief of Naval Operations from December 1945, to December 1947. With his primary and immediate objective the difficult task of reducing the most powerful Navy in history to a fraction of its wartime peak, Fleet Admiral Nimitz administered not only the rapid demobilization of vast numbers of personnel and vessels, but also the programs for the establishment and maintenance of Active and Reserve Fleets with the potential strength and readiness required to support our national policy. Responsible for the organizational readjustment and training in all fields of Naval interest, Fleet Admiral Nimitz rendered distinguished service to his country during this critical period by insuring to the greatest possible extent the Navy's ability to maintain and further the security of the Nation.

HARRY S. TRUMAN

NOTE: The presentation was made by the President in a ceremony at the White House at 3:30 p.m.

---

234   Statement by the President on the Need for Preserving Freedom and Independence in Italy.   *December 13, 1947*

ALTHOUGH the United States is withdrawing its troops from Italy in fulfillment of its obligations under the treaty of peace, this country continues its interest in the preservation of a free and independent Italy. If, in the course of events, it becomes apparent that the freedom and independence of Italy upon which the peace settlement is based are being threatened directly or indirectly, the United States, as a signatory of the peace treaty and as a member of the United Nations, will be obliged to consider what measures would be appropriate for the maintenance of peace and security.

235 Statement by the President Making Public a Report of the Commission on Higher Education. *December* 15, 1947

THE PRESIDENT'S Commission on Higher Education has submitted the first volume of its report. I look forward to studying this report and I hope that our citizens will also examine it carefully.

Higher education in our Nation is confronted today with tremendous responsibilities. Colleges and universities are burdened by great overcrowding and a shortage of teachers. Most importantly, however, we are challenged by the need to insure that higher education shall take its proper place in our national effort to strengthen democracy at home and to improve our understanding of our friends and neighbors everywhere in the world. It was for these compelling reasons that I asked this Commission to report to me and to the Nation. I am confident that the report will help all of us to understand this challenge. I am equally confident that it will prove to be of great value in meeting the challenge successfully.

A carefully developed program to strengthen higher education, taken together with a program for the support of elementary and secondary education, will inevitably strengthen our Nation and enrich the lives of our citizens.

The members of the Commission have worked diligently. They have taken time from their many tasks willingly, in order to lay before the people of the country their judgments on the great problems to be met by higher education. All of us should be grateful to them for their work.

NOTE: The report "Establishing the Goals," dated December 11, 1947 (Government Printing Office, 103 pp.), is the first of six volumes in a series entitled "Higher Education for American Democracy." The report was prepared by the President's Commission on Higher Education, of which George F. Zook served as chairman.

The report proposes sweeping changes in higher education. Specific recommendations include the abandonment of European concepts of education and the development of a curriculum attuned to the needs of a democracy; the doubling of college attendance by 1960; the integration of vocational and liberal education; the extension of free public education through the first 2 years of college for all youth who can profit from such education; the elimination of racial and religious discrimination; revision of the goals of graduate and professional school education to make them effective in training well-rounded persons as well as research specialists and technicians; and the expansion of Federal support for higher education through scholarships, fellowships, and general aid.

In conclusion the report urges establishment of community colleges; the expansion of adult education programs; and the distribution of Federal aid to education in such a manner that the poorer States can bring their educational systems closer to the quality of the wealthier States.

On December 21 the White House released volume II of the series, entitled "Equalizing and Expanding Educational Opportunity" (Government Printing Office, 69 pp.). Other reports in the series were released in 1948, as follows: vol. III, "Organizing Higher Education," released January 12; vol. IV, "Staffing Higher Education," January 25; vol. V, "Financing Higher Education," February 1; vol. VI, "Resource Data," March 21.

236 The President's News Conference of *December* 18, 1947

THE PRESIDENT. [1.] I have some things to talk to you about today. First, I want to make a short statement on the final report of the Luckman committee, and this is mimeographed and will be available—no, it isn't, either. You will have to make your notes. [*To Mr. Ross*] This one isn't?

Mr. Ross: But it is printed.

THE PRESIDENT. It is printed. You will receive the report.

[*Reading, not literally*] "I received today the final report of the Citizens Food Committee,[1] headed by Mr. Charles Luckman, and I wish again to thank the Committee for its effective work in the emergency phases of our food conservation program. The report will be released for publication shortly. I think you will find it extremely interesting.

"I wish to call your attention particularly to the statement about the number of men thrown out of work by the temporary shutdown of the distilleries. I believe you will find a good story there.

"You will recall the estimates that fifty to one hundred thousand employees would be thrown out of jobs. Later it appeared that a maximum of some three thousand might be affected. The report now shows that 965 workers were actually laid off because of that shutdown, and that the United States Employment Service was able to place 551 of these in new jobs. The result is that only 414 of the distillery workers are now out of work—414 as contrasted with the hysterical estimate of more than fifty thousand"—as are most of these estimates.

[2.] The Honorable David A. Reed resigned from the Battle Monuments Commission, and I have today appointed Adm. Edward C. Kalbfus of the Naval School at Newport, R.I.

[3.] Under the Labor Management Relations Act, created under the Federal Mediation and Conciliation Service, I am appointing the following, who will serve as the National Labor-Management Panel. Their function is to "advise in the avoidance of industrial controversies and the manner in which mediation and voluntary adjustments shall be administered, particularly

with reference to controversies affecting the general welfare of the country." And this list will be available, along with a short statement in regard to it, as you go out.

Mr. James Black, president, Pacific Gas and Electric Company—these are from management—Mr. Benjamin F. Fairless, president, United States Steel Corporation; Mr. Paul G. Hoffman, president, Studebaker Corporation; Mr. George M. Humphrey, president, M. A. Hanna Company; Lewis Lapham, president, American-Hawaiian Steamship Company; Charles E. Wilson, president, General Electric Company.

From labor: Mr. Harvey W. Brown, president, International Association of Machinists; Clinton S. Golden, Chief of the Labor Division of the American Mission for Aid to Greece; William Green, president, American Federation of Labor; Allan S. Haywood, vice president, Congress of Industrial Organizations; William L. Hutcheson, president, American Federation of Labor Carpenters Union; and Philip Murray, president, Congress of Industrial Organizations.

Now there will be a statement handed to you with that list that will cover the situation.

Q. Does that mean that Clint Golden is on his way home now?

THE PRESIDENT. Not necessarily. If he is, I don't know it.

[4.] And I have a short statement with reference to Mr. Anderson's appearance before the congressional committee.

[*Reading, not literally*] "With reference to the question regarding the publication of the list of speculators in commodity markets, I think that such list should be made public.

"However, the Congress has provided by law that information furnished to the agencies of the Government on a confidential basis shall not be divulged. Since the Congress itself has so provided, it is necessary

---

[1] The 83-page report is dated December 18, 1947.

that the Congress take some action removing this restriction. The Secretary of Agriculture could then make the list public.

"A resolution giving such authority to the Secretary of Agriculture has already been introduced and could quickly be adopted.

"I would approve such a resolution immediately.[1]

"At the hearing this morning before the Senate Appropriations Committee, the Secretary further stated that he would furnish the list to the committee, if so directed, provided the meeting was held in public and the list was made available to the public. The committee refused to take this course of action. Instead, the committee adopted a resolution that the list should be furnished to it at a secret session and behind closed doors.

"The Secretary properly rejected this proposal.

"I fully support the position of the Secretary of Agriculture.

"I have already made my position clear with reference to speculation on the commodity exchanges, and I hope that the Congress will act promptly so that the facts in this situation can be known to all."

Any questions?

Q. Is that statement mimeographed, sir?

THE PRESIDENT. That statement is mimeographed and will be available to you.

[5.] Q. Mr. President, on the Roy Harper judgeship out in Missouri, is it your understanding that when Congress adjourns tomorrow the recess appointment expires, and if so will you send a new recess appointment?

THE PRESIDENT. I will meet that situation when it comes up.

[6.] Q. Mr. President, it has been pointed out in the press that at the Yalta and Potsdam conferences when differences arose between foreign ministers they were resolved by meetings between the heads of state. Would you be agreeable to a meeting with General Stalin in order to smooth out the differences which have developed?

THE PRESIDENT. I would be most happy to see General Stalin in Washington, if he wants to come here. I have said that time and again. But I want to say to you, and clear you up entirely, that the meeting at Yalta and at Potsdam was of the heads of the states and not the foreign ministers. The foreign ministers conference was organized at Potsdam, so the foreign ministers didn't have anything to fall out about at those meetings.

Q. I was referring to the meetings which they used to hold in the mornings.

THE PRESIDENT. That was only preliminary. That was only preliminary to the meetings of the heads of states. They made no decisions.

Q. Along that line, Mr. President, have you had any direct communication with Marshal Stalin?

THE PRESIDENT. Why, no, not recently.

Q. What was the question?

THE PRESIDENT. He wanted to know if I had any communications from Premier Stalin lately, and I said no I had not.

Q. Have you had any with him?

THE PRESIDENT. No, I have not.

Q. Mr. President, is there anywhere else that you would meet him besides Washington?

THE PRESIDENT. I would be glad to see him in Washington. Period. [*Laughter*]

[7.] Q. Mr. President, I would like to ask a question about the Philippines. There is a report that we have in mind abandoning the treaty with them by which they could get preferential tariff duties in this country?

---

[1] On December 19, 1947, the President approved a joint resolution authorizing the Secretary of Agriculture to publish the names of persons transacting business on the boards of trade and to furnish such names to committees of Congress upon request (61 Stat. 941).

THE PRESIDENT. Where did you get that notion?

Q. Came from Havana.

THE PRESIDENT. There isn't a word of truth in it. Not so long as I am President it won't be abandoned.

[8.] Q. Mr. President, in the debate this afternoon in the Senate, on the provisions for voluntary agreements which would permit agreements between businessmen on allocations and priorities, Senator Morse of Oregon said the effect of this action would be to pass the political buck to the President of the United States. Would you care to comment on that, sir?

THE PRESIDENT. I think that has been very well commented on by Senator Morse. [*Laughter*]

[9.] Q. Mr. President, if there is a budget surplus of $7 billion in the Treasury, as reported, do you think that would justify tax reduction?

THE PRESIDENT. I do not.

Q. Mr. President, does that mean you are against any tax reduction next year?

THE PRESIDENT. I will come to that after the first of the year. You will hear about that in the Message on the State of the Union. I simply answered this question.

[10.] Q. The new crop report is out on winter wheat prospects, which says we can expect a 20-percent decrease next year.

THE PRESIDENT. Is it as much as that? I thought it was a billion, 240 million? No,

that was the last year's crop, wasn't it?

Q. Yes. This is winter wheat, which is the major part of the crop.

THE PRESIDENT. I haven't seen that. I haven't seen that last report.

Q. Came out at 3 o'clock.

THE PRESIDENT. Well, I haven't had a chance to see it, and I can't comment on it, but I know just exactly what it provides. That should take into consideration all the other small grains, as well as wheat.

[11.] Q. Mr. President, what would you say, in your opinion, is the present outlook for peace, as a result of the failure of the London conference?

THE PRESIDENT. I am not at all down-hearted about the peace. I think we will eventually get it.

Q. Peace with Germany?

THE PRESIDENT. Peace in the world.

Q. Have you any comment on the breakup of the London conference?

THE PRESIDENT. General Marshall will answer that question tomorrow night, at 10 o'clock on the radio.[1]

Reporter: Thank you, Mr. President.

THE PRESIDENT. You're entirely welcome.

NOTE: President Truman's one hundred and thirtieth news conference was held in his office at the White House at 4 o'clock on Thursday afternoon, December 18, 1947.

---

[1] Secretary Marshall's address is printed in the Department of State Bulletin (vol. 17, p. 1244).

237 Statement by the President Announcing Appointment of Members of the National Labor-Management Panel. *December* 18, 1947

I HAVE TODAY appointed 12 members of the National Labor-Management Panel— 6 representatives of management and 6 representatives of labor, as required by section

205 of the Labor Management Relations Act. When requested by the Director of the Federal Mediation and Conciliation Service, the panel will "advise in the avoidance of indus-

trial controversies and the manner in which mediation and voluntary adjustment shall be administered, particularly with reference to controversies affecting the general welfare of the country.

Appointment to public office, even on a part-time basis, calls for a considerable expenditure of time and energy, and a consequent sacrifice of private responsibilities and interests. On several occasions I have spoken of the difficulty of filling public posts with men of insight and broad experience. The willingness by these outstanding leaders of management and labor to serve on the National Labor-Management Panel should not only be of considerable assistance to Director Cyrus S. Ching of the Federal Mediation and Conciliation Service, but should furnish an example to others to place themselves, when needed, at the service of their country.

The appointments and the terms of office are as follows:

From management: Term expires Dec. 18

James Black, President, Pacific Gas and Electric Co.......................... 1948
Benjamin F. Fairless, President, U.S. Steel Corporation......................... 1950
Paul G. Hoffman, President, Studebaker Corporation......................... 1948
George M. Humphrey, President, M. A. Hanna Co........................... 1949
Lewis Lapham, President, American-Hawaiian SS Co........................ 1949
Charles E. Wilson, President, General Electric Co............................ 1950

From labor: Term expires Dec. 18

Harvey W. Brown, President, International Machinists Union.................... 1948
Clinton S. Golden, Chief of the Labor Division of the American Mission for Aid to Greece............................. 1949
William Green, President, American Federation of Labor.................... 1950
Allan S. Haywood, Vice President, Congress of Industrial Organizations............ 1948
William L. Hutcheson, President, American Federation of Labor Carpenters Union... 1949
Philip Murray, President, Congress of Industrial Organizations................... 1950

238   Special Message to the Congress on the Marshall Plan. *December* 19, 1947

To the Congress of the United States:

A principal concern of the people of the United States is the creation of conditions of enduring peace throughout the world. In company with other peace-loving nations, the United States is striving to insure that there will never be a World War III. In the words of the Charter of the United Nations, we are "determined to save succeeding generations from the scourge of war."

We seek lasting peace in a world where freedom and justice are secure and where there is equal opportunity for the economic well-being of all peoples.

To this end, the United States played a leading role in the founding of the United Nations. We have supported that organization at all times to the best of our ability and we have advanced a number of proposals for increasing its effectiveness in maintaining peace and security and in establishing the economic, social and moral foundations of peace.

We are working in the United Nations toward the limitation and control of armaments and, in a step without precedent or parallel, have offered to place our most powerful weapon under international control provided that other nations agree to effective and enforceable safeguards against its use for destructive purposes.

The United States, in the conviction that a prerequisite to peace in the future is the just settlement of past differences, has labored to obtain fair and workable treaties of peace for former enemy states so that they may resume their places in the family of nations.

The United States has taken the lead in world-wide efforts to promote industrial and agricultural reconstruction and a revival of world commerce, for we know that enduring peace must be based upon increased production and an expanding flow of goods and materials among nations for the benefit of all.

Since the surrender of the Axis powers, we have provided more than $15 billion, in the form of grants and loans, for aid to victims of the war, to prevent starvation, disease, and suffering; to aid in the restoration of transportation and communications; and to assist in rebuilding war-devastated economies. This assistance has averted stark tragedy and has aided progress toward recovery in many areas of the world.

In these and many other ways, the people of the United States have abundantly demonstrated their desire for world peace and the freedom and well-being of all nations.

We must now make a grave and significant decision relating to our further efforts to create the conditions of peace. We must decide whether or not we will complete the job of helping the free nations of Europe to recover from the devastation of the war. Our decision will determine in large part the future of the people of that continent. It will also determine in large part whether the free nations of the world can look forward with hope to a peaceful and prosperous future as independent states, or whether they must live in poverty and in fear of selfish totalitarian aggression.

INTEREST OF THE UNITED STATES IN EUROPEAN
RECOVERY

It is of vital importance to the United States that European recovery be continued to ultimate success. The American tradition of extending a helping hand to people in distress, our concern for the building of a healthy world economy which can make possible ever-increasing standards of living for our people, and our overwhelming concern for the maintenance of a civilization of free men and free institutions, all combine to give us this great interest in European recovery.

The people of the United States have shown, by generous contributions since the end of hostilities, their great sympathy and concern for the many millions in Europe who underwent the trials of war and enemy occupation. Our sympathy is undiminished, but we know that we cannot give relief indefinitely, and so we seek practical measures which will eliminate Europe's need for further relief.

Considered in terms of our own economy, European recovery is essential. The last two decades have taught us the bitter lesson that no economy, not even one so strong as our own, can remain healthy and prosperous in a world of poverty and want.

In the past, the flow of raw materials and manufactured products between Western Europe, Latin America, Canada and the United States has integrated these areas in a great trading system. In the same manner, Far Eastern exports to the United States have helped pay for the goods shipped from Europe to the Far East. Europe is thus an essential part of a world trading network. The failure to revive fully this vast trading system, which has begun to function again since the end of the war, would result in economic deterioration throughout the world. The United States, in common with other nations, would suffer.

Our deepest concern with European recovery, however, is that it is essential to the maintenance of the civilization in which the American way of life is rooted. It is the only assurance of the continued independence and integrity of a group of nations who constitute a bulwark for the principles of freedom, justice and the dignity of the individual.

The economic plight in which Europe now finds itself has intensified a political struggle between those who wish to remain free men living under the rule of law and those who would use economic distress as a pretext for the establishment of a totalitarian state.

The next few years can determine whether the free countries of Europe will be able to preserve their heritage of freedom. If Europe fails to recover, the peoples of these countries might be driven to the philosophy of despair—the philosophy which contends that their basic wants can be met only by the surrender of their basic rights to totalitarian control.

Such a turn of events would constitute a shattering blow to peace and stability in the world. It might well compel us to modify our own economic system and to forego, for the sake of our own security, the enjoyment of many of our freedoms and privileges.

It is for these reasons that the United States has so vital an interest in strengthening the belief of the people of Europe that freedom from fear and want will be achieved under free and democratic governments.

ORIGINS OF THE EUROPEAN RECOVERY
PROGRAM

The end of the fighting in Europe left that continent physically devastated and its economy temporarily paralyzed. The immediate problem was to prevent widespread starvation and disease and to make a start toward economic recovery. In the first year and a half after V–E day, the people of Western Europe, by their own diligent efforts and with the aid of the United States and other nations, made remarkable progress toward these objectives.

At the beginning of 1947, however, they were still short of the goal of economic recovery. Their difficulties were greatly increased during the present year, chiefly by a bitter winter followed by floods and droughts, which cut Western Europe's grain crop to the lowest figure in generations and hampered production of many other products.

Nevertheless, it was clear by last spring that Europe had achieved sufficient political and economic stability to make possible an overall plan for recovery.

European recovery is essentially a problem for the nations of Europe. It was therefore apparent that it could not be solved, even with outside aid, unless the European nations themselves would find a joint solution and accept joint responsibility for its execution. Such a cooperative plan would serve to release the full productive resources of Europe and provide a proper basis for measuring the need and effectiveness of further aid from outside Europe, and in particular from the United States.

These considerations led to the suggestion by the Secretary of State on June 5, 1947, that further help from the United States should be given only after the countries of Europe had agreed upon their basic requirements and the steps which they would take in order to give proper effect to additional aid from us.

In response to this suggestion, representatives of sixteen European nations assembled in Paris in July, at the invitation of the British and French Governments, to draw up a cooperative program of European recovery. They formed a Committee of European Economic Cooperation. The countries represented were: Austria, Belgium, Denmark, France, Greece, Iceland, Ireland, Italy, Luxembourg, the Netherlands, Norway, Portugal, Sweden, Switzerland, Turkey and the United Kingdom. Although Western Germany was not formally represented on the Committee, its requirements as well as its ability to contribute to European economic recovery were considered by the Committee.

THE RECOVERY PROGRAM PROPOSED BY THE
EUROPEAN COUNTRIES

The report of the European Committee was transmitted to the Government of the United States late in September. The report describes the present economic situation of Europe and the extent to which the participating countries can solve their problem by individual and joint efforts. After taking into account these recovery efforts, the report estimates the extent to which the sixteen countries will be unable to pay for the imports they must have.

The report points out that the peoples of Western Europe depend for their support upon international trade. It has been possible for some 270 million people, occupying this relatively small area, to enjoy a good standard of living only by manufacturing imported raw materials and exporting the finished products to the rest of the world. They must also import foodstuffs in large volume, for there is not enough farm land in Western Europe to support its population even with intensive cultivation and with favorable weather. They cannot produce adequate amounts of cotton, oil and other raw materials. Unless these deficiencies are met by imports, the productive centers of Europe can function only at low efficiency, if at all.

In the past these necessary imports were paid for by exports from Europe, by the performance of services such as shipping and banking, and by income from capital investments abroad. All these elements of international trade were so badly disrupted by the war that the people of Western Europe have been unable to produce in their own countries, or to purchase elsewhere, the goods essential to their livelihood. Shortages of raw materials, productive capacity, and exportable commodities have set up vicious circles of increasing scarcities and lowered standards of living.

The economic recovery of Western European countries depends upon breaking through these vicious circles by increasing production to a point where exports and services can pay for the imports they must have. The basic problem in making Europe self-supporting is to increase European production.

The sixteen nations presented in their report a recovery program designed to enable them, and Western Germany, to become economically self-supporting within a period of four years and thereafter to maintain a reasonable minimum standard of living for their people without special help from others. The program rests upon four basic points:

(1) A strong production effort by each of the participating countries.

(2) Creation of internal financial stability by each country.

(3) Maximum and continuing cooperation among the participating countries.

(4) A solution of the problem of the participating countries' trading deficit with the American continents, particularly by increasing European exports.

The nations represented on the European Committee agreed at Paris to do everything in their power to achieve these four aims. They agreed to take definite measures leading to financial, economic and monetary stability, the reduction of trade barriers, the removal of obstacles to the free movement of persons within Europe, and a joint effort to use their common resources to the best advantage.

These agreements are a source of great

encouragement. When the representatives of sixteen sovereign nations, with diverse peoples, histories and institutions, jointly determine to achieve closer economic ties among themselves and to break away from the self-defeating actions of narrow nationalism, the obstacles in the way of recovery appear less formidable.

The report takes into account the productive capacities of the participating nations and their ability to obtain supplies from other parts of the world. It also takes into account the possibilities of obtaining funds through the International Bank for Reconstruction and Development, through private investment, and in some instances by the sale of existing foreign assets. The participating countries recognized that some commodities, particularly food, will remain scarce for years to come, and the diet they have set as their goal for 1951 is less adequate in most cases than their pre-war diet. The report assumes that many countries will continue restrictions on the distribution of shortage items such as food, clothing and fuel.

When all these factors had been considered, the European Committee concluded that there will still be a requirement for large quantities of food, fuel, raw materials and capital equipment for which the financial resources of the participating countries will be inadequate. With successful execution of the European recovery program, this requirement will diminish in each of the four years ahead, and the Committee anticipated that by 1952 Europe could again meet its needs without special aid.

APPRAISAL OF THE EUROPEAN PROBLEM

The problem of economic recovery in Western Europe is basically of the character described in the report of the sixteen nations. A successful European recovery program will depend upon two essentials. The first

is that each nation separately and all the nations together should take vigorous action to help themselves. The second essential is that sufficient outside aid should be made available to provide the margin of victory for the recovery program.

The necessary imports which the sixteen countries cannot finance without assistance constitute only a small proportion, in terms of value, of their total national production— some 5 percent over the four years of the program. These imports, however, are of crucial importance in generating recovery. They represent the difference between ever-deepening stagnation and progressive improvement.

Most of the necessary outside aid, if it is to come at all, must come from the United States. It is a simple fact that we are the only nation with sufficient economic strength to bridge the temporary gap between minimum European needs and war-diminished European resources.

We expect that other countries which have it within their power will also give what assistance they can to Europe. Canada, for example, has been lending assistance to Europe fully as great in proportion to its capacity as that which we have given. We also expect that international institutions, particularly the International Bank, will provide such assistance as they can within their charters. But the fact remains—only the United States can provide the bulk of the aid needed by Europe over the next four years.

It is necessarily a complex and difficult task to determine the extent and nature of this aid.

In some respects, the situation has changed significantly since the report of the sixteen countries was completed. Some of these changes have been unfavorable, including price increases in the United States and other countries where Europe makes purchases, a serious drought in Europe, and aggressive activities by communists and communist-inspired groups aimed directly at the prevention of European recovery.

There have also been favorable changes. In the last few months coal production in the Ruhr district of Western Germany has increased from 230,000 tons a day to 290,000 tons a day. Similarly, coal production in the United Kingdom has risen markedly in recent weeks. Iron and steel production has correspondingly increased. Such increases in production, which lie at the heart of industrial recovery, are of far-reaching importance.

Further changes in the situation, now unpredictable, are to be expected as European recovery progresses.

All our plans and actions must be founded on the fact that the situation we are dealing with is flexible and not fixed, and we must be prepared to make adjustments whenever necessary.

Weather conditions will largely determine whether agricultural goals can be met.

Political events in Europe and in the rest of the world cannot be accurately foreseen. We must not be blind to the fact that the communists have announced determined opposition to any effort to help Europe get back on its feet. There will unquestionably be further incitements to strike, not for the purpose of redressing the legitimate grievances of particular groups, but for the purpose of bringing chaos in the hope that it will pave the way for totalitarian control.

On the other hand, if confidence and optimism are reestablished soon, the spark they provide can kindle united efforts to a degree which would substantially accelerate the progress of European recovery.

Despite these many imponderables, the dimensions of the necessary assistance by the United States can now be determined within reasonable limits. We can evaluate the probable success of a bold concept of assistance to the European economy. We can determine the principles upon which American aid should be based. We can estimate the probable magnitude of the assistance required and judge whether we can, safely and wisely, provide that assistance.

Extensive consideration has been given to these problems. Congressional committees and individual Members of the Congress have studied them at home and abroad during the recent Congressional recess. The report of the European nations has been carefully analyzed by officials of our Government. Committees of the Executive Branch and a group of distinguished private citizens have given their best thought to the relationship between Europe's needs and our resources.

PROGRAM FOR UNITED STATES AID

In the light of all these factors, an integrated program for United States aid to European recovery has been prepared for submission to the Congress.

In developing this program, certain basic considerations have been kept in mind:

First, the program is designed to make genuine recovery possible within a definite period of time, and not merely to continue relief indefinitely.

Second, the program is designed to insure that the funds and goods which we furnish will be used most effectively for European recovery.

Third, the program is designed to minimize the financial cost to the United States, but at the same time to avoid imposing on the European countries crushing financial burdens which they could not carry in the long run.

Fourth, the program is designed with due regard for conserving the physical resources of the United States and minimizing the impact on our economy of furnishing aid to Europe.

Fifth, the program is designed to be consistent with other international relationships and responsibilities of the United States.

Sixth, the administration of the program is designed to carry out wisely and efficiently this great enterprise of our foreign policy.

I shall discuss each of these basic considerations in turn.

RECOVERY—NOT RELIEF

The program is designed to assist the participating European countries in obtaining imports essential to genuine economic recovery which they cannot finance from their own resources. It is based on the expectation that with this assistance European recovery can be substantially completed in about four years.

The aid which will be required from the United States for the first fifteen months—from April 1, 1948, to June 30, 1949—is now estimated at $6.8 billion.

These funds represent careful estimates of the cost of the goods and services which will be required during this period to start Europe on the road to genuine economic recovery. The European requirements as they were stated in the Paris report have been closely reviewed and scaled downward where they appeared to include non-essentials or where limited supplies will prevent their full satisfaction.

The requirements of the remaining three years of the program are more difficult to estimate now, but they are expected to decrease year by year as progress is made toward recovery. Obviously, price changes, weather and crop conditions and other unpredictable factors will influence the overall cost of our aid. Nevertheless, the inherent nature of this enterprise and the long-range planning necessary to put it into effect on both sides of the Atlantic require that this Government indicate its plans for the duration and the general magnitude of the program, without committing itself to specific amounts in future years. The best estimates we can now make indicate that appropriations of about $10.2 billion will be required for the last three years.

I recommend that legislation providing for United States aid in support of the European recovery program authorize the appropriation of $17 billion from April 1, 1948, to June 30, 1952. Appropriation for the period from April 1, 1948, to June 30, 1949, should be made in time for the program to be put into effect by April 1, 1948. Appropriations for the later years should be considered subsequently by the Congress on an annual basis.

The funds we make available will enable the countries of Europe to purchase goods which will achieve two purposes—to lift the standard of living in Europe closer to a decent level, and at the same time to enlarge European capacity for production. Our funds will enable them to import grain for current consumption, and fertilizer and agricultural machinery to increase their food production. They will import fuel for current use, and mining machinery to increase their coal output. In addition they will obtain raw materials, such as cotton, for current production, and some manufacturing and transportation equipment to increase their productive capacity.

The industrial goods we supply will be primarily to relieve critical shortages at a few strategic points which are now curtailing the great productive powers of Europe's industrial system.

The fundamental objective of further United States aid to European countries is to help them achieve economic self-support and to contribute their full share to a peaceful and prosperous world. Our aid must be adequate to this end. If we provide only half-hearted and half-way help, our efforts will be dissipated and the chances for political and economic stability in Europe are likely to be lost.

INSURING PROPER USE OF UNITED STATES AID

A second basic consideration with regard to this program is the means by which we can insure that our aid will be used to achieve its real purposes—that our goods and our dollars will contribute most effectively to European recovery. Appropriate agreements among the participating countries and with the United States are essential to this end.

At the Paris conference the European nations pledged themselves to take specific individual and cooperative actions to accomplish genuine recovery. While some modification or amplification of these pledges may prove desirable, mutual undertakings of this nature are essential. They will give unity of purpose and effective coordination to the endeavors of the peoples of the sixteen nations.

In addition, each of the countries receiving aid will be expected to enter into an agreement with the United States affirming the pledges which it has given to the other participating countries, and making additional commitments.

Under these agreements, each country would pledge itself to take the following actions, except where they are inapplicable to the country concerned:

(1) To promote increased industrial and agricultural production in order to enable the participating country to become inde-

pendent of abnormal outside economic assistance.

(2) To take financial and monetary measures necessary to stabilize its currency, establish or maintain a proper rate of exchange, and generally to restore or maintain confidence in its monetary system.

(3) To cooperate with other participating countries to reduce barriers to trade among themselves and with other countries, and to stimulate an increasing interchange of goods and services.

(4) To make efficient use, within the framework of a joint program for European recovery, of the resources of the participating country, and to take the necessary steps to assure efficient use in the interest of European economic recovery of all goods and services made available through United States aid.

(5) To stimulate the production of specified raw materials, as may be mutually agreed upon, and to facilitate the procurement of such raw materials by the United States for stockpiling purposes from the excess above the reasonable domestic usage and commercial export requirements of the source country.

(6) To deposit in a special account the local currency equivalent of aid furnished in the form of grants, to be used only in a manner mutually agreed between the two governments.

(7) To publish domestically and to furnish to the United States appropriate information concerning the use made of our aid and the progress made under the agreements with other participating countries and with the United States.

The United States will, of course, retain the right to determine whether aid to any country is to be continued if our previous assistance has not been used effectively.

FINANCIAL ARRANGEMENTS

A third basic consideration in formulating the program of United States aid relates to the financial arrangements under which our aid is to be provided.

One of the problems in achieving the greatest benefit from United States aid is the extent to which funds should be made available in the form of grants as contrasted with loans. It is clear that we should require repayment to the extent that it is feasible and consistent with the objectives of the program, in order that no unnecessary burden be imposed upon the people of the United States. It is equally clear that we should not require repayment where it would impose paralyzing financial obligations on the people of Europe and thus defeat the basic purpose of making Europe self-supporting.

Recovery for Europe will not be achieved until its people are able to pay for their necessary imports with foreign exchange obtained through the export of goods and services. If they were to have additional burdens to bear in the form of interest and amortization payments in future years, they would have to plan for an even higher level of exports to meet these obligations. This would necessarily increase the requirements of the recovery program, and delay the achievement of economic stability.

It is also important that an increasing portion of the financial needs of Europe be met by dollar loans from the International Bank, and by the revival of private financing. This prospect would be seriously jeopardized if the United States, as part of the recovery program, were to impose all that the traffic will bear in the form of debt obligations.

I recommend that our aid should be extended partly in the form of grants and partly in the form of loans, depending primarily upon the capacity of each country to make repayments, and the effect of additional international debt upon the accomplishment of genuine recovery. No grants should be made to countries able to pay cash for all imports or to repay loans.

At a later date it may prove desirable to make available to some of the European countries special loans to assist them in attaining monetary stability. I am not now requesting authorization for such loans, since it is not possible at this time to determine when or to what extent such loans should be made.

As economic conditions in Europe improve and political conditions become more stable, private financing can be expected to play an increasingly important role. The recommended program of United States aid includes provisions to encourage private financing and investments.

IMPACT ON THE UNITED STATES ECONOMY

A fourth basic consideration is the effect of further aid for Europe upon the physical resources of the United States and upon our economy.

The essential import requirements of the 270 million people of Western Europe cover a wide range of products. Many of these requirements can be met by the United States and other countries without substantial difficulty. However, a number of the commodities which are most essential to European recovery are the same commodities for which there is an unsatisfied demand in the United States.

Sharing these commodities with the people of Europe will require some self-denial by the people of the United States. I believe that our people recognize the vital importance of our aid program and are prepared to share their goods to insure its success.

While the burden on our people should not be ignored or minimized, neither should it be exaggerated. The program of aid to Europe which I am recommending is well within our capacity to undertake.

Its total cost, though large, will be only about five percent of the cost of our effort in the recent war.

It will cost less than three percent of our national income during the life of the program.

As an investment toward the peace and security of the world and toward the realization of hope and confidence in a better way of life for the future, this cost is small indeed.

A committee under the chairmanship of the Secretary of the Interior was appointed last summer to study the effect of a foreign aid program upon the natural resources of our country. Its study has shown that our resources can safely meet the demands of a program such as I am now recommending. Such demands could not, however, be supplied indefinitely. Our program of aid to Europe recognizes this fact. Our exports to Europe will decrease during the succeeding years of the program as trade is revived along realistic patterns which will make available from other sources an increasing share of Europe's requirements.

Actually, our position with respect to some raw materials of which we have inadequate domestic resources will be improved since, under our program of aid to Europe, an increased amount of these materials will be made available to us.

During recent months the Council of Economic Advisers made an intensive study of the impact of foreign aid on our domestic economy. The Council concluded that a program of the size now contemplated is well within our productive capacity and need not produce a dangerous strain on our economy.

At the same time, a group of distinguished private citizens under the chairmanship of the Secretary of Commerce considered the extent and nature of foreign aid which the United States can and should provide. The conclusion of this group was that a program of the scope I am recommending is a proper, wise and necessary use of United States resources.

The reports submitted to me by the Council of Economic Advisers and the committees under the chairmanship of the Secretary of the Interior and the Secretary of Commerce all emphasized that specific measures should be taken to prevent our foreign aid program from imposing unnecessary burdens on our economy.

If the United States were to supply from its own production all the essential commodities needed to meet European requirements, unnecessary scarcities and unnecessary inflationary pressures would be created within our economy. It is far wiser to assist in financing the procurement of certain of these commodities from other countries, particularly the other food-producing countries in the Western Hemisphere. The funds we make available to aid European recovery therefore should not be restricted to purchases within the United States.

Under the proposed program of aid to Europe, the total exports to the whole world from this country during the next year are expected to be no greater than our total exports during the past twelve months.

This level of exports will nevertheless have an important impact on our markets. The measures I have already proposed to the Congress to fight general domestic inflation will be useful, as well, in cushioning the impact of the European aid program.

The effect of aid to Europe upon our economy, as well as its financial cost, will be significantly affected by the arrangements we make for meeting shipping requirements.

The interest of the United States will be served best by permitting the sale or temporary transfer of some of our war-built merchant ships to the European countries. Because of world steel shortages, the sale or temporary transfer of ships should be linked with a reduction or deferment of the projected shipbuilding schedules of the participating countries. These arrangements should be consistent with their long-range merchant marine requirements. They should also be consistent with our long-range objectives of maintaining an adequate merchant marine and shipbuilding industry for the United States.

Making these vessels available to the European countries will materially reduce the cost of United States aid both by lowering shipping costs and by reducing the use of scarce materials for new ship construction overseas.

RELATIONSHIP TO OTHER INTERNATIONAL
QUESTIONS

A fifth basic consideration is the relationship of our aid to the European recovery program to other international questions.

I have already mentioned that the requirements and resources of Western Germany were included in the considerations of the sixteen countries at Paris. Our program of United States aid also includes Western Germany.

The productive capacity of the highly industrialized areas of Western Germany can contribute substantially to the general cooperative effort required for European recovery. It is essential that this productive capacity be effectively utilized, and it is especially important that the coal production of the Ruhr continue to increase rapidly.

Every precaution must of course be taken against a resurgence of military power in Germany. The United States has made

clear on many occasions its determination that Germany shall never again threaten to dominate Europe or endanger the peace of the world. The inclusion of Western Germany in the European recovery program will not weaken this determination.

As an occupying power in Western Germany, the United States has a responsibility to provide minimum essentials necessary to prevent disease and unrest. Separate appropriations will be requested for this purpose for the period through June 30, 1949.

Above this minimum level, amounts needed to assist in the rehabilitation of Western Germany are included in the over-all estimates for aid to European recovery.

Another significant area of the world which has been considered in developing the recovery program is Eastern Europe. A number of the governments of Eastern Europe which were invited to participate in the work of the Paris Conference on Economic Cooperation chose not to do so. Their failure to join in the concerted effort for recovery makes this effort more difficult and will undoubtedly prolong their own economic difficulties.

This should not, however, prevent the restoration of trade between Eastern and Western Europe to the mutual advantage of both areas. Both the report of the sixteen nations and the program now submitted to the Congress are based on the belief that over the next few years the normal pattern of trade between Eastern and Western Europe will be gradually restored. As this restoration of trade is achieved, the abnormal demands on the Western Hemisphere, particularly for food and fuel, should diminish.

The relationship between this program and the United Nations deserves special emphasis because of the central importance in our foreign policy of support of the United Nations. Our support of European recovery is in full accord with our support of the United Nations. The success of the United Nations depends upon the independent strength of its members and their determination and ability to adhere to the ideals and principles embodied in the Charter. The purposes of the European recovery program are in complete harmony with the purposes of the Charter—to insure a peaceful world through the joint efforts of free nations. Attempts by any nation to prevent or sabotage European recovery for selfish ends are clearly contrary to these purposes.

It is not feasible to carry out the recovery program exclusively through the United Nations. Five of the participating countries are not yet Members of the United Nations. Furthermore, some European Members are not participating in the program.

We expect, however, that the greatest practicable use will be made of the facilities of the United Nations and its related agencies in the execution of the program. This view is shared by all the participating countries.

Our intention to undertake a program of aid for European recovery does not signify any lessening of our interest in other areas of the world. Instead, it is the means by which we can make the quickest and most effective contribution to the general improvement of economic conditions throughout the world. The workshops of Europe, with their great reservoir of skilled workers, must produce the goods to support peoples of many other nations.

I wish to make especially clear that our concentration on the task in Western Europe at this time will not lessen our long-established interest in economic cooperation with our neighbors in the Western Hemisphere. We are first of all a member of an American community of nations, in which cooperative action, similar to that which the European nations are now undertaking, is

required to increase production, to promote financial stability, and to remove barriers to trade. Fortunately we in the Americas are further advanced along this road, but we must not overlook any opportunity to make additional progress. The European recovery program will require procurement of supplies in many nations of this hemisphere. This will act as a stimulant to production and business activity and promote the reestablishment of world trade upon which the prosperity of all of us depends.

While our present efforts must be devoted primarily to Western Europe, as the most important area in the world at this time for the future of peace, we also have a special concern for the war torn areas of Asia. In Japan and Korea, the United States has supplied extensive aid to support life and commence reconstruction. Since the war's end, we have provided China with varied and important assistance which has aided that nation substantially.

The United States should continue to do all it appropriately can to assist in the restoration of economic stability as a basis for recovery in the Far East. Extensive study has been given during the last few months to the means by which we might best aid in meeting the special needs for relief and rehabilitation in China. I expect to make recommendations on that subject to the Congress during its next session.

ADMINISTRATIVE ARRANGEMENTS

I have set forth several basic considerations which should govern our aid to the recovery of Europe. One further consideration which vitally affects all the others is the necessity for effective administrative arrangements adapted to the particular requirements of the program. If the work to be done is not well organized and managed, the benefits of our aid could be largely dissipated.

The administration of our aid will involve the performance of several major functions. The needs of the participating countries must be reviewed in close cooperation with them. Continued relationships must be maintained with the United Nations and with an organization of the participating nations. The requirements for each commodity or service under the program must be carefully evaluated in relation to United States supplies and domestic needs and to the resources of other nations which can help. Decisions must be reached as to the best means of supplying aid and the conditions of aid for each country. Assistance must be given to facilitate the procurement, transportation, and efficient use of goods. A constant review must be maintained over the use of our aid and the execution of agreements. The results of the program must be evaluated and reported to all concerned—the President, the Congress, and the people.

While these activities are complex, they are not comparable in magnitude or in character to our wartime supply activities. Under this program, most of the operations can be carried out through private channels and existing Government agencies.

Nevertheless, the scope and importance of the program warrant the creation of a new organization to provide central direction and leadership. I therefore recommend the establishment of a new and separate agency, the Economic Cooperation Administration, for this purpose. It should be headed by an Administrator, appointed by the President and directly responsible to him. The Administrator should be subject to confirmation by the Senate.

The Economic Cooperation Administration will sponsor the European aid requirements as they are reviewed and adjusted with other governmental agencies, to form a practical program in the light of available supplies and capacities. The Economic Cooperation Administration will be responsible for initiating the approved program project by project and nation by nation and for regulations as to supervision, cooperative assistance, and other policy matters which will guide the program at every point. In keeping with the importance and nature of its task, the new agency should have flexibility in the determination of operating methods, the use of funds, and the hiring of key personnel.

The relationship of the Economic Cooperation Administration to the existing governmental establishment is of crucial importance. In the determination of programs for the several countries, the assessment of individual projects, and many other matters involving our activities abroad, the Economic Cooperation Administration must work closely with the Department of State. Similarly on many actions affecting our domestic economy the Administration must work with, rather than supplant, existing agencies. For example, the Department of Agriculture should be relied upon for any required government action in the procurement and allocation of food, and the Department of Commerce for the allocation of certain other commodities in short supply, and for continued administration of export controls. The facilities of these agencies will in some cases need to be strengthened, but no major changes in governmental organization to perform important domestic functions will be required.

Under these circumstances, I expect that the Economic Cooperation Administration will need only a small staff. No vast new agency or corporation is needed to perform functions for which government facilities now exist.

It is essential to realize that this program is much more than a commercial operation. It represents a major segment of our foreign policy. Day in and day out its operations will affect and be affected by foreign policy judgments. We shall be dealing with a number of countries in which there are complex and widely varying economic and political situations. This program will affect our relationships with them in matters far beyond the outline of the program itself. Its administration must therefore be fully responsive to our foreign policy. The Administrator must be subject to the direction of the Secretary of State on decisions and actions affecting our foreign policy.

The United States activities in Europe under the program will constitute essentially an extension of our present relationships with the participating countries. In order to maintain unity of United States representation abroad, our ambassador in each country must retain responsibility for all matters requiring contacts with the government to which he is accredited, including operations under this program. Some additional personnel, technically qualified to perform specialized functions arising out of the program, should be placed in the embassies to represent and carry out the responsibilities of the Economic Cooperation Administration abroad.

In addition, I recommend that provision be made for a special United States Representative for the European Recovery Program. He would represent the United States at any continuing organization of the participating countries and he would exercise general coordination of our operations in Europe under the program. He should be appointed by the President, subject to confirmation by the Senate, and have Ambassadorial rank. Because of the joint interest of the Secretary of State and the Administrator in his activities, the special Representative must serve both as the President may direct. The activities of this

Representative in promoting mutual self-help among the European nations will be of the utmost importance in achieving the success of the European recovery program.

The administrative arrangements I have described are in keeping with the character of the job to be done and will provide the most efficient and economical means for its performance.

CONCLUSION

In proposing that the Congress enact a program of aid to Europe, I am proposing that this Nation contribute to world peace and to its own security by assisting in the recovery of sixteen countries which, like the United States, are devoted to the preservation of free institutions and enduring peace among nations.

It is my belief that United States support of the European recovery program will enable the free nations of Europe to devote their great energies to the reconstruction of their economies. On this depend the restoration of a decent standard of living for their peoples, the development of a sound world economy, and continued support for the ideals of individual liberty and justice.

In providing aid to Europe we must share more than goods and funds. We must give our moral support to those nations in their struggle to rekindle the fires of hope and strengthen the will of their peoples to overcome their adversities. We must develop a feeling of teamwork in our common cause of combatting the suspicions, prejudicies, and fabrications which undermine cooperative effort, both at home and abroad.

This joint undertaking of the United States and a group of European nations, in devotion to the principles of the Charter of the United Nations, is proof that free men can effectively join together to defend their free institutions against totalitarian pressures, and to promote better standards of life for all their peoples.

I have been heartened by the widespread support which the citizens of the United States have given to the concept underlying the proposed aid to European recovery. Workers, farmers, businessmen and other major groups have all given evidence of their confidence in its noble purpose and have shown their willingness to give it full support.

I know that the Members of the Congress have already given much thoughtful consideration to the grave issues now before us. I know that the Congress will, as it should, consider with great care the legisla-

tion necessary to put the program into effect. This consideration should proceed as rapidly as possible in order that the program may become effective by April 1, 1948. It is for this reason that I am presenting my recommendations to the Congress now, rather than awaiting its reconvening in January.

I recommend this program of United States support for European recovery to the Congress in full confidence of its wisdom and necessity as a major step in our Nation's quest for a just and lasting peace.

HARRY S. TRUMAN

NOTE: On February 3, 1948, the President approved an act providing for United States support of a program for European recovery (62 Stat. 137).

239 Exchange of Messages With Prime Minister de Gasperi of Italy. *December* 20, 1947

[Released December 20, 1947. Dated December 19, 1947]

I AM GRATEFUL for your message on the occasion of the departure from Italy of Allied troops. I know that the Italian Government and people are dedicated to the preservation and protection of the freedoms which they have regained, and I am confident that I speak for the American people when I say that we are heartened by the knowledge that Italy stands with the other freedom loving nations of the world in the defense of liberty and democracy everywhere.

HARRY S. TRUMAN

[His Excellency, Alcide de Gasperi, President of the Council of Ministers, Rome]

NOTE: Prime Minister de Gasperi's message, dated December 16, follows:

The President
The White House

At the moment when all Allied troops have left our soil I wish to assure you that the Italians will forever retain the memory of their liberating action and the brotherhood of arms which united them afterwards with our regular and voluntary forces. Your troops fought in Italy for the cause of liberty and democracy. I shall be grateful to you if you will inform them that the common ideals for which they shed so much noble blood remain the supreme law of the Italian Republic.

DE GASPERI

240 Address at the Lighting of the National Community Christmas Tree on the White House Grounds. *December 24, 1947*

[Broadcast nationally at 5:15 p.m.]

My fellow countrymen:

We are met on the south lawn of the White House. Above the barren treetops rises the towering shaft of the Washington Monument. The scene is peaceful and tranquil. The shadows deepen and the Holy Night falls gently over the National Capital as we gather around our Christmas tree.

Down the ages from the first Christmas through all the years of nineteen centuries, mankind in its weary pilgrimage through a changing world has been cheered and strengthened by the message of Christmas.

The angels sang for joy at the first Christmas in faraway Bethlehem. Their song has echoed through the corridors of time and will continue to sustain the heart of man through eternity.

Let us not forget that the first Christmas was a homeless one. A humble man and woman had gone up from Galilee out of the City of Nazareth to Bethlehem. There is a sense of desolation in St. Luke's brief chronicle that Mary "brought forth her firstborn son, wrapped Him in swaddling clothes, and laid Him in a manger; because there was no room for them in the inn."

For many of our brethren in Europe and Asia this too will be a homeless Christmas. There can be little happiness for those who will keep another Christmas in poverty and exile and in separation from their loved ones. As we prepare to celebrate our Christmas this year in a land of plenty, we would be heartless indeed if we were indifferent to the plight of less fortunate peoples overseas.

We must not forget that our Revolutionary fathers also knew a Christmas of suffering and desolation. Washington wrote from Valley Forge 2 days before Christmas in 1777: "We have this day no less than 2,873 men in camp unfit for duty because they are barefooted and otherwise naked."

We can be thankful that our people have risen today, as did our forefathers in Washington's time, to our obligation and our opportunity.

At this point in the world's history, the words of St. Paul have greater significance than ever before. He said:

"And now abideth faith, hope, charity, these three; but the greatest of these is charity."

We believe this. We accept it as a basic principle of our lives. The great heart of the American people has been moved to compassion by the needs of those in other lands who are cold and hungry.

We have supplied a part of their needs and we shall do more. In this, we are maintaining the American tradition.

In extending aid to our less fortunate brothers we are developing in their hearts the return of "hope." Because of our efforts, the people of other lands see the advent of a new day in which they can lead lives free from the harrowing fear of starvation and want.

With the return of hope to these peoples will come renewed faith—faith in the dignity of the individual and the brotherhood of man.

The world grows old but the spirit of

Christmas is ever young.

Happily for all mankind, the spirit of Christmas survives travail and suffering because it fills us with hope of better things to come. Let us then put our trust in the unerring Star which guided the Wise Men to the Manger of Bethlehem. Let us hearken again to the Angel Choir singing: "Glory to God in the highest, and on earth peace, good will toward men."

With hope for the future and with faith in God, I wish all my countrymen a very Merry Christmas.

241   Statement by the President Upon Signing Order Establishing the Interdepartmental Committee for Scientific Research and Development. *December* 24, 1947

I HAVE today signed an Executive order establishing an Interdepartmental Committee for Scientific Research and Development. This Committee will maintain a continuing study of various aspects of the Federal Government's scientific programs and will recommend ways to make them most effective in promoting the national welfare. Its members will represent the Departments of Agriculture, Commerce, and Interior; the Army, the Navy, the Air Force, and the National Military Establishment; the Federal Security Agency; the Atomic Energy Commission; the National Advisory Committee for Aeronautics; the Veterans Administration; and the Smithsonian Institution.

The need for this Committee was emphasized in the recent report of the Chairman of the President's Scientific Research Board. The survey indicated there is no central group equipped to advise on the relationships among the numerous and complex Federal scientific activities, or to take leadership in the solution of administrative problems common to different agencies. The relationship of the Federal research program to our national welfare, and the great sums annually spent for research by the Government, make the establishment of such a group a matter of national importance.

The Interdepartmental Committee will perform for the entire Federal establishment functions similar to those now performed by committees and boards which coordinate research programs within single departments or among limited groups of departments. These functions will include review of administrative policies and techniques to increase the efficiency of scientific operations and examination of current policies and practices relating to Federal support of research carried on outside the Government. The Committee will encourage cooperation among the scientists of the various Government agencies and develop means by which information on research can be most effectively disseminated.

The Assistant to the President, John R. Steelman, will provide liaison between the President and the Interdepartmental Committee and between the office of the President and the Nation's scientists and their learned societies.

NOTE: The text of Executive Order 9912 "Establishing the Interdepartmental Committee on Scientific Research and Development" (3 CFR, 1943–1948 Comp., p. 676) was released with the President's statement.

242 Statement on the Resolution Enacted in Response to the President's Message of November 17. *December* 28, 1947

I AM SIGNING Senate Joint Resolution 167 with a sense of deep disappointment that the Congress has seen fit to take such feeble steps toward the control of inflation.

At a time when nearly everyone in this Nation is feeling the pressure of exorbitant prices, the Congress has enacted a bill that is pitifully inadequate as a weapon against the high cost of living.

I sign the bill reluctantly, but feel that I must do so because it contains some measures that are needed now.

On November 17, 1947, I recommended to the Congress a 10-point anti-inflation program. I emphasized that all 10 points were essential to an effective program to win the battle against inflation.

Senate Joint Resolution 167 contains appropriate legislation with respect to only 3 of the 10 points that were recommended. And these 3 points are of minor importance compared with the others.

This bill fails to include the key measures which are essential to an effective anti-inflation program.

This bill will not reduce the high cost of living and it will not keep prices from going even higher.

The meager authority contained in the bill will be utilized to the fullest extent by the Government, but the public must not be misled into believing that this bill will do the job. I would be shirking my responsibility if I did not protest against the obvious insufficiency of this legislation.

The 3 points, out of the November 17 10-point program, which this bill covers are: extension of export controls, extension of allocation authority over transportation facilities and equipment, and authorization for expansion of the Department of Agriculture program of encouraging conservation practices in this country and authorization of measures designed to increase the production of food in certain foreign countries. The bill also includes authority to limit the use of grain for distilled liquors, but only for a period of 5 weeks.

The bill contains, in sections 2 and 6, provisions which are not in accord with my recommendations. These provisions are of doubtful value at best. If they are used as an excuse for delaying the enactment of a sound anti-inflation program, they will do far more harm than good.

Section 2 undertakes to authorize a system of voluntary agreements among businessmen for the allocation of transportation facilities and equipment, for the allocation and inventory control of scarce commodities, and for the regulation of speculative trading on commodity exchanges. These agreements, if approved by the Attorney General, would be accompanied with an exemption from liability under the antitrust laws.

As the report of the Senate Committee on this legislation pointed out, "It should be definitely understood that this part of the program is purely voluntary. No representatives of industry, business, and agriculture would be compelled to consult with the President. Neither would they be compelled after consultation to enter into any agreement."

The inability of the Government to protect the interests of the people under this section is apparent.

If the members of an industry refuse to make an agreement, there is nothing the Government can do to see that a program is developed for the industry.

If the members of an industry reach an agreement which is inadequate or contrary to the public interest, there is nothing the Government can do to improve it.

If some members of an industry refuse to enter an agreement, or refuse to carry it out when it has been made, there is nothing the Government can do to assist the public-spirited members of the industry to make the agreement effective throughout the industry.

Every effort will be made, of course, to achieve whatever results are possible under this system of voluntary agreements. It is far too late in the fight against inflation, however, to place our main reliance upon voluntary action.

Efforts to obtain voluntary action by businessmen have already been extensively tried. Repeatedly during the past year I have urged voluntary price reductions. Other Government officials have attempted in many conferences with business leaders to persuade them of the necessity for making voluntary price reductions. While these efforts to obtain voluntary price reductions have produced some results, they have been wholly insufficient to stem the tide of rising prices.

The Government has also made intensive efforts to encourage conservation practices which help to reduce inflationary pressures. These efforts have accomplished much good, but they have demonstrated that voluntary measures are not sufficient to insure a fair sharing and the most effective use of vital commodities which are critically scarce.

The voluntary methods authorized by section 2, in the absence of reserve powers to back them up, can therefore be expected to accomplish little.

Another part of the bill which gives me great concern in section 6. This section proposes that the President submit to the Congress extremely detailed and specific recommendations for mandatory conservation measures for scarce commodities. Presumably the Congress would then determine in each case whether the conservation measures proposed by the President should be adopted, and what the details of the measures should be, and pass legislation authorizing them to be put into effect.

It has long been an established practice for the Congress to enact regulatory measures in general terms, leaving it to the administrative agencies to determine when the measures should be applied on the basis of the standards and conditions established by the Congress. This has proved to be a practicable and workable system. Section 6 of this bill now proposes substantially to reverse this historic process.

Under the provisions of this section, the recommendations which the President is to submit to the Congress can be prepared in the prescribed manner only when the need for mandatory conservation measures is so acute that they should be put into effect immediately. Under the normal operation of our governmental system, when an administrative agency had made this kind of determination, it would put the measures into effect at once. But the only course of action authorized under this section is for the President to submit recommendations to the Congress.

Even if the Congress should pass legislation in accordance with the recommendations it would take considerable time. Then, it would still be necessary to establish the administrative machinery which would put the conservation measures into effect. If rationing were authorized, for example, it would still take some months to print and distribute the necessary forms and documents. Furthermore, lengthy congressional discussion of specific controls would invite speculation, hoarding, dumping, and other actions to circumvent whatever program might be established.

If the procedure under section 6 is to be relied upon for dealing with critical shortages, it is hardly possible that effective measures can be taken in time.

The 10-point program which I presented to the Congress on November 17 requested basic authority to deal with inflation. It included a request for authority to regulate consumer credit and business credit; authority to regulate the distribution of scarce commodities which basically affect the cost of living or industrial production; authority to extend and strengthen rent control; and authority to utilize, on a selective basis, rationing and price control for essential cost of living items and essential industrial products.

The bill which the Congress has enacted fails to include any of these necessary elements.

During the 6 weeks since I addressed the Congress on November 17, and pointed out the alarming course of inflation, prices have continued to rise.

When I spoke to the Congress, a pound of butter in Washington, D.C., cost 88 cents. Last week, here in Washington, butter reached a new high price of $1.05.

In the last six weeks, men's street shoes in Pittsburgh have gone up from an average of $8.72 a pair to $9.38.

In this same period the price of hogs in Chicago has risen from $24.75 a hundred pounds to $26.40.

A few days ago in Omaha the price of steers reached a new alltime high of $40 a hundred pounds.

Since November 17 the price of gasoline has risen in Los Angeles from 21.5 cents a gallon to 23.3 cents.

Inflation and the high cost of living confront the American people—all the American people—with a grave danger. Unchecked inflation can bring on a serious depression that can cause untold hardship.

The legislative and executive branches of the Government must work together if this grave peril is to be conquered.

The American people look to the Congress to pass legislation adequate to perform this all-important task.

I trust that when the Congress returns it will promptly enact an effective, workable program.

NOTE: On December 30, 1947, the President signed S.J. Res. 167 "To aid in the stabilization of commodity prices, to aid in further stabilizing the economy of the United States, and for other purposes" (61 Stat. 945).

243   The President's News Conference of *December* 31, 1947

THE PRESIDENT.. [1.] Ladies and gentlemen of the press conference, I thought it would be more convenient for us to have a conference on the day before New Year's, rather than at 8 o'clock on New Year's morning, or the day after New Year's—[*laughter*]— so we set it. Since we missed last week, we thought you would want one for this week.

I want to wish all of you a happy and prosperous 1948, and to say to you that I think 1947 has been a good year—not as good as we would like to have it, none of

them ever are—and that I am still confidently looking forward to a world peace on which all the nations can agree, and the proper implementation of the United Nations.

I always think of the Constitution of the United States and the difficulties that took place in the Colonies between 1781 and 1789, and then the difficulties that took place between 1789 and 1809. If you carefully look over that situation, you will find that they had tremendous difficulties in those days, almost exactly the same situation with which we are faced now, both in Europe and here, and that it took just about 80 years, really, to get the Constitution properly implemented. In fact, it was not the Constitution of the United States until 1865.

So I don't think we ought to be discouraged at things that sometimes get in our way in making this tremendous peace organization work. I did not intend to make you a speech, but I am very much interested in that situation, and I have every faith in the final working of the United Nations as a means of general world peace, for the simple reason that we can't afford anything else. It is to our selfish interests and to the selfish interests of every country in the world that we do have a workable world peace.

Q. Mr. President, that is a very good speech. Could we have the text of that for direct quotes?

THE PRESIDENT. Yes——

Q. It's quite well worth it.

THE PRESIDENT.——I didn't intend to make you a speech, but I am highly interested in that, and that's all I have been working for since September 1945.

Now if you have any questions that I can answer, I will be glad to hear from you.

[2.] Q. I would like to ask you a question about the General Electric Company's cut. Have you any comment on their promise of reduction in prices to help reverse the spiral?

THE PRESIDENT. I will read you a telegram I have here to Mr. Wilson,[1] who happens to be a personal friend of mine.

[*Reading*] "The Company's announcement of a price reduction for consumer goods is extremely heartening in the Nation's fight against inflation. Should other industries follow your example, a real bulwark will be

---

[1] Charles E. Wilson, president of the General Electric Co.

built against rising prices."

Mr. Wilson, as you know, was here all during the war, with the War Production Board, and he was chairman of the committee which wrote the report on the bill of rights.

Q. Mr. President, did he get in touch with you personally before he made the cut?

THE PRESIDENT. No, he didn't talk to me at all. He did not talk to me at all. I didn't know it was going to happen until I heard about it this morning.

[3.] Q. Have you decided whether or not to reappoint Guy Mason for District Commissioner?

THE PRESIDENT. No I have not. I will make that announcement when I come to the conclusion of it.

Q. Mr. President——

[4.] Q. Mr. President, there are now two vacancies on the CAB——

THE PRESIDENT. Just a moment, let me get Mr. Wright's——

James L. Wright, Buffalo Evening News: That was the same question I was going to ask, so let him ask it.

Q. Two vacancies on the CAB?

THE PRESIDENT. Two?

Q. Yes. Mr. Landis and Young.

THE PRESIDENT. Oh yes, that's right. Well, I am going to fill those just as quickly as I can.

Q. Mr. President, would you give us the reason why you are not going to reappoint Mr. Landis?

THE PRESIDENT. I have no comment to make on that.

Q. Mr. President, one other question related to that. I believe it is the rule that the President appoints only for action January 31st the Chairman and the Vice Chairman of the Board.

THE PRESIDENT. Well, there is a Vice Chairman who will act as Chairman now until the Chairman is appointed, which will be done just as quickly as I can get around to it.

[5.] Q. Mr. President, just one more question.

THE PRESIDENT. Fire away.

Q. I understand that the safety report has been made to you?

THE PRESIDENT. It hasn't reached me yet. I understand that it is finally finished, but that report has not reached me yet.

Q. Will that be made public after——

THE PRESIDENT. It will, as soon as I have seen it.

[6.] Q. Mr. President, is Jim Mead under consideration for one of these vacancies, can you tell us?

THE PRESIDENT. No, I do not want to answer that question in the affirmative or in the negative. I am considering Jim Mead for several positions, but not particularly for these two.

[7.] Q. Mr. President, have you set a date for the transmittal of the message to Congress?

THE PRESIDENT. The Message on the State of the Union will go down on January 7th, the Economic Message on the 9th, and the Budget Message probably the following Monday. We have to get all those things ready, and it's a tremendous job.

[8.] Q. Mr. President, what effect do you think Henry Wallace's action [1] will have on the 1948 political picture?

THE PRESIDENT. No comment on that.

Q. Mr. President, do you think the Democrats will have a happy new year?

THE PRESIDENT. Sure they will. *I* am having one. [*Laughter*]

[9.] Q. Mr. President, can you say anything to us about what your conversation with Secretary Morgenthau—former Secretary Morgenthau was about?

THE PRESIDENT. We discussed various matters, and I think he announced to you all

that was of importance in that conversation when he went out the door.

[10.] Q. Mr. President, will you go to Congress in person with any of these messages?

THE PRESIDENT. I can't answer that yet. I will let you know in plenty of time.

[11.] Q. Mr. President, did Mr. Morgenthau tell you whether or not he was in the market—commodities market?

THE PRESIDENT. We didn't discuss that.

Q. Mr. President, in connection with the commodities market, in October when you criticized gambling in grain futures, I wonder if you could tell us what line you drew between what is called greedy speculation and legitimate trading?

THE PRESIDENT. It's easy enough for you to draw that line, Smitty,[1] but I think I had better write you an essay on it. It's a very complicated subject; and I will do that some day. [*Laughter*]

Q. Mr. President, do you consider that Dr. Graham [2] did anything wrong in his speculation——

THE PRESIDENT. I don't think he did.

Q. Mr. President, do you know of any other member of your official family who has been trading extensively in the commodities exchange?

THE PRESIDENT. No, I do not know of any, and I didn't know that Dr. Graham was trading until the morning of the day that I announced that the names must be published. That is as soon as I found it out.

Q. Did he tell you that——

THE PRESIDENT. I didn't even know Mr. Pauley was in the market until I heard them tell about it.

Q. Did Dr. Graham tell you on that day that he made——

---

[1] On December 29, 1947, Mr. Wallace announced his decision to run for President in 1948.

[1] Merriman Smith of the United Press Association.
[2] Brig. Gen. Wallace H. Graham, Physician to the President.

THE PRESIDENT. That morning, yes. He told me that morning.

[12.] Q. Mr. President, would you care to discuss reports that the Democrats have a proposal to offset the Republican tax measure?

THE PRESIDENT. I don't know anything about it. I couldn't discuss it.

[13.] Q. Mr. President, it is customary to make resolutions——

THE PRESIDENT. I beg your pardon?

Q. It is customary, or used to be at this time, to make resolutions. Are you making any?

THE PRESIDENT. I think a lot of people ought to make some resolutions. I don't intend to make any.[1]

Q. What people particularly?

THE PRESIDENT. Well, I will let you name them, Bert.[2] You and I would probably name the same people.

[14.] Q. Mr. President, in view of the increasingly bad military situation in Greece, are any steps planned by this Government——

THE PRESIDENT. The State Department I think gave out an answer to that yesterday afternoon at 4 o'clock, did they not? They should have, if they didn't. I have no comment to make further than the statement that the State Department made yesterday afternoon at the press conference.[3]

[15.] Q. Mr. President, have you decided what course you are going to follow on taxes this next year? I am not trying to get you to tell me.

THE PRESIDENT. I will give you that answer in the Message on the State of the Union. I don't like to quote it in advance.

[16.] Q. Mr. President, Senator Maybank received a letter from you saying that you are going to forward a message dealing with the fuel oil shortage. Could you tell us what might be done?

THE PRESIDENT. General Fleming has been working on that situation, and I think will have an announcement to make shortly.

[17.] Q. Mr. President, Henry Wallace said that the Democratic Party is not a peace party. Any comment on that?

THE PRESIDENT. I do not comment on anything Mr. Wallace says.

Q. Not even when he says that you can't tell the Trumans from the Republicans?

THE PRESIDENT. Now Bert! [*Laughter*] I don't answer leading questions either, Bert. [*More laughter*]

[18.] Q. Mr. President, the TVA report which you received today shows tremendous gains, in most instances new records being made in the TVA in the past fiscal year. In the light of that report, will you again this year urge river valley developments, such as the MVA and the Columbia River——

THE PRESIDENT. Not necessarily in the light of that report. I would urge them anyway. I haven't seen the report, so I can't comment on it, but I am for river valley authorities.

---

[1] At this point the White House Official Reporter noted that there was laughter, especially from Margaret Truman and members of the Wallace family who were attending the news conference.

[2] Bert Andrews of the New York Herald Tribune.

[3] The statement, released by the Department of State on December 30, follows:

"The claim of certain Communist guerrilla leaders that they have established at some unknown point a 'First Provisional Democratic Government of Free Greece' is a transparent device, the true purpose of which will be clear to everyone. It is only a phase in the familiar effort of certain elements to overthrow the legitimate and recognized Greek Government and to threaten the territorial integrity and political independence of Greece. It came as no sur-

prise. In itself, it would not materially change the existing situation.

"But if other countries were to recognize the group, this step would have serious implications. It would be clearly contrary to the principles of the United Nations Charter. And if the country concerned were one of Greece's neighbors to the north, the act would constitute an open disregard of the recent recommendations of the United Nations Assembly, as set forth in the resolution of last October."

Q. Mr. President, will you include the St. Lawrence Seaway in your messages?

THE PRESIDENT. The St. Lawrence Seaway I think I sent a special message on last year.[1] I may do the same thing this year.

[19.] Q. Mr. President, does your budget for next year contemplate any funds for Greece?

THE PRESIDENT. I will let the budget speak for itself when it comes out, and I will show it to you and talk to you about it. It isn't ready yet.

[20.] Q. Mr. President, have you found the original of that half-a-loaf anti-inflation bill yet?

THE PRESIDENT. What's that?

Q. Have you found the original of that half-a-loaf——

THE PRESIDENT. No. No. [*Laughter*] Half a loaf! I think you are getting it— I don't think it was hardly one slice. [*More laughter*] It was lost. We couldn't find it. As it turned out, we signed a duplicate of it.

Reporter: Happy New Year, and thank you, Mr. President!

NOTE: President Truman's one hundred and thirty-first news conference was held in his office at the White House at 10:30 a.m. on Wednesday, December 31, 1947.

---

[1] See 1945 volume, this series, Item 155.

Appendix A—White House Press Releases, 1947

NOTE: Includes releases covering matters with which the President was closely concerned, except announcements of Presidential personnel appointments and approvals of legislation with which there was no accompanying statement.

Releases relating to Proclamations and Executive orders have not been included. These documents are separately listed in Appendix B.

For list of Press and Radio Conferences, see subject index under "News conferences."

January

2 White House announcement of first meeting of the President's Scientific Research Board

2 Letter accepting resignation of John G. Winant as U.S. Representative in Economic and Social Council of United Nations

3 Statement by the President upon announcing the calling of a National Conference on Fire Prevention

4 Letter accepting resignation of Bernard M. Baruch as U.S. Representative on the United Nations Atomic Energy Commission

4 Letter from Secretary Byrnes to Bernard Baruch concerning his resignation

6 Annual message to the Congress on the State of the Union

7 Letter accepting resignation of James F. Byrnes as Secretary of State

8 Special message to the Congress: the President's first economic report

8 Annual message to the Congress transmitting report on Foreign Service retirement system

8 Special message to the Congress transmitting report under Property Requisitioning Act

8 Message to the Congress transmitting annual report of Commission on Erection of Memorials in Arlington Amphitheater

8 Message to the Congress transmitting annual report of Civil Service Commission

8 Memorandum concerning the Red Cross campaign

8 Statement by the President at the budget seminar

10 Annual Budget Message to the Congress: Fiscal Year 1948

10 Special message to the Senate transmitting a tax convention with France

January

11 White House release concerning meeting of President's Advisory Commission on Universal Training

11 Letter from John R. Steelman to the Administrator, Office of Temporary Controls, concerning the rubber problem

13 Special message to the Congress transmitting report on U.S. participation in International Bank for Reconstruction and Development and in International Monetary Fund

15 Statement by the President on highway safety

15 Remarks to members of the President's Committee on Civil Rights

16 Letter to Secretary Patterson and Secretary Forrestal concerning unification of the armed services

16 White House release concerning meeting of President's Advisory Commission on Universal Training

17 White House statement concerning the President's recommendation of an additional repeal of authorized appropriations

18 Letter to the President of the Senate and to the Speaker of the House concerning creation of a Department of National Defense

20 Special message to the Senate transmitting protocol extending the Inter-American Coffee Agreement

20 Letter to Richard S. Whaley approving his retirement as Chief Justice, U.S. Court of Claims

22 Exchange of messages with the President of France

25 Letter to the President of Italy following Prime Minister de Gasperi's visit to the United States

25 White House release concerning meeting of President's Advisory Commission on Universal Training

539

Appendix A

Appendix A

Appendix A

542

May

14 Citation accompanying Medal for Merit awarded to John Wesley Snyder

14 Report to the President on guaranteed wages by the OWMR Advisory Board

15 Letter accepting resignation of Joseph D. Nunan as Commissioner of Internal Revenue

16 Letter to Senator Wherry concerning the moratorium on reclamation projects and other Federal construction

16 Letter to Secretary Anderson calling a conference on farm real estate prices

19 Special message to the Congress on health and disability insurance

19 Veto of bill relating to lands on the Crow Indian Reservation (Congressional Record, vol. 93, p. 5489)

22 Special message to the Congress recommending extension of the Second War Powers Act

22 Statement by the President upon signing bill endorsing the Truman Doctrine

26 Special message to the Congress on military collaboration with other American states

27 Special message to the Congress transmitting Reorganization Plan 3 of 1947

30 Statement by the President upon signing orders relating to meritorious awards for wartime services

June

1 Report of the President's Advisory Commission on Universal Training

2 Message to the Congress transmitting annual report of Railroad Retirement Board

2 Special message to the Congress transmitting agreement extending interstate compact to conserve oil and gas

2 Letter accepting resignation of J. P. Wenchel as Assistant General Counsel, Bureau of Internal Revenue

2 White House announcement of the President's forthcoming visit to Canada

3 Joint statement following discussions with Ambassador Ivanissevich of Argentina

4 Special message to the Senate transmitting convention between the United States and the Republic of the Philippines

4 Letter accepting resignation of Spruille Braden as Assistant Secretary of State

June

4 Letter to the President of the Senate and to the Speaker of the House transmitting report of the Advisory Commission on Universal Training

5 Statement by the President on Palestine

5 Statement by the President on the general price situation

7 Statement by the President upon receiving the Attorney General's Report on Governmental Patent Practices and Policies

7 Address in Kansas City at the 35th Division reunion memorial service

11 Address before the Canadian Parliament in Ottawa

13 Letter by John R. Steelman accepting resignation of Aaron Lewittes as his legal adviser

14 Statement by the President upon ratification of the peace treaty with Italy

14 Statement by the President upon ratification of peace treaties with Hungary, Rumania, and Bulgaria

14 Letter accepting resignation of Ralph J. Bunche as U.S. Commissioner on the Caribbean Commission

14 White House announcement of appointment of William H. Hastie as U.S. Commissioner on the Caribbean Commission

15 Letter appointing members of a Special Board of Inquiry on Air Safety

16 Message to the Congress transmitting annual report of Panama Railroad Company

16 Veto of bill to reduce income taxes

17 Commencement address at Princeton University

18 Message to the Congress transmitting annual report on the work of the D.C. Juvenile Court

18 Address opening the President's Second Highway Safety Conference

19 Letter accepting resignation of S. D. Sanders as Cooperative Bank Commissioner in the Farm Credit Administration

19 Letter to the President of the Senate and to the Speaker of the House on the administration of Guam, Samoa, and the former Japanese mandated islands

20 Veto of the Taft-Hartley labor bill

20 Letter accepting resignation of Maj. Gen. J. H. Hilldring as Assistant Secretary of State

Appendix A

July

14 Letter accepting resignation of Howard C. Petersen, Assistant Secretary of War

15 Statement by the President upon signing the Second Decontrol Act

16 Special message to the Congress on flood control in the Mississippi River Basin

16 Letter from John R. Steelman to the Chairman, Reconstruction Finance Corporation, on the sale of cordage fibers

17 Special message to the Senate transmitting Inter-American Convention on Rights of the Author in Literary, Scientific and Artistic Works

17 Veto of bill relating to sale of Fidelity Building, Kansas City, Mo. (Congressional Record, vol. 93, p. 9120)

17 White House announcement of appointment of members of Board of Foreign Scholarships

17 Letter to members of the Commission on Organization of the Executive Branch

18 Veto of second bill to reduce income taxes

18 Letter appointing members to the Air Policy Commission

18 Letter to the Chairman of the Air Coordinating Committee

18 White House announcement of forthcoming inspection of troops and installations by Gen. Omar N. Bradley

18 Letter accepting resignation of Joseph J. O'Connell, Jr., as General Counsel, Treasury Department

18 Letter accepting resignation of Robert P. Patterson as Secretary of War

19 Report on coal exports by the Coordinator of Emergency Export Programs

19 Statement by the President upon signing resolution authorizing approval of trusteeship agreement for the Trust Territory of the Pacific Islands

21 Letter accepting resignation of Benjamin V. Cohen as Counselor, Department of State

21 The President's Midyear Economic Report to the Congress

22 Statement by the President: The Jewish New Year

23 Letter to the President of the Senate and to the Speaker of the House concerning a proposed statue of Commodore John Barry

24 Veto of bill for the relief of Myrtle Ruth Osborne, Marion Walts, and Jessie A. Walts (Congressional Record, vol. 93, p. 10039)

July

25 Veto of bill authorizing issuance of patent in fee to Gideon Peon (Congressional Record, vol. 93, p. 10107)

25 Veto of bill authorizing issuance of patent in fee to Joseph J. Pickett (Congressional Record, vol. 93, p. 10106)

25 Statement by the President upon signing resolution terminating additional emergency powers

25 Statement by the President on the dangers of explosive-type war souvenirs

25 Letter accepting resignation of Keen Johnson as Under Secretary of Labor

26 Statement by the President upon signing bill authorizing redemption of veterans terminal leave bonds

30 Memorandum of disapproval of bill to amend the Interstate Commerce Act

30 Memorandum of disapproval of bill for the relief of Herman Trahn (Congressional Record, vol. 93, p. 10587)

30 Statement by the President upon approving resolution providing for congressional study of aviation problems

31 Memorandum of disapproval of bill authorizing commemorative coins

31 Memorandum of disapproval of bill relating to refund of taxes illegally paid by Indian citizens

August

1 Memorandum of disapproval of bill for the relief of Mrs. Mary Jane Sherman and W. D. Sherman (Congressional Record, vol. 93, p. 10586)

1 Letter from the Chairman of the President's Special Board of Inquiry on Air Safety

5 Memorandum of disapproval of bill reimbursing the District of Columbia for expenses of U.S. Park Police

5 Memorandum of disapproval of bill for the relief of Harry V. Ball (Congressional Record, vol. 93, p. 10590)

5 Letter to Governor Pinero of Puerto Rico upon signing bill providing for an elected governor

6 White House announcement of the President's forthcoming visit to Brazil

6 Memorandum of disapproval of bill repealing the Ship Warrants Act

6 Memorandum of disapproval of bill to permit part-time referees in bankruptcy to act for claimants against the United States

Appendix A

August

6 Memorandum of disapproval of bill for the relief of Public Utility District 1 of Cowlitz County, Washington (Congressional Record, vol. 93, p. 10590)

6 Memorandum of disapproval of bill for the relief of Frank F. Miles (Congressional Record, vol. 93, p. 10585)

6 Memorandum of disapproval of bill for the relief of Mrs. Beulah Hart (Congressional Record, vol. 93, p. 10588)

6 Memorandum of disapproval of the National Science Foundation Bill

6 Memorandum of disapproval of bill for the relief of Graff, Washbourne, and Dunn (Congressional Record, vol. 93, p. 10587)

6 Memorandum of disapproval of bill to exclude newspaper and magazine vendors from the social security system

7 Memorandum of disapproval of bill relating to garbage originating outside the continental United States

7 Memorandum of disapproval of bill for the construction of a bridge across the St. Lawrence River

7 Statement by the President on the new Housing and Home Finance Agency

7 Statement by the President on the effect of congressional changes in the budget

7 Letter accepting resignation of Katherine C. Blackburn as Acting Director, Office of Government Reports

8 Memorandum of disapproval of bill relating to claims of Fidelity Trust Co. of Baltimore (Congressional Record, vol. 93, p. 10569)

8 Memorandum of disapproval of bill to continue certain mining subsidies

8 Statement by the President upon approving resolution continuing regulation of consumer credit

8 Letter from Secretary Marshall concerning the Sugar Act

15 Statement by the President on Myron C. Taylor's mission to the Vatican

16 Fifth interim report of the President's Special Board of Inquiry on Air Safety

18 Statement of policies prepared for the President by the Air Coordinating Committee

August

19 Letter accepting resignation of Watson B. Miller as Federal Security Administrator and appointing him Commissioner of Immigration and Naturalization

20 Statement by the President on the review of the 1948 budget

20 Statement by the President reviewing the 1948 budget as approved by the Congress

20 Citation accompanying Medal for Merit awarded to David K. Niles

23 Letter accepting resignation of Casper W. Ooms as Commissioner of Patents

25 Emergency board report on labor dispute involving the Terminal Railroad Association

27 Report by the Chairman of the President's Scientific Research Board

27 Statement by the President upon receiving report of his Scientific Research Board

27 Letter to Secretary Schwellenbach on employment of the physically handicapped

28 Exchange of messages with Pope Pius XII

29 Letter to Secretary Krug on the forthcoming International Conference on Natural Resources

29 White House statement concerning order restricting competition to veterans in examinations for substitute railway postal clerks

30 Statement by the Assistant to the President: Labor Day

30 Statement by the President: Labor Day

September

2 Address before the Rio de Janeiro Inter-American Conference for the Maintenance of Continental Peace and Security

5 Address in Rio de Janeiro before a joint session of the Congress of Brazil

17 Letter to the President, National Federation of Federal Employees

22 Letter accepting resignation of Frank P. Corrigan as Ambassador to Brazil

22 Letter to the Administrator, Federal Works Agency, authorizing disaster aid to Mississippi and Louisiana

24 Statement by John R. Steelman concerning disposal of Government-owned iron and steel scrap

24 Letter accepting resignation of William Benton as Assistant Secretary of State

Appendix A

Appendix A

Appendix A

Appendix B—Presidential Documents Published in the Federal Register, 1947

PROCLAMATIONS

Appendix B

EXECUTIVE ORDERS

Appendix B

[1] Not published; noted only.

[1] Not published; noted only.

Appendix B

Appendix B

[1] Not published; noted only.

Appendix B

PRESIDENTIAL DOCUMENTS OTHER THAN PROCLAMATIONS AND EXECUTIVE ORDERS

Appendix C—Presidential Reports to the Congress, 1947

Subject	Published 80th Congress	Sent to the Congress	Date of White House release
Economic Report	H. Doc. 49	Jan. 8	Jan. 8
Civil Service Commission—63rd Annual Report	. . . . . .	Jan. 8	Jan. 8
Report of all receipts and disbursements of the Foreign Service retirement and disability system for fiscal year ended June 30, 1946.	. . . . . .	Jan. 8	Jan. 8
Commission on the Erection of Memorials and Entombment of Bodies in the Arlington Memorial Amphitheater—Annual Report.	. . . . . .	Jan. 8	Jan. 8
Report of operations under the Property Requisitioning Act of October 16, 1941, as amended, for the period from April 16, 1946 through June 30, 1946.	. . . . . .	Jan. 8	Jan. 8
Report by the National Advisory Council on International Monetary and Financial Problems with respect to the participation of the United States in the International Bank for Reconstruction and Development and in the International Monetary Fund to October 31, 1946.	H. Doc. 53	Jan. 13	Jan. 13
Report on the Activities of the United Nations and the participation of the United States therein for the calendar year 1946.	H. Doc. 81	Feb. 5	. . . .
National Capital Housing Authority for the fiscal year ended June 30, 1946.	. . . . . .	Feb. 26	Feb. 26
First Report of the Air Coordinating Committee, for the calendar year 1946.	H. Doc. 148	Feb. 26	Feb. 26
National Advisory Committee for Aeronautics 32nd Annual Report, covering the fiscal year 1946, and containing a review of the unreported war years.	. . . . . .	Feb. 28	Feb. 28
Report on the operations of the Department of State under section 32(b) (2) of Public Law 584, 79th Congress, covering the period August 1, 1946, through December 31, 1946.	H. Doc. 167	Mar. 10	Mar. 10
Governor of the Panama Canal—Annual Report for fiscal year ended June 30, 1946.	. . . . . .	Mar. 20	Mar. 20
Final Report prepared by the American Red Cross reflecting all foreign war relief operations which have been conducted since July 1, 1940, from appropriations for foreign war relief.	. . . . . .	Mar. 21 [a]	. . . .
United States Participation in Operations of UNRRA:			
Tenth Report, quarter ending December 31, 1946	H. Doc. 254	May 15	. . . .
Eleventh Report, quarter ending March 31, 1947	H. Doc. 438	Aug. 29 [a]	. . . .
Railroad Retirement Board—fiscal year ended June 30, 1946	H. Doc. 289	June 2	June 2
Panama Railroad Company—96th Annual Report	. . . . . .	June 16	June 16
Report covering the work of the Juvenile Court for the fiscal year ended June 30, 1946.	H. Doc. 329	June 18	June 18

[a] Delivered to the President pro tempore of the Senate and to the Speaker of the House.

Appendix C

Subject	Published 80th Congress	Sent to the Congress	Date of White House release
Report of the National Advisory Council on Participation of the United States in the International Monetary Fund and the International Reconstruction and Development covering its operations from February 28, 1946, to March 31, 1947.	H. Doc. 365	June 26	June 26
Seventh and Final Report of the U.S. High Commissioner to the Philippine Islands covering the period from September 14, 1945, to July 4, 1946.	H. Doc. 389	July 8	July 8
Report and Recommendations of the Joint Philippine-American Finance Commission.	H. Doc. 390	July 8 [a]	July 7
Midyear Economic Report	H. Doc. 409	July 21	. . . .
Lend-Lease Operations—24th Report	H. Doc. 437	Nov. 10 [b]	. . . .
First Report on Assistance to Greece and Turkey for period ended September 30, 1947.	. . . . . .	Nov. 10 [a]	. . . .
United States Foreign Relief Program—First quarterly report covering the period from the commencement of the program through September 30, 1947.	H. Doc. 466	Nov. 24	. . . .
Annual Report for the Office of Alien Property Custodian for the fiscal year ended June 30, 1946.	H. Doc. 465	Nov. 24	Nov. 24
Report by the Governor of the Panama Canal on Means of Increasing the Capacity and Security of the Panama Canal.	. . . . . .	Dec. 1 (S) Dec. 2 (H)	Dec. 1

[a] Delivered to the President pro tempore of the Senate and to the Speaker of the House.
[b] Delivered to the Secretary of the Senate and to the Clerk of the House.

Appendix D—Rules Governing This Publication

[Reprinted from the Federal Register, vol. 24, p. 2354, dated March 26, 1959]

TITLE I—GENERAL PROVISIONS

Chapter I—Administrative Committee of the Federal Register

PART 32—PUBLIC PAPERS OF THE PRESIDENTS OF THE UNITED STATES

PUBLICATION AND FORMAT

Sec.

32.1   Publication required.
32.2   Coverage of prior years.
32.3   Format, indexes, ancillaries.

SCOPE

32.10   Basic criteria.
32.11   Sources.

FREE DISTRIBUTION

32.15   Members of Congress.
32.16   The Supreme Court.
32.17   Executive agencies.

PAID DISTRIBUTION

32.20   Agency requisitions.
32.21   Extra copies.
32.22   Sale to public.

AUTHORITY: §§ 32.1 to 32.22 issued under sec. 6, 49 Stat. 501, as amended; 44 U.S.C. 306.

PUBLICATION AND FORMAT

§ 32.1 *Publication required.* There shall be published forthwith at the end of each calendar year, beginning with the year 1957, a special edition of the FEDERAL REGISTER designated "Public Papers of the Presidents of the United States." Each volume shall cover one calendar year and shall be identified further by the name of the President and the year covered.

§ 32.2 *Coverage of prior years.* After conferring with the National Historical Publications Commission with respect to the need therefor, the Administrative Committee may from time to time authorize the publication of similar volumes covering specified calendar years prior to 1957.

§ 32.3 *Format, indexes, ancillaries.* Each annual volume, divided into books whenever appropriate, shall be separately published in the binding and style deemed by the Administrative Committee to be suitable to the dignity of the office of President of the United States. Each volume shall be appropriately indexed and shall contain appropriate ancillary information respecting significant Presidential documents not published in full text.

SCOPE

§ 32.10 *Basic criteria.* The basic text of the volumes shall consist of oral utterances by the President or of writings subscribed by him. All materials selected for inclusion under these criteria must also be in the public domain by virtue of White House press release or otherwise.

§ 32.11 *Sources.* (a) The basic text of the volumes shall be selected from the official text of: (1) Communications to the Congress, (2) public addresses, (3) transcripts of press conferences, (4) public letters, (5) messages to heads of state, (6) statements released on miscellaneous subjects, and (7) formal executive documents promulgated in accordance with law.

(b) Ancillary text, notes, and tables shall be derived from official sources only.

FREE DISTRIBUTION

§ 32.15 *Members of Congress.* Each Member of Congress, during his term of office, shall be entitled to one copy of each annual volume published during such term; *Provided*, That authorization for furnishing such copies shall be submitted in writing to the Director and signed by the authorizing Member. [As amended effective Dec. 30, 1960, 25 F.R. 14009]

§ 32.16 *The Supreme Court*. The Supreme Court of the United States shall be entitled to twelve copies of the annual volumes.

§ 32.17 *Executive agencies*. The head of each department and the head of each independent agency in the executive branch of the Government shall be entitled to one copy of each annual volume upon application therefor in writing to the Director.

PAID DISTRIBUTION

§ 32.20 *Agency requisitions*. Each Federal agency shall be entitled to obtain at cost copies of the annual volumes for official use upon the timely submission to the Government Printing Office of a printing and binding requisition (Standard Form No. 1).

§ 32.21 *Extra copies*. All requests for extra copies of the annual volumes shall be addressed to the Superintendent of Documents, Government Printing Office, Washington 25, D.C. Extra copies shall be paid for by the agency or official requesting them.

§ 32.22 *Sale to public*. The annual volumes shall be placed on sale to the public by the Superintendent of Documents at prices determined by him under the general direction of the Administrative Committee.

* * * * *

ADMINISTRATIVE COMMITTEE OF
THE FEDERAL REGISTER,

WAYNE C. GROVER,
*Archivist of the United States,
Chairman.*
RAYMOND BLATTENBERGER,
*The Public Printer,
Member.*
WILLIAM O. BURTNER,
*Representative of the
Attorney General, Member.*

Approved March 20, 1959.

WILLIAM P. ROGERS,
Attorney General.
FRANKLIN FLOETE,
Administrator of General Services.

[F.R. Doc. 59–2517; Filed, Mar. 25, 1959;
8:45 a.m.]

INDEX

[Main references are to items except as otherwise indicated]

Index

Index

Index

[Main references are to items except as otherwise indicated]

Index

[Main references are to items except as otherwise indicated]

Index

Index

Index

[Main references are to items except as otherwise indicated]

Index

[Main references are to items except as otherwise indicated]

Index

Index

Index

[Main references are to items except as otherwise indicated]

Index

Index

[Main references are to items except as otherwise indicated]

Index

Index

Index

[Main references are to items except as otherwise indicated]

Index

[Main references are to items except as otherwise indicated]

Index

Index

[Main references are to items except as otherwise indicated]

Index

Index

Index

Index

[Main references are to items except as otherwise indicated]

Index

[Main references are to items except as otherwise indicated]

Index

[Main references are to items except as otherwise indicated]

Index

Index

[Main references are to items except as otherwise indicated]

[Main references are to items except as otherwise indicated]

Index

Index

Index

Index

Index

War dead, return from overseas, 7 (p. 91)

War Department, 2 (p. 11), 6 [11, 14, 27, 32, 34, 39], 7 (pp. 56, 64, 85, 86, 91, 93), 11, 18, 35, 36 [24], 39, 47, 50, 75, 80, 92, 144, 150, 157, 181 (pp. 401, 403, 404), 195, 226 [1, 3]

War Department Act, 182 [1]

War emergency, 2 (p. 2), 6 [16], 14 [13], 35, 80

War expenditures, 181 [1], 210 [1]

War industries, 18

War information, utilization, 18

War Labor Disputes Act, 87, 120

War Manpower Commission, 81

War materials, 72, 181 (p. 402)

War Mobilization and Reconversion, Office of, 18, 24, 35, 53, 80, 96, 200

War Mobilization and Reconversion Act of 1944, 96

War of 1812, 111

War Plants Corporation, Smaller, 181 (pp. 400, 406)

War powers, termination, 35, 156

War Powers Act, First, 18, 80, 81, 102

War Powers Act, Second, 18, 24, 36 [18], 47, 58, 99

War Production Board, 179, 243 [2]

War Shipping Administration, 167, 181 (p. 404)

War souvenirs, danger of, 157

War structures, use as temporary housing, 44

Warm Springs, Ga., 78 [1]

Warner, Albert, 90 n.

Warren, Earl, 31 [10]

Warrior River Terminal Company, 7 (p. 95)

Washington, Booker T., commemorative coin, 162

Washington, D.C. *See* District of Columbia

Washington, George, 30, 68, 110, 240

Washington, Gov. Mon C. Wallgren, 95 [8]

Washington Evening Star, 107 [8], 221 [16]

Washington Monument, 240

Water carriers, 18

Water pollution, 78 [11], 171

Water resources development, 7 (pp. 58, 59), 31 [10], 68, 110, 144

Waters, Enoch P., 48 n.

WBBM, radio station, 48 n.

Weapons, 21, 101, 194
  Atomic. *See* Atomic bomb
  Poison gas, 36 [3]
  Trade in, 72

Weather Bureau, 7 (p. 59)

Webb, James E. *See* Budget, Bureau of the, Director

Wedemeyer, Lt. Gen. Albert C., 209 [4]

Welfare, Department of, proposed, 2 (p. 8)

Welfare funds, labor unions, 120, 142

Welfare programs, 4 (pp. 35, 36), 7 (pp. 58, 71, 92), 152, 181 (p. 405)

West Executive Avenue, removal of pillars, 95 [1]

West Virginia, 104

Western Hemisphere, 30, 51, 73, 112
  Defense, 101
  Economic development, 79
  European exports to, 238
  Livestock disease control, 45
  Marshall Plan participation, question of, 177 [22]
  Military cooperation, 127 [17]
  Mutual security, 188

Western nations, federation, proposed, 205 [16]

Wheat, 217
  Crops, 210 [3], 236 [10]
  Exports, 7 (p. 78), 155 [6], 210 [3]
  For overseas relief, 15, 29, 47, 107 [3], 191 [7], 209 [11]
  Marketing quota, 35
  Price control, 218 [6]
  Price supports, 76
  Speculation in, 196

Wheeler, Burton K., 78 [14, 19]

Wheeler, Lt. Gen. Raymond A., 141 [2]

Index

Index

U.S. PRESIDENT   1947
**PUBLIC PAPERS OF THE
PRESIDENTS: HARRY S. TRUMAN.**

DATE DUE

GAYLORD   PRINTED IN U.S.A.